Artificial Intelligence Technologies and the Evolution of Web 3.0

Tomayess Issa
Curtin University, Australia

Pedro Isaías
Universidade Aberta (Portuguese Open University), Portugal

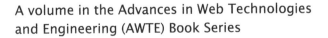
A volume in the Advances in Web Technologies
and Engineering (AWTE) Book Series

Information Science
REFERENCE
An Imprint of IGI Global

Managing Director:	Lindsay Johnston
Managing Editor:	Austin DeMarco
Director of Intellectual Property & Contracts:	Jan Travers
Acquisitions Editor:	Kayla Wolfe
Production Editor:	Christina Henning
Development Editor:	Caitlyn Martin
Typesetter:	Cody Page
Cover Design:	Jason Mull

Published in the United States of America by
Information Science Reference (an imprint of IGI Global)
701 E. Chocolate Avenue
Hershey PA, USA 17033
Tel: 717-533-8845
Fax: 717-533-8661
E-mail: cust@igi-global.com
Web site: http://www.igi-global.com

Library of Congress Cataloging-in-Publication Data

CIP Data
Artificial intelligence technologies and the evolution of Web 3.0 / Tomayess Issa and Pedro Isaias, editors.
    pages cm
  Includes bibliographical references and index.
  ISBN 978-1-4666-8147-7 (hardcover) -- ISBN 978-1-4666-8148-4 (ebook) 1. Semantic Web. 2. Artificial intelligence. 3. Web databases. 4. Educational Web sites. I. Issa, Tomayess, editor of compilation. II. Isaias, Pedro, editor of compilation.
  TK5105.88815.A78 2015
  006.3--dc23
                          2015000393

This book is published in the IGI Global book series Advances in Web Technologies and Engineering (AWTE) (ISSN: Pending; eISSN: pending)

British Cataloguing in Publication Data
A Cataloguing in Publication record for this book is available from the British Library.

All work contributed to this book is new, previously-unpublished material. The views expressed in this book are those of the authors, but not necessarily of the publisher.

For electronic access to this publication, please contact: eresources@igi-global.com.

Advances in Web Technologies and Engineering (AWTE) Book Series

Ghazi I. Alkhatib
Princess Sumaya University for Technology, Jordan
David C. Rine
George Mason University, USA

ISSN: Pending
EISSN: pending

MISSION

The **Advances in Web Technologies and Engineering (AWTE) Book Series** aims to provide a platform for research in the area of Information Technology (IT) concepts, tools, methodologies, and ethnography, in the contexts of global communication systems and Web engineered applications. Organizations are continuously overwhelmed by a variety of new information technologies, many are Web based. These new technologies are capitalizing on the widespread use of network and communication technologies for seamless integration of various issues in information and knowledge sharing within and among organizations. This emphasis on integrated approaches is unique to this book series and dictates cross platform and multidisciplinary strategy to research and practice.

The **Advances in Web Technologies and Engineering (AWTE) Book Series** seeks to create a stage where comprehensive publications are distributed for the objective of bettering and expanding the field of web systems, knowledge capture, and communication technologies. The series will provide researchers and practitioners with solutions for improving how technology is utilized for the purpose of a growing awareness of the importance of web applications and engineering.

COVERAGE

- Data Analytics for Business and Government Organizations
- Metrics-Based Performance Measurement of IT-Based and Web-Based Organizations
- Security, Integrity, Privacy, and Policy Issues
- Quality Of Service and Service Level Agreement Issues Among Integrated Systems
- Integrated Heterogeneous and Homogeneous Workflows and Databases within and Across Organizations and with Suppliers and Customers
- IT Readiness and Technology Transfer Studies
- Web Systems Performance Engineering Studies
- Data and Knowledge Validation and Verification
- Information Filtering and Display Adaptation Techniques for Wireless Devices
- IT Education and Training

IGI Global is currently accepting manuscripts for publication within this series. To submit a proposal for a volume in this series, please contact our Acquisition Editors at Acquisitions@igi-global.com or visit: http://www.igi-global.com/publish/.

Titles in this Series

For a list of additional titles in this series, please visit: www.igi-global.com

Frameworks, Methodologies, and Tools for Developing Rich Internet Applications
Giner Alor-Hernández (Instituto Tecnológico de Orizaba, Mexico) Viviana Yarel Rosales-Morales (Instituto Tecnológico de Orizaba, Mexico) and Luis Omar Colombo-Mendoza (Instituto Tecnológico de Orizaba, Mexico)
Information Science Reference • copyright 2015 • 366pp • H/C (ISBN: 9781466664371) • US $195.00 (our price)

Handbook of Research on Demand-Driven Web Services Theory, Technologies, and Applications
Zhaohao Sun (University of Ballarat, Australia & Hebei Normal University, China) and John Yearwood (Federation University, Australia)
Information Science Reference • copyright 2014 • 474pp • H/C (ISBN: 9781466658844) • US $325.00 (our price)

Evaluating Websites and Web Services Interdisciplinary Perspectives on User Satisfaction
Denis Yannacopoulos (Technological Educational Institute of Piraeus, Greece) Panagiotis Manolitzas (Technical University of Crete, Greece) Nikolaos Matsatsinis (Technical University of Crete, Greece) and Evangelos Grigoroudis (Technical University of Crete, Greece)
Information Science Reference • copyright 2014 • 354pp • H/C (ISBN: 9781466651296) • US $215.00 (our price)

Solutions for Sustaining Scalability in Internet Growth
Mohamed Boucadair (France Telecom-Orange Labs, France) and David Binet (France Telecom, France)
Information Science Reference • copyright 2014 • 288pp • H/C (ISBN: 9781466643055) • US $190.00 (our price)

Adaptive Web Services for Modular and Reusable Software Development Tactics and Solutions
Guadalupe Ortiz (University of Cádiz, Spain) and Javier Cubo (University of Málaga, Spain)
Information Science Reference • copyright 2013 • 415pp • H/C (ISBN: 9781466620896) • US $195.00 (our price)

Public Service, Governance and Web 2.0 Technologies Future Trends in Social Media
Ed Downey (State University of New York, College at Brockport, USA) and Matthew A. Jones (Portland State University, USA)
Information Science Reference • copyright 2012 • 369pp • H/C (ISBN: 9781466600713) • US $190.00 (our price)

Performance and Dependability in Service Computing Concepts, Techniques and Research Directions
Valeria Cardellini (Universita di Roma, Italy) Emiliano Casalicchio (Universita di Roma, Italy) Kalinka Regina Lucas Jaquie Castelo Branco (Universidade de São Paulo, Brazil) Júlio Cezar Estrella (Universidade de São Paulo, Brazil) and Francisco José Monaco (Universidade de São Paulo, Brazil)
Information Science Reference • copyright 2012 • 477pp • H/C (ISBN: 9781609607944) • US $195.00 (our price)

DISSEMINATOR OF KNOWLEDGE

www.igi-global.com

701 E. Chocolate Ave., Hershey, PA 17033
Order online at www.igi-global.com or call 717-533-8845 x100
To place a standing order for titles released in this series, contact: cust@igi-global.com
Mon-Fri 8:00 am - 5:00 pm (est) or fax 24 hours a day 717-533-8661

Table of Contents

Section 1
Smart Technology in Higher Education and for Human Beings

Section 2
Smart Technology in Design

Section 3
E-Government and ICT

Detailed Table of Contents

Section 1
Smart Technology in Higher Education and for Human Beings

This chapter discusses major changes in the traditional roles of teachers in Higher Education triggered by digital transformation in learning and teaching by Web 2.0 and Web 3.0. The purpose of university teaching is explored, together with the key characteristics of digital learning technologies associated with Web 2.0 and current and prospective changes linked to the notion of Web 3.0. Role labels found in the literature are reviewed against these changes and four dimensions of role change are identified, together with suggestions for preparing teachers for these changes.

Web 3.0 creates the potential for implementation of new teaching strategies and new forms of teachers' professional pedagogical activities. Today, it is possible to assume the trends of Web 3.0 development. Most of these trends have been already revealed in the analysis of the current state of modern network technologies. New educational practices require both awareness of new opportunities in networking and acceptance and understanding of new educational strategies of learners. The chapter describes a concept of teachers' professional goals transformation in terms of Web 3.0, stressing movement towards learners' needs. The first pedagogical objective is to design the information educational environment. The second objective is to perceive a student via the informational environment. The third objective is to interact with other members of the informational environment. The fourth objective is to arrange the learning process. The fifth objective is to ensure professional self-development.

Chapter 3

*Renan Rodrigues de Oliveira, Instituto Federal de Educação, Ciência e Tecnologia de Goiás
(IFG), Brazil*
Fábio Moreira Costa, Universidade Federal de Goiás (UFG), Brazil
Cedric Luiz de Carvalho, Universidade Federal de Goiás (UFG), Brazil
Ana Paula Ambròsio, Universidade Federal de Goiás (UFG), Brazil

Virtual learning environments represent an important step in enabling distance and blended education. Moodle's structure for content enables the identification of well-defined learning contexts. Nevertheless, Moodle currently does not provide standard features to leverage the use of such contextual information, nor does it provide a standard built-in search facility. This chapter presents a context-sensitive Moodle plug-in for the search of external resources that allows semantic-based retrieval of documents from any external repository that offers an OAI-PMH standard compliant interface. As a way to increase their potential use, the plug-in also retrieves Twitter messages (known as tweets), since social networks are shown as an important tool to support education. Retrieved resources are presented in order of importance according to both the query terms provided by the user and the current context derived from the Moodle content structure. Searches are semantically expanded by evaluating the query terms according to a specific ontology associated with the context.

Chapter 4

Raadila Bibi Mahmud Hajee Ahmud-Boodoo, Curtin University, Australia

A number of 3.0 e-learning systems have been proposed in the literature to capture the numerous benefits that the Semantic Web has to offer to the higher education sector. These 3.0 e-learning systems identify some essential Semantic Web characteristics that are either discussed as stand-alone factors or tend to revolve around the complexities of the Semantic Web technology and its implementation, often disregarding users' needs. Conversely, a comprehensive analysis of e-learning models for higher education in the literature revealed several Critical Success Factors (CSFs) that are relevant to the Semantic Web but often overlooked in 3.0 e-learning models. Consequently, this chapter provides an overview of the CSFs of e-learning relevant to 3.0 e-learning systems as well as an overview of the main Semantic Web characteristics for e-learning to define a new and combined set of 3.0 e-learning characteristics that will holistically represent 3.0 e-learning systems capturing the needs and expectations of users. The new initial 3.0 e-learning model proposed is evaluated within the higher education sector in Mauritius.

Chapter 5

Amit Chauhan, Florida State University, USA

The annals of the Web have been a defining moment in the evolution of education and e-Learning. The evolution of Web 1.0 almost three decades ago has been a precursor to Web 3.0 that has reshaped education and learning today. The evolution to Web 3.0 has been synonymous with "Semantic Web" or "Artificial Intelligence" (AI). AI makes it possible to deliver custom content to the learners based on their learning behavior and preferences. As a result of these developments, the learners have been empowered and have at their disposal a range of Web tools and technology powered by AI to pursue and accomplish their learning goals. This chapter traces the evolution and impact of Web 3.0 and AI on e-Learning and its role in empowering the learner and transforming the future of education and learning. This chapter will be of interest to educators and learners in exploring techniques that improve the quality of education and learning outcomes.

Chapter 6

Yoshinari Hachisu, Nanzan University, Japan
Atsushi Yoshida, Nanzan University, Japan

In this chapter, the authors propose a system for generating error correction questions of programs, which are suitable for developing debugging skills in programming education. The system generates HTML files for answering questions and CGI programs for checking answers. They are deployed on a Web server, and learners read and answer questions on Web browsers. It provides an intuitive user interface; a learner can edit codes in place at the text. To make programs including errors for learning debugging, the authors analyze types of errors and define the processes of error injection as code transformation patterns. If learners can edit any codes freely, it is difficult to check all possible answers. Instead, the authors adopt a strategy to restrict editable points and possible answers from the educational view. A demonstration of error correction questions of the C language is available at http://ecq.tebasaki.jp/.

Chapter 7

Declan Tuite, Dublin City University, Ireland

This chapter presents research from a study of novice older adult users of ICTs and the Internet from Ireland. Through the concept of digital keepsakes, this chapter connects with theorising around greater mobility and more dissipated extended families. In particular, connections can be seen with current research themes, which explore how citizens may extend the use of ICT communication act so that digital artifacts may offer emotional containment, extended time for reflection, through comments reinterpretations and sharing of experience and meaning. The value and benefit of digital artifacts can extend beyond a personal onscreen experience. Respondents reported valuing both portability and having a record of the good intentions. Such messages consisted of wishes of good luck, sympathy, or empathy.

Chapter 8

Lena Paulo Kushnir, OCAD University, Canada
Kenneth Berry, OCAD University, Canada

Advancements in technology and innovations in education allow universities to entertain new ways of teaching and learning. This chapter presents quasi-experimental data of how various online tools and teaching strategies impact student learning outcomes, satisfaction, and engagement. Specific variables impacting social presence, affect, cognition, etc., were tested to determine their impact on different student outcomes such as grades, feelings of isolation, student engagement, and perceived authenticity of course materials in a second-year Introductory Psychology course. Findings suggest that, despite the literature, only some factors had a significant impact on student outcomes and that while some course activities transferred well online, others did not; peer activities and participation in some course components particularly were hindered online. Considered here are students' experiences with online learning, including hybrid and inverted courses, and teaching strategies that help meet challenges in different higher-education learning contexts.

Section 2
Smart Technology in Design

Chapter 9

Byounghyun Yoo, Korea Institute of Science and Technology, South Korea

This chapter investigates how the visualization of sensor resources on a 3D Web-based globe organized by level-of-detail can enhance search and exploration of information by easing the formulation of geospatial queries against the metadata of sensor systems. The case study provides an approach inspired by geographical mashups in which freely available functionality and data are flexibly combined. The authors use PostgreSQL, PostGIS, PHP, X3D-Earth, and X3DOM to allow the Web3D standard and its geospatial component to be used for visual exploration and level-of-detail control of a dynamic scene. The proposed approach facilitates the dynamic exploration of the Sensor Web and allows the user to seamlessly focus in on a particular sensor system from a set of registered sensor networks deployed across the globe. In this chapter, the authors present a prototype metadata exploration system featuring levels-of-detail for a multi-scaled Sensor Web and use it to visually explore sensor data of weather stations.

Chapter 10

João Vieira, Lisbon School of Economics and Management, Portugal
Pedro Isaías, Universidade Aberta (Portuguese Open University), Portugal

The Web 3.0 has revolutionized the Internet in the last years and its benefits are still being studied. The way that websites are being developed is also changing because of this Web evolution, giving to Web developers new technologies where computers can better understand and give meaning to content. This chapter presents an overview of technologies considered to be included on the Web 3.0 concept. The main objective of the chapter is to introduce a conceptual framework of Web 3.0, or Semantic Web, technologies that can be used for developing a website. This review of literature introduces the evolution of each of the technologies mentioned, as well as their functions. Some examples and opportunities for use are also presented. The chapter offers a current state-of-the-art and an opportunity for future relevant research in the Web development area.

Section 3
E-Government and ICT

Chapter 11

Ruben C. Huacarpuma, University of Brasília, Brazil
Daniel da C. Rodrigues, University of Brasília, Brazil
Antonio M. Rubio Serrano, University of Brasília, Brazil
João Paulo C. Lustosa da Costa, University of Brasília, Brazil
Rafael T. de Sousa Júnior, University of Brasília, Brazil
Lizane Leite, University of Brasilia, Brazil
Edward Ribeiro, University of Brasilia, Brazil
Maristela Holanda, University of Brasilia, Brazil
Aleteia P. F. Araujo, University of Brasilia, Brazil

The Brazilian Ministry of Planning, Budget, and Management (MP) manages enormous amounts of data that is generated on a daily basis. Processing all of this data more efficiently can reduce operating costs, thereby making better use of public resources. In this chapter, the authors construct a Big Data framework to deal with data loading and querying problems in distributed data processing. They evaluate the proposed Big Data processes by comparing them with the current centralized process used by MP in its Integrated System for Human Resources Management (in Portuguese: Sistema Integrado de Administração de Pessoal – SIAPE). This study focuses primarily on a NoSQL solution using HBase and Cassandra, which is compared to the relational PostgreSQL implementation used as a baseline. The inclusion of Big Data technologies in the proposed solution noticeably increases the performance of loading and querying time.

Chapter 12
Rebecca Angeles, University of New Brunswick Fredericton, Canada

The chapter focuses on the use of information provided by an Online Environmental Infomediary (OEI), GoodGuide.com, to advise consumers on the overall and specific sustainability attributes of personal care and household chemical and food products. This chapter seeks to predict the willingness of consumers to be influenced by GoodGuide.com information in their purchases and to influence others as well with this information using the Value-Belief-Norm (VBN) theory and the New Environmental Paradigm (NEP) scale. An experiment was applied to a sample of both undergraduate and graduate students at the Faculty of Business Administration, University of New Brunswick Fredericton, Canada. Data analysis using a series of stepwise multiple regressions was used in this study. Study results indicate the usefulness of both theoretical frameworks in understanding consumer predisposition to use OEI-provided information and the potential of social networking and use of mobile devices and apps in facilitating access and use of green information.

Chapter 13

Knut Ekker, Nord-Trøndelag University College, Norway

The chapter first presents a background review of the application of computer technology in simulations of natural hazard situations. The chapter then presents the efforts of researchers at Mid Sweden University and Nord-Trøndelag University College to build a comprehensive emergency training tool with funding from the Interreg/EU ERDF (European Regional Development Fund). The main part of the chapter reports empirical data from this project GSS (Gaining Security Symbiosis). The project developed the tool for training emergency personnel (police, fire, ambulance, and local officials) in handling crises in the border region between Norway and Sweden. The Web-based software incorporated complex scenarios that the emergency personnel had to contend with during 3-hour training sessions. The participants included employees at the operator, tactical, and strategic level of the organizations. The training tool recorded all communications among participants which primarily was text based. The rich data source was analyzed "on-the-fly" with the software from the R Project for statistical computing and the SNA package (Social Network Analysis package). The statistical software provided detailed graphs of the social networking of communications among the participants on both sides of the national border in central Scandinavia. The chapter concludes with a presentation of ideas towards using the social networking data as input into simulation models based on system dynamics. The empirical data from the project will naturally provide data for future training sessions. A planned future model of the comprehensive training tool—netAgora—will use experiential data in a Virtual Responder component in the training sessions of emergency personnel.

Section 4
Businesses and Smart Technology

Chapter 14

Nuno Pombo, University of Beira Interior, Portugal
Nuno Garcia, University of Beira Interior, Portugal
Kouamana Bousson, University of Beira Interior, Portugal
Virginie Felizardo, University of Beira Interior, Portugal

The complexity of the clinical context requires systems with the capability to make decisions based on reduced sets of data. Moreover, the adoption of mobile and ubiquitous devices could provide personal health-related information. In line with this, eHealth application faces several challenges so as to provide accurate and reliable data to both healthcare professionals and patients. This chapter focuses on computational learning on the healthcare systems presenting different classification processes to obtain knowledge from data. Finally, a case study based on a radial basis function neural network aiming the estimation of ECG waveform is explained. The presented model revealed its adaptability and suitability to support clinical decision making. However, complementary studies should be addressed to enable the model to predict the upper and lower points related to upward and downward deflections.

The Web has become one of the most effective means of communication, and electronic marketing is rapidly transforming the way organizations communicate and operate in many areas. This chapter describes the Internet evolution; in fact, it is no longer just an information tool but has become a new dimension, allowing firms to learn more about their customers, communicate more effectively, promote and market products, services, companies, and brands. The evolution of the Internet, from Web 1.0 to Web 3.0, has resulted in a radical change in marketing strategies and tools in many businesses.

Based on ontological principles enunciated by Plato more than 2300 years ago, yet at a time when Web 3.0 technology is seen to impact the management of organizations and especially the management of organizational performance, the authors propose in this chapter to characterize the IT artefact with an approach that returns the user perspective to the forefront. As an illustration, the Performance Measurement Systems (PMS) of 16 Small and Medium-Sized Enterprises (SMEs) are investigated and characterized from their users' perspective in terms of their specific attributes as systems dedicated to managing organizational performance in the Web 3.0 era. The variety of contexts and configurations of these systems is of particular interest while looking for the principles that underlie their empirical manifestations. Results provide a framework of reference for the characterization, design, and evaluation of IT artefacts that is applicable in particular within a Web 3.0 technological context.

Above average analytical and mathematical ability are highly sought-after human attributes required from IT professionals at work in the Systems Development Life Cycle (SDLC). These attributes are perceived to be ingredients for a successful career in Information Technology (IT). When companies hire IT professionals, they often focus on the "hard" skills needed to perform the work (Joseph, Ang, Chang, & Slaughter, 2010). There is a growing awareness that technical skills alone are insufficient for success in IT. Technical skills and experience are becoming an entry-level requirement. Being technically competent is no longer enough. For IT professionals, to improve business, a wider set of skills are required. This research aimed to determine what the human attributes are that contribute most to the improvement of business, namely IT alignment. It was found that Emotional Intelligence (EI) of business analysts, systems analysts, and project managers does play a role in the non-delivery of business needs by the IT department. Further, human attributes found to contribute to business-IT alignment were experience, communication skills, professionalism, and collaboration skills. A taxonomy of IT alignment intelligence for business analysts, systems analysts, and project managers is proposed.

Foreword

As in Wikipedia, living systems get constant feedback from their external environment. Imagine that you are a principal at a high school. It is raining. A student walks into the school and almost slips in front of the door. You are very busy with other administrative work, but you make a mental note: "I must put a mat in front of the door." About a minute later, another student comes in and she also slips. You immediately need to take an action against the next dilemma.

Your students—or if you have a business, your customers—are slipping but, because you don't see them slip, you don't take any action. Web 3.0 gives you an opportunity to take an action according to your students'/customers' needs. This book is like a recipe to understand what the impacts of Web 2.0 and Web 3.0 are in education and in work. You will also get a chance to learn more about new teaching strategies to transform professional activities through Semantic Web. Semantic Web is beginning to play a significant role in many diverse areas, marking a turning point in the evolution of the Web.

Artificial Intelligence Technologies and the Evolution of Web 3.0 provide various perspectives of the use of these technologies in different sectors. The book discusses how Web 3.0 changes the academic role, how to include Semantic Web in Learning Management Systems, what is proposed in 3.0 e-Learning and Semantic Web literature, computational learning in healthcare systems, how Web 3.0 has changed marketing strategies, evolution and impact of Web 3.0 and Artificial Intelligence on e-Learning, and how to use Big Data in training sessions.

This book addresses Web 3.0 across sectors in detail and presents the most current research on the effectiveness of Web 3.0. This book gives a broader perspective from different sectors such as education, marketing, health, and industry. I welcome this collection of chapters on Web 3.0 and Artificial Intelligence and commend the contributors for their valuable work.

I believe that this book will be of interest to educators, learners, and other professionals in exploring techniques that improve the quality of work, education and learning outcomes using Web 3.0.

Sehnaz Baltaci Goktalay
Uludag University, Turkey

Sehnaz Baltacı Goktalay *completed her MSc on Instructional Design, Development, and Evaluation at Syracuse University, NY, and PhD on Instructional Technology at SUNY, Albany, NY. She has been working at Uludag University, Turkey as an assistant professor of Department of Computer Education and Instructional Technologies and the Associate Dean of the Faculty of Education. Her research interests are e-learning and integration of Web 2.0 technologies in education, social networking, clinical supervision model, and best practices in teacher education. She is involved in several national, international, and European Union projects on Web 2.0 technologies and new teacher education.*

Preface

Technology and ICT (Information and Communication Technology) have become an essential and absolute in business, education, government, health, entertainment, and others. Technology adoption will improve performance and productivity and make businesses and individual more unique in their work as well as study. Technology is ranged from devices, systems, as well applications.

Currently, massive numbers of people around the world globally and locally are using the Internet to communicate, collaborate, and cooperate via cables and wireless signals. To work with the Internet successfully, users must use software, which is called the World Wide Web or "Web," and the Web is viewed by using free software called Web browsers. There are three types of Web, Web 1.0, Web 2.0, and now Web 3.0. Web 1.0 is a read-only Web, in other words, it allows users to search for information and read it via the browsers. However, Web 2.0 is read-write Web; particularly, it involves writing, editing, and socializing. Finally, the Web 3.0 known as Semantic Web, as an illustration, allow users to read, manage, personalize, collaborate, and interact with more data in the Web. Web 3.0 is very interesting, exciting, and appealing to users, since it uses content management systems along with artificial intelligence. Web 3.0 is capable of answering users' questions as it can think and find the answers to his/her query. Web 3.0 is a new future of the Internet.

This book covers several topics in relation to Web 3.0, particularly Web 3.0 and technologies, e-learning and teaching, e-business, e-government, e-marketing and social networking, media, knowledge management, and Internet future. This book will assist various sectors, specifically education, businesses, government, etc. on how Web 3.0 will improve their performance and productivity. Furthermore, this book aims to support researchers and academics' work and sharing the latest technologies among their students nationally and internationally in the higher-education sector.

This book comprises 17 chapters divided by 4 sections, as described next.

SECTION 1: SMART TECHNOLOGY IN HIGHER EDUCATION AND FOR HUMAN BEINGS

Chapter 1, with the title "The Impact of Web 2.0 and Web 3.0 on Academic Roles in Higher Education," authored by Greener, argues about the key changes in the traditional academic roles in Higher Education generated by digital transformation in learning and teaching by Web 2.0 and Web 3.0, focusing on the teachers' roles. The purpose of this chapter is to investigate a succession of questions concerning the changes that Web 2.0 and Web 3.0 caused in the context of Higher Education. It is examined what kinds of new technology are available to teachers, exploring how Web 2.0 influenced theses changes. Also, the author seeks to question whether Web 3.0 is adequately different to guarantee further changes in teaching and learning behaviors. In addition, it is questioned how teachers (in this case Higher Education teachers) are prepared to handle these changes.

Chapter 2, entitled "Web 3.0 Technologies and Transformation of Pedagogical Activities," by Noskova, Pavlova, and Iakovleva, focuses on the notion that Web 3.0 technologies can bring new teaching strategies and new forms of pedagogical activities. To that end, the authors present a concept of teachers' professional ambitions transformation in the context of Web 3.0, focusing on learners' necessities. It is evident that Web 3.0 technologies are altering the educational context and this requires a renovation of educational activities, requires that teachers become more prepare for major developments of networking, Web-based information technologies, and especially, more aware regarding the new needs and behaviors of the learners.

In Chapter 3, "Semantic Retrieval of Documents from Digital Repositories and Twitter Integration in the Moodle Environment," authored by Oliveira, Costa, Carvalho, and Ambròsio, describes a context-sensitive Moodle (Modular Object-Oriented Distance Learning) plug-in for the search of external resources that allows semantic-based retrieval of documents from any external repository that offers an OAI-PMH (Open Archives Initiative – Protocol for Metadata Harvesting) standard interface and also retrieves Twitter messages. This plug-in allows the semantic retrieval of documents from any digital repository, contributing to a better resource retrieval capability in the context of distance learning. The authors argue that the use of tools that facilitate the implementation of data providers can be used to expose metadata from any source of information, such as distributed databases, unstructured files directories, therefore supporting the learning environment through the distribution of digital content between repositories with a low cost.

In Chapter 4, "E-Learning and the Semantic Web: A Descriptive Literature Review," written by Ahmud-Boodoo, presents a general idea of the Critical Success Factors (CSFs) regarding e-learning, which are important to 3.0 e-learning systems. In this chapter, the author reviews e-learning models for higher education found in the literature and identifies several critical success factors relevant to the Semantic Web. The author tries to identify and integrate crucial e-learning and Semantic Web characteristics from the current literature to develop a new 3.0 e-learning model. Consequently, it is characterized a new and combined group of 3.0 e-learning features that will represent 3.0 e-learning systems taking in consideration the needs and expectations of users and, therefore, it is proposed a 3.0 e-learning model.

Chapter 5, entitled "Web 3.0 and E-Learning: The Empowered Learner," authored by Chauhan, discusses the evolution and importance of Web 3.0 and Artificial Intelligence (AI) on e-Learning, its role in empowering the learner, and transforming the future of education and learning. It is explored how the Web 3.0 has developed and how this evolution has capacitate the learner. The application of Web 3.0 and AI tools and technology has created new opportunities to educators, instructors, and learners to innovate, share, and collaborate. Furthermore, with the evolution and growth of the Web have emerged new opportunities in education. The author concludes that taking into consideration the Web 3.0 development, education systems must be recreated to achieve the learning style of the Web 3.0 learners.

Chapter 6, entitled "A Web-Based System for Error Correction Questions in Programming Exercise," by Hachisu and Yoshida, suggests a system for generating error correction questions of programs and checking the correctness. This system creates HTML files for answering questions and CGI programs for checking answers. They are installed on a Web server and learners can read and answer the questions on Web browsers. Additionally, it offers an intuitive user interface. The purpose of this research is to present a framework of automatic generation and checking answers of error correction questions for debugging exercises. On the framework, the errors are identified as code transformation patterns, making it easy for teachers to add new programs and errors.

Chapter 7, entitled "Digital Keepsakes: Older Adults and the Extended Use of ICTs and Digital Artifacts," authored by Tuite, describes a research from an Irish study of beginner older adult users of ICTs and the Internet. In this chapter is included a review of literature of key issues concerning older adults and engagement with ICTs and the Internet. The author reflects on certain barriers that older users engage with technology at different levels of usage. In this context, the idea of digital keepsakes, where individuals store and re-engage with messages or other digital artifacts that provide support in times of need, offers insight into the use and reuse of ICT and Internet communications.

Chapter 8, entitled "Saving Face in Online Learning: New Directions in Teaching and E-Learning," written by Kushnir and Berry, reports on a quasi-experimental data of how various online tools and teaching strategies impact student learning outcomes, satisfaction and engagement. Specific variables impacting social presence, affect, cognition, etc. were examined to establish their force on different student results such as grades, feelings of isolation, student engagement, and perceived authenticity of course materials in a second-year Introductory Psychology course. This chapter considers issues that relate to how teachers teach and how learners learn given technological developments and educational improvements.

SECTION 2: SMART TECHNOLOGY IN DESIGN

Chapter 9, entitled "Web-Based Information Exploration of Sensor Web Using the HTML5/X3D Integration Model," written by Yoo, reports on a case study that examines how the visualization of sensor resources on a 3D Web-based globe organized by level-of-detail can improve search and exploration of information by easing the formulation of geospatial queries against the metadata of sensor systems. This case study describes an approach inspired by geographical mashups in which freely available functionality and data are flexibly merged. The presented approach makes possible the dynamic exploration of the Sensor Web and permits the user to effortlessly focus on a particular sensor system from a set of registered sensor networks deployed across the globe.

Chapter 10, entitled "Web 3.0 in Web Development," by Vieira and Isaías, presents a general review of technologies considered to be included on the Web 3.0 conception. The presented review of literature establishes the evolution of several Web 3.0 technologies, as well as their purpose and functions. The main purpose of this chapter is to describe a conceptual framework of Web 3.0 (Semantic Web) technologies that can be used when designing and developing a website. It is notorious that Semantic Web presents many opportunities concerning Web development, offering new technologies that can support websites to better interact with users, and where users can have experience that better fit them, consequently increasing their satisfaction and willingness to use a specific website again.

SECTION 3: E-GOVERNMENT AND ICT

Chapter 11, entitled "Evaluating NoSQL Databases for Big Data Processing within the Brazilian Ministry of Planning, Budget, and Management," authored by Huacarpuma, Rodrigues, Serrano, Costa, Sousa Júnior, Leite, Ribeiro, Holanda, and Araujo, reports on the design of a big data framework to manage data loading and querying problems in distributed data processing. The authors propose the use of Big Data technology to solve the limitations regarding data processing, which the Brazilian Ministry of Planning, Budget, and Management (MPOG) encounters when dealing with massive amounts of data that is generated on a daily basis. A case study was performed with the purpose of examining Brazilian federal employee data using NoSQL databases (HBase and Cassandra) and a relational database (PostgreSQL).

Chapter 12, entitled "Predicting Use of GoodGuide.com Consumer Product Sustainability Information Using VBN Theory and NEP Scale," by Angeles, explores the use of information provided by an Online Environmental Infomediary (OEI) called GoodGuide.com to recommend consumers on the overall and specific sustainability attributes of personal care and household chemical and food products. The author seeks to anticipate the motivation of consumers to be influenced by GoodGuide.com information in their shopping and to persuade others also with this information using the Value-Belief-Norm (VBN) theory and the New Environmental Paradigm (NEP) scale. Additionally, in this chapter is studied the results of an empirical study of consumers that has the purpose to predict their readiness to be influenced by the information posted on GoodGuide.com in different ways in making their purchases of household goods.

Chapter 13, entitled "Emergency Management Training and Social Network Analysis: Providing Experiential Data for Virtual Responders," by Ekker, reflects on empirical data from an Interreg/EU-funded project, which developed a software for training emergency personnel (police, fire, ambulance, and local officials) in managing crises in the border region between Norway and Sweden. This chapter presents an emergency-response training system software that was developed by a team of researchers at Mid-Sweden University and Nord-Trøndelag University in Norway during a 3-year project from 2010-2013. The presented software included complex scenarios that the emergency personnel had to compete with during 3-hour training sessions.

SECTION 4: BUSINESSES AND SMART TECHNOLOGY

Chapter 14, entitled "Artificial Neural Learning Based on Big Data Process for eHealth Applications," by Pombo, Garcia, Felizardo, and Bousson, reports on computational learning on the healthcare systems presenting different classification process to achieve knowledge from data. To that end, a case study based on a radial basis function neural network aiming the estimation of ECG waveform is presented and explained. It is shown the significance of using methodologies for acquiring knowledge based on reduced data and, consequently, enabling a system to create decisions based on a small amount of data. The authors concluded that the presented model is accurate and suitable when applied on healthcare environments providing flexibility and oriented learning according with the patient's personal data.

Chapter 15, entitled "Marketing Strategies in the Age of Web 3.0," authored by Ferrari, focuses on Web Marketing in the context of Web 3.0. It describes the impact of ICT on marketing by presenting the evolution of the Web in the last decades and how it is affecting firms' strategies and organization together with customers' behavior and buying process. Also, it presents the Web 3.0 concept and its implications, discussing the important role that nowadays is played by social media in several areas such as marketing.

Chapter 16 with the title "Characterizing the IT Artefact through Plato's Ontology: Performance Measurement Systems in the Web 3.0 Era," written by Marchand and Raymond, provides a characterization of performance measurement systems and presents an empirical analysis. To illustrate this characterization, the Performance Measurement Systems (PMS) of 16 Small and Medium-Sized Enterprises (SMEs) are explored and characterized using the users' perspective in terms of their specific attributes as systems dedicated to managing performance. In this context, following the users' perspective, the reported results have outlined the key attributes of PMS artefacts in SMEs.

In Chapter 17, "IT Alignment Intelligence: The Role of Emotional Intelligence in Business and IT Alignment," by van Blerk, de la Harpe, and Cronje, the authors seek to establish which human attributes are the one that add most value to the improvement of business, namely in IT environments. To that end, it suggests a taxonomy of IT alignment intelligence for business analysts, systems analysts, and project managers. It was found that Emotional Intelligence (EI) of business analysts, systems analysts, and project managers does play a part in the non-delivery of business needs by the IT department. Furthermore, the human attributes identified that can be of importance to business-IT alignment were experience, communication skills, professionalism, and collaboration skills.

Tomayess Issa
Curtin University, Australia

Pedro Isaias
Universidade Aberta (Portuguese Open University), Portugal

Section 1
Smart Technology in Higher Education and for Human Beings

Chapter 1
The Impact of Web 2.0 and Web 3.0 on Academic Roles in Higher Education

Sue Greener
University of Brighton, UK

ABSTRACT

This chapter discusses major changes in the traditional roles of teachers in Higher Education triggered by digital transformation in learning and teaching by Web 2.0 and Web 3.0. The purpose of university teaching is explored, together with the key characteristics of digital learning technologies associated with Web 2.0 and current and prospective changes linked to the notion of Web 3.0. Role labels found in the literature are reviewed against these changes and four dimensions of role change are identified, together with suggestions for preparing teachers for these changes.

INTRODUCTION

Since the 1970s, when Paulo Freire was writing about the need to change the role of educators, shaking up the traditional conception of a teacher who encourages conformist behaviour in students and advocating for an equality between learner and teacher, there has been significant re-examination of teaching in both compulsory and post-compulsory education. However this re-examination has been in the realm of pedagogy and philosophy of education; many university teachers are all too aware that there remains a fallback position for

their profession which relates back to their own education, their understanding of what teachers at university did and still do, which has more in common with the idea of the student as a vessel waiting to be filled, than an equal partner in the dance of learning.

For many university teachers, it has taken more than discussions on pedagogy and philosophical debates to stimulate a sea-change in practice. It has taken the explosive advent of web-based technology to force us to face the fundamentals of the teaching role. It is not that teachers have been blindly following traditional practice, so much

DOI: 10.4018/978-1-4666-8147-7.ch001

as the combined pressures of greatly increasing student numbers, driven by Government policies which demand wider educational opportunities for the majority of the population, and a pervasive paradigm in university teaching which holds that teachers at this level do not need to examine their teaching, so much as maintain and develop their scholarship. Provided we are making original contributions to knowledge through research, students will somehow benefit.

This last point held good for generations; it comes from an understanding that universities are for the development of new knowledge, a late 19th century idea, rather than for the service of their communities or the development of students who can take an effective and leading role in society (Bourner 2008). However several factors have begun to change this over-riding emphasis on the advancement of knowledge as the main purpose of the university: they include global economic difficulties which have constrained opportunities available to graduates forcing a greater emphasis on fitting students for employment, and the ubiquity of Web 2.0 which is giving students voice and choice in how they achieve their learning and the growing drive of Web 3.0 synchronising data and meaning to provide complex responses beyond the reach of individual teachers.

The re-examination of the teacher's role appears as we find ourselves once more pressed by external factors: namely the need to provide clear value to students, who pay increasing amounts for the opportunity to study. As students try to work out the potential benefits of Higher Education, when faced with debts reaching into their future in exchange for this experience, the increasing availability of online and blended learning opportunities world-wide, particularly manifested currently in MOOCs, seems to give them an alternative. Why pay to study at a particular university, when the world-wide web offers some of the best faculty world-wide; why settle for less than the best teachers and a regime of set learning

outcomes and passive consumption of knowledge, when Web 2.0 offers the chance to construct a bespoke learning package available at the student's convenience? Why not just ask complex questions of the semantic Web and solve problems in a just-in-time, need-to-know-now fashion? Papert and Harel's constructionism (1991), putting a focus on learning rather than teaching, and learners who are supported to build ideas in public view, or at least in social view, seems to start to address these external pressures. Here is a pedagogy which supports the active role of the learner in their Higher Education, which is now enabled effectively by digital technology fostering sharing and collaboration in social learning networks and contexts.

This chapter will review the evidence of changing academic roles and changing notions of learning in a world of machine-generated or peer-generated answers. A literature review will be included which explores technology related journal articles on this topic since 2006, looking at drivers for change in academic roles, current and developing online pedagogies, and particularly at the rather haphazard way in which academic roles in Higher Education are categorized and looking for pointers to the impact of Web 3.0 on classroom and online learning practice.

The aim of the chapter is to explore a series of questions, beginning with the kinds of technology available to teachers, exploring how Web 2.0 has marked a step change. We will review the traditional understanding of the roles of teachers in Higher Education, and determine the characteristics of Web 2.0 which have forced change in teachers' roles. From this point in time we seek to question whether Web 3.0 is sufficiently different to warrant further changes in teaching and learning behaviours. Finally we consider the transformation of teacher roles, looking for opportunities and challenges for both staff and students, and we question how HE teachers may be prepared to deal with these changes.

BACKGROUND: THERE HAS ALWAYS BEEN LEARNING TECHNOLOGY – WHY IS WEB 2.0 ANY DIFFERENT?

Today we talk about Technology Enhanced Learning as if this is a brand new invention, and of course, if we are referring to the impact of the computer on learning, then we really are talking about a recent revolution. Back in the 1950s, despite the advent of first generation mainframe computers, schools and colleges were likely to use chalkboards, wall posters, books and the occasional television broadcast in classes. These technologies were totally under the control of the teacher and focused on the transmission of information. Pedagogies were less likely to involve interaction given the socio-cultural expectation of teacher authority and student discipline. Higher Education was the domain of the lucky few – at the start of the twentieth century only half a million students attended HE worldwide, while at the end of that century, the figure was closer to 100 million (UNESCO 2004).

In the 1960s, B.F. Skinner, a professor at Harvard University, invented a teaching machine which was designed to offer programmed instruction to students. Using the principles of operant conditioning, the machine rewarded learners when they responded with correct answers to questions. The teaching machine offered a number of characteristics that we continue to use and consider appropriate in teaching: immediate feedback to the learner produced automatically, working at the learner's own pace, involvement in the learning process by the student, and the design of a relevant learning sequence of activities. Skinner had seen that in normal classroom practice, students were rewarded for attending the class, by entertaining teaching or activities, rather than being rewarded for learning. His machine offered a different approach in which the student had a degree of control of learning, and was rewarded for learning, not attending.

Computing only really impacted education when the first PCs were developed in the 1970s, although various programming languages were being taught in universities in the 60s (e.g. BASIC and Fortran). However, it was the advent of the World Wide Web in 1991 linking information through hypertext and URLs which set the course for technology enhanced learning, even though the internet itself was used in academia in the 1980s.

Today almost 40% of the world's population regularly uses social media, and the most popular 25 social media platforms involve 6.3 billion accounts between them (Johnson, Adams Becker, Estrada, Freeman, 2014). The implications of social media for scholarly research through communities of practice, as well as for learning through peer to peer and learner to teacher relationships cannot be ignored. In institutions, technology infrastructure is having to embrace supercomputing, data centres, research data management, high capacity mass storage systems, interactive visualization and so on. Every educational institution is operating virtual learning environments as a minimum, with increasing numbers of applications for learning both embedded within the VLEs and sitting alongside. The prospects of using big data for the support of individual students through sophisticated analysis of learning progress and interactions with content and assessment are just around the corner, with some systems already being tested. The ECAR report (2013) based on student surveys suggests that 76% of students in their sample felt that technology helped them to achieve academic outcomes. Between 2012 and 2013 surveys, there had been a 14% increase in the ownership of smartphones among students – now up to 76% - and a 15% increase in tablet ownership – now up to 31%. This is the early twenty-first century in which manifestations of computer technology are already changing our way of life as well as our way of learning.

The notion of the "teaching machine" has a modern face in developments such as MyLabs - learning programs from Pearson Education.

Web 2.0 characteristics, such as connectivity, 24/7 access to learning resources, opportunities for interactive collaboration and participation in communities and user-generated content, continue to allow learners more control over their learning pace and chosen activities, as well as offering social components to learning through online relationships. So what does this mean for teachers? Those teachers who keep pace with the technologies on offer, who have passion for learning and are prepared continually to improve and develop their curricula and learning activities can achieve personalized responses despite very large teaching groups through the technology. Programmed instruction can still play a part in e-learning and blended learning, particularly where learners are not experienced in a particular discipline or study domain. However there is a big difference between programmed instruction as conceived by Skinner and scaffolding students into new subject learning using Web 2.0. The notion of student control in Web 2.0 is much wider, offering students non-linear pathways for learning, and freedom not just to work at their own pace, but to find their own resources to supplement or even replace those provided by the teacher.

SO HOW DO WE UNDERSTAND THE ROLE OF THE TEACHER?

Given the pervasive impact of Web 2.0, particularly since 2006, the subsequent six years have offered plenty of opportunity to teachers in Higher Education to re-assess their role, but how much has it really changed? In this section of the chapter, we discuss a study of the literature since 2006 which was undertaken to understand the outcomes of re-assessment as presented in the peer-reviewed academic literature relating to educational technology. Twenty-six relevant journals were identified, as shown in the table below, and searches made of their papers since 2006 which related in some way to faculty role

development brought about in response to digital technology in general and Web 2.0 in particular. If the university teacher's role was to be debated in relation to these technology imperatives, it was considered likely that this discussion would be found in educational technology journals, which had seemed to proliferate over this period, particularly with journals increasing the number of issues to cope with the increased output of papers concerning educational technology. Table 1 lists the educational technology journals searched.

While the above list of journals (Table 1) is not claimed to be comprehensive, the list represents most of the widely available educational technology journals currently published, and includes those which are fully online, print only and both print and online. In the latter case, it is the norm to publish online swiftly and follow up later with the print edition. The list is intended to support both this particular search strategy and to be of use for other potential searches in the discipline. Inevitably new journals appear quite regularly and others change name, amalgamate or close, so this is a current list for reference, although currency beyond the date of publication cannot be guaranteed.

Searches were made initially through the ERIC database (The Education Resources Information Center) and subsequently through a Google Scholar search on the following keyword combinations:

- "Web 2.0" and "staff development"
- "Web 2.0" and "Higher Education"
- "staff development" and "technology"
- "academic role" and "technology"
- "faculty development" and "technology"

These keywords had been chosen by a preliminary search for relevant titles and terminology in the author's institutional library.

A total of 23 articles were found in the search plus a Special Issue (JALN Vol 16, No. 12 2012) devoted specifically to faculty development for

Table 1. Educational technology journals searched, by alphabetical order of title

Journal	Frequency of Publication	Publisher
Action in Teacher Education	6	Routledge
Australasian Journal of Educational Technology	6	ASCILITE
British Journal of Education Technology	6	BERA
Computers in Education	8	Elsevier
Contemporary issues in Technology & Teacher Education	4	Society for Information Technology and Teacher Education
Educational Technology and Society	4	International Forum of Educational Technology & Society
Educational Technology Research and development	6	Springer for Association for Educational Communications & Technology
EDUCAUSE review	6	EDUCAUSE
Electronic Journal of E-Learning	4	Academic Publishing Ltd.
European Journal of Open, Distance and e-Learning	2	EDEN
Innovations in Education and Teaching International	4	Routledge for SEDA
Interactive Learning Environments	6	Routledge
International Journal of Computer-Supported Collaborative Learning	4	Springer for International Society for the Learning Sciences
International Review of Research in Open and Distance Learning	3-6	IRRODL
Journal Of Asynchronous Learning Networks	4	Sloan Consortium
Journal of Computer Assisted Learning	6	Wiley
Journal of Computing in Higher Education	3	Springer
Journal of Interactive Media in Education	3	OU, UK
Journal of Online Learning and Teaching	4	MERLOT
Journal of University Teaching and Learning Practice	3	University of Wollongong, Australia
Learning, Media & Technology	4	Routledge
Open Learning: The journal of open, distance and e-learning	3	Routledge
Research in Learning Technology	3	ALT-J
Teaching in Higher Education	6	Routledge
Technology Pedagogy & Education	3	Routledge
The Internet and Higher Education	4	Elsevier

online teaching which included a further ten articles. Research methods produced primarily qualitative data and methods of analysis. Methods used included auto-ethnography, action research including interviews, journaling and observation, self-reported data through survey, phenomenogra-phy, case study, content analysis of self-reported experience and discourse analysis.

A consistent theme through the papers was an emphasis on how faculty development could be achieved, with many papers looking in detail at evaluating programmes. Faculty development was achieved in these papers by a wide range of methods including mentoring, intensive staff development programmes, applying principles of andragogy, online community of practice, training, peer evaluation, trial and error learning, 24/7 access to proprietory online tutorials, tutor support networks, virtual workshop, centrally supported "e-developers" to assist faculty and technology-enhanced lifelong learning communities.

University teacher roles were likened to "creator, developer and deliverer of the educational groceries", content expert, learning facilitator (Sappey & Relf, 2010) and facilitator, teacher, advisor, mentor, and researcher (Diaz et al., 2009). There was a clear sense of the widespread view that teacher-centred approaches were no longer helpful in the context of increasing knowledge and information and its immediate access through technology, together with the emphasis in Web 2.0 on co-creation of knowledge. While this is not particularly surprising, the terms mentioned seem to be used with little care. Facilitator, for example, carries with it implications of "guide on the side" and a modest, less visible role for the teacher. Is that really what is meant? Sappey and Relf's notion of content expert does not seem to fit with a less than visible facilitator. However that role descriptor too is potentially misleading. How can a teacher be a content expert when they are faced with a world full of experts through their students' laptops and tablets in the classroom? Mentor is another role term which carries connotations of holder of knowledge, yet teachers often learned the frameworks of their knowledge in a completely different world (in terms of knowledge dimensions and accessibility) from that of their students. What value can a mentor have for students in this brave new world? We do not seek to suggest that teachers are irrelevant to today's students; this simply underlines the inexact use of common terms for teacher roles.

The papers reviewed spent much time identifying lists of factors which were affecting teachers' roles and driving change. In relation to Web 2.0

technology some of those factors which teachers had to address were:

1. Diminished control over teaching and learning process.
2. Working in teams to develop learning resources rather than being sole arbiter of content, development and delivery.
3. 24/7 monitoring of blogs, email, forums, discussion boards, wikis and personalised student support.
4. The potential for teachers to become isolated and invisible within the team/technology (Sappey & Relf, 2010).
5. The need for a "committed local champion" (Jenkins, Browne, Walker & Hewitt, 2011).
6. Changes in practice driven by the use of e-portfolios and Open Educational Resources which necessitated considerable delivery change as well as personal learning for tutors.
7. Constraints on availability of or access to technology/software.
8. Understanding how digital resource use affected copyright issues and intellectual property.
9. "Above-campus" shared IT services among Higher Education Institutions (Wheeler & Waggener, 2009).
10. "Situative e-development" (Ooms, Burke, Linsey, & Heaton-Shrestha, 2008).
11. The model or understanding of and beliefs about learning held by the teacher (Connolly & Jones, 2007).
12. Mobile learning.

This systematic literature search for discussions of changing academic roles in relation to Web 2.0 or online/distance/blended and flexible learning supported by technology focussed only on peer-reviewed journal articles, but that meant there were some key resources missing. For example George Siemens, a prolific writer on Web 2.0 and the learning theory he and Stephen Downes advocate: connectivism where knowledge resides in networks, has promoted widely suggested academic roles as Amplifying, Curating, Way-finding and socially-driven sensemaking, Aggregating, Filtering, Modelling and Persistent presence (Siemens, 2010: np) and discusses the role of a teacher as "curatorial" (Siemens, 2007 np). The report produced by Conole and Alevizou (2010) for the Higher Education Academy in the UK also provides a useful summary of the educator's role and pressures on it to change (pp 85-87).

This brief review raises a number of questions. For example, although a broad sense of teacher role change is a common thread here, there is little precise understanding of what that role is, how it can be defined, even acknowledging that the role will always need to be adaptive in terms of context and learner group as well as subject discussed. Does this matter? I would suggest it does. As new teachers enter the profession, what kind of role models will they experience and how should they begin to construct a personal and professional notion of their roles and how those roles may develop, if there are very unclear guidelines in current use in the literature?

Also, the wide range of factors identified, which drive change in teacher roles, should be explored in more detail. It would be helpful to understand the relative impact of these factors and whether they all push in one direction concerning teacher roles, i.e. to loosen teachers' control of design and delivery and empower students to create knowledge, or perhaps whether there are counterbalances to these changes. An urgent question should also be explored concerning the changing role and interpretation of that role in relation to a teacher's influence on students' employability and preparation for employment or self-employment. It would be too easy for a teacher to step back from clear values and ensuring key topics were covered in a way which allowed the student to be evaluative and creative, yet made sure that graduates leave the Higher Education Institution able and

questioning, rather than unsure about the security and evidence base of their acquired knowledge. Whatever kind of role they adopt as technology changes the world of Higher Education, teachers' behaviours will still be copied and adapted by students: we need to make sure that what we model in relation to Web 2.0 is not diffidence or hostility, or even an inferiority complex driving defensiveness; we need to model good learning.

WHAT ARE THE CHARACTERISTICS OF WEB 2.0 WHICH HAVE FORCED CHANGE IN TEACHERS' ROLES?

One of the key changes Web 2.0 has brought about for teachers is the growth in distance learning and open online courses. Scale makes a major difference. Where once a teacher in HE may have had the luxury of a group of 20 students or fewer sitting around a table in a classroom debating ideas or listening to teacher-imparted information but capable of interrupting, the Web has put geographical or physical distance between teacher and learner and potentially has increased the ratio of learners to teacher hugely. This shifts the focus of the teacher away from content which must be delivered, to the process of designing and offering resources and activities for learning, and the processes by which the learners learn. In a Web 2.0 context, the teacher is one of many potential sources of information. While students are increasingly comfortable with digital technology in their private lives, they remain less able than most teachers to work out how to use this technology for their own learning (ECAR, 2012). The problem of learning to learn with technology is particularly acute in relation to the criticality, evaluation and synthesis of information. Teachers are having to face a brand new activity, that of intermediary between students and resources (Beaudoin, 1990) and this forces the pace for teachers to be able to monitor fast-changing resources, as well as developing skills in picking and choosing the best applications and software for their specific learning purposes (rather than falling prey to the latest gimmick). Furthermore, teachers have to maintain a hold on the fundamental principles of academic skills, which continue to be as rare among undergraduates as they ever were before Web 2.0. In fact, current technologies make it so easy to "cut and paste", and harvest relevant resources and information, that traditional academic skills of analysis, précis and logical argumentation are becoming less widely used in the student body. Where information is at the fingertips through mobile smart devices, it becomes harder to sift through and search for key arguments and put ideas together in a logical order, when they have been gathered from a wide range of web pages – it is much simpler for the student to string these together than to form them into a considered and cohesive whole.

As students become increasingly adept at media meshing (while using one device to receive content, the use of additional devices to search for supplementary information or connect with others about the content) and media stacking (using multiple devices at the same time for different purposes, for example checking email while watching TV or micro-blogging while watching video or other learning content), so the likelihood of sustained attention span on single PowerPoint slidesets in a classroom, or single learning activities within an online learning context decreases. In the UK, the Ofcom Communications Market Report 2013 found that 53% of adults are media multi-taskers (either stacking or meshing), while this applies to 81% of those owning a tablet device. However this is not particularly bad news. Students who are capable of media multi-tasking may use particularly creative ways to access and produce information in relation to academic tasks.

Another key feature with which teachers must grapple is the mobility of smart devices, whether or not we may consider laptops and tablets to be mobile devices, there is no doubt that a debate

has crystallised over the use of mobile devices in physical classroom spaces. What do students use their mobile devices for in terms of learning? The ECAR student survey (2013) suggests they use them to look up information, photograph information (e.g. slides being projected), to access digital resources such as videos, to record teachers and to take part in digital activities (such as polling for example). Clearly mobile devices can be used for learning anywhere, or at least anywhere with wifi. This enables out of classroom project based learning, the use of augmented reality and the opportunity to connect with learning beyond set class times. However, for students on campus, 74% of those students surveyed said that teachers banned or discouraged smartphone use in the classroom (equivalent figures for tablets were 30% and laptops 19%). This seems strange unless teachers are still simply frightened of students not attending to session teaching. Yet the appropriate use of these devices can add considerable value to learning – even in the classroom. For example, Laurillard (2012) neatly summarises types of learning and their relationships with digital technologies. She writes of learning through acquisition of knowledge by reading, listening and watching – all of which can be done physically and virtually – e.g. ebooks and videos on tablets. She also identifies learning through inquiry, where digital tools can be used to collect, analyse and evaluate data, learning through practice using simulations or virtual field trips, learning through production/creation, such as e-portfolios, photos, curation of ideas, and learning through discussion and collaboration using forums, wikis and video-conferencing. All these learning opportunities demonstrate that mobile learning using smart devices is not simply about a miniaturized version of portable e-learning. They can enable a greater connection with the environment, as well as connected classroom learning, personalized information management and digital literacy development (Kukulska-Hulme & Traxler, 2007).

DOES WEB 3.0 MAKE A FURTHER DIFFERENCE TO HOW TEACHERS TEACH AND HOW STUDENTS LEARN?

As the Web grows in volume and sophistication and increasingly complex algorithms take over more of the tasks we have been used to doing ourselves, so the nature and opportunities for learning change still further for students and teachers. The more we use the Web, the more is known and collected about our habits, our preferences and our behaviours. While this can sound scary, there is potential here to construct increasingly sophisticated dialogue with the Web and minimize routine tasks, particularly search tasks.

While it is difficult still to find a helpful and user-friendly definition of Web 3.0, this third generation notion can usefully describe a Web beyond document linkages which features machine-readable descriptions of documents and items, natural language searching, data-mining, and in particular database mining and artificial intelligence technologies.

How does and will such a Web affect learning and teaching? In one sense it is clear that learners (and, of course, teachers) will find it easier to track down sources and explanations of any concept or theory or application. Research careers built on mining quantitative data from different sources are likely to stumble when this activity can be machine-driven. We could take the cynical view and argue that all that is left for learners and teachers is to consume what the Web offers. As Massive Online Open Courses grow in sophistication, it will become much easier to pick up knowledge in a Just-In-Time fashion, making the traditional degree an unnecessary rite of passage.

However, there seem to be two areas in which degrees, or accreditations of packages of skills and knowledge and achievements, would still be important. The first relates to the early stage learning in any subject discipline, or multi-disciplinary contexts, where the learner lacks the vocabulary and knowledge structures to function effectively. Bodies of knowledge will not stop growing and the pressures on learners and teachers to become involved in new fields will increase. This introductory or early stage learning, on the basis of Vygotsky's ideas, suggests the need for an intermediary to facilitate learning in new fields. In some cases, Wikipedia happily fits the bill as intermediary, since its ever-growing connections and referenced information can offer rapid familiarization with new terminology. However this assumes a basis on which to construct knowledge, and getting to this point is better facilitated by a responsive teacher who has considerable expertise in the field and can design learning processes which take advantage of online resources at the same time ensuring that information is not simply collected, but is debated and constructed and applied.

The second area in which Higher Education can offer value is the process orientation discussed earlier. HE is not purely an end in itself, in its undergraduate form and increasingly postgraduate and doctoral forms, it exists to help learners prepare for the next stage of learning and activity in their lives – whether this is further learning or (self-)employment. In a paper in Higher Education Review (2011), Bourner, Greener and Rospigliosi discuss their notion of New Vocationalism. Whereas traditionally, the main aim of university education has been to acquire and ultimately to produce new knowledge, the New Vocationalism position is that the aim of university education is preparedness for learning, and knowledge acquisition and evaluation is only the means to that end. This is where pedagogy meets technology. Web 3.0 will be more than capable of delivering knowledge through natural questioning and dialogue with multiple sources and databases using machine-readable metadata. However the questioning, evaluating and creative process associated with higher order learning cannot be so simply delivered by a third party to the learning process. This remains a vital pre-occupation of university teachers and links back to the point made earlier that students are highly able with digital tools, but much less able to understand or intuit how to learn with them.

IN WHAT WAYS ARE HE TEACHER ROLES NOW TRANSFORMING?

In the earlier section of this chapter, which reviewed recent literature on HE teacher roles, the proposition was made that the names of roles were multiplying, but a clear understanding of what those roles actually meant was lacking. There appeared to be some consensus in the literature that the direction of change was to loosen teachers' control of the learning process and to empower students to take up control themselves. And this is mirrored in the literature demonstrating favourable outcomes to students who can learn to adopt self-directed strategies when working with blended or online courses. It is evident that a teacher in Higher Education is no longer the entire source of knowledge or expertise relating to what the student needs or wants to know. We have grown used to an increased pace of scholarship updating, as every academic field accumulates knowledge at an accelerating pace. Indeed, academics now find Web 2.0 technology vital to maintain and build knowledge networks with other academics across the globe and to communicate with students and colleagues and develop learning resources. In addition, Web 3.0 technology is increasingly helpful to track research impact, citations, and funding opportunities as well as organizing the infrastructure of teaching (such as timetabling, contracting, assessment, validation and review and sequential versions of materials).

There is an important issue here about role-modelling. There has been a tendency to see HE teachers prioritise materials presentation in classroom teaching and superb slidesets and videos are increasingly offered. This is clearly preferable to using poor slidesets, but there is a danger that

what teachers are modelling to their students is the art of presentation and entertainment, rather than the practice of learning. To some extent, the pace of change of knowledge and the increased user-friendliness of content development software has led teachers to focus on producing better and better slides, hyper-links, videos, podcasts, virtual reality scenarios etc etc. The problem this leads to is that students see finished articles and may fail to work out how they may be constructed and what happens when technology does not work according to plan, or delivers inappropriate or poor quality resources to their searches. If students need to learn academic process and skills of learning, then there has to be room for teachers to model these processes. This can help students to become more creative in and out of class; to make sense of a sometimes painful process of learning and to develop learning agility and resilience. I do not make a case for poor lecturing here, nor incomplete preparation. I do make a case for teachers being open to new directions proposed by students, setting up activities with open outcomes rather than closed right answers, and if necessary to model change of response where convincing arguments are put forward (Greener, 2009). Problem-based learning is one pedagogic approach which is increasing in popularity in HE but can really stretch the teacher's ingenuity and openness to learning, as students' learning, appropriately scaffolded, is encouraged through creativity and collaboration, not necessarily to achieve the teacher's view of problem solution, but to experience a process of problem-solving which is personally motivating and stimulates an appetite to learn. In problem-based learning, as discussed for example by Barrows and Tamblyn (1980), the teacher's role involves significant preparation of suitable triggers or tasks, and initially some structured facilitation, but through the process a gradual release of control, leading to strong supportive and stimulating teaching behaviours.

A paper by Harrison and Killion (2007) focuses on the leadership challenges for teachers, listing ten roles which may be helpful: resource provider, instructional specialist, curriculum specialist, classroom supporter, learning facilitator, mentor, school leader, data coach, catalyst for change, and finally, learner. Underlying this approach to role definition is a sense that teachers must grow into wider more open behaviours which work effectively with other sources of information and resources offered through the Web by many other experts. We cannot all be superheroes in teaching and we will have preferences for differing aspects of our roles, but the fundamental shift caused by Web technology's capabilities and affordances for learning does not just move the teacher's role from x to y, for example from expert presenter and controller of learning ("sage on the stage") to facilitator of learning ("guide on the side"). Instead there are several dimensions of role change to be addressed.

1. Sole author to curator
2. Loner to team player
3. Follower of tradition to creative accreditor of learning
4. Subject expert to owner and demonstrator of multiple skillsets

The move from sole author to curator is a simple outcome of the explosion of knowledge and the enabling affordances of technology to allow us to monitor and track scholarship developments and lateral connections between our own fields and others. As we learn to curate knowledge from multiple sources for the benefit of our students, we can use the help of expert communities in social networks, mailing lists, forums etc and use tools such as e-portfolio software to keep track of our activities and information, sharing the results with both students and colleagues and demonstrating these skills to others at the same time.

The move from loner to team player may seem like the opposite of reality for many teachers who feel stressed out in classrooms or in virtual environments, seemingly coping with endless new

software applications, routines and passwords just in order to deliver the basics of institutional e-learning demands. The only way forward is to break out from the solitude of trying to cope with steep learning curves on new technologies as well as increased professional demands and form teams and partnerships with other academic colleagues, learning technologists, student facilitators and advisors, so that together, the team can produce an outstanding learning experience for students.

The move from follower of tradition to creative accreditor of learning is a response to changed flexible learning patterns. For most teachers currently working in HE, the way we learned cannot be adequately reproduced today, given the massive changes introduced through technology in education. We have to move on. As we find excellent resources from across the world which can benefit our students, and as students are increasingly tempted to plagiarise from online sources, so our role moves towards increasingly creative ways of assessing knowledge and learning capability. Ultimately many universities may become simple accreditors of learning, with students learning much more flexibly from many institutions online and coming to us for accreditation of that experience. This still leaves plenty of room for academic development and teaching, provided it competes well with excellent standards worldwide.

Finally the move from single subject expert to owner and demonstrator of multiple skillsets is one which is echoed across many other professions. Technology may make many of our tasks easier, but at the same time, we have to learn how to use technology solutions to best advantage. This means that even if we are part of a teaching team and able to access specialist help, we have to gain an appreciation of the value of a wide range of technologies as well as learning to take a more multidisciplinary approach to Higher Education. This is challenging for all teachers, as we all enjoy certain comfort zones and would prefer to stay inside them.

FUTURE RESEARCH DIRECTIONS AND CONCLUDING COMMENTS

This chapter has discussed the wide-ranging impact of Web 2.0 and Web 3.0 on academic roles in Higher Education. We have looked at a series of questions, trying to identify traditional understanding of teacher roles and what exactly has happened through Web technologies which has so affected these roles. There is no doubt that there are advantages and disadvantages to both students and teachers from these learning technologies. Students, like teachers, are having to learn differently, particularly in increasingly favoured blended or fully online learning contexts. They, like teachers, are facing an avalanche of information which has somehow to be analysed and evaluated before it can become useful. Younger students, such as the Net Generation, may have lived their lives against a background of digital technology, unlike mature students and many teachers, but that does not mean they are any more capable of instantly grasping the learning opportunities afforded by the technology.

We have identified therefore the need for teachers to "stick to their knitting", to use a phrase borrowed from Peters and Waterman in their book In Search of Excellence. What good teachers know and continue to learn about pedagogy still counts and is still the most important contribution we can make to support today's learners. What we cannot do is stand still and ignore the waves of change from Web 2.0 and Web 3.0. It is one thing to acknowledge this personally as a teacher, but another to encourage institutions to change time-honoured ways of training university teachers. Digital technology is already enabling senior academic managers to track and audit capability of teachers, as well as student achievement, but the use of this information is sketchy at present. The traditional route for developing university teachers remains the gaining of a full-time PhD. This route was always intended to be a stepping stone either to further research or to take a teaching and research

place in the academy. However, the behaviours it develops and encourages are associated with the former roles of university teachers – to become sole authors, lone thinkers, followers of traditional academic practices and deep subject experts. I have made a case in this chapter for change in HE teaching roles, but this is unlikely to happen without substantial change in the way we prepare teachers for their roles. There are some excellent professional development courses in universities now which fully acknowledge the impact and opportunities of digital tools and techniques for teaching and learning. However there is still an insistence, in fact a growing one, on the rite of passage to academe which is the PhD. While a professional doctorate route into teaching is also possible, and desirable, the take-up of these part-taught doctorates with additional practitioner outcomes on top of normal doctoral requirements is low and dropout rates high. The way forward must be a significant review of the PhD tradition, not to relax standards in any way, but to develop research capability alongside teaching capability, and to do this with wide awareness of the demands of Web 2.0 and Web 3.0 technology for learning.

REFERENCES

Barrows, H. S., & Tamblyn, R. M. (1980). *Problem-based learning: An approach to medical education.* New York: Springer Publishing Company.

Beaudoin, M. (1990). The instructor's changing role in distance education. *American Journal of Distance Education, 4*(2), 21–29. doi:10.1080/08923649009526701

Bourner, T. (2008). The fully functioning university. *Higher Education Review, 40*(2), 26–46.

Bourner, T., Greener, S., & Rospigliosi, A. (2011). Graduate employability and the propensity to learn in employment: A new vocationalism. *Higher Education Review*, *43*(3), 5–30.

Connolly, M., Jones, C., & Jones, N. (2007). New approaches, new vision: Capturing teacher experiences in a brave new online world. *Open Learning*, *22*(1), 43–56. doi:10.1080/02680510601100150

Conole, G., & Alevizou, P. (2010). *A literature review of the use of web 2.0 tools in higher education*. Milton Keynes, UK: HEA.

Diaz, V., Garrett, P. B., Kinley, E. R., Moore, J. F., Schwartz, C. M., & Kohrman, P. (2009, May-June). Faculty development for the 21st century. *EDUCAUSE Review*, *44*(3), 46–55.

ECAR. (2012). *National study of undergraduate students and information technology*. Retrieved April 30th 2014, from http://www.educause.edu/ecar

ECAR. (2013). *National study of undergraduate students and information technology*. Retrieved 30th April 2014 from http://www.educause.edu/ecar

Greener, S. L. (2009). E-modelling – Helping learners to develop sound e-learning behaviours. *Electronic Journal of e-Learning, 7*(3), 265–272. Retrieved 8th June 2010 from http://www.ejel.org

Jenkins, M., Browne, T., Walker, R., & Hewitt, R. (2011). The development of technology enhanced learning: Findings from a 2008 survey of UK Higher Education Institutions. *Interactive Learning Environments*, *19*(5), 447–465. doi:10.1080/10494820903484429

Johnson, L., Adams Becker, S., Estrada, V., & Freeman, A. (2014). *NMC horizon report: 2014 higher education edition*. Austin, TX: The New Media Consortium.

Kukulska-Hulme, A., & Traxler, J. (2007). Designing for mobile and wireless learning. In H. Beetham & R. Sharpe (Eds.), *Rethinking pedagogy for a digital age: designing and delivering e-learning* (pp. 180–192). London, UK: Routledge.

Laurillard, D. (2012). *Teaching as a design science*. New York: Routledge.

Ooms, A., Burke, L., Linsey, T., & Heaton-Shrestha, C. (2008). Introducing e-developers to support a university's blended learning developments. *Research in Learning Technology*, *16*(2), 111–122. doi:10.1080/09687760802316307

Papert, S., & Harel, I. (1991). *Constructionism*. New York: Ablex Publishing Corporation.

Sappey, J., & Relf, S. (2010). Digital technology education and its impact on traditional academic roles and practice. *Journal of University Teaching and Learning Practice*, *7*(1). Retrieved from http://ro.uow.edu.au/jutlp/vol7/iss1/3

Siemens, G. (2007). *Networks, ecologies, and curatorial teaching*. Retrieved 8th January 2010 from http://www.connectivism.ca/blog/2007/08/networks_ecologies_and_curator.html

Siemens, G. (2010). Teaching in social and technological networks. *Connectivism blog*. Retrieved 20th April 2014 from http://www.connectivism.ca/?p=220/

UNESCO. (2004). *UNESCO online database*. Montreal, Canada: UNESCO Institute for Statistics. Retrieved 20th April 2014 from http://www.uis.unesco.org

Wheeler, B., & Waggener, S. (2009). Above-campus services: Shaping the promise of cloud computing for higher education. *EDUCAUSE Review*, *44*(6), 52.

ADDITIONAL READING

Beetham, H., & Sharpe, R. (2007). (Eds.) Rethinking pedagogy for a digital age: designing and delivering e-learning. London, UK: Routledge

Bourner, T., Greener, S., & Rospigliosi, A. (2011). Graduate employability and the propensity to learn in employment: A new vocationalism. *Higher Education Review, 43*(3), 5–30.

Bower, M., Hedberg, J. G., & Kuswara, A. (2010). A framework for Web 2.0 learning design. *Educational Media International, 47*(3), 177–198. doi:10.1080/09523987.2010.518811

British Journal of Educational Technology. Published by Wiley Available at: http://onlinelibrary.wiley.com/journal/10.1111/(ISSN)1467-8535

Clarke T., (2013). The advance of the MOOCs (massive open online courses): The impending globalisation of business education? *Education + Training, 55*(4), 403–413.

Cochrane, T., & Bateman, R. (2010). Smartphones give you wings: Pedagogical affordances of mobile Web 2.0. *Australasian Journal of Educational Technology, 26*(1), 1–14.

Conole, G. The seven C's of learning design Available at: http://www2.le.ac.uk/departments/beyond-distance-research-alliance/7Cs

Dron, J. (2007). *Control and constraint in e-learning.* IGI Global. doi:10.4018/978-1-59904-390-6

Dron, J., & Anderson, T. (2014). *Teaching crowds: learning and social media.* Au Press/Ubc Press.

ECAR (2013). *National study of undergraduate students and information technology,* 2013 Report (2013)

Greener, S. L. (2010). Plasticity: the online learning environment's potential to support varied learning styles and approaches. *Campus-Wide Information Systems 27*(4) 254-262 Emerald Group Publishing Limited. *Interactive Learning Environments.* A Routledge Open Access Journal published by Taylor and Francis. Available at: http://www.tandfonline.com/action/journalInformation?show=aimsScope&journalCode=nile20#.VBAtblRwaJA

Laurillard, D. (2002). *Rethinking university teaching. a conversational framework for the effective use of learning technologies.* London: Routledge. doi:10.4324/9780203304846

London, M. (2013). Generative team learning in Web 2.0 environments. *Journal of Management Development, 32*(1), 73–95. doi:10.1108/02621711311287035

Mallia, G. (2014). *The social classroom.* IGI Global. Information available at: http://www.gorgmallia.com/TheSocialClassroom_Editor.htm

Michael, K. (2012). Virtual classroom: Reflections of online learning. *Campus-Wide Information Systems, 29*(3), 156–165. doi:10.1108/10650741211243175

Miller, G., Benke, M., Chaloux, B., Ragan, L., & Schroeder, R. (2013). *Leading the e-learning transformation of Higher Education: meeting the challenges of technology and distance education.* Stylus Publishing.

NMC Horizon Report 2014 Higher Education. Available at: http://www.nmc.org/publications/2014-horizon-report-higher-ed

Owens, T. (2012). Hitting the nail on the head: The importance of specific staff development for effective blended learning. *Innovations in Education and Teaching International, 49*(4), 389–400. doi:10.1080/14703297.2012.728877

Siemens, G. Various publications on Technology Enhanced Learning and Learning Technologies. Available at: http://www.elearnspace.org/about.htm

Simuth, J., & Sarmany-Schuller, I. (2012). Principles for e-pedagogy. *Procedia: Social and Behavioral Sciences*, *46*, 4454–4456. doi:10.1016/j.sbspro.2012.06.274

KEY TERMS AND DEFINITIONS

Connectivism: A theoretical concept of learning for the digital age devised by Stephen Downes and George Siemens. Siemens' definition is "Connectivism is the integration of principles explored by chaos, network, and complexity and self-organization theories. Learning is a process that occurs within nebulous environments of shifting core elements – not entirely under the control of the individual. Learning (defined as actionable knowledge) can reside outside of ourselves (within an organization or a database), is focused on connecting specialized information sets, and the connections that enable us to learn more are more important than our current state of knowing. Connectivism is driven by the understanding that decisions are based on rapidly altering foundations. New information is continually being acquired. The ability to draw distinctions between important and unimportant information is vital. The ability to recognize when new information alters the landscape based on decisions made yesterday is also critical."

Constructionism: A learning theory from Seymour Papert based on Piaget's constructivism. Papert's definition is "Constructionism—the N word as opposed to the V word— shares contructivism's view of learning as "building knowledge structures" through progressive internalization of actions… It then adds the idea that this happens especially felicitously in a context where the learner is consciously engaged in constructing a public entity, whether it's a sand castle on the beach or a theory of the universe".

ECAR: Educause Center for Analysis and Research. Educause mission and objectives are available at http://www.educause.edu/about/mission-and-organization.

MOOC: Massive Online Open Course. This is a model of educational delivery which is normally structured in a similar way to traditional online higher education courses. Students watch lectures, read assigned material, participate in online discussions and forums, and complete quizzes and tests on the course material. MOOCs are usually provided by higher education institutions and partners, examples include Coursera, edX, and Udacity.

New Vocationalism: A re-definition of an approach to graduate employability where learning is the goal and the acquisition of knowledge is the means to that goal. The orientation is towards developing students' capacity and disposition to learn. Details available at: www.newvocationalism.org.

Web 2.0: A stage of World Wide Web development which includes features allowing user interaction, such as social networking, collaboration sites, image and video-sharing sites, wikis, and blogs.

Web 3.0: A further development stage of the World Wide Web attributed to John Markoff of the New York Times in 2006 based on standardization of data formats on the Web allowing machine processing of connections between documents (using the Resource Description Framework (RDF). Tim Berners-Lee proposed the name Semantic Web for such a Web of data linkages in 2001 and Semantic Web is often used as a synonym for Web 3.0. However the third generation Web is also facilitated by other developments such as ubiquitous connectivity and artificial intelligence technologies.

Chapter 2
Web 3.0 Technologies and Transformation of Pedagogical Activities

Tatyana Noskova
Herzen State Pedagogical University of Russia, Russia

Tatyana Pavlova
Herzen State Pedagogical University of Russia, Russia

Olga Iakovleva
Herzen State Pedagogical University of Russia, Russia

ABSTRACT

Web 3.0 creates the potential for implementation of new teaching strategies and new forms of teachers' professional pedagogical activities. Today, it is possible to assume the trends of Web 3.0 development. Most of these trends have been already revealed in the analysis of the current state of modern network technologies. New educational practices require both awareness of new opportunities in networking and acceptance and understanding of new educational strategies of learners. The chapter describes a concept of teachers' professional goals transformation in terms of Web 3.0, stressing movement towards learners' needs. The first pedagogical objective is to design the information educational environment. The second objective is to perceive a student via the informational environment. The third objective is to interact with other members of the informational environment. The fourth objective is to arrange the learning process. The fifth objective is to ensure professional self-development.

INTRODUCTION

During the last decade the issues of the web technologies have been actively discussed. The main reasons for the development of the web technologies - from Web 1.0 to Web 2.0 have been considered and identified. Today, however, there are witnessed some changes that allow to draw conclusions about the development of *Web 3.0*.

The basis of the Web 3.0 concept aims to implement possibilities of machining the information available on World Wide Web in various forms:

DOI: 10.4018/978-1-4666-8147-7.ch002

Semantic Web, 3D and mobile content, data hubs. This idea is at the crossroads of studies on artificial intelligence and Internet technologies. It raises new problems of knowledge spaces organization in the Internet, methods and tools for knowledge extraction from natural language texts, as well as the use of knowledge to create spaces of applied intelligent systems operating in the Internet.

Internet users in the contemporary environment of Web 2.0 are active not only in the information retrieval, but they are also included in the social communities and collaborative networking activities. We can assume that *Web 3.0* technologies will provide an opportunity for a user to modify and configure different electronic recourses, to increase own network environment, to personalize, to collaborate, to manage knowledge resources, to perform the new role of an expert in network societies. That means that a user will become an "expert" of his/her own information activities and needs.

The chapter aims to focus on the question: how pedagogical activities will be transformed in the context of Web 3.0? It is obvious that the main groups of professional teacher's objectives will change in terms of Web 3.0 technologies, so it is necessary to outline the main trends in this way. Besides, the position of a learner in the high-tech knowledge society will change drastically: a learner needs to be prepared to act as an active personality, to be able to choose an individual educational route, to adopt the strategy of *lifelong learning*. The chapter is based on different areas of contemporary surveys in the field of Web.3, with the special focus on the ideas of Russian researchers.

RESEARCH BACKGROUND. WEB 3.0: THE NEW FORM OF REPRESENTATION, COMPREHENSION, AND USE OF INFORMATION. DISCUSSIONS ON THE TOPIC

Researchers have not come to a consensus about the concept of Web 3.0 yet. For some researchers it is more important to understand the processes unfolding in the Internet space from the position of developing information technology: the use of knowledge to create applied intelligent systems, adaptive content systems, and virtual reality systems operating in the Internet. For other researchers it is the behavior of Internet users that attracts attention: for example, the processes related to the accounting request and customer behavior.

Thus, A. Dolgin, the creator of the customized recommendations website imhonet.ru, believes that the social aspects of *Web 3.0* should come to the foreground. In his opinion the main difference between Web 3.0 and Web 2.0 is that users do not only generate content themselves, but they also certify it: note what needs attention of reference groups and communities they are involved (Dolgin, 2008). This idea is valuable precisely for its focus on protecting the interests of consumers, but it is contrary to the more common description of the term "Web 3.0" given by J. Calacanis (American Internet entrepreneur and blogger): Web 3.0 is a combination of high-quality content and services that are created by talented professionals on the technology platform Web 2.0. Web 3.0 is the Internet concept which involves the synthesis of the strengths of Web 1.0 and Web 2.0: Internet projects uniting professionals, but built on a network, polycentric principle (Calacanis, 2007).

Contradiction between these two approaches to Web 3.0 (Web 3.0 as a self-organizing system of consumers' recommendations and Web 3.0

as a system of content and services generation produced by a network of professionals) may be withdrawn within the concept of knowledge management (Andreeva, 2013). Web 3.0 should be understood as a new profession for people and new tools for people. This new profession - knowledge manager - should become a link between Web 1.0 (content) and Web 2.0 (communities and communication services). Thus, Web 3.0 can be understood as a hierarchical version of Web 2.0, based on the principles of self-organization, but with a class of professional experts. For example, this means the formation of consumer community forums discussing the quality of various product groups around the informational core of a portal. In this work, the forum should be monitored by representatives of the portal that will provide an effective control and moderation of irresponsible ideas and advice. Thus, all advantages of Web 2.0 are summarized in the collective experience of a large number of users.

We can say that we witness the development of a new class of technologies that allow identifying a user not as an abstract visitor, but as a person, for whom more detailed information is given in accordance with the specific request.

For example, when a person asks a stranger's advice about how to act in some situations, it is important to give more details about the situation. After all, the more information is given the better is the advice. But if a person is drawn to a close friend known for many years, the one is unlikely to require additional information. It is similar with the *Semantic Web*: the more information a user tells about oneself, the more accurate solution will be given from the online services. The system constantly monitors the choices and actions of users, so data is constantly being collected. Consequently, Web 3.0 is a completely different conceptual model of the functioning of the Internet.

Here are examples of existing and rapidly developing *semantic tools*:

- Tools for virtual collaboration, co-creation and annotation of documents, including semantic wiki (AceWiki, Cicero, Mymory, Kiwi, Compendium, Debategraph, PROWE);
- Semantic information search tools (Swoogle, VisiNav, Twine, Watson, ArnetMiner);
- Repositories and virtual learning environments that import and export their data into semantic formats (Freebase, DBpedia, Project Gutenberg, MyExperiment);
- Repositories for scientific resources that can provide metadata in RDF (DSpace, EPrints);
- Tools and services that allow publishing databases interoperable semantic formats (D2R Server, TALIS, Virtuoso, RKBexplorer, Yahoo! SearchMonkey).

One of the projects on exploring the possibilities of Web 3.0 technologies, their application in education is the Ensemble project, UK (Martinez-Garcia & Morris, 2012). The project "Ensemble: Semantic Technologies for the Enhancement of Case Based Learning" is one of eight projects co-funded by ESRC (Economic and Social Research Council, the British Council Economic and Social Research) and EPSRC (Engineering and Physical Sciences Research Council, the British Council of Engineering and physical Sciences Research) in the framework of teaching and Learning Research Programme (TLRP, teaching and learning program of the Council for economic and Social Research). This research project started in October 2008, and series of follow-up projects started in 2011 and 2012. The project was oriented toward developing of better understanding of the nature of case-based learning in different settings, with the special focus on the potential for *Semantic Web* technologies to support, enhance, and transform existing practice. The idea of learners is engaged not only with existing cases written by teachers or other experts, but also in the construction and reconstruction of the cases themselves corresponds to the basic logic of Web 3.0.

WEB 3.0 AND NEW TEACHING STRATEGIES

Web 3.0 creates the potential for implementation of new teaching strategies and new forms of teachers' *professional activities*. New educational practices require both awareness of new technical opportunities in networking, the movement towards learners' also needs both acceptance and understanding of new informational behavior of students and young people. Our concept distinguishes five groups of professional teacher's objectives changing in terms of Web 3.0. The first objective is to design the information educational environment, primarily its resources (for example, with the use of micro formats and semantic search, virtual learning objects, *Open Educational Resources*). The second objective is to perceive a student via the informational environment, via the informational traces and his behavior in network collaboration. In this case there can be used such instruments as semantic profile of resource acquisition, social network communications profile, individual educational needs monitoring, positions and interests detection, interaction style analysis. The third objective is to interact with different members of the information environment: colleagues, social partners. Such interactions can take place on the base of trans-disciplinary semantic knowledge networks; social communities of innovators; communities of professional experience exchange. The fourth objective is to arrange the learning process. In this case the most perspective are computer-aided tools and non-linear communication based on the information request of youth, individualization and personalization. The fifth objective is to ensure professional self-development: learning new IT, new educational practices, self-development in a virtual environment. Let us consider the above

problems. It is obvious that today we can only assume the trends of Web 3.0 development. However, most of these trends have been already revealed in the analysis of the current state of modern network technologies.

Objective 1: WEB 3.0 in Design of the Information Educational Environment

It should be understood that the development of technologies does not occur in isolation. There is an influence on individual as the main *consumer* and transducer of technologies. In educational activities the use of Web 3.0 presupposes understanding of the processes taking place in the Internet space in terms of both information technologies and behavior of Internet users. In this environment there is an entirely new function of knowledge which radically changes the approaches to the creation of an electronic resource as the base of the educational process in the Web 3.0 space (Noskova & Pavlova, 2013). Traditionally, educational environment contains a set of prepared *digital educational resources*, complemented with results of individual information retrieval. Moreover, the latter does not play a significant role in the educational activity, because it involves a huge number of poorly structured, fragmented, not always adequate and relevant information. Web 3.0 technologies contribute to the new information organization for learner, for greater account of his individual request. Accordingly, new elements must be taken into account in design of virtual learning environments such as semantic search tools, tools for virtual collaboration, repositories using data in semantic formats, open repositories, virtual reality multimedia environments. Educational environment as a set of educational resources for all students is transformed into a set of individual educational environments and environments for collective interaction. In such changing conditions of professional activity the teacher on the one hand appears an expert accompanying students in their interaction with numerous, adaptable educational resources. On the other hand the teacher must realize that other experts who have contributed to the creation of electronic resources can be involved in this process as well.

Information search nowadays is one of the main changing processes. Modern trends in the development of search tools are: the inclusion of features that enable the automatic adaptation of the system taking into account the level of knowledge and specific queries; the possibilities to perceive the natural language queries; the use of artificial intelligence in order to give relevant information and pertinence. But such human machine interactions become effective only with a clear understanding of a user adaptation functions and the intelligent application of problem solving. In particular, modern information retrieval systems use "intelligent agents" - small programs that have the ability to educate themselves and act independently. Having a connection with a user's computer, they act as personal assistants performing series of tasks and using knowledge of needs and interests of a particular user. Intelligent robots are independent net-search agents, and some of them do not only analyze keywords, but also carry out semantic analysis of online information, revealing the degree of semantic relevance. A special group of search automation is associated with user's interaction with the resources of full-text databases. They are based on the use of technologies of syntactic and morphological analysis of a text (on the breakdown of the elements that are recognized by the program) and online processing of natural language texts. These methods are used to find specific facts, statistics, etc., which cannot be found in other ways. Usually a search in full-text databases is performed with the use of morphological analyzers which allow finding automatically existing word forms by fragments of a word, or a phrase.

Still up to 85% of new knowledge analysts get by studying texts. In the near future the systems with maximum automated ETL-processes of

structuring content will become the most popular (ETL – "extract, transform, load"). An important feature of such systems is a function of the operational analysis of information obtained on request to select the future direction of research documents (autopilot research directions), performed with the help of text mining techniques. The most urgent facilities include: text mining technology for isolation of factual information about the objects in view with the help of anaphoric references to them (pronoun reference to the object named in the text); indecipherable search; thematic and tonal (accurate and complete) rubrics creation; cluster analysis of documents collections; selection of key topics; construction of annotations; construction of multidimensional frequency distributions of documents and their study using OLAP- technologies; text mining techniques to determine the direction of research in significant documents collections and to extract new knowledge.

Open sources of information make available a huge number of publications and thus pose the problem of efficient processing of large volumes of documents. *Automatic annotation* provides compressed sense of primary sources in the form of summaries, and thus several times increases the speed of analysis. However, experience shows that the annotations as static results are used in the analysis of the "paper" documents. So, during the analysis of electronic documents collections more demonstrative and structured presentation of the content is provided by an interactive map of semantic interrelations of documents. Modern tools of text processing analysis have automatic systems of abstract compilation. Moreover, there are two approaches to solving this problem. In the first approach, the annotator program extracts from the original a small amount of fragments in which the content of the document is represented most completely: containing query terms; sentence fragments with the environment in a few words and terms, etc. In more advanced systems, the key themes of the document are directly distinguished (but not co-reference links to them). In the second approach an abstract represents a document with a brief synthesized content. Abstract formed in accordance with the first approach is qualitatively behind the second one, resulting from the synthesis. To improve the quality of annotation it is necessary to solve the problem of processing co reference links in the Russian language (Kapitonov & Tyutyunnik, 2013). Another problem encountered in the synthesis of annotation is the lack of means of semantic analysis and synthesis of text in Russian, so annotation services oriented either to the narrow subject area, or require human intervention. Most programs annotators are based on the principle of text fragments selection. However, the research systems focused on Web-documents annotation are turning out to be more efficient. Each document is calculated by "weight" (volume), based on information about the keywords, relevant phrases, and their place in the text and in the query. After that all the results are ranked, and an abstract is made out of a few sentences of a maximum "weight". The system "Analytical Courier" abstracts automatically fragments from documents on the base of the main themes of the document.

Very often the *dynamic analysis of thematic structure of publications* is needed. Unlike auto rubrics, running in the background, analysis of thematic structure of obtained documents is produced quickly. The cluster analysis method is used to analyze new problems or events in which the thematic structure is dynamic and unstable. When there are a large number of publications concerning the problem, it is important to identify the main and the most representative groups - clusters. So, in the news stream "Yandex.News" messages are automatically grouped into clusters corresponding to the main events. It must be remembered that in the processing of pages by search services only a small part of all text messages is taken into an account, and this leads to a significant noise in the analytical treatment. However, in contrast to news sites, the purpose of which is to make a summary of daily news, in the information-analytical

systems a user needs to understand the archive is often collected within a few years. For example, in the "Analytical Courier" when combined in a cluster common vocabulary and field values cards of documents are considered. Clusters may overlap, indicating their relationship, so a list of documents of any cluster or separate documents can be analyzed.

Clustering allows dividing a selection of documents into statistical semantic groups, but often a more subtle tool to detect rare but important linkages between themes collection is needed. So, *semantic maps of documents collections* are used. In this case, the object of analysis is the semantic map of documents interrelations, not the documents themselves. Map is a directed graph, in which the size of the nodes and the thickness of lines correspond to the relative weight of them. Links can be either typical (defined semantic type connection) or logical (installed fact of their existence). Arrows show the connection of cause and effect relationship between topics – the more particular topic indicated by an arrow. The thickness of arrows between themes reflects the importance. Selecting a node on the map analyst immersed in topics directly related to the subject, increasing the scale of the map and centering the map on the topic. Then the composition of the map will change: there will be topics that are most closely associated with the selected. This method of analysis is often used for joint analysis of multiple maps, search for similar situations or semantic patterns in different maps and other tasks.

Widespread use of artificial intelligence methods allows generating hypotheses - suggestions for further research. In this case *data mining* is used (Berry, 2004). Typical technology of problem linkages analysis includes the following phases: preparation of document lists upon request; semantic maps acquisition; documents view due selected order; cluster analysis of these documents; analysis of documents relevant clusters; a summary of the communication structure of topics. Specialists in many areas need to work in the information converted to a form of its involvement in the implementation of productive professional actions.

There are alternative opportunities of information retrieval, which a user also needs to master. Mechanisms using cluster analysis (data clustering) provide better presentation of search results, because they are organized into a structure. This method helps to assign certain categories or topics of documents and search results. Cluster is understood as a complex, a bunch, or a group. Clustering is aimed at - as far as possible - sorting the search results into one or more groups, and thus retrieving the results from all groups. A successful result depends on predefined groups and categories, themes or layers, which in turn determine the keywords and professional terms. The document must be properly classified so it can be assigned to a group. Reaching this goal is not always simple. To do it, the search engine reads and then examines the data and metadata documents, analyzes the contents of the document on the basis of statistical calculations (taking into account the frequency of occurrence of letters, syllables and words, the order of phrases, as well as the length of words and sentences), or uses linguistic analysis algorithms. The more accurate the data are, the more accurately can a document be selected from a particular group.

Specific search tools allow a user to interpret the results, starting from the issued clusters - categories. For example, information retrieval system Carrot Search (http://search.carrotsearch.com) graphically produces clusters of search results (bookmark FoamTree).

Visual search tools and visual search engines are a group of search tools based on concept maps (Concept-Mapping Search Engines). It is closely associated with the semantic search approach, which tries to break the data area into the semantic area, with the possibility of any degree of detail. This is the list of the most successful and well-known visual search engines, which are based on the ideology of maps: LivePlasma - liveplasma.

com, Quintura - quintura.com, Spezify - spezify.com, Kartoo - kartoo.com. Basically they do not give the traditional links on the search results, instead they generate links to nodes of concept maps (some of this is almost equivalent to the well-known concept of "tag clouds"), which are dynamically generated by the search. After that, a user is encouraged to follow one of the above topics for further detail and immersion in topics of interest issue. The appropriate cloud search results can be embedded in a web-site or shared via e-mail with other users (in the form of Flash). The Kartoo system shows the connection between the concepts of objects. Kartoo is an attempt to create a "mini-map" of the Internet, so the system has great prospects. The constructed concept maps can be saved, printed or filtered with special filters to quickly select relevant semantic zones. The results of such information retrieval are effectively handled in the same graphical forms.

Processing of information, obtained in the result of a search, determines its effectiveness in a variety of professional tasks. Effectiveness of information can be detected only in an adequate information system. Out of such system any information is absolutely passive. However, when information is included into an appropriate system according to its semantics it can be used to construct a particular information action.

For example, the issues of electronic educational resources structuring and building based on *micro format* are very important. The main aim of micro format is to make web pages as comfortable as possible for semantic analysis methods of text mining. The technologies allow use micro formats tags to mark a web page by highlighting the text elements and denoting their parameters: sentence, word, figure, table, formula, title, paragraph, collocation, new term, part of speech, causal relationships. This layout of the proposals greatly improves the reliability of professional search information on the Internet.

In the creation of the resource base of the educational process there can be used a concept of a disciplinary semantic network that meets the requirements of modern educational systems. Another approach may develop multidisciplinary web resources based on ontology knowledge and thesaurus (Boykov, Zakharov, Karyaeva & Sokolov, 2013). Thesaurus is a web resource, including domain-specific directory, information retrieval tools and tools for further analyzes (Sitnic, Vagarina & Melnikova, 2011). There are many resources to address the specified objectives. In particular thesaurus WordNet, which is represented in many languages, is designed for structuring parts of speech. Feature serves as a resource map of words with a similar meaning as synonymous series. In addition, the popular thesaurus Mesh, indexing articles on medicine, is a unique systematic resource in terms of organization of knowledge.

Currently *virtual reality* technologies are actively developing. Consequently, it is possible that *Web 3.0* will widely use virtual reality technologies. There are several ways of "immersion" in virtual reality:

- Cab Simulators (a user is in a moving cab, equipped with a surround sound system, fully simulating the internal arrangement of the cockpit or land vehicle. Cab windows replaced with high-resolution computer monitors);
- Projected Reality (virtual objects are projected onto a large screen, as if a user becomes a participant of a film);
- Augmented Reality (graphical information is projected onto a transparent screen through which a user can see the real-world objects, thus obtaining information on the additional details);
- Tele-presence (using cameras and microphones that transmit information via the communication channels, a user watches the scene from a distance. Such technology is used in telemedicine);

- Desktop virtual reality (modeled objects are displayed on a PC monitor with the use of a combination of three-dimensional graphics and stereo);
- Visually Coupled Displays (helmet, which houses screens capable of carrying conventional image, and separately for the left and right eye to create a stereo effect. Special tracking device coordinate space the user's head, according to which the visible image is changed).

In the near future the following areas of applications of virtual reality systems will develop most intensively:

- Entertainment (3D video movies, 3D rides, 3D games, 3D photos, etc.);
- Educational systems (virtual storytelling system accelerated learning, etc.);
- Scientific applications (induced reality display of scientific data, for example, nanotechnology, micro-world, physical processes, etc.);
- Military applications (simulators, case rooms, control centers, etc.);
- Business applications (VIP-demonstration, exhibition technology mapping multidimensional management information, etc.).

Virtual reality technologies are widely used in simulators for pilots, astronauts, rescuers, doctors, drivers of heavy vehicles, in those cases where training in the real environment is too expensive and dangerous. Areas of virtual reality use also can be mentioned such as the applications of complex engineering structures visualization (nuclear power plants, ships and submarines), simulation of emergencies and disasters while eliminating their consequences, medical imaging, simulation of spacecraft and the creation of virtual laboratories in space, design and build complex machines.

In education, virtual reality systems have very good prospects, for example, in the creation of virtual tutorials and laboratories. Techniques and so-called virtual narrative can be implemented with the help of virtual reality systems. For example, it can be a virtual planetarium in which student "moves on a starship" from planet to planet and issues text, sound and graphic representation of planets. Thus, a student becomes a participant of a story - these technologies are called virtual storytelling or virtual narrative.

The most promising areas in the field of business applications are the applications related to decision support systems and brainstorming. Business information is contained in the multidimensional data arrays. When there is a lot of information it is practically impossible to analyze data in a numerical form. And even the form of planar graphs is not sufficient. But if several flat presentation slides are combined in one three-dimensional scene, it becomes easier to understand the behavior of the object of study.

Professional activities with the use of virtual reality require psychological, technological readiness to the fulfillment of professional tasks in similar circumstances. It also is associated with the change in distribution and concentration, increase in the proportion of self-control and mutual control (joint activities in virtual environments).

Objective 2: The Perception of a Student via the Informational Environment

All information and communication actions of each student are saved in the network environment. It is possible that *Web 3.0* will provide teachers special tools for creating semantic and social portraits of distant learners. Through the machine and "hand" analyze methods there can be formed users' "portraits" to evaluate competences. This approach is the basis of pedagogical "vision" of a learner who interacts with the network educational resources and initiates remote communication for their adoption and mastering. During the remote and separated in time interactions there can be built

a user's image in various aspects: semantic profile and social profile. By the analysis of an electronic portfolio it is possible to assess the productivity of the learning activities, the personal characteristics of a student – learning goals and strategies, learning problems and, consequently, provide timely help in resolving the arising difficulties.

Teacher who uses traditional methodology does not require such information. The process of students' activities in a virtual environment is not significant for such a teacher, who is interested in results students demonstrate in classroom or in their completed works. The virtual learning environment using Web 3.0 technologies is based on a flexible user interaction with a variety of adaptable resources and *collaboration* in online communities with experts support. Accordingly, students' educational outcomes, challenges and achievements can be shown only in the network space. A teacher, along with the perception of student in the classroom interaction must learn to exercise perception in a new space of educational activity, via the informational environment. There are contrasting approaches to the use of information tools for perception, monitoring and correction of learner's educational behavior in a virtual environment: learner activated e-portfolio and more automated tracking of learner activities.

The process of creating a learner's *semantic profile* in the context of actions with the electronic resources of the environment can be considered on the basis of modern algorithms of the Internet search engines (Banokin & Vichugov, 2012). Behavior and user's preferences have become increasingly important in the exploratory analysis of web applications. Algorithms of websites ranking have become able to consider a user's behavior on a separate web page. There is a need to provide better and more relevant content to user's preferences, as well as a general rise in the level of satisfaction from using an application. Such tasks of web application developers have made possible to provide information relevant to user's preferences, improving behavior metrics. Usually there are the following metrics for the analysis of user's behavior on the web site: depth of view, duration of the visit, referrer, device type, geographical location. Customizing the appearance and content of a single page, in accordance with user's interests, is one of the effective solutions to achieve this goal. Semantic analyzer, executable on the client side, and generator and semantic attributes, executable on the server side can make semantic analysis of the information and dynamically adjust the location and layout of the content in accordance with the needs of a particular user. Prospective applications of this architecture can be applications that run on the principle of social networks and the large heterogeneity of different users' interests.

The process of creating a learner's *social profile* is also very important (Noskova, Kulikova, Pavlova & Yakovleva, 2013). Unlike semantic profile, social profile exhibits personal communication and social activity in the educational network environment interactions: with whom, how much, for what purpose a learner interacts; how the tasks are solved to reach planned educational purposes. This allows to some extent to identify the user's communication circuit connections. The network structure of these systems allows, on the one hand, to organize a private communication space, on the other hand – to make it possible to track human contacts and to establish informal networks of common "friends", to identify interaction leaders and to trace what problems are solved jointly by members of the group. For example, a reputation in the implementation of information effects can be researched. A number of network models allow formulating and solving the problem of information management. In the social networks agents often do not have sufficient information to make decisions or cannot handle it alone, so their decisions can be based on observed their decisions or representations of other agents (social influence). Social networks play a major role in the dissemination of information and ideas among their members.

In the process of student's electronic educational network interactions there accumulates a portfolio that a teacher can track to quickly correct student's activities. In general, this is the *network electronic portfolio*. Different types of portfolios can be accumulated. An educational electronic portfolio can be defined as a collection of works that a student has collected and organized. Such a portfolio reflects the learning process in order to present the results of a student's achievements and show learning progress over time (Barrett, 2011). *Work Portfolio* can be defined as a collection of digital archives of personal information, a reflective journal of own materials. A proceeding of the working part of the electronic portfolio is not necessarily to be published online. It can be stored on the server and be accessible only to the owner; access can be restricted partially or completely by the decision of the author. *Career Portfolio* can be defined as a tool for maintenance and presentation of the learning results, achievements and future plans with the help of the latest technologies. In this way an electronic portfolio allows both the teacher and the learner analyze and evaluate the achievements and make plans for the future on this basis.

The idea of *personal learning environment* is closely connected with the contemporary state of Web development (Johnson & Sherlock, 2014; Zubrinic & Kalpic, 2008). Individual, personalized learning environment of student's network activities accumulated and processed all information resources, communication resources as products of communication operations. Information stored in the networked environment can be marked by dates and time of occurrence. This is a special resource management - the subject of systematic analysis and sequencing of educational activities for students. Network portfolio, which stores all results, the products of student's activity during the course of development allows analyzing and assessing progress in the educational activities.

Objective 3: The Interaction with Other Members of the Information Environment

The change of the interaction with other members of the information environment is obvious in the context of *Web 3.0*. There can be numbered several key features of this new interaction in the process of solving educational problems: the use of a variety of sign systems, the implementation of information exchanges, the possession of a wide range of linguistic resources, the change of perception in the information environment.

The first feature is the use of a variety of sign systems to solve professional problems. In general sign system is an ordered set of uniformly interpreted messages, signals that can be exchanged during the interaction. Sometimes sign systems help structure the process of interaction with the purpose of giving some adequacy in terms of the reactions of the participants on different "signs". The most obvious example of such a sign system is a traditional language (in the written or in the oral form). But there are other examples of iconic systems: proposals of scientific theories, pieces of art, alarm systems in society and nature, systems of states, input and output signals of various machines and automats, programs, and algorithms for the man-machine "dialogue". As sign systems also can be considered "languages" of Fine Arts, theater, film and music, as well as any complex control systems, viewed from the standpoint of cybernetics, devices and circuits, living organisms and their subsystems (e.g., central nervous system), production and social associations and the society in general.

Thus, a person in the information environment needs to operate various sign systems and perform transcoding information from one sign system to another. Semiotic competence plays a very important role (Goncharov, Goncharova & Koroleva, 2008). For example, this competence is required in such situations as carrying out a verbal description of multimedia materials (in particular, for their

annotation), writing and making changes to a program codes, representing arrays of written texts in visual form, making a visual thesaurus. Modern information environment sets new parameters of visual form: interactivity, cross-references, data visualization, and communication visualization. The principle of using abstract data as a form of visual design is widely used in various types of art projects. In particular, the building of the Jewish Museum in Berlin (D. Libeskind's project) was designed by combining the geographic map residence of Jews living in the vicinity of the museum during the Second World War and the surface of the building (Starostova, 2013).

The second feature is the implementation of information exchanges. A person should be ready to implement information exchanges and communication with the basic requirements and characteristics of the information environment (Noskova, 2011, 2013). What are the basic requirements to be met by information exchanges?

The first requirement is the audience coverage. The information needs to be compliant with the target audience of its consumers, and possible to be released to the global audience. Modern information feature is the available set of content production points. This trend is most clearly presented on the basis of social services, where the information is available to the public, usually for free.

The second requirement is usability. It means that content production (in particular, on the basis of social media), does not require special skills and training. Any user with access to the Internet and signed up for a social network or blog can produce a content.

The third requirement is the speed of response. Information environment allows to publish information and to receive a response almost immediately.

The fourth requirement is the variability of messages. Message can be edited unlimited number of times online.

Posts of the authors in the information environment based on social media are viewed by thousands of subscribers. News and photos post are actively discussed, distributed in the network in other blogs and often quoted in the media, or serve as materials for journalistic publications. It is therefore necessary to select two areas of professional competence: the first is connected with the ability to navigate the social media space; second is the readiness to act as a source of information.

The third feature is the possession of a wide range of linguistic resources. An important characteristic of the communicative component of a professional competence is the concept of a "linguistic personality". Linguistic personality in the broadest sense is interpreted as a set of abilities and characteristics which helps a person to create and perceive texts. Linguistic personality is composed of several components: verbal-semantic (vocabulary), cognitive (speech and intellectual activity), pragmatic (motivations, intentions, and attitudes). On the formation of a linguistic personality affect such characteristics as: social status, occupation, gender, age, native language.

The informational environment has the affordances to encourage the rapid vocabulary expansion (due to the breadth of communication links), the development of coherent speech, mastering different styles of speech and writing (business speech, artistic speech), mastering skills of solving educational, extracurricular, professional tasks in oral form (discussions in the Internet, dialogue with colleagues, parents). Moreover, teacher today needs to understand that along with the usual factors affecting the development of child's speech (communication with peers, reading, adult personal pattern) there is a very important information environment, containing a rich variety of communication samples. In the virtual environment a personality is often replaced by a produced text, not only written but also oral and audiovisual. It is therefore important to direct child's attention to the diversity of speech samples in the information environment: news reports, audio, texts of writers and poets (blogs, radio and television programs), and speech developing online games. It is necessary to demonstrate the correct speech examples in child's daily life.

The fourth feature is the change of perception in the information environment. Communication tasks in the information environment have certain specifics. The transformation of many components of verbal communication occurs: the reduction of paralinguistic communication components, the change of lexical and grammatical features of speech. Text editing programs perform a routine part of writing activity, but not substitute for the development of written communicative skills (literacy, spelling, style of speech).

Solving communication tasks in the information environment is widespread today, for example, in remote psychological counseling (cyber consulting). Psychological counseling via the Internet is taking place when qualified psychological assistance is necessary. Some people are much easier to communicate at a distance than in the office of a psychologist: in familiar home environment people feel much more comfortable and protected than in the psychologist reception. If during a long life period a person experiences stress, confusion or uncertainty of the decisions correctness, modern information technology offers not only the traditional appointment with a psychologist, but gaining psychological counseling, proceeding online on the professional advisory web-sites Internet. So, a person (a client) gains an Internet psychologist's help.

Objective 4: The Arrangement of the Learning Process

With the development of Web 2.0 there have been formed the prerequisites for the new approaches of the educational process design change. Greatest conversions in this area have been associated with the use of social media in the learning process.

Social media is a relatively new phenomenon interesting for its nature: the users themselves, in joint activities, provide the overall content. Thus, the educational process transforms with the influence of media environment in two ways: on the one hand, the reflection of external social processes; on the other hand, the activity of each person. Today, the term "social media" is used to describe new forms of communication between content producers and its consumers. Such forms of communication determine the importance of co-productive content as the final product of users' activities. For example, a reader or subscriber of a blog can serve as a commenter, reporter, photographer and editor of this service. Social media is a set of online technologies that allow users to communicate with each other: users can share their views, experiences and knowledge, interact, and establish contacts, share news, information, videos, photos, music, and links. Up to these features users obtains the main advantages of information access: not only speed, but possibility of immediate response and the ability to interact directly with content creators.

In Web 2.0 there occur some limitations in educational process: multiple duplicate content; low bound of the allocated content despite hyperlinked space; failure to do an exhaustive sampling of some topics. Solving this problem involves the use of ontologies, *semantic web* that helps a user to operate in the dense information space. *Web 3.0* technologies tend not to reject, but enrich the opportunities of Web 2.0 for example by the intellectual mediation. This requires changes in resource equipping of educational process with semantic interoperability based on a common data representation domain. The use of ontological approach to provide a choice of optimum training tactics can be developed. Ontological specification of information resources allows creating personalized training collection. Conceptual foundation of training courses should be represented in ontological model domains.

In educational communication appears a bi-moderating phenomenon: students become both expert managers and authors. Small online communities of learners become system units of the educational process to conduct proactive information and communication activities, to create personally meaningful and authentic content. There is a new kind of interaction of students and teachers as participants of learning network space in which there are conditions for individual and collective socialization and self-realization in order of solve educational tasks.

Educational management in network space requires specific pedagogical skills and abilities (organizational, technical and pedagogical), based on understanding the characteristics of the network community and differences between moderated and no moderated network space. Understanding the architecture of the communication space, structuring information, educational goals and objectives, communication activities are the aspects of the curriculum based on categorization of knowledge.

The development of social media allows finding out social solutions for a wide range of educational objectives. It's not just the possibility to share files, use communication services, and update person's status in information process. According to distinctive features and basic principles of social media (Peskova, 2011) there appears the opportunity to change main features of educational process: interactivity, replication, content on demand, engagement, reach of audience and accessibility, usability, immediacy or speed of response. Thus, these trends are characteristic of contemporary educational process. Learners aim to have common interests, share knowledge, exchange experience and be involved in mutual learning.

Cloud technologies are the "ecosystem" of social media. In 2012, the research agency Gartner published materials, which have proved the relationship of social media, cloud and mobile technologies: Mobile devices, cloud computing and social media form a new ecosystem of information technology, where the main driving forces are the end users. Indeed, the main educational profit of this kind of tools is the learning activity and creativity of students.

The fundamental difference of the social situation of modern mankind is the expansion of the information and socio-cultural space that has no meaningful structural and logical connections. This space is based on the concept of hypertext and hypermedia, where each element is associated with a number of others. Modern electronic environment provides an independent, personalized, mobile access to multi-format information and communication services. To prepare person to lifelong study and self-education in such conditions, the institutional based study process should reflect these features. It is important that in a virtual educational environment, anyone can become a source of information, taking in account that youth shows high activity in social media and apparently would be involved in specific Web 3.0 communication.

Nowadays *lifelong learning* is often named as one of the main educational goals. This means that learning is not necessarily age-dependent. However, it is also assumed that youth are the most active learners. That is why the general features of modern youth should be taken into consideration while arranging the learning process for this age group. For example, according to the International Centre for advertising research (World Advertising Research Center) there can be noted a number of the leading characteristics of today's youth (De Chenecey, 2005):

- Pursuit of impressions;
- Variety of activities;
- Desire to achieve success in different areas;
- Variety of self-actualization;
- Importance of communities (virtual communities and more advanced and less valuable);
- Pursuit of quick results.

The distinctive features of modern youth connected with the study process organization are: dynamic needs, interests, active involvement in what is happening as well as independence and autonomy, freedom to express their views and desire for independence, innovation, creativity. In the formation of these characteristics mass communication often plays the leading role. In a networked environment there appear and develop special forms of social activity of youth. Learning networking where teachers act as experts make knowledge not a product but a process. It is the social process that is associated with distributed activities. Knowledge is created in cooperation of a virtual community. Starting point is a knowledge gap, which activate the process of solving this problem. *Semantic Web*, intellectual search and other advantages of modern technologies allow implementing strategies for knowledge management based on communication - oriented approach (personalization and social interaction).

At the individual level knowledge management will be realized through interpersonal exchange of knowledge (often subjectively evaluated and interpreted). The specific context of the emergence of new knowledge (discourse, stage work) would be constructed using information tools that allow optimizing this process, there may be a decision support web-system, or expert systems. At the group level, knowledge management can be implemented through inter-group knowledge sharing (on the model of "many-to-many"), and the subjectivity of assessment will depend on the overall context of social interaction groups. The information tools that allow optimizing this process may be social networking, wikis, and wide virtual discussion platforms. *Web 3.0* technologies tend for erasing boundaries between online and off-line communication. Some situations require a problems translation in machine-readable form and this mediation is provided by a special organizing center, or knowledge broker. Modern software applications for mobile devices allow including innovative elements: games, virtual and augmented reality simulators. Using such tools in educational process allows erasing the borderline between classroom and virtual educational environment.

Objective 5: Professional Self-development

The important area of professional self-development is the formation of new competencies which are necessary to conduct professional activities in Web 3.0. On the other side Web 3.0 occurs to be the powerful tool for self-learning and collaboration in professional community. Modern teacher should be able to adapt own activities to dynamically changing conditions of virtual environment in order to achieve new quality of educational results.

Transformation (conversion) of the structural components of professional competencies occurs in various areas. *The first direction is the advanced, professional breakthrough thinking*, realized on the basis of global perception of the world, the modern characters of information and enhanced system of "coordinates" (technical, social, space-time, etc.), taking in account a wide range of factors and social contexts that affect the positive and negative aspects of educational communication. This line of professional self-development is ensured by constant striving not only to keep abreast of technology trends and *information educational environment*, but also willing to comprehend fundamentally new ways of information exchange, while systems assist users in various tasks in the process of smart and personalized web. As *Web 3.0* contributes for changing the main traditional methods of educational activities related to knowledge acquisition, representation, generation and educational collaboration, it is necessary to form a flexible teacher's professional attitude, a willingness to innovate.

The second direction is the integration of new skills and competences in an actual system of pedagogical practice in order to achieve a higher level of training quality. In this aspect the professional self-development leads to the change in the overall understanding of the educational process quality. To achieve this competency a teacher has to move gradually from the advanced Web 3.0 tools evaluation to the practice of acquisition of own resources. It is possible to become a member of diverse professional communities in global information environment and take advantage of the help and expertise of their members. The formation of new competencies occurs during structuring of personalized information environment for the purpose of professional self-development. Self-setting of new educational tasks and objectives, adequate for this generation of technology is only possible with the understanding the value of various educational activities in the wider information environment. Professional self-development includes the conversion of pedagogical position associated with the strengthening of a teacher's role as an agent (expert) and a mediator in the virtual learning environment with a significant role of Intelligent Agents.

The third direction is the design of innovative professional objective, on the basis of advanced thinking and balanced technological skills (using *Semantic Web*, mobility, virtualization). Web 3.0 helps to reduce time for the labor implementation of routine operations and switch to more productive, creative activity. In the context of the Web 3.0 the most meaningful skills are connected with knowledge management. Semantic Web can be viewed as a community of knowledge sharing. Teachers today are actively involved in this process. Especially secondary school teachers are very active in implementing the concept of co-management and knowledge-sharing. This is due to a number of objective reasons: regulation of the activity of a teacher (for example preparation for certification), a numerous organizations and web recourses for advanced training in period of educational standard changing. Therefore, teachers have a good opportunity to gain practical experience of interaction in virtual environments.

Modern development is possible only in a joint venture (Elmaa, 2013) with online communities, workshops constructing knowledge), in environment that allows to design their own content; evaluate their own activities, focusing on the experience of colleagues.

Examples of teacher's networking can be grouped as professional blogs, teacher's sites, online communities, media channels.

Teacher's blogs (for example http://modernpedagog.ru/) are the area for the emergence of creative ideas and conceptual projects. Exchanging comments a teacher can optimally quickly find like-minded people. It is important that the virtual space is formed not only around a blogger, but in the whole blogosphere. Entering into a dialogue in one blog, a user gets different opportunities for self-presentation. Among them are: filling the necessary personal profile information, feedback from other users. Blogs offer wide opportunities for self-identification. Blog 3.0 is regarded as the Internet area to create collective knowledge, collective semantics, new connections and meta-connections.

Online communities and mutual exchange of experience (http://nsportal.ru/). The aim of the network is the development of content relevant to education and personally meaningful for each participant. Many of them are using the wiki technology. Wiki gives an opportunity to see the work of others (completed tasks), and to compare it with own work. Thus, users can see the advantages and disadvantages, and identify ways to improve results. It is possible to get a sample of work, see all changes and contributions to the work in the final result. *Web 3.0* technologies help to integrate useful experience and knowledge in

response to a user request, to find the answer for the professional questions, to act in contact with experts or to find like-minded people.

The approach of the educational data hubs, for example Linked Educational Cloud (http://data.linkededucation.org/) is also very effective. The main aim is the identification and promotion of innovative success approaches and educational scenarios. These projects primarily require *Web 3.0* technologies to customize their capabilities to the needs of a particular user. Development of new generation of Internet technology in teaching practice can occur only through the understanding of their essence, testing them, discussing in professional society. After that they may be the productively implemented in the educational process.

Opportunities for Further Research: Web 3.0 and its Possible Social Effects

The most important characteristic of Web 2.0 and Web 3.0 is their social nature. The essence of the changes taking place is a social force which produces changes in society and in educational practices. With new forms of communication consumers, subjects of the educational process, partners, turn into a social force that forms fundamentally new conditions for deployment of the educational process: transparency of social and educational interactions reduce costs for individuals. A new educational inquiry of youth is being formed on the basis of the network environment interactions (information and *communication*) with the access to open educational resources, technology, and learning materials on the web to supplement personalized knowledge and learning.

The development of *Web 3.0* requires further study of future professionals' formation in the educational interactions for lifelong learners.

CONCLUSION

Currently, the development of web technologies in an educational context has passed several stages. Technology Web 1.0 was based on "linear" processes of information transfer by remote in time and space users. In the educational activities it served as a basis for the transfer of traditional classroom teaching experience in a virtual environment. However, a teacher was the center of direct and reverse flows of information, the initiator of information experiences, and opinion exchange between the teacher and the student, and the organizer of the educational process on the whole.

Web 2.0 technologies enabled the drastic change of the education interactions course with the possibility to use technology-based social networks. The educational potential expanded through nonlinear communications, complex social interactions, decentralized educational interaction, creating a sophisticated communication connections within learning communities (social services, network projects, knowledge sharing community).

Prospects for use of Web 3.0 technology seem to be aimed primarily at new forms of knowledge representation. High granularity of information elements, their marking, Meta descriptions, allow changing the semantic relationships between elements of information structure that can adapt to the needs of the system user. Thus, a feature of the functioning of the new knowledge spaces on the web is not only the construction of nonlinear *communication* in social networks carried on the user's request, but also nonlinear relationships within the information structures of knowledge, realized intelligent systems based on analysis of user behavior information resource. It contributes for the implementation of students' new educational strategies. The overall educational strategy nowadays is the development of Web technology opportunities related to the increasing importance of the active position of a person: personal educational activities, interactions, cooperation.

In the center of Web 3.0 technologies there is a learner who acts as an active personality, with the individual choice of educational route, the manifestation of independence, the adoption and implementation of the strategy of *lifelong learning* in the high-tech knowledge society.

Web 3.0 technologies are changing the educational environment and require transformation of educational activities, require teachers' awareness of major developments of networking, web-based information technologies, and especially awareness of new information behavior of users. Educational environment as a set of educational resources for all students is transformed into a set of individual educational environments and environments for collective interaction. There are contrasting approaches to the use of information tools for perception, monitoring and correction of learner's educational behavior in a virtual environment: learner activated *e-portfolio* and more automated tracking of learner activities. The pedagogical interaction with other members of the information environment is changing significantly in the context of *Web 3.0* with the use of a variety of sign systems, the implementation of information exchanges, the possession of a wide range of linguistic resources, the change of perception in the information environment. The pedagogical activities on arrangement of the learning process in new conditions requires specific pedagogical skills and abilities (organizational, technical and pedagogical), based on understanding the characteristics of the network community and differences between moderated and no moderated network space. At the individual level pedagogical knowledge management has to be realized through interpersonal exchange of knowledge (subjectively evaluated and interpreted). The decisive role in the transformation of educational activities and the acquisition of new competencies plays a teacher's professional self-development in Web 3.0 information space, as Web 3.0 occurs to be the powerful tool for self-learning and collaboration in a professional community.

REFERENCES

Andreeva, T., Kianto, A., & Pavlov, Y. (2013). The impact of intellectual capital management on company competitiveness and financial performance. *Knowledge Management Research & Practice, 11*(2), 112–122. doi:10.1057/kmrp.2013.9

Barrett, H. (2011). *Balancing the two faces of e-portfolios*. Retrieved April 15, 2014 from http://electronicportfolios.org/balance/Balancing2.htm

Berry, M. W. (2004). *Survey of text mining: Clustering, classification, and retrieval*. Berlin, Germany: Springer-Verlag.

Boykov, V., Zakharov, V., Karyaeva, M., & Sokolov, V. (2013). Thesaurus poetics as a tool for information retrieval and knowledge collection. *Modeling and Analysis of Information Systems, 20*(4), 125–135.

Calacanis, J. (2007). *Web 3.0, the "official" definition*. Retrieved April 15, 2014 from http://calacanis.com/2007/10/03/web-3-0-the-official-definition/

Chih-Hsiung, T. (2012). The integration of personal learning environments & open network learning environments. *TechTrends, 56*(3), 13–19. doi:10.1007/s11528-012-0571-7

De Chenecey, S. P. (2005). Branding in an entertainment culture. *Young Consumers, 2*(3), 20–22. doi:10.1108/17473610510701151

Dolgin, A. (2008, April). *Runet: The game in advance: What is web 3.0?* Retrieved April 15, 2014 from http://polit.ru/article/2008/04/02/web3/

Elmaa, Y. (2013). Horizontal training in open environments, new forms of professional development of teachers. In *Proceedings of the Information Technology for the New School Conference* (Vol. 3, pp. 15-18). St. Petersburg, Russia: Regional Centre for Education Quality Assessment and Information Technologies.

Galkin, V., Zhuravleva, T., & Stoylik Y. (2013). Improving the quality of customer support information on technical regulations based on the technology of the Internet portal. *Transportation business in Russia, 4,* 160-161.

Goncharov, S. A., Goncharova, O. M., & Koroleva, N. N. (2008). *Symbol, person, meaning: An interdisciplinary reflection space*. St. Petersburg, Russia: HSPU Publishing House.

Johnson, M. W., & Sherlock, D. (2014). Beyond the personal learning environment: Attachment and control in the classroom of the future. *Interactive Learning Environments, 22*(2), 146–164. doi:10.1080/10494820.2012.745434

Kapitonov, O. & Tyutyunnik, V. (2013). Logical-linguistic model of semantic markup web pages. *Fundamental Research, 1*(3), 714-717.

Martinez-Garcia, A., Morris, S., Tscholl, M., Tracy, F., & Carmichael, P. (2012). Case-based learning, pedagogical innovation, and semantic web technologies. *IEEE Transactions on Learning Technologies, 5*(2), 104–116. doi:10.1109/TLT.2011.34

Melnikova, N., & Vagarina, N. (2013). The adaptation of foreign experience of semantic web technologies in education. *Engineering: Theory into Practice, 24,* 21–27.

Noskova, T. (2011). *Network educational communication*. St. Petersburg, Russia: HSPU Publishing House.

Noskova, T. (2013). *Century challenges: Pedagogy of the network environment*. St. Petersburg, Russia: HSPU Publishing House.

Noskova, T., Kulikova, S., Pavlova, T., & Yakovleva, O. (2013). *New conditions for the formation of information culture for the XXI century specialist*. St. Petersburg, Russia: HSPU Publishing House.

Noskova, T., & Pavlova, T. (2013). Electronic resources as a basis of promising professional competence. *Bulletin of the St. Petersburg University of the Russian Interior Ministry, 3*(59), 133-137.

Peskova, O. (2011). Social media as a platform for technology PR 2.0. In *Government and business: Communication resources* (pp. 57–82). Moscow, Russia: Higher School of Economics.

Sitnic, A., Vagarina, N., & Melnikova, N. (2011). Ontological description multimedia resources in the context of semantic web technologies. *Vestnik SGTU, 4*(60), 202–207.

Starostova, L. (2013). Digital technology as a factor in the transformation of aesthetic experience. In *Proceedings of the International Conference Science Culture in Perspective of "Digital Humanities"* (pp. 48-55). St. Petersburg, Russia: Asterion.

Zubrinic, K., & Kalpic, D. (2008). The web as personal learning environment. *International Journal of Emerging Technologies in Learning, 3*, 45–58.

ADDITIONAL READING

Banokin, P., & Vichugov, V. (2012). Semantic system optimization of web site content based on user preferences. *Izvestyja of Tomsk Polytechnic University, 325*(5), 93–97.

Chang, S.-K., Kapoor, A., Santhanakrishnan, G., & Vaidya, C. (2005). The design and prototyping of the chronobot system for time and knowledge exchange [IJDET]. *International Journal of Distance Education Technologies, 3*(3), 18–33. doi:10.4018/jdet.2005070102

Chee-Kit, L. (2005). *Frontiers in artificial intelligence and applications.* Washington, DC: IOS Press.

Collins-Camargo, C., Chad, D., & Lester, C. (2012). Measuring organizational effectiveness to develop strategies to promote retention in public child welfare. *Children and Youth Services Review, 34*(1), 289–295.

Fellbaum, C. (1998). *WordNet. An electronic lexical database.* Cambridge, UK: MIT Press.

Fensel, D., Wahlster, W., Lieberman, H., & Hendler, J. L. (2003). *Spinning the Semantic Web. Bringing the World Wide Web to its full potential.* Cambridge, UK: MIT Press.

Fuchs-Kittowski, F., & Prinz, W. (2005). *Interaktionsorientiertes Wissensmanagement.* Frankfurt, Germany: Peter Lang Verlag.

Greer, G., Mizoguchi, R., & Dicheva, D. (2009). *Semantic Web technologies for E-learning.* Amsterdam, Netherlands: Ios Press.

Jovanovic, J., Gassevic, D., Torniaic, C., & Hatala, M. (2009, December). The social Semantic Web in intelligent learning environments: State of the art and future challenges. *Interactive Learning Environments, 17*(4), 273–309. doi:10.1080/10494820903195140

Kaplan, A. M., & Heinlein, M. (2010). Users of the world, unite! The challenges and opportunities of social media. *Business Horizons, 53*(1), 59–68. doi:10.1016/j.bushor.2009.09.003

Kulikova, S., & Yakovleva, O. (2013). The virtual environment influence on the socialization of today's youth. *ARPN Journal of Science and Technology, 3*(4), 386–389.

Lebedeva, M., & Shilova, O. (2004). What is an ICT competence of pedagogical university students and how to form it? *Science and education, 3*, 95–99.

Noskova, T. (2007). *Psychodidactics of the educational environment.* St. Petersburg, Russia: HSPU Publishing House.

Noskova, T., Pavlova, T. (2012). New priorities of the educational activities in the educational environment of the modern university. *Scientific and technical journal SPBSPU, 2,* 329 – 335.

Noskova, T., Pavlova, T., & Yakovleva, O. (2013). High school teachers' information competencies in the virtual learning environment. In E. Smyrnova-Trybulska (Eds.), E-learning & Lifelong Learning (pp. 215-221). University of Silesia, Poland: Studio-Nova.

Noskova, T., & Yakovleva, O. (2012). Mass media and up-bringing in a university corporative environment. *Materials of V Congress of Russian Psychological Society* (Vol.3, pp. 365-366).

Panov, V. (2004). *Ecological psychology. Experience in building methodology.* Moscow, Russia: Science.

PISA. 2012 Results. (2012). What Makes Schools Successful? Retrieved April 15, 2014 from http://www.oecd.org/pisa/keyfindings/pisa-2012-results-volume-IV.pdf

Pocheptsov, G. (2000). *Communication technologies of the twentieth century.* Moscow, Russia: Vakler.

Robertson, S. E., & Jones, K. S. (1997). Simple, proven approaches to text retrieval. *Cambridge Technical Report UCAM-CL-TR-356.* Retrieved March 10, 2014, from http://www.cl.cam.ac.uk/techreports/UCAM-CL-TR-356.pdf

Rosina, I. (2004). *Educational and professional communication in the academic Internet communities. Actual problems of the theory of communication* (pp. 314–331). St. Petersburg, Russia: Publishing House of STU.

Salton, G., Fox, E., & Wu, H. (2001). Extended Boolean information retrieval. *Communications of the ACM, 26*(4), 35–43.

Savicke, J., & Juceviciene, P. (2012). Educating students in museums: Possibilities for forming Personal Learning Environments. *Socialiniai Mokslai, 4*(78), 75–83.

Sedov, K. (2004). *Discourse and identity: The evolution of communicative competence.* Moscow, Russia: Labyrinth.

UNESCO. (1998, October 9). World declaration on higher education for the twenty-first century: Vision and action. *World Conference on Higher Education.* Retrieved April 15, 2014, from http://www.unesco.org/education/educprog/wche/declaration_eng.htm

Weller, K. (2010). *Knowledge & Information.* New York, NY: De Gruyter Saur.

KEY TERMS AND DEFINITIONS

Digital Educational Resources: A set of software, information, technical and organizational support, that reflects a certain subject area and implements the technology for its study by different learning activities.

Information Educational Environment: Software telecommunications environment, which provides technological means to conduct the educational process, its information support and documentation in the Internet to any number of educational institutions, regardless of their professional expertise and level of education.

Pedagogical Activities: Relations that arise between people in the process of transmission spiritual and practical experience from generation to generation.

Pedagogical Objective: An elementary unit of the pedagogical process; to solve each pedagogical objective pedagogical interaction is organized.

Personal Learning Environment: Individual, personalized information and communication surrounding of a person; learning environment of a student's network activities accumulates and processes all information resources and all communication resources as products of communication operations.

Portfolio: A form of monitoring and evaluation of student achievement, and their characteristics, evidence of progress in learning, the materialized products on learning and cognitive activity, including self-estimation.

Semantic Web: Direction of network technologies development; the main ideas are: to provide information in a form most suitable for machine processing, to develop methods and tools for knowledge extraction from natural language texts, to use knowledge for creating spaces of applied intelligent systems operating in the Internet.

Web 3.0: The idea of a new phase of World Wide Web development. The concept aims to implement possibilities of machining the information available on World Wide Web in various forms: Semantic Web, 3D and mobile content, data hubs. This idea is at the crossroads of studies on artificial intelligence and Internet technologies.

Chapter 3

Semantic Retrieval of Documents from Digital Repositories and Twitter Integration in the Moodle Environment

Renan Rodrigues de Oliveira
Instituto Federal de Educação, Ciência e Tecnologia de Goiás (IFG), Brazil

Fábio Moreira Costa
Universidade Federal de Goiás (UFG), Brazil

Cedric Luiz de Carvalho
Universidade Federal de Goiás (UFG), Brazil

Ana Paula Ambròsio
Universidade Federal de Goiás (UFG), Brazil

ABSTRACT

Virtual learning environments represent an important step in enabling distance and blended education. Moodle's structure for content enables the identification of well-defined learning contexts. Nevertheless, Moodle currently does not provide standard features to leverage the use of such contextual information, nor does it provide a standard built-in search facility. This chapter presents a context-sensitive Moodle plug-in for the search of external resources that allows semantic-based retrieval of documents from any external repository that offers an OAI-PMH standard compliant interface. As a way to increase their potential use, the plug-in also retrieves Twitter messages (known as tweets), since social networks are shown as an important tool to support education. Retrieved resources are presented in order of importance according to both the query terms provided by the user and the current context derived from the Moodle content structure. Searches are semantically expanded by evaluating the query terms according to a specific ontology associated with the context.

INTRODUCTION

Virtual learning environments represent an important step in enabling distance and blended education. Moodle's structure for content enables the identification of well-defined learning contexts. Nevertheless, Moodle currently does not provide standard features to leverage the use of such contextual information, nor does it provide a standard built-in search facility. This work presents

DOI: 10.4018/978-1-4666-8147-7.ch003

a context-sensitive Moodle plug-in for the search of external resources that allows semantic-based retrieval of documents from any external repository that offers an OAI-PMH standard compliant interface. As a way to increase their potential use, the plug-in also retrieves Twitter messages (known as tweets), since social networks are shown as an important tool to support education. Retrieved resources are presented in order of importance according to both the query terms provided by the user and the current context derived from the Moodle content structure. Searches are semantically expanded by evaluating the query terms according to a specific ontology associated with the context.

Moodle (Modular Object Oriented Distance Learning) (Moodle, 2014) is an open source system that enables learning in virtual environments and is widely used around the world. It supports the administration of educational activities aimed at creating online communities in virtual environments with a focus on collaborative learning. Through online courses, Moodle allows iteration between students and teachers in a very simplified way. Furthermore, it has a set of tools that enables the use and publication of resources for collective use. However, these are limited to the resources introduced by the teacher for that specific course.

Social networks have proved to be important tools to support the educational process, since they bring the reality of today's world connected to the classroom. Twitter in particular has a number of useful features that enhance its use as a tool to support education. We know that Twitter messages (known as tweets) have several metadata that allows a good level of recovery and organization, including the date, location, information about the responsibility of the message and may have hashtags that allow catalog and connect tweets related to a specific topic.

However, semantic analysis allows new possibilities related to recovery of tweets to be achieved. As each tweet has a limited number of characters (140 characters), the semantic analysis process can be something quite promising and challenging.

This work describes the implementation of a context-sensitive Moodle plug-in for the search of external resources, which allows the semantic retrieval of documents from any digital repository that offers an OAI-PMH (Open Archives Initiative – Protocol for Metadata Harvesting) standard compliant interface (OAI, 2014). As a way to increase their potential use, the plug-in also retrieves Twitter messages, since social networks are shown as an important tool to support education. The document retrieval process in this proposal is performed considering the Portuguese language. However, the proposed approach also applies to other languages with similar characteristics (e.g. western languages).

The defined context-sensitive Moodle plug-in retrieves a list of tweets and documents from several external digital repositories. User supplied queries are semantically expanded to take into account the Moodle context in which the user is currently interacting. This expansion is performed using an ontology associated to that specific context.

In this work, context is defined using Moodle's own structure (organized in courses, subjects, topics etc.), which allows the identification of well-defined contexts, and ontologies. An ontology is a data model that represents a set of concepts and their relationships within a knowledge domain. They allow computer-based systems to "understand" the context of a term, allowing a semantic perspective for real world situations.

The rest of this text is organized as follows: Section 1 presents the related work. Section 2 presents the distance education and Moodle as a teaching tool. Section 3 presents a discussion on the retrieval of information using ontology that are useful artifacts in the specification of knowledge domains. Section 4 presents Moodle and its framework for context definition. Section 5 presents an overview of the Open Archives Initiative and the OAI-PMH protocol for integration of digital repositories. Section 6 presents Twitter as a tool to support education and retrieval of tweets as an information resource in Moodle. Section 7 presents the integration process of digital repositories and use of tweets as an information resource. Section 8 presents the overall system architecture of the context-sensitive Moodle plug-in. Section 9 presents the implementation of user interfaces for the Moodle plug-in, with several ways in which users can interact with the developed system. Section 10 describes experiments using the Moodle plug-in in classroom environments, followed by our conclusions and future research.

1. RELATED WORK

Since most Internet search engines return a large amount of records as the result of queries, the user can never be sure whether the information desired is among the first returned results. Thus he must analyze a large number of records to see which really meet his expectations. According to Lancaster (Lancaster, 1993), the majority of system searches, for any specific information need, will recover many more items that have no significance or relevance to the subject than items that do. Therefore, the main function of an information retrieval system is to enable the user to locate the largest possible number of relevant items (Feitosa, 2006).

In this context, difficulties of access and retrieval of relevant information become more evident. Thus, the search for better methods to store, search and retrieve information in this environment becomes a challenge to the scientific community. Since the analysis of context is essential for the proper understanding of terms used in searches, automatic mechanisms of contextualization must be defined to help narrow the search and retrieve only relevant documents. Indeed, one of the main problems of automatic document contextualization is related to the process of context formal definition, i.e., how to create contexts for the automatic classification of documents.

Ontologies allow a formal and shared understanding in a given domain. They play an important role in knowledge exchange by providing a semantic structure to the data domain in question. However, an ontology only defines the relations within a restricted domain. Thus, to be able to use the correct ontology, one must identify the domain in which we wish to work, i.e., the context.

In this work, our interest in ontologies is for their use as a mechanism for specifying knowledge domains, making them useful in the process of categorization and calculation of similarity of terms. Wu et al. (2003) deal with categorization of texts based on domain ontologies. According to the authors, the advantage of using ontologies, compared with other mechanisms of knowledge representation is that they can be read, interpreted and edited by humans. Errors can be detected and thus the description can be improved. Another advantage is the possibility of sharing an ontology among multiple applications.

Rigo et al. (2007) proposes a methodology for text classification using linguistic information described in a domain ontology. This ontology has the information necessary to identify the structure and concepts of the documents associated with a specific class. Bloehdorn et al. (2006) make use of features extracted from ontologies to improve the text classification task. The approach is based on the distribution hypothesis, i.e., during the process of classification, it is checked whether the terms are semantically similar to the context in which they are shared. Thiagarajan et al. (2008) propose a method for calculating the semantic similarity using ontologies. The method consists in adding terms that are close to the original term used to describe an entity, extending the notion of semantic similarity by considering the relationships between concepts.

The use of ontologies in the information retrieval process can also facilitate the search for learning resources. Understanding the potential of ontologies in the educational scenario is an important step towards the development of innovative applications which may contribute to the learning process. Bittencourt et al. (2007) present an overview of the Semantic Web (Berners-Lee, Hendler, & Lassila, 2001) in Education, considering some of the main research challenges (i.e., architecture and standards) and showing how the use of ontologies can enhance student learning. The authors argue that education systems are gradually incorporating semantic web technologies aiming to provide a more adaptable and personalized service, within an intelligent environment.

Roa et al. (2010) present a semantic search system for digital repositories through a case study using DSpace (DSpace, 2014) and Moodle. They introduced the use of an ontology layer to classify learning resources and a search engine based on semantic search. They define a semantic search engine for DSpace based on web services and its integration with Moodle to enhance the authoring process of educational material. Dufresne and Rouatbi (2007) present the use of ontologies as a bridge between e-learning applications. The authors emphasize how digital libraries are important information resources that have been widely used as support for education.

Social networks are being used increasingly in the educational field as a pedagogical tool or means of communication between students and their teachers. A social network is defined as a set of two elements: the actors (individuals, groups or institutions) and their connections (interactions or social ties) (Degenne & Forsé, 1999). Twitter in particular has a number of useful features that enhance its use as a tool to support education (Grossecmk & Holotescu, 2008):

- Since the message is limited to only 140 characters, it requires a significant synthesis capacity to express thought;
- Allows quick publishing of content directed to a group of stakeholders;

- Allows monitoring and participation in a discussion on a particular subject, through the collaboration of all involved (in this case, teachers, students and other interested persons);
- Teachers can provide lecture notes, tips, errands, among others, having the opportunity to receive feedback from students in real time;
- Allows students and teachers to maintain favorable situations for learning outside the classroom.

In this context, McCool (2011) presents a work that discusses how Twitter can be used pedagogically to help students' communication, collaboration and participation. The author argues that because Twitter is a free service, providing a number of free applications, it has been properly used for educational purposes. Bristol (2010) states that staying connected virtually became a mainstay of modern American culture. In his work, the author explores the use of Twitter in health and education.

With a strong background in the use of Web 2.0 technologies in education, Grosseck and Holotescu (2008) present arguments for the use of Twitter as a social networking platform in education, emphasizing its advantages, but also possible negatives. The paper also presents an application related to the use of Twitter in education.

2. DISTANCE EDUCATION AND MOODLE AS A TEACHING TOOL

The adoption of technologies in education has created new opportunities for interaction in teaching and learning activities. Although the term "distance education" has been commonly used in recent years, several definitions have been formulated to refer to the same educational experience.

Garrison (Garrison, 1993) proposes a definition for distance education quite succinctly: distance education is, in the final analysis, education. The only real difference is that the majority of communications between teacher and student is mediated. Distance education, is less a philosophy and more a method of education. Students can study in their own time, at the place of their choice (home, work, or learning center), and without face-to-face contact with a teacher. Technology is a critical element of distance education (Bates, 2005).

Virtual learning environments are computational systems intended to support activities mediated by information and communication technologies. They enable integration multiple media resources and present information in an organized manner, providing interactions between people and objects of knowledge, to contribute to the learning of a group of persons.

Moodle (Modular Object-Oriented Dynamic Learning Environment) is a virtual learning environment that allows you to produce and manage educational activities using the Internet. It is a software package designed to help educators achieve a high standard of quality in their educational activities online. Moodle was developed in PHP (a recursive acronym for "PHP: Hypertext Preprocessor") (PHP, 2014) and freely available as free software (under the GNU Public License). It is collaboratively developed by a community that brings together programmers, systems administrators, teachers, designers and users from around the world.

3. INFORMATION RETRIEVAL USING ONTOLOGIES

Since most Internet search engines return a large amount of records as the result of queries, the user is never sure exactly which information is desired among the first returned results. Thus, it is left for the user the task of analyzing a large number of records to see which of them really meet the expectations.

In this context, difficulties of access and retrieval of relevant information become apparent. Thus, the search for better methods to store, search and retrieve information in this environment becomes a challenge.

Since the analysis of context is essential for the proper understanding of the terms used in searches, automatic mechanisms for contextualization need to allow only relevant documents to be retrieved based on user interest.

One of the main problems of automatic contextualization of documents is related to the process of formal definition of contexts, i.e., how to create contexts for the automatic classification of documents. Ontologies enable a common and shared understanding in a field, playing an important role in knowledge exchange by providing a semantic structure to the data domain in question. One of the most cited definitions in the literature is that of Gruber (Gruber, 1993), which defines ontology as: "An ontology is a formal specification, explicit and a shared conceptualization."

Later Studer, Benjamins and Fensel (1998) analyzed each of the terms of this definition:

- **Conceptualization:** Refers to an abstract model of some phenomenon in the world, the identification of relevant concepts of that phenomenon;
- **Explicit:** It means that the type of concept used and its restrictions are explicitly defined;
- **Formal:** Refers to the fact that the ontology can be understood by machines;
- **Shared:** Refers to the notion that an ontology captures knowledge accepted by a group of people and not the knowledge of a particular individual.

In general, ontologies are especially useful in the management of knowledge for information retrieval since unifies terms, concepts, categories and relationships of a single domain, enabling reuse. The advantages highlighted in the use of ontologies in the process of information retrieval within a well-defined context can also facilitate the search for learning resources. Understanding the potential use of ontologies in educational settings is an important step towards the development of educational applications and web-based integration with distributed resources in the Internet.

4. MOODLE AND ITS FRAMEWORK FOR CONTEXT DEFINITION

Moodle is organized around courses. Basically, these courses are pages within Moodle where teachers can present learning resources and activities available for students to develop. The courses may have different layouts, but they usually include sections where the materials are displayed as side blocks, offering information or extra resources.

Courses may contain content for lessons that last a semester, a single session or any other variant depending on the teacher and the institution that maintains the environment. These courses can be used by a single teacher or shared by a group of teachers. The courses are organized into categories. For example, for the Science category, you can have the courses in Physics, Chemistry and Biology.

Several features of the organization of Moodle can suggest well-defined contexts. For example, if a user is accessing the category Science, this suggests that the resources they wish to recover must be related to Physics, Chemistry, Biology or any other discipline in this category. In this case, it would make no sense to show, as a result of user queries, resources from external repositories (for example, a Digital Library) that relate solely to the category of Mathematics (for example, courses in Algebra, Geometry and Number Theory).

Similarly, for a user who is accessing a Biology course on Moodle (a more specific level in the Science category), the context suggests that all represented courses must relate to matters of biology. Also, it makes no sense to have other resources that relate solely to other disciplines in the same category (for example, Physics and Chemistry) or even worse, resources related to other categories.

As shown in Figure 1, a Moodle user that accesses a particular discipline can interact with the center section where materials are displayed in blocks, or with the side frames that provide extra features. Figure 1 also shows that specific topics of a given discipline can be added for discussion in the section entitled "Course Calendar". In this case, for the Biology course, the following topics have been added: Cell Biology, Molecular Genetics and Human Physiology (more specific levels with respect to the discipline of biology).

Thus, for a user that is accessing the Cell Biology topic (a sublevel of the discipline of Biology that in turn is a sublevel of category Science), the context suggests that all queries must be related to issues of Cell Biology.

Given the above, we argue that the addition of context based on the very nature of the Moodle organization, together with ontologies of to the corresponding knowledge domains, can significantly improve the recovery of relevant documents from external repositories, which in turn can contribute to students' learning process.

5. OPEN ARCHIVES INITIATIVE

The Open Archives model emerged as a need to provide interoperability between digital repositories, enabling access to the collection of information contained therein, in an integrated manner by users. Digital repositories are developed with different architectures and technologies, are managed by different organizations, subjected to different quality standards, etc. This distributed and heterogeneous environment introduces a high degree of complexity in achieving an integrated view of digital collections.

The general idea of integration and interoperability in digital repositories is on providing

Figure 1. (1) Categories of courses (2) Current course (3) Course schedule

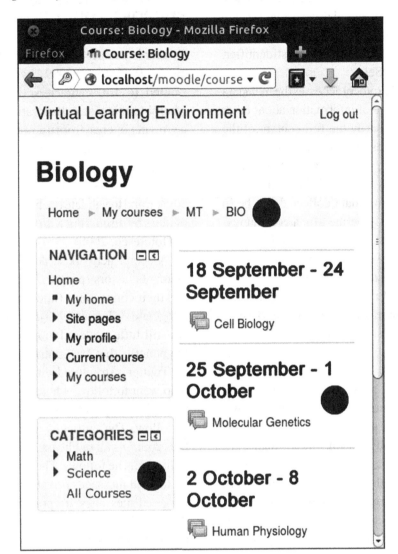

recovery of heterogeneous information resources stored in different repositories, using a single interface service. Thus, integration is the ability to provide a single interface to access the information in different digital repositories. For users, no matter where or how these resources are stored. Interoperability is the ability of digital repositories to exchange and share information and services.

In order to enable interoperability and integration in this environment, several protocols have been developed. The OAI-PMH (Open Archives Initiative – Protocol for Metadata Harvesting) (OAI-PMH, 2014) is a protocol that allows the efficient dissemination of content from digital repositories, enabling participants of the OAI initiative (Open Archives Initiative) to share their metadata with external applications that are interested in collecting such data.

Communication is performed via HTTP requests, based on request-response. The response of each request is returned in XML format. An OAI-PMH request has six verbs (commands transmitted to the repository), which can be used to collect metadata from digital repositories that are in accordance with the protocol. They are: Identify, ListMetadataFormats, ListRecord, ListIdentifier, GetRecord and ListSets.

The OAI-PMH protocol accesses the metadata (descriptive structure of information about other data) and not necessarily the full content of the repository's resources. However, by retrieving the resource's metadata, you can have full access to their real content by a URI with the address of this resource. The metadata collected can be in any format previously defined by a community, although the Dublin Core standard is specified to provide a basic level of interoperability.

Probably the greatest contribution of OAI was the development of the OAI-PMH protocol. To facilitate understanding we present some concepts and definitions related to the Open Archives architecture.

Data providers are systems that use the OAI-PMH protocol as a means to expose their metadata. These providers also may (but not necessarily) provide open access to full texts and other resources, being responsible for managing objects, exposing their metadata for collection. Data providers are the creators and maintainers of metadata and resources in their repositories.

The harvesters are programs that use the interface provided by the OAI-PMH protocol to perform the metadata collection. They import the metadata from data providers and offer the possibility of building new services on these collected metadata .

Service providers use the metadata collected by harvesters as a basis for building new services. As an example of a new service, take a system that collects metadata from several data providers, offering a single interface, that is search friendly and transparent to the end user. Figure 2, presents an example of information flow in service providers.

In this example, the service provider requests metadata to data providers, obtaining an answer in accordance with the OAI-PMH.

6. TWITTER AS A TOOL TO SUPPORT EDUCATION

Twitter is a microblogging social network (Honeycutt & Herring, 2009), where messages are limited to 140 characters (known as tweets). Microblogging is a collaborative technology with a growing interest from users coming from different domains, from e-Learning and education in general too. People use Twitter to communicate, to ask questions, to ask for directions, support, advice, and to validate open-ended interpretations or ideas by discussing with the others (Grossecmk & Holotescu, 2008).

A social network is defined as a set of two elements: actors (people, institutions or groups) and their connections (interactions or social ties) (Degenne & Forsé, 1999). However, these tools are still little explored in the classroom, despite the benefits that can contribute to a course.

Twitter is structured with followers and people who want to follow, where each user can be followed by other users, and choose who you want to follow. The particular window of each user, thus contains all public messages issued by those individuals he follows. There is also the possibility to send messages privately to other members. Targeted messages are possible with the use of the "@" before the name of the recipient. Each particular page can be customized by the user by building a small profile (Recuero, 2009). Apart from short texts, other interesting content can also be shared via forwarding tweets and links to videos, websites, blogs, etc.

Twitter can be used between teachers and students, students and students in the same class, students and students in another country, as a tool for the entire class or for pair/group work. Work on Twitter can take place in the classroom or outside (home computer, mobile devices, etc.). Tweets can also be used to ask questions and hunt for instant points of view. For teachers, Twitter can allow them to boost task-based learning, interactivity and collaborative learning which encourage the

Figure 2. Flow of information on service providers

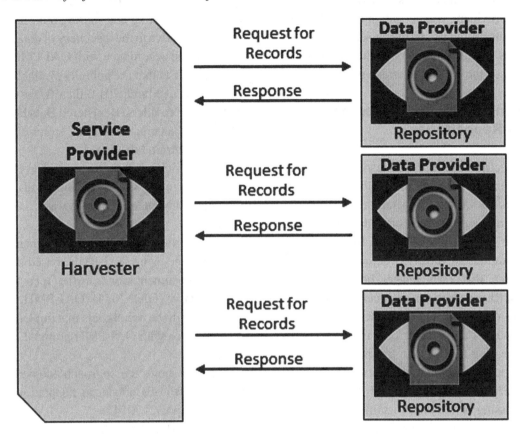

students to "achieve common learning goals by working together rather than with the teacher". Thus the teacher can play the role of a facilitator and guide rather than the "know-it-all supervisor". The renewed contacts between the students and the teacher through Twitter can also boost their respective trust and lead to increased motivation and trigger a more informal level of conversation (which is not always "negative") (Harmandaoglu, 2012).

It can catalog and connect tweets related to a particular topic through the use of hashtags, which function as an index of tweets. To create a hashtag simply use the # symbol before a word. For example, the hashtag #ufg can be used as a reference for what makes a tweet regarding the Federal University of Goiás. Hashtags thus be-

come an efficient way of finding tweets related to a particular topic.

7. INTEGRATE DIGITAL REPOSITORIES AND USING TWEETS AS AN INFORMATION RESOURCE

Using suggestions from well-defined contexts that are provided by the characteristics of the organization of Moodle, along with ontologies that refer to these fields of knowledge, we can significantly improve the process of information retrieval of relevant tweets or other documents from external repositories that can contribute to student learning.

Following is the process of integrating external data providers, which contain metadata from several data providers and tweets sent via Moodle plugin, as well as through any other external interface (i.e., the Twitter interface itself).

7.1 Using OAI-PMH to Integrate Digital Repositories

The collection and access of resource metadata from several digital repositories allows the viability of a wide variety of operations that can add value to the learning environment in which the student is placed. In this context, the most common operations are the discovery and acquisition of resources that can be images, books, art work, music, URLs, papers, among many others.

In the context of this work, the integration of data providers aims to perform integration and pre-processing of metadata for digital libraries, repositories, distributed databases, unstructured text files directories, etc. The goal of the metadata preprocessing is to reduce the dimensionality of textual information and help to reduce the computational effort related to the subsequent process of information retrieval.

In this work, the process of metadata collection is performed using the URL for metadata request existing in digital libraries and repositories that offer an implementation of the OAI-PMH as a means for exhibiting and sharing their metadata.

An alternative to the discovery of data providers that are in accordance with OAI-PMH URLs is to search lists that are publicly available on the Internet. As of March 2014, the official registry of OAI data providers (Registered Data Providers OAI, 2014) had more than 2.233 stores in various institutions around the world.

For repositories that do not have an interface conforming to the OAI-PMH protocol, we can implement this interface in two ways:

1. Through the complete development of the interface using OAI-PMH, based on available documentation from the Open Archives Initiative (OAI, 2014) (OAI-PMH, 2014);
2. Through the use of tools that implement the interface with OAI-PMH protocol.

Figure 3 shows the approach adopted in this work, which is based on an adaptation of the phpoai2 (phpoai2, 2014).

Figure 4 shows the general process scheme used in this work for integration of data providers. As seen in Figure 4, the metadata from various data providers are collected by a harvester, using the request primitive of the OAI-PMH protocol.

Figure 3. Process adopted for the exposure of metadata from repositories that do not have an interface implementation of the OAI-PMH protocol

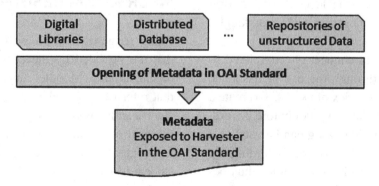

Figure 4. General scheme used in the integration process of data providers

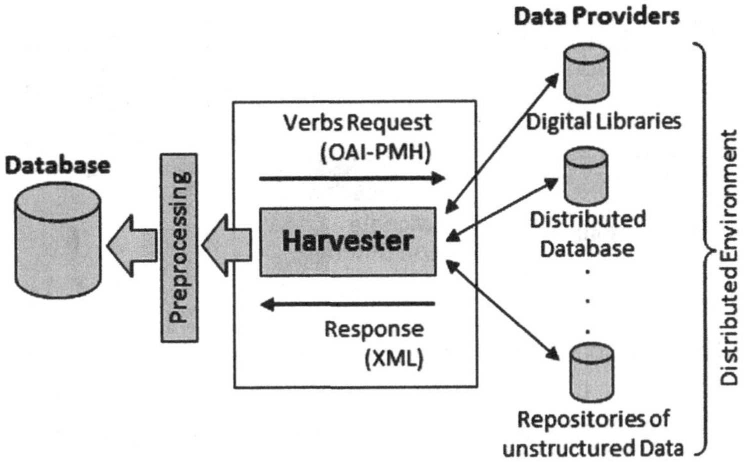

In pre-processing of metadata, the following activities are performed: removal of stopwords (irrelevant terms); stemming (reduction of semantically related terms to the same radical); removal of scores; removal of misspelled terms (according to the Portuguese language); removal of terms that are not part of the Portuguese language.

For the identification of stopwords we used a list of irrelevant terms. To implement the process of stemming we used an opensource implementation of the Porter algorithm for the Portuguese language, called PTStemmer (PTStemmer, 2014). To identify misspelled words or words that are not part of the Portuguese language, we used the open source project Jazzy (Java Spell Check API) (Jazzy, 2014), and adapted it to use a dictionary of the Portuguese language, br.ispell (br.ispell, 2014). Some terms that are important and which are not part of the Portuguese language were added to a positive list, so that they were not removed.

7.2 Tweets as an Information Resource in Moodle

Using the suggestions of well-defined contexts that are characteristic of the Moodle organization and with ontologies that refer to these fields of knowledge, can significantly improve the process of retrieval of relevant information contained in tweets or other external document repositories that may contribute to student learning. Figure 5, shows the general scheme used for the generation of the tweets database.

As seen in Figure 5, the tweets database contains messages submitted through the Moodle plug-in, as well as through any other external interface (i.e., the Twitter interface itself). Each Moodle course must have a list on Twitter, for all messages sent by the Moodle plug-in are posted on this list. The tweeter list helps in several ways, the most obvious being to create a group.

Furthermore, the list is a perfect way to "categorize" the tweets of a large amount of users without having to see all these tweets on the main page. The lists act as binder tabs, where each list refers to a specific theme.

At the end of all messages sent by Moodle plug-in, a hashtag is added that refers to the Moodle course in which the user is interacting. Hashtags allow you to catalog and connect tweets related to a particular topic, because it works as an index of tweets. To create a hashtag simply use the # symbol before a word.

In Figure 5, it is observed that the amount of characters allowed for any message is 136 characters, because the course hashtag has 4 characters

Figure 5. General scheme used in the process of generating database of tweets

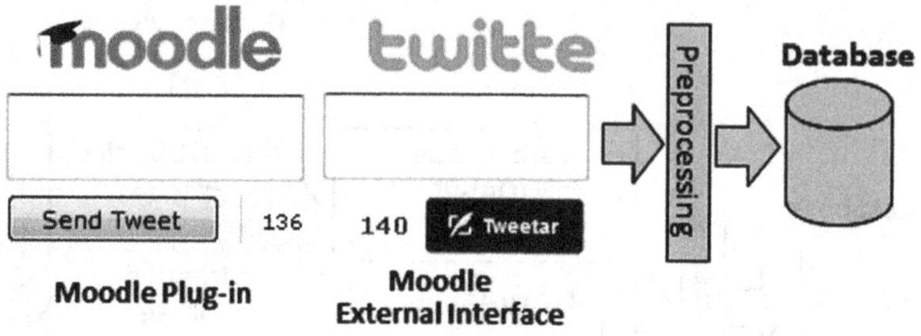

(in this case, #PC1). The inclusion of the hashtag by the Moodle plugin allows to monitor the progress of each hashtag in search systems and tracking tweets through various websites available on the Internet. The identification of the course in which the student is interacting by the Moodle plugin, defines the access list and hashtag related to this course.

The tweets that are generated outside of the Moodle plugin must be posted within the specific list of the Moodle course which you want to reference and should have, anywhere in the message, the hashtag referring to this same Moodle course. In this case, the tweets are imported by the application (through the use of the Twitter API) and subsequently subjected to the pre-processing step.

8. GENERAL SYSTEM ARCHITECTURE

This section presents the overall Moodle plug-in architecture. As seen in Figure 6, through the context-sensitive Moodle plug-in for the search of external resources users can formulate their queries by entering words that describe their topic of interest. For the construction of the core of the context-sensitive Moodle plug-in for the search of external resources, we use the Java programming language to implement the modules responsible for the integration of data providers, as well as, the process of external resources retrieval.

However, because Moodle is developed in the PHP programming language, all communication with the core of the context-sensitive Moodle plug-in for the search of external resources is accomplished through web services interface. Thus, any system capable of performing HTTP requests and handle XML can use the services of the information retrieval system that was developed in this work.

The plug-in identifies the area in which it is instantiated through the course's URLs. Each course in which the plug-in is instantiated is associated to an ontology as an artifact for specifying its knowledge domain.

As already shown in Figures 4 and 5, these features are an integrated database containing metadata from several data providers and tweets sent through Moodle plugin, as well as through any other external interface (i.e., the Twitter interface itself).

Still analyzing Figure 6, we highlight two important steps:

- **Query Analyzer:** This step aims to perform pre-processing and expanding user queries. In the pre-processing of the query, the stop words are removed and stemming of terms is performed. In query expansion, its terms are compared with the ontology. For each identified concept, the presence of equivalent concepts in this ontology is verified, adding them to the original query.

Figure 6. Procedure adopted for the recovery of resources

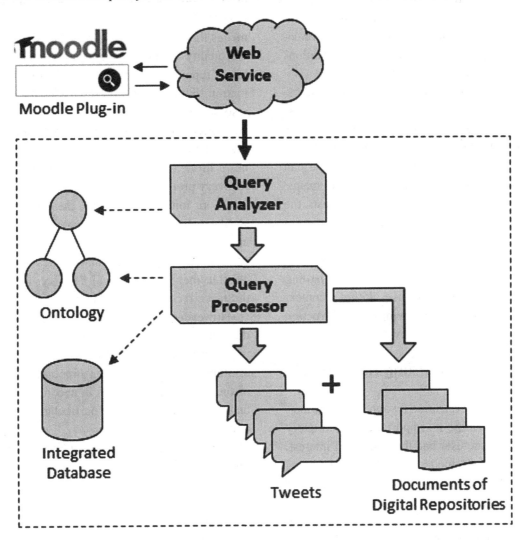

By using Jena for handling ontologies, given a certain concept it is possible to identify all concepts and their equivalents.

- **Query Processor:** After the query is pre-processed and expanded, the processing is performed for the recovery of resources. At this stage, resources are retrieved from the integrated database, making a comparison between the expanded query terms and the terms of each resource.

Since the definition of ontologies is a complex task that should be undertaken by a domain expert, and is not the main objetive of our work, we have defined ontology fragments in our knowledge domain that will serve to demonstrate the importance of ontologies in our context, and test our tool. These ontology fragments were developed without a formal methodology but they do represent a fair description of the chosen domain (computer science).

These ontologies have been implemented in OWL (Web Ontology Language) (OWL, 2014). For the creation and editing of ontologies we used Protégé (Protégé, 2014) that has an environment for creating and editing ontologies and knowledge bases. For navigation and inferences on ontologies, we used the Jena (Semantic Web Framework for Java) (Jena, 2014). Jena is an open source framework developed by HP Labs to build applications that target the Semantic Web.

For the recovery of resources, the terms of the expanded query are organized as a boolean expression. The boolean expression is executed over a structured database, using SQL (Structured Query Language). Since this integrated database can store documents from several knowledge domains, covering a wide range of topics and interests, the list of retrieved documents may contain several documents that are not of the user's interest.

So the next step is to identify the degree of similarity of each document retrieved regarding the query provided by the user within a context specified by ontology, allowing the construction of a ranking in order of relevance.

8.1 Generating Ranking Resources

In this step, each retrieved resource must be analyzed to determine its importance to the query provided by the user and the context of interest. Contexts are defined using characteristics of the Moodle's organization with the support of ontology.

The identification of the course in which the student is interacting with the Moodle plugin allows access to the ontology that specifies the knowledge domain. For each ontology of a Moodle course there should be an explicit XML file with the relations that are relevant. The relationships must have a weight that defines their importance. This file must be built by the expert who developed (or understands) the ontology. Figure 7 presents an excerpt from the specification of the relationships relevant to a particular ontology.

There are several techniques to establish measurements of similarity for documents. Most of these measures are produced by comparing vectors of terms that represent their content. In this work, external documents may originate from any reposi-

tory that provides an interface conforming to the OAI-PMH protocol and Twitter messages. This means that it is not always possible to guarantee the quality of the metadata of the repositories. Some repositories provide metadata with information that does not correctly describe a given resource, or even offer these same metadata in a very brief and incomplete form, not conforming to a particular metadata standard. Also, each tweet has a limited number of characters, making the recovery process more complex.

In our initial experiments, the calculation of similarity between the query provided by the user and the documents of several repositories was performed using conventional metrics such as the TF-IDF metric (Salton and Buckley, 1998) and the Jaccard coefficient (Manning, 2009).

However, in this work we chose to analyze the complete content description of the document metadata and Twitter messages to verify the existence of concept relationships and the weight of these concepts/relations in accordance to the ontology that specifies a particular knowledge domain.

For example, for a "Computer Programming in Java" course, a user may want to search for external documents (e.g., digital books, articles, tutorials, tweets, etc.) on a particular topic in order to assist in his learning. If a student needs to learn about arrays (a data structure that can store a series of data elements of the same size and data type), then a document with the following description may be recovered: Handout of *arrays* in *Java*: *declaration*, use of *indexes* and good *programming* practices.

Thus, using ontology for the domain of "Computer Programming", the following relationships can be identified: matrix and array are equivalent concepts; array is a concept of a programming language; Java is a programming language; array has a declaration and an index; programming is a concept in the ontology.

The occurrence of a set of terms in the description of a retrieved document which are also part of the ontology is a good indication that

Figure 7. Excerpt from the statement of the relevant relationships for a given ontology

```
1    <lists_of_properties>
2        <property_standards>
3          <property>
4              <name> has_query </name>
5              <weight> 5.0 </weight>
6          </property>
7          <property>
8              <name> has_ontology </name>
9              <weight> 2.0 </weight>
10         </property>
11         <property>
12             <name> subclass </name>
13             <weight> 3.0 </weight>
14         </property>
15       </property_standards>
16       <new_properties>
17         <property>
18             <name> has_a </name>
19             <weight> 2.0 </weight>
20         </property>
21         <property>
22             <name> resorce_of </name>
23             <weight> 2.0 </weight>
24         </property>
25       </new_properties>
26   </lists_of_properties>
```

this document is a part of the knowledge domain specified by the ontology.

After analyzing the contents of each resource for each relation identified in the ontology, we attribute the weights defined in Figure 7. The sum of the weights is the final value of relevance of this resource. Finally, these resources are sorted by relevance value (from highest to lowest). Tweets are displayed at the top of this list, followed by the documents in the digital repositories.

9. INTERFACE OF THE CONTEXT-SENSITIVE MOODLE PLUG-IN FOR THE SEARCH OF EXTERNAL RESOURCES

To develop a module for Moodle there are steps and rules that must be respected so that the application recognizes that group of files as a module. As Moodle is developed in PHP (a recursive acronym for "PHP: Hypertext Preprocessor"), the interface of the context-sensitive Moodle plug-in was also developed in this language. However, the core of the system was developed using the Java programming language, highlighting the modules responsible for the processes of integration of resources, pre-processing and information retrieval.

All communication from the Moodle plug-in interface with the core of the system is performed through requests through web services. A web service is a software system identified by a URI (Uniform Resource Identifier), in which public contracts and interfaces are defined and described in XML. The interface hides the implementation details of the service, allowing it to be used independently of the hardware or software platform on which it is implemented and the programming language it was written. To enable the provision of their services, web services need to be active and listening for requests. In this work, we used the Apache Tomcat (Apache Tomcat, 2014) as a Java application server for the web, running Apache Axis (Apache Axis, 2014) as a web services framework.

All experiments were carried out considering the recovery of resources (documents of digital repositories and tweets) in Portuguese language. However, the proposed approach also applies to other languages with similar characteristics (e.g., the western languages). To maintain the standard in the remaining of this text, the textual content of the interface images of the Moodle plug-in were translated into English.

Figure 8 presents the interface of the Moodle plug-in. The plugin instance refers to the subject "Computer Programming 1". The identification of the discipline in which the student is interacting allows Moodle plug-in access several information about the discipline. In the list vertical scroll type, the user can view the most recent tweets that refer to the discipline. By clicking on the "Search" link, one can perform semantic search, generating a ranking of the most relevant resources according to the user query.

To send a tweet, the user must authenticate by clicking the "Sign In with Twitter". In Figure 9, it is observed that the authentication is performed externally to the Moodle plug-in via OAuth protocol. The main goal of OAuth is to allow an application to authenticate to another "on behalf of a user" without access password of this user. Basically, the application requests access permission for that user and the user grants permission or not, without having to enter the password. This permission does not depend on a password. Even if the password is changed permission remains valid. In addition, permission given to the client application can be revoked at any time.

After doing the authentication, the system is redirected to the interface of Figure 10. In this interface, it is observed that a hyperlink is provided for logout, a text box for typing the tweet and a "Send Tweet" button to post to Twitter.

All messages sent by Moodle plug-in are posted on a Twitter list and a hashtag associated to the Moodle course in which the user is interacting is attached. In Figure 10, it is observed that the amount of characters allowed is 136 characters, because the discipline hashtag has 4 characters (in this case, it is the hashtag # PC1). Clicking on the hyperlink "View More" of the Moodle plugin, the user can see all the tweets that relate to the discipline.

To perform semantic search for resources, you must click on the hyperlink "Search". Figure 11 presents the Moodle plug-in search interface. There are two search modes:

- **Semantic Search:** Performs semantic search for resources (tweets and external documents within digital repositories) on the integrated database, with the support of an ontology;
- **Search Twitter Directly:** Performs the default Twitter search (using the API, without semantic processing).

Figure 8. Interface of the Moodle plug-in

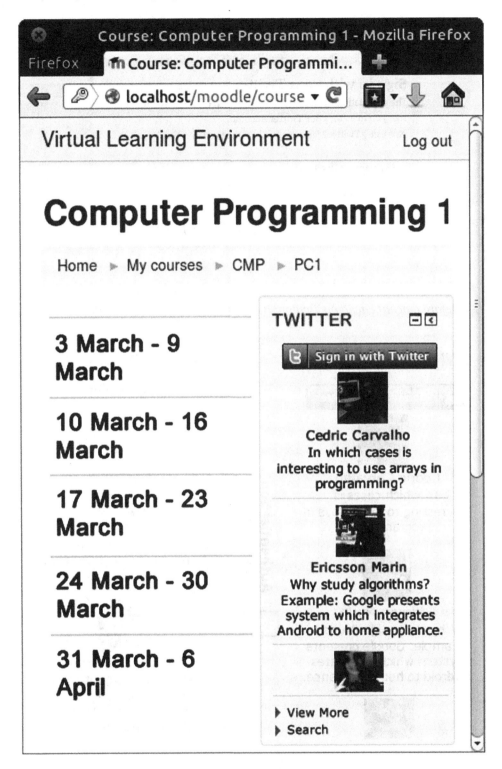

Figure 9. Authentication in Twitter through OAuth protocol

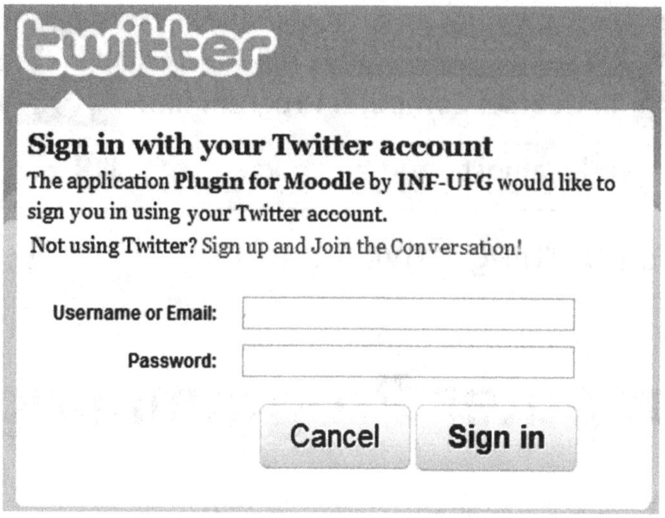

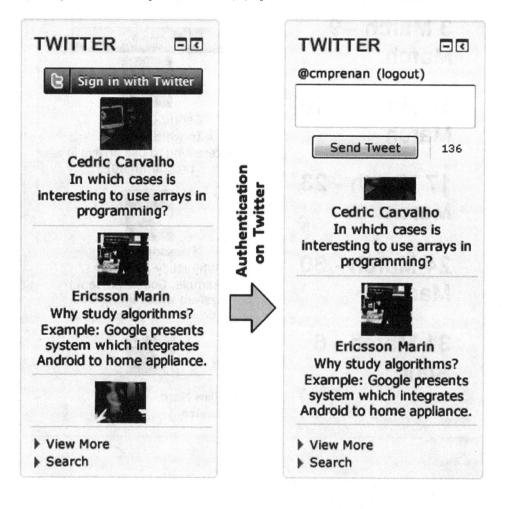

Figure 10. (A) Before autentincação on Twitter (B) After authentication on Twitter

Figure 11. Search interface of Moodle plug-in

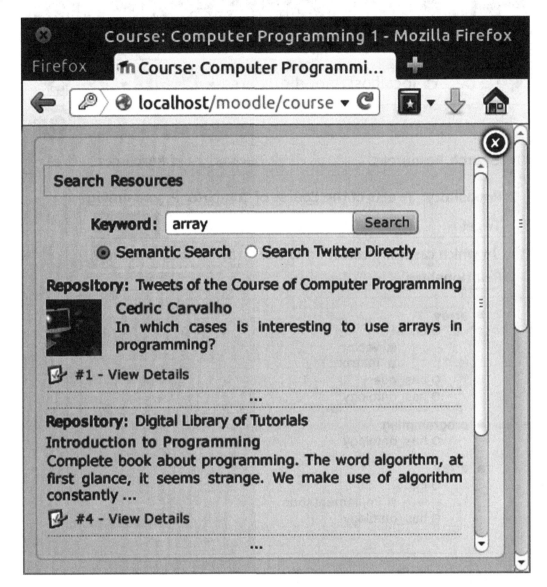

In Figure 11, the example searches for resources that refer to the term "array" in the "Computer Programming 1" context. The search result is a list of relevant resources, ordered according to the similarity they have to the query and to the domain knowledge. At the top of this list are the most relevant tweets followed by the external documents. In the example, resource #1 is the most relevant tweet identified by the system. Resource #4 is the most relevant document retrieved from digital repositories.

To view extra information on a given resource, you need to click on the "View Details" hyperlink. Figure 12, presents information about the resource identified as tweet #1.

Figure 12. Details of a tweet recovered by Moodle plug-in

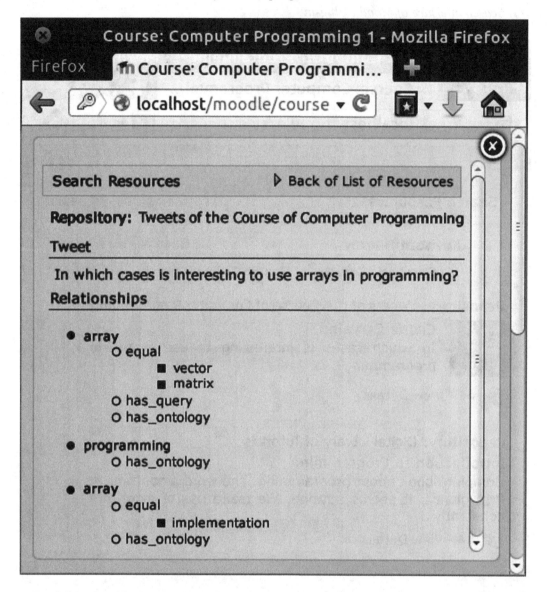

In Figure 12, there is the presentation of the content of the tweet and its relationship to the query and the ontology that specifies the domain knowledge. In this case, the relationships are as follows:

- Array
  - Equal
    - Vector
    - Matrix
  - Has_query
  - Has_ontology
- Program
  - Has_ontology
- Programming
  - Equal
    - Implementation
  - Has_ontology

Thus, we have:

- **Array:** The array term is equivalent to vector and array term. The array term is present in the user's query and also in ontology that specifies the domain knowledge;
- **Program:** The program term is present in the ontology;
- **Programming:** The programming term is equivalent to implementation term and is present in the ontology.

Figures 13 and 14 show detailed information of a digital repository document, identified as resource #4, which was recovered by the developed system. It contains information describing the document (for example: title, description, author and identifier) and its relationship to the query as well as the ontology that specifies the domain knowledge. In this case, the relationships are as follows:

- Array
  - Equal
    - Vector
    - Matrix
  - Has_query
  - Has_ontology
  - Has_a
    - Index
- Program
  - Has_ontology
- Programmer
  - Has_ontology
- Programming
  - Equals
    - Implementation
  - Has_ontology
- Algorithm
  - Has_ontology
- Index
  - Has_ontology
- Repetition
  - Has_ontology

Thus, we have:

- **Array:** The array concept is equivalent to vector and matrix. The array concept appears in the user's query and also in the knowledge domain ontology. The array concept is related to the index concept through a has_a relation (which appears in the description of the document), that is, an array has an index;
- **Program:** The program concept appears in the ontology;
- **Programmer:** The programmer concept appears in the ontology;
- **Programming:** The programming concept is equivalent to implementation and appears in the ontology.
- **Algorithm:** The algorithm concept appears in the ontology;
- **Index:** The index concept appears in the ontology;
- **Repetition:** The repetition concept appears in the ontology.

For the digital repository resources, an "Object Access" hyperlink is provided, which allows access to the full document in the online source repository.

10. ANALYSIS OF USE OF THE MOODLE PLUG-IN IN INTEGRATION WITH TWITTER

To test the Moodle plug-in, it was used as a learning tool in the "Artificial Intelligence", "Computer Programming I", "Computer Programming II" and "Mathematical Logic" courses of the Computer Science program at the Federal University of Goiás - Brazil. Both "Computer Programming I" and "Mathematical Logic" are courses taken by students in their first semester, while "Computer Programming II" is taken in their second semester and "Artificial Intelligence" in their fifth semester. All these courses are given in 2 hour classes, twice a week for 16 weeks, in a total of 64 hours per

Figure 13. Details of a document recovered by Moodle plug-in

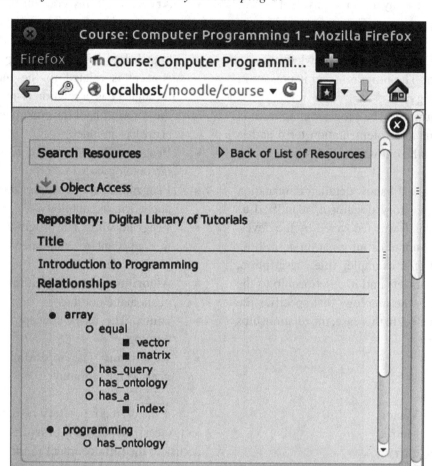

course. Two teachers participated in the experiment. A total of 131 students took these courses.

Table 1 presents a summary of the overall numbers generated from Moodle plug-in test in respect to integration with Twitter. Statistical analysis of the data shows that there is no Pearson correlation between the number of tweets and the final grade of the students, r = -.12, p = .186. Furthermore, there were no significant differences between students that failed their courses and those that were approved, t(128) = 1.26, p = .212 in relation to the number of tweets.

Analysis of the data shows that the teachers were the ones to post the larger number of tweets in each course. Students with small exceptions did not make many tweets. However, the number of

tweets increased with the course semester. This may imply that tweets demand more maturity or a greater involvement with the course. Even when rewards were given for using the tool, use was low. It must be observed that Twitter is not highly used by teenagers in Brazil. Different from the rest of the world, most users in Brazil use it in the "passive mode", to read what others post and rarely tweet. It serves mostly as a news feed. This could explain their behaviour in the courses. Unfortunately no information was obtained regarding the access and use of these tweets as news feed.

Another interesting observation is that considering the total number of students, 53.70% of students passed the courses in which they were enrolled and only 30.30% of students used Twit-

Figure 14. Details of a document recovered by Moodle plug-in (continuation)

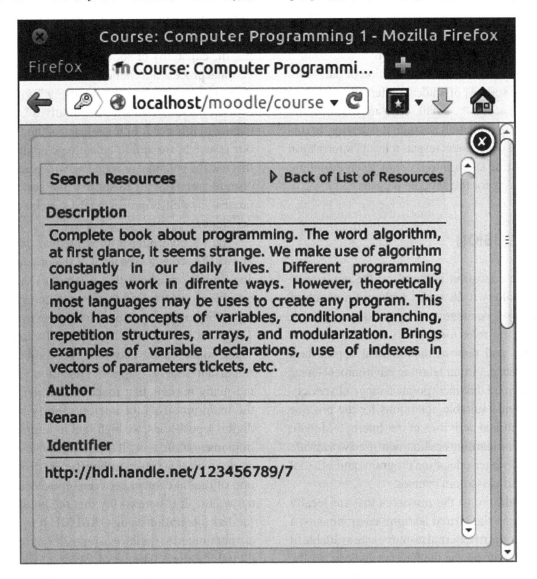

Table 1. Tweets from Moodle plug-in

Course	No. of Teacher Tweets	Greatest No. of Tweets by One of the Students	Total Tweets in Course	No. of Students that Submitted at Least One Tweet	No. of Students	Mean Tweets per Student	% of Students that Tweeted
AI	53	43	77	11	16	4.81	68.75
CP2	32	5	24	12	35	0.69	34.29
CP1	18	2	8	7	35	0.23	20.00
ML	14	1	5	5	45	0.11	11.11

Course: (AI) Artificial Intelligence (CP1) Computer Programming 1 (CP2) Computer Programming 2 (ML) Mathematical Logic ter. However, 67.44% of students who passed their course used the Moodle plug-in to share information through tweets.

Furthermore, we cannot forget that from a research perspective, the collection of data from different sources of students interaction, such as twitter, Facebook, email, etc., are important to understand and analyze student behavior. In this sense, the experiment reveals relevant information that must be taken into account when designing further uses for the Moodle plug-in.

CONCLUSION

Distance education is based on the application of technology to learning, without limitation of place, time, occupation or age of the students. It implies new roles for students and teachers, new attitudes and new methodological approaches. In this sense, virtual learning environments have been defined that incorporate a range of services that provide suitable conditions for the practice of educational activities in the Internet. Moodle is an online learning environment used worldwide both in distance education programs and as a tool to support classroom courses.

In addition, to the resources that are locally available in the virtual learning environments, a large amount of external resources are available in other repositories on the Internet and can also be retrieved and used in a student's learning process. These include content generated and shared in social networks, which can be treated as important repositories that contain information that may be useful in the educational process, since they bring the reality of the connected world to the classroom. Learning to use these resources appropriately and with responsibility is part of the goals of modern education. Through experience gained in this work, it is believed that Twitter is a tool that allows an important interaction between teachers and students. Even outside of the classroom (with Internet access and a laptop, cell phone, etc.), it is

possible to discuss relevant issues that contribute to reflection and learning for interested persons.

Indeed, the development of applications that use the capability of social networks in the educational process is a challenge. However, the case study presented in this article (using Twitter and Moodle), shows that simple initiatives can contribute to this need. In this sense, as the focus of our research, we aim to create new applications that use the potential of social networks and other current technologies to support the educational process, as well as improving the systems already developed.

The Moodle plug-in presented in this work allows the semantic retrieval of documents from any digital repository that offers an OAI-PMH interface, contributing to the resource retrieval capability of this type of learning environment. The Moodle plug-in also retrieves Twitter messages, since social networks are shown as an important tool to support education. Among the many reasons that make OAI-PMH one of the main protocols for interoperability between digital repositories, we highlight its simplicity of implementation, as well as the existence of open source tools that facilitate the efficient dissemination of digital content between repositories with a low cost. It is noteworthy that the possibilities for data integration using OAI-PMH repositories are not limited to traditional repositories (e.g., the digital libraries). The use of tools that enable the implementation of data providers can be used to expose metadata from any source of information, such as distributed databases, unstructured files directories, etc.

However, the ability to recover a greater number of resources may lead to problems due to information overload. The students may become overwhelmed by the amount of documents recovered, and by the effort necessary to select the relevant ones. This problem can be reduced by filtering the recovered documents according to the context in which the original query was made. Many features of the Moodle structure (organized in courses, subjects, topics etc.), suggest well-defined contexts. These characteristics were used to implement a context-sensitive Moodle plug-in for the search of external resources. This plug-in retrieves a list of resources from miscellaneous external repositories based on a query provided by the user. The recovered resources (documents and tweets) are analyzed to verify if they belong to the context in which the query was performed. This is done by identifying in the documents concepts and relations from the context specified in an ontology associated to the Moodle area where the user is interacting. Using the weights associated to these relations, a ranking of the documents is carried out.

Although the experiments using the tool in class environments did not yield significant improvements in the students' learning, we believe this is due to characteristics of the Brazilian use of Twitter and merit further investigation. Never the less, the tool did fulfill its purpose of recovering relevant information for the users as well as creating a database of information that can be further analyzed to obtain a clearer view of the type of doubts the students have and what type of information they seek. Also, an investigation of Twitter as a news feed and its impact on learning should be verified.

FUTURE RESEARCH

From the literature review and the tool developed in this work, we can highlight the following future research:

- Expand the use of the characteristics of the structure of Moodle for the contexts definition.
- Encourage the use of tools that enable the opening of metadata in accordance with the OAI;

- Develop application based on ontologies to model educational domains for the creation and retrieval of learning objects.
- Exploiting the potential of the semantics of Twitter hashtags, as well as the inclusion of semantic metadata as a way of indexing.
- Create new applications that use the potential of social networks and other current technologies in support of educational process as well as improving the systems already developed.

REFERENCES

Apache Axis. (2014). *Apache Axis*. Retrieved March 27, 2014, from http://ws.apache.org/axis

Apache Tomcat. (2014). *Apache Tomcat*. Retrieved March 27, 2014, from http://tomcat.apache.org

Berners-Lee, T., Hendler, J., & Lassila, O. (2001). Web semantic: A new form of web content that is meaningful to computers will unleash a revolution of new possibilities. *Scientific American, 284*(5), 34–43. doi:10.1038/scientificamerican0501-34 PMID:11396337

Bittencourt, I., Isotani, S., Costa, E., & Mizoguchi, R. (2007). Research directions on semantic web and education. *Scientia: Interdisciplinary Studies in Computer Science, 19*(1), 59–66.

Bloehdorn, S., Cimiano, P., & Hotho, A. (2006). Learning ontologies to improve text clustering and classification. In *From data and information analysis to knowledge engineering* (pp. 334–341). Berlin: Springer Berlin Heidelberg.

br.ispell. (2014). *Dictionary br.ispell*. Retrieved March 27, 2014, from http://www.ime.usp. br/~ueda/br.ispell

Bristol, T. J. (2010). Twitter: Consider the possibilities for continuing nursing education. *Journal of Continuing Education in Nursing, 41*(5), 199–200. doi:10.3928/00220124-20100423-09 PMID:20481418

Degenne, A., & Forsé, M. (1999). *Introducing social network*. London: Sage.

DSpace. (2014). *Digital repository software*. Retrieved March 27, 2014, from http://www.openarchives.org

Dufresne, A., & Rouatbi, M. (2007). Ontologies, applications integration and support to users in learning objects repositories. In Proceedings of SWEL'07: Ontologies and Semantic Web Services for Intelligent Distributed Educational Systems (pp. 30-35). Academic Press.

Feitosa, A. (2006). *Organização da informação na web: Das tags à web semântica*. Brasília, Brasil: Editora Thesaurus.

Grossecmk, G., & Holotescu, C. (2008). Can we use Twitter for educational activities? In *Proceedings of 4th International Scientific Conference eLSE eLearning and Software for Education*. Retrieved from http://www.cblt.soton.ac.uk/multimedia/PDFsMM09/Can we use twitter for educational activities.pdf

Gruber, T. R. (1993). *A translation approach to portable ontology specifications: Knowledge systems laboratory technical report KSL 92-71*. Computer Science Department, Stanford University.

Harmandaoglu, E. (2012). The use of twitter in language learning and teaching. In *Proceedings of International Conference "ICT for Language Learning"*. Retrieved from http://conference.pixel-online.net/ICT4LL2012/common/download/Paper_pdf/211-IBT41-FP-Harmandaoglu-ICT2012.pdf

Honeycutt, C., & Herring, S. C. (2009). Beyond microblogging: Conversation and collaboration via Twitter. In *Proceedings of Forty-Second Hawaii International Conference on System Sciences* (pp. 1-10). IEEE.

Jazzy. (2014). *Java spell check API*. Retrieved March 27, 2014, from http://sourceforge.net/projects/jazzy

Jena. (2014). *A semantic web framework for Java*. Retrieved March 27, 2014, from http://jena.sourceforge

Lancaster, F. W. (1993). *Indexação e resumos: Teoria e prática*. Brasília, Brasil: Briquet de Lemos Livros.

Manning, C. D. (2009). *An introduction to information retrieval*. Cambridge, England: Cambridge University Press.

McCool, L.B. (2011). *The pedagogical use of Twitter in the university classroom*. Graduate Theses and Dissertations. Retrieved from Graduate College at Digital Repository (Paper 11947).

Moodle. (2014, March 27). *Modular object oriented distance learning*. Retrieved March 27, 2014, from http://moodle.org

OAI. (2014). *Open archives initiative*. Retrieved March 27, 2014, from http://www.openarchives.org

OAI-PMH. (2014). *Open archives initiative – Protocol for metadata harvesting*. Retrieved March 27, 2014, from http://www.openarchives.org/pmh

OWL. (2014). *OWL web ontology language*. Retrieved March 27, 2014, from http://www.w3.org/TR/owlref PHP (2014). PHP

phpoai2. (2014). *PHP data provider*. Retrieved March 27, 2014, from http://physnet.uni-oldenburg.de/oai

Protégé. (2014). *Ontology editor and knowledge acquisition system*. Retrieved March 27, 2014, from http://protege.stanford.edu

PTStemmer. (2014). *A Java stemming toolkit for the Portuguese language*. Retrieved March 27, 2014, from http://code.google.com/p/ptstemmer

Recuero, R. (2009). *Redes sociais na internet*. Porto Alegre, Brasil: Editora Sulina.

Registered Data Providers, O. A. I. (2014). *List of the registered data providers OAI*. Retrieved March 27, 2014, from http://www.openarchives.org

Rigo, S. J., de Oliveira, J. P., & Barbieri, C. (2007). Classificação de textos baseada em ontologias de domínio. In *Proceedings of Anais do XXVII Congresso da SBC – V Workshop em Tecnologia da Informação e da Linguagem Humana*. Retrieved from http://www.nilc.icmc.usp.br/til/til2007_English/arq0169.pdf

Roa, D. I. J., Lapo, P. S., & Rodríguez-Artacho, M. (2010). Semantic search in institutional repositories: A case study using DSpace and Moodle. In *Proceedings of International Conference on E-Learning, E-Business, Enterprise Information Systems, & E-Government* (pp. 356-365). Academic Press.

Salton, G., & Buckley, C. (1998). Term-weighting approaches in automatic retrieval. *Information Processing & Management*, *24*(5), 513–523. doi:10.1016/0306-4573(88)90021-0

Studer, R., Benjamims, V. R., & Fensel, D. (1998). Knowledge engineering: Principles and methods. *Data & Knowledge Engineering*, *25*(1-2), 161–197. doi:10.1016/S0169-023X(97)00056-6

Thiagarajan, R., Manjunath, G., & Stumptner, M. (2008). Computing semantic similarity using ontologies. In *Proceedings of International Semantic Web Conference*. Retrieved from http://www.hpl.hp.com/techreports/2008/HPL-2008-87.pdf

Wu, S., Tsait, & Hsu, W. (2003). Text categorization using automatically acquired domain ontology. In *Proceedings of 16th International Workshop on Information Retrieval with Asian Languages* (vol. 11, pp. 138-145). Academic Press. doi:10.3115/1118935.1118953

ADDITIONAL READING

Al-Khalifa, H., & Davis, H. (2006). The evolution of metadata from standards to semantics in e-learning applications. *17th ACM Conference on Hypertext and Hypermedia*, pp. 69-72.

Alexopoulos, A. F., Koutsomitropoulos, D., Papatheodorou, T. S., & Solomou, G. D. (2009). Digital repositories and the semantic web: semantic search and navigation for DSpace. *4th International Conference on Open Repositories*. Retrieved from https://gupea.ub.gu.se/handle/2077/21339

Anistyasari, & Y. Sarno, R. (2011). Weighted ontology for subject search in learning content management system. *Electrical Engineering and Informatics*, pp. 1-4.

Aroyo, L., & Dicheva, D. (2004). The new challenges for e-learning: The educational semantic web. *Journal of Educational Technology & Society*, *7*(4), 59–69.

Baeza Yates. R., & Ribeiro Neto, B. (1999). Modern information retrieval. Harlow, UK: Addison-Wesley.

Borau, K., Ullrich, C., Feng, J., & Shen, R. (2009). Microblogging for language learning: using Twitter to train communicative and cultural competence. In Spaniol, M., Li, Q., Klamma, R., & Lau, R. W. H. (Eds.), *From Advances in Web Based Learning – ICWL - 8th International Conference*, 78-87. Aachen, Germany: Springer Berlin Heidelberg. doi:10.1007/978-3-642-03426-8_10

Brown, P. G. An experiment in using Twitter in teaching a student affairs practicum course. The *Journal of Technology in Student Affairs. Summer 2013 Edition.* Retrieved from https://www.studentaffairs.com/ejournal/Summer_2013/AnExperimentInUsingTwitter.pdf

Celorrio, C., & Verdejo, M. F. (2008). An interoperable, extensible and configurable service architecture for an integrated educational networking infrastructure. *ICALT '08 Proceedings of the 2008 Eighth IEEE International Conference on Advanced Learning Technologies*, pp. 207-211.

Cohen, A., & Duchan, G. (2012). The usage characteristics of Twitter in the learning process. *Interdisciplinary Journal of E-Learning and Learning Objects*, 8, 149–163.

Ferreira, M., & Baptista, A. A. (2005). The use of taxonomies as a way to achieve interoperability and improved resource discovery in Dspace-based repositories. *XATA - XML: Aplicações e Tecnologias Associadas.* Retrieved from http://repositorium.sdum.uminho.pt/bitstream/1822/873/1/paper-25.pdf

Fertalj, K., Hoic-Bozic, N., & Jerković, H. (2010). The integration of learning object repositories and learning management systems. *Computer Science and Information Systems*, 7(3), 387–407. doi:10.2298/CSIS081127001F

González, M. A. C., García-Peñalvo, F. J., Piguillem, J., Guerrero, M. J. C., & Forment, M. A. (2012). Interoperability in e-learning contexts. Interaction between LMS and PLE. *1st Symposium on Languages, Applications and Technologies*, pp. 205-223.

Jiang, L., Zhang, H., Yang, X., & Xie, N. (2013). Research on semantic text mining based on domain ontology. In Li, Daoliang, Chen, Yingyi (Eds.), From Computer and Computing Technologies in Agriculture VI, 336-343. Zhangjiajie, China: Springer Berlin Heidelberg. doi:10.1007/978-3-642-36124-1_40

Jovanov, M., Gushev, M., Martinovikj, D., & Spasovski, S. (2013). Moodle implementation of activity for on-line collaborative ontology building. *10th Conference for Informatics and Information Technology.* Retrieved from http://ciit.finki.ukim.mk/data/papers/10CiiT/10CiiT-06.pdf

Jovanovic, J., Devedzic, V., Gasevic, D., Hatala, M., Eap, T., Richards, G., & Brooks, C. (2007). Using semantic web technologies to analyze learning content. *IEEE Internet Computing*, 11(5), 45–53. doi:10.1109/MIC.2007.116

Kholief, M., Nada, N., & Khedr, W. (2012). Ontology-oriented inference-basead learning content management system. *International Journal of Web & Semantic Technology*, 3(3), 131–142. doi:10.5121/ijwest.2012.3309

Lagoze, C., & Van de Sompel, H. (2001). The open archives initiative: building a low-barrier interoperability framework. *ACM/IEEE Joint Conference on Digital Libraries*, pp. 54-62. doi:10.1145/379437.379449

Lorenzo, E. J., Centeno, R., & Rodríguez-Artacho, M. (2013). A framework for helping developers in the integration of external tools into virtual learning environments. *First International Conference on Technological Ecosystem for Enhancing Multiculturality*, pp. 127-132. doi:10.1145/2536536.2536556

Martínez, A., Dimitriadis, Y., Rubia, B., Gómez, E., Garrachón, I., & Marcos, J. A. (2003). Combining qualitative evaluation and social network analysis for the study of classroom social interactions. *Computers & Education - Documenting Collaborative Interactions. Issues and Approaches, 41*(4), 353–368.

Mathews, L. M. (2011). An overview: Semantic web based education. *International Journal of Computers and Applications, 26*(2), 18–22. doi:10.5120/3076-4206

Rinaldo, S. B., Tapp, S., & Laverie, D. A. (2011). Learning by tweeting: Using Twitter as a pedagogical tool. *Journal of Marketing Education, 33*(2), 193–203. doi:10.1177/0273475311410852

Segaran, T., Evans, C., & Taylor, J. (2009). *Programming the semantic web*. Sebastopol, California: O'Reilly Media.

Suleman, H. (2001). Enforcing interoperability with the open archives initiative repository explorer. *ACM/IEEE Joint Conference on Digital Libraries*, pp. 63-64. doi:10.1145/379437.379450

Usman, A., & Khan, S. (2012). Exploiting semantics in subject-based searching of Dspace. In H. Chen & C. Chowdhury (Eds.), *The Outreach of Digital Libraries: A Globalized Resource Network* (pp. 29–38). doi:10.1007/978-3-642-34752-8_4

Yusof, N., & Mansur, A. B. F. (2013). Ontology development of e-learning Moodle for social learning network analysis. *World Academy of Science. Engineering and Technology, 7*(6), 2050–2055.

Chapter 4
E–Learning and the Semantic Web:
A Descriptive Literature Review

Raadila Bibi Mahmud Hajee Ahmud-Boodoo
Curtin University, Australia

ABSTRACT

A number of 3.0 e-learning systems have been proposed in the literature to capture the numerous benefits that the Semantic Web has to offer to the higher education sector. These 3.0 e-learning systems identify some essential Semantic Web characteristics that are either discussed as stand-alone factors or tend to revolve around the complexities of the Semantic Web technology and its implementation, often disregarding users' needs. Conversely, a comprehensive analysis of e-learning models for higher education in the literature revealed several Critical Success Factors (CSFs) that are relevant to the Semantic Web but often overlooked in 3.0 e-learning models. Consequently, this chapter provides an overview of the CSFs of e-learning relevant to 3.0 e-learning systems as well as an overview of the main Semantic Web characteristics for e-learning to define a new and combined set of 3.0 e-learning characteristics that will holistically represent 3.0 e-learning systems capturing the needs and expectations of users. The new initial 3.0 e-learning model proposed is evaluated within the higher education sector in Mauritius.

INTRODUCTION

E-learning has been integrated in many universities as a modern, efficient and effective alternative to learning, especially to assist in the increased demand in higher education. With the rapid development of information and communication technologies (ICT) and the increasing needs for empowering students with critical thinking and analytical skills, it is considered a must to revolutionise current e-learning practices (Karunasena, Deng & Zhang, 2012). Efforts are being directed at building 3.0 E-learning systems in line with the Semantic Web. In fact, *Semantic Web* is seen as a promising technology to meet E-learning requirements, as it promises the best capabilities for composition and reuse of materials and contexts within E-learning. This chapter seeks to identify and integrate essential *E-learning* and *Semantic Web characteristics* from the current literature

DOI: 10.4018/978-1-4666-8147-7.ch004

to develop a new *3.0 E-learning model* which aims to provide a holistic representation of 3.0 E-learning. A comprehensive literature review will be conducted on current E-learning models as well as current Semantic E-learning models to identify a new and collective set of 3.0 *E-learning characteristics* from users' perspectives.

E-LEARNING AND THE SEMANTIC WEB: LITERATURE REVIEW

Effect of Technology on Teaching and Learning

Constant development in Information and Communication Technology (ICT) has significantly enhanced teaching and learning processes. Students are no longer regarded as consumers of information provided to them by instructors and undertaking academic activities in isolation or in isolated local groups (Keats & Schmidt, 2007). Rather, the shift is towards more interaction between students and lecturers and between peer-to-peer students. The key to supporting this evolving learning environment is the Internet. In fact, the Internet is believed to have transformed, if not revolutionised teaching and learning processes (Mering & Robbie, 2004). It has paved the way to a web-based education system and provides the platform for numerous technologies to assist in enhancing the teaching and learning process.

Evolution of the Web

The World Wide Web (WWW) has seen some important changes over the last few years. It has changed from being "an access technology" into a "participating technology" with the advent of Web 2.0 (Keats & Schmidt, 2007, p. 2). While Web 1.0, commonly considered as the 'Read Only' web, is considered as the first generation of the web, Web 2.0 or the 'read-write web' refers

to a loose collection of technologies (podcasting, blogs, wikis, social networking services, social book marking, file sharing) designed to facilitate collaboration and sharing between users(Kennedy et al., 2007; Naik & Shivalingaiah, 2008). With recent developments in web technologies, efforts are now being directed to make the web more intelligent to provide higher-level services to users - namely Web 3.0 (also referred to as the Semantic Web). This undeniably has several implications for the educational world, especially with regards to web-based education.

Web-Based Education System

Web-based system to higher education has numerous advantages, including classroom and platform independence, availability of authoring tools to develop web-based courseware, cheap and efficient storage and distribution of materials, hyperlinks to suggested readings and digital libraries" (Devedzic, 2004, p. 165). However, efforts are ongoing to improve such a system to meet some of its challenges, namely more adaptivity and intelligence. While intelligent web-based educational systems introduce some amount of adaptivity and intelligence in web-based teaching and learning, it is believed that the Semantic Web will further contribute in meeting these challenges (Devedzic, 2004).

The Semantic Web

Semantic Web encompasses efforts to build a WWW architecture where content is enhanced with formal semantics, creating an environment where automated agents are able to perform tasks efficiently on behalf of users (Stojanovic, Staab & Studer, 2001). The motivation behind the Semantic Web is largely because the current web is "not smart enough" to provide users with required information (Devedzic, 2004, p. 166). This is due to the large amount of information available on the web and the lack of structure of these resources making it increasingly difficult for users to search for learning content. As a matter of fact, users are accustomed to a network where search engines provide thousands of potential hits (if not more) and yet their ability to retrieve, manipulate and organize online materials is still rudimentary (Anderson & Whitelock, 2004). Hence, the need to make the learning process faster with well-organised learning materials specific to learner's needs and customised on-line services initiated by user profiles is deemed essential (Huang et al., 2006).However, everything on the web is machine readable but not machine-understandable (Lassila, 1998). This is where the Semantic Web is seen to have potential in providing machine-interpretable and precise information ready to be used by software agents (Devedzic, 2004). *Semantic Web* allows content to become "aware of itself" by allowing users and agents to query and infer knowledge from information quickly and automatically (Anderson & Whitelock, 2004). Web contents will be enhanced with formal semantics enabling automated agents to reason about the content and to carry out more intelligent tasks on behalf of users (Huang et al., 2006). This will facilitate access to learning materials by providing a rich set of services that can personalise content as well as provide a structured database for better knowledge handling by machines (Bucos, Dragulescu & Veltan, 2010). In fact, *ontologies*, which allow learning domains to be described from different perspectives thus allowing for a richer description and retrieval of learning contents, are considered as the backbone of the Semantic Web (Castellanos-Nieves, Fernández-Breis, Valencia-García, Martínez-Béjar & Iniesta-Moreno, 2011).

E-Learning and the Semantic Web

Many strategies have been devised over the years to improve E-learning effectiveness. While these strategies assist students in their knowledge

construction, they also create the problem of information overloading due to the large amount of learning resources generated. Semantic web technologies and the use of ontologies promise to enable intelligent web-based information processing to resolve the information overload problem and as such realise the vision of having the right information in the right context with the right level of details to the right person at the right time (Berners-Lee, Hendler & Lassila, 2001). Concepts and theories behind the Semantic Web will provide opportunities to expand the scope and ability to provide learning opportunities "unbounded by geographic, temporal, or economic distance" (Anderson & Whitelock, 2004, p. 2). In fact, the *Semantic Web* is seen as a powerful approach to meet E-learning requirements (Stojanovic et al., 2001). Consequently, a lot of work has been done in this regard with different *3.0 E-learning systems* proposed to integrate the Semantic Web within e-learning with ontologies acting as a key enabler. In fact, different aspects of E-learning have been considered in the literature with respect to the Semantic Web. Among them are content management and personalised learning with ontology-based technology (Snae & Brueckner, 2007; Ghaleb et al., 2006; Bucos et al., 2010; Devedzic, 2004; Stojanovic et al., 2001). The literature also addresses course sequencing, making use of ontologies as the basis to achieve personalised learning (De Nicola, Missikoff & Schiappelli, 2004; Srimathi & Srivatsa, 2008; Wang, 2008; Neri, 2005; Wiley, 2003; Neri & Colombetti, 2009; Brusilovsky & Vassileva, 2003). Additionally, work has also been done to support more specific aspects of E-learning, including assessment and better feedback service (Castellanos-Nieves et al., 2011; Moreale & Vargas-Vera, 2004). Trust within the Semantic Web has also been highly discussed but always in isolation from other aspects of E-learning and 3.0 E-learning (von Kortzfleisch, FO & Winand, 2000; Golbeck, Parsia & Hendler, 2003; Golbeck & Hendler, 2006; Shekarpour, Katebi & Katebi,

2009; O'Hara, Alani, Kalfoglou & Shadbolt, 2004; Cloran, 2007). Other factors such as collaboration, support, accessibility, while often implied in 3.0 E-learning systems, are seldom exhibited as major aspects to achieving effective 3.0 E-learning (Paxton, 2003; Jump & Jump, 2006).

RESEARCH METHODOLOGY

A Descriptive Literature Review

The descriptive literature review approach adopted in this chapter requires the author to conduct a comprehensive literature search in order to collect as many relevant papers as possible in the area being investigated – in this case E-learning and 3.0 E-learning models for higher education. In fact, a descriptive review focuses on revealing an interpretable pattern from the existing literature following a systematic procedure of searching, filtering and classifying (Guzzo, Jackson & Katzell, 1987). This approach is deemed appropriate as the objective of this chapter is to outline the main characteristics of a 3.0 E-learning model from identified characteristics of existing E-learning and Semantic E-learning models. Webster and Watson (2002) recommended a structured approach to determine the source materials for a review following a 3 stage process namely

- Starting with leading journals,
- Using citations from articles identified in stage 1 to determine prior articles to be considered, and
- Identifying key articles which cite articles in stage 1 and 2 to see if any of them are relevant to the review.

The following processes were adopted to identify relevant materials in the literature for this chapter.

The Searching Process

A comprehensive analysis of the literature on existing *E-learning* and *3.0 E-learning models* for higher education is required before a new and combined set of *3.0 E-learning characteristics* can be identified. As a result, the first step to this review is to identify relevant literature through both computer and manual searches. In fact, online databases search is a dominant approach for research related to contemporary phenomenon in the field of Information systems (Petter & Mclean, 2009; Sabherwal, Jeyaraj & Chowa, 2006; Hwang & Thorn, 1999). With the Semantic Web being a recently emerging technology, the focus of this research is mostly on online databases rather than manual searches.

Based on this, a keyword search on Google search engine with the following phrases namely – "Semantic Web", "Semantic Web and E-learning", "Web 3.0 and E-learning" were first conducted with focus on scholarly articles. This was followed by the keyword "Semantic Web and ontologies" and "ontologies" since most article related to the Semantic Web have mention of the particular term 'ontology'.

This process was repeated using the following keywords: "E-learning models", "Critical Success Factors for E-learning" and "E-learning critical success factors in higher education" in order to gather articles for essential higher education E-learning characteristics relevant to the Semantic Web.

Some articles were not easily accessible via the Google search engine for different reasons such as requirements for membership login details and articles to be purchased. In such cases, the online Curtin University library was used as the search database to gain access to most of these articles.

Filtering Process

Articles from the searching process were then analysed for relevance to the chapter objectives.

They were initially selected based on the chapter title. The abstract of the selected articles were then reviewed to ensure that the articles relate to the chapter objectives. Following this, the full texts of the selected ones were reviewed to gather only the articles that are related to *Semantic Web* and *E-learning models* and characteristics. Articles where essential Semantic Web 3.0 and E-learning characteristics were not discussed were discarded.

Citations in selected articles were also used as a means to find more relevant materials that could be reviewed for the chapter. Additionally, other articles which cited the selected ones were reviewed for relevance using first the title as a starting point, followed by the abstract and then a full text review where there was indication of relevance to the chapter objectives.

Classification Process

Following a full text review of the selected articles from the filtering process, a list of essential *Semantic Web characteristics* as well as *E-learning characteristics* for higher education was identified. These characteristics were grouped into eight main categories with each category having some sub-categories based on the research interest of the articles. Each article was then reviewed to identify the presence of these main characteristics and sub characteristics as outlined in Appendix A – A comparative Analysis of E-learning Characteristic.

Table 1 outlines the new set of combined Semantic Web and E-learning characteristics for a *holistic 3.0 E-learning model*.

1. **Content Management:** A systematic approach to managing knowledge is considered to be an essential pre-requisite for knowledge seekers to access relevant learning materials as and when required (Pah, Maniu, Maniu & Damian, 2007). As such content management which refers to the maintenance and manipulation of learning materials on 3.0 E-learning systems is seen as a key char-

acteristic for a 3.0 E-learning model. It can be further grouped into the following five sub-characteristics:

a. **Content Creation:** This refers to the creation of learning materials based on their different degree of difficulty and knowledge levels of students (Bucos et al., 2010). Learning content can be newly created or composed based on different elements of existing materials that can be reused.

b. **Content Retrieval:** Students will access learning materials for the learning process to take place. Lecturers and administrators will access materials for organising, maintaining, updating and integrating information as and when required (Karunasena et al., 2012).

c. **Content Reuse:** Where learning materials are broken down into elements or learning objects that can be reused for new learning content creation. Learning objects are those elements of the learning materials that can be used, re-used or referenced during technology supported learning (Snae & Brueckner, 2007).

d. **Knowledge Representation:** *Ontologies* allow for knowledge representation which is crucial for the automatic processing of Information on the Web as they provide a formal representation of learning content essential for its retrieval and reuse (Monachesi, Simov, Mossel, Osenova & Lemnitzer, 2008). In fact, *ontologies*, which allow learning domains to be described from different perspectives thus allowing for a richer description and retrieval of learning contents, are considered as the backbone of the Semantic Web (Castellanos-Nieves et al., 2011). Thus knowledge representation is a key characteristic to a 3.0 E-learning model.

Table 1. New set of combined semantic web and e-learning characteristics for a holistic 3.0 e-learning model – Prepared by the author

Main Characteristic		Sub-Characteristic
Content Management		Content Creation
		Content Retrieval
		Content Reuse
		Knowledge Representation
		Search
Usability and Accessibility		Interface Design
		Technology
		Student Centered Learning
		Collaboration
Collaboration		Student-Lecturer
		Peer-Peer
		Resource Sharing
		Group Activities
		Feedback
Teaching Principles	Curriculum	Syllabus
		Course Sequencing
	Pedagogy	Instructional Method
		Context
		Delivery Instrument
		Learning Theories
		Teaching Strategies
Personalised Learning		Student Model
		Learning and Cognitive Style
		Educational Goals
		Learning Participation
Support	Instructional	Activities
		Help
		Feedback
		Collaboration
	System	Student Centered Learning
		Organisation Support
		Technology
		Training
		Infrastructure
Trust		Student-Lecturer
		Peer-Peer
		Technology
		System
		Security
Web 3.0 Ontology-Based Technology		Ontologies Database
		Content Database
		Records Database
		Hardware
		Software
		System Infrastructure

e. **Search:** Searching of learning materials within the 3.0 E-learning environment will be enhanced with the use of ontologies.

2. **Usability and Accessibility:** Ease of use and accessibility of the 3.0 E-learning system is an essential characteristic as didactics will not matter to users especially students if their needs are not met in terms of the right and timely information and learning content being delivered to them in the easiest possible way (Pah et al., 2007). It has the following four sub characteristics:

a. **Interface Design:** The interface is the essential point of access to the 3.0 E-learning system. Users of the system will access, upload and modify information according to their roles and level of authority via the Interface. Properly designing the interface is therefore critical to ensure that learning contents are easily and effectively managed and accessed.

b. **Technology:** Technology being used should be appropriate and simple to use to promote ease of access and navigation and interaction (Masoumi, 2006).

c. **Student Centered Learning:** The 3.0 E-learning system should provide students with different tools that make navigation through the learning space easy and effective. Similarly, information being delivered to students should be contextualised and based on the student model to match the skills sets and knowledge level of each student to allow for *individualised learning* to take place (Šimić, Gašević & Devedžić, 2004).

d. **Collaboration:** Central to usability and accessibility are collaboration activities between students in terms of knowledge exchange, working on

common projects together, sharing of resources and problem solving in group (Pah et al., 2007). Additionally, students and lecturers can behave as collaborative partners away from the traditional class room model where teachers were the only providers of learning content (von Kortzfleisch & Winand, 2000).

3. **Collaboration:** To promote an effective E-learning environment requires some form of interaction and collaboration (Selim 2007). These interactive and collaborative activities can be between the student and the learning content, between peer to peer students or between students and lecturers. Collaboration can be grouped into the following five sub characteristics:

a. **Student-Lecturer:** Student interaction with the lecturer is considered as an essential component of effective E-learning (Selim, 2007).

b. **Peer-Peer:** Studies indicate that peer to peer interactions is a critical success factor when measuring student satisfaction with E-learning based courses (Selim, 2007).

c. **Resource Sharing:** Sharing resources among peers as well as between student and lecturers is an essential activity to support collaboration within an E-learning environment.

d. **Group Activities:** Group activities promote learning as well as contribute to build trust between peers thereby fostering a more dynamic learning environment.

e. **Feedback:** Timely, frequent and constructive feedback should be provided to students to facilitate learning. Similarly, students should also be able to provide feedback on their learning experience.

4. **Teaching Principles – Curriculum and Pedagogy:** While delivering learning contents to students is central to teaching, teaching principles as a 3.0 E-learning characteristic focuses on ensuring that students get the most out of their E-learning experiences. It is divided into Curriculum and Pedagogy as follows:

5. **Teaching Principles – Curriculum:** Courses need to be structured in such a way to ensure that all course objectives are clearly outlined. Lessons can be outlined based on knowledge level of students to allow them to control the level and process of their lessons (Snae & Brueckner, 2007). Curriculum has the following two sub characteristics.

   a. **Syllabus:** Modules descriptions and objectives of the course need to be detailed, assessments, assessment objectives and marking criteria need to be outlined, and teaching strategies as well as learning outcomes should be clearly stated (Snae & Brueckner, 2007).

   b. **Course Sequencing:** Learning content are provided to students in the proper sequencing based on the student model which reflect student's learning and cognitive style, motivation and needs and skills and knowledge levels for individualised delivery of learning materials (Bucos et al., 2010; Rokou, Rokou & Rokos, 2004; Snae & Brueckner, 2007).

6. **Teaching Principles – Pedagogy:** The most appropriate pedagogical strategies need to be selected based on students' learning models, educational goals and specific learning subject to allow students to acquire knowledge and particular skills (Rokou et al., 2004). Pedagogy has the following five sub characteristics:

   a. **Instructional Method:** A number of teaching methods can be employed by lecturers to deliver learning contents namely lectures, discussions, demonstrations, case studies, problem solving activities, group activities etc.

7. **Context:** Learning materials can be presented in various learning or presentation contexts (Stojanovic et al., 2001). Depending on student's learning style, content can be adapted in the right context to ensure effective learning. Such context can be an analysis, an introduction, a discussion, a presentation, a diagram (Dutta, 2006).

8. **Delivery Instrument:** Based on the instructional method, lecturers should ensure the most appropriate delivery instrument is used to ensure that learning is taking place efficiently. Student's learning preferences can also be taken into account to cater for individualised learning.

9. **Learning Theories:** Understanding how each student learns optimally can allow for the best pedagogical strategies to be put in place for life-long learning.

10. **Teaching Strategies:** Teaching strategies (e.g. learning by example, learning by doing) combined with the most appropriate learning theories promotes lifelong and student centered learning (Rokou et al., 2004).

11. **Personalised Learning:** Where students are provided with learning content which meet their specific needs and motivations as well as knowledge and skills level based on their particular learning and cognitive styles (Rokou et al., 2004). *Personalised learning* has the following four sub characteristics:

    a. **Student Model:** The student model describes how each student learns optimally (Rokou et al., 2004). Data on students, such as the learning styles, level of knowledge and skills, needs and motivations are gathered to allow for the provision of individualised learning. The 3.0 E-learning system should be able to capture student interests, favourites, predisposition and real skills to facilitate the generation of the student model (Šimić et al., 2004).

b. **Learning and Cognitive Style:** Understanding the learning styles and preferences of students can assist in learning materials delivery being customised to meet students' needs.

c. **Educational Goals:** These are the learning goals for each individual student related to the specific teaching subject and materials as well as some general goals related to the type of skills students want/need to acquire (Rokou et al., 2004)

d. **Learning Participation:** Occurs though collaborative activities between peers to promote life-long learning.

12. **Support – Instructional and System:** Users should be provided with the necessary support at all levels to ensure that the teaching and learning process is facilitated to meet users' needs and requirements. Support is divided into instructional support and system support as follows:

13. **Support – Instructional:** Where students are provided with assistance in their learning process for *learner centered learning* via activities such as the use of multiple teaching supports, lecturer support and motivation, assessments and the provision of feedbacks (Karunasena et al. 2012). It can be further grouped into the following four sub categories:

a. **Activities:** These could be individual activities to students based on their skills and knowledge levels and learning and cognitive styles as well as group activities to promote collaborative learning which enhances the learning process.

b. **Help:** Where students have access to help facilities such as frequently asked questions, discussion forums, emails to lecturers with prompt responses to assist them in their learning process.

c. **Feedback:** Needs to be prompt and motivate learners to improve their learning. Through feedback, individual differences in learning styles and motivations can be addressed, meaningful learning activities can be agreed on and appropriate high and challenging standards can be set (Paxton, 2003).

d. **Collaboration:** Through the sharing of resources among peers and between students and lecturers as well as participation in group activities and discussion.

14. **Support – System:** Users need support from their institutions (e.g. universities), support for the platform, effective technical infrastructures as well as timely and ongoing training (Pah et al., 2007). It has the following five sub characteristics:

a. **Student Centered Learning:** Courses should be designed in such a way that *individualised learning* can take place to meet the needs of specific students based on skills and knowledge levels as well as motivations and learning preferences.

b. **Organisation Support:** The higher education institution must be ready to invest in the right technology, training and infrastructure to facilitate effective implementation, use and management of the 3.0 E-learning system.

c. **Technology:** The model requires that the right level of technological support is provided at all levels to ensure effective use of the system. Additionally, the technology being used should be reliable and robust with ease of access and 24/7 availability (Masoumi, 2006).

d. **Training:** System training should be provided to users to mitigate frustrations and promotes optimum use of the system (Masoumi, 2006).

e. **Infrastructure:** A rich, reliable and capable infrastructure within which the 3.0 E-learning system operates will foster an effective E-learning environment to make the learning process a smooth one (Selim, 2007).

15. **Trust:** The establishment of trust is fundamental to the goal of facilitating learning as it promotes the creation of a stimulating, successful and enriching online learning environment (Paxton, 2003). It has the following five sub characteristics:

a. **Student-Lecturer:** For effective learning to take place, students and lecturers need to be able to discuss openly about the learning process. Feedback is vital to trust building between students and lecturers and to allow for the setting up of new challenges.

b. **Peer-Peer:** Trusting information from peers within an E-learning environment is essential for collaborative activities to take place. While it is easier to trust peers that one has a direction connection to, the challenge is to infer trust between peers that are not directly connected to each other. The trust module of the Friend-Of-A-Friend (FOAF) project which is a semantic web project where millions of users' data are distributed across the web (Golbeck & Hendler, 2006) can be adapted for the 3.0 E-learning model to promote trust between peers.

c. **Technology:** The efficient and effective use of technology in delivering E-learning based components of a course is critical to the success and users' acceptance of E-learning (Selim, 2007).

d. **System:** Users must trust the E-learning system to want to use it. This includes access to the right learning content at the right time with the proper support

whether instructional, technical or pedagogical.

e. **Security:** Security measures such as system login need to be set up to allow different level of access to different users.

16. **Web 3.0 Ontology-Based Technology:** Refers to e-learning based on Semantic technologies that support user-generated contents, content sharing, content reuse, collaborative resource management as well as student centered learning (Karunasena et al., 2012). Web 3.0 ontology-based technology can be further grouped into the following six sub characteristics:

a. **Ontologies Database:** *Ontology* is the key-enabler of the Semantic Web. The ontologies database will consist of different ontologies such as the Concept ontology, pedagogical relations ontology, pedagogical ontology and instructional ontology to enable effective delivery of learning content based on students' needs and teaching principles.

b. **Content Database:** Where learning materials are stored for access and manipulation.

c. **Records Database:** Where students records are kept such as student details, assessment scores, student learning preferences etc.

d. **Hardware:** The general hardware required to run the 3.0 E-learning system.

e. **Software:** The general software required to run the 3.0 E-learning system.

f. **System Infrastructure:** Reliable technical infrastructures need to be in place to ensure the 3.0 E-learning environment is meeting users' needs.

RESEARCH ANALYSIS AND GAPS

Each selected article in the review was carefully analysed to determine if the characteristics and sub characteristics identified for a holistic 3.0 E-learning model were included as key criteria within the article. Appendix A shows a clear outline of the availability/presence of the holistic 3.0 E-learning characteristics in the articles being reviewed. Clearly, none of the articles being reviewed covered all identified 3.0 E-learning characteristics.

Semantic Web Articles

It can be seen from Appendix A that essential *E-learning characteristics* such as usability and accessibility, teaching principles, personalised learning and collaboration that are still very relevant to the Semantic Web have often been omitted or seldom integrated into existing 3.0 E-learning models. The focus is more on Semantic Web technologies and its implementation via the use of ontologies although in many cases this aspect is also not discussed comprehensively. Additionally, essential *Semantic Web characteristics* such as trust are discussed in isolation as a stand-alone factor rather than being integrated into the 3.0 E-learning models. In fact, following the review, it is clear that existing 3.0 E-learning models have not established a collective set of characteristics for an effective implementation and use of a 3.0 E-learning system for higher education from users' perspective.

E-Learning Articles

It is further discussed that an effective 3.0 E-learning environment requires that essential factors related specifically to the *Semantic Web* and to an effective E-learning, environment in general are considered. With this in mind, the identified *holistic 3.0 E-learning characteristics* also took into consideration the critical success factors to a quality higher education E-learning system. From Appendix A, it can be clearly seen that many of these CSFs are overlooked into existing 3.0 E-learning models.

Initial Set of Collective 3.0 E-Learning Characteristics

In an attempt to provide a holistic representation of a 3.0 E-learning model, the researcher is putting forward a new holistic 3.0 E-learning model based on the combined characteristics of the Semantic Web and E-learning. Figure 1 shows the new *3.0 E-learning model* proposed in this chapter as an initial step towards a holistic representation of a 3.0 E-learning model capturing the needs and expectations of users.

DISCUSSION OF THE NEW INTIIAL HOLISTIC 3.0 E-LEARNING MODEL AND FUTURE WORKS

The proposed *initial holistic 3.0 E-learning* in Figure 1 aims to provide an initial outline of the main *3.0 E-learning characteristics* that will holistically represent a *3.0 E-learning model* taking into account both essential *Semantic web* and *E-learning characteristics* from the literature. The model provides an overview of the CSFs of E-learning relevant to 3.0 E-learning systems as well as an overview of the main Semantic Web characteristics for E-learning. However, for any E-learning system to be effective, users' perceptions and needs must be taken into consideration. As a result, this review cannot be claimed to be exhaustive. In order to ensure that the new model meets the needs and expectations of higher education E-learning users namely students, lecturers and the administrators, the model needs to be evaluated. For this purpose, the proposed model will be evaluated within the higher education sector in Mauritius.

Figure 1. Proposed Initial Holistic 3.0 E-learning Model – Prepared by the author

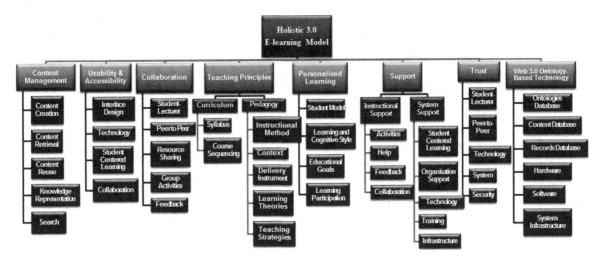

Mauritius is still in the nurturing stage of E-learning and is only just beginning to build and implement a fully workable E-learning platform that will be optimally used. However, with the growth of personal computer ownership and connection to a broadband Internet facility, E-learning in higher education is gaining momentum in the country as an alternative mode to traditional teaching and learning method. In fact, part of the Government's plan to make Mauritius into an Intelligent Mauritius (i-Mauritius) is via investments in and promotions of E-learning in the country (Oolun, Ramgolam & Dorasami, 2012). However, Mauritius still lacks a clear E-learning model and existing e-learning platforms such as, i-learn are merely static ways of delivery information over the Internet with little or no user interaction learning (Santally, 2012; Puduruth, Moloo, Mantaye & Jannoo, 2010; Kanaksabee, Odit & Ramdoyal, 2011). As a result, there is an urgent need to review the E-learning concept in the country as being a web-based delivery (uploading and downloading) of course material to include other critical aspects such as pedagogy, instructional design, support and expertise as well as student-centered and life-long learning (Puduruth et al. 2010). With the Semantic Web considered as a power-

ful approach to satisfy E-learning requirements (Stojanovic et al., 2001), a 3.0 E-learning model which take into consideration the needs of users will assist the country in its transformation into a knowledge hub and a centre of higher learning as well as providing the country with a head start in its first 3.0 E-learning system.

The author suggests that interviews and online surveys can be organised with participants from the Mauritian higher education sector namely students, lecturers and administrators to evaluate the proposed model. It is believed that following the evaluation of the proposed holistic 3.0 E-learning model, the characteristics and sub characteristics identified will be refined with possibility of new ones being identified by users as essential for a 3.0 E-Learning model. The model proposed will then be modified accordingly to reflect needs and expectations of users.

The evaluation of the initial proposed model can also be carried out within other countries. The resulting 3.0 E-learning model will have slight changes to reflect each country's individual needs and expectations from users' perspectives.

CONCLUSION

In the research and development world, there is great stress upon the need to develop educational models that will meet the expectations of the higher-education community. With the Semantic Web representing a promising technology to meet E-learning requirements, there have been ongoing efforts to build 3.0 E-learning systems, especially for the higher-education sector. Unfortunately, as identified in this chapter, there are a number of gaps in the literature with respect to existing 3.0 E-learning models. Most of the literature relating to the Semantic Web within E-learning deal principally with Semantic technologies (namely ontologies). Other essential aspects of E-learning are either overlooked or seldom integrated into 3.0 E-learning models available. This research is significant in that it aims to develop a new and combined set of 3.0 E-learning characteristics which will provide a clear representation of the Semantic Web and E-learning. Additionally, the effective integration of E-learning into a learning environment often requires a shift in the mind-set of the users away from the traditional face to face teacher-centered learning environment. With this in mind, as a future research direction, the author will seek to further ensure that the perceptions higher education E-learning users namely students, lecturers and administrators are captured in the proposed holistic 3.0 E-learning model to meet their needs and expectations.

REFERENCES

Anderson, T., & Whitelock, D. M. (2004). The educational semantic web: Visioning and practicing the future of education. *Journal of Interactive Media in Education, 2004*(1), 1–15. doi:10.5334/2004-1

Berners-Lee, T., Hendler, J., & Lassila, O. (2001). The semantic web. *Scientific American, 284*(5), 28–37. doi:10.1038/scientificamerican0501-34 PMID:11341160

Brusilovsky, P., & Vassileva, J. (2003). Course sequencing techniques for large-scale web-based education. *International Journal of Continuing Engineering Education and Lifelong Learning, 13*(1), 75–94. doi:10.1504/IJCEELL.2003.002154

Bucos, M., Dragulescu, B., & Veltan, M. (2010). Designing a semantic web ontology for e-learning in higher education. In *Proceedings of Electronics and Telecommunications (ISETC)* (pp. 415-418). IEEE. doi:10.1109/ISETC.2010.5679298

Castellanos-Nieves, D., Fernández-Breis, J. T., Valencia-García, R., Martínez-Béjar, R., & Iniesta-Moreno, M. (2011). Semantic web technologies for supporting learning assessment. *Information Sciences, 181*(9), 1517–1537. doi:10.1016/j.ins.2011.01.010

Cloran, R. A. (2007). Trust on the semantic web. Grahamstown: Rhodes University. Retrieved from http://icsa.cs.up.ac.za/issa/2005/Proceedings/Full/025_Article.pdf

De Nicola, A., Missikoff, M., & Schiappelli, F. (2004).Towards an ontological support for eLearning courses. In *Proceedings of On the Move to Meaningful Internet Systems 2004: OTM 2004 Workshops* (pp. 773-777). Springer Berlin Heidelberg. Retrieved from http://www.starlab.vub.ac.be/events/OTM04WOSE/papers/20.pdf

Devedzic, V. (2004). Education and the semantic web. *International Journal of Artificial Intelligence in Education, 14*(2), 165–191. Retrieved from http://iospress.metapress.com/content/hr4v08qm6vy8y3t7/fulltext.pdf?page=1

Dutta, B. (2006). *Semantic web based e-learning.* Retrieved from https://drtc.isibang.ac.in/bitstream/handle/1849/223/PaperP-Biswanath.pdf?sequence=1

Ghaleb, F., Daoud, S., Hasna, A., ALJa'am, J. M., El-Seoud, S. A., & El-Sofany, H. (2006). E-learning model based on semantic web technology. *International Journal of Computing & Information Sciences, 4*(2), 63-71. Retrieved from http://www.ijcis.info/Vol4N2/pp63-71.pdf

Golbeck, J., & Hendler, J. (2006). Inferring binary trust relationships in web-based social networks. *ACM Transactions on Internet Technology, 6*(4), 497–529. doi:10.1145/1183463.1183470

Golbeck, J., Parsia, B., & Hendler, J. (2003). Trust networks on the semantic web. Springer Berlin Heidelberg. Retrieved from http://pdf.aminer.org/000/674/092/trust_networks_on_the_semantic_web.pdf

Guzzo, R. A., Jackson, S. E., & Katzell, R. A. (1987). Meta-analysis analysis. *Research in Organizational Behavior, 9*, 407–442.

Huang, T., Yang, Z., Liu, Q., Li, X., Wu, B., Liu, S., & Zhao, G. (2006). Semantic web-based educational knowledge service system (EKSS) for e-learning. In *Proceedings of Communications and Networking in China* (pp. 1-5). IEEE. doi:10.1109/CHINACOM.2006.344834

Hwang, M. I., & Thorn, R. G. (1999). The effect of user engagement on system success: A meta-analytical integration of research findings. *Information & Management, 35*(4), 229–236. doi:10.1016/S0378-7206(98)00092-5

Jump, L., & Jump, R. (2006). Learning academic skills online: Student perceptions of the learning process. In *Proceedings of the First International LAMS Conference*. Retrieved from http://lamsfoundation.org/lams2006/pdfs/Jump_Jump_LAMS06.pdf

Kanaksabee, P., Odit, M. P., & Ramdoyal, A. (2011). A standard-based model for adaptive e-Learning platform for Mauritian academic institutions. *Journal of International Education Research, 7*(1). Retrieved from http://journals.cluteonline.com/index.php/JIER/article/view/3541/3588

Karunasena, A., Deng, H., & Zhang, X. (2012). A web 2.0 based e-learning success model in higher education. In *Proceedings of 2nd International Conference on Future Computers in Education.* Retrieved from http://www.ier-institute.org/2070-1918/lnit23/v23/177.pdf

Keats, D., & Schmidt, J. P. (2007). The genesis and emergence of education 3.0 in higher education and its potential for Africa. *First Monday, 12*(3). doi:10.5210/fm.v12i3.1625

Kennedy, G., Dalgarno, B., Gray, K., Judd, T., Waycott, J., Bennett, S. J., . . . Churchwood, A. (2007). *The net generation are not big users of web 2.0 technologies: Preliminary findings.* Retrieved from http://www.ascilite.org.au/conferences/singapore07/procs/kennedy.pdf

Lassila, O. (1998). Web metadata: A matter of semantics. *IEEE Internet Computing, 2*(4), 30–37. doi:10.1109/4236.707688

Masoumi, D. (2006). *Critical factors for effective e-learning.* Retrieved from http://asianvu.com/digital-library/elearning/Critical_factors_for_effective_e-learning_by_DMasoumi[1].pdf

McPherson, M. A., & Nunes, J. M. (2008). Critical issues for e-learning delivery: What may seem obvious is not always put into practice. *Journal of Computer Assisted Learning, 24*(5), 433–445. doi:10.1111/j.1365-2729.2008.00281.x

Mering, J., & Robbie, D. (2004). Education and electronic learning-Does online learning assist learners and how can it be continuously improved. In *Proceedings of the Higher Education Research and Development Society of Australasia (HERSDA 2004) Conference*. Retrieved from http://www. google.com.au/url?sa=t&rct=j&q=how%20 did%20internet%20assist%20in%20higher%20 education&source=web&cd=4&cad=rja&ve d=0CC8QFjAD&url=http%3A%2F%2Fresea rchbank.swinburne.edu.au%2Fvital%2Faccess %2Fservices%2FDownload%2Fswin%3A340 9%2FSOURCE1&ei=yhJxUPKHDKmhigeP_ YGYAw&usg=AFQjCNHr4NurG4N_wV3eN-RG3RdiC2lerLQ

Monachesi, P., Simov, K., Mossel, E., Osenova, P., & Lemnitzer, L. (2008). What ontologies can do for eLearning. In *Proceedings of IMCL 2008*. Retrived from http://www.let.uu.nl/lt4el/content/ files/IMCL08Final.pdf

Moreale, E., & Vargas-Vera, M. (2004). Semantic services in e-learning: An argumentation case study. *Journal of Educational Technology & Society, 7*(4), 112–128. Retrieved from http://ifets. info/journals/7_4/ets_7_4.pdf#page=117

Naik, U., & Shivalingaiah, D. (2008). Comparative study of web 1.0, web 2.0 and web 3.0. *International CALIBER, 499-507*. Retrieved from http:// ir.inflibnet.ac.in/bitstream/1944/1285/1/54.pdf

Neri, M. A. (2005). *Ontology-based learning objects sequencing*. Dipartimento di Elettronica e Informazione, Politecnico di Milano, Italy. Retrieved from http://unikode.me/attach/Pub-blicazioni/ELearn06.pdf

Neri, M. A., & Colombetti, M. (2009). Ontology-based learning objects search and courses generation. *Applied Artificial Intelligence, 23*(3), 233–260. doi:10.1080/08839510802715134

O'Hara, K., Alani, H., Kalfoglou, Y., & Shad-bolt, N. (2004). *Trust strategies for the semantic web*. Retrieved from http://eprints.soton. ac.uk/260029/1/ISWC04-OHara-final.pdf

Oliver, R. (2001). *Assuring the quality of online learning in Australian higher education*. Retrieved from http://ro.ecu.edu.au/cgi/viewcontent.cgi?ar ticle=5791&context=ecuworks

Oolun, K., Ramgolam, S., & Dorasami, I. V. (2012). The making of a digital nation: toward i-Mauritius. *The Global Information Technology Report 2012*. Retrieved from http://www3. weforum.org/docs/GITR/2012/GITR_Chap-ter2.2_2012.pdf

Pah, I., Maniu, I., Maniu, G., & Damian, S. (2007). A conceptual framework based on ontologies for knowledge management in e-learning systems. In *Proc. of the 6th WSEAS International Conference on Education and Educational Technology* (pp. 283-286). Retrieved from http://www.wseas.us/e-library/conferences/2007venice/papers/570-623. pdf

Papp, R. (2000). Critical success factors for distance learning. In *Proceedings of AMCIS 2000*. Retrieved from http://aisel.aisnet.org/am-cis2000/104/

Paxton, P. (2003). Meeting the challenges of on-line learning through invitational education. In *Proceedings of 2003 Educause in Australasia: Expanding the Learning Community–Meeting the Challenges*. Academic Press.

Petter, S., & McLean, E. R. (2009). A meta-analytic assessment of the DeLone and McLean IS success model: An examination of IS success at the individual level. *Information & Management, 46*(3), 159–166. doi:10.1016/j.im.2008.12.006

Pudaruth, S., Moloo, R. K., Mantaye, A., & Jannoo, N. B. (2010). A survey of e-learning platforms in Mauritius. In *Proceedings of the World Congress on Engineering* (Vol. 1). Retrieved from http://www.iaeng.org/publication/WCE2010/WCE2010_pp415-420.pdf

Rashid, S., Khan, R., & Ahmed, F. (2013). *A proposed model of e-learning management system using semantic web technology.* Retrieved from http://www.semantic-web-journal.net/sites/default/files/swj234.pdf

Rokou, F. P., Rokou, E., & Rokos, Y. (2004). Modeling web-based educational systems: Process design teaching model. *Journal of Educational Technology & Society*, *7*(1), 42–50. Retrieved from http://www.ifets.info/others/journals/7_1/ets_7_1.pdf#page=47

Sabherwal, R., Jeyaraj, A., & Chowa, C. (2006). Information system success: Individual and organizational determinants. *Management Science*, *52*(12), 1849–1864. doi:10.1287/mnsc.1060.0583

Santally, M. I. (2012). *Innovative learning technologies and pedagogies.* Retrieved from http://vcilt.blogspot.com.au/2012/07/open-university-of-mauritius.html

Selim, H. M. (2007). E-learning critical success factors: An exploratory investigation of student perceptions. *International Journal of Technology Marketing*, *2*(2), 157–182. doi:10.1504/IJTMKT.2007.014791

Shekarpour, S., Katebi, M., & Katebi, S. D. (2009). *A trust model for semantic web.* Retrieved from http://ijssst.info/Vol-10/No-2/paper2.pdf

Šimić, G., Gašević, D., & Devedžić, V. (2004). Semantic web and intelligent learning management systems. In *Proceedings of Workshop on Applications of Semantic Web Technologies for e-Learning.* Retrieved from http://www.win.tue.nl/SW-EL/2004/ITS-SWEL-Camera-ready/SWEL-ITS-Proceedings/SWEL04-ITS04-proceedings.pdf

Snae, C., & Brüeckner, M. (2007). Ontology-driven e-learning system based on roles and activities for Thai learning environment. *Interdisciplinary Journal of E-Learning and Learning Objects*, *3*(1), 1-17. Retrieved from http://www.ijello.org/Volume3/IJKLOv3p001-017Snae.pdf

Srimathi, H. (2010). Knowledge representation of LMS using ontology. *International Journal of Computers and Applications*, *6*(3). Retrieved from http://citeseerx.ist.psu.edu/viewdoc/download?doi=10.1.1.206.4163&rep=rep1&type=pdf

Srimathi, H., & Srivatsa, S. K. (2008). *Identification of ontology based learning object using instructional design.* Retrieved from http://pdf.aminer.org/000/269/789/enhancing_learning_object_content_on_the_semantic_web.pdf

Stojanovic, L., Staab, S., & Studer, R. (2001). eLearning based on the semantic web. In *Proceedings of WebNet2001-World Conference on the WWW and Internet* (pp. 23-27). Retrieved from http://pdf.aminer.org/000/306/170/semantic_e_learning_agents_supporting_elearning_by_semantic_web_and.pdf

Volery, T., & Lord, D. (2000). Critical success factors in online education. *International Journal of Educational Management*, *14*(5), 216–223. doi:10.1108/09513540010344731 von Kortzfleisch, H. F., & Winand, U. (2000). Trust in electronic learning and teaching relationships: The case of WINFO-Line. ECIS. Retrieved from http://csrc.lse.ac.uk/asp/aspecis/20000136.pdf

Wang, S. (2008). Ontology of learning objects repository for pedagogical knowledge sharing. *Interdisciplinary Journal of E-Learning and Learning Objects, 4*(1), 1-12. Retrieved from http://ijklo.org/Volume4/IJELLOv4p001-012Wang200.pdf

Webster, J., & Watson, R. T. (2002). Analyzing the past to prepare for the future: Writing a literature review. *Management Information Systems Quarterly, 26*(2), 3. Retrieved from http://raptor1.bizlab.mtsu.edu/S-Drive/JCLARK/INFS6980/Articles/6980-LitReview.pdf

Wiley, D. A. (2003). Connecting learning objects to instructional design theory: A definition, a metaphor, and a taxonomy. Logan, UT: The Edumetrics Institute. Retrieved from http://wesrac.usc.edu/wired/bldg-7_file/wiley.pdf

ADDITIONAL READING

Abrami, P. C., Bernard, R., Wade, A., Schmid, R. F., Borokhovski, E., Tamin, R., ... Peretiatkowicz, A. (2008). A review of e-learning in Canada: A rough sketch of the evidence, gaps and promising directions. *Canadian Journal of Learning and Technology/La revue canadienne de l'apprentissage et de la technologie, 32*(3).

Alsultanny, Y. A. (2006). E-learning system overview based on semantic web. *The Electronic journal of e-Learning, 4*(2), 111-118.

Aroyo, L., & Dicheva, D. (2004). The new challenges for e-learning: The educational semantic web. *Journal of Educational Technology & Society, 7*(4), 59–69.

Balog-Crisan, R., Roxin, I., & Smeureanu, I. (2008, June). e-Learning platforms for semantic web. In *World Conference on Educational Multimedia, Hypermedia and Telecommunications* (Vol. 2008, No. 1, pp. 1695-1699).

Baumann, M. (2009). Web 3.0: The next step for the Internet. *Information Today, 26*(5), 1.

Bhuasiri, W., Xaymoungkhoun, O., Zo, H., Rho, J. J., & Ciganek, A. P. (2012). Critical success factors for e-learning in developing countries: A comparative analysis between ICT experts and faculty. *Computers & Education, 58*(2), 843–855. doi:10.1016/j.compedu.2011.10.010

Bittencourt, I. I., Isotani, S., Costa, E., & Mizoguchi, R. (2008). Research directions on semantic web and education. *Interdisciplinary Studies in Computer Science, 19*(1), 60–67.

Burki, E., & Savitsky, J. J. (2001). E-learning in higher education. *College and University, 77*(2), 39.

Buzzetto-More, N. (2008). Student perceptions of various e-learning components. *Interdisciplinary Journal of E-Learning and Learning Objects, 4*(1), 113–135.

Chandrasekaran, B., Josephson, J. R., & Benjamins, V. R. (1999). What are ontologies, and why do we need them? *IEEE Intelligent Systems, 14*(1), 20–26. doi:10.1109/5254.747902

Ding, L., Kolari, P., Ding, Z., & Avancha, S. (2007). *Using ontologies in the semantic web: a survey* (pp. 79–113). Springer, US: Ontologies.

Dolog, P., Henze, N., Nejdl, W., & Sintek, M. (2004, January). The personal reader: personalizing and enriching learning resources using semantic web technologies. In *Adaptive Hypermedia and Adaptive Web-Based Systems* (pp. 85–94). Springer Berlin Heidelberg. doi:10.1007/978-3-540-27780-4_12

Ellis, R. A., Ginns, P., & Piggott, L. (2009). E-learning in higher education: Some key aspects and their relationship to approaches to study. *Higher Education Research & Development, 28*(3), 303–318. doi:10.1080/07294360902839909

Engelbrecht, E. (2003). A look at e-learning models: Investigating their value for developing an e-learning strategy. *Progressio, 25*(2), p-38.

Gaeta, M., Orciuoli, F., Paolozzi, S., & Salerno, S. (2011). Ontology extraction for knowledge reuse: The e-learning perspective. *Systems, Man and Cybernetics, Part A: Systems and Humans. IEEE Transactions on, 41*(4), 798–809.

Govindasamy, T. (2001). Successful implementation of e-learning: Pedagogical considerations. *The Internet and Higher Education, 4*(3), 287–299. doi:10.1016/S1096-7516(01)00071-9

Hendler, J. (2009). Web 3.0 emerging. *Computer, 42*(1), 111–113. doi:10.1109/MC.2009.30

Henze, N., Dolog, P., & Nejdl, W. (2004). Reasoning and ontologies for personalized e-learning in the semantic web. *Journal of Educational Technology & Society, 7*(4), 82–97.

Holohan, E., Melia, M., McMullen, D., & Pahl, C. (2005). Adaptive e-learning content generation based on semantic web technology.

Huang, W., Webster, D., Wood, D., & Ishaya, T. (2006). An intelligent semantic e-learning framework using context-aware Semantic Web technologies. *British Journal of Educational Technology, 37*(3), 351–373. doi:10.1111/j.1467-8535.2006.00610.x

Johnson, R. D., Hornik, S., & Salas, E. (2008). An empirical examination of factors contributing to the creation of successful e-learning environments. *International Journal of Human-Computer Studies, 66*(5), 356–369. doi:10.1016/j.ijhcs.2007.11.003

Kelly, B., Phipps, L., & Swift, E. (2004). Developing a holistic approach for e-learning accessibility. *Canadian Journal of Learning and Technology/ La revue canadienne de l'apprentissage et de la technologie, 30*(3).

Kolovski, V., & Galletly, J. (2003, June). Towards e-learning via the semantic web. In *International Conference on Computer Systems and Technologies-CompSysTech* (p. 2).

Koper, R. (2004). Use of the semantic web to solve some basic problems in education: Increase flexible, distributed lifelong learning; decrease teacher's workload. *Journal of Interactive Media in Education, 2004*(1), 5. doi:10.5334/2004-6-koper

Lassila, O., & Hendler, J. (2007). Embracing" Web 3.0. *IEEE Internet Computing, 11*(3), 90–93. doi:10.1109/MIC.2007.52

Lytras, M., Tsilira, A., & Themistocleous, M. (2003). Towards the semantic e-learning: An ontological oriented discussion of the new research agenda in e-learning. *AMCIS 2003 Proceedings*, 388.

Mayes, T., & De Freitas, S. (2004). Review of e-learning theories, frameworks and models. *JISC e-learning models desk study*, (1).

Mohan, P., & Brooks, C. (2003, July). Learning objects on the semantic web. In *Advanced Learning Technologies, 2003. Proceedings. The 3rd IEEE International Conference on* (pp. 195-199). IEEE. doi:10.1109/ICALT.2003.1215055

Morris, R. D. (2011). Web 3.0: Implications for online learning. *TechTrends, 55*(1), 42–46. doi:10.1007/s11528-011-0469-9

Naeve, A., Nilsson, M., & Palmér, M. (2001, October). E-learning in the semantic age. In *The 2nd European Web-based Learning, Environments Conference.*

Naidu, S. (2003). *E-learning: A guidebook of principles, procedures and practices. Commonwealth Educational Media Centre for Asia.* CEMCA.

Njenga, J. K., & Fourie, L. C. H. (2010). The myths about e-learning in higher education. *British Journal of Educational Technology, 41*(2), 199–212. doi:10.1111/j.1467-8535.2008.00910.x

Paechter, M., Maier, B., & Macher, D. (2010). Students' expectations of, and experiences in e-learning: Their relation to learning achievements and course satisfaction. *Computers & Education, 54*(1), 222–229. doi:10.1016/j.compedu.2009.08.005

Pahl, C., & Holohan, E. (2009). Applications of semantic web technology to support learning content development. *Interdisciplinary Journal of E-Learning and Learning Objects, 5.*

Romiszowski, A. J. (2004). How's the e-learning baby? Factors leading to success or failure of an educational technology innovation. *Educational Technology-Saddle Brook Then Englewood Cliffs NJ, 44*(1), 5–27.

Rosenberg, M. J. (2001). *E-learning: Strategies for delivering knowledge in the digital age* (Vol. 9). New York: McGraw-Hill.

Sampson, D. G., Lytras, M. D., Wagner, G., & Diaz, P. (2004). Ontologies and the semantic web for e-learning. *Journal of Educational Technology & Society, 7*(4), 26–28.

Shadbolt, N., Hall, W., & Berners-Lee, T. (2006). The semantic web revisited. *IEEE Intelligent Systems, 21*(3), 96–101. doi:10.1109/MIS.2006.62

Sharpe, R., & Benfield, G. (2005). The student experience of e-learning in higher education. *Brookes eJournal of Learning and Teaching, 1*(3).

Sun, P. C., Tsai, R. J., Finger, G., Chen, Y. Y., & Yeh, D. (2008). What drives a successful e-Learning? An empirical investigation of the critical factors influencing learner satisfaction. *Computers & Education, 50*(4), 1183–1202. doi:10.1016/j.compedu.2006.11.007

Tahajod, M., Iranmehr, A., & Khozooyi, N. (2009, December). Trust management for semantic web. In *Computer and Electrical Engineering, 2009. ICCEE'09. Second International Conference on* (Vol. 2, pp. 3-6). IEEE. doi:10.1109/ICCEE.2009.241

Torniai, C., Jovanovic, J., Gasevic, D., Bateman, S., & Hatala, M. (2008, July). E-learning meets the social semantic web. In *Advanced Learning Technologies, 2008. ICALT'08. Eighth IEEE International Conference on* (pp. 389-393). IEEE. doi:10.1109/ICALT.2008.20

Wahlster, W., Dengel, A., Telekom, D., Dengel, W., Dengler, C. D., Heckmann, D., . . . Sintek, M. (2006). Web 3.0: Convergence of web 2.0 and the semantic web. In In Technology Radar, Feature Paper, 2nd ed.; Deutsche Telekom Laboratories.

White, S. (2007). Critical success factors for e-learning and institutional change—some organisational perspectives on campus-wide e-learning. *British Journal of Educational Technology, 38*(5), 840–850. doi:10.1111/j.1467-8535.2007.00760.x

KEY TERMS AND DEFINITIONS

E-Learning Critical Success Factors (CSFs): Key features that are required to be present in an E-learning environment to foster effective E-learning.

E-Learning System: Is a learning environment which occurs via the Internet where users interact with each using their own personal computers and where learning content is created, stored, retrieved and shared online.

Holistic Representation: A complete and integrated view which captures different perspectives.

Ontology: Allows for the different representations of the same thing from different perspectives thus making information retrieval faster.

Personalised Learning: Learning customised to student's needs based on the student's learning style preference, motivations and existing knowledge of the subject .ppendix A – A Comparative Analysis of E-learning Characteristics.

Semantic Web Characteristics: Key features of the Semantic Web which are relevant to an E-learning environment.

Semantic Web: Where learning content is enhanced with formal semantics to provide more detailed meaning thus allowing for easier and faster content retrieval and reuse.

APPENDIX

Table 2.

Existing work on E-Learning and 3.0 E-Learning	Author(s) & Year	Content Management					Usability & Accessibility			
		Content Creation	Content Retrieval	Content Reuse	Knowledge Representation	Search	Interface Design	Technology	Student Centered Learning	Collaboration
Ontology-Driven E-Learning System	Snae & Brueckner (2007)	√	√	×	×	×	√	√	×	×
E-Learning Model based on the Semantic Web Technology	Ghaleb et al. (2006)	√	√	√	√	√	√	×	×	×
A Proposed Model of E-Learning Management System Using Semantic Web Technology	Rashid, Khan and Ahmed (2013)	√	√	√	√	√	×	×	√	√
Semantic Services in E-Learning	Moreale & Vargas-Vera (2004)	√	√	×	×	√	×	×	×	×
E-Learning based on the Semantic Web	Stojanovic, Staab & Studer (2001)	√	√	√	√	√	×	×	×	×
Semantic Web and Intelligent Management Systems (ILMS)	Simic, Gasevic & Devedzic (2004)	√	√	√	√	×	×	×	√	×
Conceptual Framework based on ontologies for knowledge management in e-learning systems	Pah, Maniu, Maniu & Damian (2007)	√	√	×	√	√	×	×	√	√
Semantic Web Ontology for E-learning in Higher Education	Bucos, Dragulescu & Veltan (2010)	√	√	×	√	×	√	×	×	×
Ontological Support for E-learning courses	De Nicola, Missikoff & Schiappelli (2004)	√	√	×	√	√	√	×	×	×

Legend: √: Characteristic Available/Present in Model ×: Characteristic Not Available/Not Present in Model

continued on following page

Table 2. Continued

Legend: √:Characteristic Available/Present in Model ×: Characteristic Not Available/Not Present in Model

Existing work on E-Learning and 3.0 E-Learning	Author(s) & Year	Content Management					Usability & Accessibility			
		Content Creation	Content Retrieval	Content Reuse	Knowledge Representation	Search	Interface Design	Technology	Student Centered Learning	Collaboration
Identification of Ontology based learning object using instructional design	Srimathi & Srivatsa (2008)	√	√	×	√	×	√	×	×	×
Knowledge representation of LMS using ontology	Srimathi (2010)	√	√	×	√	×	√	×	×	×
Ontology of Learning objects Repository for Pedagogical Knowledge Sharing	Wang (2008)	√	√	×	√	×	×	×	×	×
Ontology-based learning objects search and course generation	Neri & Colombetti (2009)	√	√	×	√	√	×	×	×	×
Ontology based learning objects sequencing	Neri (2005)	√	√	×	√	√	×	×	×	×
Course sequencing techniques for large-scale web-based education	Brusilovsky & Vassileva (2003)	√	√	×	×	×	×	×	×	×

continued on following page

Table 2. Continued

Existing work on E-Learning and 3.0 E-Learning	Author(s) & Year	Content Management					Usability & Accessibility			
		Content Creation	Content Retrieval	Content Reuse	Knowledge Representation	Search	Interface Design	Technology	Student Centered Learning	Collaboration
A Web 2.0 Based e-Learning Success Model in Higher Education	Karunasena, Deng & Zhang (2012)	√	√	√	√	√	√	√	×	√
Critical Success Factors in online education	Volery & Lord (2000)	×	×	×	×	×	√	√	√	√
Critical success factors for distance learning	Papp (2000)	√	√	×	√	×	√	√	×	×
Critical success factors for on-line course resources	Soong, Chan, Chua & Loh (2001)	×	×	×	×	×	×	×	×	√
Strategies for assuring the quality of online learning in Australian higher education	Oliver (2001)	√	√	√	√	√	√	√	√	×
E-learning critical success factors	Selim (2007)	√	√	×	√	×	×	√	×	√
A taxonomy of factors to promote quality web-supported learning	Frasen (2007)	√	√	√	√	√	√	√	√	√
Critical issues for e-learning delivery	McPherson & Nunes 2008	×	×	×	×	×	√	√	√	√

Legend: √:Characteristic Available/Present in Model ×: Characteristic Not Available/Not Present in Model

continued on following page

Table 2. Continued

Existing work on E-Learning and 3.0 E-Learning	Author(s) & Year	Content Management					Usability & Accessibility			
		Content Creation	Content Retrieval	Content Reuse	Knowledge Representation	Search	Interface Design	Technology	Student Centered Learning	Collaboration
Legend: √:Characteristic Available/Present in Model ×: Characteristic Not Available/Not Present in Model										
Modeling Web-based educational systems	Rokou, Rokou & Rokos (2004)	×	×	×	×	×	×	×	×	×
Trust in electronic learning and teaching relationships	von Kortzfleisch, FO & Winand (2000)	×	×	×	×	×	×	×	×	×
Trust Networks on the Semantic Web	Golbeck, Parsia & Hendler (2003)	×	×	×	×	×	×	×	×	×
Trust relationships in Web-based social networks	Golbeck & Hendler (2006)	×	×	×	×	×	×	×	×	×
Trust on the Semantic Web	Cloran (2007)	×	×	×	×	×	×	×	×	×
Trust Model for Semantic Web	Shekarpour, Katebi & Katebi (2009)	×	×	×	×	×	×	×	×	×

Table 3.

Legend: √:Characteristic Available/Present in Model ×: Characteristic Not Available/Not Present in Model

Existing work on E-Learning and 3.0 E-Learning	Author(s) & Year	Collaboration					Teaching Principles						
							Curriculum				Pedagogy		
		Student-Lecturer	Peer to Peer	Resource Sharing	Group Activities	Feedback	Syllabus	Course sequencing	Instructional Method	Context	Delivery Instrument	Learning Theories	Teaching Strategies
Ontology-Driven E-Learning System	Snae & Brueckner (2007)	×	×	√	√	√	√	×	√	×	√	×	√
E-Learning Model based on the Semantic Web Technology	Ghaleb et al. (2006)	×	×	√	√	√	√	×	×	×	×	×	×
A Proposed Model of E-Learning Management System Using Semantic Web Technology	Rashid, Khan and Ahmed (2013)	√	√	√	√	√	√	√	×	×	×	×	×
Semantic Services in E-Learning	Moreale & Vargas-Vera (2004)	×	×	√	×	√	√	×	×	×	×	×	×
E-Learning based on the Semantic Web	Stojanovic, Staab & Studer (2001)	×	×	×	×	×	×	×	×	√	√	×	×
Semantic Web and Intelligent Management Systems (ILMS)	Simic, Gasevic & Devedzic (2004)	×	×	×	×	√	√	√	√	√	√	×	√
Conceptual Framework based on ontologies for knowledge management in e-learning systems	Pah, Maniu, Maniu & Damian (2007)	√	×	√	√	√	×	×	√	×	√	×	√

continued on following page

Table 3. Continued

Legend: √:Characteristic Available/Present in Model x: Characteristic Not Available/Not Present in Model

Existing work on E-Learning and 3.0 E-Learning	Author(s) & Year	Teaching Principles											
		Collaboration					Curriculum				Pedagogy		
		Student-Lecturer	Peer to Peer	Resource Sharing	Group Activities	Feedback	Syllabus	Course sequencing	Instructional Method	Context	Delivery Instrument	Learning Theories	Teaching Strategies
Semantic Web Ontology for E-learning in Higher Education	Bucos, Dragulescu & Veltan (2010)	√	√	√	√	√	X	X	X	X	X	X	X
Ontological Support for E-learning courses	De Nicola, Missikoff & Schiappelli (2004)	X	X	X	X	X	X	X	X	X	X	X	X
Identification of Ontology based learning object using instructional design	Srimathi & Srivatsa (2008)	X	X	X	X	X	X	√	X	X	√	√	√
Knowledge representation of LMS using ontology	Srimathi (2010)	X	X	X	X	X	X	√	X	X	√	√	√
Ontology of Learning objects Repository for Pedagogical Knowledge Sharing	Wang (2008)	X	X	X	X	X	X	X	√	√	√	√	√
Ontology-based learning objects search and course generation	Neri & Colombetti (2009)	X	X	X	X	X	X	X	X	X	X	X	X
Ontology based learning objects sequencing	Neri (2005)	X	X	X	X	X	X	√	X	X	X	X	X

continued on following page

Table 3. Continued

Legend: √:Characteristic Available/Present in Model ×: Characteristic Not Available/Not Present in Model

| Existing work on E-Learning and 3.0 E-Learning | Author(s) & Year | Collaboration | | | | | Teaching Principles | | | | | | |
| | | | | | | | Curriculum | | | | Pedagogy | | |
		Student-Lecturer	Peer to Peer	Resource Sharing	Group Activities	Feedback	Syllabus	Course sequencing	Instructional Method	Context	Delivery Instrument	Learning Theories	Teaching Strategies
Course sequencing techniques for large-scale web-based education	Brusilovsky & Vassileva (2003)	×	×	×	×	×	×	√	√	√	√	√	√
A Web 2.0 Based e-Learning Success Model in Higher Education	Karunasena, Deng & Zhang (2012)	√	√	√	√	√	×	×	×	×	√	×	√
Critical Success Factors in online education	Volery & Lord (2000)	√	√	×	×	×	×	×	√	×	√	×	√
Critical success factors for distance learning	Papp (2000)	×	×	×	×	×	×	×	×	×	×	×	×
Critical success factors for on-line course resources	Soong, Chan, Chua & Loh (2001)	√	√	√	√	√	×	×	×	×	×	×	×
Strategies for assuring the quality of online learning in Australian higher education	Oliver (2001)	×	×	×	×	×	√	×	×	×	×	×	×

continued on following page

Table 3. Continued

Legend: √:Characteristic Available/Present in Model ×: Characteristic Not Available/Not Present in Model

Existing work on E-Learning and 3.0 E-Learning	Author(s) & Year	Teaching Principles											
		Collaboration					Curriculum				Pedagogy		
		Student-Lecturer	Peer to Peer	Resource Sharing	Group Activities	Feedback	Syllabus	Course sequencing	Instructional Method	Context	Delivery Instrument	Learning Theories	Teaching Strategies
E-learning critical success factors	Selim (2007)	√	√	√	√	√	√	×	√	×	√	√	√
A taxonomy of factors to promote quality web-supported learning	Frasen (2007)	√	√	√	√	√	√	√	√	√	√	√	√
Critical issues for e-learning delivery	McPherson & Nunes 2008	√	√	√	√	√	√	×	√	×	√	√	√
Modeling Web-based educational systems	Rokou, Rokou & Rokos (2004)	×	×	×	×	×	×	√	√	√	√	√	√
Trust in electronic learning and teaching relationships	von Kortzfleisch FO & Winand (2000)	×	√	√	√	√	×	×	×	×	×	√	√
Trust Networks on the Semantic Web	Golbeck, Parsia & Hendler (2003)	×	×	×	×	×	×	×	×	×	×	×	×
Trust relationships in Web-based social networks	Golbeck & Hendler (2006)	×	×	×	×	×	×	×	×	×	×	×	×
Trust on the Semantic Web	Cloran (2007)	×	×	×	×	×	×	×	×	×	×	×	×
Trust Model for Semantic Web	Shekarpour, Katebi & Katebi (2009)	×	×	×	×	×	×	×	×	×	×	×	×

Table 4.

Legend: √:Characteristic Available/Present in Model x: Characteristic Not Available/Not Present in Model

Existing work on E-learning and 3.0 E-learning	Author(s) & Year	Personalised Learning				Instructional Support					System Support			Support
		Student Model	Learning and cognitive style	Educational Goals	Learning Participation	Activities	Help	Feedback	Collaboration	Student Centered Learning	Organisation Support	Technology	Training	Infrastructure
Ontology-Driven E-Learning System	Snae & Brueckner (2007)	x	x	x	x	√	√	√	x	x	x	x	x	√
E-Learning Model based on the Semantic Web Technology	Ghaleb et al. (2006)	x	x	x	x	√	√	√	x	x	x	√	x	x
A Proposed Model of E-Learning Management System Using Semantic Web Technology	Rashid, Khan and Ahmed (2013)	√	√	x	x	√	√	√	√	√	x	√	x	x
Semantic Services in E-Learning	Moreale & Vargas-Vera (2004)	x	x	x	x	√	x	√	x	x	x	x	x	√
E-Learning based on the Semantic Web	Stojanovic, Staab & Studer (2001)	√	x	√	x	x	x	x	x	x	x	x	x	x
Semantic Web and Intelligent Management Systems (ILMS)	Simic, Gasevic & Devedzic (2004)	√	√	√	√	x	x	√	x	√	x	x	x	x
Conceptual Framework based on ontologies for knowledge management in e-learning systems	Pah, Maniu, Maniu & Damian (2007)	√	x	x	x	√	x	√	√	√	√	√	√	√
Semantic Web Ontology for E-learning in Higher Education	Bucos, Dragulescu & Veltan (2010)	x	x	x	x	√	√	√	√	x	x	x	x	x
Ontological Support for E-learning courses	De Nicola, Missikoff & Schiappelli (2004)	x	x	x	x	x	x	x	x	x	x	x	x	x

continued on following page

Table 4. Continued

Legend: √:Characteristic Available/Present in Model x: Characteristic Not Available/Not Present in Model

Existing work on E-learning and 3.0 E-learning	Author(s) & Year	Personalised Learning			Learning		Instructional Support					Organisation Support	System Support		Support
		Student Model	Learning and cognitive style	Educational Goals	Participation	Activities	Help	Feedback	Collaboration	Student Centered Learning			Technology	Training	Infrastructure
Identification of Ontology based learning object using instructional design	Srimathi & Srivatsa (2008)	√	√	x	x	x	x	x	x	x	x	x	x	x
Knowledge representation of LMS using ontology	Srimathi (2010)	√	√	x	x	x	x	x	x	x	x	x	x	x
Ontology of Learning objects Repository for Pedagogical Knowledge Sharing	Wang (2008)	x	x	x	x	x	x	x	x	x	x	x	x	x
Ontology-based learning objects search and course generation	Neri & Colombetti (2009)	x	x	x	x	x	x	x	x	x	x	x	x	x
Ontology based learning objects sequencing	Neri (2005)	x	x	x	x	x	x	x	x	x	x	x	x	x
Course sequencing techniques for large-scale web-based education	Brusilovsky & Vassileva (2003)	√	√	√	x	x	x	x	x	x	x	x	x	x
A Web 2.0 Based e-Learning Success Model in Higher Education	Karunasena, Deng & Zhang (2012)	x	x	x	x	√	√	√	√	x	x	√	x	x
Critical Success Factors in online education	Volery & Lord (2000)	x	x	x	x	x	x	x	√	√	x	x	x	x

continued on following page

Table 4. Continued

Legend: √:Characteristic Available/Present in Model x: Characteristic Not Available/Not Present in Model

Existing work on E-learning and 3.0 E-learning	Author(s) & Year	Personalised Learning				Instructional Support					Organisation Support	System Support		Support
		Student Model	Learning and cognitive style	Educational Goals	Learning Participation	Activities	Help	Feedback	Collaboration	Student Centered Learning		Technology	Training	Infrastructure
Critical success factors for distance learning	Papp (2000)	×	×	×	×	×	×	×	×	×	×	×	×	√
Critical success factors for on-line course resources	Soong, Chan, Chua & Loh (2001)	×	×	×	×	√	√	√	√	×	×	√	×	√
Strategies for assuring the quality of online learning in Australian higher education	Oliver (2001)	×	×	√	√	×	×	×	×	×	×	√	√	√
E-learning critical success factors	Selim (2007)	×	×	×	×	√	√	√	√	√	√	√	√	√
A taxonomy of factors to promote quality web-supported learning	Frasen (2007)	√	√	√	√	√	√	√	√	√	√	√	√	√
Critical issues for e-learning delivery	McPherson & Nunes 2008	√	√	√	√	√	√	√	√	√	√	√	√	√
Modeling Web-based educational systems	Rokou, Rokou & Rokos (2004)	√	√	√	√	×	×	×	×	×	×	×	×	×
Trust in electronic learning and teaching relationships	von Kortzfleisch, FO & Winand (2000)	√	√	√	√	√	√	√	√	×	×	×	×	×

continued on following page

Table 4. Continued

Legend: √: Characteristic Available/Present in Model x: Characteristic Not Available/Not Present in Model

| Existing work on E-learning and 3.0 E-learning | Author(s) & Year | Personalised Learning | | | | Instructional Support | | | | | Organisation Support | System Support | | Support |
		Student Model	Learning and cognitive style	Educational Goals	Learning Participation	Activities	Help	Feedback	Collaboration	Student Centered Learning		Technology	Training	Infrastructure
Trust Networks on the Semantic Web	Golbeck, Parsia & Hendler (2003)	×	×	×	×	×	×	×	×	×	×	×	×	×
Trust relationships in Web-based social networks	Golbeck & Hendler (2006)	×	×	×	×	×	×	×	×	×	×	×	×	×
Trust on the Semantic Web	Cloran (2007)	×	×	×	×	×	×	×	×	×	×	×	×	×
Trust Model for Semantic Web	Shekarpour, Katebi & Katebi (2009)	×	×	×	×	×	×	×	×	×	×	×	×	×

Table 5.

Existing work on E-Learning and 3.0 E-Learning	Author(s) & Year	Web 3.0 Ontology Based Technology				Security	Ontologies Database	Content Database	Records Database	Trust		
		Student-Lecturer	Peer to Peer	Technology	System					Hardware	Software	System Infrastructure
Ontology-Driven E-Learning System	Snae & Brueckner (2007)	×	×	×	×	√	×	√	√	√	√	√
E-Learning Model based on the Semantic Web Technology	Ghaleb et al. (2006)	×	×	×	×	√	√	√	√	√	√	√
A Proposed Model of E-Learning Management System Using Semantic Web Technology	Rashid, Khan and Ahmed (2013)	×	×	×	×	√	√	√	√	√	√	√
Semantic Services in E-Learning	Moreale & Vargas-Vera (2004)	×	×	×	×	√	√	√	√	×	×	×
E-Learning based on the Semantic Web	Stojanovic, Staab & Studer (2001)	×	×	×	×	×	√	√	√	√	√	√
Semantic Web and Intelligent Management Systems (ILMS)	Simic, Gasevic & Devedzic (2004)	×	×	×	×	√	√	√	√	√	√	√
Conceptual Framework based on ontologies for knowledge management in e-learning systems	Pah, Maniu, Maniu & Damian (2007)	×	×	×	×	×	√	√	√	×	×	×
Semantic Web Ontology for E-learning in Higher Education	Bucos, Dragulescu & Veltan (2010)	×	×	×	×	√	√	√	√	×	×	×
Ontological Support for E-learning courses	De Nicola, Missikoff & Schiappelli (2004)	×	×	×	×	×	√	√	×	×	×	×

Legend: √:Characteristic Available/Present in Model ×: Characteristic Not Available/Not Present in Model

continued on following page

Table 5. Continued

Legend: √:Characteristic Available/Present in Model ×: Characteristic Not Available/Not Present in Model

Existing work on E-Learning and 3.0 E-Learning	Author(s) & Year	Web 3.0 Ontology Based Technology								Trust		
		Student-Lecturer	Peer to Peer	Technology	System	Security	Ontologies Database	Content Database	Records Database	Hardware	Software	System Infrastructure
Identification of Ontology based learning object using instructional design	Srimathi & Srivatsa (2008)	×	×	×	×	×	√	√	×	×	×	×
Knowledge representation of LMS using ontology	Srimathi (2010)	×	×	×	×	×	√	√	×	×	×	×
Ontology of Learning objects Repository for Pedagogical Knowledge Sharing	Wang (2008)	×	×	×	×	×	√	√	×	×	×	×
Ontology-based learning objects search and course generation	Neri & Colombetti (2009)	×	×	×	×	×	√	√	√	×	×	√
Ontology based learning objects sequencing	Neri (2005)	×	×	×	×	×	√	√	√	×	×	√
Course sequencing techniques for large-scale web-based education	Brusilovsky & Vassileva (2003)	×	×	×	×	×	×	√	×	×	×	√
A Web 2.0 Based e-Learning Success Model in Higher Education	Karunasena, Deng & Zhang (2012)	×	×	×	×	×	×	√	√	√	√	√
Critical Success Factors in online education	Volery & Lord (2000)	×	×	×	×	×	×	×	×	×	×	×
Critical success factors for distance learning	Papp (2000)	×	×	×	×	×	×	×	×	×	×	×
Critical success factors for on-line course resources	Soong, Chan, Chua & Loh (2001)	×	×	×	×	×	×	×	×	×	×	×

continued on following page

Table 5. Continued

Legend: √:Characteristic Available/Present in Model ×: Characteristic Not Available/Not Present in Model

Existing work on E-Learning and 3.0 E-Learning	Author(s) & Year	Web 3.0 Ontology Based Technology								Trust		
		Student-Lecturer	Peer to Peer	Technology	System	Security	Ontologies Database	Content Database	Records Database	Hardware	Software	System Infrastructure
Strategies for assuring the quality of online learning in Australian higher education	Oliver (2001)	×	×	×	×	×	×	×	×	√	√	√
E-learning critical success factors	Selim (2007)	×	×	×	×	×	×	×	×	×	×	×
A taxonomy of factors to promote quality web-supported learning	Frasen (2007)	×	×	×	×	×	×	√	√	√	√	√
Critical issues for e-learning delivery	McPherson & Nunes 2008	×	×	√	√	√	×	×	×	√	√	√
Modeling Web-based educational systems	Rokou, Rokou & Rokos (2004)	×	×	×	×	×	×	×	×	×	×	×
Trust in electronic learning and teaching relationships	von Kortzfleisch, FO & Winand (2000)	√	×	√	×	×	×	×	×	×	×	×
Trust Networks on the Semantic Web	Golbeck, Parsia & Hendler (2003)	√	√	√	×	×	×	×	×	×	×	×
Trust relationships in Web-based social networks	Golbeck & Hendler (2006)	√	√	×	×	×	√	×	×	×	×	×
Trust on the Semantic Web	Cloran (2007)	√	√	√	√	√	√	×	×	×	×	×
Trust Model for Semantic Web	Shekarpour, Katebi & Katebi (2009)	√	√	×	×	×	×	×	×	×	×	×

Chapter 5
Web 3.0 and E-Learning:
The Empowered Learner

Amit Chauhan
Florida State University, USA

ABSTRACT

The annals of the Web have been a defining moment in the evolution of education and e-Learning. The evolution of Web 1.0 almost three decades ago has been a precursor to Web 3.0 that has reshaped education and learning today. The evolution to Web 3.0 has been synonymous with "Semantic Web" or "Artificial Intelligence" (AI). AI makes it possible to deliver custom content to the learners based on their learning behavior and preferences. As a result of these developments, the learners have been empowered and have at their disposal a range of Web tools and technology powered by AI to pursue and accomplish their learning goals. This chapter traces the evolution and impact of Web 3.0 and AI on e-Learning and its role in empowering the learner and transforming the future of education and learning. This chapter will be of interest to educators and learners in exploring techniques that improve the quality of education and learning outcomes.

INTRODUCTION

The evolution of the Web 1.0 to Web 3.0 in the last three decades has had a tremendous impact on the growth and the future of education and e-Learning. Web 3.0 or the *"Semantic Web"* builds on Web 2.0 or the *"Social Web"* which is characterized by learner interaction and participation on the web. As the third generation of the web, Web 3.0 uses data from learner interaction on the web to generate and deliver customized content to the learners. Computer algorithms form the basis of Web 3.0 which makes it possible for machines, tools, and application to exhibit Artificial Intelligence (AI).

BACKGROUND

The evolution of Web 1.0 to Web 3.0 has divided the world into *'Digital Natives'* and *'Digital Immigrants'*. *'Digital Immigrants'* utilize traditional classroom pedagogy and communication methods in the classroom (Prenksy, 2001b). They went to school and graduated without *Google* or *Wikis* and

DOI: 10.4018/978-1-4666-8147-7.ch005

have closely witnessed this epoch of technology revolution in education. In this sense, '*Digital Immigrants*' primarily include educators, educational administrators, parents and life-long learners who have been forced to adopt technology for education and learning.

How has the role of teachers transformed with the evolution of Web 3.0 and growth of AI? How can learners effectively use web tools for learning and education? What role will traditional institutions of learning play in this age of AI? What are the learning objectives and learning domains for Web 3.0? This chapter aims to explore current trends in the evolution of Web 3.0. and its overlap with the application and use of Artificial Intelligence (AI) in education and learning. This chapter will be of interest to educators and learners in exploring techniques that improve the quality of education and learning outcomes.

What is Artificial Intelligence?

The term Artificial Intelligence (AI) was first used by John McCarthy in 1955 for ascribing intelligence to machine and software. AI includes intelligent agents that are programmed with computer algorithms to maximize the potential and chances of success (Poole, Goebel, & Mackworth, 1998; Russell & Norvig, 2003). These intelligent agent or AI systems perform several tasks as computation; database query and retrieval; information search on the Internet; search engine functionality and features; and a current emerging trend – *Learning Analytics*. AI shares certain common features with Web 3.0 or the *semantic web* (Berners-Lee, 2001) which empower the learner. These features can be described as follows:

1. **Open and Cross-Platform:** AI and semantic web utilize several Application Programming Interface (APIs) that makes it possible to use them across different applications and Operating Systems (OS) platforms. Both AI and semantic web utilize

Open-source Software (OSS) for developing, sharing, and customization of applications for global use and application. Since the Web 3.0 learners are a diverse lot in terms of geography, location, language and experience with technology, the availability and use of open and cross-platform educational resources helps in maximizing learning outcomes.

2. **Data Mining:** AI and semantic web have built-in algorithms to analyze and interpret large volumes of data. This data can be used to analyze and predict learner behavior for a personalized learning experience.

3. **3D Virtualization:** Another commonality between Web 3.0 and the semantic web is the use of virtual and augmented reality learning tools and technology. These tools can be used to simulate learning processes which provide the learners visualize real-world scenarios for learning and cognition.

4. **Cloud Computing:** With cloud computing, learners have the ability to store, view, retrieve, exchange, and access computing services, files and applications over the Internet.

EVOLUTION OF THE WEB AND GROWTH OF E-LEARNING

The gradual transition of Web 1.0 to Web 3.0 over the last three decades has had a tremendous impact on education. One such impact has been the growth of eLearning. eLearning is defined as the use and application of computers and Internet to deliver information (Welsh, Wanberg, Brown & Simmering, 2003). To further analyze the impact of eLearning and how it has transformed education, it is important to look at the timeline of the web and Internet.

Web 1.0 is the first generation of the web and saw the advent and birth of the Internet. Learning in Web 1.0 was limited to four-walled classroom with limited participants and student participation. Web 1.0 did not support learner-content or learner-learner interaction on the web and was referred to as the *"Static Web"* (Berners-Lee, Hendler, & Lassila, 2001). eLearning did not become popular until the progression to Web 2.0 and Web 3.0. This was mainly because of the limited availability and use of computers and access to the Internet. The 1990s gave a tremendous boost to eLearning with the growth of the Internet; availability of broadband and affordability of computers (Teahan, 2006). The 1990s were characterized by the evolution of next generation of web, namely, Web 2.0 and Web 1.0 have moved learning out of the traditional classroom and made anywhere, anytime learning via the Internet or e-Learning a distinct possibility.

The term Web 2.0, or the second generation of web, was coined at a brainstorming session of the Web 2.0 conference, 2004 (O'Reilly, 2005). Web 2.0 is also known as the *participative* or *'Social Web'*. Web 2.0 evolved at the turn of the 21st century allowing user-interaction on the web and sharing of media-rich content online. Users can navigate web pages, links, post comments, create, edit, publish and share their own content. Users can also bookmark content and socialize via building online communities, networks, and collaborate online to accomplish common goals.

Web 3.0, also known as the *'Semantic Web'*, is the third generation of the World Wide Web (Markoff, 2006). Web 3.0 allows users to generate customized web content based on their profile and preferences. The Web 3.0 relies heavily on user-generated data such as likes, shares, comments to create search algorithms for enhancing user experience of the web. Web 3.0 is heavily geared towards the design and development of business strategies and web applications for e-commerce and Big Data analytics.

The social and semantic web together have empowered the learners since learning now extends into a global classroom with virtual collaboration through the use of free and access to open

educational resources, technology, and learning materials on the web to supplement knowledge and learning. A variety of media tools and technology make real time communication and collaboration possible with multiple opportunities for instant feedback and interaction. With this progression of the web from Web 1.0 to Web 3.0, the role of brick and mortar institutions has undergone significant development and change because of the evolution of e-Learning. It is important to analyze the impact of e-Learning on education and the transformation of the roles of administrators, educators, and learners in shaping and improving learning outcomes.

Web 1.0 – Web 3.0 (1980-2010)

In the mid-to-late 80s, as the Web 1.0 continued to evolve slowly, few websites began hosting content online. However, searching information on web was a bit overwhelming since there was no search engine that could index and retrieve search results based on search algorithms. Much of the information could be accessed and downloaded only via File Transfer Protocol (FTP) links. The links were not available publicly and could only be shared via email or a posting on the forums (Wiley, 2002a).

The year 1990 marked the dawn of an era with the launch of the first search engine – *Archie*. Initially conceived of as "archives", it was soon rechristened to *"Archie."* Archie became a central repository by indexing filenames and allowed users to search for specific files online (Sonnenreich, 1997). The development of Gopher in 1991 (Lee, 1999) marks yet another epoch in the evolution of the web for information search, storage and retrieval. These developments coincide with the evolution of Web 1.0 which was initially as designed as a simple interface to the *Semantic Web* as we know it today. Gopher developed at a time when the Internet was still in its nascent stage. Developed by Mark P. McCahillin and his team of researchers at the University of Minnesota, Gopher was a precursor to the Hypertext Transfer Protocol (HTTP) and allowed to send, transmit, receive, and display information on the World Wide Web (Lee, 1991). Gopher displayed information hierarchically on the web and together with the search engines – *Archie* and *Veronica* (Lee, 1991), heralded a new era of information search, storage and retrieval.

As the Web 1.0 began expanding, online learning started to make its presence felt and computers were viewed as an important extension of education and learning. There are many reasons that can be attributed to the advent of online courses and learning during this time. Hurn (2005) posited that there was a need to focus on learning and pedagogy away from the hardware. It was the dawn of a new era as online learning soon began to find its place in institutional settings. The online courses were teacher centered and followed the traditional classroom model. Vygotsky (1978) noted lack of instructor guidance in early online courses. Other researchers (Schauble, 1990; Hammer 1997) have also found that the early online environments included Web 1.0 instructors who did not provide timely feedback. As the Web progressed and transitioned into Web 2.0 at the turn of the twentieth century and now to Web 3.0, these developments led to learner empowerment and control. As we transition into Web 3.0, learning becomes more learner-centric providing even more learner autonomy and control.

WEB 3.0 and AI (2010 - Present)

Web 3.0 shifts the focus entirely on the learner in the sense that learners do not owe any allegiance or affiliation to any specific institution, school or university for furthering their knowledge and skills. Education 3.0 is synonymous with Web 3.0., also known as the 'Semantic Web', or the third generation of the World Wide Web (Markoff, 2006). Learning is customized to learner background, skills and they have a host of options to define, pursue, and choose from to accomplish

their learning goals. An essential characteristic of Web 3.0 is that learner-content interaction takes a prominence over learner-learner and learner instructor interaction. In fact, there are several educational applications that do not require an instructor (Brusilovsky, Eklund, & Schwarz, 1998). The learner-content interaction uses AI for providing automatic feedback to the learners and also allowing them to customize and personalize learning based on their preferences. The learners in Web 3.0 are diverse and comprise different age groups with distinct characteristics. Web 3.0 also allows learners multiple opportunities for life-long learning by forming groups and communities to accomplish their learning goals. The learners in Web 3.0 do not owe any allegiance or affiliation to a specific university or institution. The learners do not pay tuition and neither is there any eligibility criterion or pre-requisite for life-long learning. Learning is self-directed and self-regulated by learner motivation, self-efficacy and goal setting.

Andragogy and Metadata

Web 3.0 comprises of self-motivated and self-regulated adult learners. The principles of Andragogy or adult learning principles propounded by Malcolm Knowles thus find increasing relevance in the design and delivery of courses. The learners have anytime, anywhere access to the web and unlike Web 1.0 or the first generation of web, Web 3.0 supports an interactive and intuitive interface that can be customized and adapted to meet the specific needs of the learners (Brusilovsky et al., 1998). The learners define their learning goals and the learner-content interaction on the web automatically suggests, searches, retrieves, and recommends learning resources to meet their learning preferences and goals. The learner behavior can be easily tracked using metadata that can be used for the design and development of adaptive learning environments based on adult learning principles that include automated feedback and assessments.

Connectivism and Learner Autonomy

The theory of *Connectivism* was put forth by Stephen Downes and George Siemens (Siemens, 2013). The concept of *Connectivisim* implies that learners contribute to and derive knowledge from networks. *Connectivism* builds on Vygotsky's Zone of Proximal Development (ZPD) and relies on connections to support and aid learning and exchange of knowledge within a network. Vygotsky's constructivist theory, known as social constructivism, postulates that the learner is much more actively involved in a joint enterprise with the teacher in creating ("constructing") new meanings or knowledge. The Zone of Proximal Development (ZPD) was introduced by Vygotsky to differentiate between what a learner can do with or without assistance. Vygotsky views peer interaction as an essential part of the learning process (Vygotsky, 1978). The learners are in complete control of their learning and have the leverage to choose and select any online medium for achieving their learning goals. Web 3.0 offers much greater control and flexibility to the learner when compared to traditional Web 1.0 classroom setting (Kop, 2011). Web 3.0 provides learner autonomy by allowing them the freedom and leverage to form networks to co-construct and share knowledge. The learners are free to choose the learning tools and resources for an optimized learning experience. *Connectivism* allows the learners to leverage the power of Web 3.0 tools and technology to build their own personal learning networks (PLNs). The networks can be continuously updated and expanded to promote life-long learning, personal growth and professional development.

The Web 3.0 Learning Environment

Web 3.0 has in-built capabilities for providing the necessary tools and technology for use and application in instructional technology for improving learning outcomes. This can be accomplished by using a variety of tools and technology for course design and delivery. Social media and collaboration tools are finding an increasing use and application in the design of instruction and instructional strategies in Web 3.0. Web 3.0 supports integration with social media and collaboration tools such as *wikis, blogs, Facebook, twitter, journals, Google Apps* etc. These social media platforms are regularly updated with several enhancements and features to keep up-to-date with the latest technology. It is important to note that while Web 2.0 is characterized by Personal Learning Environments (PLE) designed and developed by the instructor, Education 3.0 features Personal Learning Network (PLN) developed by the learners themselves. The integration of Web 2.0 and Web 3.0 tools in Personal Learning Environments (PLE) and Personal Learning Network (PLN) can assist the learners in improving learning outcomes. There are several learning technologies that are integral to Web 3.0. These can be summarized as follows:

1. **Ontologies:** Considered as the basis of the semantic web, ontology comprises of a set of specific terms which can be attributed to a string of words for an easy reference and access (Hendler, 2001). Ontologies are closely intertwined with the semantic web (Fensel, van Harmelen, Horrocks, McGuinness & Patel-Schneider, 2001) and provide the necessary information for building knowledge bases (Swartout & Tate, 1999) and provide a guiding framework for structuring information on the web. They provide a standard basis for sharing and reuse of information. Web 3.0 has provided new set of tools and techniques to collect, analyze, and make sense of the data for making informed decisions.

2. **Cloud Computing:** There is no common definition of cloud computing (Grossman, 2009; Voas & Zhang, 2009). Cloud computing uses Internet as the delivery medium to deliver and on-demand services without the

need for installing hardware or software on local computers. The services and technology infrastructure to provide on-demand services is hosted remotely and provides an easy exchange medium on information and services to be accessed over the Internet. Cloud computing makes it possible to leverage educational resources for improving learning outcomes by using three main types of services:

a. **Infrastructure as a Service (IaaS):** This includes the online delivery of computer hardware.

b. **Platform as a Service (PaaS):** This type of cloud computing allows to build and configure remote applications. PaaS can be utilized by institutions to host applications in the cloud and not worry to much about costs or space to locally build these applications.

c. **Software as a Service (SaaS):** SaaS makes it possible to run applications without installing any software on local

machines. The software can be installed remotely on the Internet and provides economy of space and costs.

THE WEB 3.0 CHALLENGE

The Internet has taken giant strides in the last three decades with the evolution of the Web 1.0 to Web 3.0 This in turn, has also coincided with similar advancements in the realm of Education 1.0 to Education 3.0 These developments can be summarized below (Figure 1):

The progression to Web 3.0 has posed a unique opportunity and challenge for the existing learner and the current education scenario. Educational institutions are currently faced with a huge task to adopt learning initiatives that capitalize on the learner knowledge and are struggling with the need and demand on infrastructure and limited resources to transition to Web 3.0. As technology becomes all pervasive, academic institutions must rely on the use of smart web applications

Figure 1. The evolution of the web and Education 123. Copyright 2014 by Amit Chauhan

	Education 1.0	Education 2.0	Education 3.0
Instruction	Face2Face	Blended / Online	Online
Instructor	Sage on the Stage	Guide on the Side	Learner
Delivery	Lectures	Flipped Classroom	Extended Classroom
Teaching	Classroom	Personal Learning Environment (PLE)	Personal Learning Network (PLN)
Interaction	Learner-Instructor	Collaboration	Social
Learning Materials	Textbooks	Online; eBooks	Online / Cloud
Affiliation	Institution	Institution; Open Learning	No Affiliation; Anyone; Everyone
Courses	Tuition	Tuition; Coursework	Free; Stand-alone
Learning	Instructor Centered	Learner Centered /Participative	Personalized Learning
Content	Read-only	Bookmarking	Social Bookmarking
Learner	Digital Immigrants	Digital Native and Digital Immigrants	Millenials / Digital Leaner
Assessments	Tests	Learning Management System (LMS)	Learning Analytics

for measuring learning outcomes. The Web 3.0 applications can help in summative assessment and also track learner behavior and performance throughout a course. The data from these web applications can be used to identify at-risk populations and corrective measures can be taken to bring such students back in the mainstream. The use of AI makes it possible to design and develop Intelligent Tutoring Systems (ITS) for scaffolding the learners and model their behavior to improve performance and learning. To tap the full potential of Web 3.0 and AI applications, it is therefore extremely important that instructors and learners must be provided with resources and the necessary support to integrate and adopt emerging technologies effectively in the classroom. There is a huge challenge for educational administration to ensure that necessary policies are formulated to support the integration of latest technology in the design and development of curriculum and pedagogy. In order to formulate and implement the necessary policies, it is also important that educators take diversity into consideration in integrating technology with curriculum (Thinyane, 2010). The institutions must have a clear focus in adoption of such technologies and their implementation must be aimed at improving learning outcomes.

In the current scenario, it is important to discuss how the educational landscape has changed with the evolution of the web and the unique challenges it faces. A discussion of the educational developments over the past three decades will help us to better understand dynamics of the web and how Web 3.0 and AI can be leveraged to further empower the learner and improve learning and assessment.

Institutions in Web 1.0

In the early 80s, 40% of elementary schools and 75% secondary schools in the US were using computers for instruction (Center for Social Organization of Schools, 1983). Computers began to gain

wide popularity in the 90s and found application for instructional purposes (Reiser, 2001). Although computers found much popularity and relevance in educational settings, their use and impact was minimal until the mid-90s. The use of computers was limited to teaching basic computer and word processing skills (Becker, 1998; Anderson & Ronnkvist, 1999). This period was soon followed by the transition to Web 2.0 that began in early 21st century and witnessed a continuous demand for integrating tools and technology in pedagogy and learning. Institutions today are expected to support and encourage the faculty students in learning of these new skills and technology.

Institutions in Web 2.0

Emerging research in the field shows that use of Web 2.0 tools and technology in institutions of higher education is gaining increased popularity. Web 2.0 provides multiple opportunities for sharing and online collaboration. It is no doubt then that institutions are making conscious efforts to create faculty and staff awareness in promoting and Web 2.0 resources such as Open Educational Resources (OER). While a culture of borrowing and sharing of resources already exists between close colleagues within a university, the faculty and staff are hesitant to the idea of putting up resources on the internet for sharing and collaboration (Rolfe, 2012). Rolfe stated that the factors that support the growth of OER include the importance of institutional staff, partnerships and communities; and a strong belief in open education and the ability of OER to enhance individual and institutional reputations and economic factors. Institutions in the UK have adopted Web 2.0 tools such wikis and blogs for achieving learning outcomes (Lund & Smørdal, 2006; Désilets & Paquet, 2005). Research has shown that the use of wikis has been effective for assessment purposes (Minocha & Thomas, 2007). Universities need to further examine the current infrastructure and management systems in institutionalizing Web 2.0 tools and technology. For institutions to successfully adopt these new technologies would also be a great opportunity to reinvent themselves (Selwyn, 2007). Virtual Learning Environments (VLEs) and Open-source Software (OSS) that integrate new web tools and technology find increasing relevance and use in institutional settings for improving learning outcomes. Another way to encourage the integration of Web 2.0 tools in learning is to promote informal learning and informal communication (Kreijns, Kierschner, Jochems & van Burren, 2007). Yet another initiative in institutions adopting new technologies is podcasting. While Education 1.0 made it possible to record lectures and interviews for later use, Education 2.0 takes it a step further by making podcasts available in digital format that can be downloaded over the Internet. Institutions are making use of resources such as iTunes U and Learning Management Systems (LMSs) such as Blackboard (http://www.blackboard.com/), Moodle (https://moodle.org/) to support learning and achievement. Several Web 2.0 tools such as wikis, blogs, RSS, and Twitter etc. can be easily integrated into LMS such as Blackboard.

Universities and institutions must provide more incentives; allocation of funds and necessary support for the integration of new technology in designing curriculum and innovative pedagogy. In addition to deploying new technologies, institutions must foster the creation and sharing of new knowledge through the integration of these technologies. This new model is in contrast to Web 1.0 where the learner is seen as a passive recipient of knowledge and learning. The technical adeptness of learners in Web 2.0 makes it easier for institutions to integrate web technologies for learning and assessment. A large population of learners in Web 2.0 comprises digital natives who are naturally inclined towards collaborative technologies (Prensky, 2001). By leveraging Web 2.0 or the "*Social Web*" for education and learn-

ing, institutions can foster social learning and collaboration and bridge the gap between formal and informal learning. The institutions can also share these free resources to create and share knowledge to lower costs of content development and improving the quality of education.

SOLUTIONS AND RECOMMENDATIONS

The previous sections have discussed the evolution of the Web 3.0 and AI, and its impact on education. This section aims to answer some lingering questions - How will learners be assessed as they increasingly depend on the web for learning and professional development to further knowledge and skills? What will be the impact on educational institutions?

Learning Analytics

Learning analytics refers to the collection, measurement, and analysis of data gathered from the learners (Siemens, Gasevic, Haythornthwaite, Dawson, Shum, Ferguson, Duval, Verbert, & d Baker, 2011). This learner data helps to identify and predict trends and patterns in the learner behavior and their interaction with the learning environment. The data can be used to optimize learning outcomes and enhance learner experiences (Campbell, Oblinger, & DeBlois, 2007). As learners get more involved and immersed in online learning environments in Web 3.0, there is more to assessing student learning and achievement than by grading tests and homework which has been a characteristic of education in Web 1.0 learning environments. The applications of learning analytics skills find increasing relevance in Web 3.0 settings. The data generated by the learners through interaction in their learning environments can be useful for understanding learner behavior and scaffolding them to achieve learning outcomes. Learning analytics as a discipline is therefore, finding increasing relevance in Technology Enhanced Learning (TEL) as it provides valuable insights into learner characteristics and learning environment (Elias, 2011).

TRAINING IN WEB 3.0 TECHNOLOGIES

The widespread use and application of Information and Communication Technologies (ICTs) in Web 3.0 is critical to develop skills in learners that are critical to achieve learning outcomes. Research has shown that *Digital Natives* are skilled in the use of technology for personal use. However, there is also a sizable population of Digital Natives and Digital Immigrants who are not adept in the use of technology (Bennett, Maton, & Kervin, 2008). The traditional educational system was not designed for learners in the digital age (Prensky, 2001a). It is therefore necessary that instructors have the necessary training to teach relevant content (Prensky, 2001a). Digital competence is still a challenge that must be integrated into the curriculum to develop cognitive skills in the *Digital Natives* (Li & Ranieri, 2010). As both learners and instructors begin to co-create knowledge in an interchange and interplay of roles, it is essential that they have the requisite training and expertise to learn and apply the requisite skills and knowledge of tools and technology to achieve the learning outcomes. While *Digital Immigrants* are tech-savvy and have a good understanding and awareness of technology, there is a need to prepare them along with the *Digital Natives* in the selection and training of specific Web 3.0 tools that can be used to successfully accomplish the learning outcomes. Bloom's revised digital taxonomy includes a set of Web 2.0 & Web 3.0 apps that can be effectively utilized to achieve learning outcomes that closely align with the Bloom's revised digital taxonomy in Web 3.0.

Bloom's Revised Digital Taxonomy and Web Tools

The learner skills and learning outcomes to be measured in Web 3.0 need to be re-evaluated for the purposes of assessment and evaluation. Bloom's taxonomy of learning which has been the standard in Web 1.0, has been revised to Bloom's Revised Digital Taxonomy to accommodate Higher Order Thinking Skills (HOTS) in Web 2.0 and Web 3.0. (Anderson & Krathwohl, 2001). A wide variety of web tools and technology can be used for improving pedagogical techniques and assessing learning outcomes based on Bloom's revised digital taxonomy. Samantha Penny's project (Figure 2) provides a brief snapshot of some tools that can be utilized for measuring learning outcomes in Web 2.0 and Web 3.0 (Penny, 2013). Most of these tools include analytic capabilities that can be used to analyze learner performance and measure learning outcomes. These tools find extensive use in educational institutions for learning and collaboration on creative projects that are being used by the instructors to improve learning outcomes. The revised taxonomy includes the following domains for learners utilizing web tools and technology in Web 2.0 & 3.0:

- **Remembering:** The learner in Education 2.0 and Education 3.0 relies on information from multiples web resources for learning and professional development. It is essential therefore, that the learner is assessed based on information recall and retrieval of both procedural and declarative knowledge from long-term memory.
  - **Web tools:** delicious (https://delicious.com/); flickr (https://www.flickr.com/); zoho (https://www.zoho.com/); Wordnik (https://www.wordnik.com/) etc.
- **Understanding:** The learner must be able to deconstruct and simplify the acquisition of knowledge and skills.

Figure 2. Bloom's digital taxonomy pyramid. Reprinted from Samantha Penney's website, S. Penney, 2014, Retrieved from http://faculty.indstate.edu/spenney/bdt.htm

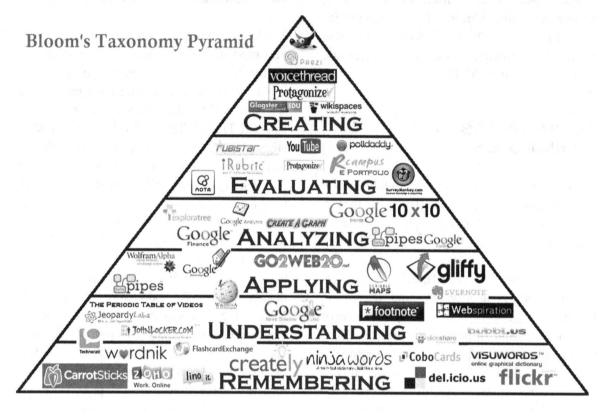

- ◦ **Sample Web tools:** Google News (https://news.google.com/); SlideShare (http://www.slideshare.net/); Technorati (http://technorati.com/); bubbl.us (https://bubbl.us/) etc.
- **Applying:** The learner must be able to apply the knowledge and skills for assessment of the learning outcomes.
  - ◦ **Sample Web tools:** Evernote (http://evernote.com/); Sketchup (http://www.sketchup.com/); Scribble Maps (http://www.scribblemaps.com/); Gliffy (http://www.gliffy.com/) etc.
- **Analyzing:** Categorization and interpretation of constituent elements.
  - ◦ **Sample Web tools:** Google Analytics (http://www.google.com/analytics/);

Google Earth (http://www.google.com/earth/); Google Finance (http://www.google.com/finance); Google Trends (http://www.google.com/trends/) etc.

- **Evaluating:** The learner must be able to derive inferences based on the standard criteria established for quality and assessment.
  - ◦ **Sample Web tools:** YouTube (http://www.youtube.com/); SurveyMonkey (https://www.surveymonkey.com/); rcampus (http://www.rcampus.com/); Protagonize (http://www.protagonize.com/); Nota (http://notaland.com/) etc.
- **Creating:** Unlike Education 1.0, the learner in Education 2.0 and Education 3.0 must

be able to create and combine knowledge by synthesizing and combining information and knowledge into new patterns or structure.

  ◦ **Sample Web tools:** Wikispaces (https://www.wikispaces.com/); Glogster (http://www.glogster.com/); Voicethread (https://voicethread.com/); Prezi (https://prezi.com/); Gimp (http://www.gimp.org/) etc.

The learners in Web 3.0 are life-long learners and are not limited to institutions granting a degree or a diploma. The learners utilize various media tools, and technology to further learning and knowledge. Most of these Web 3.0 tools that find application and use in learning have an intuitive interface and do not require extensive training. Most Web 3.0 tools and technology that find application in the Bloom's revised taxonomy have short instructional videos available on their home page that can be referenced to learn the skills and knowledge required to apply these skills. In addition, several Learning Management Systems (LMSs) tools such as Blackboard (http://www.blackboard.com/), Moodle (https://moodle.org/) which find extensive use and application in institutional settings require training workshops to be conducted to train the instructors and learners. It is important for instructors and educators to learn these skills since graduates today are required to be proficient in tools and technology to make the most of the available career prospects and opportunities. The Byron report (Byron, 2008) details how the youth today are proficient in the use of technology but are not prepared or unaware of its potential Internet hazards. The report advocates integrating Internet safety into curriculum and providing the necessary training to educators in this area. The administrative policies must include trainings in its purview the policies adopted by institutions to enhance learner experience using innovative tools and technology. It is extremely important that educators and administrators have a clear vision of incorporating these tools and are willing to take on the challenges of managing the whole new educational experience.

With the revised criterion being implemented for measuring learning outcomes and assessing learner success and achievement, the next pertinent question that comes to the fore is the role of traditional institutions and educators in Web 3.0.

Learners in Web 3.0

The learners in Web 3.0 are self-motivated and lifelong learners. They have at their disposal, a variety of tools and technology to adapt their learning, measure time-on-task and utilize performance metric to improve learning outcomes. The learners have different styles which can be easily tracked and adapted to match learner pace, knowledge levels and affective state (Khan, Weippl, & Tjoa, 2009). Web 3.0 identifies each learner as unique with different cognitive styles, background, expertise and skills in the area. The detection of individual learning styles is helps to track performance, identify critical areas which need attention and can be improved with timely intervention. The use and adaptability of Web 3.0 tools and technology has made the learners more aware and conscious of their performance and also provided tools that can be used to improve performance. The learners create, share, and build new knowledge in a network. Personalization is seen as the hallmark of Web 3.0 to address learner needs (Ebner, Schön, Taraghi, Drachsler, & Tsang, 2011). The learners can create their own Personal Learning Networks to cultivate and build their network for lifelong learning. Emerging research in the field has identified a variety of learners based on their learning style and preferences. This is unlike the traditional educational system where learners were solely identified on the basis of grades and broadly categorized as pass or fail. Web 3.0 also identifies and recognizes as lurkers who may not be actively participating in the learning activities but contribute in their way by sharing and liking content on the web. Jackson Learning Styles Profiler categorizes learners in five different categories such as conscientious achiever or a sensation seeker (Popescu, Badica, & Moraret, 2010).

Institutions in Web 3.0

Institutions must ensure that curriculum is customizable to incorporate emerging technologies that characterizes Web 3.0. Emerging research on Intelligent Learning Environments (ILE) that utilizes learner interaction on the "*Social Web*" to design custom learning experiences provides yet another opportunity for institutions to leverage the '*Semantic Web*' in optimizing learning outcomes. As learning becomes increasingly decentralized with more control and autonomy to the learner, the *Semantic Web* allows learners to create their own Personal Learning Environments (PLEs) to engage in active learning. Learning can be personalized and adapted to learner characteristics to achieve learning goals (Koper, 2004). With universities making concerted efforts to make more courses available online and firming educational alliances, there is a need for change in the educational setup. There is an increasing demand for courses that are flexible and adopt automated learning and assessment strategies. Educators can build course prototypes that utilize the *Semantic Web* to create and share effective pedagogical techniques (Bergin, Eckstein, Manns, Sharp, & Voelter, 2000). "*Semantic Web*" can provide support for analyzing learner-learner; and learner-content interactions. The analytics from learner interactions can be used for a detailed analysis of time-on-task, course navigation, the total number of clicks, lecture views, videos etc. The data analysis can help track learner performance and improve learning outcomes. "*Semantic Web*" can instantiate workflow management and optimal

allocation of resources to support learners, staff, and faculty (Koper, 2004).

While a shift to accommodate the necessary institutional and social change has gained momentum over the years, concerted efforts by the institutions and educational administrators is required to make a lasting impact. Institutions must provide the necessary technological resources and administrative leadership to teach, assess, and prepare students to compete and excel in real world settings. With institutions adopting new tools and technology for learning, it is critical to train both the educators and learners on the use of web media, tools, and technology. The next section discusses training in web tools and technologies.

Educators in Web 3.0

With the evolution of the web, the role of both the educators and learners in Web 3.0 has undergone tremendous change. Web 1.0 or the traditional classroom vested complete authority and control in the instructor with the proverbial "*Sage on the Stage*" holding true for educators. Initially perceived as the "*Global Village*," the web continued to grow even further with the internet density steadily increasing and now comprises of close-knit communities that are based on mutual and common interests. This made it convenient for educators to share learning resources with the students which can be accessed anywhere, anytime. Homework and assignments can be submitted and graded electronically. In that sense, there has been a paradigm shift in the use of technology in education and continues to evolve even further. Education in Web 1.0 was much more directed towards the learners as consumers of knowledge. Web 3.0 on the other hand focuses on creating and sharing knowledge. The role of the educator in Web 3.0 is characterized by co-constructivism (Moravec, 2009). The instructor co-constructs knowledge with the learner in an interchange and interplay of the roles between the instructor and the learner. It includes instructors who innovate, create, and share knowledge by learning along with others. The instructors assisting learners closely aligns with the notion of meaningful learning (Vygotsky, 1978). The co-construction of knowledge has thus, replaced the one-way learning style which has been the norm in Web 1.0. In addition, Web 3.0 and AI have made available plentiful web resources, tools and technology available to the educator to track and measure student learning and achievement. Educators are continuously required to redesign curriculum to align with the skills required for the professional development and growth in the knowledge economy. Educators also have the benefit of using analytics to identify "at-risk" students and take preventive measures to bring them into the mainstream and ensure learner success. The instructor involvement wherever required, can encourage the participatory environment by providing feedback and helping the student in accomplishing the learning objectives (Nir-Gal, 2002).

Adopting innovative pedagogical techniques using Web 3.0 technologies and AI may often involve charting an unfamiliar territory. Educators are going to be apprehensive of the learning outcomes accomplished with excessive reliance on technology. Since faculty will require extra time and resources for new technology trainings, and preparing learning materials a pertinent question is why would the educators want to invest time and resources in learning new technology? This is especially true when there is a general perception that existing pedagogy might be just as well effective in achieving learning outcomes. There will be an increasing focus on the adoption of new technology and there is a fear and suspicion that this would result in loosening of control by instructors (Crook, Fisher, Graber, Harrison, Lewin, Logan, Luckin, Oliver, & Sharples, 2008). Technology would also empower the learners in gaining anywhere, anytime access to multiple educational resources to achieve their learning goals. There might be an apprehension that the future role of instructors might be endangered with the adoption of technology (Crook et al., 2008). As the instructor role in becomes more of a "*guide on the side*" than "*sage on the stage*", instructors will have to upgrade and train in the necessary skills for a more learner centric pedagogy. It must be noted however that Web 3.0 does not imply that the role of the instructor is non-existent or no longer required. Instructors today are finding increasing relevance and significance in inspiring, motivating, and providing guidance to learners in the safe use of web tools, and technology. Instructors can inspire learners in this digital age to create, collaborate, and share knowledge and resources online to enrich their learning. In turn, instructors can also feel inspired by the creative ability and ingenuity of the learners.

For instructors to continue to support the self-motivated learners in Web 3.0, they must be provided with support and the necessary resources, tools, and technology to teach and train the digital natives in the effective use of technology for achieving their learning goals. Integrating technology into curriculum will provide the necessary institutional backing and support to use technology to maximize learning outcomes. Bloom's revised digital taxonomy (Anderson & Krathwohl, 2001) provides robust criteria to measure and assess learning outcomes. Bloom's revised digital taxonomy provides a set of web tools and technology that can be used by both instructors and learners to teach and demonstrate mastery of learning.

Web 3.0 has thrown open new opportunities and challenges for managing and improving quality of education. Any innovation in pedagogy and transfer of learning is not possible without the able guidance and support of educators (Crook et al., 2008). Educators must be provided with necessary incentives to mentor and support learners and they in turn, must receive adequate support from administrators and policy makers to promote research and creativity in the application of new tools and technology.

DISCUSSION

In this chapter, we have explored Web 3.0 and how it has empowered the learner. As much as Web 3.0 tools and AI have enhanced learning experiences, their use in education must be based on empirical research that investigates the use of pedagogical techniques to create meaningful learning experiences and outcomes. The use and application of Web 3.0 and AI media, tools, and technology has provided new opportunities to educators, instructors, and learners to innovate, share and collaborate. The evolution of the web has provided with new opportunities and frontiers in education. A major area that has seen tremendous growth is lifelong learning. Web tools and technology have made it possible and convenient to connect learners all around the world for creating and sharing knowledge, and collaboration. Web 3.0 has empowered the learners to access learning resources anywhere, anytime. Besides learners taking control of their learning, Web 3.0 has provided automated response and feedback systems that use AI to improve knowledge and learning. Web 3.0 provides the opportunity to collaborate and share content and learning resources online. Institutions are increasing relying on web tools to train and track learner performance and improve learning outcomes. As much as focus has shifted to tools and technology in recent years, it must be however emphasized that technology can only be a means to design and deliver quality education and not an ends in itself.

Emerging technologies such as Web 3.0 and AI provide for ever growing innovation and creativity in pedagogical techniques and the need for integrating these technologies into curriculum cannot be overemphasized to improve learning outcomes. It is extremely critical that institutions have the necessary logistics, finance, and administrative support to apply Web 3.0 technologies in pedagogy and assessment. Learners need adequate training and support for effectively using technology for lifelong learning. This requires an optimal use of educational resources for improving the overall quality of education and lifelong learning.

Web 3.0 has provided several opportunities and challenges for institutions to the extent that either they must adapt or risk being left behind in this age of the global classroom. Institutions must deliberate policies that not only facilitate the implementation but also support the use of innovative pedagogical techniques in learning and education. Additional safeguards regarding safety and security of data and privacy of information must be ensured to make learning and collaboration on the web a rewarding experience. It is only natural that as with any change, there is going to be resistance initially. It will require the concerted efforts of policy makers and administrators to provide leadership and direction in preparing a roadmap for implementing technology for improving the quality of education

FUTURE RESEARCH DIRECTIONS

Future research in the field must analyze large pools of data using data mining techniques to generate algorithms that have the ability to offer translation services in real time. Since Web 3.0 comprises learners from all around the world, such data mining techniques can help learners who are struggling with the language and lack the requisite knowledge to participate in the learning activities. Sensing the need for standards in the adoption and use of technology, the institutional bodies around the world have delineated benchmarks to measure learner success for certification and accreditation specific to their country. There is also a need to evolve common curriculum standards and performance measuring systems to improve learning outcomes. In addition to common curriculum and accreditation standards, there is a need for next generation SCORM system to evolve common standards for learners around the world. Web 3.0

ontologies can be used to design and develop learning objects and best practices in learning to further empower the learner.

CONCLUSION

In the light of Web 3.0 developments, education systems must reinvent to meet the learning style of the Web 3.0 learners. The web continues to evolve and offers a host of technology choices to the educators. The learners must be digitally competent to tap the potential of Web 3.0 to achieve the learning objectives. The wide use and application of Web 3.0 tools, technology, and media makes it somewhat convenient to leverage technology for improving learning outcomes. In order for the learners to maximize benefits of educational technology and maximize learning outcomes, the educational institutions must ensure the availability of resources to use Web 3.0 technologies effectively for improving learning and education.

REFERENCES

Anderson, R. E., & Ronnkvist, A. (1999). The presence of computers in American schools: Teaching, learning and computing: 1998 national survey (Report #2). Irvine, CA: Center for Research on Information Technology and Organizations. (ERIC Document Reproduction Service No. ED 430 548).

Becker, H. J. (1998). Running to catch a moving train: Schools and information technologies. *Theory into Practice*, *37*(1), 20–30. doi:10.1080/00405849809543782

Bennett, S., Maton, K., & Kervin, L. (2008). The 'digital natives' debate: A critical review of the evidence. *British Journal of Educational Technology*, *39*(5), 775–786. doi:10.1111/j.1467-8535.2007.00793.x

Bergin, J., Eckstein, J., Manns, M., Sharp, H., & Voelter, M. (2000). *The pedagogical pattern project*. Retrieved June 12, 2014, from http://www.pedagogicalpatterns.org

Berners-Lee, T., Hendler, J., & Lassila, O. (2001). The semantic web. *Scientific American*, 28–37. PMID:11323639

Brusilovsky, P., Eklund, J., & Schwarz, E. (1998). Web-based education for all: A tool for development adaptive courseware. *Computer Networks and ISDN Systems*, *30*(1), 291–300. doi:10.1016/S0169-7552(98)00082-8

Byron, T. (2008). Safer children in a digital world: The report of the Byron Review. Department for Children, Schools and Families, and the Department for Culture, Media and Sport.

Campbell, J. P., Oblinger, D. G., & DeBlois, P. B. (2007). Academic analytics: A new tool for a new era. *EDUCAUSE Review*, *42*, 40–57.

Center for Social Organization of Schools. (1983). *School uses of microcomputers: Reports from a national survey (Issue no. 1)*. Baltimore, MD: Johns Hopkins University, Center for Social Organization of School.

Crook, C., Fisher, T., Graber, R., Harrison, C., Lewin, C., Logan, C., Luckin, R., Oliver, M., & Sharples, M. (2008). *Web 2.0 technologies for learning: The current landscape - Opportunities, challenges and tensions*. BECTA Research Report.

Désilets, A., & Paquet, S. (2005). Wiki as a tool for web-based collaborative story telling in primary school: a Case Study. In KommersP.RichardsG. (Eds.), *Proceedings of World Conference on Educational Multimedia, Hypermedia and Telecommunications* (pp. 770-777). Chesapeake, VA: AACE.

Ebner, M., Schön, S., Taraghi, B., Drachsler, H., & Tsang, P. (2011). First steps towards an integrated personal learning environment at the university level. In Enhancing learning through technology: Education unplugged: Mobile technologies and web 2.0 (pp. 22-36). Springer Berlin Heidelberg. doi:10.1007/978-3-642-22383-9_3

Elias, T. (2011, January). *Learning analytics: Definitions, processes and potential*. Retrieved September 15, 2013 from http://learninganalytics.net/LearningAnalyticsDefinitionsProcessesPotential.pdf

Fensel, D., van Harmelen, F., Horrocks, I., McGuinness, D. L., & Patel-Schneider, P. F. (2001). OIL: An ontology infrastructure for the semantic web. *IEEE Intelligent Systems*, *16*(2), 38–45. doi:10.1109/5254.920598

Grossman, R. (2009). The case for cloud computing. *IT Professional*, *11*(2), 23–27. doi:10.1109/MITP.2009.40

Hammer, D. (1997). Discovery learning and discovery teaching. *Cognition and Instruction*, *15*(4), 485–529. doi:10.1207/s1532690xci1504_2

Hurn, J. E. (2005). Beyond point and click: Taking web based pedagogy to a new level. Paper presented at the Association of Small Computer Users in Education (ASCUE), Myrtle Beach, SC.

Khan, F. A., Weippl, E. R., & Tjoa, A. M. (2009). Integrated approach for the detection of learning styles and affective states. In *Proceedings of World Conference on Educational Multimedia, Hypermedia and Telecommunications* (pp. 753-761). Academic Press.

Kop, R. (2011). The challenges to connectivist learning on open online networks: Learning experiences during a massive open online course. *International Review of Research in Open and Distance Learning*, *12*(3).

Koper, R. (2004). Use of the semantic web to solve some basic problems in education: Increase flexible, distributed lifelong learning, decrease teacher's workload. *Journal of Interactive Media in Education*, *2004*(6).

Kreijns, K., Kirschner, P., Jochems, W., & van Buuren, H. (2007). Measuring perceived sociability of computer-supported collaborative environments. *Computers & Education*, *49*(2), 176–192. doi:10.1016/j.compedu.2005.05.004

Lee, C. (1999). *Where have all the gophers gone? Why the web beat gopher in the battle for protocol mind share*. Retrieved from School of Information and Library Science, University of North Carolina website: http://ils.unc.edu/callee/gopherpaper.htm

Li, Y., & Ranieri, M. (2010). Are 'digital natives' really digitally competent? A study on Chinese teenagers. *British Journal of Educational Technology*, *41*(6), 1029–1042. doi:10.1111/j.1467-8535.2009.01053.x

Lund, A., & Smørdal, O. (2006). *Is there a space for the teacher in a WIKI?* Paper presented at WikiSym'06, Odense, Denmark. doi:10.1145/1149453.1149466

Markoff, J. (2006, November 12). Entrepreneurs see a web guided by common sense. *The New York Times*. Retrieved from http://dt123.com/datagrid/datagridwebsitev1a/PDFs/NYT_111306_Web30.pdf

Minocha, S., & Thomas, P. G. (2007). Collaborative learning in a wiki environment: Experiences from a software engineering course. *New Review of Hypermedia and Multimedia, 13*(2), 187–209. doi:10.1080/13614560701712667

Moravec, J. (2009). *The role of teachers in education 3.0.* Retrieved from http://www.education-futures.com/2009/05/10/the-role-of-teachers-in-education-30/

Nir-Gal, O. (2002). Distance learning: The role of the teacher in a virtual learning environment. *Ma'of u-Ma'aseh, 8,* 23-50.

O'Reilly, T. (2005). *What is web 2.0?* Retrieved August 29, 2013, from http://www.oreillynet.com/pub/a/oreilly/tim/news/2005/09/30/what-is-web-20.html#mememap

Poole, D. I., Goebel, R. G., & Mackworth, A. K. (1998). *Computational intelligence.* Oxford, UK: Oxford University Press.

Popescu, E., Badica, C., & Moraret, L. (2010). Accommodating learning styles in an adaptive educational system. *Informatica (Slovenia), 34*(4), 451–462.

Prenksy, M. (2001a). Digital natives, digital immigrants. *On the Horizon, 9*(5).

Prensky, M. (2001a). *Do they really think differently?* Retrieved from http://www.emeraldinsight.com/journals.htm?articleid=1532747&show=pdf

Reiser, R. A. (2001). A history of instructional design and technology: Part I: A history of instructional media. *Educational Technology Research and Development, 49*(1), 53–64. doi:10.1007/BF02504506

Rolfe, V. (2012). Open educational resources: Staff attitudes and awareness. *The Journal of the Association of Learning Technology, 20.* doi:10.3402/rlt.v20i0/14395

Russell, S., & Norvig, P. (2003). *Artificial Intelligence: A modern approach* (3rd ed.). Prentice Hall.

Schauble, L. (1990). Belief revision in children: The role of prior knowledge and strategies for generating evidence. *Journal of Experimental Child Psychology, 49*(1), 31–57. doi:10.1016/0022-0965(90)90048-D PMID:2303776

Selwyn, N. (2007). The use of computer technology in university teaching and learning: A critical perspective. *Journal of Computer Assisted Learning, 23*(2), 83–94. doi:10.1111/j.1365-2729.2006.00204.x

Siemens, G. (2013). Massive open online courses: Innovation in education? In R. McGreal, W. Kinuthia, & S. Marshall (Eds.), *Open educational resources: Innovation, research and practice* (pp. 5–15). Athabasca, Canada: Athabasca University Press.

Siemens, G., Gasevic, D., Haythornthwaite, C., Dawson, S., Shum, S. B., Ferguson, R., Duval, E., Verbert, K., & Baker, R. S. (2011*). Open learning analytics: An integrated & modularized platform.* Proposal to design, implement and evaluate an open platform to integrate heterogeneous learning analytics techniques.

Sonnenreich, W. (1997). *A history of search engines.* Retrieved from http://www.wiley.com/compbooks/sonnenreich/history.html

Swartout, W., & Tate, A. (1999). Ontologies, guest editors' introduction. *IEEE Intelligent Systems, 14*(1), 18–19. doi:10.1109/MIS.1999.747901

Teahan, J. (2006). Teaching with an ever-spinning web: Instructional uses of web 2.0. *NCSSSMST Journal, 12,* 26–27.

Thinyane, H. (2010). Are digital natives a world-wide phenomenon? An investigation into South African first year students' use and experience with technology. *Computers & Education*, *55*(1), 406–414. doi:10.1016/j.compedu.2010.02.005

Voas, J., & Zhang, J. (2009). Cloud computing: New wine or just a new bottle, "cloud computing: New wine or just a new bottle? *IT Professional*, *11*(2), 15–17. doi:10.1109/MITP.2009.23

Vygotsky, L. S. (1978). *Mind in society: The development of higher psychological processes*. Cambridge, MA: Harvard University Press.

Welsh, E., Wanberg, C., Brown, K., & Simmering, M. (2003). E-learning: Emerging uses, empirical results and future directions. *International Journal of Training and Development*, *4*(7), 245–258. doi:10.1046/j.1360-3736.2003.00184.x

Wiley, D. A. (2002a). Connecting learning objects to instructional design theory: A definition, a metaphor, and a taxonomy. In D. A. Wiley (Ed.), *The instructional use of learning objects*. Bloomington, IN: Agency for Instructional Technology and Association for Educational Communications and Technology.

ADDITIONAL READING

P21 [Partnership for 21st century learning] (2009). *P21 framework definitions*. Tucson, AZ: P21. Retrieved from http://www.p21.org/storage/documents/P21_Framework_Definitions.pdf

Airasian, P. W., Cruikshank, K. A., Mayer, R. E., Pintrich, P. R., Raths, J., & Wittrock, M. C. (2001). *A taxonomy for learning, teaching, and assessing: A revision of Bloom's taxonomy of educational objectives (Complete edition)*. New York: Longman.

Alexander, B. (2006). Web 2.0: A new wave of innovation for teaching and learning? *EDUCAUSE Review*, *41*(2), 32.

Alexander, B., & Levine, A. (2008). Web 2.0 storytelling: Emergence of a new genre. *EDUCAUSE Review*, *43*(6), 40–56.

Anderson, T. (2008). Towards a theory of online learning. *Theory and practice of online learning,*, 45-74.

Aroyo, L., & Dicheva, D. (2004). The new challenges for c-learning: The educational semantic web. *Journal of Educational Technology & Society*, *7*(4), 59–69.

Artino, A. R., & Stephens, J. M. (2006). Learning online: Motivated to self-regulate. *Academic Exchange Quarterly*, *10*(4), 176–182.

Astin, W. (1992). *What Matters in College? Four Critical Years Revisited*. SanFrancisco, CA: Josey-Bass.

Attwell, G. (2007). Personal Learning Environments-the future of eLearning? *eLearning Papers*, *2*(1), 1-8.

Azevedo, R., Guthrie, J. T., & Seibert, D. (2004). The role of self-regulated learning in fostering students' conceptual understanding of complex systems with hypermedia. *Journal of Educational Computing Research*, *30*(1), 87–111. doi:10.2190/DVWX-GM1T-6THQ-5WC7

Benbunan-Fich, R., & Arbaugh, J. B. (2006). Separating the effects of knowledge construction and group collaboration in learning outcomes of web-based courses. *Information & Management*, *43*(6), 778–793. doi:10.1016/j.im.2005.09.001

Berge, Z. L. (1999). Interaction in post-secondary, web-based learning and teaching. *Educational Technology*, *39*(1), 5–11.

Berge, Z. L. (2002). Active, interactive, and reflective elearning. *Quarterly Review of Distance Education*, *3*(2), 181–190.

Berlanga, A., & Garcia, F. J. (2005). Learning technology specifications: Semantic objects for adaptive learning environments. *International Journal of Learning Technology*, *1*(4), 458–472. doi:10.1504/IJLT.2005.007155

Berners-Lee, T., & Hendler, J. (2001). Publishing on the semantic web. *Nature*, *410*(6832), 1023–1024. doi:10.1038/35074206 PMID:11323639

Bittencourt, I. I., Isotani, S., Costa, E., & Mizoguchi, R. (2008). Research directions on semantic web and education. *Interdisciplinary Studies in Computer Science*, *19*(1), 60–67.

Bossert, S. T. (1988). Cooperative activities in the classroom. *Review of Educational Research*, *15*, 225–250.

Boulos, M. N., Maramba, I., & Wheeler, S. (2006). Wikis, blogs and podcasts: A new generation of Web-based tools for virtual collaborative clinical practice and education. *BMC Medical Education*, *6*(1), 41. doi:10.1186/1472-6920-6-41 PMID:16911779

Brewer, P. D., & Brewer, K. L. (2010). Knowledge management, human resource management, and higher education: A theoretical model. *Journal of Education for Business*, *85*(6), 330–335. doi:10.1080/08832321003604938

Brown, B., Chui, M., & Manyika, J. (2011). Are you ready for the era of 'Big Data'? McKinsey Global Institute. Retrieved August 26, 2014, from http://www.mckinsey.com/insights/strategy/are_you_ready_for_the_era_of_big_data

Chang, M. M. (2005). Applying self-regulated learning strategies in a web-based instruction—An investigation of motivation perception. *Computer Assisted Language Learning*, *18*(3), 217–230. doi:10.1080/09588220500178939

Churches, A. (2008). Bloom's taxonomy blooms digitally. *Tech & Learning, 1*.

Churchill, D. (2009). Educational applications of Web 2.0: Using blogs to support teaching and learning. *British Journal of Educational Technology*, *40*(1), 179–183. doi:10.1111/j.1467-8535.2008.00865.x

Clark, K., Parsia, B., & Hendler, J. (2004). Will the semantic web change education? *Journal of Interactive Media in Education*, *2004*(1), 8. doi:10.5334/2004-3-clark

Cristea, A. I. (2004). What can the semantic web do for adaptive educational hypermedia? *Journal of Educational Technology & Society*, *7*(4), 40–58.

Dabbagh, N., & Kitsantas, A. (2004). Supporting self-regulation in student-centered web-based learning environments. *International Journal on E-Learning*, *3*(1), 40–47.

Devedžić, V. (2004). Web intelligence and Artificial Intelligence in education. *Journal of Educational Technology & Society*, *7*(4), 29–39.

Devedžić, V. (2004). Education and the semantic web. *International Journal of Artificial Intelligence in Education*, *14*(2), 165–191.

Dlouhá, J., & Dlouhý, J. (2009). Use of Wiki tools for raising the communicative aspect of learning. In *Proceedings of the 8th European Conference on e-Learning. NR Reading: Academic Conferences Ltd* (pp. 165-173).

Doan, A., Madhavan, J., Dhamankar, R., Domingos, P., & Halevy, A. (2003). Learning to match ontologies on the semantic web. *The International Journal on Very Large Data Bases*, *12*(4), 303–319. doi:10.1007/s00778-003-0104-2

Downes, S. (2009, February 16). Access2OER: The CCK08 solution [Web log post] Retrieved from http://halfanhour.blogspot.com/2009/02/access2oer-cck08-solution.html

Educause (2010). 7 Things you should know about analytics, *EDUCAUSE 7 things you should know series*. Retrieved September 15, 2013 from http://www.educause.edu/ir/library/pdf/ELI7059.pdf

Fini, A. (2009). The technological dimension of a massive open online course: The case of the CCK08 course tools. *International Review of Research in Open and Distance Learning*, *10*(5). Retrieved from http://www.irrodl.org/index.php/irrodl/article/view/643/1402

Ghaleb, F., Daoud, S., & Hasna, A., ALJa'am, J. M., El-Seoud, S. A., & El-Sofany, H. (2006). E-learning model based on semantic web technology. *International Journal of Computing & Information Sciences*, *4*(2), 63–71.

Gillies, R., Ashman, A., & Terwel, J. (Eds.). (2008). *The teacher's role in implementing cooperative learning in the classroom. Computer supported collaborative learning series* (Vol. 8). New York, NY: Springer. doi:10.1007/978-0-387-70892-8

Greenhow, C., Robelia, B., & Hughes, J. E. (2009). Learning, teaching, and scholarship in a digital age: Web 2.0 and classroom research: What path should we take now? *Educational Researcher*, *38*(4), 246–259. doi:10.3102/0013189X09336671

Halawi, L. A., McCarthy, R. V., & Pires, S. (2009). An evaluation of e-learning on the basis of Bloom's taxonomy: An exploratory study. *Journal of Education for Business*, *84*(6), 374–380. doi:10.3200/JOEB.84.6.374-380

Hamid, S., Chang, S., & Kurnia, S. (2009, December). Identifying the use of online social networking in higher education. In ASCILITE 2009 conference, December (pp. 6-9).

Henze, N., Dolog, P., & Nejdl, W. (2004). Reasoning and ontologies for personalized e-learning in the semantic web. *Journal of Educational Technology & Society*, *7*(4), 82–97.

Huang, W., Webster, D., Wood, D., & Ishaya, T. (2006). An intelligent semantic e-learning framework using context-aware semantic web technologies. *British Journal of Educational Technology*, *37*(3), 351–373. doi:10.1111/j.1467-8535.2006.00610.x

Imig, D. G., & Imig, S. R. (2006). The teacher effectiveness movement. How 80 years of essentialist control have shaped the teacher education profession. *Journal of Teacher Education*, *57*(2), 167–180. doi:10.1177/0022487105285672

Jacobson, M. J., & Archodidou, A. (2000). The design of hypermedia tools for learning: Fostering conceptual change and transfer of complex scientific knowledge. *Journal of the Learning Sciences*, *9*(2), 145–199. doi:10.1207/s15327809jls0902_2

Kauffman, D. F. (2004). Self-regulated learning in web-based environments: Instructional tools designed to facilitate cognitive strategy use, meta-cognitive processing, and motivational beliefs. *Journal of Educational Computing Research*, *30*(1), 139–161. doi:10.2190/AX2D-Y9VM-V7PX-0TAD

Kauffman, D. F., Ge, X., Xie, K., & Chen, C. H. (2008). Prompting in web-based environments: Supporting self-monitoring and problem solving skills in college students. *Journal of Educational Computing Research*, *38*(2), 115–137. doi:10.2190/EC.38.2.a

Keats, D., & Schmidt, J. P. (2007). The genesis and emergence of Education 3.0 in higher education and its potential for Africa. *First Monday*, *12*(3). doi:10.5210/fm.v12i3.1625

Kolovski, V., & Galletly, J. (2003, June). Towards e-learning via the semantic web. In *International Conference on Computer Systems and Technologies-CompSysTech* (p. 2).

Koper, R. (2003). Combining re-usable learning resources and services to pedagogical purposeful units of learning. *Reusing online resources: A sustainable approach to eLearning*, 46-59.

Light, D. (2011). Do Web 2.0 right. *Learning and Leading with Technology*, *38*(5), 10.

Lytras, M., & Naeve, A. (2006). Semantic e-learning: Synthesising fantasies. *British Journal of Educational Technology*, *37*(3), 479–491. doi:10.1111/j.1467-8535.2006.00617.x

Mackness, J., Mak, S., & Williams, R. (2010). The ideals and reality of participating in a MOOC. In: *Proceedings of the 7th International Conference on Networked Learning 2010*. University of Lancaster, Lancaster, pp. 266-275.

McLoughlin, C., & Lee, M. J. W. (2007). Listen and learn: A systematic review of the evidence that podcasting supports learning in higher education. In MontgomerieC.SealeJ. (Eds), *Proceedings of World Conference on Educational Multimedia, Hypermedia and Telecommunications 2007* (pp. 1669-1677). Chesapeake, VA: AACE.

Meyer, K. A. (2010). A comparison of Web 2.0 tools in a doctoral course. *The Internet and Higher Education*, *13*(4), 226–232. doi:10.1016/j.iheduc.2010.02.002

Miyazoe, T., & Anderson, T. (2010). Learning outcomes and students' perceptions of online writing: Simultaneous implementation of a forum, blog, and wiki in an EFL blended learning setting. *System*, *38*(2), 185–199. doi:10.1016/j.system.2010.03.006

Mohan, P., & Brooks, C. (2003, July). Learning objects on the semantic web. In *Advanced Learning Technologies, 2003. Proceedings. The 3rd IEEE International Conference on* (pp. 195-199). IEEE. doi:10.1109/ICALT.2003.1215055

Moore, M. G. (1993). Three types of interaction. In K. Harry, M. John, & D. Keegan (Eds.), *Distance education: New perspective*. London: Routledge.

Moreale, E., & Vargas-Vera, M. (2004). Semantic services in e-learning: An argumentation case study. *Journal of Educational Technology & Society*, *7*(4), 112–128.

Morris, R. D. (2011). Web 3.0: Implications for online learning. *TechTrends*, *55*(1), 42–46. doi:10.1007/s11528-011-0469-9

Näsström, G. (2009). Interpretation of standards with Bloom's revised taxonomy: A comparison of teachers and assessment experts. *International Journal of Research & Method in Education*, *32*(1), 39–51. doi:10.1080/17437270902749262

Norman, G., & Schmidt, H. (1993). Effectiveness of problem-based learning curricula: Theory, practice and paper darts. *Medical Education*, *34*(20), 721–728. PMID:10972750

Ohler, J. (2008). The semantic web in education. *EDUCAUSE Quarterly*, *31*(4), 7–9.

Pang, L. (2009). A survey of Web 2.0 technologies for classroom learning. *International Journal of Learning*, *16*(9).

Penny, S. (2013). Bloom's digital taxonomy pyramid [Online image]. Retrieved July 16, 2014 from http://faculty.indstate.edu/spenney/bdt.htm

Piccoli, G., Ahmad, R., & Ives, B. (2001). Web-based virtual learning environments: A research framework and a preliminary assessment of effectiveness in basic IT skills training. *Management Information Systems Quarterly*, *25*(4), 401–426. doi:10.2307/3250989

Richardson, W. (2010). Blogs, wikis, podcasts, and other powerful web tools for classrooms. *Sage (Atlanta, Ga.)*.

Robertson, I. (2008). Learners' attitudes to Wiki technology in problem based, blended learning for vocational teacher education. *Australasian Journal of Educational Technology*, *24*(4), 425–441.

Sandars, J. (2010). Social software and digital competences. *InnovAiT: The RCGP Journal for Associates in Training*, *3*(5), 306–309.

Schaffhauser, D. (2010). The Super-secret, never-before-revealed guide to Web 2.0 in the Classroom. *Campus Technology*, *24*(2), 26–35.

Schmidt, A., & Winterhalter, C. (2004). User context aware delivery of e-learning material: Approach and architecture. *Journal of Universal Computer Science*, *10*(1), 28–36.

Schroeder, A., Minocha, S., & Schneider, C. (2010). The strengths, weaknesses, opportunities and threats of using social software in higher and further education teaching and learning. *Journal of Computer Assisted Learning*, *26*(3), 159–174. doi:10.1111/j.1365-2729.2010.00347.x

Sendall, P., Ceccucci, W., & Peslak, A. (2008). Web 2.0 matters: An analysis of implementing Web 2.0 in the classroom. *Information Systems Education Journal*, *6*(64), 1–17.

Shah, N. K. (2012). E-Learning and Semantic Web. *International Journal of e-Education, e-Business, e-. Management Learning*, *2*(2), 113–116.

Sicilia, M. A., & Lytras, M. D. (2005). The semantic learning organization. *The Learning Organization*, *12*(5), 402–410. doi:10.1108/09696470510611375

Solomon, G., & Schrum, L. (2007). *Web 2.0: New tools, new schools*. International Society for Technology in Education. Retrieved July 28, 2014 from http://www.iste.org/docs/excerpts/NEWTOO-excerpt.pdf

Stojanovic, L., Staab, S., & Studer, R. (2001) eLearning based on the Semantic Web. *Proceedings of WebNet2001 - World Conference on the WWW and Internet*, Orlando, Florida

Stutt, A., & Motta, E. (2004). Semantic learning webs. *Journal of Interactive Media in Education*, *2004*(1), 2. doi:10.5334/2004-10-stutt

Tane, J., Schmitz, C., & Stumme, G. (2004, May). Semantic resource management for the web: An e-learning application. In Proceedings of the 13th international *World Wide Web conference on Alternate Track Papers & Posters* (pp. 1-10). ACM.

Trilling, B., & Fadel, C. (2009). *21st century learning skills*. San Francisco, CA: John Wiley & Sons.

Valtonen, T., Koponen, T., & Vesisenaho, M. (2011). Linking school's learning environment to students' personal online environments: Students' experiences. In Proceedings of the *4th International Network-Based Education 2011 Conference, The Social Media in the Middle of Nowhere* (pp. 146-153).

Wheeler, S. (2009). Learning space mashups: Combining Web 2.0 tools to create collaborative and reflective learning spaces. *Future Internet*, *1*(1), 3–13. doi:10.3390/fi1010003

Yang, S. J. (2006). Context aware ubiquitous learning environments for peer-to-peer collaborative learning. *Journal of Educational Technology & Society*, *9*(1).

Zhang, H., & Almeroth, K. (2010). Moodog: Tracking student activity in online course management systems. *Journal of Interactive Learning Research*, *21*(3), 407–429.

KEY TERMS AND DEFINITIONS

Andragogy: Adult learning principles that are based on the assumption that learner is self-motivated and self-directed to guide learning on the web.

Connectivism: Knowledge is created and distributed in networks.

Digital Immigrants: Those born before the computer age with little or no exposure to technology.

Digital Natives: Those born in the computer age with early exposure to technology.

Education 123: The developments in education that coincided with the evolution of Web 1.0 to Web 3.0.

E-Learning: Any learning using Internet tools and web technology.

Essentialism: Refers to the teacher-centric classroom.

Traditional Classroom: Brick and mortar classrooms with face-to-face classroom.

Web 1.0: Referred to as the "*Static Web*". Web 1.0 is a term used for the web as it existed in 1980-2000.

Web 2.0: Referred to as the "*Participative Web*". Web 2.0 is a term used for the web as it existed in 2000-2010.

Web 3.0: Referred to as the "*Semantic or personalized Web*". Web 3.0 is a term used for the web as it exists today (2010- present).

Chapter 6
A Web–Based System for Error Correction Questions in Programming Exercise

Yoshinari Hachisu
Nanzan University, Japan

Atsushi Yoshida
Nanzan University, Japan

ABSTRACT

In this chapter, the authors propose a system for generating error correction questions of programs, which are suitable for developing debugging skills in programming education. The system generates HTML files for answering questions and CGI programs for checking answers. They are deployed on a Web server, and learners read and answer questions on Web browsers. It provides an intuitive user interface; a learner can edit codes in place at the text. To make programs including errors for learning debugging, the authors analyze types of errors and define the processes of error injection as code transformation patterns. If learners can edit any codes freely, it is difficult to check all possible answers. Instead, the authors adopt a strategy to restrict editable points and possible answers from the educational view. A demonstration of error correction questions of the C language is available at http://ecq.tebasaki.jp/.

INTRODUCTION

In programming courses, students learn skills for coding, code reading, and debugging through various kinds of exercises. Although debugging is important for actual software development, it is difficult for students, even who have good understandings of programming, to acquire debugging skills effectively (Ahmadzadeh, Elliman, & Higgins, 2005; Chmiel & Loui, 2004; Lahtinen, Ala-Mutka, & Järvinen, 2005). In this chapter, we focus on a Web-based learning support system for debugging, whose controlled exercises are difficult to be provided.

Three types of exercises are often used in programming courses: describing full codes, filling empty boxes embedded in the texts of codes (fill-in-the-blank questions), and error correction questions. The last one is suitable for debugging. Describing full codes is a most typical way of

DOI: 10.4018/978-1-4666-8147-7.ch006

exercises, and through them learners find errors and inevitably try to debug for detecting faults. Experiences of debugging, however, are different for each learner, and teachers cannot control experiences for them to use all necessary debugging skills. In exercises with fill-in-the-blank questions, learners may not have chances to debug because the codes they read do not include any errors, and they can fill answers without compiling and testing. In the case of error correction questions, teachers can select errors for injecting to a correct program according to debugging skills to be learned. Learners need to detect and correct errors that are injected purposely.

To adopt error correction questions in actual programming exercises, we need to solve two problems: a user interface of a question and answering system and the cost of making questions. Some researches propose systems for generating error correction questions (Hachisu & Yoshida, 2013, 2014; Itoh, Nagataki, Ooshita, Kakugawa, & Masuzawa, 2007; Suganuma, Mine, & Shoudai, 2005). Suganuma et al. have proposed the Web-based system, but its interface is not intuitive. It shows an incorrect program and some texts are marked with id numbers to show the candidates of errors. When learners find errors, they need to write id numbers and correct texts in boxes that are displayed apart from the program; they cannot correct them on the spot. Marked texts give clear hints of answers to learners. On the other hand, when learners can edit any texts freely, some answers may be unexpected ones for teachers; in an extreme case, learners may make a whole new program whose input and output are identical to the original one. Consequently, making error correction questions requires a fair amount of work for teachers. It requires injecting various errors in code fragments and check the correctness of all possible answers, some of which may be unexpected one but correct. Itoh et al. have proposed a method for generating programs containing errors for learning algorithms, but it

doesn't provide a way to check the answers; it is supposed to be used for oral examinations. The key questions about constructing the systems for error correction questions are what kind of user interface is suitable, how to manage error injection into codes, and how to cover all possible answers in correctness checking.

In this chapter, we propose a system for generating error correction questions and checking the correctness. The system generates HTML files including editable text forms for answering questions and CGI programs for checking answers. They are deployed on a Web server, and learners read and answer questions on Web browsers. It provides an intuitive user interface; a learner can edit codes in place at the text. Editable texts are restricted and hidden from learners by using a jQuery plug-in, JEIP (Scott 2014). For management of error injection, we have analyzed types of errors and defined the processes of error injection as code transformation patterns, which we call error patterns. The system synthesizes code fragments including errors by transforming correct code fragments according to selected error patterns. If the system allows learners to edit any texts in codes, it needs to accept all possible correct answers. Full coverage of all possible answers is difficult. Instead, we adopt a strategy to restrict possible answers to the ones that are reasonable for learning objectives, which mean the syntax and semantics of the language, typical program descriptions, and algorithms that learners should understand. We have analyzed types of possible answers and proposed constraints of editable places in codes on answering questions. For evaluating the system, we have implemented a prototype of the system and made an experiment of the programming exercise using the generated questions. Our system can generate questions that widely cover the syntax and semantics of the C language such as variables, types, conditional branches, loops, arrays, functions, strings, pointers, and structures, and some algorithms such as sorting and searching. In the exercise using the questions, we found a few unexpected answers. Though we use the C language in this chapter, our key ideas are not restricted to the language. A demonstration of error correction questions is available at http://ecq.tebasaki.jp/.

The main contribution of this research is to provide a fundamental framework of automatic generation and checking answers of error correction questions for debugging exercises. On the framework, the errors are defined as code transformation patterns, and this makes it easy for teachers to add new programs and errors. We hope that the discussion about what errors and programs are effective in terms of acquiring debugging skills and how we collect errors in practical programming exercises is opened.

BACKGROUND

Error Correction Question of Program

An error correction question contains a program code including errors and requires learners to modify them correctly. We show an example in Figure 1, whose specification is "Calculate the average value while reading integer values, and then print the number of values that are greater than the average." Program (a) in Figure 1 is a correct program, and program (b) includes four errors: in Line 12, (1) the function name *scan* is a misspell of *scanf* and (2) an address operator & is missing in an argument; in Line 21, (3) the initializer and the condition in the *for* loop do not match to the range of the array referred in the loop; in Line 23, (4) variable *count* is referred without initialization. The underlined italic texts are editable elements, that is, learners can modify them. The blank lines at Line 9, 17, 20, and 28 are also editable, where learners can add a statement. When a question has many editable elements, it tends to become diffi-

cult and to allow unexpected answers. In the later section, we discuss the restriction of editable code elements from the educational view. Figure 1 is a question designed for beginners of programming who learn the syntax and semantics of conditional branches, loops, and arrays. Learning objectives of this question are usage of the *scanf* function, necessity of variable initialization, and a typical loop to scan an array.

We show another example in Figure 2. It is a more complicated program using pointers, structures, and the selection sorting algorithm; the structure person represents a personal physical datum for each person and the function *sort_by_height* sorts an array of the structure. The sort function gets an array by the parameter p and its size by the parameter *size*, and sorts p in ascending order of members *height* with the selection sort algorithm. It contains five errors: (1) in Line 6 and 8, the type of function *swap's* parameters and local variable *tmp* must be *struct person*; (2) in Line 19, the condition of the *for* loop must be $j < size$; in Line 24, (3) address operator &s are missing for both arguments; (4) the index j of array p must be i; (5) the member references to *height* are unnecessary.

These examples imply that error correction questions are more difficult than fill-in-the-blank questions for learners. Figure 3 shows an error correction question about strings in (a), and a fill-in-the-blank one in (b). The function *strncopy* copies the first **n**-letters of the string **s** to the string *d;* for example, on s*trncopy("Hello World!", d, 3), d* becomes *"Hel"*, and on *strncopy("Hello World!", d, 16), d* becomes *"Hello World!"*. The program (a) includes three errors: in Line 5, (1) the logical OR operator ǁ must be the AND operator *&&,* (2) the character *'0'* should be *'\0',* and (3) in Line 8, an assignment of the null character *(d[i] = '\0';)* is missing. In our experiences, error (3) is relatively difficult to find at a glance, although this program is simple and short. Sometimes, the bugs of this type still remain after test processes because the program can be executed normally

Figure 1. Error correction question (1): input, condition, loop, and array

```
 1: #include <stdio.h>
 2: #define MAXSIZE 128
 3:
 4: int main(void)
 5: {
 6:   int data[MAXSIZE];
 7:   int size, sum, count, i;
 8:   double avg;
 9:
10:   sum = 0;
11:   size = 0;
12:   while (scanf("%d", &data[size])
13:             != EOF) {
14:     sum += data[size];
15:     size++;
16:   }
17:
18:   avg =  (double) sum / size;
19:   printf("avg = %f\n", avg);
20:
21:   count = 0;
22:   for (i = 0; i < size; i++) {
23:     if (data[i] > avg) {
24:         count++;
25:     }
26:   }
27:   printf("greater than avg: %d\n",
28:           count);
29:
30:   return 0;
31: }
```

(a) a correct program

```
 1: #include <stdio.h>
 2: #define MAXSIZE 128
 3:
 4: int main(void)
 5: {
 6:   int data[MAXSIZE];
 7:   int size, sum, count, i;
 8:   double avg;
 9:
10:   sum = 0;
11:   size = 0;
12:   while (scan("%d", _data[size])
13:             != EOF) {
14:     sum += data[size];
15:     size++;
16:   }
17:
18:   avg =  (double) sum / size;
19:   printf("avg = %f\n", _avg);
20:
21:   for (i = 1; i <= size; i++) {
22:     if (data[i] >= avg) {
23:         count++;
24:     }
25:   }
26:   printf("greater than avg: %d\n",
27:           _count);
28:
29:   return 0;
30: }
```

(b) a program including errors

Figure 2. Error correction question (2): a sort program of an array of a structure

```
 1: struct person {
 2:     char name[64];
 3:     double height, weight;
 4: };
 5:
 6: void swap(double *a, double *b)
 7: {
 8:     double _tmp;
 9:     tmp = *a; *a = *b; *b = tmp;
10: }
11:
```

```
12: void sort_by_height(
13:         struct person p[], int size)
14: {
15:   int min, i, j;
16:
17:   for (i = 0; i < size-1; i++) {
18:     min = i;
19:     for (j = i+1; j < size-1; j++) {
20:       if (p[j].heihgt <= p[min].height) {
21:             min = j;
22:       }
23:     }
24:     swap(_p[j].height, _p[min].height);
25:   }
26: }
```

in some computer systems. In general, a learner answers an error correction question in following three steps: he/she reads a program, he/she finds errors, and he/she corrects the codes, that is, adding, deleting, replacing, or moving codes. Finding and correcting errors require understanding the control flows, data flows, and logics of programs in addition to the syntax of the language. On the other hand, fill-in-the-blank questions such as (b) explicitly show blank boxes where a learner writes correct codes. He/she may write correct codes without understanding programs. The blank box in Line 8 is a clear hint; definitely a statement is missing.

Readability of codes is important for error correction questions because unnatural descriptions in programs may give undesirable hints to learners. Codes should have comprehensive structures such as the units of inputs, main processes, and outputs. We have adopted the following coding styles: (S1) a variable is used for one purpose; (S2) the initialization of a variable that is used in a loop should locate just before the loop; (S3) two semantic process units are separated by a blank line; (S4) no successive blank lines are allowed. On injecting errors, removing a statement may cause two successive blank lines in codes. They should be integrated into one blank line because they indicate a definite lack of a statement. For example, in Figure 1 (a), when we remove the assignment statement in Line 21, we also remove the following new line because Line 20 is a blank line.

Related Works

AEGIS (Automatic Exercise Generator based on the Intelligence of Students) is a system to generate questions from XML documents and supports three types of questions: multiple-choice, fill-in-the-blank, and error correction (Suganuma et al., 2005). An error correction question is generated from a multiple-choice question by fusing an incorrect choice to the code. AEGIS requires teachers to describe a full XML description of questions, including codes and errors. Our system separates descriptions of correct codes and error patterns and synthesizes questions from them. AEGIS is the Web-based system and its interface to learners is simple. Some texts, which may be errors, are marked with id numbers. Learners select ids, whose texts are error codes, and write their correct codes in boxes that are displayed apart from the program. The interface is not intuitive and marked texts give clear hints of answers to them. In our proposing system, which is also Web-based, although editable codes are restricted in the same way of AEGIS, they are not explicitly shown to learners and learners can edit texts on the spot. Our system provides an exercise environment similar to the traditional ones with papers and pens; learners check error places and modifies them in the places.

Itoh et al. have proposed a method for generating error correction exercises for learning algorithms (Itoh et al., 2007). It determines the fault

Figure 3. Error correction question and fill-in-the-blank question: strings

```
1: void strncopy(char s[], char d[], int n)
2: {
3:     int i;
4:
5:     for (i=0; i<n || s[i] != '0'; i++) {
6:         d[i] = s[i];
7:     }
8:
9: }
```

(a) an error correction question

```
1: void strncopy(char s[], char d[], int n)
2: {
3:     int i;
4:
5:     for (i=0; i<n[  ]s[i] != [  ]; i++) {
6:         d[i] = s[i];
7:     }
8:     [                    ]
9: }
```

(b) a fill-in-the-blank question

positions by the algorithm design paradigm and injects faults by the syntax-directed faults patterns, which are specific to the algorithm education. By specifying a set of correct programs, an algorithm design paradigm such as divide-and-conquer, the number of errors to be injected, and the number of source code files to be generated, the system generates source codes including errors automatically. Though it supports error injection, it does not propose a method for the correctness checking; it is supposed that error correction questions are used in oral examinations, that is, a learner explains its errors to a teacher directly. Our system supports automatic correct checking. It also allows injecting an error at any positions, and it does not depend on specific domains of program educations.

From the view of code transformation, injecting errors is a kind of mutation system (Agrawal et al., 1984; Jia & Harma, 2011). A mutation system generates multiple variants of a code by adding small changes to its copies. The distinctive application is the test set evaluation in which test sets are tested how many variants they can detect as errors. Mutant systems add changes randomly, but our system adds changes in a restricted manner for learning debugging.

Lee et al. have proposed a *debugging-first* approach for computer education (Lee et al. 2014; Lee & Ko, 2014). They have proposed an online debugging game, to teach novices computer programming concepts in an engaging way. They have created faulty programs, which are set up to teach specific concepts. Learners (online game players) must debug them to progress through the game. They focus on teaching programming concepts using Python-like programming language designed specifically for the game. On the other hand, our aim is that learners acquire practical skills to debug actual programs written in practical programming languages like C.

While we focus on how to generate error correction questions in this chapter, categorizing programs used in education is also useful for setting up questions. Mine et al. have proposed a

method to categorize questions in AEGIS based on their ontology model created from materials in the lectures (Mine, Suganuma, & Shoudai, 2002). Some researches have proposed knowledge bases of the programming language C based on ontology-based approach (Hu, Hu, & Guo, 2013; Pierrakeas, Solomou, & Kameas, 2012). Our question generating system can make questions including errors covering wide area of knowledge bases (see the later section, "generality of error patterns").

SUPPORT SYSTEM OF ERROR CORRECTION QUESTION

The first of this section, we show an overview of our support system that consists of a question presentation system and a question generation system. Secondly, we show some typical errors for developing debugging skills. And then we explain how to design error correction questions from the views of edit operations for injecting errors, editable points, and possible answers. Finally, we explain an error pattern, which is a kind of code transformation pattern and an input of our question generation system.

Overview of Support System

We have developed a supporting system of error correction questions. Figure 4 shows an overview of the system. The system consists of two components. One is a presentation system that provides a set of error correction questions to learners. Their answers are checked by the system, and the results are returned to them. It is implemented as a Web system, i.e., a set of HTML files, JavaScript programs and Perl CGI scripts that are deployed on a Web server. Learners read and answer questions on Web browsers. The other component of the system is a generating system of error correction questions. A teacher, who is a user of the generating system, selects a correct program and error patterns, which are code transformation patterns. The system applies the patterns to the correct program and generates both of an HTML file of the question and a CGI program for checking answers. The HTML file contains a program including injected errors and editable points.

The presentation system provides an intuitive user interface; learners can edit a code on the spot and editable points are hidden from learners. If all editable points explicitly appear on a question page, learners may guess the answers without understanding. For this requirement, we have adopted JEIP (Scott, 2008), a plug-in of jQuery, which makes any texts tagged by the special attribute be editable and hides there from users unless they move the mouse over the texts on them. If they click an editable point, an input field appears at the point. After changing all editable points where they needs to modify, they submit their answers to the system by pressing the submit button. Pairs of the id of an editable point and the edited text are sent to the Web server with AJAX by calling the jQuery.ajax function. The CGI program checks answers and returns its results to the Web browser.

Figure 5 and 6 show screen shots of the error correction question of Figure 3 on a Web browser. A program is shown as usual texts in Figure 5. When a learner moves the mouse cursor over an editable point, the background color of it is changed (Figure 6 (a)). He/she clicks there, and then a text field appears on the spot like as Figure 6 (b). When he/she changes the text and push the save button, the new text is reflected to browser's window immediately. After he/she pushes the submit button, the result of his/her answers is shown on the result area; for example, the message "correct answers: 4 /5" shows that there are 5 editable points and 4 points are edited correctly.

Figure 7 shows a source HTML code of an error correction question. An editable point is surrounded by <span> and </span> tags with the "editable" class attribute.

Errors for Questions

We have collected errors in our programming courses and the related papers (Ahmadzadeh et al., 2005; Hristova, Misra, Rutter, & Mercuri, 2003; Jackson, Cobb, & Carver, 2005; Tuugalei

Figure 4. An overview of the supporting system for error correction questions

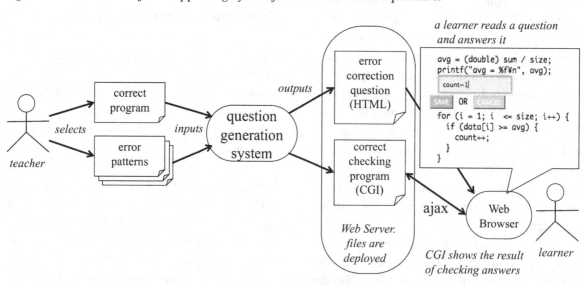

Figure 5. Screen shot of error correction question on the Web

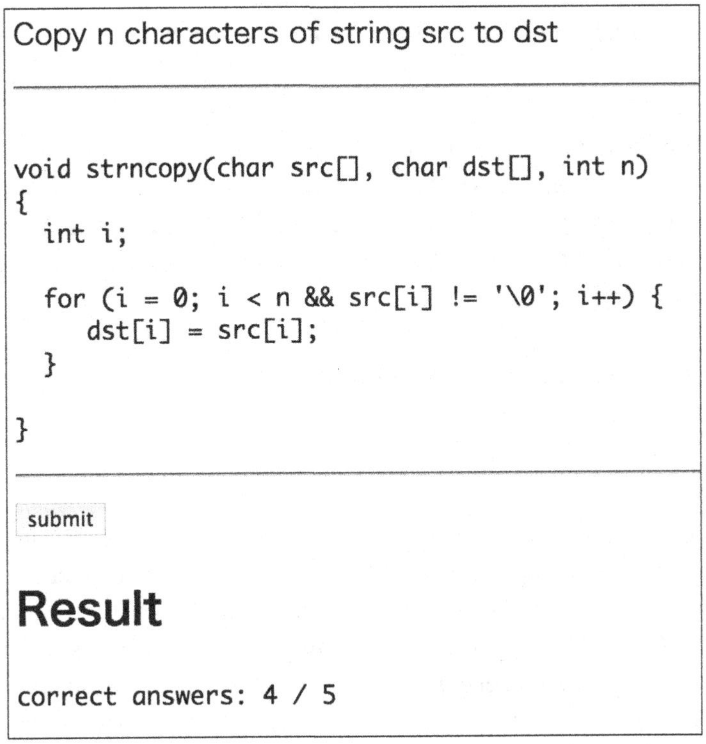

Copy n characters of string src to dst

```
void strncopy(char src[], char dst[], int n)
{
  int i;

  for (i = 0; i < n && src[i] != '\0'; i++) {
     dst[i] = src[i];
  }

}
```

submit

Result

correct answers: 4 / 5

Figure 6. Screen shots of editing texts on the Web

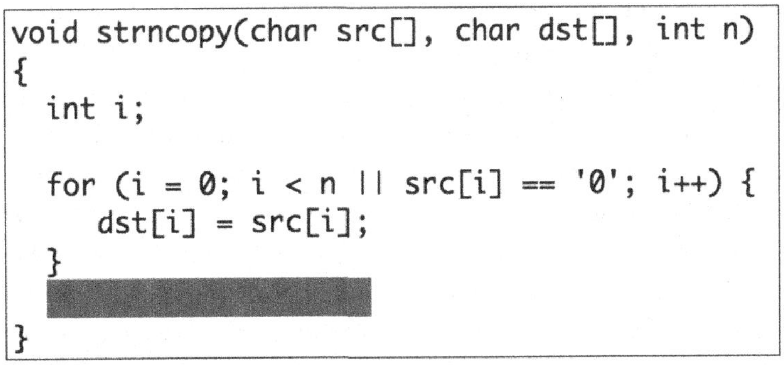

```
void strncopy(char src[], char dst[], int n)
{
  int i;

  for (i = 0; i < n || src[i] == '0'; i++) {
     dst[i] = src[i];
  }

}
```

(a) the background color is changed,
when mouse cursor is moved over an editable point

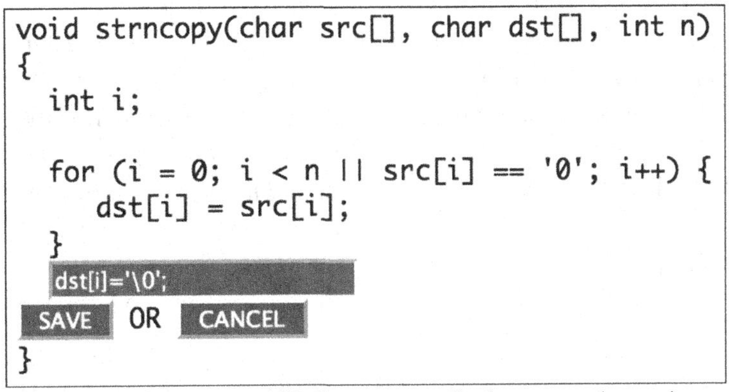

```
void strncopy(char src[], char dst[], int n)
{
  int i;

  for (i = 0; i < n || src[i] == '0'; i++) {
     dst[i] = src[i];
  }
  dst[i]='\0';
  SAVE   OR   CANCEL
}
```

(b) click there, a text filed appears. edit the text and save it.

131

Figure 7. Source HTML code

```
void strncopy(char src[], char dst[], int n)
{
  int i;
  <span class="editable" id="e1">            </span>
  for (i=0; i < n <span class="editable" id="e2">||</span>
        src[i] <span class="editable" id="e3">!=</span>
        <span class="editable" id="e4">'0'</span>; i++) {
    dst[i] = src[i];
  }
  <span class="editable" id="e5">            </span>
}
```

& Mow, 2012), for analyzing types of errors used in error correction questions. These papers reports that the students often make syntactical mistakes such as missing a semicolon and lacking one of a pair of curly braces or parentheses. In general, it is relatively easy for students to correct syntactical errors because a compiler detects them and shows error messages with line numbers. We have collected logical errors such as using a variable without initialization, wrong types, wrong data flows, and so on. These errors significantly contribute development of debugging skills because compilers do not detect them, and learners need to read programs carefully and understand its logic.

We show examples of errors and the learning objectives of them in Table 1. We have analyzed these errors in terms of edit operations, the numbers of correctable points, and possible representation. A correctable point means an editable point at which we can write a possible representation. A possible representation is one of the code fragments that are acceptable as correct answers. It may be semantically different from the original.

Edit Operations for Injecting Errors

We have analyzed edit operations for injecting errors to code fragments and classified into four types: *insert, delete, replace,* and *move*. The column of the edit operation in Table 1 shows operations for each error. Though an operation *move* is considered as a combination of *delete* and *insert*, we have identified it as a primitive because the two operations should be occurred simultaneously.

The errors injected by deleting code fragments or replacing code fragments with others are the most typical ones. A missing assignment of an initial value and a wrong relational operator in a loop condition are examples. They are caused by deleting the assignment or replacing the operator with another one. Error correction questions of these types are relatively easy to prepare. The number of these errors we found is greater than the ones of others. On the other hand, the errors of *insert* and *move* are restricted. Though it is not difficult to insert or move an element in code fragments, these errors would happen rarely because they tend to become unnatural programs such as unnecessary statements breaking data flows and it is easy for learners to find them. A typical error of moving is about recursive functions. The recursive function *putstrrev* in Figure 8 puts the string **s** in reverse order. By moving the statement calling the *putchar* function before the recursive call, the function *putstrrev* puts the string in ordinary order.

Table 1. Samples of errors for error correction questions of programs

Learning Objective	Error	Edit Operation	Correctable Point(s)	Possible Represen- tation(s)	Type
Reading primitive values with *scanf* function	Missing an address operator & before an argument (Fig. 1 err. (2))	delete	one	one	(a)
Reading strings with *scanf* function	An unnecessary address operator & before an argument (*char []*)	insert	one	one	(a)
Operator	A wrong operator (Fig. 3 err. (1))	replace	one	one	(a)
Conditional Branch	Missing else	delete	one	one	(a)
Typical loop to scan an array	Wrong initialization and condition for scanning an array (Fig.1 err. (3))	replace	one	multiple	(b)
Type	Wrong type (Fig. 2 err. (1))	replace	one	one	(a)
Structure	Unnecessary member references (Fig. 2 err. (5))	insert	one	one	(a)
Data flows of variables and initialization	Using a variable without initialization (Fig. 1 err. (4))	delete	multiple	one	(c)
Data flows in a loop	Moving an assignment into the loop (Fig. 12)	move	multiple	one	(c)
Function definition	No return value in a non-void function	delete	one	one	(a)
Function call	Wrong order of arguments of a calling function	replace	one	one	(a)
Recursive function	Wrong argument of calling recursive function (Fig. 10)	replace	one	one	(a)
Recursive function	Moving a print statement around the calling recursive function (Fig. 8)	move	one	one	(a)
String Construction	Missing an assignment of the null character '\0' (Fig. 3 err. (3))	delete	one	one	(a)
File Processing	Illegal check of the return value of the *fopen* function	replace	one	one	(a)
The elements to be swapped in the selection sort algorithm	Using wrong indexes on swapping elements in an array (Fig. 2 err (4))	replace	one	one	(a)

If we may not consider all possible answers, checking the correctness of answers is easy to be implemented; the system needs only to check that each modified element is same with the original one. The difficulty is to cover all possible answers, and we discuss it in the next section.

The Number of Correctable Points and Possible Representation

We have analyzed correctable points and possible answers that we found. Possible answers mean a set of answers whose positions in codes and representations are different from the original correct program. We ignore differences of white spaces and the differences of the representations of syntactical equivalent expressions, such as a difference of $a+b$ and $b+a$. It is possible to generate alternative representations of expressions systematically in practical time because the expressions of the answers are small in our system. We also ignore unnatural answers, such as $a+0$ for a and $8-8$ for 0, from the educational view.

Figure 8. Sample error of moving

```
 1: void putstrrev(char *s)
 2: {
 3:
 4:   if (*s == '\0') return;
 5:   else {
 6:       putstrrev(s+1);
 7:       putchar(*s);
 8:   }
 9:
10: }
```

(a) a correct program

```
 1: void putstrrev(char *s)
 2: {
 3:
 4:   if (*s == '\0') return;
 5:   else {
 6:       putchar(*s);
 7:       putstrrev(s+1);
 8:
 9:   }
10:
11: }
```

(b) a program including an error of moving

We consider the possible answers whose position and/or semantics are different. The results of the analysis are shown in Table 1 as the correctable points and the possible representations. For considering the difficulty of the correctness checking, we categorize errors into four types: (a) one correctable point and one representation, i.e., not existing any other answer, (b) one correctable point and multiple possible representations, (c) multiple correctable points and one representation, and (d) multiple correctable points and multiple possible representations.

Type (a) represents an error for which the original position and code fragment is the unique answer. The correctness checking CGI checks only one position and one fragment for each error and is easy to be implemented.

Type (b) represents an error for which the original position is the unique answer, but there are variations in code fragments to be placed. For example, an *n*-times loop including an error, *for (i=1; i<n; i++)* can be corrected as either *for (i=0; i<n; i++)* or *for (i=1; i<=n; i++)*. They cannot be checked syntactically, and this correctness depends on contexts of a program.

Type (c) represents an error for which the original code fragment is the unique answer, but positions to be placed it are not fixed to the unique position. An error of this type occurs when a statement is removed. For example, in Figure 1 (b), the initialization of the variable *count* can be inserted at any lines between Line 9 and 20.

Type (d), which does not appear in Table 1, represents an error that has multiple answers in both of positions and code fragments. In errors of this type, the answers other than the original one tend to be unnatural and inadequate from the educational view. For example, we can correct the errors at Line 21 in Figure 1 (b) by replacing *data[i]* with *data[i-1]* in Line 22. However, the code *for (i=1; i<=size; i++) data[i-1]* is misleading and undesirable for scanning an array from the first to the last. If we restrict the correctable points of the above example to Line 21, this modification is not allowed and the error becomes type (a), which is the simplest type. This example suggests us that restriction of acceptable answers is a reasonable approach.

Restriction of Correctable Points and Editable Points

How to restrict correctable points is a difficult question because they depend on the semantics of errors and target codes. One of the simplest ways is to restrict to the original positions and code fragments, as type (a). The errors in type (b) can be changed to type (a) by restricting correctable points. For example, in an error code fragment of an *n*-times loop, *for (i=1;i<n;i++),* by allowing

modification of the operator < in the condition, only *for (i=1;i<=n;i++)* can be acceptable. For accomplishing this, the question generating system needs the ability to modify fine-grained elements.

Strong restrictions, however, provide clear hints to learners and easily lead them to the answers. To avoid correctable points becoming clear hints, we introduce editable points. Editable points exist at positions similar to correctable points in program contexts and learners cannot distinguish them on the question presentation system. For example, in Figure 1 (b), the correctable point of a lacking operator *&* is at the front of the second argument at Line 12, and the editable points are at the front of the second arguments in the *printf* functions at Line 19 and 27. The function name *scan* at Line 12 is a correctable point and the function names *printf* at Line 19 and 27 are editable points. Editable points include correctable points. The difference between them is the modification of texts. When they are injected to the codes, the texts at the correctable points are replaced with error ones, but the ones at the other editable points are not changed. This introduction of editable points embraces the contradiction that they increase possible answers, which have been excluded by the restriction of correctable points. Unfortunately, this contradiction is not able to resolve systematically. How to select patterns for editable points are responsible for the users as teachers.

An error with multiple correctable points, like type (c), may occur when an assignment is deleted. The error can be corrected by adding the original assignment at any point unless a modified program preserves the original data flows. Strictly speaking, the correctness checking of type (c) requires data flow analysis, which makes the system complicated. To keep the system simple, for type (c), we introduce the reasonable constraints for the educational view: (1) only assignments for initialization can be deleted; (2) editable points where learners can insert a statement are restricted to blank lines. The rule (1) is introduced because

missing initializations are typical errors. The rule (2) prevents learners from confusing by multiple possible answers. Under these constraints and the coding style (S1) and (S2), we can identify the valid correctable points without data flow analysis, which are blank lines located between sibling statements before the deleted assignment. For example, in Figure 1 (b), the correctable points are the blank lines at Line 9, 17, and 20; the one at Line 28 is not a correctable point.

Please note that deleting an assignment is not always type (c). In Figure 3, deleting the assignment of the null character is a type (a) error because the assignment must be placed at the last of the function; adding the statement at any other places, for example at Line 4 in Figure 3, does not preserve data flows. In general, deleting a statement causes a type (a) or (c) error. In our system, teachers select an error type manually because it is difficult to detect which type of an error occurs automatically.

The errors of type (d) are problematic, but they are minor in our experiences. The purpose of the error correction questions is to develop skills for detecting typical errors. The errors of type (d) deeply depend on semantics of programs, and they are not typical. We should avoid this type of errors or try to change it to type (a) or (c) by restriction of editable points. We do not discuss this type anymore.

Error Patterns

From the above analysis, we have developed a question generation system as a kind of code transformation system. For managing correct programs and errors separately, we define errors as code transformation patterns. This separation makes it easy to add another correct program and another type of errors. We also define editable points in the same way of errors, which do not modify programs in practice. We have implemented the system on a program transformation, called TEBA (Yoshida,

Hachisu, Sawada, Chang, & Noro, 2012), which has a parser of code fragments including additional symbols, such as program patterns. TEBA also provides a transformation system on token-based syntax trees, and it allows modifying the fine-grained elements.

We show examples of error patterns in Figure 9. An error pattern consists of two parts, the before-part and the after-part. The before-part, described between %*before* and %*after,* represents a pattern of target codes to be modified. The after-part, described between %*after* and %*end,* represents a pattern of new codes as a replacement. For abstraction of syntactic elements, typed pattern variables can be used. A token beginning with $ means a pattern variable and the name of it is surrounded by curly braces { }. In the before-part, a type of a variable is described after colon. Types are *ID_FVAR* (identifiers such as functions and variables), *EXPR* (expressions), *LIT* (literals), *OPE* (operators), *STMT* (statements), and so on. The meta symbol, asterisk *, following a type

means that tokens of the type occur more than zero times. In the after-part, a variable refers to tokens matched by the variables of the same name in the before-part. For example, in Figure 9 (a), *${s:STMT*}* in the before-part matches a sequence of statements and they are referred by *${s}* in the after-part. Target tokens to be changed in the before-part and changed tokens in the after-part are surrounded by the special tags, <@ and @>. For example, in Figure 9 (a), the operator token != in <@ @> is changed to == as errors. Like this example, we can specify a context on which target tokens appear. In Figure 9 (b), an assignment is specified by the relative position of the *for* loop as a context. In an error pattern of *delete* type like Figure 9 (b), the tags in the after-part surround an empty token since error tokens never exist. When an error pattern for deleting a statement is applied, the line where the tags exist becomes a blank line. In contrast, the target tokens in the before-part are empty in an error pattern of *insert* type (Figure 9 (c)). In

Figure 9. Error patterns as code transformation

```
%before
while (${e1:EXPR} <@ != @> ${e2:EXPR})
  ${s:STMT*} $;
%after
whle (${e1} <@ == @> ${e2})
  ${s} $;
%end
```

(a) replacing != in **while** condition to ==

```
% before
<@ ${var:ID_FVAR} = ${lit:LITERAL}; @>
for (${e1:EXPR}; ${e2:EXPR}; ${e3:EXPR} )
     ${s:STMT*} $;
% after
<@ @>
for (${e1}; ${e2}; ${e3} )
  ${s} $;
% end
```

(b) deleting the assignment just before a **for** statement (Fig. 1 error (4))

```
%before
swap(${a1:EXPR}<@ @>,${a2:EXPR}<@ @>);
%after
swap(${a1}<@ .height @>,
     ${a2}<@ .height @>);
%end
```

(c) inserting unnecessary member references **.height** (Fig 2. error(5))

```
%before
<@ @>
putstrrev(s+1);
<@ putchar(*s); @>
%after
<@ putchar(*s); @>
putstrrev(s+1);
<@ @>
%end
```

(d) moving **putchar** function call (Fig. 8)

one of *move* type like Figure 9 (d), a pattern is described as a combination of *delete* and *insert* operations. That is, at least there are two pairs of special tags for each part, one for deleting and the other for inserting, and one of them contains no token. We describe an injection of editable points as an error pattern whose before-part and after-part are identical and tokens surrounded by the special tags become editable.

DISCUSSION

Generality of Error Patterns

To confirm that the system can generate error correction questions, we have defined 33 error patterns for injecting errors (23 replacing errors, 8 deleting errors, 2 inserting errors, and 2 moving errors) and 14 patterns for setting editable points, and applied them to 10 sample programs: Figure 1, Figure 2, Figure 3, Figure 8, recursive functions such as a factorial and the length of a string (Figure 10 and 11), file processing such as copying a file, a binary search function (Figure 12), and so on. Sample programs widely cover the syntax and semantics of the C language such as variable initialization, types, if-else branches, for or while loops, logical conditions, arrays, functions, structures, pointers, strings, file processing, and some algorithms such as sorting and searching. Generated questions are available at http://ecq.tebasaki.jp/.

The error patterns we defined are varied in generality. From our experiences, the error patterns for learning the syntax and semantics of the language tend to be general, and the ones for learning algorithms tend to be specific. For example, a pattern of removing an addressing operator *&* on calling the *scanf* function can be applied to any programs that read an integer or real value with the *scanf* function. The error pattern, Figure 9 (c) is less general, which depends on the function *swap* and the structure person. In our patterns, 12 of 47 patterns are specialized for the target programs.

These patterns are difficult to be reused, but they are useful for generating questions optimized for learning objectives. For example, in Figure 2, when we have described an error pattern for inserting unnecessary references (Figure 9 (c)), we have selected the member name, height, because the specification of the program requires to sort data by the member. We have set an editable point on the indexes *of p[j]*, but not the ones *of p[min]*. If both of them are editable, another answer becomes acceptable; the answers, *p[min].height > p[j]. height* in Line 20 and *swap(&p[min], &p[j])* in Line 24, are valid. We also have made the space in front of the variable *tmp* in Line 8 editable because we expect that learners may insert * in the same way of the parameters **a* and **b* without understanding meanings deeply.

Variation of Error Correction Questions

By using error patterns, we can generate multiple questions from one correct program. We show two questions of the recursive factorial function in Figure 10 (b) (c). The function **fact** in Figure 10 (a) calculates the factorial number of the non-negative number **n** (note that 0! = 1). For understanding recursive functions, learners have to understand inductive steps and the base case. When a teacher wants to make learners learn inductive step, that is, the argument is reduced on calling the function recursively, he/she selects the pattern (d) in Figure 10, which changes an argument **n-1** to **n**. On the other hand, for understanding the base case, he/she selects the pattern (e) in Figure 10, which changes a condition for terminating function calls, or the pattern (f), which changes a returned value at the base case. We can generate different questions for learning objectives from the one program. We also note that these error patterns are reusable. They can be applied to other recursive functions, for example, calculating the summation from 0 to a non-negative number. Especially, since the pattern (d) does not depend on the specific values

Figure 10. Recursive function and error patterns

```
int fact(int n)
{
    if (n == 0) return 1;
    else return n * fact(n-1);
}
```

(a) a recursive function calculating n!

```
int fact(int n)
{
    if (n == 0) return 1;
    else return n * fact(n);
}
```

(b) an error correction question
for learning inductive steps

```
int fact(int n)
{
    if (n == 1) return 0;
    else return n * fact(n-1);
}
```

(c) an error correction question
for learning the base case

```
%before
return ${e1:EXPR} ${op1:OPE}
  ${f:ID_FVAR}(<@ ${n:ID_FVAR} ${op2:OPE}
                   ${e2:EXPR} @>) ;
%after
return ${e1} ${op1} ${f}(<@ ${n} @>);
%end
```

(d) an error pattern changing the
argument of recursive function call

```
%before
if (${e:EXPR} ${op:OPE} <@ 0 @>)
   ${s:STMT*} $;
%after
if (${e} ${op} <@ 1 @>) ${s} $;
%end
```

(e) an error pattern changing the condition

```
%before
return <@ 1 @>;
%after
return <@ 0 @>;
%end
```

(f) an error pattern changing the returned value

Figure 11. Recursive function strlength

```
int strlength(char *s)
{
    if (*s == '\0') return 0;
    else return 1 + strlength(s + 1);
}
```

Figure 12. Error moving the variable initialization into the loop

```
sum = 0;
for (i = 0; i < size; i++) {
   sum = sum + data[i];
}
```

(a) a correct program

```
for (i = 0; i < size; i++) {
    sum = 0;
    sum = sum + data[i];
}
```

(b) a program including an error of moving

```
for (i = 0; i < size; i++) {
    if (i == 0) sum = 0;
    sum = sum + data[i];
}
```

(c) an unexpected answer

and variables, we can apply it to the recursive function *strlength* in Figure 11, which calculates the length of a string.

Experiment and Evaluation

We have made an experiment of the programming exercise using the generated error correction questions. The subjects are 17 undergraduate students in the third and fourth grade, who had taken programming courses and have the skills for developing small programs. The purpose of the experiment is to find unexpected answers. As a result, we have found unexpected answers that have the same output as the original correct programs.

One of them is *strlength(++s) for strlength(s+1)* in Figure 11. Both evaluated values of expressions *++s* and *s+1* are same, but the semantics are different; the former changes the value of the variable **s**, and the latter doesn't. In this program, *strlength(++s)* works appropriately because the variable **s** is never referred after calling the function. Although *s+1* is better than *++s* because *++s* changes the value of the parameter, using the expression *++s* instead of *s+1* is not so much unnatural and is acceptable from the educational view. However, *--size* instead of *size-1* at Line 19 in Figure 2 is not a correct answer because the value of **size** is used after that. Whether *++a for a+1* or *--a for a-1* is correct or not depends on a context, that is, data flows. If our system analyzes data flows of correct programs, it can be checked. The system, however, becomes complicated. Instead, we are planning to write an alternative answer in an error pattern. For example, in afterpart, an alternative is surrounded by the special tags <| |> like as *strlength(<@ s <|++s|> @>)*.

We show another unexpected answer in Figure 12. A question is about the summation of an array and an error is moving variable initialization into the loop. An unexpected answer is Figure 12 (c), that is, initialization in the loop is executed on only the first repetition, *i==0*. It is not good

codes because the condition is checked on every repetition. From the educational view, we treat it as incorrect.

We have also found redundant answers. For example, a student inserted the unnecessary statement *avg = 0;* at Line 9 in Figure 1 (b). The variable *avg* is never referred before the assignment at Line 18, and no initialization is needed. In the question of Figure 2, there was an answer that the condition of the *for* at Line 17 was changed to *i<size*. Though it executes the redundant process on *i==size-1*, it produces the same result as the original program. How to treat redundant answers depends on the purpose of the exercises. Our system cannot support the case that the teachers want to judge redundant answers as correct because the correctness checking is implemented based on text matching. For checking redundant answers, it may be effective to compare the results of the original program and the answered program by tests for the sufficient coverage of inputs, while it makes the system more complicated and requires more efforts for teachers to prepare adequate test sets.

FUTURE RESEARCH DIRECTIONS

We show future works of our research in this section. For learners, there is room for improvement of the user interface of the question presentation system. To make teachers' work lighter, support systems for making questions and collecting learners' errors are future works.

Improvement of User Interface

Our presentation system restricts editable points for reducing possible answers and hides them from learners to avoid providing undesirable hints. However, an empty line at the last of a function may become a hint. For example, in Figure 3 (a), the empty line at Line 8, which is caused by deleting the assignment *d[i]= '\0';,* may seem strange to learners. There is room for improvement of the user interface. In this case, a better idea is that the question generating system deletes an empty line before a right curly brace } and the presentation system provides a function of adding a new line at that point by learners. The presentation system becomes a kind of structure editor on which users can edit texts at restricted points.

In the experimental exercise, when students didn't find errors after some consideration, they tried to search for editable points by moving a mouse. This is not desirable. It may be better to provide a help function; for example, editable points or correctable points are shown explicitly over the time limit.

Support for Making Questions

In our system, to make questions, teachers write correct programs and select error patterns manually. A support method for selecting patterns is a future work. Patterns should be selected from the multiple views such as learning objectives, the difficulty of questions, the level of learners' understanding, and so on. Some e-Learning system using fill-in-the-blank questions dynamically evaluates both an achievement level of each learner and a difficulty level of each question, and generates appropriate questions for each learner (Mine et al., 2002; Suganuma et al., 2005; Zhao & Wakahara, 2011). In our system, we can estimate weak categories for each learner from errors that he/she cannot modify correctly. It is helpful to select error patterns.

Teachers can describe error patterns for satisfying their learning objectives. The format of error patterns is relatively easy to learn; it is a kind of program code including some pattern variables to specify types. For easier description, a method for automatic generation of error patterns is a future work. We consider that we can generate patterns from the differences between correct programs and error programs. It is similar to a program *patch*, which updates source programs, generated from

differences between old and new versions of programs. For example, a simple error about calling the recursive factorial function is the code *return n*fact(n);* instead of *return n*fact(n-1);,* and we can generate the error pattern by representing the different tokens with special tags: *fact(<@ n-1 @>)* in the before-part and *fact(<@ n @>)in* the after-part. Replacing the function name and the operator to pattern variables makes a pattern general, *return n ${op:OPE} ${f:ID_FVAR}(<@ n-1 @>);.* It can be applied to a recursive summation function. When variables and operators are replaced to pattern variables, it becomes the more general pattern, Figure 10 (d). In this pattern, the variable that does not occur on arguments is replaced to an expression pattern variable for generality. To collect heuristic knowledge like this replacement is a future work, too. For further improvement of the reusability of error patterns, it may be possible to describe the contexts of applying patterns and its edit operations separately. Though the contexts depend on programs, we expect operations can be described in general styles.

Detecting unexpected answers is a difficult problem. We show an example question of a binary search function in Figure 13. The function *bsearch* searches the value x in the ascending ordered array, *from a[left] to a[right].* When the value is found, it returns the index of the array, and when not found, it returns **-1.** To understand how to narrow a range for searching, errors are injected to branch conditions and arguments on recursive function calls. When the operator < in Line 10 is editable like as other conditions in Line 6 and 8, there is another answer; modifying *x>a[min]* in Line 10 and swapping statements in Line 11 and 13 of the original program. This is a typical case that many editable points cause alternative answers. This answer is not allowed, when the operator < in Line 10 is not editable or when one of arguments in Line 11 and 13 is not editable. Support for automatic detection of alternative answers is a big challenge.

Figure 13. Error correction question of binary search

```
1: int bsearch(int a[],
2:            int left, int right, int x)
3: {
4:   int mid;
5:
6:   if (left > right) return -1;
7   mid = (left + right) / 2;
8:   if (a[mid] == x)
9:      return mid;
10:   else if (x < a[mid])
11:      return bsearch(a, left, mid-1, x);
12:   else
13:      return bsearch(a, mid+1, right, x);
14: }
```

(a) a correct program

```
1: int bsearch(int a[],
2:            int left, int right, int x)
3: {
4:   int mid;
5:
6:   if (left == right) return -1;
7   mid = (right - left) / 2;
8:   if (a[mid] == x)
9:      return mid;
10:   else if (x <= a[mid])
11:      return bsearch(a, left, mid, x);
12:   else
13:      return bsearch(a, mid, right, x);
14: }
```

(b) a program including errors

Collecting Errors

Collecting other errors that are effective for acquiring debugging skills is also a future work. Although some researches have reported syntax errors by novice programmers (Ahmadzadeh et al., 2005; Hristova et al., 2003; Jackson et al., 2005; Tuugalei & Mow, 2012), a few logical errors are known. While we can collect syntax errors by logging compile errors, to collect logical ones we need to investigate programming processes; we have an interest in how they correct faulty programs, for which compilers report no error. Work-in-progress codes and input data they select to test programs may be helpful for teachers to analyze their errors. An integrated development environment for education is one of the suitable systems to preserve learners' processes (Hachisu, Yoshida, & Agusa, 2014; Liang, Kui, & Wang, 2011).

CONCLUSION

We have proposed a support system for generating error correction questions and checking answers. On the system, we can describe error patterns of injecting errors to codes, and the system synthesizes HTML files as questions from them. The system also generates CGI programs for checking answers. If learners can edit any codes freely, it is difficult to check all possible answers. Instead, we have adopted a strategy to restrict editable points and possible answers from the educational view. If all editable points explicitly appear on a question page, learners may guess the answers without comprehension. Our system provides an intuitive user interface using the jQuery plug-in, JEIP; a learner can edit a code in place and editable points are hidden from learners. We have collected typical errors in programming and written them as error patterns. We have generated questions from them and shown the validity of our system. We hope that discussion about learning support for debugging using error correction questions is opened.

Improvement of the user interface of questions on the Web system, a support system for making questions, and how to treat unexpected answers are future works. Automatic detection of alternative answers also remains as a big challenge.

REFERENCES

Agrawal, H., DeMillo, R. A., Hathaway, B., Hsu, W., Hsu, W., Krauser, E. W. ... Spafford, E. (1984). *Design of mutant operators for the C programming language*. Technical Report SERC-TR41-P. Purdue University.

Ahmadzadeh, M., Elliman, D., & Higgins, C. (2005). An analysis of patterns of debugging among novice computer science students. In *Proceedings of the 10th Annual SIGCSE Conference on Innovation and Technology in Computer Science Education* (pp. 84-88). ACM. doi:10.1145/1067445.1067472

Chmiel, R., & Loui, M. C. (2004). Debugging: From novice to expert. In *Proceedings of the 35th SIGCSE Technical Symposium on Computer Science Education* (pp. 17-21). ACM. doi:10.1145/971300.971310

Hachisu, Y., & Yoshida, A. (2013). Generation of error correction questions for beginners of programming (in Japanese). In Proceedings of Foundation of Software Engineering XX (FOSE2013). Kaga, Japan: Academic Press.

Hachisu, Y., & Yoshida, A. (2014). A support system for error correction questions in programming education. In *Proceedings of the International Conference e-Learning 2014* (pp. 249-258). Academic Press.

Hachisu, Y., Yoshida, A., & Agusa, K. (2014). Understanding coding processes in programming exercises (in Japanese). *IEICE Technical Report 2014-CE-125(3)*. Hakodate, Japan: IEICE.

Hristova, M., Misra, A., Rutter, M., & Mercuri, R. (2003). Identifying and correcting Java programming errors for introductory computer science students. In *Proceedings of the 34th SIGCSE Technical Symposium on Computer Science Education* (pp. 153-156). ACM. doi:10.1145/611892.611956

Hu, Y., Hu, Y., & Guo, L. (2013). Construction of C programming language based on ontology knowledge base. In *Proceedings of the Second International Conference on Innovative Computing and Cloud Computing* (pp. 23-25). Academic Press. doi:10.1145/2556871.2556877

Itoh, R., Nagataki, H., Ooshita, F., Kakugawa, H., & Masuzawa, T. (2007). A fault injection method for generating error-correction exercises in algorithm learning. In *Proceedings of the 8th International Conference on Information Technology Based Higher Education and Training* (pp. 200-205). Academic Press.

Jackson, J., Cobb, M., & Carver, C. (2005). Identifying top Java errors for novice programmers. In *Proceedings Frontiers in Education 35th Annual Conference*. Academic Press. doi:10.1109/FIE.2005.1611967

Jia, Y., & Harman, M. (2011). An analysis and survey of the development of mutation testing. *IEEE Transactions on Software Engineering, 37*(5), 649–678. doi:10.1109/TSE.2010.62

Lahtinen, E., Ala-Mutka, K., & Jrvinen, H. (2005). A study of the difficulties of novice programmers. In *Proceedings of the 10th Annual SIGCSE Conference on Innovation and Technology in Computer Science Education* (pp. 14-18). ACM. doi:10.1145/1067445.1067453

Lee, M. J., Bahmani, F., Kwan, I., LaFerte, J., Charters, P., Horvath, A., … Ko, A.J. (2014). Principles of a debugging-first puzzle game for computing education. In *Proceedings of 2014 IEEE Symposium on Visual Languages and Human-Centric Computing* (pp. 57-64). IEEE. doi:10.1109/VLHCC.2014.6883023

Lee, M. J., & Ko, A. J. (2014). A demonstration of Gidget, a debugging game for computing education. In *Proceedings of 2014 IEEE Symposium on Visual Languages and Human-Centric Computing* (pp. 211-212). IEEE. doi:10.1109/VLHCC.2014.6883060

Mine, T., Suganuma, A., & Shoudai, T. (2002). Categorizing questions according to a navigation list for a web-based self-teaching system: AEGIS. In *Proceedings of the International Conference on Computers in Education* (pp. 1245-1249). Academic Press. doi:10.1109/CIE.2002.1186203

Pierrakeas, C., Solomou, G., & Kameas, A. (2012). An ontology-based approach in learning programming languages. In *Proceedings of 16th Panhellenic Conference on Informatics* (pp. 393-398). Academic Press. doi:10.1109/PCi.2012.78

Scott, J. (2008). *jQuery edit in place (JEIP)*. Retrieved September 3, 2014 from http://josephscott.org/code/javascript/jquery-edit-in-place/

Suganuma, A., Mine, T., & Shoudai, T. (2005). Automatic exercise generating system that dynamically evaluates both students' and questions' levels [in Japanese]. *Journal of Information Processing Society of Japan*, *46*(7), 1810–1818.

Tuugalei, I., & Mow, C. (2012). Analyses of student programming errors in Java programming courses. *Journal of Emerging Trends in Computing and Information Sciences*, *3*(5), 739–749.

Wu, L., Liang, G., Kui, S., & Wang, Q. (2011). CEclipse: An online IDE for programming in the cloud. In *Proceedings of 2011 IEEE World Congress on Services*. IEEE. doi:10.1109/SERVICES.2011.74

Yoshida, A., Hachisu, Y., Sawada, A., Chang, H. M., & Noro, M. (2012). A source code rewriting system based on attributed token sequence [in Japanese]. *Journal of Information Processing Society of Japan*, *53*(7), 1832–1849.

Zhao, W., & Wakahara, T. (2011). A support system using Moodle for improving students understanding. In *Proceedings of Third International Conference on Intelligent Networking and Collaborative Systems* (pp. 478-483). Academic Press. doi:10.1109/INCoS.2011.43

KEY TERMS AND DEFINITIONS

AJAX: It is implementation techniques for asynchronous communication between a Web browser and a Web server. A Web application using AJAX can update contents of the page without reloading.

Error Correction Question: Texts including errors are shown as a question to a learner. He/she finds error texts and corrects them.

Error Pattern: It is code transformation pattern for injecting errors to correct programs.

Fill-in-the-Blank Question: Texts including empty boxes are shown as a question to a learner. He/she finds appropriate texts by himself/herself and fills them in boxes.

jQuery: It is a JavaScript library to enhance functionality and usability of Web browsers.

Learning Objective: It means knowledge or skill that learners should understand in the course. In programming courses, it is the syntax and semantics of the language, typical program descriptions, and algorithms that learners should understand.

Multiple-Choice Question: Texts including empty boxes are shown as a question to a learner. Unlike a fill-in-the-blank question, multiple texts, one of which is the appropriate text, are shown to a learner. He/she selects appropriate texts in boxes.

Chapter 7
Digital Keepsakes:
Older Adults and the Extended Use of ICTs and Digital Artifacts

Declan Tuite
Dublin City University, Ireland

ABSTRACT

This chapter presents research from a study of novice older adult users of ICTs and the Internet from Ireland. Through the concept of digital keepsakes, this chapter connects with theorising around greater mobility and more dissipated extended families. In particular, connections can be seen with current research themes, which explore how citizens may extend the use of ICT communication act so that digital artifacts may offer emotional containment, extended time for reflection, through comments reinterpretations and sharing of experience and meaning. The value and benefit of digital artifacts can extend beyond a personal onscreen experience. Respondents reported valuing both portability and having a record of the good intentions. Such messages consisted of wishes of good luck, sympathy, or empathy.

INTRODUCTION

The primary aim of the research was to shed light on how people who have never used the Internet before as adults take up the technology and what they do with it. Within this attention was paid to the effects of engaging with ICT's on social networks, social capital and the behaviours and attitudes the older adults developed having embedded ICTs' into everyday life.

The motivation for this research arose from reviewing the outcomes of eInclusion projects directed at a key group perceived to be outside the information society, namely older adults. It

seemed curious that while many projects had taken place and indeed there were reports on the outcomes they did not study the longer-term effects of the training courses. The reports were positive about the older peoples experiences and attitudes to both ICT's and the training however these reports mostly taken from surveys which were carried out very close to end date of the older peoples participation in training either at the end of the training or up to six weeks later.

This raised questions as to if these new skills were maintained and even embedded into everyday life once the training was over and what did the older adults do with these new skills. Could any

DOI: 10.4018/978-1-4666-8147-7.ch007

differences in the use by older adults as oppose to other generations be found and how did being an older adult effect their longer term use of the Internet due to what ever meaning (attitudes, perceptions, assumption and experiences) ICT's have for older adults?

Consequently, research was undertaken to better understand how the older adults may have embedded their newly learned ICT skills into their everyday life. The research uses in-depth semi-structured interviews, name generators and critical incident technique to gather data. The participants were interviewed seven to eighteen months after completing their courses. To gain deeper and richer 'thick' descriptions from the respondents, the use of questions and scenarios around social support was incorporated in the study. Everyday scenarios around health issues and domestic situations provided the opportunity for the participants to recount their behaviors, experiences and perceptions, in relation to ICT use. The use of a name generator afforded mapping the social networks of the respondent with attention to tie strength which used descriptors such as, kin links and identifying those whom the respondents would discuss important matters with to help identify tie strength.

The sample reflects the characteristics of older Irish adults who were targeted for training via the *BenefIT* eInclusion programmes not the general population. Twenty-seven older adults aged sixty to seventy-two who participated in ICT and Internet training course were interviewed. Older adults made up the greatest segment of those who participated in the training programme. The sample consists of people from rural (40%), urban (40%) and city (20%) contexts in the same proportion as participation rates in the training schemes (Jordan, 2010). More women participated in the training programmes than men. the sample reflects this particpantation rate with one third of participants in this study being men. Most of the participants had left formal education at second

level with just three of the sample having third level qualifications.

The sample does not reflect the general population in regarding gender composition, but mirrors the participation rates on the training programmes. The sample is made up of older adults who participated in targeted training courses and does not represent all Irish older adults

This chapter will present a review of literature of key regarding older adults and engagement with ICT's and the Internet. This will be expanded to include more general uses of the ICT's and the Internet regarding that offer deeper insight into the perceived value ICTs and Internet use by older adults such as media multiplexity, co-presence and the important of ICT mediated communications in relationship maintenance. Factors such as the strengths and weakness of various mediated communication channels are discussed. By using the concept of digital keepsakes, where individuals store and re-engage with messages or other digital artifacts that offer comfort or support in times of need, offers insight into the use and reuse of ICT and Internet communications, the original findings of the study are then presented and discuss in relations to the current literature.

Finally the outcomes of the findings are drawn out to suggest both future possible avenues of research an how these enhanced understandings of older adults behavior and attitudes may inform us regarding future uses of ICTs as they become even more embedded and invisible in peoples daily lives.

BACKGROUND

To enable a rounded discussion of the extended uses of ICT enabled communications by older adults the literature review will present both background on specific literature and research focused on use of the Internet and ICTs by older adults and compliment this with research focused on more general uses and the associated behaviours.

Firstly a background of older adults and the Internet will be presented. This will develop to highlight the particular favoured uses of mediated communications by older adults and the associated benefits engaging in online mediated communication for older adults, particularly close social ties and family members at a distance. From this point particular attention is paid to the findings from research which focuses on behaviours and activities by older adults online and in mediated contexts. The final part of the literature review discusses strategies for managing the array of ICTs available, and the value associated with communicating via different online platforms, whether synchronous, asynchronous, text based or full screen video. The opportunities, which certain online communications tools allow for reviewing and reminiscing, will be highlighted.

Older Adults, the Internet and ICT's

Much of the research around older adults and the Internet revolves about the barriers and rejection of new technologies (Warburton, Cowan, & Bathgate, 2013; Barnard, Bradley, Hodgson, & Lloyd, 2013; González, Ramirez, & Viadel, 2012; Neves and Amaro, 2012;) or the immediate acts in which the older adults take part in (Feist, Parker, & Hugo., 2012; Xie, 2008; Sum, Mathews, & Hughes, 2009; Fast, Gierveld, & Keating, 2008).

A principle barrier is a lack of training and facilitation (Barnard et al., 2013; Bailey & Ngwenyama, 2010). When training exists there is a noted need for continued and regular support for developing these newly learned skills (Gardner, Kamber, & Netherland, 2012; Feist et al, 2010) which needs to be tailored to the older adults and localized (Feist et al., 2010). Along with this the cost of equipment and ISP subscriptions, a lack of knowledge regarding potential benefits of ICT use (Melenhorst, Rogers, & Bouwhuis, 2006) and anxiety about the technology (Warburton et al., 2013; Selwyn & Facer, 2007) provide impediments to older adults engaging with ICTs. Lee

and Coughlin (2014) have recently proposed a inclusive and holistic set of ten factors which influence older adults adoption of technology; value, usability, affordability, accessibility, technical support, social support, emotion, independence, experience, and confidence.

Russell, Campbell and Hughes (2008) offers a classifications of users depending on frequency of user, type of use and those who the older user may communicate with online. Suggested are four types of uses; rejectors, utilisers, browsers and augmenters.

Rejectors are seen to make a deliberate choice not to engage but still can have use of the Internet by proxy, usually via family members. Their main information sources are offline and their frequency of use of the Internet by proxy is at most weekly but more usually several weeks apart. Utilizers use the Internet more frequently up to several times a week and use the Internet as a supplementary source of information and social contact. When using the Internet to source information they tend to find a source and stick with that source. They will communicate online sparingly with those they already know offline. Browsers spend a lot of time online usually daily. They will consolidate information from multiple sources and do not need to stick to a resource they find useful and are willing to explore alternative sources. They will communicate with those they already know but will so do with reasonable comfort. Augmenters behave like digital natives (Prensky, 2005) and as Tapscott (2008) notes have technology as part of their lives and use ICT and the Internet constantly and they source information from a variety of online sources. They communicate with those they already know offline and are willing to communicate with strangers.

Use of ICT by Older Adults

When investigating behaviours of older users, Nahm and Resnick (2001) noted that as they grow old, people may be less socially active and may be living at considerable distance from family members. They argue that ICT use enhances social communication and wellbeing in seniors as the Internet can create virtual social networks that can cross generations and may include family, friends and others outside the immediate family, which proved to lead to a reported enhanced sense of social connectedness and well-being in older adults (Nahm & Resnick, 2001). Nimrod (2012) supports these findings and augments this by noting that social connections are not the only perceived benefit of Internet use by older users and that being able to independently look up information regarding health, travel and hobbies is valued highly.

There is body of research that concurs and places looking up health information in particular as motivating factor in Internet use by older adults (Czaja, et al., 2013; Rideout & Newman, 2005; McMillan & Macias, 2008). Fox (2004) reports that more than two-thirds of those in the study searched for information on health issues, noting that searching for greater detail on prescribed drugs being the most usual search (Fox, 2004; Jones & Fox, 2009). They state that "*older Internet users are significantly more likely than younger generations to look online for health information. [...]. Researching health information is the third most popular online activity with the most senior age group, after email and online search.*" (Jones & Fox, 2009, p.3). Noteworthy is the level of perceived trustworthiness of health information online by older adults, with the Internet being considered a more trustworthy source of information on health matters than traditional media apart from printed books (Rideout & Newman, 2005).

Early research by Fox (2001) studied the use of ICTs by older adults, finding that while older adults are the least likely to be online those that have engaged with ICT and in particular email have 'fallen in love with' the Internet and particularly email. More than any other age group they will have access to the Internet from home.

Furthermore they found that within older users it is more likely that they will be men, highly educated, married and have a relatively high retirement income. They found that their motivation to go online was to maintain contact with their children and grandchildren, and that they had received encouragement from family member to go online (Fox, 2001).

Older adults are likely to engage with many forms of ICTs including email, instant messaging, online fora and video messages (Wagner, Hassanein & Head, 2010; Xie, 2008). Sum et al., (2009) suggest that for older people the Internet supplements rather than replaces more face-to-face modes of communication and connection (Sum et al., 2009). Fast et al., (2008) find that along with health issues, older people rank social networks highly; as people get older they value strong emotionally rewarding relationships, primarily kin and established friendships (Charles & Carstensen, 2010; Cornwell 2011). Gato and Tak (2008) state that contact and communication with family and friends is reported by older people to be the most important perceived benefit of using the Internet. There is a consistency in research in that connectivity with family and friends is the most important factor giving quality to their lives (Farquhar, 1995; Antonucci, 2001). This is mirrored with findings from Victor *et al.* (2005) that reduced quality of life is associated with reduced social contact, isolation and feelings of loneliness (Victor, Scambler, Bowling, & Bond, 2005). This has been noted of particular use in in difficult or stressful times (Opalinski, 2001) such as times of transition (Mikal, Rice, Abeyta, & DeVilbiss, J, 2013; Norval, 2012).

As people get older they focus more on strong emotionally rewarding relationships, primarily kin and longer established friendships (Charles & Carstensen, 2010; Cornwell, Laumann & Schumm, 2008; Cornwell and Waite, 2009). So that, as Cornwell, Laumann and Schumm, (2008) found, as people age the size of their social network decreases. However, gender differences have been found in studies of older adults. Older women are more likely to have wider social networks (Cornwell, 2011), including both kin and non-kin, so that they are more likely than their male contemporaries to have greater bridging capital (McPherson, Smith-Lovin, & Brashears, 2006). McPherson et al., (2006) found that generally older women had larger social networks and invest more in ties outside the household. These weaker ties may have instrumental advantages for these older women and offer great control in their everyday lives and a sense of independence (Cornwell, 2011).

Contact and communication with family and friends is reported by older people to be the most important perceived benefit of using the Internet. Through correspondence via email with their family and friends the older adults who took part in the study reported a greater feeling of connectedness (Cotten, Anderson, & McCullough, 2013; Gatto & Tak, 2008). Connecting with family and friends, especially grandchildren (Forghani, Neustaedter, & Schiphorst, 2013; Weatherall, 2000) has been found to be a benefit of ICT use for older people and using ICT to access help and support in difficult times such as coping with grief (Opalinski, 2001). These potential benefits may afford greater connectivity as research has found that the level of social capital in older people generally declines with age (Forsman, Herberts, Nyqvist, Wahlbeck, & Schierenbeck, 2013).

Benefits of Being Connected

There is a consensus that with older people social isolation is a strong predictor of poorer health and linked to cardiovascular disease (Hawkley & Cacioppo, 2013). Isolation is also found to be linked to premature mortality, depression, poorer nutrition and the likelihood of older adults to delay seeking care or help (Nyqvist, Forsman, Giuntoli, & Cattan, 2013; Cacioppo, Hughes,

Waite, Hawkley, & Thisted, 2006). So that being part of a supportive social network makes people feel cared for, valued, loved and esteemed, which has very beneficial effects on health (Wilkinson & Marmot, 2003).

Early research focusing on the use older adults learning ICT skills suggests that engaging with the training and the use of ICT can increase the self-confidence and ability to learn and aid with memory retention of older people (Ogozalek, 1991; Groves & Slack, 1994). This suggests that older adults who can effectively use the Internet, email in particular can address issues of loneliness, boredom, helplessness and the decline of mental skill. A later study by McConatha (2002) found that older people who learned to use ICT has provided increased in the level of life satisfaction and reduced levels of depression (McConatha, 2002). While more recently Xie (2008) offers that those learning ICT and engaging in Internet use reported a more meaningful retirement and that they had developed their own self-evaluations and noted changes in the views of other of them (Xie, 2008). Hendrix (2000) extends these outcomes with older people reporting enhanced self-efficacy; fun and mental stimulation; enhanced personal control and self-determination; improved education and skills development (e.g., monitor their health status); and increased social interaction (Hendrix, 2000).

The main uses of ICT and the Internet by older users were finding information on health issues and maintaining social connections. The benefits of older adults conducting independent research online and learning of these new skills are seen to be positive resulting in improved self-esteem and cognitive function. The increased opportunities to connect socially with family and friends have been associated with lower levels of loneliness and a perceived increase in quality of life. The use of ICT cannot only empower older people to receive but also to provide support.

Recent research by Huber *et al.* (2012) found that even if the two-way communication is through ambient devices which track movement, the older person and the caregiver can feel more connected. They noted that, for older adults, even if mediated indirectly through technologies the having the information that 'all is well' provides comfort and reassurance (Huber *et al.*, 2012).

Family at a Distance

With increased mobility and greater ease in migration, families are using ICTs to remain connected across and within countries. The potential 'death of distance' (Cairncross, 1997) which ICTs may provide is been played out through near ubiquity and lowering cost if ICTs. Families that live geographically dispersed may remain connected through transnational networks (Mahler, 2001). Research addressing the impact of Internet and ICT use for migration processes and the maintenance of relationships between the migrants and the non-migrant family members and friends at home is growing (Hiller & Franz 2004; Diminescu, 2008; Komito, 2011, Komito & Bates, 2012; Madianou and Miller 2012). This area of research and scholarship is useful as many of the participants in this research project had experienced recent changes in proximity of family members due to the rise in immigration in Ireland following the economic crisis. Maintaining family connections then becomes more feasible with the introduction of ICT and Internet mediated communications both synchronous and asynchronous.

Wilding (2006) finds that many migrants describe recent developments such as cheap affordable transnational calls or Internet enabled emails as 'miracles' (Wilding, 2006), as communications, which allow a continued presence in family members lives who may be living at thousands of miles distance. ICTs and the Internet enable the migrant to be both 'there' and 'here' simultaneously, helping lessen the sense of physical separation (Pertierra, 2006). The use of ICTs to offset the absence of close family members

may blur the boundaries between absence and presence, due to a pattern of continuous mediated interactions (Licoppe, 2004). Where not just the content of messages but the act of communicating is perceived as important (Licoppe & Smoreda, 2005). This offers the increased opportunity for phatic communication (Malinowski, 1923) where the objective is the social interaction itself and not as with instrumental communication trying to accomplish a task outside the communication.

Yet having a sense of constant presence in the lives of family members is not always perceived as preferential as with parents' attempts to maintain regular in contact to show love and provide care can be perceived by older children as a form of surveillance or control (Horst, 2006). With more modes of commination and these modes being interconnected and 'on' more of the time, creating social distance for those who want to break away is more difficult (Wilding, 2006).

Online media play a more crucial role in maintaining family ties between geographically dispersed family. There can be greater use of visual communication, as with using video-chat or sharing photographs, which may be either by direct email or via social networking sites (Dekker & Engbersen, 2012).

Skrbiš (2008) highlights the importance emotions in the transnational family experience, that separation bears a cost on the migrants by dissociating the migrant from both family and friends and their other social significant referents (Skrbiš, 2008). The migration process is laden with emotional disruptions and disconnections (Huang & Yeoh, 2007; Baldassar, 2008; Mahler, 2001) and usually also bears with it losses such as financial (Baldassar, 2007). With the perceived emotional and social cost of migration lessened the threshold of migration may too be lowered due to ICT and Internet communications (Dekker & Engberson, 2012). As suggested by Komito (2011), both emotional and social costs of migration can be somewhat abated via ICT and Internet communications, social media in particular.

Wilding (2006) has commented on the capacity of ICTs to construct a 'connected presence', however is cautious in noting that ICT connections are incorporated into a preexisting set of family relationships which also had preexisting practices and expectations in communications. Whereby, if sibling relationships had been strained before the availability of ICT communication they continued to be strained afterwards. Similarly if a parent-child relationship had been intimate before communicating via email it remained intimate afterwards (Wilding, 2006).

From Events to Ambience

Koskinen (2004) found that initially senders of messages online made a drama out of posting of pictures or text, each post becoming an event, something newsworthy. But as greater familiarity with the technology grows and the possibility of leaving connections on for longer periods of time or in some cases permanently on, there can be a move from event to ambience. Ito (2005) finds that the use of more mundane photos of ambient visual information can act as *'thinking of you'* messages; rich media *'sweet nothings'*. Cohen (2005) has noted that, not only what may be perceived as special events but more mundane everyday occurrences offering a stream of mundane mementos. The development of some of the key technologies such as laptops to include built-in cameras, speakers and microphones, and thus removing the need to 'plug-in', has afforded greater ease and greater choice in location of use, when and where to connect with others. Which theoretically can move toward *'perpetual contact'* as proposed by Katz and Aakhus (2002) regarding mobile phones. (Katz & Aakhus, 2002).

While studying the use of ICTs to maintain social connections in Canada; Milliken, O'Donnell, Gibson, and Daniels (2012) found that seeing the person with whom there are communicating has the effect of improving the sense of connection. Like earlier research (Biocca, Burgoon, Harm, & Stoner, 2003) investigating the how ICTs may afford social presence, Milliken et al., (2012) find that older adults placed great value the visual element and increased the level of engagement in the communication. Not only was being able to see the other person noted as having great value but also being seen themselves was noted as important that they would 'suffer through' interruptions in connection or poor audio quality (Milliken et al., 2012). Similarly Judge and Neustaedter (2010) and Ames, Kaye and Spasojevic (2010) found that the perceived extra value of communication being synchronous and having a greater level of social cues was viewed as being worth the extra work needed to manage the choice of media used to communicate (Judge & Neustaedter, 2010; Ames et al., 2010).

So that while ICTs may present the isolation paradox - always being in touch but never together, Bauman (2008) asserts that ICTs through their ability to afford co-presence can lead to perceived attunement and offer a repair function to relationships. With more instant communication and more ambient communication, particularly though social media family ties can become a more intimate part of everyday life for those living at a distance (Brekke, 2008; Madianou & Miller 2012).

Each medium brings with it certain 'social affordances'. While depending on post, an asynchronous medium, migrants may have to wait days or weeks before receiving a reply. Typically letters sent fortnightly and a response started on the day of receiving them (Wilding, 2006). Yet letters by post not only serve as communication, they may be stored, reread and become valued as symbols of unity and connectedness. Letters also may be judged to be a more personal form of communication, as they can be perceived as being crafted with dedication and devotion (Madianou & Miller 2012). Similarly audio cassettes, sent home or to the family members at a distance, could be listened too many times, and offer the emotional immediacy of the voice and can have advantages over letters where literacy may be an issue (Madianou & Miller 2012).

The use of ICTs to offset the absence of close family members may blur the boundaries between absence and presence, due to a pattern of continuous mediated interactions (Licoppe, 2004). Where not just the content of messages but the act of communicating is perceived as important (Licoppe & Smoreda, 2005).

The array of choices, which bring with them an array of potential benefits or drawbacks require a level of understanding and sophistication as well as management of the communications by those family members living at a distance who wish to stay in contact. This may lead to choices being made by those communicating via ICTs and the Internet on which mode to use depending on intimacy of relationship, the perceived appropriateness of a mode for the message, cost, living in the same time zones, which has been described as either polymedia (Madianou and Miller, 2012) or media multiplexity (Haythornthwaite, 2001; Mesch, 2009).

STRATEGIES FOR NETWORKING: MEDIA AND COMMUNICATION MULTIPLEXITY

Swidler (1986) has argued that derived from their cultural backgrounds individuals have a set of habits and skills which they have at their disposal for managing the social world in everyday life. Individuals having as such "a repertoire or 'tool kit' of habits, skills, and styles from which people construct 'strategies of action'" (Swidler 1986, p. 273). The notion of a 'repertoire' of available strategies and possible actions is useful in framing an individual's behaviour when engaging in ICT mediated communications. Firstly habitual use of certain 'strategies of action' which for Swidler

(1986) are defined by "persistent ways of ordering action through time" (Swidler 1986, p. 273) may result in individuals relying on the same few ways of communicating via ICTs through habit that may lead to reduced options. If considering the use of ICTs, the habitual set of practiced options may be put into place again and again in a way perhaps reducing the communication options employed. Secondly, using the metaphor of 'toolkits', each individual may have different sets of skills and knowledge within their own 'toolkit' leading to different available options. This is linked to the notion that these 'toolkits' reside inside larger 'toolboxes' from which individuals may draw on to manage their social world, however the toolboxes of some may contain more repertoires than others (Swidler 1986).

Developing from Swidler's notion of cultural toolkits and cultural toolboxes, Hogan (2009) describes the combination of ICT used by individuals and the strategies they employ as a 'networking repertoire' (Hogan 2009). Hogan (2009) suggests that, while they may differ from individual to individual, as a repertoire of media uses they are both rhythmic and habitual (Hogan 2009). The identification of a 'networking repertoire' is not dissimilar to models of networking presented by Burt (1997, 1992) of 'information brokering' or Wellman (2002) of 'networked individualism'.

From research focusing on the social uses of ICT, it has been found that not only can people use multiple ICTs in combination but that they also choose which combination to use for which message or contact. This can be done by using their choice of ICTs simultaneously or sequentially (Kim *et al.*, 2007; Stephens *et al.*, 2008). As Quan-Haase and Wellman (2006) have stated regarding the combination of computer mediated communication, face-to-face contact and the telephone, they "serve different communication purposes, often working in synergy and not in competition with one another" (Quan-Haase and Wellman 2006, p.299).

Hogan (2009), from surveying and interviewing Canadian citizens, found that they use multiple forms of ICT to connect with their social network. However it was noted that for the interviewees, being a close contact (stronger tie) was not as much an indicator of who they would communicate with as was the perceived level of social accessibility they had of their contact. The greater the level of social accessibility the more likely they would be in regular contact with them.

Choosing which ICT to use for a certain message or which set of ICTs to mix and match requires knowledge of the capabilities and perceived pros and cons of each mode, leading to the phenomenon of media or communication multiplexity, where multiple ICTs are used to maintain social relationships (Haythornthwaite, 2001; Baym, Zhang, & Lin, 2004; Mesch, 2009; Xie, 2008).

Mesch (2009) found that several factors influence an individual's choice of which ICT enabled communication channel, or set of communication channels to use, such as the location in which the communication takes place, the perceived closeness of the contact, the knowledge of the variety of options the person had to communicate via ICT and the content of the message (Mesch, 2009). Like Kennedy and Wellman (2007), Mesch (2009) found that the location of where the communication was taking place had an effect of whether to text, instant message, video chat or email. For example as with Kennedy and Wellman (2007) the location of a computer in the home indicates which of form of ICT communication are deemed most appropriate (Kennedy & Wellman, 2007).

Yet Hogan (2009) posits that the managing of communication multiplexity can become a burden. That not only do individuals need to develop skills to use ICT to communicate with their network they also need to negotiate which form of ICT they will use with their social network for communication. Neustaedter and Greenberg (2012), while investigating the use of video chat in intimate relationships, found that negotiating suitable times when both parties may be available

and have access to the computer, required the use of other media. Favoured forms of ICTs that were used to check the availability of the communication partner were text messages, instant messages or phone calls (Neustaedter & Greenberg, 2012).

More Valued Forms of ICTs

Discussion around the value placed on live and synchronous communications suggests that the more instantaneous the communication the greater value it will have (Walther & Parks, 2002). Early literature regarding the value and use of ICTs for relationship maintenance suggested that lack of social and visual cues in certain types of ICT enable communications may lead to less rewarding communication with less opportunity for emotional content (Cummings, Butler & Kraut, 2002).

McKenna, Green and Gleason (2002) posit that while the asynchronicity of email does not allow for immediate feedback, email offers the chance for those replying to invest in deeper reflection on their responses and to compose their response more carefully (McKenna, Green and Gleason, 2002). Rettie (2007) noted a preference for less rich media, when studying the uses of Instant Messenger, email, text messages and mobile phones. Opposing previous research which suggested that more social presence and more visual cues lead to a gratifying communication experience, Rettie (2007), found that each of the four technologies were viewed to have advantages, such as abbreviation, length of time invested in reply or the absence of social niceties.

Licoppe and Smoreda, (2004) propose that use of ICT may afford a 'connected presence', so that people manage a combination of mediated communications simultaneously or one after another. Nardi (2005) offers that this readiness to communicate gives others the sign of availability and indicates to them an awareness of the other, resulting in a shared social context or 'common ground' (Licoppe & Smoreda, 2005; Nardi 2005). Boase, Horrigan, Wellman and Rainie (2006), from a large national survey of Internet users in the United States, found that the frequency of the use of media is related to the frequency of communication with personal contacts, the more an individual uses ICT for information seeking, entertainment or educational purposes the more they will connected using ICT with others (Boase, Horrigan, Wellman & Rainie 2006).

The instantaneous and synchronous traits of certain ICTs offer an immediate connection, for example with video-chat, with the inclusion of a visual element it offers the subtleties inherent in face-to-face communications. The potential of an instantaneous connection via ICTs can offer reassurance when an intimate tie is at some distance. However ICTs offer the potential of storing and later retrieval of messages from others. Elliot and Urry (2010) have noted, that within a family context these messages can offer intimacy producing 'shared histories'. And as ICTs, in particular social media sites, by offering shared opportunities such as collaborative uploading can facilitate dialogues memories or histories. For example a photograph may be uploaded, which may then be commented on or amended to by another via adding related photographs and messages. So that while ICTs offer relationship maintenance and repair function, they can also offer a form of containment (Bauman, 2008; Elliot & Urry, 2010).

Photographs in particular have been noted to tell the family story regarding relationships between family members and within the family itself. Photographs themselves both being a family cultural artifact and something, which can shape family life (Sarvas & Frohlich, 2011; Frohlich, 2004). Traditionally photographs in families recorded events which were viewed as celebrations, such as weddings and christenings, but not major family events such as funerals or divorces (Merz, 1988). Within the study of photographs on view in households they were nearly all of family with very few of friends, colleagues or strangers (Halle, 1991).

Petrelli and Whittaker (2010) note that along with important family events such as weddings or births significant periods in a person's life were positioned as important mementos such as time attending university. Research on digital photo sharing tells that families are inclined to mostly share through email, it was found that the extended conversion and feedback around the photos were as valued as highly as the receiving the photos themselves (Frohlich, 2004; Miller & Edwards 2007).

Graham, Satchell and Rouncefield (2007) describe how individuals are producing 'digital documents of life' where they write about and take photographs of their current locations offering reflection through ICTs such as mobile blogs. Cohen (2005) has noted that, not only what may be perceived as special events but more mundane everyday occurrences such as casual meetings or meals are being recorded visually and posted online, offering a stream of mundane mementos (Cohen, 2005). When shared using ICTs such as social network site these may be seen and commented on by people who are close intimate ties as well as those who are weaker ties, as Donath and boyd (2004) note both personal and social communicative acts. So that what may initiate as a personal memory may move toward 'distributed presence' where personal picture of everyday life, even if unintentionally be achieved, commented on and subsequently shared ending up be 'pictures for life' (van Dijick, 2008).

Reflecting, Reminiscing, and Sharing

The potential of an instantaneous connection via ICTs can offer reassurance when an intimate tie is at some distance and ICTs offer both relationship maintenance and repair functions (Bauman, 2008). However, certain ICTs offer the potential of storing and later retrieval of messages from others. Individuals who store digital artifacts such as SMSs, photographs or emails allow themselves the opportunity of subsequent viewing, reassessment or reprocessing of the message or photograph. These acts offer a form of emotional containment (Elliot & Urry, 2010).

Research on digital photo sharing tells that families are inclined to mostly share through email, it was found that the extended conversion and feedback around the photos were as valued as highly as the receiving the photos themselves (Miller & Edwards, 2007).

By recollecting, individuals may retrace steps of past experiences. Also if in a group setting, it can be both pleasurable and an opportunity to share personal or family history. On a more personal level, stored digital artifacts may facilitate reflection on past events and give the opportunity to looking at their past experiences from different perspectives (Peesapati *et al.,* 2010).

EXTENDED USES OF DIGITAL ARTIFACTS

The literature regarding the uses of ICTs by older adults offers a picture of older adults, which is largely, based on either the instantaneous acts of communication itself. Finding from the research study presented here augment this by highlighting and detailing uses and value placed on ICT communications and the subsequent value yielded by the storage and retrieval of the associated digital artifacts. The participants in this study emphasized the importance or emotional support they received form the initial communications, and of particular importance here, later on via the text and images they could review.

The affordances provided by ICT use for giving and receiving emotional support became apparent especially around health issues and other longer running personal issues. Emotional support could be received in what were perceived as a 'difficult time'. When dealing with longer running illnesses, the time during the recovery from a medical procedure or the time spent grieving, the respondents spoke of particularly valuing ICT messages such as emails and SMSs.

Email Communication

The asynchronous nature of email was seen as a benefit in that an inquiry of how someone was doing could be read and importantly saved. Initially, emails and texts offered *'thinking of you'* style reminders to the family member with the health condition. With emails being read and composed by both parties at times that suited them. Catherine described how emails where of comfort to her "I had a problem in the last year and people emailed me all the time...it's very supportive...I could read them again if I was down...it really helps you know".

When sending messages to others, the respondents reported that they could send supportive messages when they had time or when they thought of their friend or family member. Their friend or family member may be at work, unable to access a phone or computer at that time or living at some distance with time zone implications leading to difficulty in a phone call of video chat. For example, thinking of someone on a Wednesday afternoon and being able to send the well wishes then instead of waiting until a time at the weekend when both parties might be free. It also signaled a level of consideration for those having a difficult time so that the need to offer support did not become intrusive. Kathleen explained "I have a friend an 'old lady' in hospital and I would text her in case would not want to interrupt her, and if she had time she would talk to me, if not at least she gets a message to see how she is."

Phone-Messages

The saving and storing of messages was seen to be an unexpected advantage of ICT communication. In particular respondents who recounted their interactions with their social network around health issues reported how texts from their social network would be kept and stored on their mobile phones. The mobile phone was seen a very private personal space. As stated by one respondent 'this is my phone not like the Internet in the library'. The stored messages became digital keepsakes. While spending her days at the hospital after her husband's stroke, Terese found having both new messages arrive and being able to re-read stored messages very supportive.

Terese:

You can't use a phone in there [the hospital ward], but I would get messages to see how their daddy was doing and how I was doing. And they'd say [the hospital staff] you should go home now and rest but I could not sleep with all that going on... but I could keep an eye on the messages and type some back if it was late. It was something to have it ...was a worry you know.

The saved message could be carried with the respondent and re-read if wanted but more importantly the respondent would '*know it's there*'. Respondents reported valuing both portability and having a record of the good intentions. Such messages consisted of wishes of good luck, sympathy or empathy.

Digital Photography

More than half of the participants (16) reported that they would often show the digital photographs on a computer screen to friends visiting at home or in a communal space with computer and Internet access, while more than two thirds of the participants (20) choose to print of photographs to show and discuss in face-to-face settings with friends and neighbors. For example Patrick used a variety of ICT enabled skills and face-to-face information gathering while investigating the whereabouts of classmates.

Patrick:

I have old school photographs and I took them on a digital camera and I put them on my computer. I'm in touch with this guy who I met at a funeral here and he was in them and I'm in touch with him now by email, he's in America. He tells me who is in them [the old photos], going back to the fifties. There are a few in the class we don't know and there's about 30 in the photo and we've tracked most of them down. We found some on Facebook and just found some websites like work or their family's or that. If any of them are back I can bring the picture with me and ask them who is that there. I can send them the picture too, to see what is the name of that fella.

DISCUSSION

Digital artifacts, such as SMS, emails and digital photos, can offer uses beyond their initial communication act. This research offers support to Frohlich (2004) and Miller and Edwards (2007) who reported that photographs shared between family members via email offer extended use and added value through conversations and comments via email around the photographs.

This study's findings suggest that the value and uses of such artifacts can extend beyond use within the family network to offline contexts. This supplements the notion, that not only the act of communicating is valued (Licoppe & Smoreda, 2005) but that having evidence of the communication and the repeated availability of the messages adds value to the communications. Being able to store, review and reread mediated communications such as emails and SMSs, as Bauman (2008) suggests, was found in this study to extend the use and offer extra value to the communication, particularly around difficult times Opalinski (2001) when coping with grief or supporting a loved one through a serious illness.

As value was attached to messages of support or empathy, which were read, reread and at times carried with the older people would suggest that Walther *et al.*'s (2002) argument, that due to reduced social cues mediated communications such as SMS and email necessarily reduce the ability to send and receive interpersonal impressions and warmth, does not hold in all cases. Moreover being able to reread, reminisce and carry with one may increase the emotional value placed on them by the receiver, and that they offer a longer life span than other forms of communications which are simultaneous and may contain full visual representations.

Two aspects are worth noting regarding these messages of support in times of distress. Firstly, they were in times of distress. During times of distress recounting the outcome of an operation or perhaps reporting the prognosis of a medical test repeatedly can be stressful in themselves. Asynchronous media may allow some space and time to compose oneself and afford a level of privacy that a phone call of videochat may not. So that associated with asynchronous communication may be a calmness or gentleness which live communication may not offer. Secondly, the individuals who participated in this study were older adults and were familiar and comfortable with written forms of communications. Their benchmark often reported being that of a family letter or a card for special events. Both letters and cards allow for rereading and portability and notably offer time to compose a response sooner that reply quickly in a reactive fashion.

The individuals who participated in this study were older adults and were familiar and comfortable with traditional forms of communications. In this way it may be suggested that these older adults have transferred both experience and practice from older media to new media.

This study augments our understanding of how older adults use digital communications. The study presents evidence and contextualization of use of digital communications and the associated artifacts beyond their initial communicative acts. This contributes to the wider research and debates regarding ICT use and social support. More specifically it sheds new light on current research themes, which seek to understand how citizens may integrate and exploit ICTs when faced with a more mobile and dissipated extended families in the twenty-first century.

FUTURE RESEARCH DIRECTIONS

As we study the uses and effects of ICT's and the Internet regarding older adults we may find that we have much to learn from those not fully integrated into the main activities of the information society. As ICTs and the Internet become more and more embedded into daily life, beyond the work place or education settings, almost to the point of invisibility it is useful to have some type of snapshot and social history of these relatively early years of adoption and use by a generation that will most likely not exist again. That is, individuals who as adults who have had little if no exposure to ICT's. As younger people are getting older and that eventually almost all older people will have been using the Internet from a young age, in Western countries at least and in the near future it will be difficult to find anyone - in Ireland certainly and the developed world more generally - who does not use the internet to communicate. To focus on a part of society like this will at least offer important social history but mostly likely original interpretations and particular uses and understandings of these new technologies.

With studies exploring possibilities of the next web developments, the potential affordances these and rates of adoption, the impact on social and importantly from the perspective of this chapter, the emotional lives of those who maintain connections via the web and other online environments will prove more and more worthy of study. So that frameworks and theories such as social shaping / domestication of technology or more technologically deterministic viewpoints of technologies, will find more areas to contrast and interplay to give our understanding of the impact and effects of ICTs and the Internet on us.

There may also be a greater call for more a longitudinal research in general but specifically of older adults engagement with ICTs and the Internet, particularly as mobile platforms become more normative.

Yet while this chapter delves into technologies and ways to communicating heralded as Web 2.0. We note with interest that what was announced and promised as a tidal wave of change, even with the current pace of change, has taken almost ten years to become embedded in substantial portions of the populations daily lives. The greater depth of sematic tagging and more vernacular colloquial and localized labeling of content on the web their may be more changes especially regarding lay person investigating things like health matters – still a top element for older adults.

Also it is key to note that many of the used and value placed against there new way so communicating seem to be based on earlier forms of communicated – the handwritten letter, the printed photograph. Will these still be useful or indeed metaphors used with the evolutions of technologies and the fact that more and more people are being exposed to these types of technologies. For example, there is increasingly greater exposure of more and more individuals to technologies, especially ICTs in their workplace setting. With greater parts of the population engaging with what would have been considered regarding of their workplaces being particularly technology focused or requiring what would have been seen as archetypal knowledge worker (Drucker, 2011) or those more ordinarily working in the information society (Webster, 2014). A person who is likely to retire in ten years from now will have had much greater opportunities to engage with ICTs both in professional, workplace and home/family settings.

CONCLUSION

The research focusing on older adults and Internet use finds that certain barriers or perceived barriers exist, which consists of lack of training, cost of equipment and ISP subscriptions, lack of knowledge regarding potential benefits of ICT use and anxiety about the technology. Older users engage with technology at different levels of use regarding time and sophistication of use. Some older adults will embed the use of ICTs into everyday lives using it daily and displaying independence and high levels of understandings of online media. Others will use them occasionally as a supplementary source of information and connection to other they already know, while others having been introduced to ICTs will revert to the use by proxy of ICTs, in particular the Internet, on an occasional basis. The effectiveness of older people participating was linked to localised support and tuition sustained over a long period.

The concept of digital keepsakes, where individuals store and re-engage with messages or other digital artifacts that offer comfort or support in times of need, offers insight into the use and reuse of ICT and Internet communications. This can be understood to have a recurring value beyond the immediate communication act and be highly regarded by individuals on emotional and social levels.

The sharing of digital artifacts on screen or printing photographs from social network sites also offers extended use of ICT and Internet communications which offer new talking points either with friends at home or within the community, extending the value and benefits of digital artifacts from a personal onscreen experience to face-to-to contexts.

REFERENCES

Ames, M. G., Go, J., Kaye, J. J., & Spasojevic, M. (2010, February). Making love in the network closet: The benefits and work of family videochat. In *Proceedings of the 2010 ACM Conference on Computer Supported Cooperative Work* (pp. 145-154). ACM. doi:10.1145/1718918.1718946

Antonucci, T. (2001). Social relations: An examination of social networks, social support, and sense of control. In Handbook of psychology of aging (5th ed.; pp. 427-453). San Diego, CA: Academic Press.

Bailey, A., & Ngwenyama, O. (2010). Bridging the generation gap in ICT use: Interrogating identity, technology and interactions in community telecenters. *Information Technology for Development*, *16*(1), 62–82. doi:10.1080/02681100903566156

Baldassar, L. (2007). Transnational families and the provision of moral and emotional support: The relationship between truth and distance. *Identities: Global Studies in Culture and Power*, *14*(4), 385–409. doi:10.1080/10702890701578423

Baldassar, L. (2008). Missing kin and longing to be together: Emotions and the construction of copresence in transnational relationships. *Journal of Intercultural Studies (Melbourne, Vic.)*, *29*(3), 247–266. doi:10.1080/07256860802169196

Barnard, Y., Bradley, M. D., Hodgson, F., & Lloyd, A. D. (2013). Learning to use new technologies by older adults: Perceived difficulties, experimentation behaviour and usability. *Computers in Human Behavior*, *29*(4), 1715–1724. doi:10.1016/j.chb.2013.02.006

Bauman, Z. (2008). *The art of life*. Cambridge, MA: Polity.

Baym, N. K., Zhang, Y. B., & Lin, M. (2004). Social interactions across media: Interpersonal communication on the internet, telephone and face-to-face. *New Media & Society*, *6*(3), 299–318. doi:10.1177/1461444804041438

Biocca, F., Burgoon, J., Harm, C., & Stoner, M. (2001). Criteria and scope conditions for a theory and measure of social presence. East Lansing, MI: Media Interface and Network Design (M.I.N.D.) Lab.

Boase, J., Horrigan, J. B., Wellman, B., & Rainie, L. (2006). *Pew report: The strength of internet ties*. Washington, DC: Pew Internet and American Life Project.

Brekke, M. (2008). Young refugees in a network society. In *Mobility and place: Enacting Northern European peripheries* (pp. 103-114). Academic Press.

Cacioppo, J. T., Hughes, M. E., Waite, L. J., Hawkley, L. C., & Thisted, R. A. (2006). Loneliness as a specific risk factor for depressive symptoms: Cross-sectional and longitudinal analyses. *Psychology and Aging*, *21*(1), 140–151. doi:10.1037/0882-7974.21.1.140 PMID:16594799

Cairncross, F. (1997). *The death of distance: How the communications revolution is changing our lives*. Boston: Harvard Business School Press.

Charles, S., & Carstensen, L. L. (2010). Social and emotional aging. *Annual Review of Psychology*, *61*(1), 383–409. doi:10.1146/annurev.psych.093008.100448 PMID:19575618

Cohen, K. R. (2005). What does the photoblog want? *Media Culture & Society*, *27*(6), 883–901. doi:10.1177/0163443705057675

Cornwell, B. (2011). Independence through social networks: Bridging potential among older women and men. *The Journals of Gerontology. Series B, Psychological Sciences and Social Sciences*, gbr111. PMID:21983039

Cornwell, B., Laumann, E. O., & Schumm, L. P. (2008). The social connectedness of older adults: A national profile. *American Sociological Review*, *73*(2), 185–203. doi:10.1177/000312240807300201 PMID:19018292

Cornwell, E. Y., & Waite, L. J. (2009). Social disconnectedness, perceived isolation, and health among older adults. *Journal of Health and Social Behavior*, *50*(1), 31–48. doi:10.1177/002214650905000103 PMID:19413133

Cotten, S. R., Anderson, W. A., & McCullough, B. M. (2013). Impact of internet use on loneliness and contact with others among older adults: Cross-sectional analysis. *Journal of Medical Internet Research*, *15*(2), e39. doi:10.2196/jmir.2306 PMID:23448864

Cummings, J. N., Butler, B., & Kraut, R. (2002). The quality of online social relationships. *Communications of the ACM*, *45*(7), 103–108. doi:10.1145/514236.514242

Czaja, S. J., Sharit, J., Lee, C. C., Nair, S. N., Hernández, M. A., Arana, N., & Fu, S. H. (2013). Factors influencing use of an e-health website in a community sample of older adults. *Journal of the American Medical Informatics Association*, *20*(2), 277–284. doi:10.1136/amiajnl-2012-000876 PMID:22802269

Dekker, R., & Engbersen, G. (2014). How social media transform migrant networks and facilitate migration. *Global Networks*, *14*(4), 401–418. doi:10.1111/glob.12040

Diminescu, D. (2008). The connected migrant: An epistemological manifesto. *Social Sciences Information. Information Sur les Sciences Sociales*, *47*(4), 565–579. doi:10.1177/0539018408096447

Donath, J., & Boyd, D. (2004). Public displays of connection. *BT Technology Journal*, *22*(4), 71-82.

Drucker, P. (2011). *The age of discontinuity: Guidelines to our changing society*. Transaction Publishers.

Elliott, A., & Urry, J. (2010). *Mobile lives*. New York: Routledge.

Farquhar, M. (1995). Definitions of quality of life: A taxonomy. *Journal of Advanced Nursing*, *22*(3), 502–508. doi:10.1046/j.1365-2648.1995.22030502.x PMID:7499618

Fast, J., Gierveld, J. D. J., & Keating, N. (2008). Ageing, disability and participation. In Rural ageing: A good place to grow old? (pp. 63-73). Bristol, MA: Polocy Press.

Feist, H. R., Parker, K., & Hugo, G. (2012). Older and online: Enhancing social connections in Australian rural places. *The Journal of Community Informatics*, *8*(1).

Forghani, A., Neustaedter, C., & Schiphorst, T. (2013). Investigating the communication patterns of distance-separated grandparents and grandchildren. In Proceedings of CHI'13 Extended Abstracts on Human Factors in Computing Systems (pp. 67-72). ACM. doi:10.1145/2468356.2468370

Forsman, A. K., Herberts, C., Nyqvist, F., Wahlbeck, K., & Schierenbeck, I. (2013). Understanding the role of social capital for mental wellbeing among older adults. *Ageing and Society*, *33*(05), 804–825. doi:10.1017/S0144686X12000256

Fox, S. (2001). *Wired seniors: A fervent few, inspired by family ties*. Pew Internet & American Life Project.

Fox, S. (2004). *Older Americans and the internet*. Washington, DC: Pew Research Center.

Frohlich, D. (2004). *Audiophotography: Bringing photos to life with sounds*. Berlin: Springer-Verlag. doi:10.1007/978-1-4020-2210-4

Gardner, P. J., Kamber, T., & Netherland, J. (2012). "Getting turned on": Using ICT training to promote active ageing in New York City. *The Journal of Community Informatics, 8*(1).

Gatto, S. L., & Tak, S. H. (2008). Computer, internet, and e-mail use among older adults: Benefits and barriers. *Educational Gerontology, 34*(9), 800–811. doi:10.1080/03601270802243697

Gonzalez, A., Ramirez, M. P., & Viadel, V. (2012). Attitudes of the elderly toward information and communications technologies. *Educational Gerontology, 38*(9), 585–594. doi:10.1080/03601277.2011.595314

Graham, C., Satchell, C., & Rouncefield, M. (2007). Sharing places: Digital content and lived life. In *Proceedings of Shared Encounters Workshop at CHI'07*. ACM.

Groves, D. L., & Slack, T. (1994). Computers and their application to senior citizen therapy within a nursing home. *Journal of Instructional Psychology*.

Halle, D. (1991). Displaying the dream: The visual presentation of family and self in the modern American household. *Journal of Comparative Family Studies*, 217–229.

Hawkley, L. C., & Cacioppo, J. T. (2013). Loneliness and health. In *Encyclopedia of behavioral medicine* (pp. 1172–1176). New York: Springer.

Haythornthwaite, C. (2001). Exploring multiplexity: Social network structures in a computer-supported distance learning class. *The Information Society, 17*(3), 211–226. doi:10.1080/01972240152493065

Hendrix, C. C. (1999). Computer use among elderly people. *Computers in Nursing, 18*(2), 62–68. PMID:10740912

Hiller, H. H., & Franz, T. M. (2004). New ties, old ties and lost ties: The use of the internet in diaspora. *New Media & Society, 6*(6), 731–752. doi:10.1177/146144804044327

Hogan, B. J. (2009). *Networking in everyday life*. (Ph.D. dissertation). Graduate Department of Sociology, University of Toronto, Toronto, Canada.

Horst, H. A. (2006). The blessings and burdens of communication: Cell phones in Jamaican transnational social fields. *Global Networks, 6*(2), 143–159. doi:10.1111/j.1471-0374.2006.00138.x

Huang, S., & Yeoh, B. S. (2007). Emotional labour and transnational domestic work: The moving geographies of 'maid abuse' in Singapore. *Mobilities, 2*(2), 195–217. doi:10.1080/17450100701381557

Huber, L. L., Shankar, K., Caine, K., Connelly, K., Camp, L. J., Walker, B. A., & Borrero, L. (2013). How in-home technologies mediate caregiving relationships in later life. *International Journal of Human-Computer Interaction, 29*(7), 441–455. doi:10.1080/10447318.2012.715990

Ito, M. (2005). Mobile phones, Japanese youth and the replacement of social contact. In R. Ling & P. Pedersen (Eds.), *Mobile communications: Renegotiation of the social sphere* (pp. 131–148). London: Springer. doi:10.1007/1-84628-248-9_9

Jones, S., & Fox, S. (2009). *Generations online in 2009*. Washington, DC: Pew Internet & American Life Project.

Jordan, A. (2010). *What benefit? The outcome of the "BenefIT" scheme*. Department of Communications, Energy & Natural Resources.

Judge, T. K., & Neustaedter, C. (2010, April). Sharing conversation and sharing life: video conferencing in the home. In *Proceedings of the SIGCHI Conference on Human Factors in Computing Systems* (pp. 655-658). ACM. doi:10.1145/1753326.1753422

Katz, J., & Aakhus, M. (Eds.). (2002). *Perpetual contact: Mobile communication, private talk, public performance.* Cambridge, UK: Cambridge University Press. doi:10.1017/CBO9780511489471

Kennedy, T. L. M., & Wellman, B. (2007). The networked household. *Information Communication and Society, 10*(5), 645–670. doi:10.1080/13691180701658012

Komito, L. (2011). Social media and migration: Virtual community 2.0. *Journal of the American Society for Information Science and Technology, 62*(6), 1075–1086. doi:10.1002/asi.21517

Komito, L., & Bates, J. (2012). Migration, community and social media. In Transnationalism in the global city. Bilbao, Spain: University of Deusto.

Koskinen, I. (2004, June). Seeing with mobile images: Towards perpetual visual contact. In *Proceedings of T-Mobile Hungary 2004 Conference.* Academic Press.

Koskinen, I. (2004, June). Seeing with mobile images: Towards perpetual visual contact. In *Proceedings of T-Mobile Hungary 2004 Conference.* Academic Press.

Lee, C., & Coughlin, J. F. (2014). Older adults' Adoption of technology: An integrated approach to identifying determinants and barriers. *Journal of Product Innovation Management.* doi:10.1111/jpim.12176

Licoppe, C. (2004). Connected presence: The emergence of a new repertoire for managing social relationships in a changing communication technoscape. *Environment and Planning. D, Society & Space, 22*(1), 135–156. doi:10.1068/d323t

Licoppe, C., & Smoreda, Z. (2005). Are social networks technologically embedded?: How networks are changing today with changes in communication technology. *Social Networks, 27*(4), 317–335. doi:10.1016/j.socnet.2004.11.001

Madianou, M., & Miller, D. (2011). *Migration and new media: Transnational families and polymedia.* New York: Routledge.

Mahler, S. J. (2001). Transnational relationships: The struggle to communicate across borders. *Identities (Yverdon), 7*(4), 583–619. doi:10.1080/1070289X.2001.9962679

Malinowski, B. (1923). The problem of meaning in primitive languages. In C. K. Ogden & I. A. Richards (Eds.), *The meaning of meaning* (pp. 296–355). London: Routledge and Kegan Paul.

McConatha, D. (2002). Aging online: Toward a theory of e-quality. In *Older adults, health information, and the world wide web* (pp. 21-41). Academic Press.

McKenna, K. Y., Green, A. S., & Gleason, M. E. (2002). Relationship formation on the internet: What's the big attraction? *The Journal of Social Issues, 58*(1), 9–31. doi:10.1111/1540-4560.00246

McMillan, S. J., & Macias, W. (2008). Strengthening the safety net for online seniors: Factors influencing differences in health information seeking among older internet users. *Journal of Health Communication, 13*(8), 778–792. doi:10.1080/10810730802487448 PMID:19051113

McPherson, M., Smith-Lovin, L., & Brashears, M. E. (2006). Social isolation in America: Changes in core discussion networks over two decades. *American Sociological Review, 71*(3), 353–375. doi:10.1177/000312240607100301

Melenhorst, A. S., Rogers, W. A., & Bouwhuis, D. G. (2006). Older adults' motivated choice for technological innovation: Evidence for benefit-driven selectivity. *Psychology and Aging, 21*(1), 190–195. doi:10.1037/0882-7974.21.1.190 PMID:16594804

Merz, C. (1988). Smile, please. *New Statesman & Society, 1*(10), 42.

Mesch, G. S. (2009). Social context and communication channels choice among adolescents. *Computers in Human Behavior, 25*(1), 244–251. doi:10.1016/j.chb.2008.09.007

Mikal, J. P., Rice, R. E., Abeyta, A., & DeVilbiss, J. (2013). Transition, stress and computer-mediated social support. *Computers in Human Behavior, 29*(5), A40–A53. doi:10.1016/j.chb.2012.12.012

Miller, A. D., & Edwards, W. K. (2007). Give and take: A study of consumer photo-sharing culture and practice. In *Proceedings of the SIGCHI Conference on Human Factors in Computing Systems* (pp. 347-356). ACM. doi:10.1145/1240624.1240682

Milliken, M., O'Donnell, S., Gibson, K., & Daniels, B. (2012). Older adults and video communications: A case study. *The Journal of Community Informatics, 8*(1).

Nahm, E. S., & Resnick, B. (2001). Homebound older adults' experiences with the internet and e-mail. *Computers in Nursing, 19*(6), 257–263. PMID:11764717

Nardi, B. A. (2005). Beyond bandwidth: Dimensions of connection in interpersonal communication. *Computer Supported Cooperative Work, 14*(2), 91–130. doi:10.1007/s10606-004-8127-9

Neustaedter, C., & Greenberg, S. (2012, May). Intimacy in long-distance relationships over video chat. In *Proceedings of the SIGCHI Conference on Human Factors in Computing Systems* (pp. 753-762). ACM. doi:10.1145/2207676.2207785

Neves, B. B., & Amaro, F. (2012). Too old for technology? How the elderly of Lisbon use and perceive ICT. *The Journal of Community Informatics, 8*(1).

Nimrod, G. (2012). Online communities as a resource in older adults' tourism. *The Journal of Community Informatics, 8*(1).

Norval, C. (2012). Understanding the incentives of older adults' participation on social networking sites. *ACM Sigaccess Accessibility and Computing*, (102), 25-29.

Nyqvist, F., Forsman, A. K., Giuntoli, G., & Cattan, M. (2013). Social capital as a resource for mental well-being in older people: A systematic review. *Aging & Mental Health, 17*(4), 394–410. doi:10.1080/13607863.2012.742490 PMID:23186534

Ogozalek, V. Z. (1991). The social impacts of computing: Computer technology and the graying of America. *Social Science Computer Review, 9*(4), 655–666. doi:10.1177/089443939100900409

Opalinski, L. (2001). Older adults and the digital divide: Assessing results of a web-based survey. *Journal of Technology in Human Services, 18*(3-4), 203–221. doi:10.1300/J017v18n03_13

Peesapati, S. T., Schwanda, V., Schultz, J., Lepage, M., Jeong, S. Y., & Cosley, D. (2010). Pensieve: supporting everyday reminiscence. In *Proceedings of the SIGCHI Conference on Human Factors in Computing Systems* (pp. 2027-2036). ACM.

Pertierra, R. (2006). *Transforming technologies: Altered selves*. Manila: De La Salle University Press.

Petrelli, D., & Whittaker, S. (2010). Family memories in the home: Contrasting physical and digital mementos. *Personal and Ubiquitous Computing, 14*(2), 153–169. doi:10.1007/s00779-009-0279-7

Prensky, M. (2005). Listen to the natives. *Educational Leadership, 63*(4).

Rettie, R. (2007). *A Comparison of four new communication technologies: Research repository.* London: Kingston University.

Rettie, R. (2008). Mobile phones as network capital: Facilitating connections. *Mobilities, 3*(2), 291–311. doi:10.1080/17450100802095346

Rideout, V., & Newman, T. (2005). *E-health and the elderly: How seniors use the internet for health information: Key findings from a national survey of older Americans.* Menlo Park, CA: Kaiser Family Foundation.

Russell, C., Campbell, A., & Hughes, I. (2008). Ageing, social capital and the Internet: Findings from an exploratory study of Australian 'silver surfers'. *Australasian Journal on Ageing, 27*(2), 78–82. doi:10.1111/j.1741-6612.2008.00284.x PMID:18713197

Sarvas, R., & Frohlich, D. M. (2011). *From snapshots to social media: The changing picture of domestic photography.* London: Springer. doi:10.1007/978-0-85729-247-6

Selwyn, N., & Facer, K. (2007). *Beyond the digital divide: Rethinking digital inclusion for the 21st century.* Bristol: FutureLab.

Skrbiš, Z. (2008). Transnational families: Theorising migration, emotions and belonging. *Journal of Intercultural Studies (Melbourne, Vic.), 29*(3), 231–246. doi:10.1080/07256860802169188

Sum, S., Mathews, R. M., & Hughes, I. (2009). Participation of older adults in cyberspace: How Australian older adults use the internet. *Australasian Journal on Ageing, 28*(4), 189–193. doi:10.1111/j.1741-6612.2009.00374.x PMID:19951340

Swidler, A. (1986). Culture in action: Symbols and strategies. *American Sociological Review, 51*(2), 273–286. doi:10.2307/2095521

Tapscott, D. (2008). *Grown up digital: How the net generation is changing your world.* New York: McGraw-Hill.

Van Dijck, J. (2008). Digital photography: Communication, identity, memory. *Visual Communication, 7*(1), 57–76. doi:10.1177/1470357207084865

Victor, C. R., Scambler, S. J., Bowling, A. N. N., & Bond, J. (2005). The prevalence of, and risk factors for, loneliness in later life: A survey of older people in Great Britain. *Ageing and Society, 25*(06), 357–375. doi:10.1017/S0144686X04003332

Wagner, N., Hassanein, K., & Head, M. (2010). Computer use by older adults: A multi-disciplinary review. *Computers in Human Behavior, 26*(5), 870–882. doi:10.1016/j.chb.2010.03.029

Walther, J. B., Loh, T., & Granka, L. (2005). Let me count the ways the interchange of verbal and nonverbal cues in computer-mediated and face-to-face affinity. *Journal of Language and Social Psychology, 24*(1), 36–65. doi:10.1177/0261927X04273036

Walther, J. B., & Parks, M. R. (2002). Cues filtered out, cues filtered. In Handbook of interpersonal communication (vol. 3, pp. 529-563). Academic Press.

Warburton, J., Cowan, S., & Bathgate, T. (2013). Building social capital among rural, older Australians through information and communication technologies: A review article. *Australasian Journal on Ageing, 32*(1), 8–14. doi:10.1111/j.1741-6612.2012.00634.x PMID:23521728

Weatherall, J. W. A. (2000). A grounded theory analysis of older adults and information technology. *Educational Gerontology, 26*(4), 371–386. doi:10.1080/036012700407857

Webster, F. (2014). *Theories of the information society.* New York: Routledge.

Wilding, R. (2006). 'Virtual' intimacies? Families communicating across transnational contexts. *Global Networks*, 6(2), 125–142. doi:10.1111/j.1471-0374.2006.00137.x

Wilkinson, R. G., & Marmot, M. G. (Eds.). (2003). *Social determinants of health: The solid facts*. World Health Organization.

Xie, B. (2008). Multimodal computer-mediated communication and social support among older Chinese internet users. *Journal of Computer-Mediated Communication*, 13(3), 728–750. doi:10.1111/j.1083-6101.2008.00417.x

ADDITIONAL READING

Adams, N., Stubbs, D., & Woods, V. (2005). Psychological barriers to Internet usage among older adults in the UK. *Informatics for Health & Social Care*, 30(1), 3–17. doi:10.1080/14639230500066876 PMID:16036626

Baldassar, L. (2007). Transnational families and aged care: The mobility of care and the migrancy of ageing. *Journal of Ethnic and Migration Studies*, 33(2), 275–297. doi:10.1080/13691830601154252

Bauman, Z. (2013). *Liquid modernity*. Cambridge: Polity Press.

Baym, N. K. (2010). *Personal connections in the digital age*. Cambridge: Polity Press.

Chen, Y., Lee, B., & Kirk, R. M. (2012). Internet Use among Older Adults: Constraints and Opportunities. *Engaging Older Adults with Modern Technology: Internet Use and Information Access Needs: Internet Use and Information Access Needs*, 124.

Czaja, S. J., & Lee, C. C. (2007). The impact of aging on access to technology. *Universal Access in the Information Society*, 5(4), 341–349. doi:10.1007/s10209-006-0060-x

Elliott, A., & Urry, J. (2010). *Mobile lives*. New York: Routledge.

Gardner, P. J., Kamber, T., & Netherland, J. (2012). "Getting Turned On": Using ICT Training To Promote Active Ageing In New York City. *The Journal of Community Informatics*, 8(1).

Garrido, M., Sey, A., Hart, T., & Santana, L. (2012). Literature review of how telecentres operate and have an impact on e-inclusion. *European Union*.

Gatto, S. L., & Tak, S. H. (2008). Computer, Internet, and e-mail use among older adults: Benefits and barriers. *Educational Gerontology*, 34(9), 800–811. doi:10.1080/03601270802243697

Hirsch, E., & Silverstone, R. (Eds.). (2003). *Consuming technologies: media and information in domestic spaces*. Routledge.

Huang, C. (2010). Internet use and psychological well-being: A meta-analysis. *Cyberpsychology, Behavior, and Social Networking*, 13(3), 241–249. doi:10.1089/cyber.2009.0217 PMID:20557242

Jones, S., & Fox, S. (2009). *Generations online in 2009* (pp. 1–9). Washington, DC: Pew Internet & American Life Project.

Komito, L. (2011). Social media and migration: Virtual community 2.0. *Journal of the American Society for Information Science and Technology*, 62(6), 1075–1086. doi:10.1002/asi.21517

Kommers, P., Isaias, P., & Issa, T. (Eds.). (2014). *Perspectives on Social Media: A Yearbook*. New York: Routledge.

Ling, R. S. (2008). *New tech, new ties*. Cambridge, MA: MIT Press.

Maaß, W. (2011). The elderly and the Internet: How senior citizens deal with online privacy. In *Privacy online* (pp. 235–249). Berlin: Springer.

Madden, M. (2010). Older adults and social media. *Pew Internet & American Life Project, 27*.

Madianou, M., & Miller, D. (2011). *Migration and new media: Transnational families and polymedia*. New York: Routledge.

Milliken, M., ODonnell, S., Gibson, K., & Daniels, B. (2012). Older adults and video communications: A case study. *The Journal of Community Informatics, 8*(1).

Olsen, J. K. B., Pedersen, S. A., & Hendricks, V. F. (2012). *A Companion to the Philosophy of Technology*. Oxford: John Wiley & Sons.

Rainie, L., & Wellman, B. (2012). *Networked: The new social operating system*. Cambridge, Mass: MIT Press.

Sayago, S., Sloan, D., & Blat, J. (2011). Everyday use of computer-mediated communication tools and its evolution over time: An ethnographical study with older people. *Interacting with Computers, 23*(5), 543–554. doi:10.1016/j.intcom.2011.06.001

Selwyn, N., Gorard, S., Furlong, J., & Madden, L. (2003). Older adults' use of information and communications technology in everyday life. *Ageing and Society, 23*(05), 561–582. doi:10.1017/S0144686X03001302

Shapira, N., Barak, A., & Gal, I. (2007). Promoting older adults' well-being through Internet training and use.

Sum, S., Mathews, R., & Hughes, I. (2009). 'Participation of older adults in cyberspace: How Australian older adults use the Internet'. *Australasian Journal on Ageing, 28*(4), 189–193. doi:10.1111/j.1741-6612.2009.00374.x PMID:19951340

Zhao, S., & Elesh, D. (2008). Copresence as 'being with'. *Information Communication and Society, 11*(4), 565–583. doi:10.1080/13691180801998995

Zheng, R., Hill, R. D., & Gardner, M. K. (2013). *Engaging Older Adults with Modern Technology: Internet Use and Information Access Needs*. Information Science Reference. doi:10.4018/978-1-4666-1966-1

KEY TERMS AND DEFINITIONS

Digital Artifact: Any type of item produced and stored as digitally or electronically. For example text document, video, images or audio. Important characteristics for this chapter is being able to readily retrieve and subsequently review the artifact. Of interest is the portably via handheld/mobile devices such as phones.

Digital Keepsakes: Where individuals store and re-engage with messages or other digital artifacts originated from mediated communications – particularly when they that offer comfort or support in times of need.

Emotional Containment: The affordance of digital artifacts and communication which offers security, reflection and an establishment of an individual's boundaries, can help establish a safe feeling or space.

Media Multiplexity: Using more than one media to communicate, which may support each other to offer management of each channel, or may be chosen by the user for specific purposes and messages because of the message conent or message recieveer.be chosen by the user.

Networked Individualism: Describes how, rather than being embedded in groups people have become networked as individuals. In place of the family, neighborhood or work it is the person who becomes the focus it is the person who is the focus.

Older Adults: Persons 65 years of age and older.

Social Affordances: The opportunities which for communication, building and maintaining relationships, and gathering information which the ICT's can offer and subsequently influence everyday life. These may include being always connected, personalization (both of incoming sources of information and outgoing represen- tations), portably (being able to communicate and gather information without being tied to a particular machine or place) or globalized con- nectivity (distance and state boundaries becoming considerably less important when communicating due to cheaper costs and both one-to-one and one-to-many).

Social History: Studies of the experiences of ordinary people in the past with emphasis on the individual or social structures and processes as opposed to political, military, diplomatic and constitutional structures.

Chapter 8
Saving Face in Online Learning:
New Directions in Teaching and E-Learning

Lena Paulo Kushnir
OCAD University, Canada

Kenneth Berry
OCAD University, Canada

ABSTRACT

Advancements in technology and innovations in education allow universities to entertain new ways of teaching and learning. This chapter presents quasi-experimental data of how various online tools and teaching strategies impact student learning outcomes, satisfaction, and engagement. Specific variables impacting social presence, affect, cognition, etc., were tested to determine their impact on different student outcomes such as grades, feelings of isolation, student engagement, and perceived authenticity of course materials in a second-year Introductory Psychology course. Findings suggest that, despite the literature, only some factors had a significant impact on student outcomes and that while some course activities transferred well online, others did not; peer activities and participation in some course components particularly were hindered online. Considered here are students' experiences with online learning, including hybrid and inverted courses, and teaching strategies that help meet challenges in different higher-education learning contexts.

INTRODUCTION

Advancements in technology and innovations in education allow universities around the world to think up new ways of teaching and learning that can sometimes help instructors avoid barriers encountered in traditional educational contexts. Technology drives and enables a lot of the new

and different methods of online teaching and innovation that we hear so much about in the media, amongst our colleagues, and across institutions. Some views of what higher education should look like today include that it be easily accessed by anyone who wants to be educated, that it cost less than it currently does, and that there be a significant increase in student engagement, student experi-

DOI: 10.4018/978-1-4666-8147-7.ch008

ence, and the quality of education. Whether for online, hybrid or blended courses, or some other learning context, instructors are often wary of using too much technology since it can be distracting. They worry that some educational technologies can take something away from their teaching or negatively impact students' learning experience. There is an argument to be made that one can use technology in ways that brings groups of learners together. For example, utilize technologies and devices in the classroom that students are using anyways (in their daily interactions), and embrace those technologies in ways that create meaningful course interactions rather than distractions, or use them in ways that empower both instructors and students, and engages them online (outside of the classroom) or even inside of the classroom.

It seems obvious that online learning technologies can help instructors to innovate, but what is the evidence that online learning, or the available tools and the teaching strategies supported by those tools, facilitate learning? Presented here are findings from a three part quasi-experiment research series that considers teaching strategies and educational technologies that push learning beyond boundaries often found in different teaching contexts. Boundaries considered here include social presence, affect, perceived authenticity of a course, student interactions, behaviour and cognition. *Study-One* of this research series (conducted in the summer of 2012), was published elsewhere (Berry & Paulo Kushnir, 2013). Data from *Study-One* compared face-to-face and online teaching and learning; in this chapter, *Study-Two* (conducted in the summer of 2013) and *Study-Three* (conducted in the summer of 2014) add new data on teaching approaches, strategies, course and curriculum design that focus only on online teaching and learning. This chapter extends our work published elsewhere (Paulo Kushnir & Berry, 2014), updating details, elaborating the content, and enhancing the results with newly obtained results (*i.e.,* data from *Study-Three*). Specific variables impacting social presence, affect,

student interactions, behaviour, cognition, *etc.,* where tested to determine their impact on different student outcomes (*e.g.,* quiz, test, and exam scores, final course grades, feelings of isolation, student engagement and satisfaction, feeling like the course, instructor and course materials were authentic, *etc.*) in a second-year Introduction to Psychology course. Results show that, despite the literature, only some factors had a significant impact on student outcomes.

LITERATURE REVIEW

Enrollments in online education continue to grow at a quicker pace than enrollments overall in higher education. As many universities and colleges struggle with issues of space, scheduling conflicts and budget cuts, some believe that online education offers cost effective alternatives to traditional classroom teaching (Allen & Seaman, 2010, 2013; Carey & Trick, 2013). In 2010 the Sloan Consortium reported that online enrollments were up 17%, compared to 12% the previous year (Parry, 2010). In 2011, at least 33% of college students had participated in at least one online course and the majority of these students (over 82%) were undergraduates (Allen & Seaman, 2011; Parry, 2010; Salcedo, 2010).

Online courses are convenient in higher education, alleviating constraints of time and space of traditional face-to-face courses, allowing institutions to offer more courses, and effectively meet the growing and changing needs of students (Allen & Seaman, 2013; Carey & Trick, 2013; Gould, 2003; Gupta & Lei, 2010; Macon, 2011). The literature is positive for the most part; some argue that it might be more cost effective for institutions to offer online courses since they often require less overhead than face-to-face courses with the necessity for physical classrooms. Others argue that online courses expand the reach of the institution, potentially attracting international students and possibly increasing institutional revenue. Some consider online courses as a way of retaining undergraduates and ensuring that they graduate on time, while others see the benefits of allowing students to learn at their own pace, the flexibility around studying and working (either part-time or full-time), the related savings on commuting, of childcare, *etc.*, (Allen & Seaman, 2013; Lei & Govra, 2010; Lockwood & Esselstein, 2013; Macon, 2011; Salcedo, 2010; Wuensch, Aziz, Ozan, Kishore & Tabrizi, 2008).

Online learning is not always viewed positively. Some curriculum committees routinely question the academic rigor of online courses (particularly science courses) and express concern about academic integrity, and worry that academic rigor is often compromised to facilitate online delivery (Schoenfeld-Tacher, McConnell, & Graham, 2001). Before institutions invest in online courses, it is important that there be added value, a positive impact on student learning and engagement, and assurances that rigor and academic integrity are maintained.

Some authors argue that the development of on online assets consumes tremendous amounts of resources, time and effort, and can increase the workload of faculty, taking 2 to 3 times more time (and in some cases more, amounting to hundreds of hours of work) to prepare and deliver compared to the time required to prepare and deliver traditional face-to-face curriculum (Campbell, Horton, Craig, & Gries, 2014; Pallof & Pratt, 2007). Most of this time is likely due to the increased effort required to develop online activities and materials (*e.g.*, coming up with engaging activities, recording and editing lecture videos, managing and uploading the resulting large files, *etc.*, Campbell *et al.*, 2014). Despite the extra work, over 30% of faculty report teaching online and this is increasing (Simson, Smaldino, Albright, & Zvacek, 2006).

Consistent with Means, Toyama, Murphy, Bakia and Jones (2009), for this study, online learning is defined as learning that takes place partially or entirely over the internet. This definition excludes purely print-based correspondence education, broadcast television or radio, video conferencing, video cassettes, and standalone educational software programs that do not have a significant internet based instructional component.

Student Engagement and Interaction in Online Courses

While the literature is generally positive about online interactions, and some authors report high levels of student engagement and interaction (Schoenfeld-Tacher *et al.*, 2001), classroom interactions and feelings of community are often the reported benefits of traditional face-to-face courses (Homberg-Wright & Wright, 2012). When considering learning outcomes and types of interactions, (*e.g.*, using Blooms Taxonomy of learning objectives), some authors report high-level interactions in online courses compared to face-to-face courses (Schoenfeld-Tacher *et al.*, 2001). Some students rate the faculty-to-student interactions in online courses to be about the same as those face-to-face courses (Allen & Seaman, 2011), but students who prefer face-to-face classes, do so because they enjoy being with the instructor and enjoy the classroom interactions (Berry & Paulo Kushnir, 2013; Daymont & Blau, 2008). Good quality online courses have to incorporate a substantial amount of student-to-student and student-to-instructor interactions (Clark-Ibáñez & Scott 2008; Summer, 2000). The level of interaction in online courses, students' satisfaction, and enjoyment in these courses, are often seen as predictors of students' perceived learning (Rovai & Barnum, 2003) and real learning, as measured by increases in students' grades (Bassili & Joordens, 2008) in online courses.

Student Satisfaction and Social Presence in Online Courses

Students' satisfaction of their experience in a course is often seen as an indicator of successful learning (Bassili & Joordens, 2008; McFarland

& Hamilton, 2005; Parkhurst *et al.,* 2008; Summers *et al.,* 2005; York, 2008). The argument being that there is a relationship between student satisfaction and students' perception of the quality of their learning (Piccoli, Rami, & Blake, 2001) and students' actual learning (Bassili & Joordens, 2008). Substantial and timely interactions between the students and instructors can reflect high levels of student satisfaction, and this high level of satisfaction can also indicate that teaching methods strongly reflect learning goals and student expectations (Moore, 2005). However, the link between student satisfaction and student learning is not clear since students might report that they are more satisfied with a course that they perceive as being easy, fun, or less demanding; these attributes may not necessarily be linked to real measure of success. Macon (2011) reported that undergraduates tend to be more satisfied with traditional face-to-face courses than with online courses, while York (2008) found that students were just as satisfied with online course work as with face-to-face course work; Fillion, Limayem, Laferriere and Mantha (2007) found online students to be more satisfied than face-to-face students. Some say that despite these competing findings, it is reasonable to expect that in a classroom where successful learning is evident, then student satisfaction will be higher (Driscoll, Jicha, Hunt, Tichavsky & Thompson, 2012), and this is especially so in inverted classes (Campbell *et al.,* 2014).

Online students who are more satisfied with their learning experience and satisfied with their instructors have been found to have a greater sense of social presence in the course (Lyons, Reysen & Pierce, 2012; Richardson & Swan, 2003). There is lots of research that suggests that it is difficult to develop online social presence, at least at a deep enough level that satisfies students. Instructors have to work very hard at creating a presence online (Hale, Mirakian & Day, 2009; Kearns, Shoaf & Summey, 2004; Richardson & Swan, 2003; Salcedo, 2010; Summers *et al.,* 2005).

Student Learning Outcomes in Online Courses

For the most part, the literature reports no statistically significant differences in learning outcomes between online and face-to-face students when grades are considered. Some authors report that online students slightly outperform their face-to-face peers in the same course (Beeckman *et al.,* 2008; Beyea *et al.,* 2008; Lim *et al.,* 2008; Parkhurst *et al.,* 2008; Salcedo, 2010); as mentioned above, academic integrity is often a serious concern (Schoenfeld-Tacher *et al.,* 2001). Some authors have found that online learning is at least as effective and robust as face-to-face learning (Brownstein *et al.,* 2008; Colvin *et al.,* 2014), therefore providing the same level of instruction (Carter & Emerson, 2012; Driscoll *et al.,* 2012; Russell, 1999; Tucker, 2001). In some cases, online instruction is reported to be less effective than face-to-face instruction (Logan, Augustyniak & Reese, 2002; Urtel, 2008) with students having difficulty keeping up with the requirements of the course (Berry & Paulo Kushnir, 2013; Keramidas, 2012). Also, some authors (*e.g.,* Horton *et al.,* 2014; Means *et al.,* 2009) report evidence that blended and hybrid instruction (*i.e.,* combining online and face-to-face elements) has a greater advantage relative to purely face-to-face instruction or purely online instruction.

There is a growing body of empirical research investigating the efficacy of online learning and the teaching strategies that impact e-learning, but much of the research still focuses on how different factors impact perceptions of learning and how students experience different e-learning contexts. A comprehensive review of the literature here suggests that there is not much evidence for learning being enhanced by different online pedagogies; more data driven research needs to be conducted with the goal to link and apply existing theoretical frameworks to data that adds to our understanding of the design and use of e-learning. This type of research linking theories to online learning is too often absent in the education literature, and Chalmers (2000), Kraus *et al* (2001), and Mayer (1997) suggest that more of this type of linking is necessary so that educators can make informed, data-based decisions about the most effective implementation of online technologies and e-learning. The research presented in this chapter was developed and organized to systematically and empirically measure the impact of various factors on online teaching and learning. Our work here helps education researchers, instructors and other education specialists to understand how specific teaching strategies can impact online learning in different higher-education contexts such as completely online, hybrid, blended, and inverted or flipped courses.

RESEARCH RATIONALE

This chapter evaluates the impact of various teaching strategies and online tools (*e.g.,* the use of lecture videos, online quizzes with rapid feedback, peer-to-peer activities, and online course assignments) on the following factors:

1. Student engagement, interaction and feelings of isolation
2. Satisfaction of learning experience, social presence (and how well students felt they got to know the instructor), and authenticity of the course materials
3. Student learning outcomes (as measured by differences in course grades)

We set out to investigate what are students' experiences online, if there are variables or teaching strategies that impact the factors listed above, and if certain strategies correlate to, and predict, better student learning outcomes.

DESIGN OF THE RESEARCH SERIES

Summary of the Research Series

In *Study-One*, half of the students completed a second-year, Introductory Psychology course in a traditional face-to-face setting while the other half completed the same course entirely online (with the exception of term tests and the final exam which were completed face-to-face to ensure academic integrity). In *Study-Two*, all students completed the same Introductory Psychology course entirely online (again with the exception of term tests and the final exam, to ensure academic integrity). One of the two groups of students in *Study-Two* received 30-60 minute lecture videos as part of the online course materials, while the other group received the same lecture videos chunked into 5-15 minute lecture video segments with embedded quizzes that popped up during the short 5-15 minute lecture clips. In *Study-Three,* all students completed the same Introductory Psychology course entirely online (as in *Study-Two*). In this third case, half of the students even wrote the term tests and final exam online using a third party service provider of live online proctoring to ensure academic integrity (a model where certified proctors invigilate students writing tests using web cams and a host of sophisticated technologies including authentication and remote access software that allows proctors access to students' computers, screen sharing technology, video and audio recordings of students, proctors and all test processes), while the other half of the students in *Study-Three* wrote term tests and the final exam face-to-face in a classroom like students in studies *One* and *Two*. Students in *Study-Three* received 30-60 minute lecture videos with embedded quizzes (*i.e.,* students did not receive shorter lecture clips as in *Study-Two*). Figure 1 below summarizes studies 1, 2, and 3, the different group variables and comparisons made between and within the different groups.

Figure 1. Summary of Research Series: Study-One, Study-Two, and Study-Three with group details and comparisons

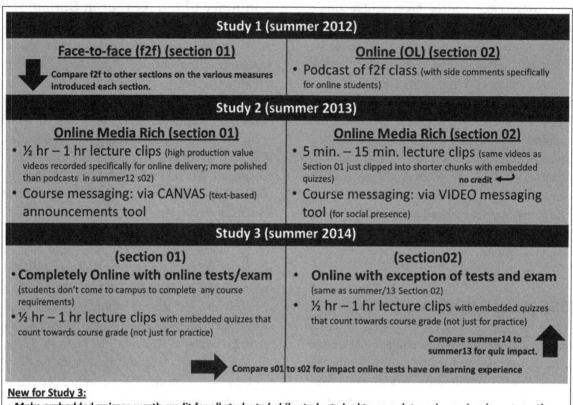

Participants and Description of the Research Series

Study 1

A total of 60 students enrolled in an introductory psychology course at a small urban university participated in *Study-One* of this research series in the summer of 2012. About half of those participants were enrolled in a face-to-face section of the course (section 01, *Study-One*; n=31). The other half were enrolled in an online section of the course that consisted of podcast recordings of the face-to-face class with side comments directed at the online students to in order to clarify issues or

direct them to section specific information (section 02, *Study-One*; n=29). The students were self-selected and allowed to choose the section of the course in which they wished to enroll; they were only restricted from switching between course sections after the final date to register in the course passed (a date set by the University Registrar's Office, and within the first week of classes).

Study 2

A total of 52 students enrolled at the same university and in the same course, participated in *Study-Two* of this research series in the summer of 2013. In this study, all students completed the course online. Similar to the first study, about half of the participants were enrolled in one section (section 01, *Study-Two*; n=25; students received 30-60 minute lecture videos, and all course messages were delivered using the text announcement tool in the institution's learning management system (LMS) and the other half of students were enrolled in another section of the same course (section 02, *Study-Two*; n=27; students received 5-15 minute lecture clips with embedded quizzes, and course messages were delivered via a video messaging tool (rather than the LMS text announcement tool) in the hopes of increasing social presence). As was the case in *Study-One*, students were self-selected and only restricted from switching course sections after the final registration date (though students in this second study had no reason to move between sections since they were unaware of any explicit differences between the groups; as far as they were concerned, there were just two online sections of the course that were available concurrently).

Study 3

A total of 53 students enrolled at the same university and in the same course as students in the first two studies, participated in *Study-Three* of this research series, in the summer of 2014. Students in this study also completed the entire course online. As in the first two studies, half of the participants were enrolled in one section (section 01, *Study-Three* ; n=28; students received 30-60 minute lecture videos with embedded quizzes, and course messages were delivered via a video messaging tool plus the text announcement tool that was available in the institution's LMS to reiterate particularly important messages and time sensitive messages); the other half of the students were enrolled in another section of the same course (section 02, *Study-Three*; n=25; students received 30-60 minute lecture clips with embedded quizzes, and course messages were delivered via a video messaging tool plus the text announcement

tool that was available in the institution's LMS to reiterate particularly important messages and time sensitive messages). As in the first two studies, students were self-selected, and again, only restricted from switching sections after the final registration date. The only distinction between groups in this third study was whether students completed their tests and exam online using live proctoring services from a third party provider (*i.e.,* section 01) or whether students completed their tests and exam face-to-face, on campus (*i.e.,* section 02).

Details Relevant to Groups in all Three Studies

A total of 165 students participated in this research series over a three year period of the summer session Introduction to Psychology course taught by the same instructor, using the same course materials, tests and exams (which were restricted and not made available to students after the tests and exam), and, generally, the same course components. Across all groups, there were no significant differences between first year university average scores, cumulative average scores, and high school entrance average scores (*i.e.,* previous grades were not a factor that differed across the groups). All online students received an introductory, *"presence"* and *"welcome"* video from the instructor. Also, all of the lecture material and course activities were available to students online and hosted on the institutional LMS. With the exception of students in section 01 of *Study-Three* (*i.e.,* online students who wrote online tests and exam using live proctoring services from a third party provider) students came to campus (*i.e.,* physically, face-to-face) three times to complete some of the requirements of their course (*i.e.,* to write two term tests and a final exam). Unlike the online students, the fully face-to-face students (*i.e.,* section 01, *Study-One*) met for lectures in a class for 3 hours, 2 times per week during a compressed summer semester of 6 weeks. The online students received the same lectures via online lecture videos available in the course LMS during the same compressed summer semester of 6 weeks in each of the relevant summer sessions. Normally, the lecture videos were also available for download to mobile devices, but for the purposes of tracking students' completion of the embedded lecture quizzes, this service was suspended for online students only in *Study-Two*. Online students in *Study-One* (*i.e.,* section 02) and both groups of students in *Study-Three* had access to the mobile downloads.

A key component in the face-face section of *Study-One* (*i.e.,* section 01) was peer activities, which were facilitated with the use of student response systems (*i.e.,* clickers) in the classroom. This particular course component was replicated in the online groups in *Study-One* (*i.e.,* section 02) and *Study-Two* (*i.e.,* sections 01 and 02) by using online quizzes and a discussion board in the institution's LMS. Initially (in *Study-One*), Adobe Connect break out rooms were used to facilitate synchronous peer activities and to replicate the face-to-face example of peer activities and clicker use, but this had to be abandoned due to a problem with the Adobe Connect tool. As a result, Adobe Connect was only used for synchronous online office hours. This particular component had to be re-developed and became an asynchronous activity when moved to the online quizzes and discussion board (*i.e.,* part-way through *Study-One* and in all of *Study-Two*). This peer activity component was abandoned in *Study-Three* as it was one of the few course components in studies 1 and 2 that did not transfer well to the online environment. As presented below, in the Results section, it is the one part of the course where students' grades dropped dramatically and about which students vehemently complained that they did not enjoy this component of the course; they found it to be the most frustrating and the most time consuming component of the course. With the exception of this peer activity component, students received the same exact course content and other course components across all sections of the courses delivered by the same instructor (*i.e.,* Summer of 2012, Summer of 2013 and Summer of 2014).

Online student experience was assessed using a half-way checking in survey that took place about half-way through the course. This survey provided valuable formative feedback on how things were going for the online students; if any serious problems existed (like the Adobe Connect problem), the instructor could take action to correct any problems immediately. All students across the three studies (face-to-face and online) received an end-of-term survey before they exited the course that was distributed after the final exam. This survey provided important summative feedback about student experience, satisfaction, engagement, feelings of isolation, and perceived authenticity of course materials, how well students felt like they got to know the instructor, and a host of other measures. Other learning outcome comparisons included grades on 6 quizzes worth 10% of the final grade, 2 term tests each worth 20% of the final grade, a final exam worth 30% of the final grade, an assignment worth 10% of the final grade, peer activities and class participation worth 10% of the final grade, and finally, overall course grades for all groups were also compared.

ANALYSES

Analysis of the data included response frequencies of the quantitative survey questions across the groups and independent *t*-Tests to measure any differences between final grades for the online and face-to-face students in *Study-One*, and between the four online groups in *Study-Two* and *Study-Three*. ANOVAs were calculated to measure any differences between all course grades across the six groups in all three studies of the research series. Qualitative analyses of the open-ended survey questions included response frequencies of the student's survey text answers across the groups and weighted word lists that were calculated and puzzled out into word clouds that were generated from the students' text answers. The word clouds represented summaries of the text that students wrote in their open-ended answers. A user generated word cloud visualizes information that is related to a specific survey question and, in essence, it depicts visually, the frequency of specific topics that students write about in their open-ended answers. The importance (or frequency) of specific words is often displayed by using font size (as in the examples below), font colour, or other attributes (see Bateman *et al.*, 2008 for an overview of word/tag clouds).

RESULTS AND DISCUSSION

Student Engagement, Interaction, and Feelings of Isolation

Class interactions and feelings of community are some of the reported benefits of traditional face-to-face courses (Homberg-Wright & Wright, 2012) and in some cases, students who prefer the face-to-face classes do so because they like interacting with the instructor and their classmates (Berry & Paulo Kushnir, 2013; Daymont & Blau, 2008). This suggests that perhaps online environments should provide lots of opportunities for engagement and interaction. In our three studies, students were asked to indicate in which part of the course they felt most engaged; as indicated in Figure 2, below, students reported that the Peer Discussions/Activities and Peer Instruction (opportunities designed in the course for students to work with one another and discuss core course material), the Science Meets Art project (a course assignment that was shared amongst classmates and included an Art Exhibition) and Quizzes were reported to provide the most engagement. Demonstration videos as well as Lecture podcasts/Lecture videos also contributed to student engagement. Online students were asked whether they wanted more interactions with their classmates, and if so, what sort of interactions they wanted.

Interestingly, the request for face-to-face interactions and study groups came up frequently in the students' responses (as shown in Figure 3 below).

The data in Figures 2 and 3 provide support for flipped or inverted classes where the lectures and usual in-class material are placed online for students to access outside of class time, and, as a result, class time can be used for activities that would normally be done at home such as homework and other assignments, but in a more engaged and interactive manner. Instructors can also free up class time for other types of interactive and engaging activities instead of just passive lectures. This teaching strategy empowers instructors to innovate in their courses, giving them and students the opportunity to have engaging, interactive sessions such as collaborative work and in-class activities that focus on higher level cognitive activities (Bull, Ferster & Kjellstrom, 2012; Brunsell & Horejsi, 2013; Lockwood & Esselstein, 2013; Mason *et al.,* 2013; Milman, 2012; Steed, 2012) and the flexibility to blend face-to-face instruction with online instruction which is often viewed as having a more positive impact on learning than any one type of instruction on its own (Campbell *et al.,* 2014; Horton *et al.,* 2014; Means *et al.,* 2009; Lookwood & Esselstein, 2013; Szpunar, Khan, & Schacter, 2013).

When students were asked if they felt isolated in the online sections of the course, students who received almost all the course announcements via video messages (*i.e.,* section 02, summer 2013, *Study-Two*) reported least often that they felt isolated in the course. Compared to this particular group, students who had some, but not all, of their course announcements via video messages (*i.e.,* sections 01 and 02, summer 2014, *Study-Three*), reported about the same or just a bit more isolation. All of these students reported less isolation compared to students who did not receive any video messages, but rather received all course announcements via a text announcement tool that was available in the course LMS (*i.e.,* section 02, summer 2012, *Study-One*, and section 01, summer

Figure 2. Course components and course activities that helped students feel most engaged

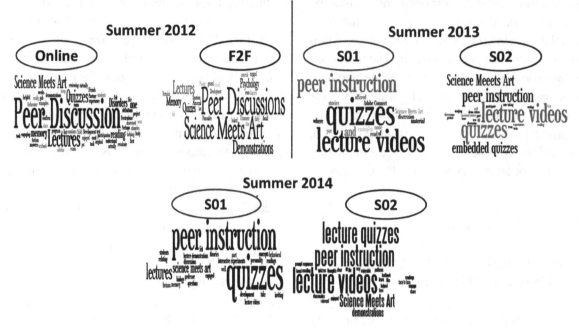

Figure 3. The sorts of interactions that online students wanted to have more of with their classmates

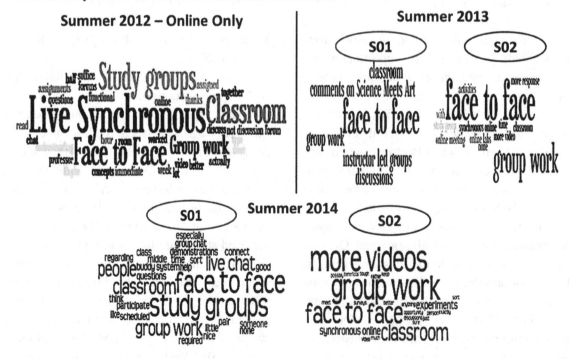

2013, *Study-Two*). Figure 4 shows students reports of feeling isolated in the online sections of the course. These findings suggest that students who received video messages felt more included and connected in the course compared to the others who seemed lonelier.

Student Satisfaction, Social Presence, and Authenticity

We asked students about what they found most satisfying about the course. Overwhelmingly, across all groups, students reported being satisfied with their learning experience and course experience; Figure 5 shows what students found most satisfying about the course. As reported earlier, online students who are more satisfied with their learning experience and satisfied with their instructors have been found to have a greater

sense of social presence in a course (Lyons *et al.,* 2012; Richardson & Swan, 2003) shown here, in Figures 6 & 7, by how well they got know the instructor, and what course factors helped them feel like they knew the instructor (see Figure 8). We also found that this had an impact on students' perceived authenticity of the course materials, and how real or artificial the course felt to students (see Figure 9). It is encouraging to see that the *"course material", "learning",* and *"feeling engaged"* appear consistently across the groups. As reported in the literature, the level of student satisfaction can be an indication of the level of student learning outcomes (Bassili & Joordens, 2008; Parkhurst *et al.,* 2008; Summers *et al.,* 2005; York, 2008).

The findings presented in figures 6 to 9, tie in nicely with the findings in Figure 4, above (about students' reports of feeling isolated in the

Figure 4. Online students' report of feeling isolated in the course

Did you feel isolated in the course?

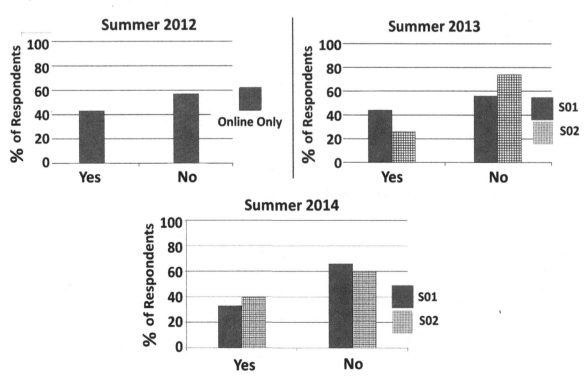

Figure 5. What satisfied students most about the course

What did you find most satisfying about the course?

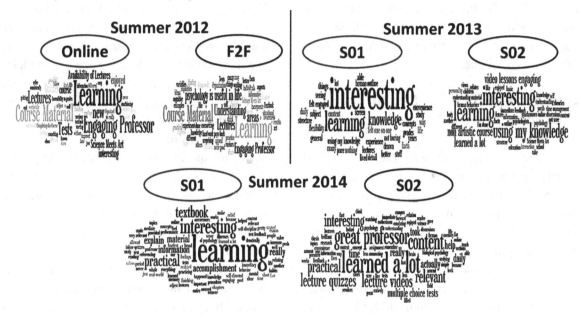

Figure 6. Students' report of whether they felt like they got to know the instructor

Considering that this was an online course with different types of interactions with the instructor than you might be used to in face-to-face courses, did you feel like you got to know the instructor?

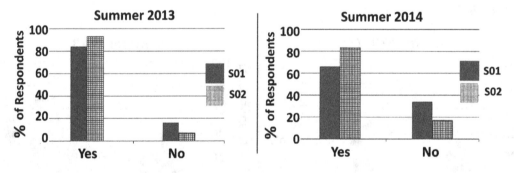

Figure 7. How well students felt like they got to know the instructor

How well did you feel like you got to know the instructor?

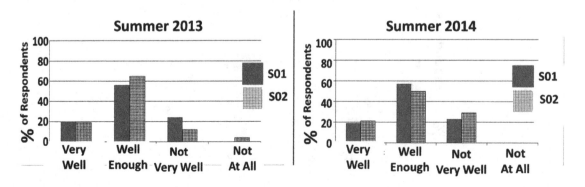

Figure 8. What aspects of the course made students feel like they got to know the instructor

(Choose all that apply to you.) Considering that this was an online course with different types of interactions, which of the following made you feel like you got to know the instructor?

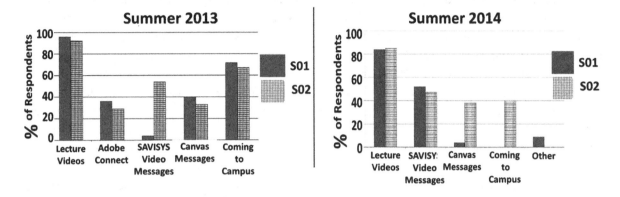

Figure 9. How authentic the course felt to students

Compared to other face-to-face courses that you have taken at this institution and considering that the lectures in this course were pre-recorded, how authentic (or real) did the lectures feel to you (*e.g.,* lecture videos seemed natural and sincere, or unnatural, a bit fake, awkward or artificial)?

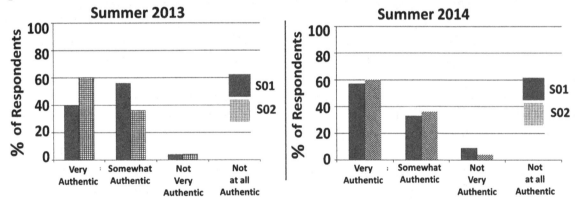

course). One possible explanation for our findings on isolation is that the personable video messages might have left students with a better sense of the instructor's online presence and this might have allowed students to connect better with the instructor (even when students never met the instructor face-to-face, like those in section 01, summer 2014, *Study-Three,* who wrote their term tests and final exam online). The video messages might also have allowed students to feel more connected to other students in the course, and made them feel that they belonged in the course, giving them a better

sense of community than if they had not received the video messages. While questions about *"if"* and *"how well"* students felt they got to know the instructor were not asked of the online students in the first study, students in the second and third studies overwhelmingly reported that they felt like they got to know the instructor well (see Figures 6 & 7); Figure 8 shows that the video messages contributed significantly to these findings, and that the course felt pretty authentic and real (see Figure 9) to most students. Feeling welcome and connected in a course is likely related to feeling satisfied with one's experience in a course (hard to imagine that these factors would contribute to a negative experience). As reported earlier, students who are more satisfied with their learning experience and satisfied with their instructors have been found to have a greater sense of social presence in the course (Lyons *et al.,* 2012; Richardson & Swan, 2003), and, at least in this study, that seems to go hand-in-hand with the course feeling *"real"* and seeming authentic.

Learning Outcomes

Students were asked what aspects of the course contributed most to their learning (see Figure 10). While students reported that the interactive quizzes and active components contributed most to their learning, they also complained that the peer activities and online quizzes (not the embedded lecture quizzes) were too demanding and time consuming; there were no significant differences between the groups of students on their grades for any of the course components (*i.e.,* across 6 quizzes, 2 term tests, final exam, course assignment, peer interactions and activities, course participation, or final course grade). While peer activity and participation grades dropped dramatically in the online groups in studies *One* and *Two,* the differences were not statistically significant. While these insignificant findings are consistent with other research discussed above, it is not to say that e-learning has no impact on student outcomes; on the contrary, it has impact on many other learning related factors, as discussed here (*e.g.,* engagement, experience, isolation, perceived authenticity, *etc.*) and as reported elsewhere (*e.g.,* Sadaghiani, 2012; Szpunar *et al.,* 2013).

LIMITATIONS, CONCLUSION, AND RECOMMENDATIONS

We set out to evaluate the impact of various online tools and teaching strategies (podcasts/lecture videos, online assignments, online quizzes, rapid feedback, discussions, and peer activities) on student learning outcomes, student engagement and student satisfaction of their learning experience. We discovered that students had similar experiences across the different groups supporting the argument that online instruction can provide at least the same level of instruction and satisfaction as face-to-face instruction (Bassili & Joordens, 2008; Driscoll *et al.,* 2012; Russell, 1999; Tucker, 2001). While we didn't empirically detect any differences in student learning, as measured by increases or decreases in student grades, we did identify many teaching strategies and e-learning factors that impacted student engagement, experience, isolation, perceived authenticity, *etc.* There are many possible explanations for why students in the different groups performed similarly on the quizzes, tests, and exams. At the time that this chapter was written, only preliminary analyses of the data had been completed. Perhaps richer, deeper and more sophisticated analyses, with thorough data mining of the empirical quiz, test, exam and overall course grade data might reveal more interesting findings.

In our study, we discovered that the teaching strategies we chose influenced the teaching tools we used, which in turn, had some influence back on our teaching strategies. It is important that online courses be built on sound pedagogical principles in order to facilitate meaningful and successful learning. We took the necessary steps to design the online course sections around our teaching and learning goals that supported our instructional needs and student learning needs and desired learning outcomes; we did not design the online course around the teaching tools that happen to be available to us. A large team of specialists invested a significant amount of time, money and resources to ensure that a good quality and meaningful online experience was created for students. As more and more university instructors look to educational media and technologies to help engage students and enrich learning environments

Figure 10. What course factors students believed helped their learning

What components of the course contributed most to your learning?

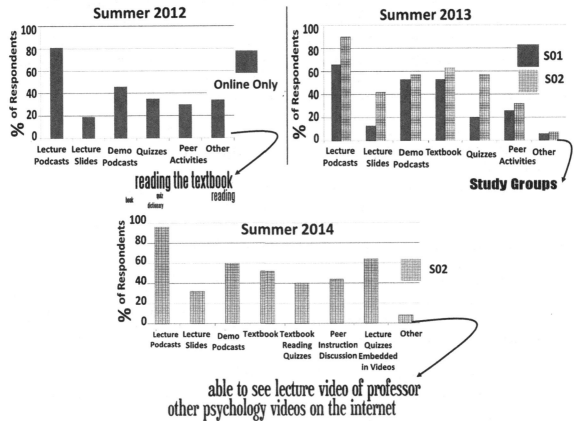

in different learning contexts (*e.g.*, fully online courses, hybrid, blended and inverted or flipped courses), it will be helpful if future research focuses on the use of different learning contexts and online innovations to facilitate different teaching strategies and learning methods, both in and out of the classroom.

While this chapter did not investigate factors directly linked to the evolution of Web 3.0, it certainly considered issues that speak to how teachers teach and how learners learn given technological advancements and educational innovations. For example, while mobile learning was not a factor that was manipulated or measured in the studies discussed here, students in all of the online sections across the three studies (with the exception of one,

as reported above) were given the opportunity for downloading the lecture videos to their personal digital assistants (PDA's) or mobile smartphones. The institutional LMS supported a variety of files types for download to accommodate different learning needs and maximize flexibility. Also, not yet investigated or analyzed in this body of data, was the impact that the embedded quizzes had on student learning outcomes. It might be that the knowledge a student gains from the rapid feedback provided from embedded video quizzes can impact learning. As reported above, the embedded quizzes had a tremendous impact on which course components students believed helped them most in their learning and helped them to feel the most engaged in the course. It is not unreasonable to believe that this technology might eventually develop to contribute to a sort of artificially intelligent directed type of feedback, where teaching and learning can be shaped by that feedback. This idea is not unlike targeted marketing that we experience on the Web more often these days. After having visited certain web sites, subsequent web visits or searches are often interrupted with targeted ads or suggestions for searches related to previous page visits and those suggestions or targeted pieces are shaped by those previous page visits.

Future research should continue to systematically and empirically investigate the impact that different e-learning pedagogies have on teaching strategies and learning outcomes, while, at the same time, varying variables of platform, learning device, and modality. There are lots of possible factors that will generate interesting discussions: impact that devices have on how students read, listen and learn, and that are more or less conducive to effective learning, given new media and technologies; type of interactions that are possible or not possible, or simply changing interactions and different types of interactions, again, given new media and technological developments – all of which look promising with the development of artificial intelligence technologies and the evolution of Web 3.0. Advancements in technology and innovations in education allow universities to think up new ways of teaching and learning. It is in understanding the pedagogy behind the technology that will get us further along in understanding how to best implement educational media and technologies to enrich e-learning.

ACKNOWLEDGMENT

The authors thank the very large and helpful team of people who provided extensive resources and tremendous support for this project, making it technically, procedurally and financially possible. We especially thank the staff in Academic Computing, the Faculty and Curriculum Development Centre, our research assistants, the Office of the Vice President, Academic, and the Office of the Dean, Faculty of Liberal Arts & Sciences and School of Interdisciplinary Studies at OCAD University.

REFERENCES

Allen, E. I., & Seaman, J. (2010). *Class differences: Online education in the United States*. Sloan Consortium. Retrieved March 19, 2014 from http://files.eric.ed.gov/fulltext/ED529952.pdf

Allen, E. I., & Seaman, J. (2011). *Going the distance: Online education in the United States, 2011*. Sloan Consortium. Retrieved March 21, 2014 from http://files.eric.ed.gov/fulltext/ED529948.pdf

Allen, E. I., & Seaman, J. (2013). *Changing course: Ten years of tracking online education in the United States*. Sloan Consortium. Retrieved September 21, 2014 from http://files.eric.ed.gov/fulltext/ED541571.pdf

Bassili, J. N., & Joordens, S. (2008). Media player tool use, satisfaction with online lectures and examination performance. *Journal of Distance Education, 22*(2), 93–108.

Bateman, S., Gutwin, C., & Nacenta, M. (2008). Seeing things in the clouds: The effect of visual features on tag cloud selections. In *Proc. of the 19th ACM conference on Hypertext and Hypermedia* (pp. 193–202). ACM Press. doi:10.1145/1379092.1379130

Beeckman, D., Schoonhoven, L., Boucqué, H., Van Maele, G., & Defloor, T. (2008). Pressure ulcers: E-learning to improve classification by nurses and nursing students. *Journal of Clinical Nursing, 17*(13), 1697–1707. doi:10.1111/j.1365-2702.2007.02200.x PMID:18592624

Berry, K., & Paulo Kushnir, L. (2013). Crossing borders: A comparison of the impact of various teaching strategies and tools in an online and face-to-face psychology course. In *Proceedings of the 25th World Conference on Educational Multimedia, Hypermedia and Telecommunications 2013* (pp. 1724-1731). Chesapeake, VA: AACE.

Beyea, J. A., Wong, E., Bromwich, M., Weston, W. W., & Fung, K. (2008). Evaluation of a particle repositioning maneuver web-based teaching module. *The Laryngoscope, 118*(1), 175–180. doi:10.1097/MLG.0b013e31814b290d PMID:18251035

Brownstein, B., Brownstein, D., & Gerlowski, D. A. (2008). Web-based vs. face-to-face MBA classes: A comparative assessment study. *Journal of College Teaching and Learning, 5*(11), 41–48.

Brunsell, E., & Horejsi, M. (2013). A flipped classroom in action. *Science Teacher (Normal, Ill.), 80*, 8.

Bull, G., Ferster, B., & Kjellstrom, W. (2012). Inventing the flipped classroom. *Learning and Leading with Technology, 40*(1), 10.

Campbell, J., Horton, D., Craig, M., & Gries, P. (2014). Evaluating an inverted CS1. In *Proceedings of the 45th ACM Technical Symposium on Computer Science Education (SIGCSE '14)*. ACM. Retrieved September 21, 2014 from http://doi.acm.org/10.1145/2538862.2538943

Carey, T., & Trick, D. (2013). *How online learning affects productivity, cost and quality in higher education: An environmental scan and review of the literature*. Toronto, Canada: Higher Education Quality Council of Ontario. Retrieved March 5, 2014 from http://www.heqco.ca/SiteCollectionDocuments/How_Online_Learning_Affects_Productivity-ENG.pdf

Carter, L. K., & Emerson, T. L. N. (2012). In-class vs. online experiments: Is there a difference? *The Journal of Economic Education, 43*(1), 4–18. doi:10.1080/00220485.2011.636699

Chalmers, P. A. (2000). User interface improvements in computer-assisted instruction, the challenge. *Computers in Human Behavior, 16*(5), 507–517. doi:10.1016/S0747-5632(00)00022-4

Clark-Ibáñez, M., & Scott, L. (2008). Learning to teach online. *Teaching Sociology, 36*(1), 34-41.

Colvin, K. F., Champaign, J., Liu, A., Zhou, Q., Fredericks, C., & Pritchard, D. E. (2014). Learning in an Introductory Physics MOOC: All cohorts learn equally, including an on-campus class. *International Review of Research in Open and Distance Learning, 15*(4). Retrieved September 21, 2014 from http://www.irrodl.org/index.php/irrodl/article/view/1902/3009

Daymont, T., & Blau, G. (2008). Student performance in online and traditional sections of an undergraduate management course. *Journal of Behavioral and Applied Management, 9*(3), 275–294.

Driscoll, A., Jicha, K., Hunt, A. N., Tichavsky, L., & Thompson, G. (2012). Can online courses deliver in-class results?: A comparison of student performance and satisfaction in an online versus a face-to-face introductory sociology course. *Teaching Sociology, 40*(4), 312–331. doi:10.1177/0092055X12446624

Fillion, G., Limayem, M., Laferriere, T., & Mantha, R. (2007). Integrating ICT into higher education: A study of onsite vs online students' perceptions. *Academy of Educational Leadership Journal, 11*(2), 45–72.

Gould, T. (2003). Hybrid classes: Maximizing institutional resources and student learning. In *Proceedings of the 2003 ASCUE Conference* (pp. 54-59). ASCUE.

Gupta, R. K., & Lei, S. A. (2010). College distance education courses: Evaluating benefits and costs from institutional, faculty and students' perspectives. *Education, 130*, 616.

Hale, L. S., Mirakian, E. A., & Day, D. B. (2009). Online vs classroom instruction: Student satisfaction and learning outcomes in an undergraduate allied health pharmacology course. *Journal of Allied Health, 38*(2), 36–42. PMID:19753411

Homberg-Wright, K, & Wright, D. J. (2012). MBA and undergraduate business student perceptions of online courses: Experienced online students versus students who have not taken an online course. *Global Education Journal,* (1), 169-186.

Horton, D., Craig, M., Campbell, J., Gries, P., & Zingaro, D. (2014). Comparing outcomes in Inverted and traditional CS1. In *Proceedings of the 19th ACM Technical Symposium on Innovation and Technology in Computer Science Education.* Retrieved September 21, 2014 from https://www.openconf.org/iticse2014/modules/request.php?module=oc_program&action=summary.php&id=1123

Kearns, L. E., Shoaf, J. R., & Summey, M. B. (2004). Performance and satisfaction of second-degree BSN students in web-based and traditional course delivery environments. *The Journal of Nursing Education, 43*(6), 280–284. PMID:15230307

Keramidas, C. G. (2012). Are undergraduate students ready for online learning? A comparison of online and face-to-face sections of a course. *Rural Special Education Quarterly, 31*(4), 25–32.

Kraus, L. A., Reed, W. M., & Fitzgerald, G. E. (2001). The effects of learning style and hypermedia prior experience on behavioral disorders knowledge and time on task: A case-based hypermedia environment. *Computers in Human Behavior, 17*(1), 125–140. doi:10.1016/S0747-5632(00)00030-3

Lim, J., Kim, M., Chen, S., & Ryder, C. (2008). An empirical investigation of student achievement and satisfaction in different learning environments. *Journal of Instructional Psychology, 35*(2), 113–119.

Lockwood, K., & Esselstein, R. (2013). The inverted classroom and the CS curriculum. In *Proceeding of the 44th ACM Technical Symposium on Computer Science Education, SIGCSE '13* (pp. 113-118). New York, NY: ACM. doi:10.1145/2445196.2445236

Logan, E., Augustyniak, R., & Rees, A. (2002). Distance education as different education: A student-centered investigation of distance learning experience. *Journal of Education for Library and Information Science, 43*(1), 32-42.

Lyons, A., Reysen, S., & Pierce, L. (2012). Video lecture format, student technological efficacy, and social presence in online courses. *Computers in Human Behavior, 28*(1), 181–186. doi:10.1016/j.chb.2011.08.025

Macon, D. K. (2011). Student satisfaction with online courses vs traditional courses: A meta-analysis. (Order No. 3447725, Northcentral University). *ProQuest Dissertations and Theses,* 88. Retrieved September 21, 2014 from http://search.proquest.com/docview/858611481?accountid=14771

Mason, G. S., Shuman, T. R., & Cook, K. E. (2013). Comparing the effectiveness of an inverted classroom to a traditional classroom in an upper-division engineering course. *IEEE Transactions on Education, 56*(4), 430–435. doi:10.1109/TE.2013.2249066

Mayer, R. E. (1997). Multimedia learning: Are we asking the right questions? *Educational Psychologist, 32*(1), 1–19. doi:10.1207/s15326985ep3201_1

McFarland, D., & Hamilton, D. (2005). Factors affecting student performance and satisfaction: Online versus traditional course delivery. *Journal of Computer Information Systems, 46*(2), 25–32.

Means, B., Toyama, Y., Murphy, R., Bakia, M., & Jones, K. (2009). *Evaluation of evidence-based practices in online learning: A meta-analysis and review of online learning studies.* US Department of Education. Available from https://www2.ed.gov/rschstat/eval/tech/evidence-based-practices/finalreport.pdf

Milman, N. B. (2012). The flipped classroom strategy: What is it and how can it best be used? *Distance Learning, 9*, 85.

Moore, J. C. (2005). *The Sloan Consortium quality framework and the five pillars.* The Sloan Consortium. Retrieved April 4, 2011 from http://sloanconsortium.org/publications/freedownloads

Pallof, R., & Pratt, K. (2007). *Building online learning communities: Effective strategies for the virtual classroom* (2nd ed.). San Francisco, CA: Jossey-Bass.

Parkhurst, R., Moskal, B. M., Lucena, J., & Downey, G. L. (2008). Engineering cultures: Comparing student learning in online and classroom based implementations. *International Journal of Engineering Education, 24*(5), 955–955.

Parry, M. (2010). *Colleges see 17 percent increase in online enrollment.* Retrieved April 16, 2013, from http://chronicle.com/blogs/wiredcampus/colleges-see-17-percent-increase-in-online-enrollment/20820

Paulo Kushnir, L., & Berry, K. C. (2014). Inside, outside, upside down: New directions in online teaching and e-learning. In *Proceedings of the 8th Annual International Conference on e-Learning (ICEL 2014)* (pp. 133-140). Academic Press.

Piccoli, G., Rami, A., & Blake, I. (2001). Web-based virtual learning environments: A research framework and a preliminary assessment of effectiveness in basic IT skills training. *Management Information Systems Quarterly, 25*(4), 401–426. doi:10.2307/3250989

Richardson, J. C., & Swan, K. (2003). Examining social presence in online courses in relation to students' perceived learning and satisfaction. *Journal of Asynchronous Learning Networks, 7*(1), 68–88.

Rovai, A. P., & Barnum, K. T. (2003). On-line course effectiveness: An analysis of student interactions and perceptions of learning. *Journal of Distance Education, 18*(1), 57–73.

Russell, T. L. (1999). *The no significant difference phenomenon*. Raleigh, NC: North Carolina State University.

Sadaghiani, H. R. (2012). Online prelectures: An alternative to textbook reading assignments. *The Physics Teacher*, *50*(5), 301. doi:10.1119/1.3703549

Salcedo, C. S. (2010). Comparative analysis of learning outcomes in face-to-face foreign language classes vs. language lab and online. *Journal of College Teaching and Learning*, *7*(2), 43–54.

Schoenfeld-Tacher, R., McConnell, S., & Graham, M. (2001). Do no harm: A comparison of the effects of on-line vs. traditional delivery media on a science course. *Journal of Science Education and Technology*, *10*(3), 257–265. doi:10.1023/A:1016690600795

Steed, A. (2012). The flipped classroom. *Teaching Business & Economics*, *16*(3), 9–11.

Summers, J. J., Waigandt, A., & Whittaker, T. A. (2005). A comparison of student achievement and satisfaction in an online versus a traditional face-to-face statistics class. *Innovative Higher Education*, *29*(3), 233–250. doi:10.1007/s10755-005-1938-x

Szpunar, K. K., Khan, N. Y., & Schacter, D. L. (2013). Interpolated memory tests reduce mind wandering and improve learning of online lectures. *Proceedings of the National Academy of Sciences of the United States of America*, *110*(16), 6313–6317. doi:10.1073/pnas.1221764110 PMID:23576743

Tucker, S. (2001). Distance education: Better, worse, or as good as traditional education? *Online Journal of Distance Learning Administration*, *4*(4). Retrieved from http://www.westga.edu/~distance/ojdla/winter44/tucker44.html

Urtel, M. G. (2008). Assessing academic performance between traditional and distance education course formats. *Journal of Educational Technology & Society*, *11*(1), 322–330.

Wuensch, K., Aziz, S., Ozan, E., Kishore, M., & Tabrizi, M. H. N. (2008). Pedagogical characteristics of online and face-to-face classes. *International Journal on E-Learning*, *7*(3), 523–532.

York, R. O. (2008). Comparing three modes of instruction in a graduate social work program. *Journal of Social Work Education*, *44*(2), 157–172. doi:10.5175/JSWE.2008.200700031

ADDITIONAL READING

EL-Deghaidy, H., & Nouby, A. (2008). Effectiveness of a blended e-learning cooperative approach in an Egyptian teacher education programme. *Computers & Education*, *51*(3), 988–1006. doi:10.1016/j.compedu.2007.10.001

Friedman, H. H., & Friedman, L. W. (2011). Crises in education: Online learning as a solution. *Creative Education*, *2*(03), 156–163. doi:10.4236/ce.2011.23022

Heilesen, S. B. (2010). What is the academic efficacy of podcasting? *Computers & Education*, *55*(3), 1063–1068. doi:10.1016/j.compedu.2010.05.002

Karppinen, P. (2005). Meaningful learning with digital and online videos: Theoretical perspectives. *AACE Journal*, *13*(3), 233–250.

Kear, K. L., & Heap, N. W. (2007). 'Sorting the wheat from the chaff': Investigating overload in educational discussion systems. *Journal of Computer Assisted Learning*, *23*(3), 235–247. doi:10.1111/j.1365-2729.2006.00212.x

Shapiro, A. (2009). An empirical study of personal response technology for improving attendance and learning in a large class. *Journal of the Scholarship of Teaching and Learning*, *9*(1), 13–26.

Simonson, M. R., Simonson, M., Smaldino, S. E., & Albright, M. (2006). *Teaching and learning at a distance: Foundations of distance education* Pearson/Merrill Prentice Hall.

Sumner, J. (2000). Serving the system: A critical history of distance education. *Open Learning*, *15*(3), 267–285. doi:10.1080/713688409

Weinschenk, S. M. (2011). *100 Things Every Designer Needs To Know About People*. Berkeley, CA: New Riders.

Yang, H. H., & Wang, S. (2013). *Cases on E-Learning Management: Development and Implementation*. Hershey, PA: IGI Global. doi:10.4018/978-1-4666-1933-3

KEY TERMS AND DEFINITIONS

Authenticity of Online Resources: Compared to face-to-face learning, how natural, sincere, or real *versus* how unnatural, awkward, fake or artificial online materials feel to students learning online or using online materials.

Empirical Research: Research based on the collection of data from systematic observations or experimentation, not based on common sense wisdom or other untestable methods.

Inverted/Flipped Class: A class where lectures and usual in-class materials or activities are placed online for students to access outside of class time, and, as a result, class time can be used for activities that would normally be done at home such as homework and other assignments, allowing instructors to free up class time for more interactive, engaging activities that focus on higher levels of cognitive activities than what one might find in passive lectures.

Isolation: In the context of e-learning, it is the lack of contact and real communications between learners and/or instructors, resulting in students feeling lonely, disconnected, not welcomed, or feeling like they are not part of a community of online learners.

Learning Outcomes: The knowledge and skills that a learner is expected to learn at the completion of a set of learning activities or instructions.

Online Learning: Networked learning activities that are supported electronically, outside of the classroom, using a variety of technologies.

Social Presence: In the context of e-learning, it is the idea that real people are part of a community of learners and they are successful at projecting their real personalities in the online environment such that learners feel like they are interacting with real people, feel like they know one another, and feel connected; almost as if to have met face-to-face.

Section 2
Smart Technology in Design

Chapter 9
Web–Based Information Exploration of Sensor Web Using the HTML5/ X3D Integration Model

Byounghyun Yoo
Korea Institute of Science and Technology, South Korea

ABSTRACT

This chapter investigates how the visualization of sensor resources on a 3D Web-based globe organized by level-of-detail can enhance search and exploration of information by easing the formulation of geospatial queries against the metadata of sensor systems. The case study provides an approach inspired by geographical mashups in which freely available functionality and data are flexibly combined. The authors use PostgreSQL, PostGIS, PHP, X3D-Earth, and X3DOM to allow the Web3D standard and its geospatial component to be used for visual exploration and level-of-detail control of a dynamic scene. The proposed approach facilitates the dynamic exploration of the Sensor Web and allows the user to seamlessly focus in on a particular sensor system from a set of registered sensor networks deployed across the globe. In this chapter, the authors present a prototype metadata exploration system featuring levels-of-detail for a multi-scaled Sensor Web and use it to visually explore sensor data of weather stations.

INTRODUCTION

While most environmental scientists rely on the sensor data portals hosted by a few large-scale government and research institutes, finding information on the Web is generally done using an ordinary text query or tree-based hierarchical text exploration interface. This approach is useful in that people routinely find sensor data from specific data portals. However, searching and exploration can be frustrating when queries return a tremendous number of sensor resources. Often the query output does not match what they are seeking. Search remains primarily textual and result lists are usually unstructured and not interactive. Therefore there is need for an efficient discovery and exploration interface for large distributed sensor resources.

DOI: 10.4018/978-1-4666-8147-7.ch009

In this chapter, we introduce an approach for sensor metadata discovery by exploring a Web-based 3D virtual globe on which the metadata of distributed sensor systems are queried and visualized through interaction with the information seeker. In order to provide a more intuitive exposure of metadata for sensor networks, we implement a dynamic 3D scene of sensor information on the globe by interactive navigation using HTML5 and X3D integration model (X3DOM) (Behr *et al.,* 2009; Behr *et al.,* 2010). Multiple levels-of-detail for metadata visualization are proposed for the display of a multi-scaled sensor network. We apply the proposed approach to the exploration of metadata of personal weather stations which are deployed across the globe in order to investigate how the visualization of metadata on a 3D Web-based globe organized by level-of-detail can enhance the search and exploration of information.

BACKGROUND

Similar to the W3C Web standards enabling the WWW, the Open Geospatial Consortium's Sensor Web Enablement (SWE) standards enable researchers and developers to make sensing resources discoverable, accessible, and re-useable via the Web. The SWE is composed of candidate specifications including Observation and Measurement (O&M), Sensor Model Language (SensorML), and Sensor Observation Service (SOS). The Sensor Instance Registry (SIR) was introduced as a web service interface for discovering sensors, collecting sensor metadata, handling sensor status information and to close the gap between the SensorML based metadata model and the information models used by Open Geospatial Consortium (OGC) Catalogs (Jirka & Nüst, 2010). A reader can refer to the recent publication (Bröring *et al.*, 2011) to get detail information about examples and applications of SWE.

A semantic approach is necessary to facilitate discovery of heterogeneous sensor resources and their datasets. Research on the Semantic Sensor Web (Sheth *et al.*, 2008) investigates the role of semantic annotation, ontologies, and reasoning to improve Sensor Web functionality including sensor discovery and sensor integration. Related work in this field includes methods for linking geosensor databases with ontologies (Hornsby & King, 2008), a semantically-enabled Sensor Observation Service (SemSOS) (Henson *et al.*, 2009) or the semantic annotation of sensor services with terms from ontologies (Babitski *et al.*, 2009).

Ontologies need to serve as the basis for semantic reasoning. Various research groups have started to specify sensor, stimuli, and observation ontologies. Examples include the Semantic Web for Earth and Environmental Terminology (SWEET) (Raskin & Pan, 2005) focusing on modeling of observed properties, observation based ontologies influenced by O&M (Probst, 2006), and a sensor-centric ontology with a strong relation to SensorML (Russomanno *et al.*, 2005). There are also domain-specific ontologies, such as the Marine Metadata Interoperability project, which is particularly designed for oceanographic sensors (Bermudez *et al.*, 2006). The observation-centric ontology was also developed in a consensus process within the W3C Semantic Sensor Network Incubator Group (Janowicz & Compton, 2010). An ontology for sensor data exchange was derived from the Content Standard for Digital Geospatial Metadata (CSDGM) (Federal Geographic Data Committee, 1998), SensorML and SWEET, and used for its prototype service (Feng & Yu, 2010). However it still has the limitation of a text-based query interface. Thus this paper focuses on enhancing the user interface for search and exploration of sensor resources.

For dynamic exploration of the Sensor Web proposed in this paper, a metadata model and ontology for sensor data are necessary. We utilize the CSDGM standard model for harvesting sensor metadata and transforming the collected metadata sets into our online database to investigate our approach. However, the metadata model and ontology for sensor data collection, which are the enabling technologies for data harvesting for our prototype system, are not the principal idea of our approach because we aim at improving the user's experience for interactive exploration of Sensor Web.

Interactive visualizations can considerably improve the exploration of data. Graphical user interface elements can enable visual information seeking via dynamic queries (Ahlberg & Shneiderman, 1994). An extension of dynamic queries can display visual overviews beyond the current query constraints and thus provides cues for how changing a query may yield a satisfying set of results (Spence & Tweedie, 1998). Coordinated visualization yields deeper insights by showing the interdependencies among the information sources (Baldonado *et al.*, 2000). For example, geographic information can be explored in an interface where two linked visualizations are provided for spatial and conceptual domains (Cai, 2002). Coordinated information visualization query widgets that make it possible for information seekers to orient themselves within Web-based information spaces and to incrementally build complex filtering queries have been developed (Dörk *et al.*, 2008).

Metadata that describe characteristics of a sensor resource are used for discovering potential datasets and evaluating their suitability for the researcher's purposes. Discovery is based on search functions relying on metadata about thematic, spatial, and temporal extents of datasets (Beard & Sharma, 1997). Previous teams have developed tools for evaluating datasets by visualization. For example, Mutton and Golbeck used 2D graphs to visualize semantic metadata and ontologies (Mutton & Golbeck, 2003), but such graphs can often be complicated and hard to comprehend. Other researchers, therefore, developed algorithms for the 3D visualization of semantic metadata models and ontologies (Papamanthou *et al.*, 2004). Gobel and Jasnoch used visualization techniques and spa-

tial metaphors to generate effective and intuitive representations of the metadata (Gobel & Jasnoch, 2001). Multiple scholars have demonstrated the usefulness of the visualization of metadata as a tool for visual analysis and reasoning and have used them to support the search for geographic resources (Ahonen-Rainio, 2005; Albertoni *et al.*, 2005). Exploratory visual analysis is useful for the preliminary investigation of large spatiotemporal datasets (Wood *et al.*, 2007). The mapping and superimposition of metadata summaries can be used to provide a supporting context for data discovery and access by the synthesis of metadata, map and feature services (Aditya & Kraak, 2007a, 2007b; NiculaMarque & Berghmans, 2008).

Previous work has shown the potential of 3D visualization using virtual globe as a tool of data exploration (Stensgaard *et al.*, 2009; Tomaszewski, 2011). The virtual globe is used for exploring geo-temporal differences of datasets (Wood *et al.*, 2007; Hoeber *et al.*, 2011) and data publication of Sensor Web (Liang *et al.*, 2010). 3D thematic mapping using the virtual globe and geobrowsers (Sandvik, 2008) offered a framework of 3D geo-visualization for statistical datasets. It provides an inspiration for 3D geo-visualization of metadata of Sensor Web. Sandvik (2008) also advocated the advantages of 3D visualization when using geographical thematic mapping in a series of articles. Multiple visual variables (e.g., color and height of 3D geometry) to present statistical indicators make comparison of information easier and much more accurate when spinning the globe and they provide freedom of navigation with 3D Digital Earth.

Behr *et al.* (2009) introduced X3DOM, which is a model that allows to directly integrate X3D nodes into HTML5 DOM content. X3DOM eases the integration of X3D in modern web applications by directly mapping and synchronizing live DOM elements to a X3D scene model. The integration model is notably evolving and used a framework for online visualization of 3D city model (Mao & Ban, 2011).

DESIGN OF METADATA VISUALIZATION

We extend data-oriented data registry of Sensor Web toward visual information exploration in the virtual globe on the Web, by developing interactive visualizations that provide dynamic exploration across multiple levels-of-detail. These are intuitive user interfaces for efficient information retrieval of metadata for large datasets of sensor resources across the globe.

Design Goals

In order to explore a number of distributed sensor resources efficiently, we have to consider the characteristics and the process of information retrieval and acquisition of human recognition. For an unskilled information seeker, finding proper sensor systems from a large amount of unstructured metadata is similar to finding a specific grain of sand in a desert. Because current web portals for data publication and sharing of deployed sensor resources are data-oriented and organized from the perspective of the data provider, it is difficult to explore information without specific knowledge about the resources. Our goal in designing metadata visualization is not to provide a system for the skilled expert who has specific information he or she is seeking, but to create an intuitive exploration environment for researchers who may be unfamiliar with the sensor resources in a particular field. These external researchers need tools to dynamically filter out unnecessary information from the system according to their interests by visually exposing a summary of the metadata from a registry of sensor systems on the virtual globe. To realize this goal, the method of visualization and the level of visualized metadata should selectively change according to the perspective view of the information seeker. The visualization system should guide an information seeker in progressively reducing candidate query results from large datasets of unfamiliar sensor resources. The specific design goals of metadata visualization system are the following:

- **Enable Casual Formulation of Geospatial Semantic Queries:** An information exploration system should support casual browsing of a large information space using semantic queries. For example, the system should enable filtering metadata according to thematic or administrative areas. The capability of defining a search area with multi-polygon and other geospatial queries should be supported. Complex queries can be constructed in conjunctive form using a combination of multiple queries. The exploration system should allow the formulation of search queries based on parameters by selecting geometric objects in a 3D scene that might be difficult to specify with textual queries. For instance, formulation of a query to select sensor resources recorded within a specific multi-polygon is not simple to describe in textual query.
- **Summarize Information Collections Visually:** The display should include a visual overview of metadata, as well as a clear indication of the currently selected and filtered items. According to the selected sensor source area, the number of items and the complexity of information, the system should represent the summarized information with proper visualization methods and level-of-detail. The level-of-detail will be explained more in the following section.
- **Use Integrated Dynamic Visualization:** The system should provide unrestricted degree-of-freedom of navigation for intuitive exploration. The data should be visualized on the 3D earth globe system.
- **Optimize the Amount of Data Transmitted to the User:** In order to avoid heavy data transmission, the system should minimize the amount of data retrieved.

Light and responsive navigation of the 3D earth globe with summarized metadata visualization is necessary.

- **Conform to Open Standards for Interoperability:** The overall architecture and technologies employed in an information exploration system as well as the markup of sensor metadata should use open standards to foster integrated exploration of heterogeneous sensor resources.

- **Provide Information Drill-Down:** The interface should provide access to an appropriate resolution of sensor information and specific sensor data. The information seeker should be able to display detailed information such as sensor description and recent history of sensor values for result items upon request. The metadata exploration system can provide direct access to the repository storing the sensor dataset.

Level-of-Detail of Metadata

In information exploration visualized on a virtual globe, the system must display not only information from the virtual globe but also metadata of sensor networks in a way that depends on the complexity of the two sets of information. For example, if the most pertinent sensor stations are deployed in a specific area while thousands of stations are recorded in the metadata registry, the local view of the 3D scene can display only specific sensor stations which are included in the viewing frustum of the current scene. However, the global view of the same information shows all the metadata in a very small region of display. If the same method of visualization is applied for both cases, the amount of information in the global view is larger than that of the local view, and there are complex occlusions among the metadata displayed in a small area. These phenomena should be avoided through the consideration of proper visualization methods for different levels-of-detail.

We summarize specific visualization methods for metadata exploration in Figure 1.

- **Statistical Visualization:** An information exploration system should be able to display a statistical visualization, which shows the distribution of sensor systems according to geographical location. It is appropriate to expose a broad view of the overall metadata registered in the system. The visualization can show a bar chart, choropleth and proportional symbol, which are geographically referenced on the globe (Figure 1b).

- **Text Tag:** A text tag shows 3D text on a specific location of the virtual globe (Figure 1c). It shows textual information with variation of size, style, and color of the text displayed. It is used to display more detail information than statistical visualization. For example, a text tag can show a sensor identification string with different color and size according to the characteristic of sensor systems.

- **3D Shape Template:** A 3D shape template can be used to display any kind of 3D object on the globe. For example, a simplified 3D model of sensor system can be a template. It can be located at any specific geographical location (Figure 1d). A 3D shape template is composed with an X3D shape object, so that any event, animation and interaction can be implemented with X3D standard node description.

- **2D Dynamic Sprite:** 2D dynamic sprite is a simple 2D image that is generated dynamically on the information exploration server. It is appropriate to draw summarized information of the sensor system in limited 3D space. The image is dynamically generated according to queries and mapped as a texture image on a 3D geometry in a 3D scene (Figure 1e).

Figure 1. A conceptual design of the proposed visualization methods. (a) Initial view, (b) Statistical visualization, (c) Text tag, (d) 3D shape template, (e) 2D dynamic sprite, (f) Graph drawing of sensor data

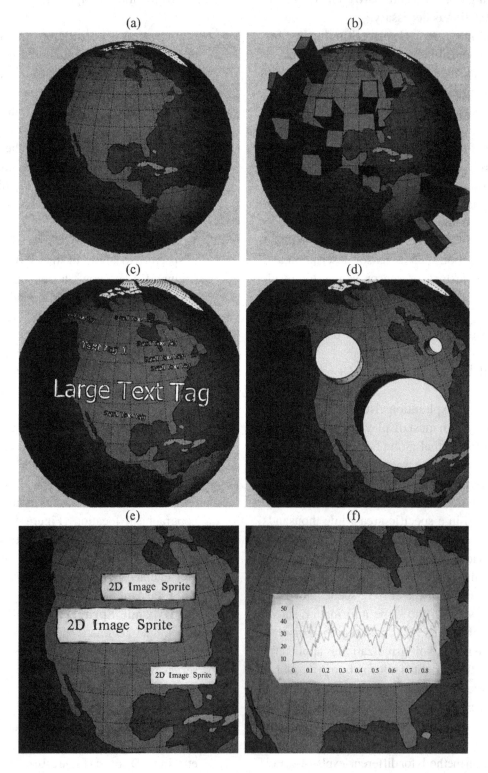

- **Graph Drawing of Sensor Data:** Practical sensor data can be displayed as a 2D or 3D graph drawing in the 3D space of the information exploration system (Figure 1f). It is useful to visualize the recent history of sensor values when the information seeker wants to access more detail of the sensor system after decreasing focus on a particular sensor system.

The types of visualization, described above, should be modified by reduction of focus range of the 3D scene in the procedural information exploration so that the amount of information exposed to the user can be managed.

Standard Web3D Technologies

The component technologies are configured to explore the massive metadata of Sensor Web. The data, applications and communication technolo-

gies used are depicted in Figure 2. It should be noted that while the following technologies are all required to build an integrated system, most of the development is involved with the generation of a dynamic X3D scene to represent an implicit query for visual exploration.

- X3D is open standard file format and runtime architecture to represent and communicate 3D scenes and objects using XML on the Web. The X3D geospatial component provides support for geographic and geospatial applications including the ability to embed geospatial coordinates in certain X3D nodes. Google Earth, Microsoft Bing Maps, NASA World Wind and ESRI ArcGIS Explorer are well-known geobrowsers, which let the user add data layers to maps and imagery. However, a comparative review of existing geobrowsers and related technologies showed that X3D

Figure 2. Data, application and communication technologies used in the proposed system

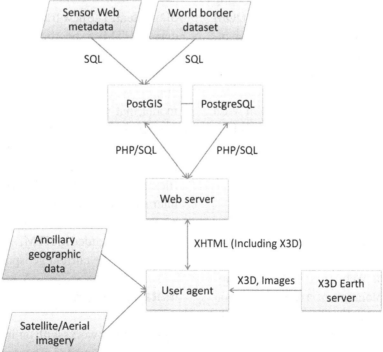

provides the largest number of competitive features in a royalty-free open standards (Yoo & Brutzman, 2009). Another comparative study of related 3D graphics capabilities among open, royalty-free standard formats, preferably based on XML, evaluated 42 graphics file formats (Crews, 2008). Taking the stated objectives for each 3D format into consideration relevant to this study's requirements, X3D provides the most comprehensive solution.

- X3D-Earth is an open standard-based technology for publishing earth globes, which includes tools to enable users to build their own globes utilizing their own data. We can build our X3D-Earth globe instance based on the specific requirements for exploring the metadata from particular sensor networks.

- X3DOM model is an open and human-readable 3D scene-graph embedded in the HTML DOM, which extends the DOM interfaces and allows the application developer to access and manipulate the 3D content by only adding, removing or changing the DOM elements via standard DOM scripting. Thus, no specific plugins or plugin interfaces like the Scene Authoring Interface (SAI) are needed. Furthermore, this seamless integration of 3D contents in the web browser integrates well with common web dynamic techniques such as DHTML and Ajax, and the web browsers already provide a complete deployment structure (Behr *et al.*, 2011).

IMPLEMENTATION

We implemented a Web-based system to support the visual exploration of a large collection of metadata from the distributed Sensor Web. The prototype performs online browsing of ap-

proximately 34,000 sensor systems from which datasets are accessible.

Architecture

The architecture of the visual metadata exploration system is divided into two parts: client-side and server-side (see Figure 3). On the Web server, data is processed and filtered to generate a dynamic X3D scene. We use PHP as an overall programming framework and PostgreSQL as the back-end database for storing processed metadata from the distributed Sensor Web. PostGIS is used to extend the geospatial capability of the database. Presentations and interactions are realized in the Web browser. We support the latest build of WebGL-enabled browsers. WebGL-enabled web browsers are available for most platforms. Mozilla Firefox and Google Chrome for any platform, and Safari for Mac OS X are compatible with our Web application. Because the W3C standards such as HTML5, CSS3 and Web-browser implementations are moving forward quickly, X3D has also been moving toward a new framework and runtime to support the integration of HTML5 and declarative 3D content. The new framework tries to fulfill the current HTML5 specifications for declarative 3D content and allows the inclusion of X3D elements as part of any HTML5 DOM tree. Therefore, we employ X3DOM as a HTML5/X3D integration model that renders the X3D scene and handles interactive events from the metadata exploration. While the basic structure of the interface is transmitted as XHTML, CSS, and JavaScript files, the actual processed and filtered data for the interactive exploration of metadata is retrieved by the browser as X3D XML encoded objects, which is embedded in HTML DOM, generated in response to the current geospatial query.

Metadata Extraction

Our prototype works with online repositories that are constantly updated. The metadata is extracted

Figure 3. Architecture of the implemented system

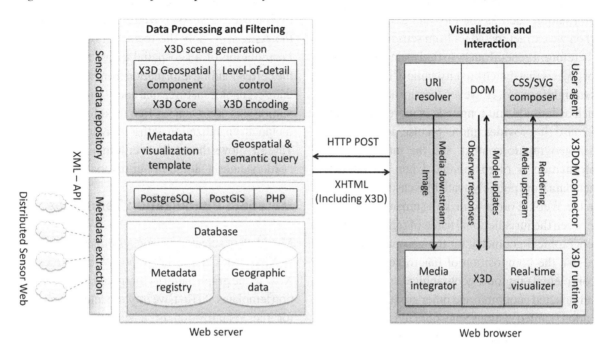

and stored in an online database, which is updated from distributed Sensor Web resources. In our work, we extract information from publicly available datasets of weather stations on the Web via the personal weather station (PWS) project managed by Weather Underground (Weather Underground, 2012). The system assumes information items have a weather station identifier (unique ID), description (text), date and time of last observation (timestamp), geographic location (longitude and latitude), jurisdictional information including city and country names, and physical properties related to weather.

The extraction of metadata is straightforward. In order to create the list of weather stations that are publicly accessible on the Web, we query the web service of Weather Underground and find weather stations, which are registered as contributors to the PWS project. The retrieved information such as unique station identifier (unique ID), text string describing neighborhood, city and country name, station type, and direct access link (URL)

are stored in our online database. The actual detailed metadata of each personal weather station is collected by formulating a query with parameters using the list of available stations. The PWS project provides an XML-based API, which gives access to the current status of weather stations. A PHP program extracts the detailed metadata and updates our online database for the information exploration system. Our online database stores description and jurisdictional information as simple attributes in the database. Date information such as timestamp, geographical information including latitude and longitude, and physical properties of weather require unit and format checking and conversion before the information is injected into our database.

Geospatial Query

A geospatial query is necessary to filter out metadata of sensor resources that are outside of the region of interest during progressive exploration and narrowing of focus. We collect jurisdictional information such as the city and country name when we extract metadata from sensor networks. Therefore, a general query to find metadata of sensor objects that match this city name or region code is straightforward. However, location information such as latitude and longitude is more important because it provides more precise information in a geographic context, and the jurisdictional information is often omitted when we collect metadata from publicly available sensor resources on the Web. In order to make a semantic relation between the jurisdictional name of region and the geographical geometry for the geospatial query, we use the composition of macro geographical (continental) regions, geographical sub-regions, and selected economic and other groupings information (United Nations Statistics Division, 2011), which are provided by the statistics division of the United Nations. The correlated region name, code, and geometry are stored into our online database and are used for formulating a casual query based on the jurisdictional region name such as city or country. For example, it is not possible

to figure out whether a sensor station is included in South-Eastern Asia, which is a sub-region of the Asia, with only the metadata of the station. Formulation of a geospatial query that refers to the corresponding information from world borders dataset enables such a casual query based on region name. This approach is often used for generating metadata visualization with a statistical summary. Table 1 shows the attribute columns of the world borders dataset stored in our database.

Metadata Visualization Templates

Metadata of selected sensor systems is visualized as X3D nodes in a scene graph. We implemented X3D scene graph patterns for metadata visualization templates. At first, we implemented a template for the visualization of a statistical summary using geo-referenced 3D bar charts. Objects can be located in arbitrary location using geospatial coordinate system according to the current X3D standard specification. The bar chart can be located at a specific geographic location by specifying the 3D shape node of the bar chart as a child node of

Table 1. Attribute columns of world borders dataset

Column	Type	Description
ID	Serial	Unique ID
FIPS	String (2)	FIPS 10-4 Country Code
ISO2	String (2)	ISO 3166-1 Alpha-2 Country Code
ISO3	String (3)	ISO 3166-1 Alpha-3 Country Code
UN	Short Integer (3)	ISO 3166-1 Numeric-3 Country Code
Name	String (50)	Name of country/area
Area	Long Integer (7)	Land area, FAO Statistics (2002)
POP2005	Double (10, 0)	Population, World Population Prospects (2005)
Region	Short Integer (3)	Macro geographical (continental region), UN Statistics
Subregion	Short Integer (3)	Geographical sub-region, UN Statistics
Lon	Float (7, 3)	Longitude
Lat	Float (7, 3)	Latitude
Geometry	Multi-polygon	Country/area border as polygons

a GeoLocation node in an X3D scene. However, the current implementation of X3DOM lacks of support for several nodes belong to the geospatial component such as GeoLocation, GeoTransform and GeoViewpoint nodes. Thus we implemented visualization templates using IndexedFaceset composed of GeoCoordinate node instead of go-referencing standard X3D objects. The rectangular shape of the bar chart can be replaced with an arbitrary 3D object, and it is possible to scale the size of the shape proportionally to attributes of metadata. In addition, the appearance such as color and luminosity can be used to visualize information of metadata attributes implicitly.

Figure 4 shows example visualizations of personal weather stations. Figure 4a shows a 3D bar chart that visualizes the number of stations registered in the database according to country border. Figure 4b shows 3D prism map which is inspired by 3D thematic mapping (Sandvik, 2008). Both examples are rendered in a standard X3D player embedded in a Web browser. In these examples, we used Google Chrome, although other browsers including Firefox and Safari should work.

The 2D image sprite is generated dynamically from our server by PHP and the GD graphics library. We employed the GD library to generate dynamic images that directly represent summarized metadata queried from our PostGIS database. The generated sprite can represent practical values of measurement as well as the status of sensor systems and the types of sensors with small icons as well as text strings. Font style, color and size of text string and size, color and shape of icon can express much detailed information in the limited space of the 2D sprite. The image sprite can be mapped on any 3D geometry in the X3D scene graph since it is used as a regular image texture.

Figure 4 shows the visualization of summarized metadata using the pseudo code. In this example, we focused our interest on the weather stations located in China. The image sprite represents identifier, city and country name, type of the weather

station, last observation date and time, composition and status of sensors, which compose the weather station. Font style and color is used to represent status of the sensors in this example. It is possible to combine multiple visualization templates and formulate more dynamic events using the X3D scene graph. For example, the image sprite can be combined with graph drawing template. In order to add event control to the 3D scene, an element. appendChild event is attached to the image sprite. The event triggered when the mouse is over the image sprite (element.onmouseover attribute) is routed to add X3D nodes that render a 2D graph. Thus the 2D graph showing the recent history of sensor data is displayed when the mouse cursor is over the image sprite as shown in Figure 4d. A 2D image of a graph of recent weather is generated from the API of PWS project of the Weather Underground. The image is mapped as an ImageTexture node of a 3D surface by element. setAttribute method. It is the most detailed information that our exploration system can display regarding the selected weather station. The final step of seamless focusing in toward the specific sensor system is that we provide a direct link to the Web page of the sensor system by Anchor node attached to the 2D graph.

USE CASE

Personal Weather Stations

In order to investigate how the visualization of metadata on a 3D Web-based globe organized by level-of-detail can enhance the search and exploration of information, we applied our development to a prototype metadata exploration system featuring levels-of-detail for a multi-scaled Sensor Web and used it to visually explore weather stations. The 34,700 personal weather stations are collected from the PWS project and registered in our online database.

Figure 4. Visualization of sensor resources on a Web-based virtual globe: (a) statistical bar chart, (b) 3D prism, (c) dynamic image sprite, and (d) graph drawing of selected sensor data

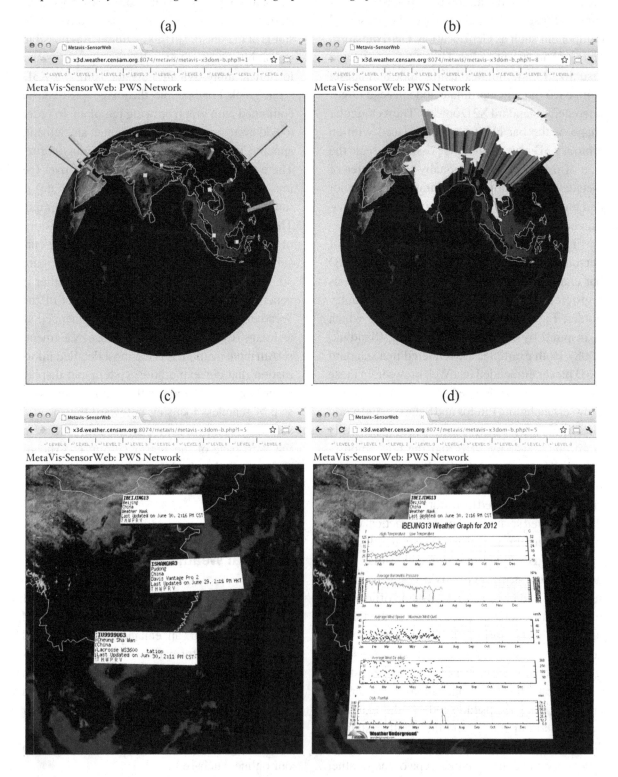

The existing data access interface of the PWS project is based on text queries that produce and result lists expressed in HTML table with hyperlinks. This interface provides no mechanism for the user to summarize data or metadata from multiple weather stations. The user's only option is to laboriously follow the link to each individual weather station. We have transitioned the information exploration process from the traditional text-based user interface to a three-dimensional space with a seamless exploration interface based on a virtual globe. Even when the information seeker does not have domain specific knowledge of the weather stations, our system provides an easy and intuitive approach to exploring the available sensor information. When the user first engages with the information exploration interface, our system shows only brief information about how many stations are distributed in jurisdictional area borders (Figure 4a). At this point, the information seeker can decide which areas he or she will explore further to retrieve more detailed information. Once a specific location such as a region border is selected then a geospatial query implicitly formulated within our system filters out unnecessary information and displays only a summarized result of the metadata within the selected region boundary using detailed metadata sprites visualized on top of the 3D scene (Figure 4c). When the user has more interest in a specific station, then he or she can trigger a mouse event to enable the overlay of detailed properties and the recent history of measurement shown in a 2D graph on top of the 3D scene (Figure 4d). If the information seeker still has specific needs for downloading sensor data from the station, our system provides direct access to the sensor system as a hyperlink.

The summarization approaches that reduce level-of-detail at broader views are not limited to summarizing the sensor metadata, but are also applicable to summarizing sensor data themselves in order to expose a broad view of the scientific properties of sensors such as temperature to the users. For example, when the user selects sensor data (e.g., temperature) instead of sensor metadata as the visualization mode, our prototype system displays average values of temperature recorded by sensors in weather stations within each country border (Figure 5a). A geospatial query, which computes average values of temperature by country from registered weather stations, is implicitly formulated within our system, and a dynamic 3D scene is generated using a statistical bar chart. The color and the height scale of the bar chart vary proportionally according to the value of the temperature. The 3D bar chart shows real values scaled to fit on a digital globe, and the user can easily assess differences in average temperature between stations. When the user has more interest in a specific region, e.g., Japan as shown in Figure 5b, the level-of-detail of the dynamic 3D scene is automatically updated by a geospatial query, which is again implicitly formulated within the system. Figure 5c shows a visualization using combination of 3D prism presenting the number of registered weather stations and bar chart presenting the summarized temperature in each country, and Figure 5d shows a dynamic 3D scene composed of various visualization templates.

Visual Exploration of Cyberinfrastructure

In order to verify the usefulness of our approach and the feasibility of the proposed visualization templates according to the LOD of sensor resources, we applied our approach to different types of sensor data sets. As we mentioned in Section 1, archived sensor data sets provided by data portals are the most reliable sensor resource for environmental researchers. We developed a cyberinfrastructure (Yoo *et al.*, 2012) to extend the longevity of sensor data, to facilitate data discovery, and to provide data access for authorized users. This Web service provides sensor

Figure 5. Visualization of sensor resources on a Web-based virtual globe: (a) a global view shows summarized temperature of weather stations in each country, (b) a local view shows separate temperature of weather stations, and (c) combination of 3D prism presenting the number of registered weather stations and bar chart presenting the summarized temperature in each country, and (d) a dynamic 3D scene composed of various visualization templates

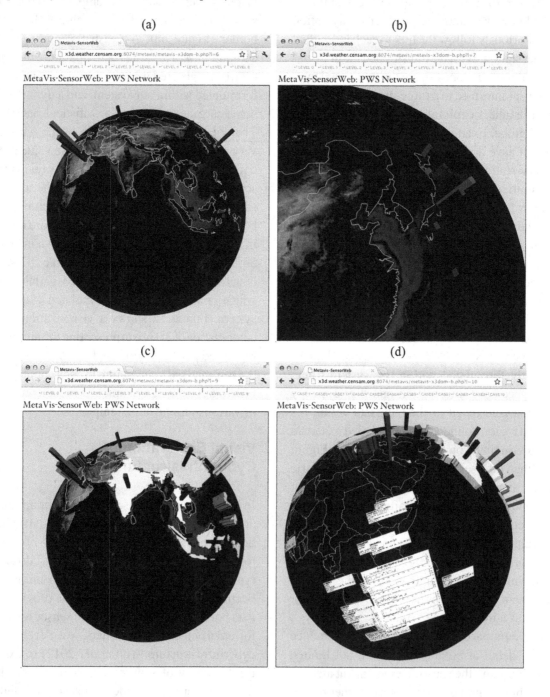

data registration, discovery and exchange using ontology-based scientific metadata (Yu and Feng 2009).

We registered a rainfall data archive that is available from the National Environment Agency (NEA) of Singapore. The archive is composed of hourly rainfall data from 33 sensor stations. The boundary boarder, water basins, and the rainfall archive of Singapore are accessible from the cyberinfrastructure; however the interface is based on text-based query. We applied our visualization template to the rainfall data archive and the results are shown in Figure 6(a) and (b). The 3D bar chart in Figure 6(a) and (b) shows values of rainfall for each water basin, and the bar chart dynamically varies according to the hourly rainfall data archived in our system. The exploration environment using the HTML/X3D integration model makes dynamic comparison of rainfall values and precise comparison without any specialized tools except our prototype Web application and standard Web browsers.

The Typhoon Center of Regional Specialized Meteorological Center (RSMC) of Japan at Tokyo provides information on tropical cyclones in the western North Pacific and the South China Sea. The aforementioned cyberinfrastructure provides a web service for spatial analysis of the tropical cyclone track data. We applied the proposed visualization templates to data exploration for the spatial analysis functions. Figure 6(c) shows a global view of a 3D shape template that visualizes the simplified information of tropical cyclones. The visualization provides intuitive understanding of the distribution of tropical cyclones for a selected period. The dynamic exploration interface including free spinning and navigation with just a standard Web browser makes data exploration easier. Figure 6(d) shows a local view of line streams, which represents the trajectories of mature hurricanes among the data sets shown in Figure 6(c).

CONCLUSION

We have introduced a visual exploration interface using 3D space for visualizing metadata of the Sensor Web. This approach transitions human processing of information during data discovery from two-dimensional space with text based search to three-dimensional space with visual media navigation. The amount of information transmitted to the user during the exploration is increased dramatically compared to the former text-based approach. Furthermore, the seamless focusing enabled by the new interface provides a less frustrating and more intuitive experience.

The main contribution of this work is the design and verification of LOD of metadata for Web-based dynamic visualization, the application of dynamic geospatial query and the use of mashups with the X3D-based earth globe to Web-based information exploration of sensor resources. The Web application based on HTML5/X3D integration model eliminated the need for third party plug-ins to enable interactive representation of 3D geospatial information. Therefore the information exploration of the Sensor Web based on an X3D Earth globe with only a standard Web browser implementation without any third party plug-in has been realized. We have designed level-of-detail for proper metadata visualization at multiple levels of exploration and implemented X3D templates for several styles of visualization methods. We have developed a PHP program that enables formulation of a dynamic geospatial query and the generation of an X3D scene for the visualization of the query result.

In the current realization, our prototype system is limited to fairly simple visual representations and query variations. This is partly due to the constrained capabilities of current Web browsers, the current implementation of X3DOM that support X3D Geospatial Component. For example, the current X3DOM still does not conform to the

Figure 6. Visualization of sensor resources on a Web-based virtual globe: (f) visualization of rainfall data for Singapore in a local view, (g) dynamic change of the 3D bar chart according to the change of rainfall data, (h) a global view of a 3D shape template used for a visualization of the summary for tropical cyclones data sets, and (i) a local view of a line set template used for a visualization of the detail trajectory of mature hurricane data

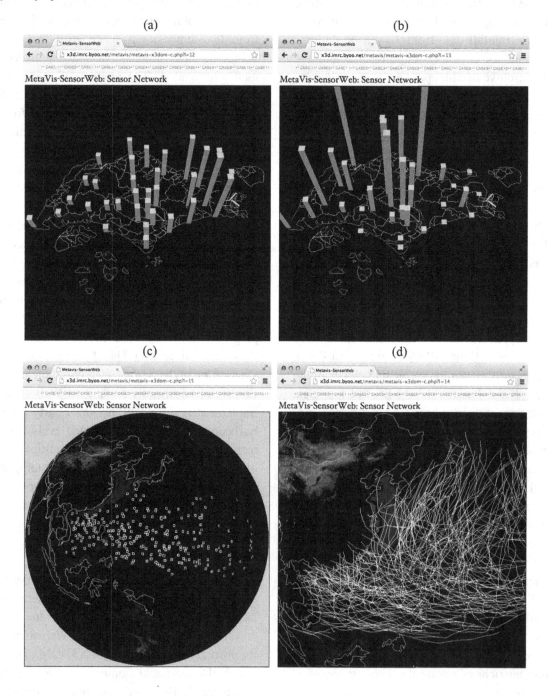

full specification of X3D standard version 3.2. We expect to extend the functionality of our prototype to facilitate the dynamic exploration of the Sensor Web and to allow the user to seamlessly focus in on a particular sensor system in more intuitive ways.

REFERENCES

Aditya, T., & Kraak, M.-J. (2007a). Aim4GDI: Facilitating the synthesis of GDI resources through mapping and superimpositions of metadata summaries. *GeoInformatica*, *11*(4), 459–478. doi:10.1007/s10707-007-0021-4

Aditya, T., & Kraak, M.-J. (2007b). A search interface for an SDI: Implementation and evaluation of metadata visualization strategies. *Transactions in GIS*, *11*(3), 413–435. doi:10.1111/j.1467-9671.2007.01053.x

Ahlberg, C., & Shneiderman, B. (1994). Visual information seeking: Tight coupling of dynamic query filters with starfield displays. In *Proceedings of the SIGCHI Conference on Human Factors in Computing Systems: Celebrating Interdependence* (pp. 313-317). Boston, MA: ACM. doi:10.1145/259963.260390

Ahonen-Rainio, P. (2005). *Visualization of geospatial metadata for selecting geographic datasets*. (Doctoral dissertation). Helsinki University of Technology, Espoo, Finland.

Albertoni, R., Bertone, A., & Martino, M. D. (2005). Visualization and semantic analysis of geographic metadata. In *Proceedings of Workshop on Geographic information retrieval* (pp. 9-16). Bremen, Germany: ACM. doi:10.1145/1096985.1096989

Babitski, G., Bergweiler, S., Hoffmann, J., Schön, D., Stasch, C., & Walkowski, A. (2009). Ontology-based integration of sensor web services in disaster management. In K. Janowicz, M. Raubal, & S. Levashkin (Eds.), *Geospatial semantics* (pp. 103–121). Berlin, Germany: Springer Berlin Heidelberg. doi:10.1007/978-3-642-10436-7_7

Baldonado, M. Q. W., Woodruff, A., & Kuchinsky, A. (2000). Guidelines for using multiple views in information visualization. In *Proceedings of the Working Conference on Advanced Visual Interfaces* (pp. 110-119). Palermo, Italy: ACM. doi:10.1145/345513.345271

Beard, K., & Sharma, V. (1997). Multidimensional ranking for data in digital spatial libraries. *International Journal on Digital Libraries*, *1*(2), 153–160. doi:10.1007/s007990050011

Behr, J., Eschler, P., Jung, Y., & Zöllner, M. (2009). X3DOM: A DOM-based HTML5/X3D integration model. In *Proceedings of International Conference on 3D Web Technology* (pp. 127-135). Darmstadt, Germany: ACM. doi:10.1145/1559764.1559784

Behr, J., Jung, Y., Drevensek, T., & Aderhold, A. (2011). Dynamic and interactive aspects of X3DOM. In *Proceedings of International Conference on 3D Web Technology* (pp. 81-87). Paris, France: ACM.

Behr, J., Jung, Y., Keil, J., Drevensek, T., Zoellner, M., Eschler, P., & Fellner, D. (2010). A scalable architecture for the HTML5/X3D integration model X3DOM. In *Proceedings of International Conference on Web 3D Technology* (pp. 185-194). Los Angeles, CA: ACM. doi:10.1145/1836049.1836077

Bermudez, L., Graybeal, J., & Arko, R. (2006). A marine platforms ontology: Experiences and lessons. In *Proceedings of Workshop on Semantic Sensor Networks (SSN 2006). Proceedings of conjunction with 5th International Semantic Web Conference (ISWC 2006)*. Athens, GA: Academic Press.

Bröring, A., Echterhoff, J., Jirka, S., Simonis, I., Everding, T., Stasch, C., & Lemmens, R. et al. (2011). New generation sensor web enablement. *Sensors (Basel, Switzerland)*, *11*(3), 2652–2699. doi:10.3390/s110302652 PMID:22163760

Cai, G. (2002). GeoVIBE: A visual interface for geographic digital libraries. In K. Börner & C. Chen (Eds.), *Visual interfaces to digital libraries* (pp. 171–187). Bremen, Germany: Springer Berlin Heidelberg. doi:10.1007/3-540-36222-3_13

Crews, N. (2008). *Comparative study of open 3D graphics standards*. Autodesk Inc.

Dörk, M., Carpendale, S., Collins, C., & Williamson, C. (2008). Visgets: Coordinated visualizations for Web-based information exploration and discovery. *IEEE Transactions on Visualization and Computer Graphics*, *14*(6), 1205–1212. doi:10.1109/TVCG.2008.175 PMID:18988965

Federal Geographic Data Committee. (1998). *Content standard for digital geospatial metadata*. Retrieved April 30, 2014, from http://www.fgdc.gov/metadata/csdgm

Feng, C.-C., & Yu, L. (2010). Ontology-based data exchange and integration: An experience in cyberinfrastructure of sensor network based monitoring system. In *Proceedings of International Conference on Advances in Semantic Processing* (pp. 83-90). Florence, Italy: Academic Press.

Gobel, S., & Jasnoch, U. (2001). Visualization techniques in metadata information systems for geospatial data. *Advances in Environmental Research*, *5*(4), 415–424. doi:10.1016/S1093-0191(01)00093-4

Henson, C. A., Pschorr, J. K., Sheth, A. P., & Thirunarayan, K. (2009). SemSOS: Semantic sensor observation service. In *Proceedings of International Symposium on Collaborative Technologies and Systems* (pp. 44-53). Baltimore, MD: Academic Press.

Hoeber, O., Wilson, G., Harding, S., Enguehard, R., & Devillers, R. (2011). Exploring geo-temporal differences using gtdiff. In *Proceedings of Pacific Visualization Symposium (PacificVis)* (pp. 139-146). Hong Kong: IEEE.

Hornsby, K. S., & King, K. (2008). Linking geosensor network data and ontologies to support transportation modeling. Lecture Notes in Computer Science, 4540, 191-209.

Janowicz, K., & Compton, M. (2010). The stimulus-sensor-observation ontology design pattern and its integration into the semantic sensor network ontology. In *Proceedings of International Workshop on Semantic Sensor Networks 2010* (pp. 7–11). Shanghai, China: Academic Press.

Jirka, S., & Nüst, D. (2010). *Sensor instance registry discussion paper*. Public Discussion Paper: Open Geospatial Consortium, Open Geospatial Consortium.

Liang, S., Chang, D., Badger, J., Rezel, R., Chen, S., Huang, C. Y., & Li, R. Y. (2010). GeoCENS: Geospatial cyberinfrastructure for environmental sensing. In *Proceedings of International Conference on Geographic Information Science*. Zurich, Switzerland: Academic Press.

Mao, B., & Ban, Y. (2011). Online visualization of 3D city model using CityGML and X3DOM. *Cartographica: The International Journal for Geographic Information and Geovisualization, 46*(2), 109–114. doi:10.3138/carto.46.2.109

Mutton, P., & Golbeck, J. (2003). Visualization of semantic metadata and ontologies. In *Proceedings of International Conference on Information Visualization* (pp. 300-305). London, UK: Academic Press.

Nicula, B., Marque, C., & Berghmans, D. (2008). Visualization of distributed solar data and metadata with the solar weather browser. *Solar Physics, 248*(2), 225–232. doi:10.1007/s11207-007-9105-4

Papamanthou, C., Tollis, I. G., & Doerr, M. (2004). 3D visualization of semantic metadata models and ontologies. *Lecture Notes in Computer Science, 3383*, 377-388.

Probst, F. (2006). Ontological analysis of observations and measurements. *Lecture Notes in Computer Science - Geographic. Information Science, 4197*, 304–320.

Raskin, R. G., & Pan, M. J. (2005). Knowledge representation in the semantic web for earth and environmental terminology (SWEET). *Computers & Geosciences, 31*(9), 1119–1125. doi:10.1016/j.cageo.2004.12.004

Russomanno, D. J., Kothari, C., & Thomas, O. (2005). Building a sensor ontology: A practical approach leveraging iso and ogc models. In *Proceedings of International Conference on Artificial Intelligence* (pp. 17-18). Las Vegas, NV: Academic Press.

Sandvik, B. (2008). *Using KML for thematic mapping*. Retrieved February 19, 2013, from: http://thematicmapping.org/downloads/Using_KML_for_Thematic_Mapping.pdf

Sheth, A., Henson, C., & Sahoo, S. S. (2008). Semantic sensor web. *IEEE Internet Computing, 12*(4), 78–83. doi:10.1109/MIC.2008.87

Spence, R., & Tweedie, L. (1998). The attribute explorer: Information synthesis via exploration. *Interacting with Computers, 11*(2), 137–146. doi:10.1016/S0953-5438(98)00022-8

Stensgaard, A.-S., Saarnak, C. F. L., Utzinger, J., Vounatsou, P., Simoonga, C., Mushinge, G., & Kristensen, T. K. et al. (2009). Virtual globes and geospatial health: The potential of new tools in the management and control of vector-borne diseases. *Geospatial Health, 3*(2), 127–141. doi:10.4081/gh.2009.216 PMID:19440958

Tomaszewski, B. (2011). Situation awareness and virtual globes: Applications for disaster management. *Computers & Geosciences, 37*(1), 86–92. doi:10.1016/j.cageo.2010.03.009

United Nations Statistics Division. (2011). *Composition of macro geographical (continental) regions, geographical sub-regions, and selected economic and other groupings*. Retrieved April 30, 2014, from http://unstats.un.org/unsd/methods/m49/m49regin.htm

Weather Underground. (2012). *The personal weather station project*. Retrieved April 30, 2014, from http://www.wunderground.com/weatherstation/index.asp

Wood, J., Dykes, J., Slingsby, A., & Clarke, K. (2007). Interactive visual exploration of a large spatio-temporal dataset: Reflections on a geovisualization mashup. *IEEE Transactions on Visualization and Computer Graphics, 13*(6), 1176–1183.

Yoo, B., & Brutzman, D. (2009). X3D earth terrain-tile production chain for georeferenced simulation. In *Proceedings of International Conference on 3D Web Technology* (pp. 159-166). Darmstadt, Germany: ACM. doi:10.1145/1559764.1559789

KEY TERMS AND DEFINITIONS

Extensible 3D: A royalty-free ISO standard XML-based file format for representing 3D computer graphics.

HTML5: A core technology markup language of the Internet used for structuring and presenting content for the World Wide Web.

Level-of-Detail: A computer graphics technique to adapt the detail of the displayed 3D object to the user needs.

Sensor Web: A type of sensor network that is especially well suited for environmental monitoring.

Web3D: Interactive 3D content and which are embedded into web pages, and that we can see through a web browser.

X3D: Acronym of Extensible 3D.

X3DOM: An open-source framework and runtime for 3D graphics on the Web.

Chapter 10
Web 3.0 in Web Development

João Vieira
Lisbon School of Economics and Management, Portugal

Pedro Isaías
Universidade Aberta (Portuguese Open University), Portugal

ABSTRACT

The Web 3.0 has revolutionized the Internet in the last years and its benefits are still being studied. The way that websites are being developed is also changing because of this Web evolution, giving to Web developers new technologies where computers can better understand and give meaning to content. This chapter presents an overview of technologies considered to be included on the Web 3.0 concept. The main objective of the chapter is to introduce a conceptual framework of Web 3.0, or Semantic Web, technologies that can be used for developing a website. This review of literature introduces the evolution of each of the technologies mentioned, as well as their functions. Some examples and opportunities for use are also presented. The chapter offers a current state-of-the-art and an opportunity for future relevant research in the Web development area.

INTRODUCTION

Websites have become an important tool for different areas such as commerce, information and education (Thyagharajan & Nayak, 2007). There has been an explosive increase in the number of users, which leads to new challenges in order to meet the needs of each user (Antoniou, Paschou, Sourla & Tsakalidis, 2010; Arora & Kant, 2012; Alpert, Karat, Karat, Brodie & Vergo 2003). The competition between web sites has also increased in recent years, which means that it is necessary to find certain competitive advantages to give

better results. Considering this scenario, new web development technologies were developed to improve the relationship between the user and the web site in order to increase user satisfaction and consequently the number of sales, access, or other measurable objectives. These technologies seek to offer customized services to meet the individual needs of each user and reduce the complexity in consumer choices (Alpert et al., 2003).

The concept of Web 3.0 is considered to be the next step in the evolution of the web, with several new ideas adding new functionalities to existing services. Some of these changes promise

DOI: 10.4018/978-1-4666-8147-7.ch010

to enhance data mining with improved search capability, bigger databases, intelligent search and recommendation options, better software agents, and new personalization techniques. The idea behind Web 3.0 is to create a form of language that the computer can understand, with the goal of processing, transforming, understanding and acting on the information received (Dwivedi, Williams, Mitra, Niranjan & Weerakkody, 2011). This is also the main reason why it is known as semantic web, as it allows the computers to understand the meaning of the information, and not just display it. Within this idea, web development is also at a time of change and constantly evolving, with new technologies being implemented and new research to be reasoned in order to transform the web according to the concept of Web 3.0 (Barassi & Treré, 2012). The main focus of Web 3.0 technologies is to encourage users to contribute information in such a way that computers can understand and act on it. In this way, web systems will assist users in various tasks such as research, recommendations, navigation, and organization, among other tasks, in particular, taking into account the needs and preferences of each user, creating a smart and personalized web. This set of technologies led to the growing interest in the new generation of web development, which leads to more business investment in these strategies, as well as studies conducted in the subject (Dwivedi et al, 2011). This chapter will therefore propose a conceptual framework of technologies that can be applied to web development via the concept of Web 3.0. The framework proposed will be a review chapter which presents some of the most popular technologies for web development. The chapter will begin to explain and give a background of several concepts essential to the meaning of Web 3.0 technologies, such as semantic web technology, user model and data mining techniques. Then, the chapter will discuss some of the issues of web development and the need to implement

the framework proposed in this chapter. After this discussion, a detailed explanation is given of each of the technologies which can be considered to be Web 3.0. It will explain how these technologies have evolved in recent years, and how they work in the present, giving known examples and cases where they can be used.

BACKGROUND

Semantic Web Technologies

Semantic technologies have been the focus of study since the earlier 2000s, and numerous studies have been conducted in order to improve and define these technologies. The concept of semantic web was created by Tim Berners-Lee with the purpose of creating a web that could recognize the meaning of the information in the web documents. Berners-Lee saw it as a way to bring a common structure to the content on web pages, allowing software agents to carry out several tasks on behalf of the user, creating a mutual cooperation between the computer and the humans (Sabucedo, Rifón, Corradini, Polzonetti & Re, 2010; Kück, 2004). With the semantic web, the machines become much better at processing and understanding the meaning of the data. For example, an agent on a clinic's web page can understand the working days of a specific doctor and the appointment times, for the user to schedule a consult (Berners-Lee, Hendler & Lassila, 2001). The technologies of semantic web are based on three trends (Martin et al, 2011):

- Knowledge representation;
- Knowledge generation through collaboration; and
- Personalization of the gathered knowledge.

Several important terms need to be explained, in order to understand semantic technologies. Ontologies are conceptual models that describe the main concepts of the domain and their relationships. An example of an ontology stated by Berners-Lee and Lassila (2001), is a rule such as "If a city code is associated with a state code, and an address uses that city code, then that address has the associated state code" (Berners-Lee, Hendler & Lassila, 2001, pp. 3). The reasoning techniques are then in charge of working with the metadata based on the ontologies (Dolog & Nejdl, 2007). The metadata capture part of the meaning of data, converting into meaningful information that is then interpreted by the software agents. There are currently two technologies for developing metadata in the semantic web: the Extensible Markup Language (XML) that defines the structure of the data, without giving meaning, and the Resource Description Framework (RDF) that defines the semantic meaning of the data structure defined by the XML. The software agents, or smart agents, will then gather all the semantic resources to make the necessary logical inferences, which are constructed according to the principles of reasoning (Kasimati & Zamani, 2011). These terms can be used in several technologies, which we will explain later in the chapter.

User Model and Data Mining Techniques

In order to meet the needs of each user and implement these technologies, the system has to look for a way to gather the information needed for the purpose. In this respect, there is a feature that allows users to be distinguished and represents the individual information of each one, known as the user model. This model can collect different types of information, depending on the strategy that a website is attempting to use, i.e. select and prioritize the most relevant information in a user's search, manipulate and organize links or display only the content that matters to each one. This model requires constant updating of the information of each user, and can make the collection of data from different sources, either by observing the interaction that the user has with the system or asking them to add their own data. In building a user model, it is necessary to take into account three essential aspects (Brusilovsky & Millán, 2007):

- The nature of the data, or its origin;
- The type of information contained in the model; and
- The methods used.

However, for a user model to be created, the system needs to gather the necessary information by using data mining techniques. The data mining approach to web development and personalization is called 'web usage mining', which can be defined as an automatic discovery and analysis of patterns of data collected and also the interactions that the user has with the websites. With this data collection and pattern discovery, the website owners can better understand their users, creating the user model, and support the decision-making that is necessary for organizing the website. In order to predict the future interests of users, the websites usually use techniques for pattern discovery with learning algorithms (Mobasher, 2007). The clustering aims to divide a data set into clusters, where each cluster has its similarities maximized. The clusters can be users or items. In user clustering, users are grouped based on their profile similarity. In items clustering, items are grouped on the similarity of the interest scores given by all users. The items can also be clustered according to the similarity of their content features or attributes.

The association rule discovery is where the algorithm can find groups of items or pages that are usually accessed or purchased together. With this technique, the websites can better organize their content. The sequence rule discovery is differentiated from the association rule because it takes into account the order and sequence in which items or pages have been accessed. With this technique, the websites can discover the frequent navigational paths (Kantardzic, 2011).

More recent, popular mostly because of the concept of Web 3.0, are the latent variable models (LVM) that use probabilistic approaches to discover the structural and semantic relationships within the data (Mobasher, 2007).

WEB 3.0 TECHNOLOGIES

Issues, Controversies, Problems

The web has evolved considerably since its creation. From the web 1.0 where it was considered to be a read-only web, where the information was stored and the users could only search and read on a website. The web 2.0 gave a new meaning to the term, turning websites more people-centric, where users could participate and not only read but also write. The social component of websites where also introduced with this new term. The web 3.0, explained earlier on the chapter, it's an evolution of the web 2.0, and it that was created to decrease human's tasks and decisions, by leaving them to the machines (Aghaei, Nematbakhsh & Farsani, 2012). There were also several improvements to be made in web development in order to address the lack of structure of the information that does not categorize, filter or interpret documents, which led researchers to develop intelligent agents (Cooley, Mobasher & Srivastava, 1997). There was a need to change to an even greater "web of people", due to the increasing value of the user (Wahlster & Dengel, 2006). There was also a need to create a more intelligent web that could understand the meaning of the information and what the user needs, by creating a personalized experience for the user. For this reason, web development needed several improvements such as offering new solutions and options to the users, and essentially decreasing the difficulty of tasks and helping users on their decisions, which due to the amount of content and information, are becoming more difficult.

For these reasons, this chapter will propose a framework that could be implemented when developing a website. These technologies are considered to be Web 3.0 because of their purpose and characteristics, and are based on personalization which we consider to be an important term to understand the Web 3.0 in web development.

SOLUTIONS AND RECOMMENDATIONS

Recommendation Systems

One of the most popular personalization systems is the recommendation system, which uses data mining techniques that analyse the behaviour of users in a particular website, and then recommend products or content that may be of interest to the user, taking into account their preferences (Wu, Im, Tremaine, Instone & Turoff, 2002). We have, has examples of these systems, websites such as Amazon, StumbleUpon, Last.fm, Movielens, Yahoo, TripAdvisor, Flickr, among many others (Montgomery & Smith, 2009). These systems may also collect information from users in two distinct forms: explicit or implicit. The first is the user that provides the information, while in the second, the website collects data indirectly. There are, however, several techniques to determine the recommendations presented.

Collaborative Filtering Recommender Systems

Collaborative filtering is the process of evaluating products (films, books, music, news, etc.) based on other people's opinions. This technique allows the various opinions from a web community to be used to generate recommendations to users who may have the same interests. If, for example, a user does not know which product to choose, he can take into account the recommendations based on ratings from that community portal (Arora & Kant, 2012). This can particularly facilitate the choice and decision of the client/user, because it takes into account the similarity that sometimes exists between different users (Ricci, Rokach & Shapira., 2011). This filtering can also be important for websites to realize the content in which they must continue to invest, taking into account the ratings and the recommendations drawn up. From the perspective of the users, the recommendations can serve not only for simple products, but also to, for example, find other people (social networks), assist in educational models (e-learning) or help in finding new locations (e.g. restaurant recommendations) (Schafer, Frankowski, Herlocker & Sen, 2007).

Content-Based Recommendation Systems

This filtering is also based on similarity, but in this case it is the similarity of the products that the system uses to generate recommendations (Camargo & Vidotti, 2007). For this purpose, the system analyses the descriptions of products, recommending those that have a closer resemblance to products in which the user has already shown interest in the past (Lops et al, 2011). On the recommendations made, the system uses the user profile, usually in order to generate the desired results. This technique can use different ways to analyse the profile (Pazzani & Billsus, 2007):

- A model of user preferences, taking into account the ratings given to various products.
- The history of user interactions with the system, which takes into account factors such as: the products previously visited,

purchased and upgraded, and even user-specific features (e.g. location of customer).

Case/Knowledge-Based Recommendations

The case-based system is another form of filtering, and attempts to use the descriptions of the products (ex: price, brand, colour, etc.) to find recommendations that meet the user's requirements (Burke, 2000). However, this system differs from others by using a database of cases, where one can find past experiences that were resolved (called cases) (Ricci et al., 2011). These cases are represented as products, and recommendations are made by collecting cases that resemble the specific query from the user. The system then searches for the description of the products and suggests those that best suit the user's query (Mandl, Felfernig, Teppan & Schubert, 2011). Take, as an example, an e-commerce website for mobile phones using a case-based recommendation system. We want to get recommendations on a cell phone through a query based on price and on the internal memory. The system will then give us a number of recommendations that represent the most similar cases that match the established specificities. This filter can have some similarities with the content-based system; however, Smyth (Smyth, 2007) presents two reasons that differentiate them:

- The representation of the case is much more structured than the content-based filtering systems, because this one uses the different characteristics of the products, instead of just using the description in text. This method makes it possible to establish specific names and values that describe the intended product, which is why it´s better suited to e-commerce.
- The assessment of similarity, allows these systems to make recommendations, even when the results do not match the exact values intended by the user, but still feature

products with values very close to the ones that they searched for. This is not the case with content filtering systems, because when these fail to find the desired products with the same similarity, no results are shown.

Hybrid Recommender Systems

A hybrid system combines multiple techniques, such as the ones referred to earlier, in order to obtain better results. These systems are mainly built to resolve recommendation problems, by mixing different techniques (Ricci et al., 2011). One of the problems that these systems seek to solve, is the so-called "cold-start" that usually occurs in collaborative filtering. When a new user starts to use a website, their profile is still quite small in information, regarding the interaction with the website. This means that the system is unable to obtain the best results, because the data, with which one has to work at the beginning, is scarce (Burke, 2007). One of the ways proposed to correct this weak start, was to combine the initial system with a technique based on knowledge, in which the system could find recommendations based on the needs and preferences of the user. Burke conducted a study that allowed him to identify different strategies of hybrid systems. This concluded that there are several forms of different techniques to complement and increase the odds of success on the recommendations. Some of the strategies found allowed, for example, the system to choose the technique depending on the problem, or that different results of two or more systems were presented in a single result (Burke, 2002).

Other Systems

The above recommendation systems are some of the most popular and where we find numerous examples already spread around the web. However, there are still more recommendation techniques that have gained in importance, although there

are not as many examples. One of the systems that have been steadily gaining popularity, mainly because of the importance that social networks have nowadays, is the community-based system. This system consists in generating recommendations through the preferences of "friends" of users, based on the ratings that they provide (Kamahara, Asakawa, Shimojo & Miyahara, 2005). The emergence of this technique is due also to the fact that certain studies have shown that people tend to rely more on recommendations from people they know, that in unknown users (Ricci et al., 2011). One example is the social network Bling, where users can share their purchases and the products that they would like to have, and also follow other users to obtain recommendations based on what others have bought.

Another technique is the demographic system that recommends products based on the demographic profile of the user, which is known through questions posed by the system. The recommendations are generated taking into account the user's personal attributes, such as nationality, age, among others. Although there is evidence that this technique can improve the performance of a system, there have been few studies on demographic systems (Ricci et al., 2011; Burke, 2007).

Adaptive Content

The purpose of this technology is to identify the relevant content for each of the users and how it should be organized, taking into account aspects such as preferences, interests, specialities and the context (Koch & Rossi, 2002). Each user should feel that this type of website adapts and focuses on their needs.

The first form of adaptive content that enables the system to make the selection of content is the page variants. Different versions of each page of the website are developed, which then will be displayed depending on the context. The mechanism of this system aims to select and submit the page that best fits the user. This is not considered to be a complex adaptation technique, but instead, it is the simplest way and the first to be developed (Kobsa, Koenemann & Pohl, 2001; Wu, Houben & Bra, 1998).

A more complex form is the fragment-variant. This one has far more detail, and involves selecting different combinations of fragments, where each fragment corresponds to a piece of information, such as paragraphs of text or images (Wu et al., 1998). These fragments can be optional, where a page is specified as a set of fragments and each of these is chosen taking into account various conditions of applicability such as the interests, knowledge and skills of the user (Bunt, Carenini & Conati, 2007). Or they can be altering fragments, where each page is considered as a set of constituents and for each of these, there is a set of corresponding fragments. The page is created by selecting for each constituent the fragment that is most appropriate for the current context of the user with the website (Bra et al. 2003). These two forms of adaptation require that the predefined pages or fragments be developed beforehand, so that the process of selection is simpler.

The techniques listed above allow a website to identify the most relevant content to the user. However, being one of the objectives of this strategy, it is also necessary to create the conditions for the presentation of the contents. For the presentation, this can take two paths: focus or context. If the system tries to prioritize focus, this will only show the user the most relevant content and prevent access to the remainder. This situation may bring some disadvantages, mainly because it takes control from the user, which is one of the most important dimensions to the success of a website. If the priority is given to the context, then the website will seek to give greater emphasis to relevant content, but still gives visibility to everything else, without distracting the user from the main objective. Many of the techniques used in context priority do not draw attention to the secondary content, although they never hide it, which allows the user to maintain full control,

having at one's disposal essential information highlighted in order to facilitate interactivity with the website. The most commonly used ways to give greater relevance to the content are, in particular, the colours, size and order of presentation (Tsandilas & Schraefel, 2004).

3D Content

In recent years, with the rapid development of technology, it has been possible to create new forms of content presentation on a website, where the 3D models stand out. These models are being used more often, because it has been proven that the technology can be useful in different areas, and that any user can use this technique with a simple personal computer (Chittaro & Ranon, 2007).

This 3D content has been presented primarily in two distinct ways: either through websites that use models of 3D objects, or based in a virtual environment. The 3D objects are generally used in e-commerce because they allow every user to examine the products through an exact representation. 3D virtual environments can also be useful for e-commerce, to the extent that a virtual store can be created where the various products are displayed. However, this type of technique is used to re-create, for example, cities, museums or other environments that are best applied to websites dedicated to tourism, culture, or online communities (Chittaro & Ranon, 2007; Celentano & Pittarello, 2004).

3D technology is applicable to different types of websites and brings advantages that make this a Web 3.0 technology. In e-commerce, a store can be created entirely in 3D, which takes the user to a closer experience of reality, and is therefore more familiar to the client (Hughes et al., 2002). This could allow consumers, as in a real store, to browse all the products closely, and to see the actual store, as if you were there. Not only does this allow the user to have a more real experience, but it also allows the user to have a far more attractive visual experience, which leads to greater customer satisfaction. These stores may also contain other customers or vendors with which users can interact and so create a more social experience. However, the most common situation in e-commerce websites is the integration of interactive 3D objects, because it is a simpler technique and also brings some of the benefits mentioned above (Lui, Piccoli & Ives, 2007).

The virtual cities allow users to move through 3D re-creations of the cities they want to visit. Most of these models focus only on showing a city, or a simple location, for the user to have a more detailed guide, and also to find and recognize the sights; hence its greater use in tourism websites. These virtual cities may also serve for the planning of a real city (Chittaro & Ranon, 2007; Rakkolainen & Vainio, 2001).

In the field of e-learning and training functions, this can also be an area to explore. With the ability to create authentic virtual worlds, 3D technology can help users learn and practise certain concepts or specific functions in a secure environment (Monahan et al., 2008; Livingstone et al., 2008). For example, it can be useful in the education of medical students, by providing 3D reconstructions of parts of the human body or 3D simulators of real cases. This is just one of the areas of study where 3D technology can be of benefit (Pankratius & Vossen, 2003).

Adaptive Navigation

With the enormous amount of information that each user can access these days, it is sometimes difficult to navigate on a website where a large variety of documents is available. If users are confronted with several links in a web page, the time consumed to meet their goal will be greater and the task will not be so easy. Having regard to this problem, the need arose to create strategies where the navigation was easy for the user. Adaptive navigation, or customization of links, aims to create a system where the web pages adapt to the objectives, needs and knowledge of the user, i.e.

as a kind of forecast of essential links (Bra et al., 1999). This system seeks to change the appearance of links on each web page, depending on each user and his/her context, giving personalized access to the information. Different techniques were developed for different types of websites, such as e-commerce and e-learning (Brusilovsky, 2007).

The first and simplest technique to be developed was the direct guidance, consisting of suggesting the next unit to visit, or an alternate step, taking into account the goals of the user and other model parameters (Mampadi, Chen, Ghinea & Chen, 2011). If the suggestion is already on the page, then the link will be highlighted so that it is obvious to the user. If not, the system can create a dynamic link that will call the attention to move on to the next step. This technique is rarely used nowadays (Brusilovsky, 2007).

Other techniques emerged and eventually fell into disuse. Among these we can mention the link ordering, in which the goal was to prioritize all the links of a page depending on the user's model and other criteria. The most relevant links were closer to the top of the page. There was also the technique of link hiding, which sought to remove the units that were considered irrelevant and thus decreasing the space of navigation (Bra, Brusilovsky & Houben, 1999).

The technology of link annotation has emerged in order to highlight the links through the use of annotations, giving additional information to the user about the state of the connection. This is a more popular technique, especially since the annotations appear by moving the mouse icon on the link (Brusilovsky, 2007). This may be a technique used for e-learning, and has already been demonstrated through visual annotations; for example, the green for links are suggested for the user, and red for cases where the user does not have the necessary knowledge (Weber & Specht, 1997).

The latest and probably the most popular in this type of system is the link generation that allows the user to create links that were not originally present on a page. The system can generate new connections in a variety of ways, either because it managed to capture other important links during the navigation of the user and then adds them to a set of existing links, or because it creates dynamic links that may be of interest to the user, regarding its context, i.e. goals, needs, interests or knowledge (Baumeister, Knapp, Koch & Zhang, 2005; Brusilovsky, 2007).

Product Customization

With the increasing competitiveness of companies, the need arose to differentiate in particular the experience that a company offers to each client, extending this to a one-to-one relationship, a concept that has become popular in recent years. The situation is similar in websites, and in order to create the desired experiences for each user, giving them a feeling of empathy for the service, the strategy focuses on offering the user the opportunity for active participation, and of course never forgetting user needs and preferences (Yang, Zhang, Liu & Xie, 2004).

Then the idea of mass customization was introduced, a term used a great deal in the last decade, that focuses on the production and provisioning of custom products in order to create products that meet user needs. Mass customization is identified as one of the most important strategies for competitive advantage (Fogliatto, Silveira & Borenstein, 2012). There are already several types of websites using this type of strategy, especially in industries such as clothing, automobiles, and computers. The websites allow users to draw their own products, giving them the opportunity to choose among a wide variety of attributes, components, prices, delivery methods and other options (Bharati & Chaudhury, 2006). As the best-known examples, we have Dell that allows the users to purchase a computer made to measure, taking into account their needs and tastes. Adidas allows its customers to draw their own shoes, with a wide variety of designs. Ikea allows users to plan and design an entire house

division, depending on their preferences. Several studies have claimed that these strategies might be one of the reasons for the increase in value in these companies, although there is no concrete data to prove this (Arora et al., 2008).

Personalized Search

With the enormous amount of information available on the internet, a simple search can become a difficult task for the user. Most search systems still employ the template "one size fits all", which will not meet the goals of the new web (Kumar & Sharan, 2014). Although the search systems still help the users, the situation has been made more difficult given that the information available is increasing, which gives rise to problems such as outdated information and the difficulty in retaining this information (Chau, Zeng & Chen, 2001). However, the main problem that the search systems needed to solve was the fact that the results of a search query were equal for different users seeking the same title, ignoring the interests and preferences of each one, and especially taking into account that a word can have different meanings.

An essential component of the personalized search is the user profile model that is based on personal information and that will influence the search results (Liang, 2011). This model can be obtained and constructed in different ways, which are described below.

Contextual search is one where the system will obtain the information from the user's current context. This context is based on different dimensions such as software or hardware used, the current location or the own user's context, where the system collects information such as demographic, cognitive and social context (Lechani, Boughanem & Daoud., 2009). This technique allows the search results to be collected on the basis of different factors that can influence the current situation of the user.

Using search histories, the system constructs the search results taking into account interests and searches made previously by the user. In this way, the system can set the user model through the behaviour that the user has when doing the search, such as content viewed on previous searches and also the words used (Matthijs & Radlinski, 2011).

The representations of user needs, unlike previous techniques, are used as explicit feedback. The users need to rank the search results in order to determine the relevant content so that the system could build the user model (Micarelli, Gasparetti, Sciarrone & Gauch, 2007). Some prototypes were constructed on the basis of this technique, but some studies have shown that techniques that use this type of feedback typically are not as well accepted due to the extra effort made by the users (Vallet & Castells, 2011).

There is also a search system with a collaborative component, where the concept of community is essential (Morris, 2013). The main objective is to register the selected pages for each user in each query and thus know the most visited pages within the community, which also means that it is possible to estimate the relevance between a web page and the query used by the user (Smyth, Balfe, Briggs, Coyle & Freyne, 2003).

Another form of personalized search is to use a technique of result clustering, so that the user has greater ease in navigating through different search results. The results are grouped into categories or groups according to their similarity which helps distinguish the relevant documents from the not relevant (Zeng et al., 2004). This technique has been primarily a target of study for informational websites, which several authors believe are the ones that return the best results, especially due to the characteristics of a news website where thousands of articles that may relate to only one query (Vadrevu et al, 2011).

Finally, and probably the best known technique, is the search system based on classification of pages, known as PageRank. Although this system is based on the classification of web pages, this ranking is not done by users, but rather by an algorithm where the goal is to measure the relevancy of a page according to the link structure (Haveliwala, 2002). The basic concept of this technique is that a page is sorted through an accounting of links that point and direct to that same page. This accounting is made not only in terms of quantity but also in quality of the link. A simple way to understand the algorithm is for example, if a page X contains a hyperlink to another page Y, then it is assigning a certain importance to that link (Haveliwala, 1999). After the appropriate calculations, the system will position the search results according to their relevance. The algorithm has undergone several enhancements and new releases, especially as it is a technique used by the Google search system.

Intelligent Agents

The software of intelligent agents, based also in the area of artificial intelligence, was developed with the objective of assisting users with different tasks, and in particular aiming to simplify them. These programs can be used in several cases where a user needs help or needs the system itself to perform a task, such as finding various information sources, filtering out information that is irrelevant, making suggestions according to user needs, assisting the user in decision-making or even collaborating in a particular function (Shaoling & Fangfang, 2009; Sycara, Decker & Pannu., 1996; Magedanz, Rothermel & Krause, 1996).

The main difference that distinguishes the intelligent agents of other systems, is the greater involvement of these with the user; however, a doubt still persists regarding whether this kind of strategy can actually facilitate a user's tasks, or improve comprehension or retention of information by a user (Hoorn et al., 2004). The use of intelligent agents who seek to create empathy with the user have already been tested in some types of websites such as Ananova which aimed to present the news, prototypes of virtual vendors, avatars to entertainment websites, among others. However, many did not achieve the desired success, or failed to prove that these emotional agents had a better reception by users (Herrera, Miguel, Castro-Schez & Glez-Morcillo, 2010; Beale & Creed, 2009; Hoorn et al., 2004).

The use of these intelligent agents has been the subject of studies pertaining to e-learning and it is primarily in this area that this strategy seems to present better results and higher capacities of success. These studies are due mainly to the fact that learning is a process where active interaction is essential. Nowadays, it is possible to create intelligent agents that show affection towards the user, managing to identify facial expressions, body language and other gestures. Moreover, it is possible to create communication skills essential for a user who wants to learn and collaborate with the software for better learning (Hoorn et al., 2004; Soliman & Guetl, 2010).

Affective Technologies

The idea behind this technology is to create systems that can interact and influence emotions or other affective parameters (Höök, 2013). It also seeks to recognize, interpret, and simulate human emotions and is considered a way to improve the quality of communication between humans and computers (Tao & Tan, 2005). The interest in affective technologies has grown in recent years, despite still being an evolving technology and where we still have a few doubts. The utility that this may have on the web, and in the way it manages to capture human emotion to create different types of systems, has shown, in several studies, that it can be an asset for the websites looking to invest on Web 3.0 technologies. E-learning is once again one of the biggest areas of interest because the influence on users ' emotions can make a big difference in learning. There were studies with models which allowed the system to detect and answer the user, taking into account his/her emotions and cognitive states. In order to capture the emotional information, essential for this process, a few methods were created where the computer

collected information through facial expressions, posture and body movements or speech. In this way, the system can capture the effects that a particular model is having on the user, and identify and create other forms of teaching that are more appropriate, and above all, improve the essential aspects that a user needs to have in an e-learning process such as interest, attention and awareness (Li, Cheng & Qian, 2008; Ma, Wang & Liang., 2008; Sheng, Zhu-ying & Wan-xin., 2010).

Other areas where this technology can take large profits are the social and community areas such as social networks, blogs or forums. There is a growing need in these fields to realize the emotions of users in order to analyse the market, or collect more specific opinions (Strapparava & Mihalcea, 2008). This led to algorithms and models that could identify emotions and affective states of users through what they write in these websites. These algorithms allow each sentence written by a user to be analysed, identifying what they regard as negative, emotional and positive words, and then distinguish positive and negative attitudes of users. The tests of these algorithms have shown positive results and were able to demonstrate that the words used by users are an important factor in the recognition of emotions (Ren & Quan, 2012; Quan, He & Ren., 2010). Despite these results, this is still a recent technology and it is still in need of improvement.

Several recent studies have also shown that recommendation systems can be integrated with affective technology. Recently, some prototypes have been proposed in order to use this technology with recommendation systems with the objective of improving its accuracy using affective parameters and emotions (González, Rosa, Montaner & Delfin., 2007). One of the prototypes allowed a system based on content to use affective metadata, and not the original metadata, which will be, in the case of a movie the genre, the actors, theme, among others. The aim of this system would be to separate relevant products from the non-relevant (Tkalcic, Kosir & Tasic, 2011). Another technique allowed the use of personality traits in a collaborative filtering system. In a collaborative system, a calculation is made to measure the similarity between users; however, using this technique, it is possible to use affective technology to measure the user's personality so that problems like the "cold start" could disappear. Several studies proposed the following ways to extract a user's personality traits in order to calculate the necessary measure (Nunes, Bezerra & Oliveira, 2012):

- **Surveys:** Use questions to trace the personality of the individual;
- **Based on Keyboard:** Seeks to understand patterns of a user typing on their keyboard and using the mouse;
- **Based on Text:** Recognizes the traces through the users text;
- **Based on Stories:** Similar to the questionnaires but using scenarios and short stories;
- **Based on Sensors:** Allows personality to be captured through the expressions and movements.

In all these prototypes, it was also possible to prove that the recommendation systems that use affective techniques obtain better results compared with the original techniques. Calculations helped to realize that the "affective recommendations" were usually more accurate (Tkalcic et al., 2011; Nunes et al., 2012).

CONCLUSION

The Web 3.0, or semantic web, offers many opportunities for the evolution of web development, providing new technologies where the websites can better interact with the users, and where the users can have their personalized experience, which increases their satisfaction. With these technologies, websites can offer personalized environments, effective information, interactivity and new collaborative ways to improve web navigation. The Web 3.0 technologies can also provide major benefits to areas like e-learning in education, electronic commerce, or information on the web. E-learning will be capable of adapting to the learning characteristics of each user in a dynamic and interactive way, improving the learning process. E-commerce can offer customized options, personalized characteristics, and a better monitoring and assistance for each user. Informational and entertainment websites can adapt their content based on context, knowledge and other user characteristics, as well as offering better visual and interactive ways of content. Search websites, can better tailor search results based on users' interests, needs and preferences. These are just some of the ways that Web 3.0 technologies can improve web development and user navigation on websites. Much research is still being conducted on Web 3.0 and its impact on web development, but there are still issues to resolve regarding the benefits of each of these technologies, because some of them are still to be proved. Hence, future research and studies are still needed. For example, it may be important to study that the technologies mentioned here can be implemented in different scenarios; however, some of these may not be suitable for certain cases because it is necessary to take into account factors such as the number of users or the content presented. For example, a news website may not have much use for 3D content. This means that studying which technologies are more effective for certain types of websites can be a great research opportunity.

REFERENCES

Aghaei, S., Nematbakhsh, M., & Farsani, H. (2012). Evolution of the world wide web: From web 1.0 to web 4.0. *International Journal of Web & Semantic Technology*, *3*(1), 1–10. doi:10.5121/ijwest.2012.3101

Alpert, S. R., Karat, J., Karat, C.-M., Brodie, C., & Vergo, J. G. (2003). User attitudes regarding a user-adaptive ecommerce web Site. *User Modeling and User-Adapted Interaction*, *13*(4), 373–396. doi:10.1023/A:1026201108015

Arora, K., & Kant, K. (2012, March). *Techniques for adaptive websites and web personalization without any user effort*. Paper presented at the Conference on Electrical, Electronics and Computer Sciences, Bophal. doi:10.1109/SCEECS.2012.6184734

Arora, N., Dreze, X., Ghose, A., Hess, J., Iyengar, R., Jing, B., & Zhang, Z. et al. (2008). Putting one-to-one marketing to work: Personalization, customization, and choice. *Marketing Letters*, *19*(3-4), 305–332. doi:10.1007/s11002-008-9056-z

Barassi, V., & Treré, E. (2012). Does web 3.0 come after web 2.0? Deconstructing theoretical assumptions through practice. *New Media & Society*, *14*(8), 1269–1285. doi:10.1177/1461444812445878

Baumeister, H., Knapp, A., Koch, N., & Zhang, G. (2005). Modelling adaptivity with aspects. In *Proceedings of International Conference on Web Engineering* (pp. 406-416). Academic Press. doi:10.1007/11531371_53

Beale, R., & Creed, C. (2009). Affective interaction: How emotional agents affect users. *International Journal of Human-Computer Studies*, *67*(9), 755–776. doi:10.1016/j.ijhcs.2009.05.001

Berners-Lee, T., Hendler, J., & Lassila, O. (2001). The semantic web. *Scientific American*, 29–37. PMID:11323639

Bharati, P., & Chaudhury, A. (2006). Product customization on the web: An empirical study of factors impacting choiceboard user satisfaction. *Management Science and Information Systems Faculty Publication Series*, 4.

Bra, P., Aerts, A., Berden, B., Lange, B., Rousseau, B., Santic, T., ... Stash, N. (2003). AHA! The adaptive hypermedia architecture. In *Proceedings of 14th Association for Computing Machinery Conference on Hypertext and Hypermedia* (pp. 81-84). Nottingham, UK: Academic Press.

Bra, P., Brusilovsky, P., & Houben, G. (1999). Adaptive hypermedia: From systems to framework. Association for Computing Machinery Computing Surveys, 31(4).

Brusilovsky, P. (2007). Adaptive navigation support. In P. Brusilovsky, A. Kobsa, & W. Nejdl (Eds.), *The adaptive web: Methods and strategies of web personalization* (pp. 263–290). Berlin: Springer. doi:10.1007/978-3-540-72079-9_8

Brusilovsky, P., & Millán, E. (2007). User models for adaptive hypermedia and adaptive educational systems. In P. Brusilovsky, A. Kobsa, & W. Nejdl (Eds.), *The adaptive web: Methods and strategies of web personalization* (pp. 3–53). Berlin: Springer. doi:10.1007/978-3-540-72079-9_1

Bunt, A., Carenini, G., & Conati, C. (2007). Adaptive content presentation for the web. In P. Brusilovsky, A. Kobsa, & W. Nejdl (Eds.), *The adaptive web: Methods and strategies of web personalization* (pp. 409–432). Berlin: Springer. doi:10.1007/978-3-540-72079-9_13

Burke, R. (2000). Knowledge-based recommender systems. In A. Kent (Ed.), *Encyclopedia of library and information systems*. New York: Marcel Dekker.

Burke, R. (2002). Hybrid recommender systems: Survey and experiments. *User Modeling and User-Adapted Interaction*, *12*(4), 331–370. doi:10.1023/A:1021240730564

Burke, R. (2007). Hybrid web recommender systems. In P. Brusilovsky, A. Kobsa, & W. Nejdl (Eds.), *The adaptive web: Methods and strategies of web personalization* (pp. 377–408). Berlin: Springer. doi:10.1007/978-3-540-72079-9_12

Camargo, L., & Vidotti, S. (2007). Personalization: A mediating service in research environments. *TransInformação*, *19*(3), 251–264. doi:10.1590/S0103-37862007000300005

Celentano, A., & Pittarello, F. (2004). Observing and adapting user behaviour in navigational 3D interfaces. *Advanced Visual Interfaces*, 275-282.

Chau, M., Zeng, D., & Chen, H. (2001). Personalized spiders for web search and analysis. In *Proceedings of 1st ACM/IEEE-CS Joint Conference on Digital Libraries* (pp. 79-87).Roanoke, VA: ACM. doi:10.1145/379437.379454

Chittaro, L., & Ranon, R. (2007). Adaptive 3D web sites. In P. Brusilovsky, A. Kobsa, & W. Nejdl (Eds.), *The adaptive web: Methods and strategies of web personalization* (pp. 433–462). Berlin: Springer. doi:10.1007/978-3-540-72079-9_14

Cooley, R., Mobasher, B., & Srivastava, J. (1997, November). *Web mining: information and pattern discovery on the world wide web*. Paper presented at 9th IEEE International Conference on Tools with Artificial Intelligence, Newport Beach, CA. doi:10.1109/TAI.1997.632303

Dolog, P., & Nejdl, W. (2007). Semantic web technologies for the adaptive web. In P. Brusilovsky, A. Kobsa, & W. Nejdl (Eds.), *The adaptive web: Methods and strategies of web personalization* (pp. 697–719). Berlin: Springer. doi:10.1007/978-3-540-72079-9_23

Dwivedi, Y., Williams, M., Mitra, A., Niranjan, S., & Weerakkody, V. (2011). Understanding advances in web technologies: Evolution from web 2.0 to web 3.0. *ECIS*, *2011*, 257.

Fogliatto, F., Silveira, G., & Borenstein, D. (2012). The mass customization decade: An updated review of the literature. *International Journal of Production Economics*, *138*(1), 14–25. doi:10.1016/j.ijpe.2012.03.002

González, G., Rosa, J., Montaner, M., & Delfin, S. (2007, April). *Embedding emotional context in recommender systems*. Paper presented at IEEE 23rd International Conference on Data Engineering Workshop, Istanbul, Turkey. doi:10.1109/ICDEW.2007.4401075

Haveliwala, T. (1999). *Efficient computation of PageRank*. Stanford University Technical Report.

Haveliwala, T. (2002). Topic-sensitive PageRank. In *Proceedings of 11th International Conference on World Wide Web (WWW'02)*, (pp. 517-526). Honolulu, HI: IEEE.

Herrera, V., Miguel, R., Castro-Schez, J., & Glez-Morcillo, C. (2010). *Using an emotional intelligent agent to support customers' searches interactively in e-marketplaces*. Paper presented at 22nd International Conference on Tools with Artificial Intelligence, Arrar.

Höök, K. (2013). Affective computing. In M. Soegaard & R. Dam (Eds.), *The encyclopedia of human-computer interaction*. Aarhus: Interaction Design Foundation.

Hoorn, J., Eliens, A., Huang, Z., Vugt, H., Konijn, E., & Visser, C. (2004). *Agents with character: Evaluation of empathic agents in digital dossiers*. Paper presented at AAMAS' 04 Workshop on Empathic Agents, New York, NY.

Hughes, S., Brusilovsky, P., & Lewis, M. (2002). Adaptive navigation support in 3D e-commerce activities. In *Proceedings of Workshop on Recommendation and Personalization in E-Commerce at the 2nd International Conference on Adaptive Hypermedia and Adaptive Web-Based Systems* (pp. 132-139). Malaga, Spain: Academic Press.

Kamahara, J., Asakawa, T., Shimojo, S., & Miyahara, H. (2005). A community-based recommendation system to reveal unexpected interests. In *Proceedings of 11ᵗʰ International Multimedia Modelling Conference (MMM)* (pp. 433-438), Melbourne, Australia: Academic Press. doi:10.1109/MMMC.2005.5

Kantardzic, M. (2011). *Data mining: Concepts, models, methods, and algorithms.* Hoboken, NJ: John Wiley & Sons, Inc. doi:10.1002/9781118029145

Kasimati, A., & Zamani, E. (2011). Education and learning in the semantic web. In *Proceedings of 15ᵗʰ Panhellenic Conference on Informatics (PCI)* (p. 338-344). Kastoria, Greece: Academic Press. doi:10.1109/PCI.2011.40

Kobsa, A., Koenemann, J., & Pohl, W. (2001). Personalised hypermedia presentation techniques for improving online customer relationships. *The Knowledge Engineering Review, 16*(2), 111–155. doi:10.1017/S0269888901000108

Koch, N., & Rossi, G. (2002). Patterns for adaptive web applications. In *Proceedings of 7ᵗʰ European Conference on Pattern Languages of Programs.* Irsee, Germany: Academic Press.

Kück, G. (2004). Tim Berners-Lee's semantic web. *South African Journal of Information Management, 6*(1).

Kumar, R., & Sharan, A. (2014, February). *Personalized web search using browsing history and domain knowledge.* Paper presented at Issues and Challenges in Intelligent Computing Techniques (ICICT), Ghaziabad. doi:10.1109/ICICICT.2014.6781332

Lechani, L., Boughanem, M., & Daoud, M. (2009). Evaluation of contextual information retrieval effectiveness: Overview of issues and research. *Journal of Knowledge and Information Systems, 24*(1), 1–34. doi:10.1007/s10115-009-0231-1

Li, L., Cheng, L., & Qian, K. (2008, August). *An e-learning system model based on affective computing.* Paper presented at International Conference on Cyberworlds, Hangzhou, China. doi:10.1109/CW.2008.41

Liang, C. (2011, March). *User profile for personalized web search.* Paper presented at 8th International Conference on Fuzzy Systems and Knowledge Discovery (FSKD), Shangai, China.

Livingstone, D., Kemp, J., & Edgar, E. (2008). From multi-user virtual environment to 3D virtual learning environment. *ALT-J. Research in Learning Technology, 16*(3), 139–150.

Lops, P., Gemmis, M., & Semeraro, G. (2011). Content-based recommender systems: State of the art and trends. In F. Ricci, L. Rokach, B. Shapira, & P. Kantor (Eds.), *Recommender systems handbook* (pp. 73–105). Berlin: Springer. doi:10.1007/978-0-387-85820-3_3

Lui, T., Piccoli, G., & Ives, B. (2007). Marketing strategies in virtual worlds. *ACM SIGMIS Database, 38*(4), 77–80. doi:10.1145/1314234.1314248

Ma, X., Wang, R., & Liang, J. (2008, August). *The e-learning system model based on affective computing.* Paper presented at 7th International Conference on Web-based Learning (ICWL), Jinhua, China. doi:10.1109/ICWL.2008.27

Magedanz, T., Rothermel, K., & Krause, S. (1996, March). *Intelligent agents: An emerging technology for next generation telecommunications.* Paper presented at INFOCOM'96, 15th Annual Joint Conference of the IEEE Computer Societies, Networking the Next Generation 2, San Francisco, CA. doi:10.1109/INFCOM.1996.493313

Mampadi, F., Chen, S., Ghinea, G., & Chen, M. (2011). Design of adaptive hypermedia learning systems: A cognitive style approach. *Computers & Education, 56*(4), 1003–1011. doi:10.1016/j.compedu.2010.11.018

Mandl, M., Felfernig, A., Teppan, E., & Schubert, M. (2011). Consumer decision making in knowledge-based recommendation. *Journal of Intelligent Information Systems*, *37*(1), 1–22. doi:10.1007/s10844-010-0134-3

Martin, S., Diaz, G., Sancristobal, E., Gil, R., Castro, M., & Peire, J. (2011). New technology trends in education: Seven years of forecasts and convergence. *Computers & Education*, *57*(3), 1893–1906. doi:10.1016/j.compedu.2011.04.003

Matthijs, N., & Radlinski, F. (2011). Personalizing web search using long term browsing history. In *Proceedings of 4th ACM International conference on Web Search and Data Mining* (pp. 25-34). Kowloon, Hong Kong: ACM. doi:10.1145/1935826.1935840

Micarelli, A., Gasparetti, F., Sciarrone, F., & Gauch, S. (2007). Personalized search on the World Wide Web. In P. Brusilovsky, A. Kobsa, & W. Nejdl (Eds.), *The adaptive web: Methods and strategies of web personalization* (pp. 195–230). Berlin: Springer. doi:10.1007/978-3-540-72079-9_6

Mobasher, B. (2007). Data mining for web personalization. In P. Brusilovsky, A. Kobsa, & W. Nejdl (Eds.), *The adaptive web: Methods and strategies of web personalization* (pp. 263–290). Berlin: Springer. doi:10.1007/978-3-540-72079-9_3

Monahan, T., McArdle, G., & Bertolotto, M. (2008). Virtual reality for collaborative e-learning. *Computers & Education*, *50*(4), 1339–1353. doi:10.1016/j.compedu.2006.12.008

Montgomery, A., & Smith, M. (2009). Prospects for personalization on the Internet. *Journal of Interactive Marketing*, *23*(2), 130–137. doi:10.1016/j.intmar.2009.02.001

Morris, M. (2013). Collaborative search revisited. In *Proceedings of 2013 Conference on Computer Supported Cooperative Work* (pp. 1181-1192). New York, NY: Academic Press.

Nunes, M., Bezerra, J., & Oliveira, A. (2012). PersonalitYML: A markup language to standardize the user personality in recommender systems. *GEINTEC Magazine*, *2*(3), 255–273. doi:10.7198/S2237-0722201200030006

Pankratius, V., & Vossen, G. (2003). Towards e-learning grids: Using grid computing in electronic learning. In *Proceedings of IEEE Workshop on Knowledge Grid and Grid Intelligence (IEEE/WIC)* (pp. 4-15). IEEE.

Pazzani, M., & Billsus, D. (2007). Content-based recommendation systems. In P. Brusilovsky, A. Kobsa, & W. Nejdl (Eds.), *The adaptive web: Methods and strategies of web personalization* (pp. 325–341). Berlin: Springer. doi:10.1007/978-3-540-72079-9_10

Quan, C., He, T., & Ren, F. (2010, August). *Emotion analysis in blogs at sentence level using a Chinese emotion corpus*. Paper presented at International Conference on Natural Language Processing and Knowledge Engineering (NLP-KE), Beijing, China. doi:10.1109/NLPKE.2010.5587790

Rakkolainen, I., & Vainio, T. (2001). A 3D city info for mobile users. *Computers & Graphics*, *25*(4), 619–625. doi:10.1016/S0097-8493(01)00090-5

Ren, F., & Quan, C. (2012). Linguistic-based emotion analysis and recognition for measuring consumer satisfaction: An application of affective computing. *Information Technology Management*, *13*(4), 321–332. doi:10.1007/s10799-012-0138-5

Ricci, F., Rokach, L., & Shapira, B. (2011). Introduction to recommender systems handbook. In F. Ricci, L. Rokach, B. Shapira, & P. Kantor (Eds.), *Recommender systems handbook* (pp. 1–35). Berlin: Springer. doi:10.1007/978-0-387-85820-3_1

Sabucedo, L., Rifón, L., Corradini, F., Polzonetti, A., & Re, B. (2010). Knowledge-based platform for e-government agents: A web-based solution using semantic technologies. *Expert Systems with Applications, 37*(5), 3647–3656. doi:10.1016/j.eswa.2009.10.026

Schafer, J., Frankowski, D., Herlocker, J., & Sen, S. (2007). Collaborative filtering recommender systems. In P. Brusilovsky, A. Kobsa, & W. Nejdl (Eds.), *The adaptive web: Methods and strategies of web personalization* (pp. 291–324). Berlin: Springer. doi:10.1007/978-3-540-72079-9_9

Shaoling, D., & Fangfang, Z. (2009, August). *Intelligent agents improving the efficiency of ubiquitous e-learning.* Paper presented at International Conference on Management and Service Science (MASS), Wuhan, China.

Sheng, Z., Zhu-ying, L., & Wan-xin, D. (2010, August). *The model of e-learning based on affective computing.* Paper presented at 3rd International Conference on Advanced Computer Theory and Engineering (ICACTE), Chengdu, China.

Smyth, B. (2007). Case-based recommendation. In P. Brusilovsky, A. Kobsa, & W. Nejdl (Eds.), *The adaptive web: Methods and strategies of web personalization* (pp. 342–376). Berlin: Springer. doi:10.1007/978-3-540-72079-9_11

Smyth, B., Balfe, E., Briggs, P., Coyle, M., & Freyne, J. (2003). Collaborative web search. In *Proceedings of International Joint Conferences on Artificial Intelligence* (pp. 1417-1419). IEEE.

Soliman, M., & Guetl, C. (2010). Intelligent pedagogical agents in immersive virtual learning environments: A review. In *Proceedings of MIPRO, 33rd International Convention* (pp. 827-832). Opatija, Croatia: Academic Press.

Strapparava, C., & Mihalcea, R. (2008). Learning to identify emotions in text. In Proceedings of SAC'08, 2008 ACM Symposium on Applied Computing (pp. 1556-1560). Ceará, Brazil: ACM.

Sycara, K., Decker, K., & Pannu, A. (1996). Distributed intelligent agents. *IEEE Expert: Intelligent Systems and their Applications, 11*(6), 36-36.

Tao, J., & Tan, T. (2005). Affective computing: A review. In J. Tao, T. Tan, & R. Picard (Eds.), *Affective computing and intelligent interaction (ACII)* (pp. 981–995). Berlin: Springer. doi:10.1007/11573548_125

Thyagharajan, K., & Nayak, R. (2007). Adaptive content creation for personalized e-learning using web services. *Journal of Applied Sciences Research, 3*(9), 828–836.

Tkalcic, M., Kosir, A., & Tasic, J. (2011). Usage of affective computing in recommender systems. *Elektrotehniski Vestnik, 78*(1-2), 12–17.

Tsandilas, T., & Schraefel, M. (2004). Usable adaptive hypermedia systems. *New Review of Hypermedia and Multimedia, 10*(1), 5–29. doi:10.1080/13614560410001728137

Vadrevu, S., Teo, C., Rajan, S., Punera, K., Dom, B., Smola, A., … Zheng, Z. (2011). WSDM'11. In *Proceedings of 4th ACM International conference on Web Search and Data Mining* (pp. 675-684). Kowloon, Hong Kong: ACM.

Vallet, D., & Castells, P. (2011). On diversifying and personalizing web search. In *Proceedings of 34th International ACM SIGIR Conference on Research and Development in Informational Retrieval.* Beijing, China: ACM.

Wahlster, W., & Dengel, A. (2006). *Web 3.0: Convergence of web 2.0 and the semantic web* (2nd ed.). Deutsche Telekom Laboratories.

Weber, G., & Specht, M. (1997). User modeling and adaptive navigation support in WWW-based tutoring systems. In *User Modeling: Proceedings of the 6th International Conference (UM97)*, (pp. 289-300). Berlin: Springer. doi:10.1007/978-3-7091-2670-7_30

Wu, D., Im, I., Tremaine, M., Instone, K., & Turoff, M. (2002). A framework for classifying personalization scheme used on e-commerce websites. In *Proceedings of 36ᵗʰ Hawaii International Conference on System Sciences (HICSS)* (pp. 222-234).Waikoloa, HI: IEEE.

Wu, H., Houben, G., & Bra, P. (1998). AHAM: A reference model to support adaptive hypermedia authoring. In Van de Zesde interdisciplinaire conferentie informatiewetenschap (pp.77-88). Academic Press.

Yang, Y., Zhang, X., Liu, F., & Xie, Q. (2004). An internet-based product customization system for CIM. *Robotics and Computer-integrated Manufacturing*, *21*(2), 109–118. doi:10.1016/j.rcim.2004.06.002

Zeng, H., He, Q., Chen, Z., Ma, W., & Ma, J. (2004). Learning to cluster web search results. In *Proceedings of SIGIR'04, 27th Annual International ACM SIGIR Conference on Research and Development in Information Retrieval* (pp. 210-217). New York, NY: ACM.

ADDITIONAL READING

Ansari, A., Essegaier, S., & Kohli, R. (2000). Internet recommendation systems. *JMR, Journal of Marketing Research*, *37*(3), 363–375. doi:10.1509/jmkr.37.3.363.18779

Cardoso, J. (2007). The semantic web vision: Where are we? *IEEE Intelligent Systems*, *22*(5), 84–88. doi:10.1109/MIS.2007.4338499

Chen, H., Finin, T., Joshi, A., Kagal, L., Perich, F., & Chakraborty, D. (2004). Intelligent agents meet the semantic web in smart spaces. *IEEE Internet Computing*, *8*(6), 69–79. doi:10.1109/MIC.2004.66

Dewan, R., Jing, B., & Seidmann, A. (2000). Adoption of Internet-based product customization and pricing strategies. *Journal of Management Information Systems*, *17*(2), 9–28.

Fayyad, U., Piatetsky-Shapiro, G., & Smyth, P. (1996). From data mining to knowledge discovery in databases. *AI Magazine*, *17*(3), 37–54.

Fuchs, C., Hofkirchner, W., Schafranek, M., Raffl, C., Sandoval, M., & Bichler, R. (2010). Theoretical foundations of the web: Cognition, communication, and co-operation. Towards an understanding of web 1.0, 2.0, 3.0. *Future Internet*, *2*(1), 41–59. doi:10.3390/fi2010041

Han, M., & Hofmeister, C. (2006). Modeling and verification of adaptive navigation in web applications. *6th International Conference on Web Engineering*, (pp. 329-336). Menlo Park, CA. doi:10.1145/1145581.1145645

Hendler, J. (2001). Agents and the semantic web. *IEEE Intelligent Systems*, *16*(2), 30–37. doi:10.1109/5254.920597

Hendler, J. (2008). Web 3.0: Chicken farms on the semantic web. *Computer*, *41*(1), 106–108. doi:10.1109/MC.2008.34

Jankowski, J., & Decker, S. (2012). A dual-mode user interface for accessing 3D content on the World Wide Web. *21st International Conference on World Wide Web*, (pp. 1047-1056). doi:10.1145/2187836.2187977

Kobsa, A. (2001). Generic user modeling Systems. *User Modeling and User-Adapted Interaction*, *11*(1), 42–63.

Lassila, O., & Hendler, J. (2007). Embracing "web 3.0". *IEEE Internet Computing*, *11*(3), 90–93. doi:10.1109/MIC.2007.52

Maedche, A., & Staab, S. (2001). Learning ontologies for the semantic web. *IEEE Intelligent Systems, 16*(2), 72–79. doi:10.1109/5254.920602

Makris, C., Panagis, Y., Sakkopoulos, E., & Tsakalidis, A. (2007). Category ranking for personalized search. *Data & Knowledge Engineering, 60*(1), 109–125. doi:10.1016/j.datak.2005.11.006

McIlraith, S., Son, T., & Zeng, H. (2001). Semantic web services. *IEEE Intelligent Systems, 16*(2), 46–53. doi:10.1109/5254.920599

Pattal, M., Li, Y., & Zeng, J. (2009). Web 3.0: A real personal web! *3rd International Conference on Next Generation Mobile Applications, Services and Technologies, (pp.* 125-128). Cardiff, Wales.

Picard, R. (2003). Affective computing: Challenges. *International Journal of Human-Computer Studies, 59*(1-2), 55–64. doi:10.1016/S1071-5819(03)00052-1

Picard, R. (2010). Affective computing: From laughter to IEEE. *IEEE Transactions on Affective Computing, 1*(1), 11–17. doi:10.1109/T-AFFC.2010.10

Pretschner, A. (1999). Ontology based personalized search. *11th IEEE International Conference on Tools with Artificial Intelligence, (pp.* 391-398). Chicago, IL.

Rahwan, I., Kowalczyk, R., & Pham, H. (2002). Intelligent agents for automated one-to-many e-commerce negotiation. *Australian Computer Science Communications, 24*(1), 197–204.

Shadbolt, N., Hall, W., & Berners-Lee, T. (2006). The semantic web revisited. *IEEE Intelligent Systems, 21*(3), 96–101. doi:10.1109/MIS.2006.62

Shen, X., Tan, B., & Zhai, C. (2007). Privacy protection in personalized search. *ACM SIGIR Forum 41*(1), 4-17.

Silva, J., Rahman, A., & Saddik, A. (2008). Web 3.0: A vision for bridging the gap between real and virtual. *1st ACM International Workshop on Communicability Design and Evaluation in Cultural and Ecological Multimedia System, (pp.* 9-14). Vancouver, BC. doi:10.1145/1462039.1462042

Speretta, M., & Gauch, S. (2005). Personalized search based on user search histories. *2005 IEEE/WIC/ACM International Conference on Web Intelligence, (pp.* 622-628). doi:10.1109/WI.2005.114

Srivastava, J., Cooley, R., Deshpande, M., & Tan, P. (2000). Web usage mining: Discovery and applications of usage patterns from web data. *ACM SIGKDD Explorations Newsletter, 1*(2), 12–23. doi:10.1145/846183.846188

KEY TERMS AND DEFINITIONS

3D Content: Represents 3 dimensional models of items, products or locations. With this content, the user can visualize and interact in a more realistic way.

Adaptive Content: Has the main purpose of selecting the relevant content for each user and organizing it, taking into account aspects such as preferences, interests, specialties and the context.

Adaptive Navigation: Adaptive navigation, or customization of links, is a system where the web pages adapt to the objectives, needs and knowledge of the user, presenting to the user the most relevant links to them.

Affective Technologies: Systems that can interact and influence emotions or other affective parameters. It also seeks to recognize, interpret, and simulate human emotions and is considered a way to improve the quality of communication between humans and computers.

Data Mining: It's the process of discovering patterns by extracting information that can be then used for analysis. It can be used, depending on the technique used, for different pattern discoveries, like groups of data records, unusual records and dependencies.

Intelligent Agents: Assists the users in different tasks and tries to simplify them. It can be used for several tasks such as, collect various information sources, filtering information that is irrelevant, make suggestions according to user needs, assist the user in decision-making or even collaborate in a particular function.

Personalized Search: Based on the user profile, and their information, the search results will be personalized to each user. It can be based on user context, needs, search histories, and others.

Product Customization: Based on the customization term, presents the user with a range of product choices, in which the user can determine the different characteristics of a product based on their preferences and needs.

Recommendation Systems: It's a web system that can generate recommendations of different items and products. The recommendations can be based on different aspects like, other users or item features.

Web 3.0: Considered to be the third phase in evolution of the web. The main objective of Web 3.0 it's to make the machines understand the meaning and the logical connections of the information stored on the web. It is essentially a more "intelligent" web.

Web Development: It's the term used for the work involved when developing a website. Web development range from simple tasks like a simple web page, to more complex and elaborate ones like recommendation systems or intelligent agents.

Section 3
E–Government and ICT

Chapter 11
Evaluating NoSQL Databases for Big Data Processing within the Brazilian Ministry of Planning, Budget, and Management

Ruben C. Huacarpuma
University of Brasília, Brazil

Daniel da C. Rodrigues
University of Brasília, Brazil

Antonio M. Rubio Serrano
University of Brasília, Brazil

João Paulo C. Lustosa da Costa
University of Brasília, Brazil

Rafael T. de Sousa Júnior
University of Brasília, Brazil

Lizane Leite
University of Brasilia, Brazil

Edward Ribeiro
University of Brasilia, Brazil

Maristela Holanda
University of Brasilia, Brazil

Aleteia P. F. Araujo
University of Brasilia, Brazil

ABSTRACT

The Brazilian Ministry of Planning, Budget, and Management (MP) manages enormous amounts of data that is generated on a daily basis. Processing all of this data more efficiently can reduce operating costs, thereby making better use of public resources. In this chapter, the authors construct a Big Data framework to deal with data loading and querying problems in distributed data processing. They evaluate the proposed Big Data processes by comparing them with the current centralized process used by MP in its Integrated System for Human Resources Management (in Portuguese: Sistema Integrado de Administração de Pessoal – SIAPE). This study focuses primarily on a NoSQL solution using HBase and Cassandra, which is compared to the relational PostgreSQL implementation used as a baseline. The inclusion of Big Data technologies in the proposed solution noticeably increases the performance of loading and querying time.

DOI: 10.4018/978-1-4666-8147-7.ch011

INTRODUCTION

Over the past years, Big Data storage and management have become challenging tasks. According to Russom (2011), when the volume of data started to grow exponentially in the early 2000s, storage and processing technologies were overwhelmed managing hundreds of terabytes of data. In addition, the heterogeneous nature of the data presents challenges that must be taken into consideration. Such characteristics can be observed in different domains such as social network operations, gene sequencing or cellular protein concentration measurement (Andrew, 2012). Moreover, improved Internet connections and new technologies, such as smartphones or tablets, require faster data storage and querying. For these reasons, organizations and enterprises are becoming more and more interested in Big Data technologies (Collet, 2011).

Along with well-known IT companies such as Google and Facebook, governments are also interested in Big Data technologies in order to process information related to education, health, energy, urban planning, financial risks and security. Efficient processing of all this data reduces operating costs, thereby economizing the investment of public resources in a more rational way (Office of Science and Technology Policy of The United States, 2012). In the same way as other governments, Brazil is starting to employ Big Data technologies in its IT systems.

In this chapter, we propose the use of Big Data technology to solve the limitations observed on the SIAPE database processing. Notably, the SIAPE system controls payroll information regarding all federal public sector employees in Brazil. Given its growth rate of 16GB per month, the SIAPE database can be characterized as a relevant Big Data case. Specifically we focus on the Extract, Transform and Load (ETL) (Jun, 2009) modules in this system, which in our proposal are modified in order to operate with NoSQL data storage, using HBase and Cassandra. Thus, the SIAPE database is used as a case study in this chapter in order to validate our proposal.

The remainder of this chapter is structured as follows: Section 2 presents basic concepts related to Big Data; in Section 3, we describe the use case including our proposed solution; Section 4 discusses our implementation results. Finally, Section 5 presents our conclusions.

BIG DATA

The current data we manage is very diverse and complex. This is a consequence of social network interactions, blog posts, tweets, photos and other shared content. Devices continuously send messages about what they or their users are doing. Scientists are generating detailed measurements of the world around us with sensors installed within devices such as mobile telephones, tablets, watches, cars, computers, etc. and finally the internet is the ultimate source of data with colossal dimensions (Marz, 2013).

Big data is exceeding the conventional database systems capacities. The data is too big, moves too fast or does not fit into existing database architectures (Dumbill, 2012). Although the literature usually defines Big Data based on the size of the data, in this work point of view, Big Data is not only defined by the size, but also according to Russom (2011), we take into account the so called by 3Vs factors, i.e. Volume, Variety and Velocity.

Volume

Data volume is the primary attribute of Big Data is the greatest challenge to conventional IT structures. With that in mind, Big Data can be quantified by counting records, transactions, tables, or files. However, most people define Big Data in terabytes (TB) and sometimes petabytes (PB) (Russom, 2011). Many companies already have large amounts of archived data such as Google,

Yahoo and Facebook. Assuming that the volume of data is larger than conventional relational database infrastructures can cope with, the options for processing become limited to a choice of massive parallel processing. For instance, Hadoop based solutions use a distributed file system (Hadoop Distributed File System – HDFS), which makes data available to multiple computing nodes.

Variety

Data can be produced and stored in multiple formats. For example, it could be text from social networks, image data, and raw feed directly from a sensor source. None of these are initially ready for integration into an application. A common use of Big Data processing is to take unstructured data and extract ordered meaning, so that it can be used as a structured input to an application or as information to decision making. In this context, specific data types suit certain classes of databases better (Dumbill, 2012). For instance, documents encoded as XML are most versatile when stored in a dedicated XML store. Social network relations are basically graphs, and in this sense this data type fits better in graph databases.

Velocity

Another describing attribute of Big Data is its velocity or the speed with which it is generated. Another way to describe can be through the frequency of data generation or frequency of data delivery. In this context, the data rate growth related to social media utilization has changed how people consume the data. On social media, users are often solely interested by their recent messages (tweets, status updates, new comments, etc). Then they frequently discard old messages and pay attention only to recent updates. The data movement is now almost real time and the update window has been reduced to fractions of a second. In this same sense, the smartphone era contributes to increasing the rate of data inflow,

by promoting a performant streaming data source (Dumbill, 2012).

There are many reasons to consider the issue of streaming the data processing. First, when the input data comes in real time, and cannot be entirely stored, then some level of analysis must occur as the data streams in, in order to keep storage requirements practical. Secondly, analyzing the input stream is needed when the application mandates an immediate response to the data. Due to the rise of mobile applications and online gaming this is an increasingly common situation.

BIG DATA TECHNOLOGIES

The astonishing growth in data has profoundly affected traditional database systems, such as relational databases. Traditional systems and data management techniques associated with them are not suitable to manage. In this context, a new set of technologies has emerged to deal with the Big Data challenges.

Hadoop (Apache Hadoop, 2014) and MapReduce (Dean, 2008) have long been mainstays of the big data movement. They emerged as newer and faster ways to extract business value from massive datasets. The Hadoop project has become one of the most popular implementations of MapReduce, supported by the Apache Foundation. Hadoop-MapReduce is a Java implementation framework created by Google. Hadoop was originally developed at Yahoo to manage and analyze Web-scale datasets and has quickly been adopted by other technical companies and industries.

The Hadoop project aims to develop open source software for distributed, scalable and reliable computing. To achieve this, the Hadoop framework runs applications on a large cluster built of commodity hardware. Hadoop implements MapReduce, a strategy where the application is divided into many small tasks, each of which may be executed or re-executed at any node in the cluster. Data is stored in a Node using the distributed file system HDFS which is the open source implementation of the Google File System (GFS). While HDFS provides a high aggregate bandwidth across the cluster, both MapReduce and the HDFS are designed so that node failures are automatically handled by the framework (Apache Hadoop, 2014).

Besides the Hadoop framework, other technologies can be grouped under the term Not-only SQL (NoSQL). These systems have the main characteristic of scaling to tackle a large number of data sets and effectively use new techniques to manage Big Data (Marz, 2013). As the use of Big Data technologies makes it possible to extract value from very large volumes of a wide variety of data by enabling high-velocity capture, discovery, and analysis, these new technologies are spreading out and, consequently, the storage, manipulation and analysis of enormous datasets are becoming cheaper and faster than ever before. In this context, database storage systems are preeminent, a fact that motivates the development of new database technologies such as NoSQL databases which as would be expected are designed mainly for storing and retrieving great quantities of data.

NoSQL Databases

NoSQL database systems have emerged in the beginning of 21st century as an alternative to traditional Relational Database Management Systems (RDBMS). They are distributed databases built to meet the demands of high scalability and fault tolerance in the management and analysis of massive amounts of data, the so called Big Data paradigm. Over the last 10 years, various NoSQL technologies have emerged, each one with its own set of peculiarities, advantages and disadvantages. Thus, we devote the first part of this section to contextualize the most representative examples of NoSQL systems currently available and their main characteristics.

In general, NoSQL comprises a class of data storage systems non-adherent to the relational model and that are useful when storing and retrieving great quantities of data is more important than managing the relationships between the elements. NoSQL systems are used on a distributed system that offers scalability by taking profit from multiple node processors. Unlike traditional relational models, NoSQL does not provide a strict consistency for the data, as defined by the Atomicity, Consistency, Isolation and Durability (ACID) principles. Indeed, this definition of consistency may be too strict and not necessary in some cases, especially if we want to work in a distributed environment. Instead of the strict ACID model, NoSQL systems are based on the Consistency, Availability and Partition Tolerance (CAP) theory (Ramakrishnan, 2012), which is applied to all the database storage systems. Consistency means that "all clients have the same view of data". Availability means that "each client can always read and write". Partition tolerance means that "the system works well despite physical network partitions". All database storage systems could present only two of those three characteristics (Ramakrishnan, 2012).

The modern relational database management system (RDMS) provides consistency and availability, but it cannot be extended to partition tolerance. On the other hand, a NoSQL database provides partition tolerance and either consistency (strong and weak) or availability, but not both. Besides that, several NoSQL databases have loosened up the requirement on consistency in order to achieve better availability and partitioning; the resulting systems are known as Basically Available, Soft-state and eventually consistent (BASE) systems (Prichett, 2008).

There are three main categories of NoSQL databases: key-value stores, column family databases and document-based stores (Padhy, 2011). These NoSQL databases are subject to the CAP theorem, being scalable and performing with an in-memory dataset and on-disk storage (designed to exist in memory for speed and can be persisted to disk) (Padhy, 2011). Each category is represented by one or more NoSQL databases written in various programming languages (Java, Erlang, C, etc), and generally available as open source software. Within the scope of this chapter, we use column family and key-values databases.

Column Family Database

A Column Family (CF) database supports the concept of tables with rows and columns. These tables need to be created at the time of defining the database schema, but despite their similarities with the relational database model, these stores follow a different architecture because column family stores do not support ACID transactions, do not follow the relational model, and do not comprise a high-level query language like SQL. The atomicity unit of a CF is a row, i.e., every read or write in one line is atomic, making it impossible for two competing operations to change the same line simultaneously. However, transactions are usually not supported.

Technically, each table in a CF database is defined as a sparse multi-dimensional distributed map. The word sparse comes from the fact that columns created in a database do not waste space if most cells are empty. They are multidimensional because they can be configured to store the last *n* versions (usually *n = 3*) of each cell, and because the database is also distributed and runs on a cluster.

Key-Value Database

The key-value database has the simplest data model among the NoSQL databases. The data is scattered in a cluster, where each node is responsible for a portion of the data. In other words, the data is automatically partitioned (or else, sharded) and evenly distributed, and replicated, among the nodes. This strategy brings the following direct advantages: higher throughput, small read & write latencies, high availability and fault tolerance. These databases favor architectural principles like availability, fault tolerance, operational simplicity, and predictable scalability.

The minimum set of operations supported by Key-Value stores is:

- **Put (Key, Value):** Given a sequence of bytes as an identifier (key), and another sequence as the data (value), the database stores the pair (key, value) in one of the cluster machines. Additionally, it replicates this same data on yet another machine to increase the availability and fault tolerance in the event of hardware and software failure of the original machine that received the data. These databases use a hash function to evenly distribute the data among the machines.
- **Get (Key):** Given the same key used in the put operation, this operation returns the correspondent data, so that it retrieves the data closest to the client machine.
- **Delete (Key):** Also, given the key, the data is removed from the node that was storing it, along with its replicas.

Thus, these databases implement a Distributed Hash Table (DHT) between various nodes of the cluster. In a traditional hash table, a hash function provides an even spread of data between the various slots of an in-memory table. In a DHT, this same hash function can be used to determine which node in the cluster will be responsible for storing the data. Through the use of a good hash function, as MD5 or SHA1, the key-value database allows an even spreading of data across the cluster, thus providing load balancing between machines, and increasing the throughput of the system, because the database will be able to perform various requests simultaneously, each directed to a separate machine. Each machine becomes the owner of a range of data, represented by part of the key space, in what is called Consistent Hashing (Karger, 1997). Also, the nodes in the cluster nodes form a peer-to-peer (p2p) network where each node performs the same function, i.e., there are no special nodes (managers or masters) that could represent a potential single point of failure. Thus, even if one or more nodes are down, the cluster is able to keep operating only suffering a graceful degradation of performance.

HBase NoSQL Database

HBase (Vora, 2011) is one of the most widely used NoSQL databases. It is an Apache open source project and aims to provide a storage system similar to Bigtable in the Hadoop distributed computing environment. HBase implements the column-oriented model as well as Bigtable. Bigtable was one of the first NoSQL systems, along with Dynamo at Amazon, but both are closed source systems not available outside their proprietary institutions. However, the articles published on the Dynamo (DeCandia, 2007) and BigTable (Chang, 2008) systems motivated the implementation of open source clones that achieved high popularity and production use.

HBase stores data in tables described as sparse multidimensional sorted maps, which are structurally different from the relations found in conventional relational databases. An HBase table stores data rows based on the row key. Thus, each row has a unique row key and an arbitrary number of columns. Several columns can be grouped in a column family. A column of a given row, which we denote as table cell, can store a list of timestamp-value pairs, where the timestamps are unique and the values may contain duplicates (Franke, 2013).

To access a particular cell in HBase it is necessary to pass the following tuple: row key, column family, column, timestamp. We must specify the timestamp because HBase can store multiple ver-

sions of the same multidimensional cell so we can use this resource as a sort of content "versioning". It is noteworthy that the content of each cell is opaque to HBase. In other words, it can be any sequence of bytes. The row key is a sequence of bytes that uniquely identifies an HBase table row. In practical terms, it is the row primary key. The row key can not be updated, and each HBase table sorts all the row keys, lexicographically ordered. The Column Family groups a set of related columns, and every column must be part of one, and only one, column family. To retrieve a given column one should inform which column family it belongs to as *column-family:column*. The column family acts as a namespace (scope) that separates not only logically, but physically, a set of related columns, because all columns belonging to a given column-family are stored contiguously on the same file on a file system. The column family is represented by a sequence of printable characters and should be declared at the time of database schema creation, but the columns, which can be any byte sequence, can be created or deleted dynamically while the database is running. A given HBase table can contain hundreds of column families and thousands of columns.

Each HBase table is partitioned into one or more adjacent sets of rows, called regions. Through replication and the partitioning of regions, HBase provides fault tolerance and high availability. An HBase cluster is divided into two types of servers: HMaster and HRegionServer. The HMaster manages the metadata of HBase tables while the HRegionServer stores and manages access to the Regions. In general, a single HMaster server and several HRegionServer machines are used as an HBase instance. The replication and high availability of data is delegated to an HDFS.

Each table in HBase is horizontally partitioned among multiple machines according to the interval and range size. The HBase does not have a query language (DML) or a metadata manipulation language (DDL), and it does not support secondary keys. All those features were left out to allow for a high performance database that can process many thousands of operations per second with high availability and fault tolerance.

The architecture of HBase (and Cassandra) is based on the concept of Log Structured Merge Tree (LSMTree). The HBase keeps a table in memory (Memtable) where operations like insertion, search, and data changes are performed. Periodically, or after the Memtable reaches a certain size (threshold), the Memtable is flushed to disk, and a clean Memtable is created. Each Memtable writing will result in an immutable indexed file called SSTable (Sorted String Table). One feature that explains the high HBase performance is that it performs this operation asynchronously and flush in the background. Before returning the acknowledgment to the user, each write request is first recorded in a command log on disk, and after that the data is inserted / changed in RAM in Memtable. The writing command log provides fault tolerance because if the machine fails before generating the SSTable then, after the machine Restarts, HBase will identify checkpoints not finalized and make a replay with the log command to reenter the data in the Memtable not affected. Obviously, a failure or corruption of the log file would make the data recovery impossible, so administrators of HBase clusters recommend storing this log on a separate fault-tolerant disk with RAID 10, for example.

In a production system, HBase should run on HDFS, so that it can provide resources such as replication and fault tolerance. On the other hand, as high availability is a requirement, it is recommended the use of a coordination module (Zookeeper) to prevent the machine from becoming unavailable given that HMaster failures can turn HBase unavailable.

Basically there are two data retrieving operations in HBase: scan table and get, the first one scanning a range of rows and retrieving the lot, while the get performing a specific operation of only retrieving a row (or column-family/column subset).

Cassandra NoSQL Database

Cassandra (Lakshman & Malik, 2009) is an open source NoSQL database created by engineers at Facebook, specifically to implement the Inbox Search feature, which allows users of the social network to search their inboxes. After releasing the system as free software in 2008, engineers at Facebook backtracked on their strategy of using Cassandra internally, but the Apache community adopted the project and has added features to this system at a constant pace, making this a remarkable active project regarding new features and bug fixes. Cassandra presents high scalability regarding data volume as well as concurrent users, high availability under failure scenarios, and high performance, mainly for writing operations. Unlike HBase, Cassandra's latest versions have the Cassandra Query Language (CQL) which derives directly from a subset of SQL.

Cassandra's architecture draws heavily on Amazon's Dynamo, a key-value database, and on Google's Bigtable column family database. Accordingly, Cassandra incorporates the concepts of tunable consistency and consistent hashing, while following the Bigtable Column Family model (also used in HBase). An instance of Cassandra is a cluster composed of machines. A keyspace is the namespace for a particular database, typically one per application. Data in a Keyspace is inserted as a row and addressed by a primary key (a byte array), called Row Key. Each row contains one or more Column Families (CFs) that are a collection of columns grouped by logical affinity. Columns can be created and removed dynamically and have an associated timestamp to deal with concurrent updates.

CASE STUDY

The case study presented in this work consists of the implementation of NoSQL storage systems using Hadoop, HBase and Cassandra technologies. The performance of the proposed solutions is compared to the PostgreSQL (PostgreSQL, 2014) implementation that is currently used on the SIAPE database. SIAPE is a national system to manage the payroll of Brazilian federal employees. This system manages every paying unit at the national level. In addition, it ensures the availability of employee data on the page siapenet.gov.br. (SIAPE, 2014) and produces a mirror file for auditing purposes, as well as for business intelligence data warehousing and open data publishing, overall comprising an anti-corruption policy.

In this context, we are interested in analyzing the loading time of the SIAPE mirror file into HBase and Cassandra compared to the same operation into a PostgreSQL database. Besides that we are interested in comparing query time performance of auditing operations over the SIAPE mirror database in order to find payroll anomalies. In order to audit this database, a set of data mining and filtering software modules, called audit trails, was developed in another correlated work (Campos, 2012).

For the present work, the hardware setup used for the relational database system consists of a Dell Inc. PowerEdge R610 with a 2xCPU Xeon 2.80GHz, 32GB RAM and a 500GB HD. The Database Management System (DBMS) used in this case is the PostgreSQL v8.4 optimized for this hardware. The HBase implementation comprises a single system that has been configured as a Master Server, while three systems are used as Region Servers, being each master and region server configured with 2xCPU Xeon 2.80GHz, 8GB RAM and a 500GB HD. Finally, for the Cassandra implementation, the cluster comprises three nodes, each one configured with 2xCPU Xeon 2.80GHz, 8GB RAM and a 500GB HD.

In the remainder of this section we explain, initially, how the mirror file is formatted before beginning with the data loading. Then the process of loading data is described and, finally, we discuss some aspects related to the resulting data storage.

SIAPE File/Database

On a monthly basis, the SIAPE system generates a mirror file, which contains a sequential copy of the SIAPE database including personal, functional and financial data of federal public workers in Brazil (Serrano, 2014). This file has information about two and half million workers, including active, inactive and retired people. The actual size of each SIAPE file per month amounts to nearly 16GB, and is growing every month. Moreover, this file contains 36 fields of personal data, 153 fields of functional data and 32 fields of financial data, totaling 221 fields. The data file structure comprises a fixed size field where the paying unit lists every personal data in the first line, and the next line contains the functional data. After the functional data, there are several lines of financial data whose number depends on the number of rubrics that the employee receives.

The number of lines for personal and functional data is about 28,696,200 lines and 167,077,000 lines for financial data. This information covers, exclusively, the 2012 fiscal year, so in both short and long-term periods, this database is prone to an important growth rate regarding operations for storing and querying data.

Modeling

For this work purposes, the first challenge was to adapt the relational model of the SIAPE database (See Figure 1) to the NoSQL model, both for HBase and Cassandra. The relational model of the SIAPE database is composed mainly of the tables "servidor_historico" (employee records), "servidor_dado_financeiro" (employee financial data), as well as auxiliary tables and the related

Figure 1. PostgreSQL data model for personal, functional, and financial data

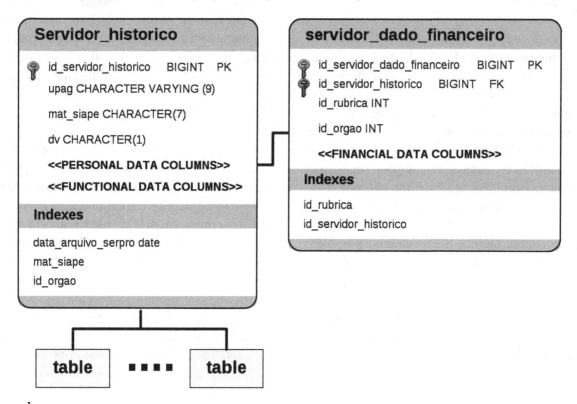

indexes for the main queries. The servidor_historico table contains 192 fields of personal and financial information of employees and servidor_dado_financeiro table has 20 fields. Figure 1 shows a part of the relational data model. The relationships between rubrica (rubrics), rubricas_pontos_controle (control point of rubrics), rubrica_pc_rubricas_incompativeis (rubric incompatibly) and ponto_controle (control point) are auxiliary tables. These relationships are related to rubrics that must not be paid simultaneously for the same employee in a month. A rubric is a classification for payment components that an employee can receive. For example, a component may be a regular salary payment or a sporadic vacation payment. A control point is a classification for every object that can be audited. For the purposes of this work the main interest is on rubric incompatibly. Figure 2 shows a part of the data model related to rubrics.

Figure 2. PostgreSQL data model for rubrics

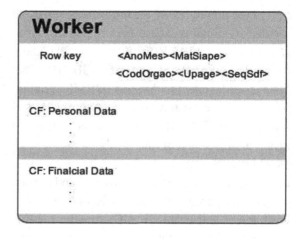

HBase Data Model

For the HBase model, the "Worker" table was defined and its row key composed of the fields "Year/Month", "MatSiape", "CodOrgao", "Upag" and "SeqSdf" to guarantee a unique identifier for every employee (see Figure 3). The creation of this row key was defined to take advantage of the HBase data structure. This row key was created according to the most common questions to be answered in the queries.

In the HBase implementation, two column families were defined: "Personal Data" and "Financial Data". The "Personal Data" is a column family to group all columns related to the employee's personal data, while the "Financial Data" is a column family to store the employee's financial data. In this sense, the last attribute (SeqSdf) of the row key contains a sequence value to represent every financial data of a specific employee. Moreover, the use of column families in HBase for storing data allows for disk usage optimization. The data structure designed for storing SIAPE data in the HBase system is shown in Figure 3.

Cassandra Data Model

The Cassandra data model is composed of family columns. The servidor_dado_financeiro column family has a composed row key comprising the columns cod_rubrica (cod_rubric), ano (year), mês (month), cod_orgao, upag e mat_siape. This row key is similar to the HBase model, though with one more field compared to HBase model, the cod_rubrica field. Consequently, the Cassandra model uses fewer fields of personal and functional information because just these few fields are used when executing payrolls. Another column family is called "rubrica" (rubric) with the composed row key comprising *ponto_controle*, *cod_rubrica* and *cod_rubrica_incompativel*. Figure 4 shows the data model implemented by Cassandra.

HBase Implementation

First, in the HBase implementation, the Cloudera Hadoop Distribution v4.0 (CHD4) was used, given that it is user friendly and has free distribution, thereby leading to the configuration of the CHD4, Zookeeper (only for the Master Server), HDFS and HBase. Secondly, we defined two steps for loading the SIAPE file: formatting the SIAPE file in a CSV format and loading the CSV files using the ETL provided by the Pentaho Data Integration (PDI) (Pulvirenti, 2011). To implement the formatting process for HBase, we used a shell script to separate the personal and functional data in a CSV file, called *servidor* (employee), as well as another CSV file containing financial data of employees, called *servidor_dados_financeiros*. The *servidor* file has 192 fields. After the formatting, this file contains almost 2.4 million rows (or employees and their personal and functional data). The *servidor_dados_financeiros* file has 20 fields and, after formatting, this file contains almost 20 million rows. In the case of Cassandra, the formatting process is the same as the HBase formatting process.

To implement the loading process the PDI software is used to load data into the "Worker" HBase table for "servidor" and "servidor_dados_financeiros" data. Figures 5 and 6 show the flow model of the loading process for the "Worker" table in the HBase database. In the first step, we treat the CSV file of "servidor" concatenating the year and month fields. In the Second step, the row key is generated for every employee by composing with the fields Year/Month, MatSiape, CodOrgao, Upage and generating the SeqSdf. In the third step, unnecessary or temporary fields are removed. Finally, we insert the output into the "Worker" HBase table. For financial data the process follows the same sequence as shown in Figure 6.

Figure 3. HBase structure for the SIAPE Database

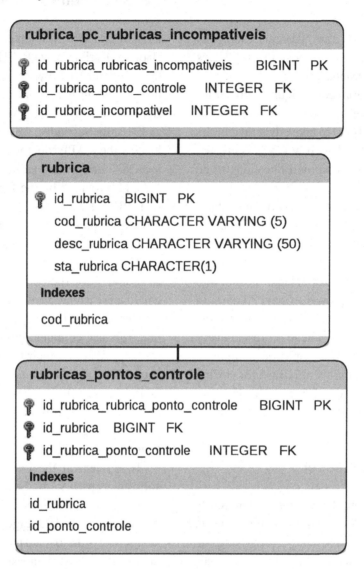

Cassandra Implementation

As stated above the data model was implemented in a cluster of 3 nodes using the Cassandra DataStax Community Edition 2.0.7. In addition, the CQLSH is used, making it possible to execute the Cassandra Query Language (CQL) which enables to use of a query syntax similar to the relational SQL language. By means of CQLSH, the keyspace "siape" is created, as well as the family columns. Subsequently, the following steps are performed:

the loading process and the querying process for rubric incompatibilities.

Cassandra Loading Process

The process used for loading data into the Cassandra database is very similar to the process used for the HBase database. First, the SIAPE file is processed by a shell script resulting two formatted files: one which contains personal and functional data and the other which contains only financial

Figure 4. Cassandra data model

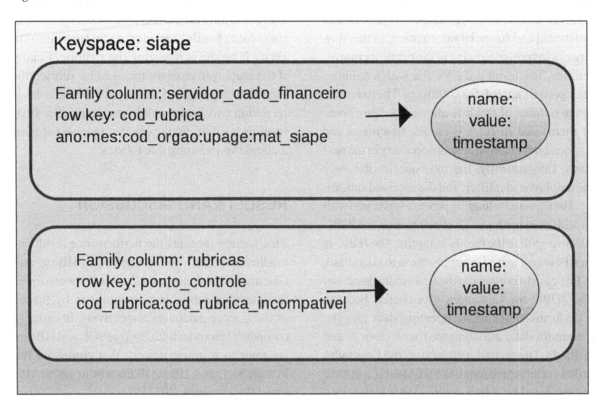

Figure 5. ETL flow for personal data

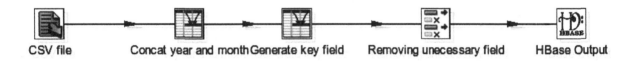

Figure 6. ETL flow for financial data

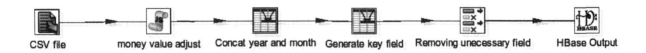

data. Secondly, the Pentaho Data Integration (PDI) is used to filter constraints over personal, functional and financial information. In this way, it performs pre-processing of the rubric incompatibilities. The result is a CSV file with 6 columns and approximately 6,500,000 lines. The reduction in the number of fields is allowed because some of them used to filter personal, functional and financial information are not necessary in the next steps. Consequently, the next queries use only the employee identifier, and the received rubrics.

The Cassandra loading process was tested with two different methods. The first one uses the JDBC API to populate the family columns. The JDBC is an API to connect a Java application to a database, in this case to connect to the Cassandra database. The JDBC for Cassandra was chosen because it performs better while inserting data into the Cassandra database compared with other tested methods. The second method uses the Cassandra Bulk Loader which requires SSTABLEs, a feature implemented by a Java application which uses a especial API called STableSimpleUnsortedWriter. After building SSTABLEs, it is necessary to use another process to load the SSTABLEs into the Cassandra database.

Cassandra Querying Process

In order to query the Cassandra implementation, a Java application was developed using the Hector API (Hector, 2014) which is used to make queries over the Cassandra database by providing functions to access, read, write, update and delete data. The application searches every x_i rubrics that has the "ponto_controle" id with relation to rubric incompatibilities into the family column "rubrica". For each rubric x_i is created a thread responsible for other queries. After that, still in the family column "rubrica", a search is done for all incompatible rubrics with the x_i rubric. For each incompatible rubric y_{ij}, the employees that receive the rubric y_{ij} in the column family "servidor_dado_financeiro" are searched for a

previously defined specific year and month. For every resulting employee, a new search is done in the column family "servidor_dado_financeiro" to verify if he/she is receiving the x_i rubric. Finally if the employee receives the y_{ij} and x_i rubric, this employee is qualified as irregular because he is receiving two incompatible payments. The final result is a set of employees that received at least a couple of incompatible rubrics.

RESULTS AND DISCUSSION

This section presents the performance results of loading data with the PostgreSQL, HBase and Cassandra databases as well as the response times for querying rubric incompatibilities by means of these three databases respectively. In order to compare Cassandra with PostgreSQL and HBase, we refer to a previous work that compared the PostgreSQL and HBase databases using SIAPE data (Huacarpuma, 2013).

Loading Data Results

Previous to testing the loading process, the source mirror file is processed once; resulting in the input CSV file. Then, the loading process was repeatedly tested using this CSV file.

The loading times for the relational and the NoSQL databases are shown in the Table 1 and Figure 7. Comparing these results, the HBase solution is clearly faster than PostgreSQL and Cassandra for many reasons. One reason is that HBase does not use the ACID principle as does PostgreSQL. While PostgreSQL spends more time and resources trying to fit the ACID properties, HBase and Cassandra are interested in fitting consistency and partition tolerance according to the CAP theorem. This is less expensive in terms of time and resources. Another aspect that may contribute to reduce the loading time for HBase is the use of the HDFS given that we store the CSV file into the HDFS with the objective of reducing the O/I during the loading process. It is important to highlight that Cassandra loading time using the BulkLoader resulted in the worst loading times. Indeed, the loading time using BulkLoader is faster than any other tested, but the previous process to get the SSTABLE is very slow. This could be explained because the Java application to build the SSTABLE is inefficient to transform the CSV file to SSTABLE.

Query Data Results

A brief comparison of some querying processing times is shown in Table 2, for three different queries, as well as in Figure 8 for one complex query (C). The query response time tests also showed better results for NoSQL databases, with performance gains (Efficiency) when comparing to the relational solution, seemingly because they are column-oriented databases. But it is not clear which NoSQL solution performs better as each one's performance depends on the type of the executed query, given that while showing almost the same result for Item A, their results are inverted for Item B and C.

These results are the consequence of many factors. First, the HBase and Cassandra models use the key to get an entire row (value). Thus, the method to build the key will impact the speed of the query. Secondly, the HBase key table is ordered, so if the key is built with the more frequently used fields, the query responses will be faster. This happens because every row is stored in order according to the key used and when the probability of the row being stored in the same HDFS DataNode is very high. This facilitates querying data very quickly because the more fields (more frequently used fields to query data) contained in the key the faster the query will be. This is the case unless the number of fields becomes too large because this may compromise the query performance. Thirdly, one reason for Cassandra's performance is the replication strategy. Besides this, data is partitioned using a consistency hashing so each data item is assigned to a node in the cluster. Finally, the HBase columns are lexicographically oriented. This allows "scan" operations to be very fast in a specific range without the necessity of using secondary indexes. By contrast, the Cassandra database uses a secondary index in each column in the column family.

HBase works differently from a relational database, since it is a column oriented database where the columns are lexicographically oriented. This allows scan operations within a specific range in a more direct and rapid way, without the necessity of using secondary indexes. On the other hand, Cassandra is not a relational database, but it has

Table 1. Loading data results

Database	Time (Minutes)
PostgreSQL	30.00
Pentaho-HBase	5.18
Cassandra (JDBC)	13.32
Cassandra (BulkLoader)	265.49

Table 2. Querying data results

	Response Time for Querying Data				
	PostgreSQL	Pentaho HBase	Efficiency (%)	Cassandra	Efficiency (%)
D. Single query by key	23 ms	16 ms	30.43	16 ms	30.43
E. All data about a worker Filtered by month and year	35 ms	17 ms	51.43	11 ms	68.57
F. Audit Trail: Incompatibility of rubric	26.67 min	8.78 min	67.06	14.04 min	47.36

Figure 7. Loading data results

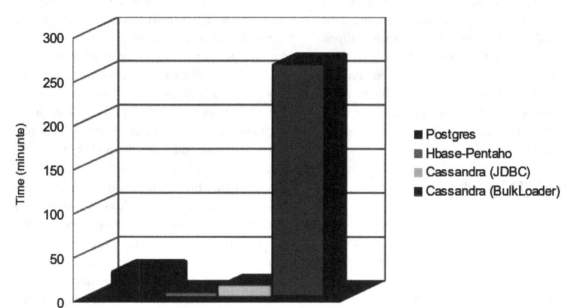

Figure 8. Query time for Audit Trail: Incompatibility of rubric

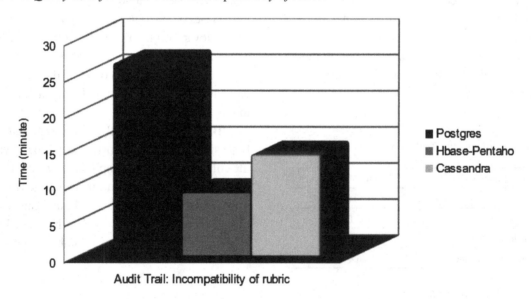

some characteristics typical of relational database such as the CQL language for querying and creating tables and secondary indexes.

Additionally, it is worth pointing out that the NoSQL database results can be improved by tuning the data store, for instance, via table scan for HBase. Currently the scan is done sequentially in the HBase database. This operation can be done in parallel for every DataNode. This allows distributing the data processing to every DataNode thus improving the table scan.

Furthermore, it is worth to consider that the HBase scalability may help managing the data growth that is expected for the future years.

FUTURE RESEARCH DIRECTIONS

There are still many research possibilities to continue this study. This chapter focused mainly on two types of databases: relational database and column-oriented databases. Nonetheless, a large number of NoSQL database exists, each one with different architectures and characteristics. Further study of other databases would also allow the identification of new design patterns, specific to each database. In this context, as a future work we intend to test loading data in a larger cluster including desktop computers with less processing and storage capacities. Also a comparison with other NoSQL technologies can be done which will show the performance of column-oriented databases, comparing them to other data storage such as Riak and mongoDB. Another interesting future work will be to test NoSQL databases not only on querying the audit trail concerning the incompatibility of rubrics but also other audit trails, using other NoSQL models.

Moreover, it would also be useful to study the capabilities when combining the Cassandra and the Hadoop cluster, since Hadoop MapReduce jobs can be used to do complex computations on the data stored into Cassandra. Cassandra can hold advantages, since the HBase uses HDFS as a file system. This study case considered a dataset of the 2012 year as example, but it could be used with a bigger data volume (2011, 2012 and the current year data).

CONCLUSION

In this work, a case study was carried out to analyze Brazilian federal payroll data using NoSQL databases (HBase and Cassandra) and a relational database (PostgreSQL). In order to compare the performance of these technologies, the load and query time was analyzed. The developed comparison might be relevant when deciding which database to use. In this context, we show how the performance is improved by using Big Data technologies. We have used the combination of HBase-Pentaho and Cassandra-JDBC-Hector to test the load and query processes. The main query analyzed was the incompatibility of rubrics in payrolls. The NoSQL technologies showed better performance in loading and querying data compared to the relational approach.

It seems undeniable that Big Data will gain importance in a lot of fields. Hadoop technology offers a powerful means of distributing and computing among commodity servers. Combined with NoSQL databases they are able to manage big data processing. In this context this work examines a relatively big database (SIAPE database), which is actually facing storage, process and query problems. These problems may put the current system at risk, in the short and the long-term. Hence, this work aims to provide valuable experience in selecting a NoSQL database and using it efficiently.

As a final observation, it is important to note that NoSQL modeling is based on queries, which has limits when compared to a relational modeling based on data. Relational models are projected to solve different queries and not only specifics ones, such as NoSQL databases. Moreover, we observed that good modeling of data can help to get better query latency.

ACKNOWLEDGMENT

The authors thank the Brazilian Ministry of Planning, Budget and Management for its support to this work, as well as the Brazilian Innovation Agency FINEP (Grant RENASIC/PROTO 01.12.0555.00).

REFERENCES

Andrew, C., Huy, L., & Aditya, P. (2012). Big data. *XRDS The ACM Magazine for Students, 19*(1), 7–8. doi:10.1145/2331042.2331045

Apache Hadoop. (2014). Retrieved September, 2014, from http://hadoop.apache.org/

Campos, S. R., Fernandes, A. A., de Sousa, R. T., Jr., de Freitas, E. P., da Costa, J. P. C. L., Serrano, A. M. R., ... Rodrigues, C. T. (2012). Ontologic audit trails mapping for detection of irregularities in payrolls. In *Proceedings of the Fourth International Conference on Computational Aspects of Social Networks* (CASoN). São Carlos, Brazil: IEEE Press.

Chang, F., Dean, J., Ghemawat, S., Hsieh, W. C., Wallach, D. A., Burrows, M., & Gruber, R. E. (2008). Bigtable: A distributed storage system for structured data. *ACM Transactions on Computer Systems, 26*(2), 1–26. doi:10.1145/1365815.1365816

Collett, S. (2011). Why Big data is a big deal. *Computerworld, 45*(20), 1–6. Retrieved from http://www.computerworld.com/article/2550147/business-intelligence/why-big-data-is-a-big-deal.html

Dean, J., & Ghemawat, S. (2008). MapReduce: Simplified data processing on large clusters. *Communications of the ACM, 51*(1), 107–113. doi:10.1145/1327452.1327492

DeCandia, G., Hastorun, D., Jampani, M., Kakulapati, G., Lakshman, A., Pilchin, A., & Vogels, W. (2007). Dynamo: Amazon's highly available key-value store. *ACM SIGOPS Operating Systems Review ACM, 41*(6), 205–220. doi:10.1145/1323293.1294281

Dumbill, E. (2012). *Planning for big data*. Sebastopol, CA: O'Reilly Media, Inc.

Franke, C., Morin, S., Chebotko, A., Abraham, J., & Brazier, P. (2013). Efficient processing of semantic web queries in HBase and mySQL cluster. *IT Professional, 15*(3), 36–43. doi:10.1109/MITP.2012.42

Hector. (2014). *Hector a high level java client for apache Cassandra*. Retrieved September, 2014, from http://hector-client.github.io/hector/build/html/index.html

Huacarpuma, R. C., Rodrigues, D. D. C., Serrano, A. M. R., da Costa, J. P. C. L., de Sousa, R. T. Jr, Holanda, M. T., & Araujo, A. P. F. (2013). Big data: A case study on data from the Brazilian ministry of planning, budgeting and management. In *Proceedings of the IADIS International Conference Applied Computing 2013*. Porto, Portugal: IADIS Press.

Jun, T., Kai, C., Yu, F., & Gang, T. (2009). The research & application of ETL tool in business intelligence project. In *Proceedings of the Information Technology and Applications* (IFITA'09). Chengdu, China: IEEE Press. doi:10.1109/IFITA.2009.48

Karger, D., Lehman, E., Leighton, T., Panigrahy, R., Levine, M., & Lewin, D. (1997). Consistent hashing and random trees: Distributed caching protocols for relieving hot spots on the world wide web. In *Proceedings of the Twenty-Ninth Annual ACM Symposium on Theory of Computing*. ACM Press. doi:10.1145/258533.258660

Lakshman, A., & Malik, P. (2009). Cassandra: Structured storage system on a P2P network. In *Proceedings of the 28th ACM Symposium on Principles of Distributed Computing* (PODC '09). New York, NY: ACM Press.

Marz, N., & Warren, J. (2013). *Big data: Principles and best practices of scalable realtime data systems*. Manning Publications.

Office of Science and Technology Policy of the United States. (2012). *Fact sheet: Big data across the federal government*. Retrieved September, 2014, from www.WhiteHouse.gov/OSTP

Padhy, R. P., Patra, M. R., & Satapathy, S. C. (2011). RDBMS to NoSQL: Reviewing some next-generation non-relational databases. *International Journal of Advanced Engineering Science and Technologies*, *11*(1), 15–30.

Postgre, S. Q. L. (2014). *PostgreSQL: The world's most advanced open source database*. Retrieved September, 2014, from http://www.postgresql.org/

Pritchett, D. (2008). BASE: An acid alternative. *Queue*, *6*(3), 48–55. doi:10.1145/1394127.1394128

Pulvirenti, A. S., & Roldan, M. C. (2011). *Pentaho data integration 4 cookbook*. Olton Birmingham, UK: Packt Publishing Ltd.

Ramakrishnan, R. (2012). CAP and cloud data management. *Computer*, *45*(2), 43–49. doi:10.1109/MC.2011.388

Russom, P. (2011). *Big data analytics: Executive summary*. Renton, WA: TDWI Research.

Serrano, A. M. R., Rodrigues, P. H. B., Huacarpuma, R. C., da Costa, J. P. C. L., de Freitas, E. P., Assis, V. L., . . . Pilon, B. H. A. (2014). Improved business intelligence solution with reimbursement tracking system for the Brazilian ministry of planning, budget and management. In *Proceedings of the 6th International Conference on Knowledge Management and Information Sharing (KMIS'14)*. Rome, Italy: SCITEPRESS. doi:10.5220/0005169104340440

SIAPE. (2014). *Siape - Sistema integrado de administração de recursos humanos*. Retrieved September, 2014, in Portuguese, from https://www.serpro.gov.br/conteudo-solucoes/produtos/administracao-federal/siape-sistema-integrado-de-administracao-de-recursos-humanos

Vora, M. N. (2011). Hadoop-HBase for large-scale data. In *Proceedings of the International Conference on Computer Science and Network Technology (ICCSNT)*. Harbin, China: IEEE Press.

KEY TERMS AND DEFINITIONS

Cassandra noSQL: Cassandra noSQL database presents high scalability regarding data volume as well as concurrent users, high availability under failure scenarios, and high performance, mainly for writing operations.

Column Family noSQL: noSQL database which supports the concept of tables with rows and columns.

Hadoop: Hadoop project aims to develop open source software for distributed, scalable and reliable computing.

HBase noSQL: It is an Apache open source project and aims to provide a storage system. HBase database implements the column-oriented model.

HDFS: Hadoop Distributed file system, which makes data available to multiple computing nodes.

MapReduce: MapReduce is a programming model where the application is divided into many small tasks, each of which may be executed or re-executed at any node in the cluster.

noSQL Database: Distributed database systems built to meet the demands of high scalability and fault tolerance in the management and analysis of massive amounts of data, an alternative to traditional Relational Database Management Systems (RDBMS).

Chapter 12

Predicting Use of GoodGuide.com Consumer Product Sustainability Information Using VBN Theory and NEP Scale

Rebecca Angeles
University of New Brunswick Fredericton, Canada

ABSTRACT

The chapter focuses on the use of information provided by an Online Environmental Infomediary (OEI), GoodGuide.com, to advise consumers on the overall and specific sustainability attributes of personal care and household chemical and food products. This chapter seeks to predict the willingness of consumers to be influenced by GoodGuide.com information in their purchases and to influence others as well with this information using the Value-Belief-Norm (VBN) theory and the New Environmental Paradigm (NEP) scale. An experiment was applied to a sample of both undergraduate and graduate students at the Faculty of Business Administration, University of New Brunswick Fredericton, Canada. Data analysis using a series of stepwise multiple regressions was used in this study. Study results indicate the usefulness of both theoretical frameworks in understanding consumer predisposition to use OEI-provided information and the potential of social networking and use of mobile devices and apps in facilitating access and use of green information.

INTRODUCTION

Concern for the environmental is one of the key issues of this time and while there has been considerable coverage of how firms can conduct themselves in a sustainable manner, there needs to be a proportionate focus on the role of consumers and how they should vote with their dollars to spur the production of green products. In this study, "environmental sustainability" of products is understood to be those attributes of physical products that render them harmless to the environment in the sense that the raw materials and the production processes used in making them, the consequences of consuming/using them in terms of the effects on individual buyers, and the processes used to

DOI: 10.4018/978-1-4666-8147-7.ch012

dispose of them or recycle them do not pose any harm to society and nature.

This study focuses on the role of individual consumers in driving the production of green products, specifically, green products used in the home to which individuals have far greater physical exposure, and thus, potential health risks. But understanding beforehand what would make consumers do so is, perhaps, more important. Thus, this study looks at what are the appropriate values, beliefs, norms, and attitudes that might predispose an individual to undertake actions that favor "green" consumer behaviors.

Generally speaking, "values" refer to something that an individual holds with respect or importance, or could represent esteemed principles or standards of behavior. "Beliefs," in general, represent a person's views of what he/she holds to be true in reality or the scheme of things. "Norms" in the context of the study refer to what a group of persons hold as appropriate in terms of how an individual should act within a specific situation. "Attitudes" are a learned predisposition to respond to people or situations that individuals learn based on their beliefs, values, and assumptions about the world. Of specific interest of this study is to find out what would predispose a consumer to use sustainability-related information on consumer products shown on GoodGuide.com, an online environmental infomediary (OEI) that specializes on products used in the home, to inform their actual purchase of "green" products.

Understanding sustainability information pertaining to products, however, is a challenge in and of itself.

Remy and Huang (2012) interviewed consumers who considered themselves environmentally informed as they went about seeking and using environmental sustainability information relevant to their purchase of electronic products. This exploration uncovered two key issues salient to the use of this kind of information in the purchase process --- the need to reduce the complexity of the relevant information needed to evaluate a product and the need to establish trust in the information. In today's marketplace, consumers are challenged to find relevant and useful information they could use in making the most routine and repetitive purchases for a wide range of items. But it is the purchase of household products and consumer packaged goods that exposes consumers' health and well being to all sorts of risks. Information technology (IT) can be used as a tool to address the need to have access to sustainability information regarding a wide range of products through the use of OEIs like GoodGuide.com. This chapter examines the results of an empirical study of consumers (i.e., both undergraduate and MBA students of a Canadian university) that seeks to predict their willingness to be influenced by the information posted on GoodGuide.com in various ways in making their purchases of ordinary and typical household goods using the Value-Belief-Norm (VBN) Theory and the New Environmental Paradigm (NEP) Scale.

ISSUE, CONTROVERSY, AND PROBLEM: SUSTAINABILITY PRODUCT INFORMATION AND THE CONSUMER

Both the need to reduce complex information and the need to trust product sustainability information are addressed by the information available from GoodGuide.com, an OEI that provides sustainability performance ratings for thousands of consumer products in a form that is useful at the point of purchase. Godfrey (2014) defines OEIs as third party information dealers that mediate between consumers and firms and provide both parties information they need and value. An OEI like GoodGuide.com is a good example of implementing Goleman's (2009) idea of "radical transparency" in the product's supply chain by revealing salient sustainability related information that informs the consumer about things like raw materials used in the production of the product and the sustainability of the business operations involved in the manufacturing process itself. OEIs like GoodGuide.com should also take advantage of social networking and mobile apps that can assist consumers make an "intelligent" green decision at the point of purchase.

Objectives of Study

This study investigates the determinants of using an OEI called GoodGuide.com in a consumer's purchase of personal care and household chemical and food products using the concepts of the VBN theory and the NEP scale. While there is great concern for the ability of firms to conduct environmentally sustainable business operations in the manufacture of physical products, there is the equally important matter of providing consumers accurate, reliable, timely, and trustworthy information they can use in buying sustainable products at the point of purchase. Both the VBN theory and NEP scale have been used previously in a wide variety of studies involving environmental sustainability. However, this is the first study to use these frameworks in determining a consumer's willingness to influence others and be influenced by the information on the sustainability of products provided by GoodGuide.com.

GoodGuide.com Environmental Sustainability Information for Consumers

Founded by Dara O'Rourke, a professor of environmental and labor policy at the University of California at Berkeley, GoodGuide.com provides consumers information about the environmental, health, and social performance of about 100,000 or more products covering primarily personal care, household chemical and food products, and to a lesser extent, pet food, paper products, lighting products, home appliances, cell phones, and cars. GoodGuide.com focuses on products that account for 80 percent of sales revenues within its product category. There is also a GoodGuide.com mobile app that is free and downloadable for consumer use at the point of purchase in groceries and/or supermarkets. Product performance information across the three dimensions is expressed in ratings in a scale from 0 to 10 --- the higher the number, the more environmentally friendly the product is. GoodGuide.com provides both an overall product rating and also drills down to the individual numerical ratings for each of the three areas of scoring.

The following is a detailed description of each of the three performance dimensions. The health rating encompasses the following aspects: (1) human health impact: provides information about the health hazards the ingredients used pose and the product's nutritional value; (2) data adequacy: informs consumer if the information needed to evaluate health risks was available for the product; (3) other negative aspect indicators: cover issues such as whether or not the firm used banned or restricted ingredients in making the product, toxic materials, or contaminants from the production process; and (4) product management indicators: cover issues related to the sustainable management of the products based on third-party certifications verifying health or environmental performance.

The environmental rating encompasses the following aspects: (1) environmental management indicators: cover issues such as the firm's overall corporate governance encompassing sustainability in its supply chain, the firm's compliance with sustainability related legislation, involvement in controversies, use of exemplary sustainability business practices, etc.; (2) transparency indicators: cover availability of relevant information from the product's firm to evaluate things like the raw materials use for manufacturing the product, water and energy use in the production process, etc.; and (3) environmental impact indicators:

cover issues relevant to the consequences of the product firm's manufacturing processes like carbon emissions, waste generation, greenhouse gas emissions, thwarting of biodiversity, etc.

The social rating encompasses the following aspects: (1) environmental management indicators: cover issues such as the firm's overall corporate governance encompassing sustainability in its supply chain, the firm's compliance with sustainability related legislation, involvement in controversies, use of exemplary sustainability business practices, etc.; (2) transparency indicators: cover availability of relevant information from the product's firm to evaluate social issues; (3) consumer indicators: cover issues pertaining to customer health and safety, product recall, labeling, and marketing practices; (4) community indicators: cover issues related to a product firm's relationships with the community, stakeholder engagement initiatives, and public policy positions; (5) worker indicators: cover issues related to the product firm's performance on occupational safety, worker health, diversity and equal opportunity in hiring, observance of human and labor rights, etc. The knowhow behind GoodGuide.com's ratings is represented by a team of scientific and technology experts in life cycle assessment, environmental engineering, chemistry, nutrition, and sociology, who analyze and organize product information data from various sources.

GoodGuide.com information for consumers is provided for free. GoodGuide.com's business has been funded by venture capital funds from New Enterprise Associates, Draper Fisher Jurvetson and Physic Ventures. Recently, however, Underwriters Laboratories, one of the biggest quality assurance firms, purchased GoodGuide.com, however the website continues to function as an independent subsidiary (Godfrey, 2014). GoodGuide.com also earns revenue from firms that purchase business intelligence related to the evaluation of the environmental sustainability of their products/services.

This business intelligence service helps client firms compare their sustainability performance expressed as the three assessment components (i.e., health, environmental, and social) vis-à-vis those of their competitors.

BACKGROUND AND LITERATURE REVIEW

Value-Belief-Norm Theory

This study uses Stern's value-belief-norm (VBN) theory, which is, thus far, the most comprehensive and empirically supported theory that connects the concepts of value theory, norm activation theory, and the New Environmental Paradigm perspective in anticipating pro-environmental behavior. In a nutshell, the VBN theory purports that the convergence of a person's values, beliefs, and personal norms drives his or her environmental behavior. Jansson et al. (2011) suggest that this theory also postulates that the relationship between values and actual behavior is mediated by behavior-specific beliefs and personal moral norms that guide a person's actions. The authors de Groot and Steg (2008) and Hansla et al. (2008) discuss that the first aspect of the VBN theory consists of three sets of values (i.e., biospheric, altruistic, and egoistic values) and research has shown that these value sets are related to proenvironmental behaviors. The second aspect of the VBN theory is that specific beliefs affect the behavior of green consumers. Thus, Stern (2000) and Bamberg and Schmidt (2003) submit that if a person is aware of the environmental consequences of certain behaviors and furthermore, is able to ascribe responsibility to themselves for taking preventive action to avoid negative effects on the environment, then, a proenvironmental norm develops which has a high probability of leading to proenvironmental behavior. Finally, Stern (2000) presents the last aspect of the VBN theory (i.e., the attitudinal factor) --- the personal environmental norm, which relates the strongest to actual proenvironmental behavior.

Stern's theoretical framework is an all-inclusive umbrella that describes how the relatively stable elements of a person's personal and belief structure link with that person's more focused beliefs about the relationships between humans and nature (i.e., NEP), that person's awareness of the consequences of his/her actions pertaining to the environment, and finally, that person's sense of responsibility for taking corrective action. This model has had strong empirical support. Stern et al. (1999) have shown, for instance, that the model predicts environmental citizenship, private-sphere behavior, and policy support.

The authors de Groot and Steg (2008), Hansla et al. (2008), and Stern et al. (1999) articulate that the values associated with environmental behavior are the altruistic, biospheric, and egoistic values. The influence of these values on an individual's green consumer decision varies. The altruistic value focuses on the perceived costs and benefits for other people. The biospheric value focuses on the perceived costs and benefits for the ecosystem and biosphere as a whole. The egoistic value focuses on whether the perceived benefits exceed the perceived costs solely for the individual concerned. Cleveland et al. (2005) and Nordlund and Garvill (2002) found that altruistic and biospheric values relate positively with green consumer behaviors, while egoistic values appear to relate negatively with the same. Also, within the moral norm-activation framework of the VBN theory, Schwartz (1977) found that a pro-environmental norm develops, which, in turn, could very likely lead to green behavior if the person is aware of the consequences of the behavior (AC), and especially so if he/she ascribes responsibility to himself/herself for taking preventive action, according to Bamberg and Schmidt (2003) and Stern (2000).

The last concept in the framework is personal norm (i.e., personal environmental norm), which translates into feelings of moral obligation to act, making the individual more willing to behave in a green manner. To develop this particular norm, an individual needs to incorporate his/her social norms into a consistent personal value system.

The following are the most recent studies that used the VBN theory within the domain of environmental sustainability research. Johansson et al. (2013) used the VBN theory to identify the extent to which landowners would differ in terms of their perceived moral obligation to protect local biodiversity after participating in conservation programs. Aguilar-Luzon et al. (2012) compared the VBN theory to the theory of planned behavior to determine which one has a better predictive power in anticipating the recycling behavior of Spanish housewives. Jansson et al. (2011) used the VBN theory to understand consumer adoption of a high involvement eco-innovation in the form of an alternative fuel vehicle powered by electricity or biofuels, using a Swedish sample of respondents.

New Environmental Paradigm (NEP) Scale

Dunlap and Van Liere (1978, 1984) introduced their conceptualization of the New Environmental Paradigm (NEP) which presents beliefs about humanity's ability to upset the balance of nature, existence of the limits to growth for human societies, and humanity's right to rule over nature and its resources. The early version of this scale proved to be robust: Dunlap and Van Liere (1978, 1984) found that the instrument's 12 items had a high internal consistency (coefficient alpha = .81) in the 1976 Washington State study which strongly distinguished known environmentalists from the general public. Thus, the authors argued that the instrument could be used as the New

Environmental Paradigm Scale for measuring environmental concern. In time, consensus among various social scientists emerged, in effect, supporting the NEP scale as representing a coherent set of beliefs constituting a worldview toward specific environmental issues (Dalton et al., 1999).

This study uses selected items from the NEP scale and a high score on this scale implies a pro-ecological orientation that is expected to lead to proenvironmental beliefs and attitudes on a wide range of issues (Pierce, Dalton, & Zaitsev, 1999; Stern, Dietz, Kalof, & Guagnano, 1995).

The following are the most recent studies using the NEP scale within the domain of environmental sustainability research. Jowett et al. (2014) used the NEP scale to measure how students' attitudes towards the environment changed after exposure to higher education experiences. Wu (2012) developed a Chinese version of the revised NEP scale and tested it on 507 Chinese students, which resulted in the modification of the instrument resulting from cultural differences between China and Western nations. Taskin (2009) used the NEP scale and the General Environmental Attitudes and Perceptions (GAP) instrument to explore the environmental attitudes of Turkish senior high school students as a basis for suggesting future curricular reforms.

RESEARCH METHOD

The research method used in this study is the experimental method combined with the survey technique. Both undergraduate and graduate students of the course, "Management Information Systems" in the Faculty of Business of the University of New Brunswick Fredericton were invited to participate in the study. There were no incentives offered and a total of 128 students chose to participate in the study. The experimental treatment consisted of exposing the students to the following elements before the written survey was administered: a lecture on the concept of "environmental sustainability" as applied to corporate supply chains; a tour of the GoodGuide.com website showing its background, services, functionalities, and explanation of the ratings used for products shown on the site; and a demonstration of the GoodGuide.com mobile app used in smartphones so that consumers could access GoodGuide.com product ratings in the grocery/supermarket.

The following items constitute the specific measures of the key dependent variable in the study, mean of the willingness to be influenced by GoodGuide.com information and willingness to influence others as well: "I think that the information available on GoodGuide.com will be useful to me in the future for purchasing green products."; "People purchasing household products should consult information on GoodGuide.com to properly identify green products."; "I would be willing to share information about green household products that I learn from GoodGuide.com with my family members and friends."; "I would be willing to share information I learn about green household products from GoodGuide.com with family members and friends via my social network account."; "If my family members and friends shared information about green products from GoodGuide.com, I would be willing to be influenced by this information in my purchase decisions."; "I find the product and firm information on GoodGuide.com reliable and trustworthy."; "I find the experts used by GoodGuide.com to produce the firm and product ratings to be reliable and trustworthy."; "I think that third party websites like GoodGuide.com are doing the consumer public a good service by providing reliable and good information on the ratings of products in terms of how 'green' they are using scores reflecting 'environment,' 'health,' and 'society' ratings."; "I think that social networking via Facebook, LinkedIn, Twitter, MySpace, etc., has the potential of helping consumers spread the good word about 'green' products."; and "I would very likely use GoodGuide.com's app for a smartphone while shopping for products in a grocery or supermarket." (Table 1).

The independent variables consist of the constructs used in the VBN theory and NEP scale. The following constructs are part of the VBN theory framework: biospheric values (4 items), altruistic values (4 items), and egoistic values (4 items); awareness of consequences (9 items); ascription of responsibility (4 items); and personal environmental norm (5 items). Appendix A shows the survey questionnaire items for these constructs. A total of 7 items were selected for the NEP scale used in this study. A series of stepwise multiple regressions were used as the data analysis method for this study.

Table 1. Selected items for dependent variable: willingness to influence others with and be influenced by GoodGuide.com information

GoodGuide.com Item	Mean*	Standard Deviation	N**
"I would be willing to purchase green products only if they are priced the same as conventional products."	5.59	1.565	128
"I would not be willing to purchase green products priced higher than conventional products.	4.26	1.689	128
"I would be willing to share information about green household products that I learn from GoodGuide.com with my family members and friends."	5.15	1.689	128
"I would be willing to share information that I learn about green household products from GoodGuide.com with my family members and friends via my social network account."	3.91	1.914	125
"If my family members and friends shared information about green products from GoodGuide.com, I would be willing to be influenced by this information in my purchase decision."	4.61	1.421	127
"I find the product and firm information on GoodGuide.com reliable and trustworthy."	4.57	1.337	127
"I find the experts used by GoodGuide.com to produce firm and product ratings to be reliable and trustworthy."	4.67	1.397	126
"I think that third party websites like Good-Guide.com are doing the consumer public a good service by providing reliable and good information on the ratings of products in terms of how 'green' they are using scores reflecting 'environment,' 'health,' and 'social' ratings."	5.50	1.368	127
"I think that social networking via Facebook, LinkedIn, Twitter, MySpace, etc., has the potential of helping consumers spread the good word about 'green' products."	5.46	1.572	128
"I would very likely use GoodGuide.com's app for a smartphone while shopping for products in a grocery or supermarket."	4.32	1.936	124

*A 7-point Likert scale was used for the questionnaire items.**Differing N values indicate missing values for a specific questionnaire item.

STUDY FINDINGS

Testing VBN Theory Using Survey Data

Before proceeding with the multiple regression analysis, the VBN theory was first tested as shown in Table 2. A number of hierarchical multiple regressions were run to test the VBN theory. Each construct was entered as a dependent variable and the other constructs were entered as independent variables in each of the regression runs. In the last step, the three value steps in addition to NEPMean, awareness of consequences, and ascription of responsibility were regressed on personal environmental norm as shown on Table 2. There were a total of four iterations of multiple regressions conducted to test the VBN theory. In the first model, the NEP scale mean is the dependent variable and three value sets were used as independent variables which explain 20.4 percent of the variance in the NEP scale beliefs. In model 2, the three value sets and the NEP scale were used as independent variables and they did not significantly predict awareness of consequences, the dependent variable. In model 3, however, the independent variables ---biospheric values, altruistic values, and awareness of consequences significantly predicted ascription of responsibility, accounting for 51.6 percent of its variance. In model 4, the three value sets, awareness of consequences, and ascription of responsibility accounted for 55.5 percent of the variance of the dependent variable, personal environmental norm. All of the models, with the exception of model 2, are significant (p<0.001) and thus, moderately corroborate the hierarchical nature of the VBN theory when applied to this study's data on the use perception of GoodGuide.com information.

Multiple Regression Results

This study sought to determine the independent variables that would predict a respondent's willingness to be influenced by GoodGuide. com information and to influence others using that same information. A number of stepwise regressions were ran using the willingness to be influenced/influence others using GoodGuide. com information as the dependent variable. Different parts of the VBN theory framework were tested as independent variables in the stepwise regression models (Table 3).

The first multiple regression model entered the three value orientations (i.e., altruistic, egoistic, and biospheric), the two types of beliefs relevant to environmental behavior (i.e., awareness of environmental consequences (AC) and ascription of responsibility (AR) for environmental consequences, and the final element, personal environmental norm, experienced as feelings of moral obligation to act in a manner that protects the environment. All in all, there were six independent variables: altruistic, biospheric, and egoistic values; awareness of consequences; ascription of responsibility; and personal environmental norm. Of these six predictors, only ascription of responsibility (p<.01) and egoistic values (p<.01) were significant predictors of an individual's willingness to be influenced by and willingness to influence others using GoodGuide.com information, the lone dependent variable. The full model of the first multiple regression explains 50.5 percent of the variance in the dependent variable (N=109, F=19.365, p < .000), using the adjusted R^2 value. There were multicollinearity issues, however, with four out of the six predictor variables: ascription of responsibility, personal environmental norm, biospheric values, and altruistic values, which are explained by the high correlations among them. The following are the correlation values among these variables: ascription of responsibility (correlation with personal environmental norm = .690; correlation with biospheric values = .703; correlation with altruistic values = .654 --- all two-tailed correlations are significant at p<.01 level). The following are the correlation values among these variables: personal environmental

Table 2. Testing the VBN theory using multiple regression

Model	B	SE Beta	Beta	p	F	Adj. R²
Model 1: DV: NEP IVs:				.000	11.070	0.204
Biospheric	.149	.072	.289	**.043**		
Altruistic	.090	.078	.163	.251		
Egoistic	.117	.043	.225	**.007**		
Model 2: DV: AwareCon IVs: Biospheric				.234	1.415	.014
Altruistic	.050	.087	.093	.564		
Egoistic	-.004	.092	-.006	.968		
NEP	-.078	.053	-.142	.139		
Model 3: DV: AscResp IVs:				.000	25.478	.516
Biospheric	.489	.118	.465	**.000**		
Altruistic	.266	.125	.236	**.036**		
Egoistic	-.003	.072	-.003	.965		
NEP	.168	.154	.080	.276		
AwareCon	.225	.129	.116	**.084**		
Model 4: DV: PerEnviron IVs:				.000	24.453	.555
Biospheric	.401	.133	.352	**.003**		
Altruistic	.090	.133	.074	.501		
Egoistic	-.091	.076	-.077	.237		
NEP	.178	.165	.075	.284		
AwareCon	.004	.138	.002	.977		
AscResp	.390	.101	.358	**.000**		

norm (correlation with ascription of responsibility = .690; correlation with biospheric values = .709; correlation with altruistic values = .641 --- all two-tailed correlations are significant at p<.01 level). The following are the correlation values among these variables: biospheric values (correlation with ascription of responsibility = .703; correlation with personal environmental norm = .709; correlation with altruistic values = .816 --- all two-tailed correlations are significant at p<.01 level). The following are the correlation values among these variables: altruistic values (correlation with ascription of responsibility = .654; correlation with personal environmental norm = .641; correlation with biospheric values =

.816 --- all two-tailed correlations are significant at p<.01 level).

The second multiple regression model entered two of the three value orientations (i.e., altruistic and egoistic), the two types of beliefs relevant to environmental behavior (i.e., awareness of environmental consequences (AC) and ascription of responsibility (AR) for environmental consequences, and the final element, personal environmental norm. Biospheric values were eliminated from the model since it correlates highly with altruistic values (correlation = .816). Of the five predictors in this second model, only ascription of responsibility (p<.000), altruistic values (p<.01), and egoistic values (p<.01) were significant

Table 3. Multiple regression statistics for seven models

	B	SE B	Beta	p	F	Adj. R²
Model 1: DV: WillingtobeInfluencedGG IVs:					19.365 (Sig = .000)	.505
Egoistic Values	.179	.067	.185	.009		
Biospheric Values	.159	.124	.170	.204		
AwareConseq	.182	.230	.067	.429		
PerEnviron	.023	.088	.028	.796		
Altruistic Values	.198	.120	.199	.101		
AscriptionResp	.326	.094	.362	.001		
Model 2: DV: WillingtobeInfluencedGG IVs:					22.770 (Sig = .000)	.502
Egoistic Values	.179	.067	.186	.009		
AwareConseq	.200	.230	.074	.385		
PerEnviron	.053	.086	.065	.539		
Altruistic Values	.289	.096	.291	.003		
AscriptionResp	.354	.092	.394	.000		
Model 3: DV: WillingtobeInfluencedGG IVs:					28.978 (Sig = .000)	.504
Egoistic Values	.170	.066	.179	.011		
AwareConseq	.213	.218	.078	.331		
Altruistic Values	.304	.092	.305	.001		
AscriptionResp	.382	.081	.426	.000		
Model 4: DV: WillingtobeInfluencedGG IVs:					14.826 (Sig = .000)	.480
NEPMean	-.057	.159	-.029	.719		
Egoistic Values	.194	.072	.201	.008		
AwareConseq	.081	.245	.029	.741		
PerEnviron	.029	.090	.036	.749		
Altruistic Values	.219	.125	.219	.084		
AscriptionResp	.310	.090	.348	.002		
Biospheric Values	.166	.127	.181	.194		
Model 5: DV: WillingtobeInfluencedGG IVs:					16.891 (Sig = .000)	.476
NEPMean	-.031	.158	-.016	.843		
Egoistic Values	.193	.072	.200	.008		
AwareConseq	.095	.246	.034	.700		
PerEnviron	.059	.087	.073	.500		
Altruistic Values	.314	.102	.315	.003		
AscriptionResp	.338	.093	.379	.000		
Model 6: DV: WillingtobeInfluencedGG IVs:					12.291 (Sig = .000)	.301
NEPMean	.126	.180	.064	.485		
Egoistic Values	.209	.083	.216	.014		
AwareConseq	.323	.279	.115	.250		
PerEnviron	.372	.080	.460	.000		
Model 7: DV: WillingtobeInfluencedGG IVs:					7.652 (Sig = .000)	.157
NEPMean	.345	.184	.181	.064		
Egoistic Values	.174	.090	.182	.885		
AwareConseq	.847	.272	.301	.002		

predictors of an individual's willingness to be influenced by and willingness to influence others using GoodGuide.com information. This second model explains 50.2 percent of the variance in the dependent variable (N=109, F=22.770, p < .000), using the adjusted R^2 value. There were multicollinearity issues, however, with ascription of responsibility and personal environmental norm, which are highly correlated (correlation = .690).

The third multiple regression model entered two of the three value orientations (i.e., altruistic and egoistic), the two types of beliefs relevant to environmental behavior (i.e., awareness of environmental consequences (AC) and ascription of responsibility (AR) for environmental consequences). The personal environmental norm variable was eliminated the model because of its high correlation with ascription of responsibility (correlation = .690) --- a move taken to eliminate future multicollinearity problems. Of the four predictors in the third model, ascription of responsibility (p<.000), altruistic values (p<.01), and egoistic values (p<.01) were significant predictors of the dependent variable. This third model explains 50.4 percent of the variance in the dependent variable (N=111, F=28.978, p<.000), using the adjusted R^2 value. There were no multicollinearity issues with this third regression model.

The fourth multiple regression model is the most comprehensive model that included the greatest number of predictors: all three value orientations, awareness of environmental consequences, ascription of responsibility, personal environmental norm, and this time adding the NEP scale. Of all the predictors in the fourth model, ascription of responsibility (p<.01), altruistic values (p<.10), and egoistic values (p<.01) were significant predictors of the dependent variable. This fourth model explains 48.0 percent of the variance in the dependent variable (N=106, F=14.826, p<.000), using the adjusted R^2 value. There were multicollinearity issues with ascription of responsibility, altruistic and egoistic values, and personal environmental norm.

The fifth multiple regression model included all predictor variables in the fourth model with the exception of biospheric values, which correlated highly with altruistic values (correlation = .815). Of all the predictors in the fifth model, ascription of responsibility (p<.000), altruistic values (p<.10), and egoistic values (p<.01) were significant predictors of the dependent variable. This fourth model explains 47.6 percent of the variance in the dependent variable (N=106, F=16.891, p<.000), using the adjusted R^2 value. There were multicollinearity issues with ascription of responsibility, altruistic values, and personal environmental norm.

The sixth multiple regression model included the predictor variables: NEPMean, egoistic values, awareness of consequences, and personal environmental norm. Two variables, ascription of responsibility and altruistic values were eliminated because the former correlated highly with personal environmental norm (correlation = .675) and altruistic values (correlation =.654). Of all the predictors in the sixth model, personal environmental norm (p<.000) and egoistic values (p<.05) were significant predictors of the dependent variable. This fourth model explains 30.1 percent of the variance in the dependent variable (N=106, F=12.291, p<.000), using the adjusted R^2 value. There were multicollinearity issues with awareness of consequences and personal environmental norm.

The seventh multiple regression model included the predictor variables: NEPMean, egoistic values, and awareness of consequences. The variable personal environmental norm was eliminated because it correlates highly with awareness of consequences (correlation = .524). All three predictor variables were significant in this seventh multiple regression model (p<.000), which explains 15.7 percent of the variance in the dependent variable (N=108, F=7.652, p<.000), using the adjusted R^2 value. There were no multicollinearity issues with this seventh multiple regression model.

T-Tests Using Significant Predictor Variables

Further analysis on the multiple regression results were conducted using T-Tests (Tables 4-7). Two groups were created using the significant predictor variables: NEP scale, personal environmental norm, awareness of consequences, and egoistic values. Categorical variables were created for these four significant predictor variables designating respondents that were high and low on the values of these variables. For independent variables using 7-point Likert scales (i.e., NEP scale, personal environmental norm, and egoistic values) group 1 members are those who had responded with values from 1 to 3.50; group 2 members are those who responded with values from 3.51 and up. Awareness of consequences was the only predictor variable using a 3-point scale, therefore group 1 members are those whose mean values for this construct were from 1 to 1.50, and group 2 members are those whose mean values for this construct were 1.51 and up.

The expectation is that respondents that belong to the "high" scoring group for a particular variable (except the groups for egoistic values) are expected to score higher as well on all the dependent variables used in this study. The T-test results for the personal environmental norm (PEN) construct are consistently significant and generally in the expected direction --- which means, group 2 members (i.e., respondents with higher PEN scores) have higher means on all dependent variables except dependent variables 15 and 16. Understandably, group 1 (i.e., respondents with lower PEN scores) has a greater mean values for dependent variable 15 (i.e., respondent willing to purchase green products only if green products are priced the same as conventional products) and dependent variable 16 (i.e., respondent is not willing to purchase green products priced higher than conventional products). Group 1 members are obviously more price sensitive than group 2 members.

The T-test results for NEP scale construct, however, are mixed. The means for dependent variables 15, 16, and 18 are not significantly different for groups 1 (i.e., respondents with lower NEP scale mean scores) and 2 (i.e., respondents with higher NEP scale mean scores). This means that both groups are price sensitive and will not spend more for green products. Also, members of both groups equally think that consumers should consult GoodGuide.com information in identifying green products. For all other dependent variables, group 2 members for the NEP scale have significantly higher means than those of group 1 members --- which is what is expected.

The T-test results for awareness of consequences are counter-intuitive and unexpected. Basically overall, there are no significant differences in the means scored for all dependent variables by both groups 1 (i.e., respondents with lower awareness of consequences scores) and 2 (i.e., respondents with higher awareness of consequences scores). Strangely enough, group 1 members have higher means on most of the dependent variables than group 2 members --- though not significantly so, except for dependent variables 16 (i.e., respondent is not willing to purchase green products priced higher than conventional products), 17 (i.e., information available on GoodGuide.com would be useful to the respondent in purchasing green products), and 18 (i.e., respondent thinks consumers should consult GoodGuide.com information to properly identify green products). Group 2 members have higher means for these three dependent variables, though not significantly so.

In terms of the descriptive statistics for awareness of consequences, 75.6 percent of the sample belongs to group 2 for awareness of consequences, meaning, a large majority of the respondents are cognitively aware of the consequences of various forms of environmental abuses. This finding clearly demonstrates that possession of knowledge alone does not automatically lead to the formation of appropriate sustainability related attitudes, beliefs, and intentions.

Table 4. T-test results for all dependent variables and personal environmental norms

Variable	Mean	SD	t	df	p
Dependent Variable 15: Respondent willing to purchase green products only if green products are priced the same as conventional products.					
Group 1* Group 2**	6.13 5.35	1.185 1.656	2.843	75.891	.01
Dependent Variable 16: Respondent is not willing to purchase green products priced higher than conventional products.					
Group 1 Group 2	4.94 4.03	1.813 1.616	2.496	49.406	.05
Dependent Variable 17: Information available on GoodGuide.com would be useful to the respondent in purchasing green products.					
Group 1 Group 2	3.56 5.51	1.523 1.198	-6.529	45.534	.000
Dependent Variable 18: Respondent thinks that consumers should consult GoodGuide.com information to properly identify green products.					
Group 1 Group 2	3.59 5.02	1.583 1.406	-4.515	49.274	.000
Dependent Variable 19: Respondent is willing to share GoodGuide.com information with family and friends.					
Group 1 Group 2	3.66 5.63	1.807 1.330	-5.652	43.402	.000
Dependent Variable 21: Respondent willing to share GoodGuide.com info with family & friends via a social network.					
Group 1 Group 2	2.41 4.44	1.456 1.745	-6.411	65.159	.000
Dependent Variable 22: Respondent willing to be influenced by family & friends with GoodGuide.com info					
Group 1 Group 2	3.53 4.96	1.436 1.237	-4.997	48.161	.000
Dependent Variable 23: Respondent finds product and firm information on GoodGuide.com reliable and trustworthy.					
Group 1 Group 2	4.03 4.74	1.492 1.214	-2.433	46.420	.05
Dependent Variable 24: Respondent finds experts used by GoodGuide.com to produce the firm and product ratings to be reliable and trustworthy.					
Group 1 Group 2	4.22 4.83	1.736 1.218	-1.840	42.463	.10
Dependent Variable 25: Respondent thinks third party websites like GoodGuide.com are doing the consumer public a good service by providing reliable and good information on the ratings of products in terms of how "green" they are using scores reflecting"environment," "health," and "society" ratings.					
Group 1 Group 2	4.91 5.71	1.614 1.220	-2.572	44.247	.05
Dependent Variable 26: Respondent thinks that social networking via Facebook, LinkedIn, Twitter, MySpace, etc., has the potential of helping consumers spread the good word about "green" products.					
Group 1 Group 2	5.00 5.59	1.901 1.437	-1.840	121	.10
Dependent Variable 29: Respondent willing to use a GoodGuide.com smartphone app when shopping for products in a grocery or supermarket.					
Group 1 Group 2	2.56 4.97	1.625 1.615	-7.176	54.745	.000

Legend:
* Group 1: sample respondents who are *have lower mean personal environmental norm scores*
** Group 2: sample respondents who *have higher mean personal environmental norm scores*

Table 5. T-test results for all dependent variables and NEP scale mean

Variable	Mean	SD	t	df	p
Dependent Variable 15: Respondent willing to purchase green products only if green products are priced the same as conventional products.					
Group 1* Group 2**	5.56 5.54	1.590 1.586	.021	121	.983
Dependent Variable 16: Respondent is not willing to purchase green products priced higher than conventional products.					
Group 1 Group 2	4.89 4.25	1.965 1.686	1.089	121	.278
Dependent Variable 17: Information available on GoodGuide.com would be useful to the respondent in purchasing green products.					
Group 1 Group 2	3.89 5.12	1.764 1.499	-2.0291	8.954	.10
Dependent Variable 18: Respondent thinks that consumers should consult GoodGuide.com information to properly identify green products.					
Group 1 Group 2	4.22 4.75	1.641 1.573	-.958	121	.340
Dependent Variable 19: Respondent is willing to share GoodGuide.com information with family and friends.					
Group 1 Group 2	3.67 5.29	2.062 1.584	-2.308	8.762	.05
Dependent Variable 21: Respondent willing to share GoodGuide.com info with family & friends via a social network.					
Group 1 Group 2	2.44 4.07	1.509 1.887	-3.048	10.126	.05
Dependent Variable 22: Respondent willing to be influenced by family & friends with GoodGuide.com info.					
Group 1 Group 2	3.67 4.71	1.871 1.361	-2.152	121	.05
Dependent Variable 23: Respondent finds product and firm information on GoodGuide.com reliable and trustworthy.					
Group 1 Group 2	3.67 4.65	1.581 1.288	-2.159	120	.05
Dependent Variable 24: Respondent finds experts used by GoodGuide.com to produce the firm and product ratings to be reliable and trustworthy.					
Group 1 Group 2	3.56 4.79	1.590 1.325	-2.259	8.916	.10
Dependent Variable 25: Respondent thinks third party websites like GoodGuide.com are doing the consumer public a good service by providing reliable and good information on the ratings of products in terms of how "green" they are using scores reflecting"environment," "health," and "society" ratings.					
Group 1 Group 2	4.56 5.62	1.740 1.256	-2.374	120	.10
Dependent Variable 26: Respondent thinks that social networking via Facebook, LinkedIn, Twitter, MySpace, etc., has the potential of helping consumers spread the good word about "green" products.					
Group 1 Group 2	4.56 5.58	1.590 1.516	-1.865	9.187	.10
Dependent Variable 29: Respondent willing to use a GoodGuide.com smartphone app when shopping for products in a grocery or supermarket.					
Group 1 Group 2	3.11 4.47	1.900 1.892	-2.062	9.333	.10

Legend:

* Group 1: sample respondents who are *have lower mean NEP scale scores*

** *Group 2: sample respondents who* have higher mean NEP scale scores

Table 6. T-test results for all dependent variables and awareness of consequences

Variable	Mean	SD	t	df	p
Dependent Variable 15: respondent willing to purchase green products only if green products are priced the same as conventional products.					
Group 1* Group 2**	5.82 5.49	1.565 1.583.	.979	122	.330
Dependent Variable 16: respondent is not willing to purchase green products priced higher than conventional products.					
Group 1 Group 2	4.21 4.28	1.686 1.727	-.181	122	.856
Dependent Variable 17: Information available on GoodGuide.com would be useful to the respondent in purchasing green products.					
Group 1 Group 2	4.93 5.01	1.654 1.513	-.247	120	.806
Dependent Variable 18: Respondent thinks that consumers should consult GoodGuide.com information to properly identify green products.					
Group 1 Group 2	4.39 4.74	1.812 1.517	-1.017	122	.311
Dependent Variable 19: Respondent is willing to share GoodGuide.com information with family and friends.					
Group 1 Group 2	5.18 5.07	1.847 1.650	.290	122	.772
Dependent Variable 21: Respondent willing to share GoodGuide.com info with family & friends via a social network.					
Group 1 Group 2	4.11 3.77	2.217 1.781	.840	120	.403
Dependent Variable 22: Respondent willing to be influenced by family & friends with GoodGuide.com info.					
Group 1 Group 2	4.79 4.49	1.618 1.330	.986	122	.326
Dependent Variable 23: Respondent finds product and firm information on GoodGuide.com reliable and trustworthy.					
Group 1 Group 2	4.61 4.48	1.499 1.270	.431	121	.667
Dependent Variable 24: Respondent finds experts used by GoodGuide.com to produce the firm and product ratings to be reliable and trustworthy.					
Group 1 Group 2	4.75 4.59	1.578 1.347	.546	120	.586
Dependent Variable 25: Respondent thinks third party websites like GoodGuide.com are doing the consumer public a good service by providing reliable and good information on the ratings of products in terms of how "green" they are using scores reflecting"environment," "health," and "society" ratings.					
Group 1 Group 2	5.57 5.41	1.574 1.301	.548	121	.585
Dependent Variable 26: Respondent thinks that social networking via Facebook, LinkedIn, Twitter, MySpace, etc., has the potential of helping consumers spread the good word about "green" products.					
Group 1 Group 2	5.54 5.39	1.795 1.517	.442	122	.659
Dependent Variable 29: Respondent willing to use a GoodGuide.com smartphone app when shopping for products in a grocery or supermarket.					
Group 1 Group 2	4.32 4.27	2.195 1.866	.125	119	.900

Legend:

* Group 1: sample respondents who are have lower mean awareness of consequences scores

** Group 2: sample respondents who have higher mean awareness of consequences scores

Table 7. T-test results for all dependent variables and egoistic values

Variable	Mean	SD	t	df	p
Dependent Variable 15: Respondent willing to purchase green products only if green products are priced the same as conventional products.					
Group 1* Group 2**	4.93 5.76	1.856 1.420	-2.245	40.169	.05
Dependent Variable 16: Respondent is not willing to purchase green products priced higher than conventional products.					
Group 1 Group 2	3.97 4.36	1.732 1.687	-1.121	124	.265
Dependent Variable 17: Information available on GoodGuide.com would be useful to the respondent in purchasing green products					
Group 1 Group 2	5.10 5.01	1.423 1.596	.274	122	.785
Dependent Variable 18: Respondent thinks that consumers should consult GoodGuide.com information to properly identify green products.					
Group 1 Group 2	4.63 4.72	1.520 1.620	-.256	124	.799
Dependent Variable 19: Respondent is willing to share GoodGuide.com information with family and friends.					
Group 1 Group 2	5.10 5.15	1.647 1.723	-.128	124	.898
Dependent Variable 21: Respondent willing to share GoodGuide.com info with family & friends via a social network.					
Group 1 Group 2	3.71 3.97	2.070 1.883	-.615	122	.540
Dependent Variable 22: Respondent willing to be influenced by family & friends with GoodGuide.com info.					
Group 1 Group 2	4.57 4.63	1.251 1.481	-.195	124	.846
Dependent Variable 23: Respondent finds product and firm information on GoodGuide.com reliable and trustworthy.					
Group 1 Group 2	4.30 4.64	1.317 1.344	-1.221	1223	.224
Dependent Variable 24: Respondent finds experts used by GoodGuide.com to produce the firm and product ratings to be reliable and trustworthy.					
Group 1 Group 2	4.21 4.80	1.449 1.365	-1.956	44.272	.10
Dependent Variable 25: Respondent thinks third party websites like GoodGuide.com are doing the consumer public a good service by providing reliable and good information on the ratings of products in terms of how "green" they are using scores reflecting"environment," "health," and "society" ratings.					
Group 1 Group 2	5.17 5.59	1.464 1.333	-1.479	123	.142
Dependent Variable 26: Respondent thinks that social networking via Facebook, LinkedIn, Twitter, MySpace, etc., has the potential of helping consumers spread the good word about "green" products.					
Group 1 Group 2	5.17 5.54	1.821 1.493	-1.138	124	.257
Dependent Variable 29: Respondent willing to use a GoodGuide.com smartphone app when shopping for products in a grocery or supermarket.					
Group 1 Group 2	4.46 4.26	1.972 1.936	.481	121	.631

Legend:

 * *Group 1: sample respondents who are* have lower mean egoistic values scores

 ** *Group 2: sample respondents who* have higher mean egoistic values scores

The T-test results for egoistic values are also quite unexpected. The expectation for egoistic value results is in reverse, in other words, group 1 members (i.e., respondents with lower egoistic value scores) are expected to have higher score values on all dependent variables compared to the scores returned by group 2 members (i.e., respondents with higher egoistic value scores). There were no significant differences in the mean values for most of the dependent variables registered by members of both groups 1 and 2. Members of group 2 returned higher mean values only for two dependent variables --- 15 (i.e., respondent willing to purchase green products only if green products are priced the same as conventional products) and 24 (i.e., respondent finds experts used by GoodGuide.com to produce the firm and product ratings to be reliable and trustworthy).

SUGGESTED SOLUTIONS

This study brought out the importance of the potential of social networking and use of mobile devices in using GoodGuide.com information on the social, health, and environmental ratings of products, which overall, indicate its environmental friendliness. GoodGuide.com is a primary example of an online electronic infomediary that espouses Goleman's (2009) principle of "radical transparency" of product attributes and manufacturing processes that should be supported in the marketplace. Online environmental infomediaries like GoodGuide.com could contribute significantly to the lack of understandable, reliable, and trustworthy information on the sustainability attributes of ordinary products consumers purchase. Through the use of downloadable apps, OEIs also could solve the logistical problem of access to this complex information needed to make repetitive purchase decisions at the point of purchase through the use of cellphones or smartphones.

The other issue with sustainability information is its trustworthiness. This can be partially addressed by using social networking influences that can play a part in allaying concerns about the reliability of the information. Sharing recommendations about the use of GoodGuide.com derived information could strengthen a consumer's confidence in the information if these recommendations or referrals come from trusted friends and family members. Another possibility for the future to increase the trustworthiness of the posted information is to post endorsements from credible agencies like the U.S. Environmental Protection Agency or EPA or non-governmental agencies like Green Peace or from a consortium of scientists and ecologists who have examined and verified information posted on the website.

In this study, the significant predictor variables to pay attention to are NEP Mean, awareness of consequences, egoistic values, and personal environmental norms. The first three predictor variables were all significant in the seventh and last model (accounting for 15.7 percent of the variance in the dependent variable), and personal environmental norms was significant in the sixth model (which together with the other three predictors, account for 30.1 percent of the variance in the dependent variable).

The implication of these findings is that different forms of educational efforts should be pursued by various organizations --- firms, the government, nongovernmental organizations, etc., to promote pro-environmental views embodied in the constructs NEP Mean, awareness of consequences, and personal environmental norm. Regarding the personal environmental norm, Schwartz 1977) and Hopper and Nielsen (1991) found this construct to be a major influence on environmentally friendly behavior since a sense of moral obligation predisposes an individual to act more in a way that leads to green product choices, search, and recycling. The personal environmental norm is an internalized social norm tied to a person's self-concept and as such is a more difficult target for persuasive efforts from the point-of-view of vested stakeholders such as public and private policymakers. It has been suggested that the use of injunctive norms that inculcate a sense of personal moral obligation from the internalization of a pre-scribed societal view of how individuals should behave as "green consumers" might work better (Schwartz, 1997; Hopper & Nielsen, 1991). For instance, public service messages could encourage "doing the right thing" via school- or church-based programs. Also, social influence strategies using widely recognized and respected opinion leaders and celebrities endorsing green behaviors could be used in a way that would appeal to feelings of guilt for noncompliance or enhanced self-esteem for behaving appropriately.

Cultivating the desired environmental world views embodied in the NEP scale and awareness of consequences items, perhaps, would be bet-ter approached through education at all levels. There is a suggestion to include concepts on global citizenship as part of the sustainability curriculum to ensure that students learn to accept social and moral responsibilities implicit in being a consumer using up the earth's natural resources (Sibbel, 2009).

The emergence of egoistic values as a signifi-cant predictor in this study is counter-intuitive, but, nevertheless, helps us understand the current state of mind of the participants in this study. Perhaps, this sample of participants is far more representative of the majority of consumers in the marketplace who are just getting acquainted with the sustainability mindset. Perhaps, stake-holders with an interest in sustainability could use this finding to slant promotional/educational sustainability materials to emphasize the benefits to the individual of becoming more earth friendly. For instance, promoters could articulate and ac-centuate how sustainable consumer products are healthier since they are toxin free. The price of green products would figure strongly in the cost/benefit analysis that consumers with dominant egoistic values in this sample would undertake and clearly would discourage consumers' purchase.

FUTURE RESEARCH DIRECTIONS

The VBN theory was validated using the survey data for this empirical study. Also, both the VBN theory and NEP Scale have been important tools in understanding an individual's willingness to influence others and be influenced by informa-tion posted on GoodGuide.com. This is the only empirical study, thus far, that has used both theo-retical frameworks to test consumers' intention to use sustainability information distributed by an online environmental infomediary to inform their purchase of green household products.

These same theoretical frameworks could be tested in a future research study using study partici-pants making actual household product purchases using GoodGuide.com information at the point of purchase, preferably using mobile devices.

The obvious limitation if this study is the use of the experimental design rather than the sur-veying of actual shoppers who used GoodGuide.com information while shopping in groceries or supermarkets. For the future, therefore, it is recommended that consumers that actually used GoodGuide.com information in their shopping trips to the grocery or supermarket, be surveyed. It would also be good to probe the influence of their social networks in their use of GoodGuide.com and if they would be interested in influencing their friends and family with this information, and if they, in fact, used the GoodGuide.com smart-phone app during their shopping trips.

CONCLUSION

This study highlights the important role played by online environmental infomediaries such as GoodGuide.com when it comes to communicating environmentally relevant information within the personal shopping context. Translating complex technical information that is needed in understand-ing the sustainability implications of products and services is a critical service that needs to be provided to individual consumers to enhance their ongoing education in this technical matter. The importance of consumer-oriented product sustainability information is indicated by the research finding that two-thirds of consumers would consider factors such as sustainability in their purchase decisions but will only go so far in seeking this information (Goleman, 2009). Online environmental infomediaries such as GoodGuide. com should target this captive market segment that is ready to use sustainability information and take appropriate action at the point of sale. Within the context of the supply chain, the practice of sustainability "radical transparency" should also be promoted in both upstream and downstream directions (Goleman, 2009). Providing consumers the tools to vote with their dollars is a promising way of aligning corporate business practices and operations with the tenets of environmental sustainability and respect for the earth's natural resources.

REFERENCES

Aguilar-Luzon, M., Garcia-Martinez, J. M. A., Calvo-Salguero, A., & Salinas, J. M. (2012). Comparative study between the theory of planned behavior and the value-belief-norm model regarding the environment, on spanish housewives' recycling behavior. *Journal of Applied Social Psychology*, *42*(11), 2797–2833. doi:10.1111/j.1559-1816.2012.00962.x

Andersson, L., Shivarajan, S., & Blau, G. (2005). Enacting ecological sustainability in the MNC: A test of an adapted value-belief-norm framework. *Journal of Business Ethics*, *59*(3), 295–305. doi:10.1007/s10551-005-3440-x

Armstrong, J. B., & Impara, J. C. (1991). The impact of an environmental education program on knowledge and attitude. *The Journal of Environmental Education*, *22*(4), 36–40. doi:10.1080/00958964.1991.9943060

Bamberg, S., & Schmidt, P. (2003). Incentives, morality, or habit? Predicting students' car use for university routes with the models of Ajzen, Schwartz, and Triandis. *Environment and Behavior*, *35*(2), 264–285. doi:10.1177/0013916502250134

Cleveland, M., Kalamas, M., & Laroche, M. (2005). Shades of green: Linking environmental locus of control and pro-environmental behaviors. *Journal of Consumer Marketing*, *22*(4), 198–212. doi:10.1108/07363760510605317

Dalton, R. J., Gontmacher, Y., Lovrich, N. P., & Pierce, J. C. (1999). Environmental attitudes and the new environmental paradigm. In R. J. Dalton, P. Garb, P. Lovrich, J. C. Pierce, & J. M. Whitely (Eds.), *Critical masses: Citizens, nuclear weapons production, and environmental destruction in the United States and Russia* (pp. 195–230). Cambridge, MA: MIT Press.

De Groot, J. I. M., & Steg, L. (2008). Value orientations to explain beliefs related to environmental significant behavior: How to measure egoistic, altruistic, and biospheric value orientation. *Environment and Behavior*, *40*(3), 330–354. doi:10.1177/0013916506297831

Dunlap, R. E., & Van Liere, K. D. (1978). The 'new environmental paradigm': A proposed measuring instrument and preliminary results. *The Journal of Environmental Education*, *9*(4), 10–19. doi:10.1080/00958964.1978.10801875

Dunlap, R. E., & Van Liere, K. D. (1984). Commitment to the dominant social paradigm and concern for environmental quality. *Social Science Quarterly*, *65*, 1013–1028.

Dunlap, R. E., Van Liere, K. D., Mertig, A. G., & Emmet Jones, R. (2000). Measuring endorsement of the new ecological paradigm: A revised NEP scale. *The Journal of Social Issues*, *56*(3), 425–439. doi:10.1111/0022-4537.00176

Fliegenschnee, M., & Schelakovsky, M. (1998). *Umweltpsychologie und Umweltbildung: eine Ein-fuhrung aus humanokologischer Sicht.* Wien: Facultas Universitats Verlag.

Godfrey, M. (2014). Environmental infomediaries in the risk society: The behavioral impact of online environmental information communication strategies. *Stream: Culture/Politics/Technology, 5*(1), 29-36.

Goleman, D. (2009). *Ecological intelligence: How knowing the hidden impacts of what webBuy can change everything.* New York, NY: Crown Business.

Hansla, A., Gamble, A., Juliusson, A., & Garling, T. (2008). The relationships between awareness of consequences, environmental concern, and value orientation. *Journal of Environmental Psychology, 28*(1), 1–9. doi:10.1016/j.jenvp.2007.08.004

Hopper, J. R., & Nielsen, J. M. (1991). Recycling as altruistic behavior: Normative and behavioral strategies to expand participation in a community recycling program. *Environment and Behavior, 23*(2), 195–220. doi:10.1177/0013916591232004

Jansson, J., Marell, A., & Nordlund, A. (2010). Green consumer behavior: Determinants of curtailment and eco-innovation adoption. *Journal of Consumer Marketing, 27*(4), 358–370. doi:10.1108/07363761011052396

Jansson, J., Marell, A., & Nordlund, A. (2011). Exploring consumer adoption of a high involvement eco-innovation using value-belief-norm theory. *Journal of Consumer Behaviour, 10*(1), 51–60. doi:10.1002/cb.346

Johansson, M., Rahm, J., & Gyllin, M. (2013). Landowners' participation in biodiversity conservation examined through the value-belief-norm theory. *Landscape Research, 38*(3), 295–311. doi:10.1080/01426397.2012.673576

Jowett, T., Harraway, J., Lovelock, B., Skeaff, S., Slooten, L., Strack, M., & Shephard, K. (2014). Multinomial-regression modeling of the environmental attitudes of higher education students based on the revised new ecological paradigm scale. *The Journal of Environmental Education, 45*(1), 1–15. doi:10.1080/00958964.2013.783777

Minton, A. P., & Rose, R. L. (1997). The effects of environmental concern on environmentally friendly consumer behavior: An exploratory study. *Journal of Business Research, 40*(1), 37–48. doi:10.1016/S0148-2963(96)00209-3

Nordlund, A. M., & Garvill, J. (2002). Value structures behind proenvironmental behavior. *Environment and Behavior, 34*(6), 740–756. doi:10.1177/001391602237244

Pierce, J. C., Dalton, R. J., & Zaitsev, A. (1999). Public perceptions of environmental conditions. In R. J. Dalton, P. Garb, P. Lovrich, J. C. Pierce, & J. M. Whitely (Eds.), *Critical masses: Citizens, nuclear weapons production, and environmental destruction in the United States and Russia* (pp. 97–129). Cambridge, MA: MIT Press.

Preuss, S. (1991). *Umweltkatastrophe Mensch. Ueber unsere Grenzen und Moeglichkeiten, oekologisch bewusst zu handeln.* Heidelberg, Germany: Roland Asanger Verlag.

Remy, C., & Huang, E. M. (2012). The complexity of information for sustainable choices. In *Proceedings Position Paper at Simple, Sustainable Living Workshop.* ACM.

Schwartz, S. (1999). *Normative influences on altruism.* In L. Berkowitz (Ed.), Advances in experimental social psychology (pp. 221–279). New York, NY: Academic Press.

Schwartz, S. H. (1977). Normative influences on altruism. *Advances in Experimental Social Psychology, 10*, 221–279. doi:10.1016/S0065-2601(08)60358-5

Sibbel, A. (2009). Pathways towards sustainability through higher education. *International Journal of Sustainability in Higher Education, 10*(1), 68–82. doi:10.1108/14676370910925262

Stern, P. C. (2000). Toward a coherent theory of environmentally significant behavior. *The Journal of Social Issues, 56*(3), 407–424. doi:10.1111/0022-4537.00175

Stern, P. C., Dietz, T., Abel, T., Guagnano, G. A., & Kalof, L. (1999). A value-belief-norm theory of support for social movements: The case of environmentalism. *Human Ecology Review, 6*(2), 81–97.

Stern, P. C., Dietz, T., Kalof, L., & Guagnano, G. A. (1995). Values, beliefs, and proenvironmental attitude formation toward emergent attitude objects. *Journal of Applied Social Psychology, 25*(18), 1611–1636. doi:10.1111/j.1559-1816.1995.tb02636.x

Taskin, O. (2009). The environmental attitudes of Turkish sénior high school students in the context of postmaterialism and the new environmental paradigm. *International Journal of Science Education, 31*(4), 481–502. doi:10.1080/09500690701691689

Wu, L. (2012). Exploring the new ecological paradigm scale for gauging children's environmental attitudes in China. *The Journal of Environmental Education, 43*(2), 107–120. doi:10.1080/00958964.2011.616554

ADDITIONAL READING

Bamberg, S. (2003). How does environmental concern influence specific environmentally related behaviors? A new answer to an old question. *Journal of Environmental Psychology, 23*(1), 21–32. doi:10.1016/S0272-4944(02)00078-6

Clark, C., Kotchen, M., & Moore, M. (2003). Internal and external influences on pro-environmental behavior: Participation in a green electricity program. *Journal of Environmental Psychology, 23*(3), 237–246. doi:10.1016/S0272-4944(02)00105-6

Cottrell, S. P. (2003). Influence of sociodemographics and environmental attitudes on general responsible environmental behavior among recreational boaters. *Environment and Behavior, 35*(3), 347–375. doi:10.1177/0013916503035003003

Degenhardt, L. (2002). Why do people act in sustainable ways? Results of an empirical survey of lifestyle Pioneers. In P. Schmuck & W. P. Schultz (Eds.), *Psychology of Sustainable Development*. Norwell, MA: Kluwer Academic Publishers. doi:10.1007/978-1-4615-0995-0_7

Diekman, A., & Preisendorfer, P. (1988). Environmental behavior: Discrepancies between aspirations and reality. *Rationality and Society, 10*(1), 79–102. doi:10.1177/104346398010001004

Diekman, A., & Preisendorfer, P. (2003). Green and greenback: The behavioral aspects of environmental attitudes in low-cost and high-cost situations. *Rationality and Society, 15*(4), 441–472. doi:10.1177/1043463103154002

Eden, S. (1993). Individual environmental responsibility and its role in public environmentalism. *Environment & Planning, 25*(12), 1743–1758. doi:10.1068/a251743

Fraj, E., & Martinez, E. (2006). Environmental values and lifestyles as determining factors of ecological consumer behaviour: An empirical analysis. *Journal of Consumer Marketing, 23*(3), 133–144. doi:10.1108/07363760610663295

Fraj, E., & Martinez, E. (2007). Ecological consumer behavior: An empirical analysis. *International Journal of Consumer Studies, 31*(1), 26–33. doi:10.1111/j.1470-6431.2006.00565.x

Garling, T., Fujii, S., Garling, A., & Jakobsson, C. (2003). Moderating effects of social value orientation on determinants of proenvironmental behavior intention. *Journal of Environmental Psychology*, *23*(1), 1–9. doi:10.1016/S0272-4944(02)00081-6

Grankvist, G., & Biel, A. (2001). The importance of beliefs and purchase criteria in the choice of eco-labeled food products. *Journal of Environmental Psychology*, *21*(4), 405–410. doi:10.1006/jevp.2001.0234

Haanpaa, L. (2007). Consumers' green commitment: Indication of a postmodern lifestyle? *International Journal of Consumer Studies*, *31*(5), 478–486. doi:10.1111/j.1470-6431.2007.00598.x

Kaiser, F., Wolfing, S., & Fuhrer, U. (1999). Environmental attitude and ecological behavior. *Journal of Environmental Psychology*, *19*(1), 1–19. doi:10.1006/jevp.1998.0107

Labay, D. G., & Kinnear, T. C. (1981). Exploring the consumer decision process in the adoption of solar energy systems. *The Journal of Consumer Research*, *8*(3), 271–278. doi:10.1086/208865

Minton, A. P., & Rose, R. L. (1997). The effects of environmental concern on environmentally friendly consumer behavior: An exploratory study. *Journal of Business Research*, *40*(1), 37–48. doi:10.1016/S0148-2963(96)00209-3

Poortinga, W., Steg, L., & Vlek, C. (2004). Values, environmental concern, and environmental behavior: A study into household energy use. *Environment and Behavior*, *36*(1), 70–93. doi:10.1177/0013916503251466

Shaw, D., Grehan, E., Shiu, E., Hassan, L., & Thomson, J. (2005). An exploration of values in ethical consumer decision making. *Journal of Consumer Behaviour*, *4*(3), 185–200. doi:10.1002/cb.3

Straughan, R. D., & Roberts, J. A. (1999). Environmental segmentation alternatives: A look at green consumer behavior in the new millennium. *Journal of Consumer Marketing*, *16*(6), 558–575. doi:10.1108/07363769910297506

Tanner, C. (1999). Constraints on environmental behavior. *Journal of Environmental Psychology*, *19*(2), 145–157. doi:10.1006/jevp.1999.0121

Thogersen, J. (2002). Direct experience and the strength of the personal norm-behavior relationship. *Psychology and Marketing*, *19*(10), 881–893. doi:10.1002/mar.10042

Vlek, C., & Steg, L. (2007). Human behavior and environmental sustainability: Problems, driving forces, and research topics. *The Journal of Social Issues*, *63*(1), 1–19. doi:10.1111/j.1540-4560.2007.00493.x

Watson, R. T., & Boudreau, M. C. (2010). Information systems and environentally sustainable development: Energy informatics and new directions for the IS community. *Management Information Systems Quarterly*, *34*(1), 23–38.

KEY TERMS AND DEFINITIONS

Consumer Behavior: The study of individuals, groups, or organizations and the processes they use to select, secure, and dispose of products, services, experiences, or ideas to satisfy their needs.

Environmental Sustainability: The Environmental Protection Agency defines "environmental sustainability" as a state in which "…humans and nature can exist in productive harmony, that permit fulfilling the social, economic and other requirements of present and future generations".

Mobile Apps: Small pieces of software accessed and operates via the Internet and are designed for use in mobile, handheld devices.

New Environmental Paradigm (NEP): Dunlap and Van Liere (1978, 1984) introduced their conceptualization of the New Environmental Paradigm (NEP) which presents beliefs about humanity's ability to upset the balance of nature, existence of the limits to growth for human societies, and humanity's right to rule over nature and its resources.

Online Environmental Informediary (OEI): OEIs are third party information dealers that mediate between consumers and firms and provide both parties information they need and value (Godfrey, 2014).

Social Networking: The practice of expanding users' business and social contacts by making connections through their mutual business and social acquaintances/friends. Social networking sites supporting social and professional communities support social networking.

Value-Belief-Norm Theory: Stern's value-belief-norm (VBN) theory is, thus far, the most comprehensive and empirically supported theory that connects the concepts of value theory, norm activation theory, and the New Environmental Paradigm perspective in anticipating pro-environmental behavior.

APPENDIX: SURVEY QUESTIONNAIRE ITEMS FOR SELECTED CONSTRUCTS

Awareness of Consequences

[**Response Options:** 3: a very serious problem, 2: somewhat of a problem, 1: won't really be a problem for me and my family]

About "Climate Change"

[AC1] I think that climate change, which is sometimes called the "greenhouse effect" will be:

About "The Loss of Tropical Forests"

[AC2] I think that the problem of loss of tropical forests will be:

About "Toxic Substances"

[AC3] I think that the problem of use of toxic substances will be:

Ascription of Responsibility

[**Response Options:** Strongly Disagree: 1 to Strongly Agree: 7]
   [AR1] I feel partly responsible for the promoting greater consumer awareness of green products by using my power to vote through my consumer dollars.
   [AR2] I feel partly responsible for global warming by buying products that are not green.
   [AR3] Not only private industry and government are responsible for increased carbon emissions and a greater carbon footprint --- I am responsible as well.
   [AR4] By purchasing products made by firms that support supply chains that are not environmentally aware, I am contributing somehow to dire state of environmental resource depletion and global warming.

Personal Environmental Norm

[**Response Options:** Strongly Disagree: 1 to Strongly Agree: 7]
   [PEN1] I feel a personal, moral obligation to buy environmentally friendly products for our household.
   [PEN2] I feel a personal, moral obligation to buy products made from recycled ingredients.
   [PEN3] I feel a personal, moral obligation to buy products made by companies known for being environmentally responsible.
   [PEN4] I feel a personal, moral obligation to read and compare labels for environmentally safe ingredients when I shop.
   [PEN5] I feel a personal, moral obligation to pay attention to advertisements about products which are safe for the environment.

New Environmental Paradigm Scale

[**Response Options:** Strongly Disagree: 1 to Strongly Agree: 7]
[NEP1] Humans are severely abusing the environment.
[NEP2] The balance of nature is strong enough to cope with the impacts of modern industrial nations.
[NEP3] The so-called "ecological crisis" facing humankind has been greatly exaggerated.
[NEP4] The earth is like a spaceship with very limited room and resources.
[NEP5] The balance of nature is very delicate and easily upset.
[NEP6] If things continue on their present course, we will soon experience a major ecological ca-tastrophe.
[NEP7] Humans have the right to modify the natural environment to suit their needs.

Biospheric Values

[**Response Options:** Not Important At All: 1 to Very Important: 7]
[BV1] Protecting the environment; preserving nature
[BV2] Preventing pollution; decreasing my own pollution
[BV3] Respecting the earth, live in harmony with other species
[BV4] Unity with nature; fitting into nature

Altruistic Values

[**Response Options:** Not Important At All: 1 to Very Important: 7]
[AV1] Social justice, correcting injustice, care for the weak
[AV2] Preventing pollution, conserving natural resources
[AV3] Equality, equal opportunity for all
[AV4] A world of peace, free of war and conflict

Egoistic Values

[**Response Options:** Not Important At All: 1 to Very Important: 7]
[EV1] Social power, control over others, dominance…
[EV2] Influential, having an impact on people and events…
[EV3] Wealth, material possessions, money…
[EV4] Authority, the right to lead or command…

Chapter 13
Emergency Management Training and Social Network Analysis:
Providing Experiential Data for Virtual Responders

Knut Ekker
Nord-Trøndelag University College, Norway

ABSTRACT

The chapter first presents a background review of the application of computer technology in simulations of natural hazard situations. The chapter then presents the efforts of researchers at Mid Sweden University and Nord-Trøndelag University College to build a comprehensive emergency training tool with funding from the Interreg/EU ERDF (European Regional Development Fund). The main part of the chapter reports empirical data from this project GSS (Gaining Security Symbiosis). The project developed the tool for training emergency personnel (police, fire, ambulance, and local officials) in handling crises in the border region between Norway and Sweden. The Web-based software incorporated complex scenarios that the emergency personnel had to contend with during 3-hour training sessions. The participants included employees at the operator, tactical, and strategic level of the organizations. The training tool recorded all communications among participants which primarily was text based. The rich data source was analyzed "on-the-fly" with the software from the R Project for statistical computing and the SNA package (Social Network Analysis package). The statistical software provided detailed graphs of the social networking of communications among the participants on both sides of the national border in central Scandinavia. The chapter concludes with a presentation of ideas towards using the social networking data as input into simulation models based on system dynamics. The empirical data from the project will naturally provide data for future training sessions. A planned future model of the comprehensive training tool—netAgora—will use experiential data in a Virtual Responder component in the training sessions of emergency personnel.

DOI: 10.4018/978-1-4666-8147-7.ch013

INTRODUCTION

This chapter describes an EU-funded research project (Interreg) which during the years 2010 – 2013 worked with emergency personnel developing software for training in handling emergencies in the mountainous border region of mid-Norway and mid-Sweden. The ideas for this project was developed with the help of colleagues in Slovenia and Greece during the autumn of 2008 and resulted in a project proposal to the 7th Framework Programme of the EU in December 2008. This proposal did not receive any funding for the four-country collaboration project, but a smaller project received funding from the Interreg Sweden-Norway programme of the EU. The chapter presents background information on research on simulations of natural hazards and the work in the project on developing software for emergency training exercises as a computerize role playing package. The empirical part of the chapter presents data from three years of simulations / role playing exercises with participants within the police, fire and ambulance emergency response personnel in both countries. The chapter concludes with presenting the plan for a comprehensive training tool – netAgora – that will be the focus of a new project by the participants of the completed research project. Nord-Trøndelag University College and Mid-Sweden University will be the principal investigators of the project planned for 2015-2018.

BACKGROUND

Over the last 40 years, the application of computer technology in order to train individuals and organizations in the handling of emergencies has been in focus as a means of making the training process more effective and realistic. During the late 1970's the Federal Emergency Management Agency in the US (FEMA) initiated a study utilizing networked computers (Terak) in studying variations in response-pattern among participants receiving a simulated tornado threat (Leik et al., 1981). In 1980, the laboratory research expanded the computerized simulations to handle human response to the threat of volcano eruptions following the eruption of Mt. St. Helens in May 1980 (Ekker, Gifford, Leik & Leik, 1988). Post and Fox (1982) has documented the programming of experiments on a Terak computer. The author participated in the programming of a set of Terak computers using UCSD Pascal from the University of California San Diego (Threedee.com, 2015). The operating system used around 1978 on these computers was a version of RT-11 (Cryptosmith. com, 2015), and it had no networking capabilities, and the FEMA funded project hired a computer scientist to implement a networking component of the RT-11. This pioneering work on the operating system RT-11 resulted in providing the project with three networked Terak computers running experiments/simulations from 1978 until 1981. The simulations were run in mobile homes in Minneapolis and in Washington State (following the Mt. St. Helens eruption in 1980), wired with a primitive implementation of a LAN (local area network). Currently there is collaborative work on a UCSD Pascal implementation as a SourceForge project (ScourceForge.net, 2015). Recently, the University of California San Diego released parts of the source code and a non-profit license.

Research on computerized training for personnel handling emergencies has focused on the challenges of inter-organizational as well as international issues. The work of Stolk, Alexandrian, Gros and Paggio (2001) focuses on training for environmental crisis based in the experiences of the GAMMA-EC Project. The project trained the staff of environmental agencies in handling emergencies emphasizing decision-making and communication within and between teams of participants.

A comprehensive study of emergency operations centers in New Zealand, Canada and USA (Sinclair, 2011) show that anecdotal data is often the base of practices related to preparedness - lacking systematic study and validation.

A study of the handling of emergencies at 400 county-level emergency management agencies hypothesizes that "The greater the problem severity for organizations, the greater the level of external collaboration" (McGuire, 2010, p. 291).

The police department in Hong Kong (HKPF) has the last few years conducted territory-wide exercises of simulated critical incidents and have found that due to the cost of such field exercises there are few officers that are able to participate in these training events. Consequently, the Police College of HKPF used an online role-play simulation platform referred to as Scenario-based Interactive Multi-player Simulation (SIMS) (Leung, 2014). The development of this simulation system started in 2009 and the results show that role-play simulations have "the potential to provide scenario planning that is a cost effective supplement to traditional face-to-face training" (Leung, 2014, p. 212).

Research at the University of Siegen (Germany) has focused on the role of improvisation in handling emergencies often requiring the coordinated responses from fire departments, police, public administration, electricity infrastructure operators and citizens (Ley, Pipek, Reuter & Wiedenhoefer, 2012).

Traditional post-disaster research often uses the "lessons learned" approach of retracing decisions during the actual emergency. Birkland (2009) identifies threats to the validity of such approaches describing the "lessons learned documents as "fantasy documents". The approach utilizing a computerized emergency training tool will allow a focus on the ongoing processes during the training session rather than an after-the-fact approach.

TOWARDS A COMPREHENSIVE EMERGENCY TRAINING TOOL

Research 2010 - 2013

In 2010, researchers at the Nord-Trøndelag University College and Mid Sweden University began designing a computerized training system for emergency response in the border region between Norway and Sweden (Trøndelag and Jämtland). The project GSS (Gaining Security Symbiosis) received funding by the Interreg program of the European Regional Development Fund and teamed up with representatives from emergency response teams and municipalities along the border. This expanded team designed scenarios of emergencies that would play out in the computerized training system. A central aim of the project was to increase the interaction across the border among emergency personnel. This paper reports on the design of the training tool and results from this project.

The project chose to utilize a three-part cycle over the three years of the project – the cycle consisting of: scenario development – training session – evaluation period. The goals of the project included training of coordinated emergency response in the border region and sharing resources among teams on both sides of the national border.

The scenarios included severe winter weather conditions with snow / freezing rain causing a number of complicated emergencies including electrical power failure, severe traffic accidents, students lost in the mountains during a skiing trip across the border and a family getting lost among steep cliffs on a cold, foggy night.

The computer based training tool consists of standard web technology with LAMP – Linux computer, Apache webserver, MySQL database server and PHP server-side programming language. The user interface was presented in standard html with CSS and JavaScript for interaction – and a range of web browsers could be utilized – Chrome, Firefox, Safari, Safari for iPad and a couple of generations of Internet Explorer. (Asproth et al., 2014).

The participants in the simulations consisted of local emergency operators from the police, fire and ambulance services as well as county and municipality representatives. The participants would log into the training tool in the role they serve in real life – thus there were representatives from the police, fire and ambulance services of both Sweden and Norway. Sweden participated with representatives from a single county (Jämtland) and in Norway two counties border with Sweden (Nord- and Sør-Trøndelag). Consequently, there are a double set of teams on the Norwegian side during the 2013 training session running a more complex scenario involving a larger geographical area, and a single team on the Norwegian side during the 2011 and 2012 training session in which the scenarios took place in a more narrow geographical area.

The participants were from all levels of the emergency teams – in 2011 primarily strategic personnel, in 2012 primarily personnel from the tactical and operational level and in 2013 from all three levels of the emergency operations. In total 101 individuals have participated in the training sessions.

In 2011, all participants gathered at the Border Rescue Council and the Norwegian participants gathered face to face in one room – while the Swedish participants gathered in an adjoining room at the Cultural Center at Stiklestad, Verdal. The communication with participants in the other country occurred through the web-based training tool and some of the intra country communication could take place as face-to-face talks at neighboring tables in the room occupied by each country.

Figure 1 shows the location of the project in the border region between Norway and Sweden. In Sweden, the region covers part of the county of Jämtland compared with Norway, in which the region covers part of the counties of Nord- and Sør-Trøndelag.

Emergency Management Tool

Figure 2 shows the presentation of the scenario and a display of the communications channel in the training tool used in the project.

Figure 1. Location in Scandinavia and region of Jämtland and Trøndelag of the research project

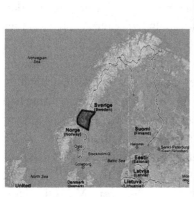
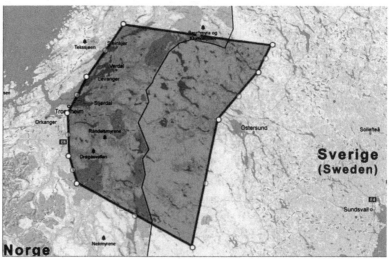

The interface for initiating communications with other participants is not shown in Figure 2 – but this "initiating contact" interface allowed a choice of "requesting information" or "giving information" and a drop-down menu for choosing recipient of the message. The training system allowed for open-ended messages with no limitation as to the number of characters submitted.

The training system allowed for relatively complex scenario messages that could include audio, video and multimedia content (see Figure 3).

Results from Training Sessions

This section presents results from the training sessions in 2011 – which also allowed face-to-face interaction among teams with a given country. The section also presents results from 2012 and 2013 – in which all participants were located at their respective workplaces.

The project utilized the R statistics package and the SNA package (Social Network Analysis package) in order to analyze the data from the training sessions (Butts, 2008). The R statistics and the SNA packages are open source statistical tools integrated into the software solutions for the current project. The training sessions provided a rich source of data summarized both for the debriefing following the training session as well as for research purposes. The R statistics package allow for a batch oriented statistical analysis "on-the-fly" of complex social network data among the participating teams of emergency personnel (Ekker, 2010). In practice that means that following a training session of a simulated emergency the project was able to provide participants with a detailed analysis of the data following the three-hour training session. Although not technically "on-the-fly" in the sense that the graphs popped up automatically, a series of programs written in

Figure 2. Scenario details on the left and communications channel on the right (in Swedish/Norwegian)

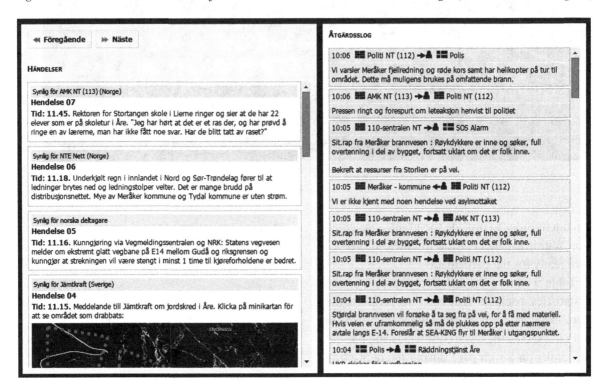

Figure 3. Multimedia and map information allowed in scenario details (in Swedish/Norwegian)

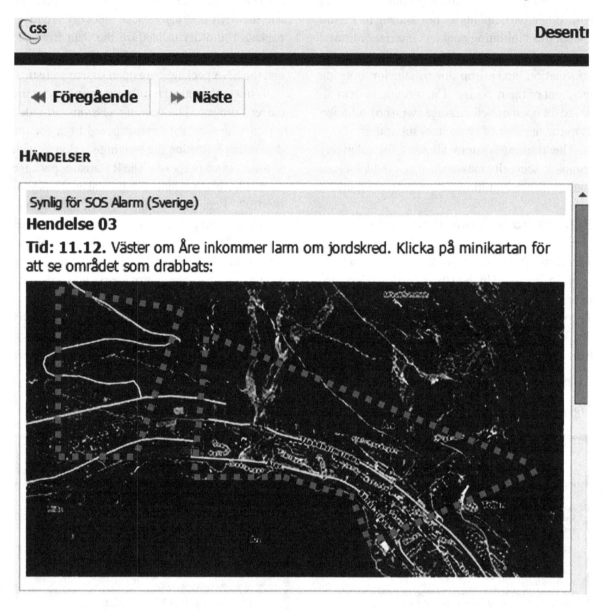

php ran in order to provide the graphs presented here. Within a matter of a few minutes, the graphs were ready for the participants.

Table 1 shows the batch commands of the R statistics package necessary to produce the social network analysis provided in Figure 4. In order to execute the batch commands and present the results on a web page during the debriefing session following the training session, the php

language execution of the R commands in Table 1 is shown below using the "plain vanilla" design of R statistics (Jocker, 2009).

```
<?php  exec ("cat  rC_network_
give_segment_1.txt | /usr/bin/R
--vanilla",$result,$error);  ?>
<img src="plot_SNA_give_segment_1.
jpg" width=600 height=420>
```

Table 1. Set of commands in R statistics package for producing the social network analysis in Figure 4

```
library("network")
set.seed(1702)
m <- matrix(scan("gss_agg_give_seg_1.txt", what="char", skip=1),ncol=9, nrow=9)
## transpose the matrix for presentation
m <- t(m)
net <- network(m, matrix.type="adjacency", loops = TRUE)
org <- network.vertex.names(net) <- list("S-municip","S-county","S-police","S-fire","S-112","N-fire","N-county","N-police","media")
summary(net)
jpeg("plot_SNA_give_segment_1.jpg", width=1000, height=700)
mai=c(1,1,1,0)
par(mfrow= c(1,1))
##Display the network
plot(net, displaylabels=TRUE, label=network.vertex.names(net),
vertex.cex=2, usearrows=TRUE,
vertex.sides=3,
boxed.labels=TRUE)
warnings()
```

Figure 4. Training 2011 – giving information early in simulation (strategic personnel primarily)

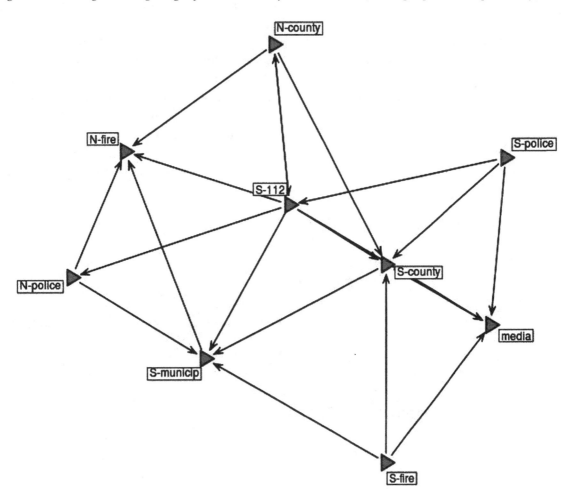

The research project developed a data-analysis presentation tool making it possible to choose among several Social Network Analysis (SNA) graphs. The tool also presents statistical analysis of the data (mostly Norwegian text) and is available at the following link: http://netgss.org/GSS_stat/2013/eng/SNN_graph_request.php.

This tool generated the figures presented in the chapter (Figures 4 – 7).

Figure 4 shows the pattern of communication among primarily strategic level personnel in the police, fire and county representatives in Norway and Sweden during the annual meeting of the Border Rescue Council where participants were meeting face to face in each nationality group. Sweden has a single alarm number – 112 – while in Norway there are three distinct alarm numbers – 110, 112 and 113 – representing fire, police and ambulances, respectively.

The police in both countries and the Swedish 112 alarm central (SOS alarm) are all disseminating information (giving information) to other groups. Arrows point towards the team offered information.

Figure 5 presents the pattern of communications during the 2012 training session. This group of participants included primarily operative personnel – and all participants were located at their regular workplaces – a decentralized training session. The Swedish police and the Swedish SOS alarm (S-112) have central roles during this session while the Swedish rescue team in Östersund (S-fireO) and the Norwegian ambulance service are communicating to a lesser degree. Arrows are pointing towards the team offered information.

During the training session in 2013, there were a total of 21 participating roles in the emergency simulation, 15 on the Norwegian side of the border and 6 on the Swedish side of the border of Mid-Scandinavia. Within each role there may be two or three colleagues sharing the experience of participating in the training session, consequently more than 40 individuals participated in the 2013 training session.

Figure 6 shows the pattern of communications among all participants in the 2013 training sessions. The communications pattern became quite complex and during the debriefing session it became necessary to break down and present communications within each country and communications across the border, separately.

Figure 7 presents the communications across the border in order to answer the question "Who connects with whom across the border?" The

Figure 5. Training 2012 - giving information early in simulation (operative personnel primarily)

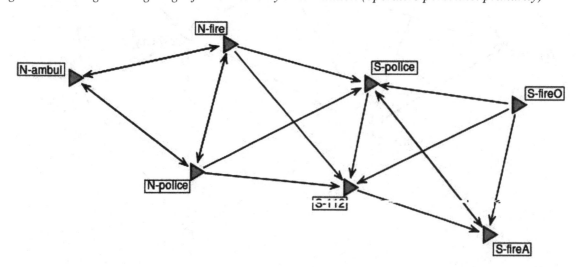

Figure 6. Training 2013 - giving information (all participants)

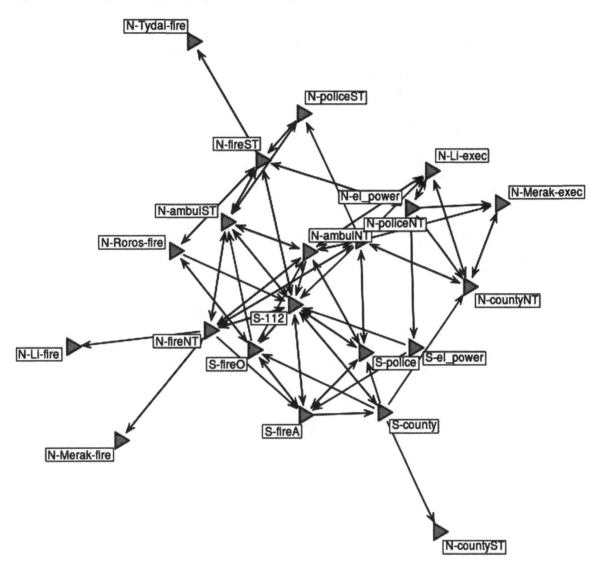

Swedish 911 (S-112) and the ambulance service of Nord-Trøndelag (N-ambulNT) play central roles in the communication across the border during this training session. We also notice that the electrical power companies (S-el_power and N-el_power) and the county administration (S-county, N-countyNT & N-countyST) communicate with their respective counterparts in the other country – but not with any other participants across the border.

Three of the four municipalities in Norway that participated in the training session in 2013 did not initiate contacts across the border (N-Li, N-Merak and N-Tydal). The fire department in Røros (N-Roros-fire) communicated with the Swedish 911 (S-112) and the Swedish rescue team in Östersund (S-fireO).

In Table 2 the number of messages produced during the 3 hour training session in 2013 is

Figure 7. Training 2013 - giving information (participants across border)

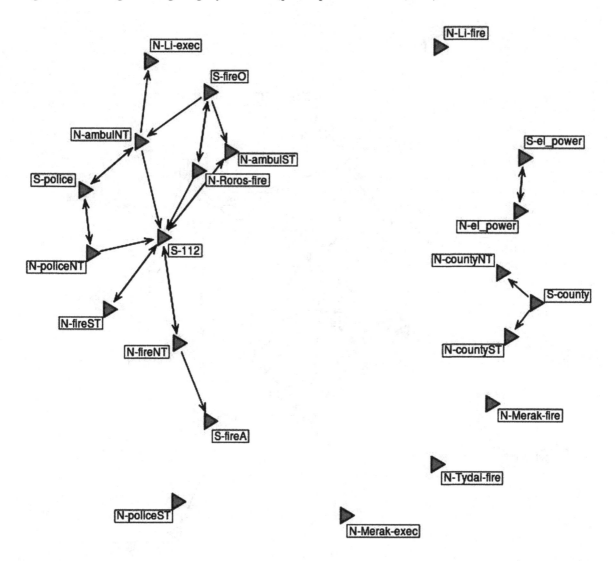

Table 2. Number of messages in 2013 producing the social network analysis in Figures 6 and 7

Number of Messages:	Sweden	Norway	Total
Internally in country	91	224	315
Across border	19	35	54
Total	110	259	369

presented. We see that 14.6% (54 of in total 369) of the messages crossed the border. In total 369 messages were used in the Figure 6 – and the 54 messages sent across the border constitutes the basis for Figure 7.

One of the advantages of the training tool was the fact that operative personnel could also participate since the training in 2012 and 2013 occurred decentralized at computers with internet connection at the workplace of the participants. Previous years only tactical and strategic level personnel were able to participate in desktop training sessions.

Of the three years of training sessions, the one in 2011 was a tabletop session with the participants located in a separate "Norway" and a "Sweden" room. Communications among teams within own country could occur face-to-face or utilizing the training tool developed by the project. Due to this situation in 2011, the proportion of communications across the border is much higher (over 50%) compared with 2012 and 2013 (percentage of communications across border is under 22%). Table 3 shows the distribution of internal vs. across the border communications for all three training sessions of the project.

Social network analysis with the R statistics package proved to be a viable approach to providing participants with a detailed debriefing session following a 3-hour training session. Providing graphs of the network of communications provide the necessary details for participants to identify bottlenecks and obstacles to communication.

Participants also expressed appreciation for the fact that operative personnel also could participate given decentralized training sessions, relatively short in time requirement and participants remained at their daily work desk. In the years prior to 2011 such training sessions were handled as table top exercises at the Border Rescue Council meetings in May each year, and the participants during these two day meetings were primarily strategic or tactical personnel. We have not been able to document an increase in the interaction across the border among emergency personnel. Figure 8 presents the distribution of the participants over the 3 years of training session and the proportion of operative personnel was higher than 30% in 2012 and 2013 compared with approximately 20% in 2011.

In a survey of the participants administered participants a few weeks before the emergency training session and another survey a few weeks following the training session across all 3 years, the participants answered questions about the awareness of who among the various emergency response teams would be the leader of the real life rescue operations.

Figure 9 shows that in 2011 – in which over 50% of the participants were from the strategic level of the organization – there is not much improvement in knowledge regarding leadership in an emergency. In 2012 and 2013, however, the level of knowledge regarding who will take charge during an emergency has increased from under 40% to over 50% following the training session.

Table 3. Communication pattern: giving information to other participants (percentage of messages)

Messages Transmitted:	2011		2012		2013	
	Sweden	Norway	Sweden	Norway	Sweden	Norway
Internally in country	42.9	46.3	100.0	78.4	82.7	86.5
Across border	57.1	53.7	0.0	21.6	17.3	13.5
Total (N)	100.0 (49)	100.0 (41)	100.0 (15)	100.0 (37)	100.0 (110)	100.0 (259)

Figure 8. Participants in the emergency training sessions in 2011, 2012 and 2013

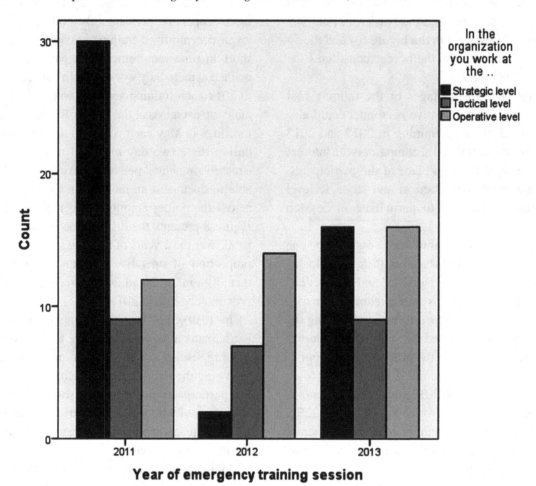

This result shows that the project achieved the goal of raising awareness regarding differences in leading emergency rescue operations in the border region.

FUTURE RESEARCH DIRECTIONS

During the preparation of an EU Framework 7 project, the participants developed an overall software model – the netAgora model presented in Figure 10. The model materialized in cooperation with colleagues in Slovenia and Greece.

The web portal netGSS.org describes the netAgora model this way:

The Virtual Situation Room (VSR) is the interaction surface toward the user. Through this surface (GUI) the user has access to all the other resources of netAgora. VSR may be freely adopted to meet the specific requirements of different user categories. There is no theoretical limit to the number of users that may simultaneously be connected to netAgora.

The Virtual Responder (VR) is a system component, which simulate the behaviour of other responders. From the point of view of the player there is no difference between a virtual actor and a real actor. This means that in netAgora there are always several actors, real or virtual ones, which you as user have to coordinate and communicate with.

Figure 9. Awareness among participants regarding leadership during real emergencies by year

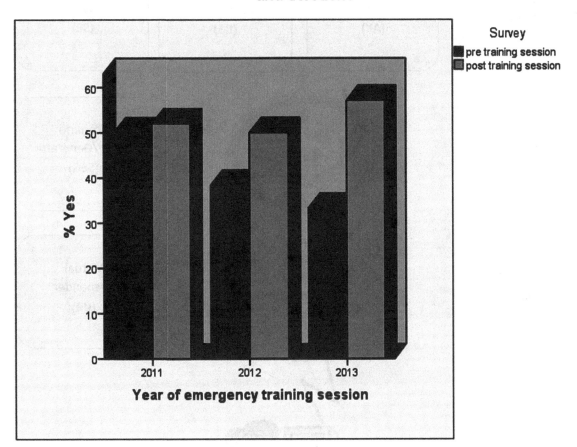

Does your organization have a plan for who will be the leader of the emergency response team in the event of an accident in the border region betwen Norway and Sweden?

The Disaster Simulator (DS) is the core of netAgora. DS can calculate (simulate) the dynamic evolution of a set of crucial disaster variables and react on different user decisions and actions. The ability to handle geographical or spatial information (GIS) is a crucial faculty of the Disaster simulator. The user can select a scenario, i.e. disaster, from the Scenario Bank (SB) or set up a new one, or change an existing one, with help of the Scenario Editor/Generator (SEG). The Assessment Kit (AK) helps the user to evaluate the decisions and actions taken during the playing of a scenario.

Experiences and Lessons Learned (ELL), at last, is a knowledge bank with tested and verified disaster and crisis knowledge. Via the Meeting and Cooperation Support (MCS) the user can interact and discuss with other disaster responders and via the Expert Panel (EP) she or he can put disaster related questions to a group of disaster experts and disaster researchers. (Source: Interreg project website 2010-2013, maintained by author of this chapter)

At the end of 2013, the Virtual Situation Room and the Disaster Simulator were completed components of netAgora and the project began

Figure 10. Overall model for future development - netAgora

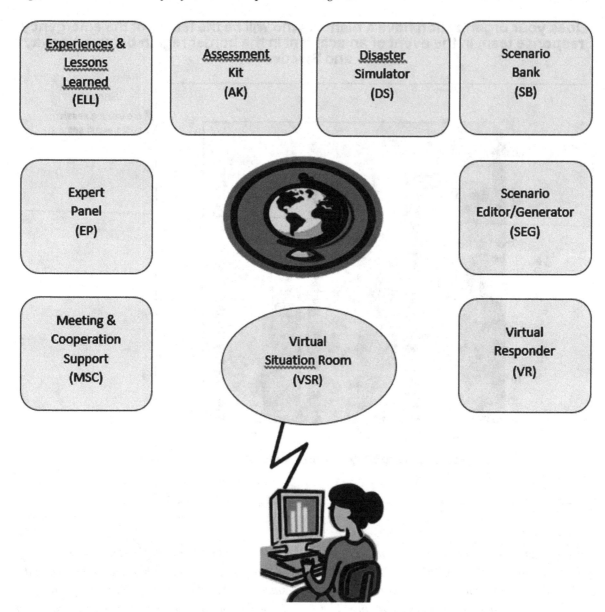

the work towards a Scenario Bank. The project developed a questionnaire - with results presented in Figure 8 and 9 – and this effort will provide the basis of the Assessment Kit and presented in the Drupal Content Management Software package. A Scenario Editor / Generator is in the initial stages of development in which elements from prior scenarios may be used in new training sessions with simulated emergencies.

Data from each completed training sessions will in the future provide data for the Virtual Responder (VR) of the netAgora training model. Two or three teams in Norway may choose to play against a virtual responder in Sweden if it is not possible to schedule "live" participants.

In another paper the research group at Mid Sweden University and Nord-Trøndelag University College (Ekker, Asproth & Holmberg 2013) has outlined the use of data from the training sessions in a system dynamics model (SD model). Figure 11 outlines such a double loop learning system using the social network empirical data as input to a system dynamics model.

The system dynamics model will provide insights into crisis management that in turn will influence the development of future scenarios for the training system. The 2013 publication (Ekker et al., 2013) outlines a first version of the system dynamics model in which the common situation awareness (CSA) is a key concept. The communication pattern empirically identified in the training sessions (Figure 4 – 7) is a rich source of data, and provides input for a future simulation model using system dynamics. From the graphs, an intense communication pattern "will support the assumption of a high CSA in the simulation model while scattered communication between security actors will indicate a lower CSA" (Ekker et al., 2013, p. 9). The number of security actors (role playing participants in the training session) is quite large and the simulation model (using system dynamics) employs with a lower number of actors by focusing on the centers of the graphs (Figure 4 – 7).

The conclusions derived from the simulation model based on systems dynamics will be available to the participants of the training sessions and may influence the handling of real emergencies in the future. Researchers in Slovenia have documented what they refer to as Group Information Feedback (Kljajić and Borštnar, 2011) indicating that a

feedback mechanism outlined in Figure 11 will provide a setting for the best possible learning and increased competence among rescue personnel. Further, the data presented in this chapter shows that the communication patterns change during the emergency presented in the training session. This fact will have an impact on the simulation model based on system dynamics.

CONCLUSION

This chapter has presented an emergency-response training system software that was developed by a team of researchers at Mid-Sweden University and Nord-Trøndelag University College in Norway during a 3-year project from 2010-2013.

The chapter has shown that training is important for emergency personnel at all levels (strategic, tactical and operation level) of the emergency teams, and such a training can easily be facilitated using a training system presented in the netAgora model. The training system records the flow of communication during the simulated emergency and this rich data source allows for analysis of behavior by the various emergency teams. The data may also indicate improvements in the procedures for handling real emergencies.

Using the social network analysis tool (SNA) of the R project (2015) is a key element for distilling useful data from the rich data source provided by the training tool. The next step will be to apply data from the social network analysis in system

Figure 11. Double loop learning between training system exercises and system dynamics modeling

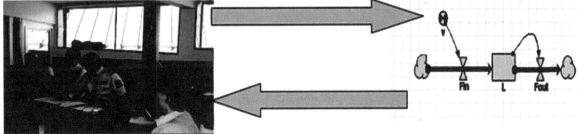

dynamics models in order to glean more insight into situations by allowing "what if" questions in the analysis of the simulations.

The data from the training sessions and data from the simulation model based on system dynamics will provide input to the Virtual Responder system component of a future implementation of the netAgora model. The project participants are planning a continuation of the project and will be applying for funding under the Horizon 2020 program of the EU during the first half of 2015. In this planned project the work on the netAgora software package will continue. The software package evolves along the lines outlined by research in Hong Kong (Leung, 2014) and draws on current research in Europe (Ley et al., 2012).

ACKNOWLEDGMENT

Interreg / European Regional Development Fund (ERDF) funded the GSS (Gaining Security Symbiosis) project.

REFERENCES

Asproth, V., Borglund, E., Danielsson, E., Ekker, K., Holand, I. S., Holmberg, S. C., ... Öberg, L. M. (2014). *Rapport från GSS: Gränsöverskridande samarbete för säkerhet (Report from GSS. Security cooperation across the border)*. Steinkjer / Östersund: Nord-Trøndelag University College and Mid Sweden University Press.

Birkland, T. A. (2009). Disasters, lessons learned, and fantasy documents. *Journal of Contingencies and Crisis Management, 17*(3), 1–12. doi:10.1111/j.1468-5973.2009.00575.x

Butts, C. T. (2008). Social network analysis with SNA. *Journal of Statistical Software, 24*(6), 1–51. PMID:18612375

Cryptosmith.com. (2015). *Digital's RT-11 file system: Tech teaching*. Retrieved January 22, 2015 from http://cryptosmith.com/2013/10/19/digitals-rt-11-file-system/

Ekker, K. (2010). Information retrieval for simulation debriefing: Statistical analysis "on the fly". In *Proceedings of World Conference on Educational Multimedia, Hypermedia and Telecommunications* (pp. 3329-3336). Academic Press.

Ekker, K., Asproth, V., & Holmberg, S. C. (2013). Debriefing with R-statistics and support for system dynamics modeling of inter regional security. In P. Kommers and P. Isaias (Eds), *Proceedings of the International Conference e-Society 2013* (pp. 3-10). Academic Press.

Ekker, K., Gifford, G., Leik, S. A., & Leik, R. K. (1988). Using microcomputer game-simulation experiments to study family response to the Mt. St. Helens eruptions. *Social Science Computer Review, 6*(1), 90–105. doi:10.1177/089443938800600109

Jocker, M. L. (2009). *Executing R in PhP*. Retrieved March 7, 2014 from http://www.matthewjockers.net//?s=Executing+R+in+php&search=Go

Kljajić, M., & Borštnar, M. K. (2011). Context-dependent modelling and anticipation the other coin in the system approach. In V. Asproth (Ed.), *Challenges for the future in an ICT context*. Mid Sweden University. Retrieved January 22, 2015 from http://miun.diva-portal.org/smash/get/diva2:478461/FULLTEXT01.pdf

Leik, R. K., Carter, T. M., Clark, J. P., Kendall, S. D., Gifford, G. A., Bielefeld, W., & Ekker, K. (1981). *Community response to natural hazard warnings: Final report*. Minneapolis, MN: University of Minnesota Press.

Leung, C. (2014). *Exploring the effectiveness of online role play simulations to reduce groupthink in crisis management training*. (Doctoral dissertation). University of Hong Kong. Retrieved March 18, 2014 from http://hub.hku.hk/handle/10722/196550

Ley, B., Pipek, V., Reuter, C., & Wiedenhoefer, T. (2012). Supporting improvisation work in inter-organizational crisis management. In *Proceedings of Computers and Human Interaction CHI'12*. Austin, TX: ACM. Retrieved March 15, 2014 from http://www.wiwi.uni-siegen.de/wirtschaftsinformatik/paper/2012/leypipekreuterwiedenh2012_improvisationwork_chi2012.pdf

Post, T. A., & Fox, J. L. (1982). Programming experiments on a TERAK 8510/A microcomputer. *Behavior Research Methods and Instrumentation*, *14*(2), 276–280. doi:10.3758/BF03202166

R Project. (2015). *The R project for statistical computing*. Retrieved January 22, 2015 from http://www.r-project.org/

SourceForge.net. (2015). *ucsd-psystem-xc 0.13*. Retrieved January 22, 2015 from http://ucsd-psystem-xc.sourceforge.net/

Stolk, D., Alexandrian, D., Gros, B., & Paggio, R. (2001). Gaming and multimedia applications for environmental crisis management training. *Computers in Human Behavior*, *17*(5-6), 627–642. doi:10.1016/S0747-5632(01)00027-9

Threedee.com. (2013). *The UCSD P-system museum*. Retrieved January 22, 2015 from http://www.threedee.com/jcm/psystem/

KEY TERMS AND DEFINITIONS

Emergency Management: The handling of a crisis either ad hoc or in reference to a preplanned procedure.

GSS: Interreg/EU funded project «Grenseoverskridende samarbeid for sikkerhet» (Across border cooperation for security).

netAgora: A comprehensive training tool for emergency response personnel developed by GSS project.

R Statistics: A statistical analysis package developed as an open source project organized as "The R Project for Statistical Computing".

Role-Play: Participants in a game assume a set of roles defined by game rules.

SNA: Social network analysis package within the R statistics package.

Social network Analysis: Analysis of the pattern of communication among individuals or groups.

Virtual Responders: A planned netAgora system component simulating the behavior of other roles.

Section 4
Businesses and Smart Technology

Chapter 14
Artificial Neural Learning Based on Big Data Process for eHealth Applications

Nuno Pombo
University of Beira Interior, Portugal

Kouamana Bousson
University of Beira Interior, Portugal

Nuno Garcia
University of Beira Interior, Portugal

Virginie Felizardo
University of Beira Interior, Portugal

ABSTRACT

The complexity of the clinical context requires systems with the capability to make decisions based on reduced sets of data. Moreover, the adoption of mobile and ubiquitous devices could provide personal health-related information. In line with this, eHealth application faces several challenges so as to provide accurate and reliable data to both healthcare professionals and patients. This chapter focuses on computational learning on the healthcare systems presenting different classification processes to obtain knowledge from data. Finally, a case study based on a radial basis function neural network aiming the estimation of ECG waveform is explained. The presented model revealed its adaptability and suitability to support clinical decision making. However, complementary studies should be addressed to enable the model to predict the upper and lower points related to upward and downward deflections.

INTRODUCTION

The ubiquity of mobile devices and the Internet raised the paradigm of the new care model based more on contacts than on visits (Escarrabill, Marti, & Torrente, 2011). The ability to interact with the system anywhere and at anytime thoroughly changes the coordinates of time and place and offers invaluable opportunities to the healthcare delivery and management which lead to many opportunities as well as many challenges arising from the availability, accessibility and plasticity of information and tools to access information. In fact, despite the Internet provide a new medium for information storage, sharing, processing and distribution, the exponential growth and heterogeneity of web information represents a complex, large-scale, dynamic and fast-changing tasks to present data on accurately and timely fashion, and therefore meeting demands for quality and

DOI: 10.4018/978-1-4666-8147-7.ch014

productivity on different applications and contexts. This topic is even more important when data is the main support for clinical knowledge and decision-making on distributed architectures delivered based on the web for many different purposes such as: screening, diagnosis, treatment and monitoring. The technological improvement that occurred in recent years enable the development of computerised decision support systems supported by three main foundations:

- **Data Acquisition:** Based on cheap and tiny sensors, microprocessors and mobile devices;
- **Data Storage:** Cheap disk storage, and storage virtualization;
- **Data Distribution:** Easier and faster delivery using Internet.

The adoption of computerised systems on healthcare highly depends on the accurate and reliable knowledge which results from the collected and processed data, mostly acquired from different sources and devices such as sensors or mobile phones. The abundance of these devices coupled with the progress made in wireless communication, lead to its adoption on healthcare systems as a preferred means to collect data. However, they are not designed to obtain a large amount of data that require its submission to remote databases and thus enable the integration and process of information in which the knowledge is based. In addition, mobile and dynamic environments require that standard data mining algorithms must be modified appropriately aiming to enable time critical intelligent, data analysis on streams of continuous data (Krishnaswamy, Loke, & Zaslavsky, 2002). On the healthcare context a user friendly systems are required not only for extracting information based with minimum input from user, but also with the capability to offer personal health related information.

Thus, seems to be promising the development of new methods and techniques with the capability

to reduce and/or synthesize the collected data and therefore, enabling the system to produce decisions based on a small amount of data. Typically, a function approximation is applied to determine the appropriate subset of data that provide representative and accurate explanation ability of the entire sample.

Therefore, this chapter focuses on computational learning on the healthcare context and presents a case study with it application. The chapter is organized as follows: The first section describes different clinical systems and their classification process to knowledge acquisition by computers. Moreover, neural networks techniques are presented and described in detail highlighting their mathematical explanation. Then, the second section presents a case study based on experimental research including a description of its mathematical concepts. Finally, the last section concludes the chapter and summarizes the main points.

BACKGROUND

Nowadays the clinical and hospital environment are equipped with several devices and services for monitoring and data acquisition that in most cases perform continuous acquisition of medical parameters. The huge amount of collected and stored data, results in a large amount of data needed for evaluation and medical treatment, and all indications are that this trend will continue to increase. The medical data are usually associated with characteristics such as high dimensionality, multiple classes, missing and noisy data, systemic and human errors, deriving from the different nature of medical information (Lavrač, 1999; Tanwani, Afridi, Shafiq, & Farooq, 2009).

In order to assist health professionals in decision support and minimizing diagnosis errors, the classification techniques have been used increasingly in medical solutions and services in various areas in order to provide rapid diagnosis and increased quality of medical treatment (Al–Shayea,

El–Refae, & Yaseen, 2013; Wasan, Bhatnagar, & Kaur, 2008). Due to this complexity, the medical databases are a major challenge to the machine learning and data mining algorithms techniques for classification (Tanwani et al., 2009). These data are, partly, a useful tool for helping to understand disease and to formulate predictive models via machine learning (Dissanayake & Corne, 2010).

In medical environment, classification techniques can be useful in different areas, including screening, diagnosis, prognosis, monitoring, therapy, survival analysis, hospital management, prediction of effectiveness of surgical procedures, medical tests, medication, and the discovery of relationships among clinical and diagnosis data (R. E. Abdel-Aal, 2004; R.E. Abdel-Aal, 2005). According (Tanwani et al., 2009) there is a great diversity of work in this subject but has not yet reached a consensus on a suitable classification technique for a specific nature of medical data. Emphasizing the importance of these techniques in screening, for example, a high percentage of false negatives increase the risk of patients not receiving an individualized diagnosis, on the other hand, a higher percentage of false positives leads to unnecessary expenditure of resources (R. E. Abdel-Aal, 2004).

There is therefore a need to improve classification accuracy for medical diagnosis. In line with this, the main variables that determine the accuracy classification are (Tanwani et al., 2009): 1) the nature of database, 2) pre-processing filter, and 3) the choice of classification scheme. This paper presents a "Guidelines to Select Machine Learning Scheme for Classification of Biomedical Datasets" and also a study on the classification of 31 different sets of biomedical data, using a diverse set of machine learning system. In (Al–Shayea et al., 2013) are evaluated the use of classification techniques in two cases: in nephritis disease, in which the data are the symptoms of the disease; and heart disease, the data are cardiac Single Proton Emission Computed Tomography (SPECT) images. Each patient is classified into

two categories as infected or not infected. In the same sense the differential diagnosis of various diseases is a challenging problem in clinical medicine because between groups of diseases there are a set of symptoms and similar signs (Radwan E. Abdel-Aal, Abdel-Halim, & Abdel-Aal, 2006). These techniques have been used to solve several multiclass classification problems. In Table 1 are shown some studies with different tasks for a specific clinical condition.

Independently of the selected technique, the ability to produce knowledge from data is based on the wise selection of the classification process which varies according to the used learning methodology. Thus, with the purpose of obtaining a function approximation, one of the following four approaches is used: supervised, semi-supervised, unsupervised learning and reinforcement learning.

- **Supervised Learning**: Assumes that the user knows beforehand the concepts, in other words the classes and the instances of each class, that is, an exhaustive database built on external sources is available. The knowledge is obtained through a process or training which includes a data set called the training sample which is structured according to the knowledge base supported by human experts as physicians in medical context, and databases. As shown in Figure 1, this sample aims at tuning the system based on the minimization of the error signal determined by the differentiator which represents the difference between the desired response (expected values) and the current response of the system (observed values). This produces an iterative learning process depending on the system environment.
- **Unsupervised Learning:** Assumes that the user is unaware of the classes due to the lack of information sufficiently available. Instead of supervised learning which aims at establishing a relationship between

Table 1. Selected studies

Study	Task	Clinical Condition
(Ramadan et al., 1991)	Differential diagnosis	Dyslexia subtypes
(Syiam, 1994)	Diagnosis	Eye disease
(Nguyen et al., 1996)	Risk assessment	Diabetic retinopathy
(Ikeda, Ito, Ishigaki, & Yamauchi, 1997)	Differential diagnosis	Pancreatic ductal adenocarcinoma and mass forming pancreatitis
(García-Pérez, Violante, & Cervantes-Pérez, 1998)	Differential diagnosis	Dementia
(Axer, Jantzen, Berks, & Keyserlingk, 2000)	Differential diagnosis	Aphasia
(Kim & Park, 2000)	Assessment	Sleep stages
(Abe et al., 2004)	Differential diagnosis	Interstitial lung diseases
(R.E. Abdel-Aal, 2005)	Differential diagnosis	Dermatology
(Serrano, Tomečková, & Zvárová, 2006)	Assessment	Atherosclerosis
(Heckerling et al., 2007)	Assessment	Urinary tract infection
(Mundra & Rajapakse, 2007)	Assessment	Prostate cancer
(Zhang, Yan, Zhao, & Zhang, 2008)	Assessment and diagnosis	Micro-calcifications in digital format mammograms
(Das, Turkoglu, & Sengur, 2009)	Diagnosis	Heart disease
(Gil, Johnsson, Chamizo, Paya, & Fernandez, 2009)	Diagnosis	Urological dysfunctions
(Lin, 2009)	Diagnosis	Liver disease
(Altunay, Telatar, Erogul, & Aydur, 2009)	Assessment and Diagnosis	Uroflowmeter signals
(Er, Yumusak, & Temurtas, 2010)	Diagnosis	Chest disease
(Al-Shayea & Bahia, 2010)	Diagnosis	Urinary diseases
(Yao & Li, 2010)	Assessment	DNA microarray
(Zhu, Jia, & Ji, 2010)	Assessment	Leukaemia and ovarian cancer
(Debnath & Kurita, 2010)	Assessment	Leukaemia
(Abas, Yusof, & Noah, 2011)	Treatment	Postoperative pain
(Jinglin, Li, & Yong, 2011)	Diagnosis	Low back pain
(Latha, Swetha, Bhavya, Geetha, & Suhasini, 2012)	Assessment	Chest pain
(Juhola, Aalto, Joutsijoki, & Hirvonen, 2013)	Diagnosis	Otoneurological patients
(Juhola, Joutsijoki, Aalto, & Hirvonen, 2014)	Diagnosis	Otoneurological patients

dependent and independent variables, unsupervised learning treats all variables the same way so as to determine the different classes based on diverse features ob-

served in the collection of unlabeled data that encompass the sample set. As shown in Figure 2, there is no feedback due to the fact that the unsupervised learning assumes that the learning system is reliable enough to produce accurate outcomes.

- **Semi-Supervised Learning:** Aims at propagating full labels to incompletely labeled data. Usually, the data set consists of a mixture of labeled data and unlabeled data. As shown in Figure 3, semi-supervised learning combines the methodology of the supervised learning to process the labeled data with the unsupervised learning to compute the unlabeled data (Singh, Nowak, & Zhu, 2008).

- **Reinforcement Learning (RL):** Is a paradigm of ML for which rewards and punishments guide the learning process. As shown in Figure 4, in RL there is an agent (learner) that acts autonomously and receives a scalar reward signal that is used to evaluate the consequences of its actions.

The classification process varies according to the used learning methodology. When supervised learning is applied, the classification refers to the mapping of data items into one of the predefined classes. On the contrary, when unsupervised learning is utilized the classification refers to the cluster analysis on the data set which offers a better understanding of the data set characteristics and providing a starting point for exploring further relationships. Choosing the right classifier is a critical step in the knowledge acquiring process. This chapter presents an eHealth application to predict the ECG waveform enabling not only the decision support making based on a reduced data set, but also alerts and messages based on the real-time collected data. The presented model is based on the artificial neural learning whose principles are explained below.

ARTIFICIAL NEURAL NETWORKS

The artificial neural networks (ANN) are composed of interconnected processing elements, called nodes, as shown in Figure 5, that carry out the classification process which was inspired in the way the brain recognizes patterns. Each element encompasses one or more inputs (signals) from other elements via the connections. These inputs represent propagation, either feedforward or backpropagation, of estimated weights through the nodes of the network so as to generate an output set where each component represents a particular classification for the input set. The net input of weighted signals received by a unit j is given by:

$$net_j = w_0 + \sum_{i=1}^{n} w_i x_i \qquad (1)$$

Figure 1. Supervised learning diagram

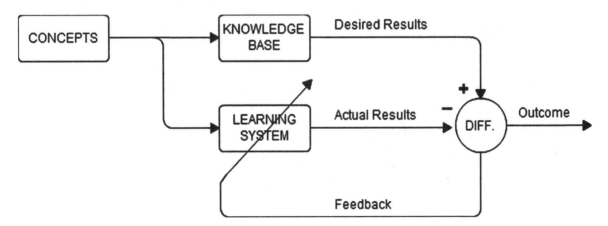

Figure 2. Unsupervised learning diagram

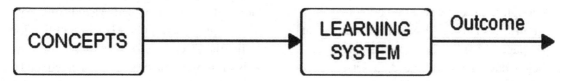

Figure 3. Semi-supervised learning diagram

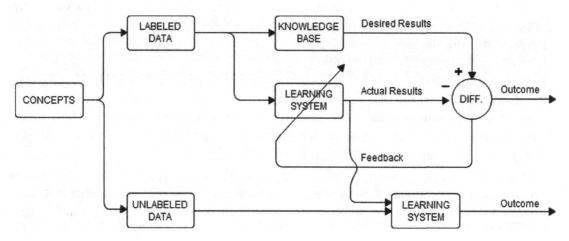

Figure 4. Reinforcement learning diagram

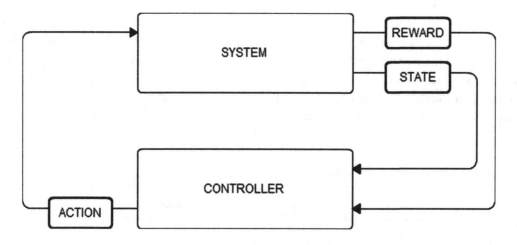

Figure 5. A single network node

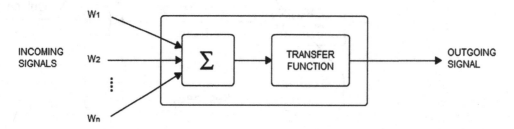

where w_0 is the biasing signal, w_i the weight on input connection ij, x_i the magnitude of signal on input connection ij and n the number of input connections to node j.

An ANN composed of a unique layer of nodes is called single-layer perceptron (SLP) whereas it is called multi-layer perceptron (MLP) when it is composed of several layers. The SLP is applied to learning from a batch of training, in a repeated way, to find the accurate vector for the entire training set, whereas MLPs aim at the separation of input instances into their appropriate categories. However, despite its robustness to noisy data and its ability to represent complex functions, its inability to explain decisions and the lack of transparency of data, presents an obstacle for its use in clinical settings. Also, determining the adequate size of the hidden layer is sensitive to poor approximations caused by lack of neurons, or overfitting from excessive nodes. Moreover, an important limitation is that ANN are highly nonlinear in the parameters and so the learning must be based on nonlinear optimization techniques. For this reason, radial basis function neural network (RBFNN) is commonly used for modeling problems. This network presents one hidden layer which performs a fixed nonlinear transformation with no adjustable parameters and it maps the input space onto a new space, and a network output obtained from the linear combination of weighted with connecting weights (Li, Tian, & Chen, 2008).

As depicted in Figure 6, a typical RBFNN structure encompasses a m-dimensional input vector x, and a n-dimensional output vector y: $x \in R^m, y \in R^n, f_r : x \rightarrow y$ according to:

$$f_r(x) = \lambda_0 + \sum_{i=1}^{n_r} \lambda_i \phi \left(\|x - c_i\| \right) \qquad (2)$$

where $\phi(.)$ is a given function from $R^+ to R$, $\| . \|$ denotes the Euclidean norm, λ_i, $0 \leq i \leq n_r$ are the weights or parameters, $c_i \in R^n, 1 \leq i \leq n_r$, are

known as RBF centers, and n_r is the number of centers (Chen, Cowan, & Grant, 1991). The functional form $\phi(.)$ and the centers c_i are assumed to have been fixed and its choices must be carefully considered in order for the RBFNN to be able to match closely the performance of the two-layer neural network.

Usually, the centers are chosen from the data points $\{x(t)\}_{i=1}^N$. The key question as occurs in almost all practical applications is therefore the choice of the relevant input variables from the data set. Thus, the approximation schema of RBF becomes:where the weighted norm is defined by:

$$f(x) = \sum_{i=1}^{n} c_i G \left(\|x - t_i\|_w \right) \qquad (3)$$

$$\|x\|_w \equiv x W^T W x \qquad (4)$$

and $G \left(\|x - t_i\|_w \right)$ is the radial basis function.

Applying Eq. 3, means that the level curves of the basis functions are not circles, but ellipses, whose axis do not need to be aligned with the coordinate axis. Then, the optimal center locations t_i satisfy the following set of nonlinear equations (Poggio & Girosi, 1990):

$$t_i = \frac{\sum_j P_j^i x_j}{\sum_j P_j^i}, \; i = 1, ... n \qquad (5)$$

where P_j^i are coefficients that depend on all the parameters of the network and ate not necessarily positive. Due to the fact that the optimal centers are a weighted sum of the example points, in some cases it may be more efficient to adjust P_j^i rather than the components of t_i.

In line with this, there are several radial basis functions such as the Gaussian function:

Figure 6. A standard RBFNN structure

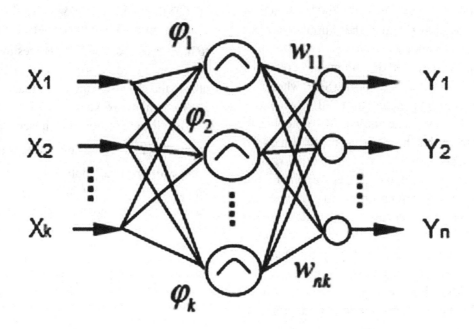

$$\varphi_j(x) = \exp\left(-\frac{\|x - \mu_j\|^2}{\sigma_j^2}\right) \qquad (6)$$

the multiquadrics function:

$$\varphi_j(x) = \sqrt{x^2 + \sigma_j^2} \qquad (7)$$

the inverse multiquadrics function:

$$\varphi_j(x) = \frac{1}{\sqrt{x^2 + \sigma_j^2}} \qquad (8)$$

and finally the thin plate splines conditionally positive definite functions:

$$\varphi_j(x) = x^{2n+1}$$
$$\varphi_j(x) = x^{2n} \ln x \qquad (9)$$

where $x = (x_1, x_2, ..., x_m)^T$ is the input vector, μ_j is the center vector, and σ_j is the radius width of the j-th hidden node. The output layer represents the outputs of the network and each input node is a linear combination of the k radial basis functions of hidden nodes:

$$y_i = \sum_{j=1}^{k} w_{ji} \varphi_j(x) \qquad (10)$$

The next section presents a case study based on experimental research consisted of several data acquisition during physical exercise in the sports physiology laboratory (Felizardo, Gaspar, Garcia, & Reis, 2011) which combines a RBFNN with a filtering method.

METHODS

Experimental Sample

The experimental sample is composed of 57 young and adult people (43 male and 14 female) aged between 18 and 44 years, with a mean age of 24.37±5.96 years, all of them physically active but not competitive. In this sample 48 subjects were soldiers belonging to the Infantry Regiment n°13 (RI13) and 9 subjects were college teachers or students of the Department of Sports Science, Exercise and Health. Anthropometric data relating to age, height, weight and fat percentage of participants in the study of both sexes was collected and are detailed in Table 2.

Exercise Plan

During the experimental protocol each subject performed an exercise series of walking and running in treadmill. The exercise plan consists in incremental velocities, for men, walking velocity was defined as 5.8 km/h and three running velocities levels were 8.4 km/h, 10.3 km/h, 11.6 km/h. For women, walking velocity was defined as 5.1 km/h and 7.7 km/h, 9 km/h, 10.3 km/h for running velocities. The duration of each exercise level was five minutes, interspersed with a period of 1 to 3 minutes for recovery.

Instrumentation

For physiological data acquisition during the exercise protocol was used the *bioPlux* acquisition system. This system have suited features such as eight acquisition channels, its sampling frequency is 1 kHz, weight of 80 g and includes a Bluetooth communication interface, thus allowing a great comfort and independence of movements during the exercise.

The *bioPlux* which is connected to a triaxial accelerometer, *xyzPlux* (measuring range ± 3g); an electrocardiogram (ECG) sensor (ECG triodes), *ecgPlux*; two sensors of electro-dermal activity (EDA), *edaPlux*; a peripheral temperature sensor, *tempPlux* (0 °C - 100 °C ± 1.5%); and an electromyography (EMG) sensor, *emgPlux*.

Collocation of Acquisition System and Sensors

The *bioPlux*, was secured to the left side of the user's waist. The sensors was connected to *bioPlux,* as shown in Figure 7, in the following way, the three ECG leads were placed in the horizontal plane precordial position (V3, V4, V5); peripheral body temperature was measured by placing the temperature sensor in the axillary region on the left side; triaxial accelerometry was collected by placing the accelerometer sensor in the suprainguinal region on the right side; the two EDA sensors were placed on the abdomen and on the left hand (index and middle fingers); and the EMG sensor in the right *rectus femoral* (anterior thigh muscle).

Organization of Data Files

The data obtained from the *bioPlux* is recorded on open ASCII format (.txt), containing data on each velocity level and the respective pauses. Each file

Table 2. Anthropometric data of study participants

Subject	Age (years)	Height (cm)	Weight (kg)	% Fat
General	24.37±5.96	171.26±9.38	69.88±12.10	16.21±4.59
Male	24.21±6.24	174.73±7.73	73.22±11.08	14.22±3.41
Female	24.86±5.19	160.60±4.87	59.62±9.18	22.33±4.91

Figure 7. Location of acquisition system and sensors (adapted from (Godfrey, Conway, Meagher, & ÓLaighin, 2008)

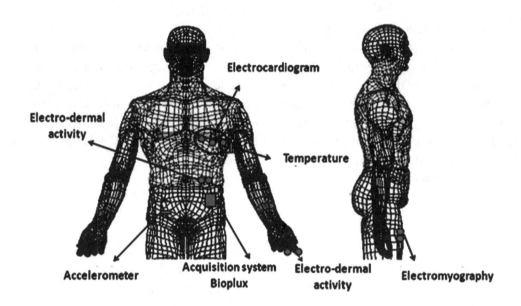

from *bioPlux* consists in 10 columns: 1 - Sequential number (repeating from 0 to 127); 2 - not used; 3 - x axes of accelerometer (vertical axes); 4 - y axes of accelerometer (medial-lateral axes); 5 - z axes of accelerometer (anterior-posterior axes); 6 – EMG; 7 – ECG; 8 - EDA (hand); 9 - EDA (abdomen); and 10 - Skin temperature.

Collected data is available for further research and result validation at the ALLab wiki website, at the following address: http://allab.it.ubi.pt/mediawiki.

RESULTS AND DISCUSSION

The experimental results are carried out in MATLAB software package 7.13 and focused on the ECG signals extracted from the individual data file of each participant. The ECG is a signal acquired from the body surface which characterizes the electrical activity of the human heart showing the regular contraction and relaxation of heart muscle. The analysis of ECG waveform is used for diagnosing the various heart abnormalities. This waveform consists of five basic waves P, Q, R, S, and T waves and sometimes U waves. The P wave represents atrial depolarization, Q, R and S wave is commonly known as QRS complex which represents the ventricular depolarization and T wave represents the repolarization of ventricle (Maglaveras, Stamkopoulos, Diamantaras, Pappas, & Strintzis, 1998).

The predictive model is based on the RBFNN combined with a filtering technique (Savitzky & Golay, 1964) for smoothing and differentiation which automatically performs the running least-squares polynomial fitting when the input signal was convolved with the filter coefficients. Due to the fact that the ECG is a quasi-periodic signal where each elementary beat is repeated over time with certain variability on the distance between contiguous beats, our case study is based on the estimation of it waveform. The original ECG waveform and the noise eliminated from the ECG after band pass filtering, are shown in Figure 8 and

Figure 9 respectively. Both figures presented a 10 seconds ECG sample representing 10000 records.

The filtering process assumes great significance because the ECG signal is often disturbed by broadband noise, mainly composed of high-frequency interferences due to electromagnetism and the grounding. Thus is important to minimize the distortion in the feature waveforms so as to keep those features that would be of most interest in terms of analysis, whilst at the same time removing the noise. Then, these filtered data are computed through a RBFNN, on a widow size of 5 milliseconds, so as to enable the system to estimate the ECG waveform. An example is shown in Figure 10 for which the sample data representing six seconds (6000 records) is divided between training and testing set. The training set is composed of 2400 records (40%) and the testing set represents 3600 records (60%). This means that the learning process offered by the proposed model occurs during 2.4 seconds of ECG data, and the testing phase is performed in order to estimate

the remaining 3.6 seconds. The optimised network structure obtained is based on two hidden layers with 18 and one node respectively. The model uses the standard RBFNN function provided in the MATLAB with the following settings: mean squared error goal: 1.0, spread of radial basis function=500, maximum number of neurons=750 and number of neurons to add between displays=25.

The proposed model processes a reduced window size (only 5 milliseconds) in order to minimize oscillations of the computed data which results on a low-frequency signal. Moreover, that could be very challenging to determine the suitable spread for a reliable learning generalization in the whole input space. Based on the experimental evaluation the most accurate system was obtained using spread=500. As shown in Figure 10, with the exception of upward and downward deflections, the predictive model revealed to be accurate and reliable to predict the ECG waveform, denoting it capability to support the healthcare decision making based on a reduced sample of clinical data.

Figure 8. Original ECG waveform

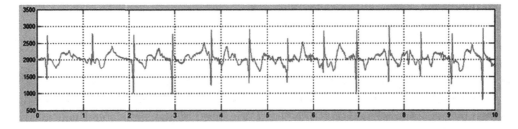

Figure 9. ECG waveform with Savitzky-Golay filter

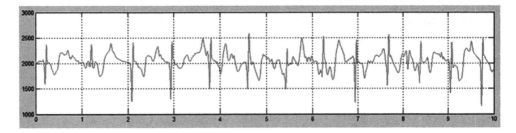

Figure 10. Estimated and original ECG

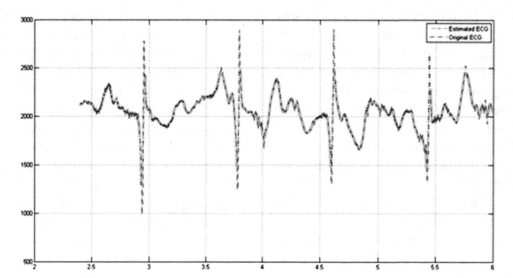

CONCLUSION

This chapter highlighted the importance of methodologies for obtaining knowledge based on reduced data and therefore, enabling the system to produce decisions based on a small amount of data. Both, real time data acquisition and offline clinical decision support systems are demanding new approaches which enable to determine the appropriate subset of data that provide representative and accurate explanation ability of the entire sample. In line with this, an overview related to neural networks focusing on complementary concepts, namely learning and classification, and supported by a case study based on RBFNN combined with a filtering technique. This model revealed to be accurate and suitable when applied on healthcare and wellbeing context providing adaptability and oriented learning according with the patient's personal data. However, future studies should be addressed to determine a model with the capability to predict upward and downward deflec-

tions more accurately. In addition, complementary studies should be focused on the inclusion of the Fourier transform into the proposed model aiming to provide a suitable degree of the polynomial used by the Savitzky-Golay filter. Besides, the method should be extended to allow real-time forecasting of ECG signal not based on batch learning but on online learning.

ACKNOWLEDGMENT

The authors acknowledge the contribution of the Instituto de Telecomunicações, R&D Unit 50008, financed by the applicable financial framework (FCT/MEC through national funds and when applicable co-funded by FEDER – PT2020 partnership agreement). The authors also acknowledge the contribution of COST Action IC1303 - AAPELE - Algorithms, Architectures and Platforms for Enhanced Living Environments.

REFERENCES

Abas, H. I., Yusof, M. M., & Noah, S. A. M. (2011). The application of ontology in a clinical decision support system for acute postoperative pain management. In *Proceedings of Semantic Technology and Information Retrieval (STAIR)* (pp. 106–112). Academic Press. doi:10.1109/STAIR.2011.5995773

Abdel-Aal, R. E. (2004). Abductive network committees for improved classification of medical data. *Methods of Information in Medicine, 43*(2), 192–201. PMID:15136869

Abdel-Aal, R. E. (2005). Improved classification of medical data using abductive network committees trained on different feature subsets. *Computer Methods and Programs in Biomedicine, 80*(2), 141–153. doi:10.1016/j.cmpb.2005.08.001 PMID:16169631

Abdel-Aal, R. E., Abdel-Halim, M. R. E., & Abdel-Aal, S. (2006). Improving the classification of multiple disorders with problem decomposition. *Journal of Biomedical Informatics, 39*(6), 612–625. doi:10.1016/j.jbi.2005.12.001 PMID:16442851

Abe, H., Ashizawa, K., Li, F., Matsuyama, N., Fukushima, A., Shiraishi, J., & Doi, K. (2004). Artificial neural networks (ANNs) for differential diagnosis of interstitial lung disease: Results of a simulation test with actual clinical cases. *Academic Radiology, 11*(1), 29–37. doi:10.1016/S1076-6332(03)00572-5 PMID:14746399

Al-Shayea, P., & Bahia, I. (2010). *Urinary system diseases diagnosis using artificial neural networks*. Academic Press.

Al–Shayea, Q., El–Refae, G., & Yaseen, S. (2013). Artificial neural networks for medical diagnosis using biomedical dataset. *International Journal of Behavioural and Healthcare Research, 4*(1), 45–63. doi:10.1504/IJBHR.2013.054519

Altunay, S., Telatar, Z., Erogul, O., & Aydur, E. (2009). A new approach to urinary system dynamics problems: Evaluation and classification of uroflowmeter signals using artificial neural networks. *Expert Systems with Applications, 36*(3), 4891–4895. doi:10.1016/j.eswa.2008.05.051

Axer, H., Jantzen, J., Berks, G., & Keyserlingk, D. G. V. (2000). *Aphasia classification using neural networks*. Academic Press.

Chen, S., Cowan, C. F. N., & Grant, P. M. (1991). Orthogonal least squares learning algorithm for radial basis function networks. *IEEE Transactions on Neural Networks, 2*(2), 302–309. doi:10.1109/72.80341

Das, R., Turkoglu, I., & Sengur, A. (2009). Effective diagnosis of heart disease through neural networks ensembles. *Expert Systems with Applications, 36*(4), 7675–7680. doi:10.1016/j.eswa.2008.09.013

Debnath, R., & Kurita, T. (2010). An evolutionary approach for gene selection and classification of microarray data based on {SVM} error-bound theories. *Bio Systems, 100*(1), 39–46. doi:10.1016/j.biosystems.2009.12.006 PMID:20045444

Dissanayake, M. S. B., & Corne, D. W. (2010). Feature selection and classification in bioscience/medical datasets: study of parameters and multi-objective approach in two-phase EA/k-NN method. In *Proceedings of Computational Intelligence (UKCI)* (pp. 1–6). Academic Press. doi:10.1109/UKCI.2010.5625581

Er, O., Yumusak, N., & Temurtas, F. (2010). Chest diseases diagnosis using artificial neural networks. *Expert Systems with Applications, 37*(12), 7648–7655. doi:10.1016/j.eswa.2010.04.078

Escarrabill, J., Marti, T., & Torrente, E. (2011). Good morning, doctor Google. *Revista Portuguesa de Pneumologia, 17*(4), 177–181. doi:10.1016/j.rppneu.2011.03.011 PMID:21600729

Felizardo, V., Gaspar, P. D., Garcia, N. M., & Reis, V. (2011). Acquisition of multiple physiological parameters during physical exercise. *International Journal of E-Health and Medical Communications*, *2*(4), 37–49. doi:10.4018/jehmc.2011100103

García-Pérez, E., Violante, A., & Cervantes-Pérez, F. (1998). Using neural networks for differential diagnosis of Alzheimer disease and vascular dementia. *Expert Systems with Applications*, *14*(1-2), 219–225. doi:10.1016/S0957-4174(97)00076-6

Gil, D., Johnsson, M., Chamizo, J. M. G., Paya, A. S., & Fernandez, D. R. (2009). Application of artificial neural networks in the diagnosis of urological dysfunctions. *Expert Systems with Applications*, *36*(3, Part 2), 5754–5760. doi:10.1016/j.eswa.2008.06.065

Godfrey, A., Conway, R., Meagher, D., & ÓLaighin, G. (2008). Direct measurement of human movement by accelerometry. *Medical Engineering & Physics*, *30*(10), 1364–1386. doi:10.1016/j.medengphy.2008.09.005

Heckerling, P. S., Canaris, G. J., Flach, S. D., Tape, T. G., Wigton, R. S., & Gerber, B. S. (2007). Predictors of urinary tract infection based on artificial neural networks and genetic algorithms. *International Journal of Medical Informatics*, *76*(4), 289–296. doi:10.1016/j.ijmedinf.2006.01.005 PMID:16469531

Ikeda, M., Ito, S., Ishigaki, T., & Yamauchi, K. (1997). Evaluation of a neural network classifier for pancreatic masses based on {CT} findings. *Computerized Medical Imaging and Graphics*, *21*(3), 175–183. doi:10.1016/S0895-6111(97)00006-2 PMID:9258595

Jinglin, Y., Li, H.-X., & Yong, H. (2011). A probabilistic SVM based decision system for pain diagnosis. *Expert Systems with Applications*, *38*(8), 9346–9351. doi:10.1016/j.eswa.2011.01.106

Juhola, M., Aalto, H., Joutsijoki, H., & Hirvonen, T. P. (2013). The classification of valid and invalid beats of three-dimensional nystagmus eye movement signals using machine learning methods. *Adv. Artif. Neu. Sys.*, *2013*, 16:16–16:16. doi:10.1155/2013/972412

Juhola, M., Joutsijoki, H., Aalto, H., & Hirvonen, T. P. (2014). On classification in the case of a medical data set with a complicated distribution. *Applied Computing and Informatics*. doi:10.1016/j.aci.2014.03.001

Kim, B. Y., & Park, K. S. (2000). Automatic sleep stage scoring system using genetic algorithms and neural network. In *Engineering in Medicine and Biology Society, 2000: Proceedings of the 22nd Annual International Conference of the IEEE* (Vol. 2, pp. 849–850). IEEE. doi:10.1109/IEMBS.2000.897848

Krishnaswamy, S., Loke, S., & Zaslavsky, A. (2002). *Towards anytime anywhere data mining e-services*. Retrieved from http://arrow.monash.edu.au/hdl/1959.1/128540

Latha, V., Swetha, P., Bhavya, M., Geetha, G., & Suhasini, D. (2012). Combined methodology of the classification rules for medical data-sets. *International Journal of Engineering Trends and Technology*, *3*(1), 32–36.

Lavrač, N. (1999). Selected techniques for data mining in medicine. *Artificial Intelligence in Medicine*, *16*(1), 3–23. doi:10.1016/S0933-3657(98)00062-1 PMID:10225344

Li, M., Tian, J., & Chen, F. (2008). Improving multiclass pattern recognition with a co-evolutionary RBFNN. *Pattern Recognition Letters*, *29*(4), 392–406. doi:10.1016/j.patrec.2007.10.019

Lin, R.-H. (2009). An intelligent model for liver disease diagnosis. *Artificial Intelligence in Medicine*, *47*(1), 53–62. doi:10.1016/j.artmed.2009.05.005 PMID:19540738

Maglaveras, N., Stamkopoulos, T., Diamantaras, K., Pappas, C., & Strintzis, M. (1998). ECG pattern recognition and classification using non-linear transformations and neural networks: A review. *International Journal of Medical Informatics, 52*(1), 191–208. doi:10.1016/S1386-5056(98)00138-5 PMID:9848416

Mundra, P., & Rajapakse, J. (2007). SVM-RFE with relevancy and redundancy criteria for gene selection. In J. Rajapakse, B. Schmidt, & G. Volkert (Eds.), *Pattern recognition in bioinformatics* (Vol. 4774, pp. 242–252). Springer Berlin Heidelberg. doi:10.1007/978-3-540-75286-8_24

Nguyen, H. T., Butler, M., Roychoudhry, A., Shannon, A. G., Flack, J., & Mitchell, P. (1996). Classification of diabetic retinopathy using neural networks. In *Engineering in Medicine and Biology Society, 1996. Bridging Disciplines for Biomedicine: Proceedings of the 18th Annual International Conference of the IEEE* (*Vol. 4*, pp. 1548–1549). IEEE. doi:10.1109/IEMBS.1996.647546

Poggio, T., & Girosi, F. (1990). Networks for approximation and learning. *Proceedings of the IEEE, 78*(9), 1481–1497. doi:10.1109/5.58326

Ramadan, Z., Ropelle, K., Myklebust, J., Goldstein, M., Feng, X., & Flynn, J. (1991). A neural network to discriminate between dyslexic subtypes. In *Engineering in Medicine and Biology Society, Proceedings of the Annual International Conference of the IEEE* (pp. 1405–1406). IEEE. doi:10.1109/IEMBS.1991.684513

Savitzky, A., & Golay, M. J. E. (1964). Smoothing and differentiation of data by simplified least squares procedures. *Analytical Chemistry, 36*(8), 1627–1639. doi:10.1021/ac60214a047

Serrano, J. I., Tomečková, M., & Zvárová, J. (2006). Machine learning methods for knowledge discovery in medical data on atherosclerosis. *European Journal for Biomedical Informatics, 1*, 6–33.

Singh, A., Nowak, R. D., & Zhu, X. (2008). Unlabeled data: Now it helps, now it doesn't. In D. Koller, D. Schuurmans, Y. Bengio, & L. Bottou (Eds.), NIPS (pp. 1513–1520). Curran Associates, Inc. Retrieved from http://dblp.uni-trier.de/db/conf/nips/nips2008.html#SinghNZ08

Syiam, M. M. (1994). A neural network expert system for diagnosing eye diseases. In *Artificial Intelligence for Applications, Proceedings of the Tenth Conference on* (pp. 491–492). doi:10.1109/CAIA.1994.323624

Tanwani, A., Afridi, J., Shafiq, M. Z., & Farooq, M. (2009). Guidelines to select machine learning scheme for classification of biomedical datasets. In C. Pizzuti, M. Ritchie, & M. Giacobini (Eds.), *Evolutionary computation, machine learning and data mining in bioinformatics* (Vol. 5483, pp. 128–139). Springer Berlin Heidelberg. doi:10.1007/978-3-642-01184-9_12

Wasan, S. K., Bhatnagar, V., & Kaur, H. (2008). The impact of data mining techniques on medical diagnostics. *Data Science Journal, 5*, 119–126. doi:10.2481/dsj.5.119

Yao, B., & Li, S. (2010). ANMM4CBR: A case-based reasoning method for gene expression data classification. *Algorithms for Molecular Biology; AMB, 5*(1), 14. doi:10.1186/1748-7188-5-14 PMID:20051140

Zhang, G., Yan, P., Zhao, H., & Zhang, X. (2008). A computer aided diagnosis system in mammography using artificial neural networks. In *Proceedings of BioMedical Engineering and Informatics* (Vol. 2, pp. 823–826). Academic Press. doi:10.1109/BMEI.2008.93

Zhu, Z., Jia, S., & Ji, Z. (2010). Towards a memetic feature selection paradigm. *Computational Intelligence Magazine, IEEE, 5*(2), 41–53. doi:10.1109/MCI.2010.936311

KEY TERMS AND DEFINITIONS

Artificial Neural Networks (ANN): Computational models inspired by brain's nervous systems which are capable of machine learning and pattern recognition. ANN are composed by simple, and highly interconnected processing elements that process information by their dynamic state response to external inputs.

Big Data: Is a term describing the storage and analysis of large and or complex data sets using a series of techniques including, but not limited to: database tools, machine learning and artificial intelligence.

Clinical Decision Support System (CDSS): Systems to assist patients and health care professionals on healthcare processes, such as triage, early detection of diseases, identification of changes in health symptoms, patients' self-reporting, evaluation of treatment, and monitoring.

ECG: Is a test that checks for problems with the electrical activity of your heart. An ECG translates the heart's electrical activity into line tracings on paper. The spikes and dips in the line tracings are called waves.

Reinforcement Learning: The knowledge is obtained using rewards and punishments which there is an agent (learner) that acts autonomously and receives a scalar reward signal that is used to evaluate the consequences of its actions.

Semi-Supervised Learning: Combines the methodology of the supervised learning to process the labeled data with the unsupervised learning to compute the unlabeled data.

Supervised Learning: The knowledge is obtained through a training which includes a data set called the training sample which is structured according to the knowledge base supported by human experts as physicians in medical context, and databases. It is assumed that the user knows beforehand the classes and the instances of each class.

Unsupervised Learning: Treats all variables the same way so as to determine the different classes based on diverse features observed in the collection of unlabeled data that encompass the sample set. It is assumed that the user is unaware of the classes due to the lack of information sufficiently available.

Chapter 15
Marketing Strategies in the Age of Web 3.0

Sonia Ferrari
University of Calabria, Italy

ABSTRACT

The Web has become one of the most effective means of communication, and electronic marketing is rapidly transforming the way organizations communicate and operate in many areas. This chapter describes the Internet evolution; in fact, it is no longer just an information tool but has become a new dimension, allowing firms to learn more about their customers, communicate more effectively, promote and market products, services, companies, and brands. The evolution of the Internet, from Web 1.0 to Web 3.0, has resulted in a radical change in marketing strategies and tools in many businesses.

INTRODUCTION

The aim of this chapter is to analyse how Web marketing has been changing in the last decades because of new communication models. In particular, a considerable section is dedicated to the evolution of marketing due to the continuous innovations on the Internet. After the age of Web 1.0 and 2.0, today the Network is shifting is towards the Web 3.0 as if to say the Semantic Web. The chapter describes the main characteristics of the Web 3.0 and how it will influence users' behaviour, consumers' attitudes and buying habits, and companies' marketing strategies.

In postmodern society the Internet has enabled consumers to enjoy a level of freedom not previously imaginable, providing a source of cheap and easily accessible information and also an instrument of socialization and learning. Thanks to a rational, but also highly emotional, more immersive and interactive use, it has reduced the information asymmetry between supply and demand of goods and services. The consumer, highly active and participatory, has become more informed and more demanding than ever before.

After the stages of the *information only* (Web 1.0) and the *relational marketing* (the phase of the so-called Web 2.0, in which companies sought to contact the users of their Websites), the Internet has entered the period of the *collaborative* or *semantic marketing*, the moment of Web 3.0. Now supply and demand can meet in an interactive way, all stakeholders and companies seek to acquire knowledge, not about the client but from

DOI: 10.4018/978-1-4666-8147-7.ch015

the client, and to work with him/her to differentiate their offerings.

For this reason, today the Web is one of the most effective means of communication, and electronic marketing is rapidly transforming the way organizations communicate and operate.

The chapter describes the impact of ICTs on marketing, illustrating the evolution of the Web in the last decades and how it is affecting firms' strategies and organizations together with customers' behaviour and buying process. Special attention is devoted to Web Marketing and how it is influencing companies' communication and promotion policies. The Web 3.0 concept and its implications are presented, together with the important role today played by social media.

INNOVATIONS IN ICTs AND MARKETING: THE NEW DIMENSIONS OF COMMUNICATION

Nowadays electronic communications (telecommunications and television) represent more than 80% of the worldwide turnover of communication industry. The gradual migration "from atom to bits" is evident if we take into account the last five years: from 2008 immaterial communications have registered an annual growth rate of over 4%, while in the same period of time publishing and postal services have lost more than a percentage point per year (Autorità per le Garanzie nelle Comunicazioni, 2013). The range of services offered through electronic communications' networks and the value generated by businesses and users of these facilities are continuously increasing.

Thanks to the spread of broadband and wireless networks, applications for mobile technologies and the emergence of mobile devices[1], the Internet has become a means to give and receive targeted and multimedia content and information, to buy and sell products and services, as well as to communicate with communities and know better the characteristics of customers[2]. As a result, the ways

to socialize, communicate, gather information and learn through the Web have changed, especially among the younger population (Sassoon, 2012). During 2012, in Europe the main services for Internet users were emails and search engines (representing the prevalent use for respectively 89% and 83% of the total), but other online activities are assuming the size of "mass" services among the Internet users. At the EU level, 61% read online newspapers, 54% use e-banking services, 52% write messages using social media and 50% use travel services (Eurostat, 2013).

As a consequence, the Internet is no longer just an information tool: it has become a new dimension, allowing firms to learn more about their customers and to communicate more effectively, as well as to promote and market products, services, companies, brands. The growing use of mobile Internet devices, such as smart phones and tablets, getting smaller and more manageable, helps to amplify the effects of the evolution of the Web 3.0, which has resulted in a radical change in marketing strategies and tools in many businesses.

Thanks to new ICTs, customers can communicate better and can become *prosumers* (Normann, 1991), participating in the creation of the right product or service for them (Kotler, Kartajaya & Setiawan, 2010). The concept was born in the service sector where, due to the contemporariness of production, consumption and sometimes also buying activities, the customer is not passive but has a productive role in the delivery process. For the customer it is a way to live an interactive experience, creating a value for him/her and for the organization it is a competitive advantage. The consumer, now a prosumer, becomes a co-creator of value, a partner and no more a target (Erragcha, 2014; Hennig-Thurau et al., 2010),

The process is enclosed in the concept of *cocreation* (Prahalad & Krishnan, 2008). The idea is that customers, through their consumer experiences, can improve future experiences and personalise them, taking into account their own needs and preferences (Kotler, et al., 2010).

THE EVOLUTION OF THE WEB AND THE BIRTH OF WEB MARKETING FROM THE WEB 1.0 TO THE WEB 3.0

During the Web 1.0 era companies communicate on the Internet by means of static pages, using one-way media without interactivity; later, with Web 2.0, communication becomes two-way and users can generate their own contents to be put on the Web. It is the birth of an interactive platform, in which you can share information and feedbacks (Noti, 2013). In Web 3.0 the interaction is between computers and the aim is to process large quantities of data and information to obtain targeted knowledge (Mistilis, 2012).

So, after an era of a marketing mainly targeted at selling, followed by an era of relationship marketing, today the time has arrived of a marketing through which firms invite customers to participate in the development of products and communication. It is the age of the "Collaborative Marketing", also called by Kotler "Marketing 3.0" (Kotler et al., 2010), in which firms need to collaborate with their shareholders, clients, employees, and partners, together with other firms.

There is not only one accepted definition of the concept of Web 3.0. It is still confused and vague, and it signifies more an attitude than a technological evolution. Anyway, the so-called *Semantic Web* has three main characteristics: to be ubiquitous, individualized, and efficient. The ubiquity is due to the possibility of being connected anywhere and anytime. The individualized character refers to the information, which is segmented and adapted to varied people and situations. Finally, Web 3.0 is efficient because it supplies information selected on the basis of individual interests to be read, understood and recognized by computers (Almeida, Santos & Monteiro, 2013).

Today, the firms have to collect and use the so called *Big Data*, an enormous amount of information and data coming from the Web. Thanks to social media, they can evaluate the use that consumers make of a product or a brand on the

Internet as well as their involvement by looking at posts, images, etc. In this way it is possible to check the electronic image and reputation of brand and products. The *cloud computing* is helping in this direction, allowing the centralized data storage and the sharing of data-processing tasks. The Semantic Web aims at helping with this type of problems, facilitating the collection and a more effective use of data.

Tim Berners-Lee, the inventor of World Wide Web, coined the concept for the first time. In 1999 he foresaw an era in which computers will communicate between themselves (Floridi, 2009), elaborating and integrating user-generated content to create a new meaning and useful knowledge for companies. Berners-Lee was thinking about an environment in which computers, people and systems would dialogue better and cooperate (Carbone, Contreras, Hernandez & Gomez-Perez, 2012).

As described by Tasner (2010), the key elements of Web 3.0 from the marketing point of view are:

- Microblogging (the sharing of users' thoughts and ideas);
- Virtual reality worlds (the existence of virtual spaces in which you can interact with other users in 3 dimensions);
- Customization/ personalization of visitors' experience;
- Mobile (the widespread use of mobile phones and other devices to surf the net and buy products);
- On-demand collaboration (users can interact in real-time sharing documents and working simultaneously on the same project).

These concepts can be summarized in the following formula:

Web 3.0=4C+P+VS

The 4Cs are: content, commerce, community and context; P means personalization and VS stands for vertical search, so to limit the number of search channels (Eftekhari & Zeynab, 2008). This formula puts together the main elements of Web 2.0 (user-generated content, e-commerce, the role of communities) with the specific target of every user of the Web (the context), aiming to personalize the offer by a focussed search (the vertical search). Through this new approach you can obtain an innovative Internet environment, the Web 3.0.

In contrast with Web 2.0, based on users' participation, Web 3.0 will be based on users' cooperation (Barassi & Treré, 2012). The major problems of Web 2.0 are connected with the following aspects (Tasner, 2010): oversaturation (as if to say too many information on the Web), misconceptions (wrong ideas about some Web characteristics and elements), time (the time is increasingly faster and people need more time to surf and know news and innovation), modes of interaction (the role of human touch is every day less essential and there is confusion and lack of adoption). Finally the openness of the Web creates problems in terms of reduction in users' personal privacy.

It is clear that the idea of going beyond Web 2.0 was born to go beyond these limits; there is also the need of firms and organizations to put together, elaborate, organize and use in a more effective and efficient mode the huge volume of information coming from the Web, especially after its wide spread use through social media during the last decades.

In Table 1 you can see the differences between Web 2.0 and Web 3.0 described so far.

The Web Marketing

Considering the data on the growing importance of national and international use of the Web to gather information, choose and buy products and/or services, as well as to communicate and exchange information and impressions on experiences of consumption, it is evident that the visibility in the Web has become a crucial factor in the competitive success of firms.

However, for the companies, to have their own Website is not enough to maximize the results. It is essential, in fact, to be easily reached, to communicate effectively with the target markets and to create a trustful and interactive relationship with online audiences by means of a right Web Marketing strategy.

Web Marketing can be defined as a set of marketing activities that, through the Internet, allows the promotion of a company or a product, as well as the offering of services such as marketing, customer relationships, information services, etc. It also allows the creation of direct marketing strategies, which aim to maximize customer

Table 1. Main differences between the Web 2.0 and the Web 3.0

	Web 2.0	Web 3.0
Type of interactions	Sharing of information between users	Sharing of information between computers
Sought results	Feedbacks from users	Targeted knowledge
Marketing model	Relationship Marketing	Collaborative Marketing
Involved subjects	People, firms	People, firms, computers, systems
Base	Users' participation	Users' cooperation
Main components	User-generated Content, E-commerce, Social Media	User Generated Content, E-commerce, Social Media, Context, Vertical Search

satisfaction and loyalty, as well as to facilitate the reaching of new markets with reduced costs.

To develop a Web Marketing campaign you need to evaluate and use the full potential of the Internet, especially in terms of interaction (communication takes place in real time, and it is instantaneous, flexible, two-way, networked), customization and communication (thanks to a direct relationship with the customer).

In recent decades the technological developments in the fields of information and telecommunication technologies have had a significant impact on all productive sectors, encouraging new marketing strategies (Noti, 2013). First of all they caused a process of disintermediation (with a growing importance of the Web as a distribution channel and a consequent reduction of barriers of market entry), as well as a customization of supply and an increase of information offer, together with a possibility of comparison between alternatives on the market.

In a world of this kind, in which the transparency of the market has grown, the consumer, who is no longer a passive recipient of one-sided communications, has more power, especially in terms of his ability to analyse and compare offers, as well as in terms of possibility of interaction with other users and with companies. Since the age of Web 2.0 this has happened not only thanks to the institutional and business tools of electronic communication, that are more and more sophisticated, numerous and heterogeneous, but also thanks to other available innovative tools, such as platforms for the sharing of digital contents, social commerce, blogs, social networks, forums, newsgroups and communities. These real independent information networks allow Web users to create their own multimedia contents and to disseminate and receive non-commercial information about products, companies, offers, and in particular, reviews and recommendations, also through review sites.

Thanks to the Web Marketing, corporate communication is no longer one-sided, as in the past, but highly interactive and bi-directional, allowing the reception from the customers of various kinds of feedback about issues such as levels of satisfaction, expectations, inefficiencies, preferences, complaints, and suggestions. For companies these are useful elements in making an assessment of the provided products and services. They also foster the development of a customer relationship much stronger than in the past, serve to increase the level of customer loyalty, and allow operators to know better their target markets and current trends. In this way, companies can communicate directly with their current and potential customers, easily identifying segments and communities that are potentially interested in their offering, adopting languages to suit the characteristics of each. In addition, they can create and send messages for specific needs, even in real time, for example to inform about events, promotions, etc. and they can contact market niches or even individual users, who may be interested in specific information or who have requested it (Sassoon, 2012).

Currently the Internet provides low cost, updated, customizable, multimedia, and comparable information (with the support of audio, video, photo, etc.) and a distribution channel that requires low investment, also accessible to small businesses. But today it has also become a means of promotional activities, as well as a support for the consumer.

Other advantages of the Web interactivity are connected with the possibility of retaining the existing customers, through specific programs and tools such as newsletters, podcasting, wikis, blogs, and contests. Besides, companies can create a contacts database, useful to perform the function of Customer Relationship Management (CRM), for periodic or occasional promotional activities, and online surveys and market research. In the era of the so-called CRM 3.0 or Social CRM (Almeida, et al., 2013) firms can use customers' conversations and relationships in the social networks to enhance their CRM processes. Thereby consumers collaborate directly or not to improve companies' offer and this is also an opportunity to create new products and services.

Finally, the Web, flexible and multimedia instrument, can be used to communicate in an innovative way, that is effective and suited to experiential products, e.g. tourism or leisure (Ferrari, 2012). Through tools such as photos, video, audio, three-dimensional and interactive maps, virtual tours, Webcams, GIS, Tags, downloaded and printed information, geological sites, online sale, GPS and smart phones, etc., the communication media grow rapidly, changing from unilateral push tools to interactive channels. Besides, the contents of communication are becoming more and more complex and specific, depending on the identity and the character of the receiver and the context of the communication (Stavrakantonakis, Gagiu, Toma & Fensel, 2013).

With all these innovations, the Internet has also become an instrument for a strong emotional involvement of the potential customer, who, through it, can imagine and create her/his own consumer experience. In fact, the new Web tools allow people to share the experience of consumption in real-time with other consumers, making their stories much more engaging, especially if they are inserted in the Web during the experience, often with the support of photos and/or videos.

The ability to gather information with greater emotional involvement is enhanced by the many opportunities offered by new technologies, which allow access via the computer or other various devices to virtual worlds, i.e. *augmented reality*, through virtual tours, geolocalizations, music, videos, photos, audios, downloadable documents, etc. The emergence of new media environments is, in fact, the result of the spread of smart phones and tablets connected to the Web, accessing multimedia instruments with innovative services and applications, favoured by the spread of wireless networks.

The possible means for a Web Marketing campaign are numerous and each one allows to reach specific goals and objectives. The results achieved through Web Marketing activities can be easily monitored and evaluated in terms of visits, contacts, sales, rankings on the major search engines, etc.

There are three essential components of Web Marketing which integrate the techniques of traditional advertising with the techniques of direct marketing online: pull instruments (affiliations, search engines, digital couponing), advertising itself, i.e. push instruments (these are more traditional tools such as banner campaigns, email marketing, pop-up, shutter, skyscraper, sponsorship) and interactive tools.

The best known and widespread tool is the search marketing, which deals with the visibility on search engines. The *search engine optimization (SEO)* aims at increasing the visibility of a website in search engines. It is based on a set of activities such as the optimization of the website structure and its URL, the accessibility of information by users' search engines, and the link optimisation (Adams, 2013). Instead the *search engine marketing (SEM)* is an instrument of Web Marketing that promotes the websites through a major visibility in search engine results pages (SERPs) by means of optimization itself and advertising.

But the most innovative and interesting tool is represented by the interactive marketing; its more established instruments are the blogs, while the new ones are the social networks. Blogs are "Web diaries" in which, through Publishing Wizard programs, you can create Web pages. There are different types of blogs, from those of current affairs to personal blogs, depending on the subjects. Now they have become, for companies, instruments to attract potential customers, promote their products, submit news, change their images, participate in forums with customers, and so on. Forums are very interesting, as sources of immediate feedback from the market.

Web Marketing techniques can be summarized in two main categories. The first, used mainly in the 90s before the advent of Web 2.0, is of a promotional type and departs only slightly from traditional marketing tools. The second category is called *viral*, because it is based on social commerce, namely on interactivity, using tools such as e-mail, video and social media (Van Belleghem, Eenhuizen & Veris, 2011; Williamson, 2011). Viral marketing is a form of electronic word of mouth that is similar to the spread of viruses on social networks. It allows the user to have a much more active and relevant role than in the past, through the creation and communication of personal contents; so the new techniques have a dual purpose: to enhance the visibility of a product, company, brand, as well as in the case of traditional marketing techniques, and to improve relationships with customers. In 2013 about 30% of European enterprises used social media (e.g. social networks, blogs, content-sharing sites and wikis), with almost three out of four of these businesses (73%) using such applications to improve or build their image and to market products and services (Eurostat, 2013).

The Role of Users

Perhaps the most important revolution since Web 2.0 era, which has put the consumer in a central location in the Web, is the opportunity given to all users to generate their own contents (*user- generated content*) to insert online with great ease and without the need for specific technical skills. The *open source content management system* connects people and contents within communities that share interests, facilitating the dissemination of information and the collaboration between different subjects. This gives rise to forms of communication that are no longer one to one or one to many, but rather many to many (Kotler et al., 2010), and gives life to the semantic marketing (Rincon, 2012). In some cases, the Internet user can become the creator of a myth or a story about a brand or a product / service that an alert company can use as an effective promotional tool to create forms of communication based on storytelling.

It means that costumers have a great power and that organizations no longer have control of their brands. As a consequence, the importance of advertising is lower and there is a growth of power, already very high, in the word of mouth approach, which is a really effective communication tool, especially in the provision of services. In fact, Web 2.0 and Web 3.0 have allowed to gradually move from word of mouth to *word of mouse*, that is a quick way to communicate and to amplify the positive or negative impact of word of mouth; e-mail, chat, forums, social networks multiply its effects. So we can say that there has been a shifting from the exchange of information to the sharing of knowledge (Erragcha, 2014) and that the Web is now for users a real experiencialscape.

Social media are the interactions among people by which they create, share, or exchange information and ideas in virtual communities and networks. The creation of social media, such as forums and blogs, can retain customers and create a kind of *tribe*, a fans community of a product, a brand or a type of experience. Often the basis of certain consumer behaviours is the desire to belong to a *communitas*, a temporary situation in which people meet outside everyday life and share something specific, with a sense of belonging to the group in an egalitarian way (Cova, 2003; Maffesoli, 1996). To get in touch with these groups, companies have to offer them, through tools such as information microblogging, elements that contribute to the rites of the tribe, creating myths, magic contents, and more (Sassoon, 2012). As Kotler et al. (2010) state: "because social media is low-cost and bias-free, it will be the future of marketing communication" (p.9).

THE IMPORTANCE OF VIRTUAL COMMUNITIES IN THE ERA OF MARKETING 3.0

Today, the emotional involvement is one of the main reasons behind certain forms of consumption related to leisure (Arnould, Price & Zinkhan, 2004; Hirshman & Holbrook, 1982). Emotional, highly immersive experiences can be lived, amplified and communicated through the participation in virtual communities and social networks (Hagel III & Armstrong, 1997).

Social networks, groups of people with different types of social ties, such as casual acquaintance, labour relations, family ties, are one of the most advanced forms of online communication. For companies it is increasingly important to dialogue with customers, even informally, through social networks; it is, in fact, a way of knowing their target market in greater detail and to interact with customers. It is also a means to create an image different from the traditional and institutional ones.

The growth of virtual social networks and all kinds of virtual communities has determined in the last few years dramatic changes in business models in terms of communication strategies and decision making processes (Garrigos-Simon, Lapiedra Alcami & Barbera Ribera, 2012). Besides they have effects also on the value chain and the structure of enterprises, creating new forms of competition. In fact, networks are precious sources of information and knowledge sharing, but also sources of creativity and innovation. Through them people can add value to firms' offers, adapting them to new trends in customers' preferences, tastes and needs, fashion and styles, changes in social patterns, etc. Networks are also powerful promotional tools.

The most cited definition of virtual community is that of Rheingold (1993): "Virtual communities are social aggregations that emerge from the Net when enough people carry on those public discussions long enough, with sufficient human feeling, to form Webs of personal relationships in cyberspace" (p.5). The virtual community is a group of people, who may or may not meet face to face and who exchange words and ideas through the mediation of computers and networks.

In a multidisciplinary approach, which takes into account sociological, technological and e-

commerce related aspects, the main characteristics of virtual communities are as follows: participants share goals, interests, needs, or activities, which are the main reason of group membership; in addition, they are involved in an active and repetitive way, and often have strong interactions between them, with high emotional involvement. Participants have regulated access to shared resources; they can mutually exchange information, support and services, as well as conversations and languages (Preece, 2000; Wang & Fesenmaier, 2002).

McMillan (1996) illustrates the four dimensions of a virtual community: *Spirit, Trust, Trade* and *Art*. The first (Spirit) is related to the sense of belonging to the group, which distinguishes each member by outsiders. It symbolises the idea of the right to be part of the group, but also the mutual trust among the members, which is the basis of the community. The Trust is the concept that the community should inculcate in its members as they do in the community itself. Today this is typical of horizontal relationships and it means that customers trust more one another than they trust the firms. As a consequence the importance of companies' advertising decreases and that of word of mouth grows (Kotler et al., 2010). The Trade embodies the idea that the purpose of the community is the sharing of needs and resources of the members. The Art means that in the group there is an emotional connection shared in time and space, which implies the exchange of experiences among the participants as the basis of the community development (Kim, Lee, & Hiemstra, 2004). For this reason, members should have similar interests and passions.

In fact, the four basic needs met by the online communities are: interest, relationship, fantasy and transaction (Hagel III & Armstrong, 1997). Putting together a group of people who have common interests and knowledge on a specific topic satisfies the first. The relationship between members who share something (life experience, interest, etc.) is created through a strong connection. The fantasy grows through the "opportunity to get together and explore new worlds of fantasy and fun." The transaction refers to the exchange of information within the group.

In addition to the functional needs (such as information, entertainment, etc.), the virtual community also meets social and psychological needs (Wang & Fesenmaier, 2002). Social needs are related to the opportunity to interact with other people and include relationship, interactivity, trust, communication and evasion. Finally, the psychological needs are connected to the desire for identification, involvement, being part of a tribe, sharing rituals, having a role, getting away from everyday life and being creative.

Virtual communities provide an interesting and fascinating environment, in which you can interact with others, and highly enriching experiences; these experiences go far beyond the desire to exchange information about products and consumer experiences (Hagel III & Armstrong, 1997). Participants in a virtual community seek, in fact, emotions and satisfaction of intrinsic needs. The community offers an enriching environment in which they come into contact with others to be part of a tribe (Cova, 1995; Maffesoli, 1996), sharing experiences, memories, passions and / or consumption rituals, savouring memories of past experiences, being reassured, creating social bonds, daydreaming, receiving stimuli and experiencing moments of anticipation about future experiences, as well as spending free time pleasantly (Jansson, 2002; Stamboulis & Skayannis, 2003; Tussyadiah & Fesenmaier, 2009). These aims are important emotional, social and psychological components, which are not always consciously and explicitly realized (Hennig-Thurau, Gwinner, Walsh & Gremler, 2004; Wang & Fesenmaier, 2004).

The participation in online communities is a tool to experience moments of *immersion* in the experience (Carù & Cova, 2004; Pine & Gilmore, 1999), namely deep experiences of inner growth and transformation, in which the subject is mentally involved. The immersion in a virtual community can be considered as one of the mediation tools of

consumption experience, tools that "facilitate and / or interpret the experience of another individual" (Tussyadiah & Fesenmaier, 2009, p.25). There are other mediation tools, both impersonal (design, setting-shape, mobile phones, Internet, etc.) and personal (other consumers, guides, etc.) (Jennings & Nickerson, 2006). They allow to live consumer experiences in a physical, virtual or imaginary way, gradually separating them from a realistic hedonism to turn towards an imaginary one, not based on experiences but on fantasies generated by the media (Campbell, 2005). Diving in these fantasies and daydreams is a pleasant experience, which is sought by certain categories of users, the so-called "imaginative hedonists". These imaginary worlds can become, therefore, a means to enhance the value of consumption and intensify it, and can be used by companies as marketing levers (Tussyadiah & Fesenmaier, 2009).

Today, the consumer experience is increasingly being designed, represented, organized, planned, measured, priced, and (often explicitly) charged to generate greater customer value through the creation of a myth. This myth can be felt in every phase of the experience. The virtual community can create myths, promote them, and keep them alive after the experience for the customer and for other people has finished.

The final stage of the consumption experience, which is dedicated to the memory, has always been rather neglected. It is, however, an important component of the experience of consumption (mainly because it is a source of promotion by word of mouth) (Clawson, 1963; Wright, 2010), which, thanks to the Web, has been re-evaluated. It is the moment in which companies can encourage visitors to "experience the experience" (Morgan, Lugosi, & Ritchie, 2010, p.130), that is to say to create stories about products and brands that allow you to relive the experience; they can also become the base element of targeted storytelling activities.

In the phase called *remembered consumption and nostalgia* (Arnoul et al., 2004), at the end of the experience, the consumer is eager to relive it, through sharing it with others and activating word of mouth. He/she can, therefore, create his/her own albums and diaries, post photos and videos, put online comments and reviews about products, brands, companies, and so on. All this information will be used by other consumers to make decisions about future purchases and by companies to determine their marketing strategies.

Being part of a community of this type may, therefore, affect the experience in all its stages and have various types of effects on the buying process in different ways because of its impact on expectations, perceptions, satisfaction levels, image of the company and/or product, and brand evaluation subsequent to consumption (Bickart & Schindler, 2001; Kim, Lee, & Hiemstra, 2004). Thanks to this, important implications emerge for business marketing.

In conclusion, the virtual community is a true media landscape or *mediascape*³, which can be known and visited before, during and after the purchase and consumption of a product. This can happen in social places or *socialscapes*: the places where social interactions occur, such as shops, airports, etc. Therefore, it becomes "a pervasive element of the entire consumer experience, from the stage of anticipation to that of action, and finally, to the reflection and the analyses subsequent the consumption" (Jennings & Nickerson, 2006, p.58); a virtual community is particularly suited to communicate the experiential elements of consumption.

WEB 3.0 IMPLICATIONS FOR BUSINESSES

Companies are not always ready to take innovations on the Web, especially those linked to the new concept of Web 3.0. This has great potentialities, some of them still little known and understood, and that scares because of the difficulty in controlling the communication, which is no more one-way but multidirectional and multi-media.

Many do not understand, therefore, the potential of the Internet, which, as shown, has now become a real *experientialscape*, a place in which to live and share experiences and emotions. There is no more, in fact, in the Web a boundary between contents' producers and those who benefit from them. Thanks to user-generated content the roles of those who exercise authority and those who control have changed and new languages and new forms of storytelling have emerged (Sassoon, 2012).

Nowadays, with the greater availability of information about customers and markets, companies need to filter and organize it better. Web 3.0 is the tool to do this and also to contextualize information by users, transforming it into knowledge. The techniques of Semantic Web allow the processing of information obtained via the Internet, to make it meaningful for firms and adapt it to the different needs of various users. Thereby firms can use the information gathered by different organizations before, during or after contact with customers by means of various techniques such as CRM, data warehousing, data mining. They can also use information coming from social media or the Web in general. This information collection is the basis for designing personalized offers, in which the role of networks is essential (Almeida et al., 2013).

In the Web 3.0 economy the companies must adapt to new and more demanding communication rules, such as new Google's ways to index and make websites relevant. They have to invest in different marketing communication channels on the Internet, that are the following: SEO, blogging, social media marketing, content marketing, email marketing, referral and review marketing, public relations marketing, and video marketing (Adams, 2013). The aim is to become more and more relevant on the Web every day.

In the future Web 3.0 will organize and put together large flows of information on the basis of main interests, themes and topics, considering various customers and users profiles. The content will be customized through a profile of users and customers who will live personalised experiences on the Web. In this way companies' communication and advertising will become more effective.

Already today through the Web customers can cooperate in every phase of the value chain, with different types of actions, from reviews on products/services to the cocreation of goods (Hennig-Thurau et al., 2010; Hoyer, Rajesh, Dorotic, Krafft & Singh, 2010; Krishnamurthy, 2009). The consumer who wants to create his/her own customized product through innovative but rather widespread tools, such as *dynamic packaging* in tourism, may do so thanks to forms of social and e-commerce; these allow to be better informed, also through non-commercial, highly reliable sources, that enhance the emotional and experiential components of products. The clients, therefore, collaborate in the creation of individualized offerings, giving information on their preferences, choosing different versions of products and services and cocreating them (Kotler et al., 2010).

Nowadays the firms try, through forms of *mass customization*, to offer products that are more and more specific, avoiding cost increase. This can be achieved by identifying the key elements of each good and making flexible the offer, in order to provide to the customer a *made-to-order* feeling without excessive costs (Almeida et al., 2013). It could be the beginning of personalised product series every day more particular until getting at the production of specific individualised goods for every customer.

The actual revolution in Web 3.0 is the importance given to customers through social media and other interactive tools. They can co-create products and firms must involve them and generate with them a positive and collaborative relationship, involving all stakeholders in the whole production process. For this reason firms have to promote the participation of people and customers through instruments like *community managers* and *crowdsourcing* techniques (Garrigos-Simon et al., 2012).

The three main objectives of community managers are: reaching better marketing results, promoting products and events and improving firm's image and customers' loyalty. They must stimulate participation and collaboration of customers and stakeholders in the social media, trying to control their activity on the Web, especially word of mouth. Today many large and innovative companies have their pages in the most important social networks and some of them have created their own social networks.

Another relevant management tool of Web 3.0 era is the *crowdsourcing*, whose importance is quickly growing. It is defined as the "outsourcing of tasks to the general Internet public" (Kleemann, Vob &

Rieder, 2008, p.5). It is the externalization of a task or a function of an organization (i.e. the development of a product or the design of a advertising campaign) to a group of people via the Internet by means of an open call. It is a very cheap way to obtain help and innovative supports. It is not the only form of collaborative initiative born thanks to the Internet.

There is also the *crowdfunding*: a process in which a group of people put together their own money to sustain persons or organizations' projects. It is a form of microcredit made possible thanks to the Web that has the role of meeting instrument for these people.

For businesses the real challenge of Web 3.0 is the ability to use the multiple information obtained from the Internet to provide clients with customized experiences and create for them a higher added value. The Web 3.0 is not only a way to become more competitive, but is also an opportunity for the creation of new businesses that offer innovative goods and services related to the management of on-line information and the customization of offers, as well as a way to address the mobility of people. It is the moment of the one-to-one marketing.

CONCLUSION AND FUTURE RESEARCH DIRECTIONS

In conclusion, the Web supports more and more every day the potential and the current client in all phases of the buying process (perception of the stimulus, recognition of need, information search, comparison of alternatives, purchase and subsequent evaluation), as well as in all moments of the experience of consumption (Arnoul et al., 2004).

In fact, the network carries out the information function, and is a place of learning and sales; in the Web you can create and share content / information, then it becomes a "square" for listening and interaction, where you can live a true multimedia experience.

As a consequence, the Internet gives aid to the consumer during the entire decision-making process. At the beginning of the process, he/she can collect, without wasting time, energy or money, detailed, personalized and multi-dimensional information, also through electronic word of mouth. Such information will allow him/her to foretaste a future consumption experience, living very pleasant moments that affect expectations, future decision, perceptions and subsequent evaluation. This represents not only a way to anticipate the future consumer experience, but also a virtual and imaginary tour, a real pleasure in itself. Being able to live these experiences is really significant, especially for buyers of *hedonic products*, such as tourism, where the phase before the purchase is considered part of the consumer experience. It is, therefore, important for companies, especially those that offer these type of products, to enrich their Websites with multimedia highly sensory and engaging content, utilizing the support of sound, music, images, videos, photos, etc.

In addition, during the consumption experience, also thanks to applications for mobile technologies, the Internet can provide a valuable aid to the consumer in getting information and better enjoy the experience; just think of the possibilities offered to the tourist to be accompanied on a meeting and discovery journey through geo-localized tours. In this way, a technology application evolves from a purely informational and promotional tool, to a place of experiences and relationships. Moreover, during the experience, the consumer can already put feedback on-line, telling and commenting on various aspects.

In this way, in the Web 3.0 era companies can learn much more about their current and future target markets, creating interactive relationships, also very close, with their customers; they can learn the habits, tastes and preferences, even of small market niches, much better than in the past, creating very careful and elaborated forms of adaptation of supply and communication to the characteristics of the target audiences, up to customization. This enhances the satisfaction and loyalty of customers, through a continuous process improving and increasing direct contacts with the market.

Finally, the Web user can create stories and myths that can become the basis for targeted communication activities; in fact, while in the past communication was one-way, today the stories of the public can become the starting point of effective advertising campaigns, real tools of storytelling, if firms are able to adequately address and enhance the user-generated content (Sassoon, 2012).

Naturally there are control difficulties: companies often fear that Web users can circulate information spoiling their images and there is the problem of the reliability and authoritativeness of information sources, which are often anonymous and do not always provide verifiable information. In addition, some users have the fear of being somehow controlled and catalogued by site owners or other subjects that store information on carried out activities, browsers' behaviour interest topics and so on. Besides, the network is still for many a difficult territory to explore, with numerous sites, links and hyperlinks, augmented reality, social networks and other tools that are likely to lead to an excess of information. That creates in users worry, anxiety and uncertainty regarding achieved results. Such great abundance of information could, in some cases, cause confusion and carelessness on the part of the user; he/she, rather than having a support in purchasing decisions, becomes more uncertain and, far from being re-assured, perceives an increasing risk during the buying process. For this reason communication should be clear, enriching and easy to read, tools and languages must be suitable to specific audiences and the Web Marketing should be flanked by other, more traditional, marketing initiatives.

Businesses and marketers should see, however, as an opportunity and not a threat, the connection with the market achieved thanks to the Web 3.0; they need not to be afraid by the loss of control of the situation, on the contrary, they must try to create a more direct relationship with the public. Only if operators are ready to listen, the way to manage the contacts typical of old media will change to take into account the specificities of Web 3.0 and consumers will become interlocutors generous with information and feedback.

The Internet is changing and the transformation of the Web is affecting the economic and political organization of our society, together with consumers' behaviour, their attitudes and needs. The great revolution of Web 3.0 is the creation of new management and marketing systems based on collaborative relationships with customers, employees and other stakeholders by means of various networks (Garrigos-Simon, 2012).

Nevertheless, the concept of Web 3.0 is not entirely clear yet. It has not exactly shown what could really offer to the world of business, to individual companies, as well as to consumers and more generally to the public of Internet users. These are, therefore, future lines of research to be addressed in the light of what will be the evolution of the Web; in particular, it would be important to study the implications of marketing one-to-one communication on the future business strategies, to understand which opportunities it offers in addition to those already identified.

REFERENCES

Adams, R. L. (2013). *Web 3.0 startups: Online marketing strategies for launching & promoting any business on the web.* Create Space Independent Publishing Platform.

Almeida, F., Santos, J. D., & Monteiro, J. A. (2013). E-commerce business models in the context of web 3.0 paradigm. *International Journal of Advanced Information Technology, 3*(6), 1–12. doi:10.5121/ijait.2013.3601

Arnould, E., Price, L., & Zinkhan, G. (2004). *Consumers* (2nd ed.). New York, NY: McGraw-Hill/Irwin.

Autorità per le garanzie nelle comunicazioni. (2013). *Relazione annuale sull'attività svolta.* Roma.

Barassi, V., & Treré, E. (2012). Does web 3.0 come after web 2.0? Deconstructing theoretical assumptions through practice. *New Media & Society, 14*(8), 1269–1285. doi:10.1177/1461444812445878

Bickart, B., & Schindler, R. M. (2001). Internet forums as influential sources of consumer information. *Journal of Interactive Marketing, 15*(3), 31–40. doi:10.1002/dir.1014

Campbell, C. (2005). The romantic ethic and the spirit of the modern consumerism. London: WritersPrintShop.

Carbone, F., Contreras, J., Hernandez, J. Z., & Gomez-Perez, J. M. (2012). Open innovation in an enterprise 3.0 framework: Three case studies. *Expert Systems with Applications, 39*(10), 8929–8939. doi:10.1016/j.eswa.2012.02.015

Carù, A., & Cova, B. (2004). How service elements wrap the consumer's experience. The case of music consumption on the Auditorium of Milan. *Finanza Marketing e Produzione, 2*, 5–28.

Clawson, M. (1963). *Land and water for recreation: Opportunities, policies and problems*. New York, NY: Rand McNally.

Cova, B. (1995). Community and consumption: towards a definition of the "linking value" of products and services. In *Proceedings of the European Marketing Academy Conference ESSEC*. Paris: ESSEC.

Cova, B. (2003). *Il marketing tribale*. Milano, Italy: Il Sole 24 Ore.

Eftekhari, M. II., & Zeynab, B. (2008). *Web 1.0 to web 3.0 evolution and its impact on tourism business development*. Working paper.

Erragcha, N. (2014). Social networks as marketing tools. *British Journal of Marketing Studies*, *2*(1), 79–88.

Eurostat. (2013). *Statistics in focus*. Author.

Ferrari, S. (2012). *Marketing del turismo: Consumatori, imprese e destinazioni nel nuovo millennio*. Padova, Italy: Cedam.

Floridi, L. (2009). Web 2.0 vs. the semantic web: A philosophical assessment. *Episteme*, *6*(1), 27–37. doi:10.3366/E174236000800052X

Garrigos-Simon, F. J., Lapiedra Alcami, R., & Barbera Ribera, T. (2012). Social networks and Web 3.0: Their impact on the management and marketing of organizations. *Management Decision*, *50*(10), 1880–1890. doi:10.1108/00251741211279657

Hagel, J. III, & Armstrong, A. G. (1997). *Net Gain: Expanding markets through virtual communities*. Harvard, MA: Harvard Business School Press.

Hennig-Thurau, T., Gwinner, K. P., Walsh, G., & Gremler, D. D. (2004). Electronic word-of-mouth via consumer-opinion platforms: What motivates consumer to articulate themselves on the Internet. *Journal of Interactive Marketing*, *18*(1), 38–52. doi:10.1002/dir.10073

Hennig-Thurau, T., Malthouse, E. C., Friege, C., Gensler, S., Lobschat, L., Rangaswamy, A., & Skiera, B. (2010). The Impact of new media on customer relationships. *Journal of Service Research*, *13*(3), 311–330. doi:10.1177/1094670510375460

Hirshman, E., & Holbrook, M. (1982). Hedonic consumption: Emerging concepts, methods and propositions. *Journal of Marketing*, *46*(3), 92–101. doi:10.2307/1251707

Hoyer, W., Rajesh, C., Dorotic, M., Krafft, M., & Singh, S. (2010). Customer participation in value creation. *Journal of Service Research*, *13*(3), 283–296. doi:10.1177/1094670510375604

Jansson, A. (2002). Spatial phantasmagoria. *European Journal of Communication*, *17*(4), 429–443. doi:10.1177/0267323102017004201

Jennings, G., & Nickerson, N. P. (2006). *Quality tourism experiences*. Oxford, UK: Elsevier, Butterwoth-Heinemann.

Kim, W. G., Lee, C., & Hiemstra, S. J. (2004). Effects of an online virtual community on customer loyalty and travel product purchases. *Tourism Management*, *25*(3), 343–355. doi:10.1016/S0261-5177(03)00142-0

Kleemann, F., Vob, G. G., & Rieder, K. (2008). Un(der)paid innovators: The commercial utilization of consumer work through crowdsourcing. *Science. Technology & Innovation Studies*, *4*(1), 5–26.

Kotler, P., Kartajaya, H., & Setiawan, I. (2010). *Marketing 3.0: From products to consumers to the human spirit*. Hoboken, NJ: John Wiley & Sons, Inc. doi:10.1002/9781118257883

Krishnamurthy, S. (2009). Mozilla vs. Godzilla – The launch of the Mozilla Firefox browser. *Journal of Interactive Marketing*, *23*(3), 259–271. doi:10.1016/j.intmar.2009.04.008

Maffesoli, M. (1996). *The time of the tribes.* London: Sage.

McMillan, D. W. (1996). Sense of community. *Journal of Community Psychology, 24*(4), 315–325. doi:10.1002/(SICI)1520-6629(199610)24:4<315::AID-JCOP2>3.0.CO;2-T

Mistilis, N. (2012). Challenges and potential of the semantic web for tourism. *E-Review of Tourism Research, 10*(2), 51-55.

Morgan, M., Lugosi, P., & Ritchie, J. R. (Eds.). (2010). *The tourism and leisure experience.* Bristol, UK: Channel View Publications.

Normann, R. (1991). *Service management: Strategy and leadership in service business.* Chichester, UK: Wiley.

Noti, E. (2013, July). Web 2.0 and its influence in the tourism sector. *European Scientific Journal,* 115-123.

Pine, B., & Gilmore, J. (1999). *The experience economy: Work is theatre & every business a stage.* Harvard, MA: Harvard Business School Press.

Prahalad, C. K., & Krishnan, M. S. (2008). *The new age of innovation: Driving co-created value through global networks.* New York, NY: Mc Graw-Hill.

Preece, J. (2000). *Online communities: Designing usability, supporting sociability.* Chichester, UK: Wiley.

Rheingold, H. (1993). *The virtual community: Homesteading on the electronic frontier.* Reading, MA: Addison-Wesley.

Rincón, J. (2012). *XML y web semántica: bases de datos en el contexto de la web semántica.* Universitat Oberta de Catalunya.

Sassoon, J. (2012). *Web storytelling.* Milano, Italy: Franco Angeli.

Stamboulis, Y., & Skayannis, P. (2003). Innovation strategies and technology for experience-based tourism. *Tourism Management, 24*(1), 35–43. doi:10.1016/S0261-5177(02)00047-X

Stavrakantonakis, I., Gagiu, A., Toma, I., & Fensel, D. (2013). Towards online engagement via the social web. In *Proceedings of WEB 2013: The First International Conference on Building and Exploring Web Based Environments* (pp.26-31). Academic Press.

Tasner, M. (2010). *Marketing in the moment: The practical guide to using Web 3.0 marketing to reach your customer first.* Upper Saddle River, NJ: Pearson Education.

Tussyadiah, I. P., & Fesenmaier, D. R. (2009). Mediating tourist experiences: Access to places via shared videos. *Annals of Tourism Research, 36*(1), 24–40. doi:10.1016/j.annals.2008.10.001

Van Belleghem, S., Eenhuizen, M., & Veris, E. (2011). *Social media around the world 2011.* InSites Consulting. Retrieved 18-11-2011 from http://www.slideshare.net/stevenvanbelleghem/social-media-aroundthe-world-2011/download?lead=394fd930572c9b62fb082021a-f5a6d0922046ec4

Wang, Y., & Fesenmaier, D. R. (2004). Modeling participation in an online travel community. *Journal of Travel Research, 42*(February), 261–270. doi:10.1177/0047287503258824

Wang, Y., Yu, Q., & Fesenmaier, D. R. (2002). Defining the virtual community: Implications for tourism marketing. *Tourism Management, 23*(4), 407–417. doi:10.1016/S0261-5177(01)00093-0

We Are Social. (2014). *Global digital statistic.* Retrieved from http://wearesocial.net/blog/

Williamson, D. A. (2011), *Worldwide social network ad spending: a rising tide.* eMarketer.com. Retrieved 26-02-2011 from http://www.emarketer.com/Report.aspx?code=emarketer_2000692

Wright, R. K. (2010). Been there, done that: Embracing our post-trip experiential recollections through the social construction and subjective consumption of personal narratives. In M. Morgan, P. Lugosi, & J. R. Ritchie (Eds.), *The tourism and leisure experience* (pp. 117–136). Bristol, UK: Channel View Publications.

Zeithaml, V., Bitner, M. J., Gremler, D. D., & Bonetti, E. (2012). *Marketing dei servizi* (3rd ed.). Milano, Italy: Mc Graw Hill.

ADDITIONAL READING

Aguiton, Ch., & Cardon, D. (2007). The strength of weak cooperation: An attempt to understand the meaning of Web 2.0. *Communications & Stratégies*, *65*, 51–65.

Akyol, S. (2013). Social media and marketing: Viral marketing. *Academic Journal of Interdisciplinary Studies*, *2*(8), 586–590.

Almeida, F., & Oliveira, J. (2011). sustainable business models for Web 3.0". *Proceedings of* Bendapudi, N., & Leone, R.P. (2003). Psychological implications of customer participation in co-production. *Journal of Marketing*, *67*, 14–28.

Bettencourt, L. A., Ostrom, A. L., Brown, S. W., & Roundtree, R. I. (2002). Client co-production in knowledge-intensive business services. *California Management Review*, *44*(4), 100–128. doi:10.2307/41166145

Blackshaw, P., & Nazzaro, M. (2004). *Consumer-generated media (cgm) 101: word of mouth is the ace of the web-fortified consumer*. Intelliseek White Paper. From http://www.intelliseek.com/whitepaper

Brabham, D. C. (2008). Crowdsourcing as a model for problem solving an introduction and 87 cases. *The International Journal of Research into New Media Technologies*. From http://www.clickadvisor.com/downloads/Brabham_Crowdsourcing_Problem_Solving.pdf

Cameraro, C., & San Jose, R. (2011). Social and attitudinal determinants of viral marketing dynamics. *Computers in Human Behavior*, *27*(6), 2292–2300. doi:10.1016/j.chb.2011.07.008

Casoto, P., Dattolo, A., Omero, P., Pudota, N., & Tasso, C. (2008). Accessing, analyzing, and extracting information. From: User Generated Contents. Handbook of Research on Web 2.0, 3.0, and X.0, (pp.312-328).

Cena, F., Farzan, R., & Lops, P. (2009). Web 3.0: merging semantic web with social web. *Proceedings of the 20th ACM conference on Hypertext and Hypermedia*, 385-386. doi:10.1145/1557914.1558002

Cheung, M. F. Y., & To, W. M. (2011). Customer involvement and perceptions: The moderating role of customer co-production. *Journal of Retailing and Consumer Services*, *18*(4), 271–277. doi:10.1016/j.jretconser.2010.12.011

Cooke, M. (2008). The new world of Web 2.0 research. *International Journal of Market Research*, *50*(5), 569–572. doi:10.2501/S147078530820002X

Cooke, M., & Buckley, N. (2008). Web 2.0, social networks and the future of market research. *International Journal of Market Research*, *50*, 267–292.

De Vries, L., Gensler, S., & Leeflang, P. S. H. (2012). Popularity of brand posts on brand fan pages: An investigation of the effects of social media marketing. *Journal of Interactive Marketing*, *26*(2), 83–91. doi:10.1016/j.intmar.2012.01.003

Fuchs C., Hofkirchner W., Schafranek M., Raffl C., Sandoval M., & Bichler R. (2010). theoretical foundations of the web: cognition, communication, and co-operation. towards an understanding of Web 1.0, 2.0, 3.0". *Future Internet,* (1), 41-59.

International Conference on Project Economic Evaluation, 86-92.

Junghun, K., Choonseong, L., Byungun, K., & Youngjoon, C. (2007). Evolution of online social networks: a conceptual framework. Toronto, Canada: Canadian Center of Science and Education Dwivedi, Y., Williams, M., Mitra, A., Niranjan, S., & Weerakkody, V. (2011). Understanding advances in Web technologies: evolution from Web 2.0 to Web 3.0. ECIS 2011 Proceedings (Paper 257).

Knapp, D. (2012). *Peer-to-Peer, the Next Business Model?* From http://abcnews.go.com/Technology/story?id=98635&page=1

Lassila, O., & Handler, J. (2007). Embracing Web 3.0. IEEE Internet Computing, 11 (3), 90-93. From.10.1109/MIC.2007.52

Maurer, K. (2008). *Storytelling as a PR tool in the tourism industry.* Saarbrucken, Germany: VDM.

Naik, U., & Shivalingaiah, D. (2008). Comparative study of Web 1.0, Web 2.0 and Web 3.0".

Newson. A., Houthon, D., & Patten, J. (2009). *Bloging and other social media: exploiting the technology and protecting the enterprise.* Farnham, Englad: Gower.

O'reilly, T. (2007). What is web 2.0: Design patterns and business models for the next generation of software. *Communications and Strategies,* 1, 17. *Proceedings of International CALIBER* (pp. 499-507).

Report, N. O. (2009). *Social networks & blogs now 4th most popular online activity, ahead of personal email.* Nielsen Reports. From http://www.nielsen.com/us/en/insights/press-room/2009/social_networks___.html

Sabbagh, K., Acker, O., Karam, D., & Rahbani, J. (2011). *Designing the transcendent Web the power of Web 3.0.* New York, NY: Booz & Company Inc.

Taylor, D. G. (2010). *I speak, therefore I am: identity and self-construction as motivation to engage in electronic word of mouth.* University of North Texas.

KEY TERMS AND DEFINITIONS

Crowdsourcing: Is the externalization of a task or a function of an organization (i.e. the development of a product or the design of a advertising campaign) to a group of people via the Internet by means of an open call. It is a very cheap way to obtain help and innovative supports. It is not the only form of collaborative initiative born thanks to the Internet. Social

Media: Are digital entities that allow web users to create their own content, disseminate it, and receive in virtual communities and networks information of non-commercial nature about products / services, companies, brands. They are blogs, social networks, forums, newsgroups and communities, which represent independent information networks.

User Generated Content: Is a digital content created by web users; they can share it online with great ease and without the need for specific technical skills.

Virtual reality (VR): Is a simulated reality, a virtual simulation created through the use of the computer.

Web Marketing: Is a set of marketing activities that, through the Internet, allows the promotion of a company or a product, as well as the offering of services such as marketing, customer relationships, information services, etc. It also allows the creation of direct marketing strategies, which aim to maximize customer satisfaction and loyalty, as well as to facilitate the reaching of new markets with reduced costs.

Web 2.0: Is an evolution of the Word Wide Web in which the communication becomes two-way and users can generate their own contents to put them on the Web. It represents the birth of an interactive platform, in which you can share information and feedbacks. It is not a technological evolution but a new way to make and use web content.

Web 3.0: It is also called Semantic Web. Its main characteristic is that the interaction is between computers and the aim is to process large quantities of data and information to obtain targeted knowledge. It has three main charac-

teristics: to be ubiquitous, individualized, and efficient. The ubiquity is due to the possibility of being connected anywhere and in anytime. The individualized character refers to the information that is segmented and adapted to varied people and situations. The Web 3.0 is more an attitude than a technological evolution.

ENDNOTES

[1] Electronic utilities are 9 billion worlwide; 5 of these arc of new generation (broadband and digital television devices). Most of the utilities are represented by mobile lines (72% of total). In the last five years, mobile lines increased by 60% (Autorità per le Garanzie nelle Comunicazioni, 2013).

[2] Internet penetration in the world is 35%, social networking penetration is 26% and mobile penetration is 93% (Jan, 2014) (We Are Social, 2014).

[3] Zeithaml called it the *virtual servicescape* (Zeithaml, Bitner, Gremler & Bonetti, 2012).

Chapter 16

Characterizing the IT Artefact through Plato's Ontology:
Performance Measurement Systems in the Web 3.0 Era

Marie Marchand
Université du Québec à Trois-Rivières, Canada

Louis Raymond
Université du Québec à Trois-Rivières, Canada

ABSTRACT

Based on ontological principles enunciated by Plato more than 2300 years ago, yet at a time when Web 3.0 technology is seen to impact the management of organizations and especially the management of organizational performance, the authors propose in this chapter to characterize the IT artefact with an approach that returns the user perspective to the forefront. As an illustration, the Performance Measurement Systems (PMS) of 16 Small and Medium-Sized Enterprises (SMEs) are investigated and characterized from their users' perspective in terms of their specific attributes as systems dedicated to managing organizational performance in the Web 3.0 era. The variety of contexts and configurations of these systems is of particular interest while looking for the principles that underlie their empirical manifestations. Results provide a framework of reference for the characterization, design, and evaluation of IT artefacts that is applicable in particular within a Web 3.0 technological context.

1. INTRODUCTION

Calls have been made repeatedly to characterize and theorize IT artefacts in IS studies (Weber, 2003). While one is regularly reminded in the IS literature of the importance of the IT artefact and of its study as such (Kling & Scacchi, 1982;

Leonardi & Barley, 2008), there exists as of yet no theorization of this artefact that is grounded in practice (Orlikowski, 2010). And notwithstanding the fact that questions related to the IT artefact are recognized as the most relevant topics in the IS research domain (Whinston & Geng, 2004), one observes that "IT artefacts are either absent,

DOI: 10.4018/978-1-4666-8147-7.ch016

black-boxed, abstracted from social life, or reduced to surrogate measures" (Orlikowski & Iacono, 2001, p. 130). The need to refocus on the IT artefact, to consider it explicitly in its material and cultural presence in the organization, and thus to conceptualize and theorize this artefact has also been underlined by other IS researchers such as Agarwal & Lucas (2005).

There thus remains a need to conceptualize and theorize the IT artefact in order to identify its true nature and its true role in an organization so as to obtain practical implications in terms of systems design, use and management, and in terms of the organizational "fit" of this artefact, that is, the extent to which it answers the needs of the organization and the individuals that compose it (Strong & Volkoff, 2010). Preoccupations expressed by many in the IS field as to the nature of IT artefacts and as to their delimitation as objects of study thus reveal an epistemo-ontological problem with regard to these specific artefacts (Merrill, 2011), and also with regard to technological artefacts in general (Barley, 1998). Now, a return to the foundations of philosophical reflection from which scientific thought originated can provide solution paths to this problem. Inspired by the ontological principles enunciated by Plato 2370 years ago (Brisson, 2001; Fine, 1993), an approach meant to facilitate the characterization of IT artefacts is proposed in this chapter. Its interest lies in the fact that it returns the *user* to the forefront, it focuses on the *function* of the IT artefact, and it allows for the theorization of this artefact in the context of its use. And at a time when Web 3.0 technology is seen to impact the management of organizations and the management of organizational performance in particular (Garrigos-Simon, Alcamí & Ribera, 2012), such a characterization is meant to be especially applicable in this new technological context.

This approach was developed empirically through the study of a particular type of IT artefact, i.e. performance measurement systems (PMS). As these systems are highly contextualized because of their strategic nature (Marchand & Raymond, 2008), their study is meant to generate relatively generalizable and useful findings with regard to their characterization as IT artefacts in the Web 3.0 era. The rest of the chapter is structured as follows: We first present PMS and the IT characterization issues that relate to these systems. We then expose the ontological foundations of our approach and develop it in order to characterize the IT artefact. The methodology is described, followed by the results of applying the approach developed, as the PMS of 16 small and medium-sized enterprises (SMEs) in different industries are investigated and characterized. Follow the implications of these results for research and practice. The chapter ends with future research avenues and concluding remarks.

2. CHARACTERIZING PERFORMANCE MEASUREMENT SYSTEMS AS AN IT ARTEFACT

In the new global economy, many business enterprises must achieve "world-class" status (Cagliano & Spina, 2002), that is, a level of excellence such that they can compete on a world-wide basis. Focusing on organizational performance in a multi-dimensional manner, performance measurement systems (PMS) may be considered as means of reaching performance objectives. Considering their support role in both tactical and strategic decision making (Kueng, Meier & Wettstein, 2001), PMS are designed for executives, although not exclusively (Turban, Aronson, Liang, & Sharda, 2007). PMS can be used collectively by the managers of the organization (Kaplan & Norton, 1996). As internal systems, they have either been acquired as packaged software or developed for the specific needs of the firm (Sharif, 2002). As external systems, they are accessible in the form of external diagnostic tools (St-Pierre & Delisle, 2006) and are used on an *ad hoc* and discretionary basis. Moreover, PMS are among the organizational information systems that can now benefit from the advent of Web 3.0 technology (Cision, 2009), including systems to be developed for – and used in – the specific context of SMEs (Binsardi, Green, & Jackson, 2013; Castro, Putnik, Cruz-Cunha, Ferreira, Shah, & Alves, 2012).

In conjunction with the evolution of information technologies, including Web-based technologies, PMS can be enriched with new system functionalities that allow them to move beyond simple measurement by providing a more extensive and customised support for decision-making in the firm. Through this enrichment, PMS now play a more important role in the organization, extending beyond control toward support for continuous improvement and managerial development (Sinclair & Zairi, 2000). Emphasis is placed on their contribution to the definition, deployment and diffusion of strategy (Kaplan and Norton, 1996), to the alignment of operations with strategic objectives (Garengo, Biazzo, & Bititci, 2005), and to organizational learning (Kueng et al., 2001), while also supporting human resource management and competitive benchmarking (De Toni & Tonchia, 2001).

While certain efforts have been made to position PMS in relation to information systems (IS) in general (Kueng et al., 2001), there has been as-of-yet no attempt to study PMS on the basis of their characterization as information systems (Marchand & Raymond, 2008). While seemingly-related systems such as executive information systems (EIS) have been the object of past IS research (Bergeron, Raymond, Rivard, & Gara, 1995), these systems have evolved differently and thus cannot be assimilated to PMS (Marchand & Raymond, 2008). PMS differ from EIS mainly by their multi-dimensional perspective of the firm's performance, reflecting the interest of various performance stakeholders.

The PMS research domain faces an ontological problem in that the object of research, namely the PMS artefact, is lacking in a widely-recognised common definition (Franco-Santos, Kennerley, Micheli, Martinez, Mason, Marr, Gray, & Neely, 2007). Moreover, existing definitions of PMS are insufficient for an information artefact whose practice in organizations one wants to understand and eventually improve. This situation does not favour the exploration of PMS whose configurations differ from the "tried-and-true" (Neely, 2005). In empirical studies, there is a problem of specifying research variables when the object of whom the usage is studied has not been previously characterized in its essential dimensions (Alter, 2006). There is a need for theorizing PMS artefacts (Hudson, Smart, & Bourne, 2001) and for ways of characterizing PMS artefacts, as expressed by the following recurring question in PMS research: What are the specific attributes of these systems (Garengo et al., 2005)?

3. ONTOLOGICAL FOUNDATION

Ontological issues are not new in the history of mankind and have engendered reflections aiming to identify and name objects. As objects created by man, artefacts have been the subject of philosophical enquiry wherein the interest lies in studying both the intention from which they originate (expected utility) and their material characteristics (Kroes & Meijers, 2006; Thomasson, 2009). Given a renewal of interest in Plato's thought and a reinterpretation of his dialogues (Brisson, 2001), this philosopher's ontological questionings as well as his distinction between the sensible world and the intelligible world appear to us to have great relevance in that the idea of a "thing", its "intelligible form" (Pradeau, 2001), arises essentially from its function, and is accessible only by the experience of that thing, implying that the person who holds that knowledge is thus its user.

In Plato's Republic, many metaphors are employed to both highlight and illustrate the user's contribution to knowledge of the object, implying and contrasting three perspectives that can be taken with regard to it, namely the imitator's, the maker's and the user's perspective. In the following excerpt, the three perspectives, represented respectively by the painter, the craftsman, and the horseman, are proposed relative to two objects, a bit and reins:

A painter, we say, will paint reins and a bit. (…). But a shoemaker and a smith will make them. (…). Then does the painter understand how the reins and the bit must be? Or does even the maker not understand the smith and the leather-cutter but only he who knows how to use them, the horseman? (…). And won't we say that it is so for everything? (…). For each thing there are these three arts one that will use, one that will make, one that will imitate. (Book X, 601c, 601d)

Plato thus invites us to consider these three ontological perspectives, while insisting that only the user, through his or her experience of the object, get to know the true nature of this object, which is essentially related to its functions. Moreover, the maker depends, within his or her craft, on the user's knowledge and risks, without any contact with user, loosing his or her capacity to make a useful object (Leroux, 2002). Hence, within a pragmatic hierarchy of expertise, first there is "one who knows how to use », then "one who knows how to make", and finally "one who knows how to imitate" the object (Leroux, 2002). Using a flute as a case in point, Plato enjoins us as follows:

It's quite necessary, then, that the man who uses each thing be most experienced and that he report to the maker what are the good or bad points, in actual use, of the instrument he uses. For example, about flutes, a flute player surely reports to the flute-maker which ones would serve him in playing, and he will prescribe how they must be made, and the other will serve him. (…). Therefore the maker of the same implement will have right trust concerning its beauty and its badness from being with the man who knows and from being compelled to listen to the man who knows, while

the user will have knowledge. (…). Therefore, with respect to beauty and badness, the imitator will neither know nor opine rightly about what he imitates. (Book X, 601d, 601e, 602a)

In using Plato's flute as a metaphor for characterizing the IT artefact, one may recall that the power of metaphors to understand phenomena has been previously used and documented in IS research (Hirschheim & Newman, 1991; Madsen, 1994). In particular, metaphors are meant to "enable rich conceptualizations" and provide a better understanding of the social context in which IT artefacts are developed and used (Oates & Fitzgerald, 2007).

3.1 Plato's Ontological Perspectives and the IT Artefact

As opposed to common-sense natural objects, artefacts are objects whose existence depends upon human activity, both mental and physical, i.e. "they would not exist were it not for the beliefs, practices, and/or intentions of the human beings who make and use them" (Thomasson, 2009, p. 193). The "artefactual function" notion hence refers to the intended function of the artefact (Millikan, 1999). The ontological status proper to the artefact is thus conferred by its function (Baker, 2004). Ascertaining the proper ontological status of artefacts is crucial to understand their role as well as to determine the appropriate methods to study their function and to design the features that are relevant to this function (Thomasson, *op. cit.*).

One may think that it is thus for IT artefacts, i.e. that to understand their nature, one must understand their function, their *raison d'être*. The three perspectives highlighted by Plato could then allow us to determine the proper ontological positioning of the IT artefact. To do so, we can match a particular ontological position to each perspective and then associate to each position the various approaches used in IS research to study IT artefacts. We may then ascertain and possibly explain the strengths and weaknesses of each approach. As presented in Table 1, each the three perspectives of the object in Plato's ontology is described in terms of the ontological value it attributes to the object, its basis for conceptualizing the object, the variables considered by the research that takes this perspective, its basis for theorizing the object, and its implications for research and practice.

3.2 User's Perspective

From the user's perspective, priority is given to the object's functions as put into practice within the context of use. For Plato, it is the position nearest to the object because its *raison d'être* resides in the use of its functions. By his or her experience of the object, the user has a deeper knowledge of it, closer to its true nature.

Ontological value, basis for conceptualizing and variables. The ontological value of the object as conceived by the user can be qualified as explicit and direct, same as the maker's perspective. The user's perspective differs however in that it considers the IT artefact as used and as influenced by its use. One is thus in the presence of an empirical - as opposed to a theoretical - artefact whose conceptualization is founded upon a functional configuration, that is, functions of the artefact actually used, be it by the maker's design or emerging from the user's adaptations. IS studies that take this perspective can examine the IT artefact on its own and analyze its role in the emergence of phenomena by focusing on the attributes of this artefact that are mobilized by the user.

Theorization of the IT artefact. In taking the user's perspective, IS research looks at an empirical IT artefact in its organizational practice, that

Table 1. Perspectives emanating from plato's ontology for studying the IT artefact

	Imitator's Perspective	Maker's Perspective	User's Perspective
Ontological Value	- Implicit and indirect consideration of the IT artefact - Absent, reduced or approximated artefact	- Explicit and direct consideration of the IT artefact - Theoretical artefact	- Explicit and direct consideration of the IT artefact - Empirical artefact
Basis for Conceptualizing the IT Artefact	- Absent artefact - Generic configuration - Substitute configuration	Technological configuraton	Functional Configuration
Variables	- Absent - Sole "technology" variable - Variables from a substitute object	Technical features of the IT artefact	Attributes of the IT artefact mobilized by its use
Basis for Theorizing the IT Artefact	- Impossible if absent - Influence of the sole "technology" variable - Influence of the substitute object	- IT artefact and its technical features - Influence of the IT artefact and of its technical features	- IT artefact and the attributes mobilized by its use - Influence of the artefact and of the attributes mobilized by its use - Influence of the context of use on the artefact and its attributes
Implications for IS Research and Practice	- Limited understanding of the role of the IT artefact - No possibility of practical improvements	- Limited understanding of the role of the IT artefact *in situ* - Obsoleteness of practical implications	- Improved understanding of the role of the IT artefact - Possibility of practical improvements to the artefact and to its use

is, within a system of influences. Of particular interest will be the influences of use (through feedback) and context of use upon the artefact's configuration (modifications, emergence of new features to preserve usefulness), that is, the process of appropriation of the object by the user. One assumes here that the IT artefact is permeable to influences and that its characteristics can be both independent and dependent variables. The true nature of the IT artefact is thus revealed in its practice, through the user's experience, as it is the object's use that determines what it is and what it must be, that defines it above and beyond what had been planned by the maker. This last perspective is echoed in the IS literature by authors who advocate the explicit consideration of the IT artefact as an object of study, including its consideration as being part of an "ensemble" or as being "embedded" in a social context (Alter, 2003; Orlikowsky, 2010). In this view, both IT-related variables and other ensemble or context variables must be accounted for if one is to achieve a truer understanding of IS phenomena.

Implications. Taking the user's perspective allows IS researchers to study the evolution of the IT artefact in practice, in the form of a constant process of alignment, in order to broaden and deepen knowledge on the role played by this artefact in the organization. For instance, uses of the artefact that were unplanned by the maker can thus be identified, as well as the modifications to the original artefact made by the user following his or her usage experience. This last perspective maintains the focus on the *why* of the IT artefact's existence, on the needs of the users (including the evolution of these needs), and on *how* these individuals use and change such an artefact in a complex and dynamic social context (Orlikowski & Iacono, 2001). Implications for practice are thus centered on the object's usefulness, that is, on the functional evolution, "customization" or "tailorability" of the IT artefact, in collaboration with the maker, in order to optimize its use (Malone, Lai, & Fry, 1995; Orlikowski, 1995).

3.3 Theorizing the IT Artefact from the User's Perspective

Given the preceding considerations, theorizing the IT artefact from the user's perspective implies that this artefact must be considered in its specific context of use, profiting from the user's experience. The attributes of the IT artefact that are mobilized by this use form the basis for its theorization, including the artefact's definition, its decomposition into variables (conceptualization) and the inclusion of these variables in a theory or theoretical model.

To enact the user's perspective, each aspect of the theorization, that is, the definition of the IT artefact, its decomposition into variables and its theoretical inclusion will be illustrated through performance measurement systems (PMS). These systems constitute appropriately illustrative examples of IT artefacts because they are highly contextualized due to their strategic nature and must be aligned with organizational and managerial requirements (Kennerley & Neely, 2003; Franco-Santos et al., 2007).

3.3.1 Definition of the IT Artefact

Reflecting different trains of thought, many definitions of the IT artefact can be found in the IS literature, presenting this artefact more or less precisely, more or less technically and more or less inclusively of organizational and social elements. For instance, Benbasat and Zmud (2003, p. 186) define an IT artefact as "the application of IT to enable or support some task(s) embedded within a structure(s) that itself is embedded within a context(s). Here, the hardware/software design of the IT artifact encapsulates the structures, routines, norms, and values implicit in the rich contexts within which the artifact is embedded."

Defining a PMS as an IT artefact thus requires identifying it, circumscribing it, i.e. determining what is part of it and what is not. In this regard, Matook and Brown (2008) have noted that IS researchers often do not provide adequate definitions of the IT artefact studied. From the user's perspective, such a definition will emanate from the function of the IT artefact, and the characteristics considered will be those that render possible this function, that is, the artefact's *functional configuration*. Summarizing PMS notions can help us here to define the PMS artefact in terms of its focus and measurement framework, and in terms of its technological aspects.

Focus and measurement framework of PMS. The definition of performance within the PMS literature tend to be founded on the firm's strategic objectives (Kaplan & Norton, 1996), and to take into account the interests and expectancies of different stakeholders such as owners/ stockholders, customers, employees, suppliers, government, extending to society and future generations (e.g., Neely, Adams, & Kennerley, 2002). Accordingly, PMS must have the capacity to evaluate the organization in its entirety and to integrate all functions/dimensions in balance with the importance given to each (Nudurupati, Bititci, Kumar, & Chan, 2011). To reflect and support such an holistic, multidimensional, balanced and integrated perspective, PMS are based on frameworks (or model) of measurement proposed to practitioners, each putting forward a specific management perspective (e.g., Kaplan and Norton's Balanced Scorecard, 1992; Neely et al.'s Performance Prism, 2002). Ideally adapted to an organization's specific "performance logic", a PMS's performance measurement framework constitutes its conceptual foundation (Marchand & Raymond, 2008).

IS aspects of PMS. Made possible by advances in IT such as data-warehousing, data-mining, expert systems and other artificial intelligence technologies, and Web-based technologies and services, the initial data capturing-processing-communicating functionalities of PMS may be enriched to include tasks such as evaluation/ diagnostic, and recommendation of action plans (Sharif, 2002). PMS can be integrated with other organizational systems such as accounting information systems and enterprise systems (De Toni & Tonchia, 2001). A PMS includes various types of information outputs usually in the form of performance indicators (PI), meant to give a balanced view of performance (Lorino, 2001), i.e., quantitative/qualitative, results/determinants, operational/strategic, internal/ external. Indicators are often aggregated by performance dimension, or by strategic business unit (Fernandez, 2005). External benchmarks may also be included (Sinclair & Zairi, 2000).

3.3.2 Decomposition of the IT Artefact

To decompose the IT artefact into variables from the user's perspective, one first needs to know what attributes of this artefact are actually mobilized by its use. In this regard, Alter (2003) pointed out the importance of making a judicious choice of IT artefact variables in order to fully understand IS-related phenomena. Now one finds in the IS literature few attempts at identifying such variables. Already in 1992, DeLone and McLean had proposed a set of subconstructs and variables for the "information quality" and "system quality" constructs. Aiming to characterize executive information systems, Bergeron and Raymond (1992) also assembled a list of attributes culled from the literature. Later, in attempting to organize IT artefact variables, Matook and Brown (2008) proposed five dimensions (static–dynamic, adaptive–non-adaptive, synchronous–asynchronous, integrated–standalone, stateless–stateful), whereas Strong and Volkoff (2010) proposed two (coverage, enablement).

As well, structuring PMS notions in main themes can be useful in decomposing the IT artefact into its variables. We thus reviewed the literature to identify the various attributes required by PMS artefacts to accomplish their function, further classifying these attributes along the three dimensions proposed by Marchand and Raymond (2008), namely 1) alignment and scope,

2) management support sophistication, and 3) IT sophistication. Figure 1 present the formative model of the PMS artefact that emerged from this exercise. Such a characterization of an IT artefact, in this instance, is meant to represents the user's perspective when it is founded on the attributes that are actually used (Gable, Sedera, & Chan, 2008).

3.3.3 Theoretical Inclusion of the IT Artefact

The theoretical inclusion of the IT artefact requires its explicit incorporation as a full-fledged construct within a theory or theoretical framework, be it for purposes of analysis, explanation, prediction, or design and action (Gregor, 2006). From the user's perspective, this incorporation will be based on the attributes of the artefact that are mobilized by its utilization. As an integral part of a system of influences, the IT artefact and its characteristics become context-bound independent and dependent constructs. The user's perspective will also consider use itself and the effects of use, including effects on the artefact encountered and observed by the user, as in Benbasat and Zmud's (2003) nomological net whose aim is effectively to guide the theoretical inclusion of the IT artefact.

It is worth recalling at this juncture that the same IT artefact can have different uses and different impacts in different contexts (Kling & Scacchi, 1982). The mixed results of previous research

Figure 1. Formative model of the PMS artefact

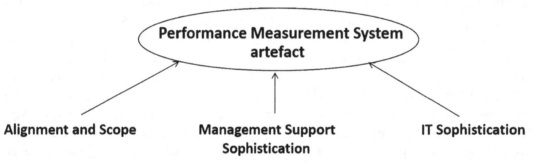

Performance Measurement System artefact

Alignment and Scope

1 Management Level
Operations level PIs
Production quality PIs
Production delays PIs
Strategic level PIs
Production flexibility PIs

2 Coverage
Prospective mgmt PIs
Organizational learning PIs
R&D PIs
Customer satisfaction PIs
Organizational climate PIs

3 Architecture
Functional PIs
Project management PIs
Process management PIs

Management Support Sophistication

4 Information Output
Graphic format
Qualitative measures

5 Organizational Role
Relative measures (ratios, gaps)
Allows for benchmarking
Shows cause-effect links
Shows operations-strategy links
Interprets contents
Formulates recommendations
Allows for scenario development

IT Sophistication

6 Access/Interface
Secured access
Customized interface
Access from outside
Interactivity of user interface

7 Integration
Horizontal integration
Vertical integration

PI: Performance Indicator

have been attributed, among other reasons, to the fact that the relationship between the IT artefact and its organizational impacts has been studied without considering the organizational context in which this artefact is deployed and used (Pinsonneault & Rivard, 1998). Thus many authors have recognized the importance of contextualizing the IT artefact in order to better understand its use and its effects on individuals, on groups and on organizations (Gregor, 2006; Orlikowski, 2010). The PMS artefact construct, as it is shown in Figure 1, is operationalized in this study through the three dimensions previously identified, each dimension aiming to capture a different aspect of the construct and the combination of the three meaning to define the construct (Petter, Straub, & Rai, 2007).

4. RESEARCH METHOD

The objective of characterizing an artefact implies the adoption of a perspective that respects the ontological value of the object to be studied. A positivist realist posture was adopted to favour the achievement of this objective (Strong & Volkoff, 2010), while at the same time taking into account the presence of the researcher *in situ* and its involvement (Miles & Huberman, 1994).

4.1 Research Design and Sampling

Contextualizing an IT artefact in space and time implies a trade-off between theoretical parsimony and explanatory power. The choice of a strategy combining depth and scope allows for taking into consideration the complexity of contexts while ensuring control of relevant variables (Robson 2002; Yin, 2003). To this effect, using a research strategy such as the multiple case study or "field study" in the sense of Stone (1978) and Boudreau et al. (2001) is appropriate, as it reduces dependence from the contexts and at the same time favours

the generalizability and transferability of results (Lee & Baskerville, 2003).

Sampling aimed to provide for a variety of contexts (Yin, 2003). The variety of contexts should involve a variety of configurations of these artefacts. Identification of potential firms had been previously done with the assistance of an industry association (Drucker-Godard, Ehlinger, & Grenier, 2003). Criteria had previously been set for the identification of the PMS artefact among the firm's organizational information system (OIS). To ensure the selection of firms with PMS meeting these criteria as well as to provide richness of experiences, phone calls and e-mails were carried on with the owner-manager before the interview. As a result, 16 SMEs (as defined by the European Commission, 2005), located in different regions of the province of Quebec, Canada, and showing a variety of contexts for the firms' size, age and industry were selected, as can be seen in Table 2.

4.2 Data Collection

Data collection was based on both structured and flexible methods, allowing for the management of a large number of different data types and their corroboration and triangulation (Boudreau et al., 2001).

Combining qualitative and quantitative approaches, extensive interviews were conducted *in situ* with the owner-managers of the firms. The owner-manager's influence in developing the SME's strategy and managing its performance is the key to informing these aspects (Spanos & Lioukas, 2001) and consequently to describe the artefact dedicated to measuring organizational performance. The interview was initiated with two open questions: What is your definition of the performance when it is about your firm? How and with what tools do you measure and manage this performance? A particular attention was given to dashboards in use. The notion of dashboard represents a succinct information presentation mode, based on the "cockpit" metaphor (e.g.,

Table 2. The 16 firms investigated

Firm ID	A	B	C	D	E	F	G	H
No. of empl.	16	43	70	39	135	250	55	65
Age of firm	30	17	28	30	32	43	35	13
Sector	Electronics /telecom.	Construction	Industrial equipment	Chemical	Industrial equipment	Chemical	Construction	Construction
PMS	different DBs: accounting/ cost, orders, production quality	organisation DB: accounting/ cost, sales, production	organisation DB: accounting/ cost, sales, HRM, production	organisation DB: accounting/ cost, sales, production	different DBs: accounting/ cost, CRM, HRM, production, engineering	organisation DB /ERP: accounting/ cost, sales, HRM, production	different DBs: accounting/ cost, orders	different DBs: accounting/ cost, clients, production
No. of empl.	75	130	96	524	25	40	23	15
Age of firm	34	30	25	65	31	18	17	47
Sector	Industrial equipment	Industrial equipment	Electronic /telecom.	Construction	Construction	Chemical	Industrial equipment	Construction
PMS	organisation DB/ERP: accounting/ cost, orders, HRM, production	different DBs: accounting/ cost, sales, HRM, production	organisation DB/ERP: accounting/ cost, sales, HRM, production	organisation DB: accounting/ cost, sales, production	organisation DB: accounting/ cost, sales, production	organisation DB: accounting/ cost, sales, HRM, production	organisation DB: accounting/ cost, sales, HRM	different DBs: accounting/ cost, orders

Legend: DB: database; ERP: enterprise resource planning; CRM: customer relationship management; HRM: human resource management.

Georges, 2002), where indicators to monitor and control the firm's progress are immediately captured through ergonomically designed graphics (Epstein & Manzoni, 1998).

To ensure a systematic capture of PMS artefacts attributes, a list of 38 characteristics was then presented to the owner-manager. Resorting to the list in the second part of the interview aimed to avoid biases that direct initial questions could introduce (Vandenbosch & Huff, 1997). This list had been built from the PMS literature review previously performed and validated through preliminary "in the field" activities. Its method was based on a tool developed and validated by Bergeron and Raymond (1992) for investigating EIS from a managerial perspective. Measures were taken to avoid any presumption of the presence or absence of characteristics, as well as to avoid giving the impression the interview was carried out for evaluation purposes.

PMS use was ascertained by adapting previous IS usage measures from the PMS literature (Bititci & Nudurupati, 2002; Bourne, Mills, Wilcox, Neely, & Platts, 2000). Five-point scales were used to measure the frequency of use in terms of the various usage purposes of a PMS. Given the diversity of the cases studied and in order to bring out the most significant results, these scales were dichotomized (Kanellis, Lycett, & Paul, 1998), thus establishing the regular or systematic presence of a specific form of use.

4.3 Data Analysis

Various methods were used for corroboration and triangulation purposes. Combined intra-site and inter-sites analyses were worked out (Miles & Huberman, 1994; Runkel, 1990). Intra-site iteration between the various types of data (annotated lists, verbatim transcriptions, post-interview notes, documents obtained from the interviewee) aimed to understand the internal logic of the site, and to validate data for the cross-site subsequent analysis. Inter-sites or cross-sites iteration aimed to clarify the dynamics and configurations of the different sites, as well as to clarify variables and to prioritize themes.

Usual qualitative data analysis methods were used, such as content analysis, coding, data reduction, synthesis around recurring themes, inter-sites matrices by theme (Yin, 2003). Items revealed unclear or misunderstood by interviewees were removed from the list of artefacts characteristics (Miles & Huberman, 1994). From the original list, 28 characteristics were retained for analysis purpose.

The data were first analyzed by using Runkel's (1990) method of relative frequencies. This method is based on the elementary calculus of probabilities, its objective being to find links between two variables or characteristics. It does so by verifying the independence of events, wherein the actual relative frequency (or proportion) of joint events is compared to the expected frequency if the events were independent of one another. In describing *variable-oriented* cross-case analysis methods, Miles and Huberman (1994) refer to Runkel's method as follows: "count cases", "do statistics", "look for clusters of conditions and actions", locate "densities of types of behavior." (p. 206). Cluster analysis and "exact" correlational analysis appropriate for small sample research were also used (Hoyle, 1999; Weerahandi, 1995).

5. RESULTS

5.1 Describing and Characterizing the PMS Artefact from the User's Perspective

Given the study's aim and the ensuing model of the PMS artefact (Figure 1), our first analytical task is one of description and characterization of this artefact from the user's perspective. Rich de-

scriptions of the 16 PMS artefacts were obtained. PMS descriptions were also obtained by means of the list handed out to the owner-managers in order to identify PMS attributes. Table 3 presents these results for the 16 PMS artefacts, ranked on the basis of the total number of attributes present per artefact.

One is first struck by the variety of PMS profiles. Indeed, the total number of attributes varies from 28, the maximum possible (P), to 7 (G). This variety of situations prevails within each of the three categories of PMS attributes, that is, "alignment and scope", "management support sophistication" and "IT sophistication" attributes. One then notes that the most frequent attributes, i.e. present in at least 14 of the 16 PMS, are related to measuring operations and production in a prospective manner (operations level PIs, production quality PIs, production delays PIs, prospective management PIs) and to measuring aspects pertaining to organizational functions (functions PIs). These attributes are for the most part in the alignment and scope category. Also present to the same extent are one management support sophistication attribute (relative measures) and one IT sophistication attribute (secured access). Less frequent attributes (present in less than half of PMS) belong to management support sophistication category and pertain to the organizational role of PMS (recommendations, scenarios development).

A closer examination reveals that even the less frequent attributes of alignment and scope category are present in most situations (10 of 16 PMS) as is the case, for example, for research and development PIs, clients' satisfaction PIs, and production flexibility PIs. Attributes of this category would allow for an extended and holistic scope in performance measurement that could be compared to what is recommended in PMS literature (e.g., Kaplan and Norton's Balanced Scorecard, 1992). Among the management support sophistication category, the most encountered attributes are mainly related to information output

Table 3. Attributes of the PMS artefacts

Dimension Attribute	PMS ARTEFACTS																Total
	P	F	M	C	Q	K	O	L	N	A	E	H	B	D	R	G	
Alignment and Scope																	
Operations level PIs	√	√	√	√	√	√	√	√	√	√	√	√	√	√	√	√	16
Production quality PIs	√	√	√	√	√	√	√	√	√	√	√	√	√	√	√		15
Prospective management PIs	√	√	√	√	√	√	√	√	√	√	√	√	√	√	√		15
Production delays PIs	√	√	√	√	√	√	√	√		√	√	√		√	√	√	14
Functions PIs	√	√	√	√	√	√	√	√	√	√	√	√		√	√		14
Strategic level PIs	√	√	√	√	√	√	√	√	√	√	√	√	√				13
Project management PIs	√	√	√	√	√	√	√	√		√	√	√		√			12
Organizational learning PIs	√	√	√	√	√	√	√	√	√	√	√						11
Process management PIs	√	√	√	√	√	√	√	√	√		√	√					11
R&D PIs	√	√	√	√	√		√	√	√		√	√					10
Production flexibility PIs	√	√	√		√		√	√	√		√	√			√		10
Clients satisfaction PIs	√	√	√	√	√			√		√	√			√	√		10
Organizational climate PIs	√	√	√		√	√	√	√	√	√	√						10
Total	13	13	13	11	13	10	12	13	10	10	13	10	4	7	7	2	
Management Support Sophistication																	
Relative measures (ratios, gaps)	√	√	√	√	√	√	√	√	√	√	√	√	√		√		14
Graphic format	√	√	√	√	√	√	√	√	√	√	√	√	√				13
Shows cause-effect links	√	√	√	√	√	√	√	√	√	√	√	√					12
Qualitative measures	√	√	√	√	√	√	√		√	√	√	√	√				12
Allows for benchmarking	√	√		√	√		√		√	√		√		√	√	√	11
Shows operations-strategy links	√	√	√	√	√	√	√			√		√	√				10
Interprets contents	√	√	√	√		√			√	√		√	√				9
Formulates recommendations	√	√	√	√						√		√					6
Allows for scenario development	√	√	√	√		√											5
Total	9	9	8	9	6	7	6	3	6	8	4	8	5	1	2	1	
IT Sophistication																	
Secured access	√		√	√	√	√	√	√	√	√	√	√	√	√	√	√	15
Customized interface	√	√	√	√	√	√	√	√	√				√	√		√	12
Access from outside	√	√	√	√	√	√	√	√	√		√		√			√	12
Horizontal integration	√	√	√	√	√	√	√	√					√	√			10
Interactivity of user interface	√	√	√			√	√	√	√				√			√	9
Vertical integration	√	√	√		√	√			√				√	√			8
Total	6	5	6	4	5	6	5	5	5	1	2	1	6	4	1	4	
Total	28	27	27	24	24	23	23	21	21	19	19	19	15	12	10	7	

quality (relative measures, graphic format, and qualitative measures). Less prevalent attributes, as indicated above, relate to the organizational role of PMS. Requiring a higher level of integration between the various PMS components, and thus important resource implications, these attributes are expected to be less present in SMEs given their resource constraints. Among the IT sophistication category, the most encountered attribute relates to security in accessing the PMS. This attribute is present in 15 of the 16 PMS. On the opposite, interactivity of the user's interface is the least encountered attribute of the category, present in 9 of the 16 PMS.

Considering cluster analysis as appropriate to classify IT artefacts by an orchestrating theme or profile, this technique was used to further characterize the observed PMS artefacts. This approach aims to group the artefacts into clusters such that each cluster's membership is highly homogeneous with respect to certain characteristics. Here, the characteristics (or clustering variables) are the seven components that form the PMS artefact construct (Figure 1), namely management level, coverage, architecture, information output, organizational role, access/interface and integration.

A four-cluster solution was found to be most parsimonious in identifying groups of PMS artefacts that could be clearly distinguished from one another, based on a meaningful pattern of relationships among the clustering variables. Table 4 presents the means of the seven clustering variables for each of the four PMS artefact profiles (clusters). In keeping with the small sample data analysis approach taken here, a comparison of mean frequencies within each cluster with the overall mean was used to evaluate the equality of variable means across the clusters and thus assess the distinctiveness of each derived cluster. Furthermore, this allowed an overall relative characterization of the four clusters along the three PMS artefact dimensions, that is, in terms of alignment and scope, management support sophistication and IT sophistication.

Returning to Table 4, one of the two clusters regrouping four PMS artefacts (B, D, G and R), was named *operational PMS*. These artefacts are characterized by a limited alignment level and scope, and limited management support sophistication. Enterprise D's OIS illustrates this, being composed of subsystems that cover the whole range of the firm's operations (accounting,

Table 4. Classification of the PMS artefacts on the basis of their attributes

Dimension Attribute (Range)	PMS Artefact Profile			
	Organizational PMS (C F M P)	Functional PMS (E K L N O Q)	Managerial PMS (A H)	Operational PMS (B D G R)
Alignment and Scope	high	high	average	low
Management level (2 – 5)	4.7	4.8	4.0	3.0
Coverage (0 – 5)	4.8	4.3	3.0	1.3
Architecture (0 – 3)	3.0	2.7	3.0	0.8
Mgmt Support Sophistication	high	average	high	low
Information output (0 – 2)	2.0	1.8	2.0	0.5
Organizational role (1 – 7)	6.8	3.5	6.0	1.8
IT Sophistication	high	average	low	average
Access/Interface (1 – 4)	3.5	3.5	1.0	2.8
Integration (0 – 2)	1.8	1.2	0.0	1.0

sales, inventory, and production) and that share a common organizational database. Each subsystem produces a daily dashboard for each manager concerned. From these dashboards, the owner-manager enters into his personal "consolidated" dashboard information relative to 15 PIs, in his own words, the "crucial information" that is the object of his daily monitoring. The monthly version of this last dashboard includes the detailed information relative to these indicators, as they are harmonized with ISO and industry association exigencies.

The other cluster comprised of two PMS artefacts (A and H), was labelled *managerial PMS*, as these two artefacts are characterized by a high level of management support sophistication. Their information processing capacity assures a more standard coverage of performance, and essentially aims at providing information that is easily usable by operational-level managers. These PMS show a low degree of IT sophistication however as their components are poorly integrated and there is thus frequent human intervention. For instance, enterprise A's OIS is comprised of independent systems that cover accounting, order entry and production. The chief executive manages on the basis of the reports provided by these systems and on a benchmarking of the firm's practices and performance provided annually by a diagnostic tool. This annual evaluation report constitutes the leader's performance management dashboard. The PMS (OIS and annual dashboard) is neither online nor accessible from outside the firm.

The cluster regrouping six PMS artefacts (E, K, L, N, O and Q) was named *functional PMS*. As these artefacts show a high degree of alignment and have a wide scope, they allow for a holistic measurement of performance, that is, both at the operational and strategic management levels, and both horizontally (organizational projects and processes) and vertically (organizational functions). In enterprise E's case, the OIS is comprised of independent systems that include sales and CRM, engineering and supply, accounting, HRM,

completed by employee and customer satisfaction surveys. Information is updated in real time and the various dashboards produced by these systems are presented to the owner-manager either weekly (orders, strategic products) or every two weeks (engineering, production, financial statements). The chief executive does not have a personal dashboard and works from the OIS dashboards that provide him with the ten PIs he considers to be "truly predominant".

The cluster comprised of four PMS artefacts (C, F, M and P), was labelled *organizational PMS*. These last artefacts are the ones that show high levels on all three PMS dimensions. Like the preceding cluster, they allow for a holistic measurement of performance (alignment and scope). This measurement is well-supported by systems that facilitate the comprehension and use of information (management support sophistication) and by state-of-the-art technology that requires no or very little human intervention (IT sophistication). More precisely, enterprise M has implemented an ERP system that assures the integration of transactions. It has also implemented an intranet-based organizational dashboard that is accessible to all personnel. This dashboard is fed by the ERP system with regard to accounting, HRM, sales/marketing and production, and from the enterprise database with regard to the strategic plan, various customer and employee surveys, market/competition analyses and other external information sources. The dashboard presents 45 PIs on one main screen, that is, "the indicators that are the most important at this juncture" in the words of the owner-manager. Each PI is hyperlinked to a page presenting its purpose, its action plan, its calculation method, its monthly results, its history and its weighting. Each PI has a "proprietor" who updates its results once per month. When the information originates from the ERP system, a single entry per indicator suffices and no human intervention is necessary. This organizational dashboard is accessible from outside the enterprise.

5.2 Validating the PMS Artefact from the User's Perspective

The second analytical task of this study is one of validation of the preceding characterization of the PMS artefact from the user's perspective, i.e. ascertaining that such a characterization is both relevant and useful with regard to PMS theory and practice. In order to do so, we must examine the relationship between this artefact and its usage in context. One basically aims here to determine whether characterizing an IT artefact from the user's perspective can help us to predict and explain the nature and extent of its use, and eventually help in prescribing its design.

The nature of PMS usage was defined through the five basic purposes for which managers are deemed to use these systems, as identified from the previous review of the PMS literature. Thus, PMS can be used by managers for purposes of continuous improvement (e.g. total quality management), operations management, strategic decision-making, strategic planning, and diffusion of strategy (to employees and other stakeholders in the firm's performance). The extent (or frequency) of this usage for each purpose can range from no use at all to systematic use. The relationship between the PMS artefact's seven attribute components and its five usage purposes is then ascertained through the correlation coefficients presented in Table 5.

The first results of note is that attributes characterizing the "alignment and scope" of the PMS artefact from the user's perspective, and "coverage" attributes in particular (e.g. organizational learning PIs), are strongly associated to the use of this artefact for strategic purposes, that is, for strategic decision-making, strategic planning and diffusion of strategy. In other words, the greater presence of such attributes or features in the design of the artefact favors such use. Secondly, "management support sophistication" attributes are seen to favor the use of PMS for strategic planning in general, with "information output" (e.g. qualitative measures) and "organizational role" (e.g. shows operations-strategy links) attributes respectively favoring strategic decision-making and the diffusion of strategy in particular. Thirdly, the PMS artefact's "IT sophistication" attributes are the only ones to enable the use of PMS for operations management purposes, with "access/interface" attributes (e.g. secured access, customized interface) also enabling strategic decision-making and the diffusion of strategy. Finally, none of the previously mentioned artefact attributes were seen to influence the use of PMS for continuous improvement purposes. Altogether, certain PMS attributes that characterize this IT artefact from the user's perspective are clearly seen to enable and influence certain of its uses.

To pursue and extend this line of analysis, the relationship between the four PMIS artefact profiles and the five usage purposes is ascertained through the relative frequencies presented in Table 6. Here, one first observes that the *organizational* PMIS artefact profile is strongly and positively associated to use in the form of planning and diffusion of strategy. For its part, the *functional* profile is strongly and positively associated to the use of the PMIS artefact for strategic decision-making, but negatively associated to its use for continuous improvement. Note that a negative relationship implies that certain attribute patterns inhibit rather than favor certain uses of the artefact. Moreover, the *managerial* profile is observed to inhibit PMIS use for operations management purposes. Finally, the *operational* artefact profile is seen to disfavor PMIS usage for strategic decision-making, strategic planning and diffusion of strategy purposes. Altogether, the attribute profiles that characterize the PMIS artefact from the user's perspective are clearly shown to influence the purpose for which – and the extent to which – this artefact is actually used.

Table 5. Relationship of the PMS artefact's attributes with its use

Dimension Attribute	Use of the PMS Artefact for:				
	Continuous Improvement	Operations Management	Strategic Decision-Making	Strategic Planning	Diffusion of Strategy
Alignment and Scope					
Management level	-.11	-.04	.31	.63**	.22
Coverage	-.24	.05	.35[a]	.73***	.41[a]
Architecture	-.07	-.32	.14	.72***	.36[a]
Management Support Sophistication					
Information output	-.21	-.27	.55**	.65**	.23
Organizational role	-.21	-.26	.27	.64**	.38[a]
IT Sophistication					
Access/Interface	.00	.41[a]	.68**	.00	.44*
Integration	.28	.44*	.26	.10	.11

Nota. Light-shaded cells indicate a significant relationship (exact Pearson correlation coefficient).
[a]$p < 0.1$ *: $p < 0.05$ **: $p < 0.01$ ***: $p < 0.001$ (one-tailed)

Table 6. Relationship of the PMIS artefact's profile with its use

PMIS Artefact Used For:	Organizational PMIS				Functional PMIS						Manag. PMIS		Operational PMIS				Total
	C	F	M	P	E	K	L	N	O	Q	A	H	B	D	G	R	
Continuous improvement	√	√	√	√		√	√		√	√	√	√	√	√	√	√	14
Operations management	√	√	√	√	√	√	√	√		√			√	√	√	√	13
Strategic decision-making	√	√	√	√	√	√	√	√	√	√		√	√		√		13
Strategic planning	√	√	√	√	√	√	√			√	√	√					11
Diffusion of strategy	√	√	√	√			√	√	√	√		√			√		10

Nota. Light-shaded cells indicate a positive relationship; dark-shaded cells indicate a negative relationship (relationships identified through Runkel's relative frequencies method).

6. IMPLICATIONS

6.1 Implications for Research on PMS

In regard to PMS, this study has attempted to fill a void in empirical knowledge (Neely, Gregory, & Platts, 1995). Whereas empirical descriptions of these systems are scarce and even the research community recognizes the critical need for a PMS definition (Franco-Santos et al., 2007), this study produces an empirical description of several PMS artefacts and brings out their inherent characteristics of systems dedicated to measuring and managing organizational performance. In regard to performance measurement systems in SMEs, this study will help to fill a gap between theory and practice (Hudson et al., 2001), whereas the inapplicability to small firms of conclusions provided by research on large corporations is recognized.

Whereas knowledge on the use of PMS in SMEs is still rather scarce (Bititci, Garengo,

Dörfler, & Nudurupati, 2012), this research provides evidence to show that SMEs develop a PMS that is aligned with their specific needs, and that owner-managers are closely involved. Moreover, while much remains to be learned on the actual use of PMS, given the few empirical investigations of this issue that have been made up to now, our work has generated knowledge on the reasons for which different types of PMS are used, and on the influence of the PMS artefact's configuration or design upon this use.

6.2 Implications for Research on Organizational IT Artefacts

In regard to organizational IT in general, this research provides an empirical description of an artefact that is of strategic importance for the modern enterprise. In the IS field, research is animated by the same questions that have guided our work, while repeated appeals are launched for a theorization of the artefact, essential to the development of the discipline (Benbasat & Zmud, 2003). Thus our work contributes to the resolution of the ontological problems that arise when one seeks to study the IT artefact in its context of use, 1) by providing a structuring approach to the characterization of the IT artefact and 2) by valuing the user's perspective of the IT artefact.

Characterization of the IT artefact. Starting with a tridimensional formative model of the PMS artefact, we have developed an approach to circumscribe this artefact in its context of use and to identify its variables. A first contribution here is that this approach extends the basis for comparison of IT artefacts with regard to their essential characteristics, structuring this comparison in the process and rendering it more transparent. Furthermore, this approach allows for a greater control of IT artefact variables in relational analyses, including analyses of the influence of specific contextual elements upon the IT artefact and analyses of the influence of the IT artefact upon use and the impacts of use. To this effect, our approach can

be combined with existing IS research models designed to study the IT artefacts in context, that is, by adapting and applying previously validated models focusing on system quality and information quality, such as the DeLone and McLean's IS success model (1992). Figure 2 presents an adaptation of this model, allowing for a contextualisation based on the artefact's characteristics and on the tasks to be performed with the support of the artefact, as actually used in organizations (DeLone & McLean, 2003; Rai et al., 2002). This would allow for a better understanding of usage problems that are specific to an organizational IT artefact and would provide actionable insights in proposing appropriate solutions to these problems.

Valuing the user's perspective. Taking the user's perspective to study the IT artefact, i.e. describing it as it is truly used as was done in this study, *de facto* incorporates in good part this artefact's context of use. In so doing, we concur with Strong and Volkoff's (2010) recommendation to take into account the "latent elements" associated with the social nature of the IT artefact. Following Kling and Scacchi (1982), our approach can also facilitate access to the IT artefact as defined or redefined over time by the user to insure its proper functioning in a specific and evolving context. Finally, by characterizing and documenting the IT artefact from the user's perspective, IS researchers can avoid the conceptual fracture that can happen when one attempts to link a theoretical artefact or an approximated artefact (through proxies) to empirically observed uses and impacts.

Ontological positioning. In the end, this study could offer to IS researchers the opportunity to clarify the ontological positioning of their work and thus provide greater coherence to their research design. Eventually, this could also facilitate the aggregation of research studies on the IT artefact into an integrated body of work. With ontological foundations that are known and can thus be shared, comparison between studies can be made more easily and the resulting knowledge of the phenomenon under study can be deepened.

Figure 2. PMS artefact research model adapted from DeLone and McLean's (2003) IS success model

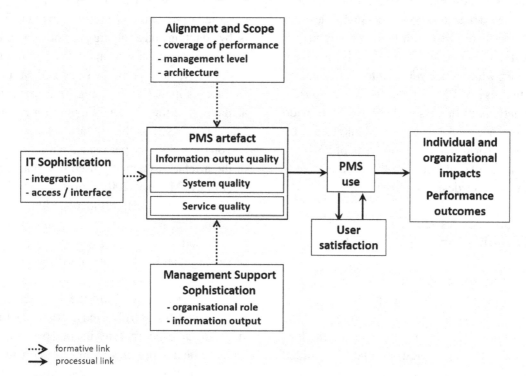

6.3 Implications for Practice: PMS Design and Evaluation

This study has some implications for owner-managers of manufacturing SMEs and for those whose mission is to provide assistance to these firms. Its results provide an empirical basis for PMS design and evaluation that is coherent of the particular context of such firms. PMS designers in SMEs may find useful to resort to the empirical description of PMS artefacts provided, for system aspects and for information output. Our results can also guide the evaluation and improvement of existing artefacts. While performing this study, we noticed the lack of benchmarks available to guide the owner-manager in decision making about the PMS artefact. Indeed, when interviews were carried on, the interviewees showed a keen interest in the list of attributes, pointing out the missing components in their system. This interest is reflected in the literature while many advocate

the benchmark of PMS artefact attributes (e.g., Bititci, Turner, & Begemann, 2000; Kennerley & Neely, 2003). Furthermore, PMS designers may now incorporate Web 3.0 technology to provide the "agile data, information and analytics capabilities" required by these systems (Delen & Demirkan, 2013, p. 359).

7. FUTURE RESEARCH AND CONCLUSION

Research on PMS will help to develop performance measurement systems that are appropriate to the specific needs of SMEs. Calls have been made in IS research to adequately identify the IS artefacts that are studied as to their design, implementation and use. Empirical research on PMS thus must continue for these firms, in response to the issues raised by many. For example, our results show that some attributes are common across firms and that others seem more related to the peculiarities of each one. To this effect, a classification framework that is focused on such artefacts becomes an indispensable theoretical and empirical tool, be it for the study of PMS as well as the study of IS in general. The classification scheme used for structuring our approach could be useful to further studies aiming to determine, for instance, classes of artefacts based on specific characteristics, and aligned on specific organizational and business environments. Also, a more precise characterization of PMS becomes even more important, given the great diversity of such systems brought about by the rapid evolution of the IT and network infrastructures that enable them.

As reported in Plato's Republic, Socrates uses the metaphor of the flute to illustrate that the idea of a thing, its "intelligible form" (ουσια), arises mainly from its function, and is accessible only by experiencing that thing. The metaphor of the flute as used by Plato reminds us of the importance of focusing on the artefact and to do so from the perspective of the user. It is by the use of a PMS that one understands its "essence", and it is the user who has the best understanding of it. Describing the IS artefact from the user's perspective has the advantage of putting the emphasis on the characteristics that matter for the user in a specific context of use, that is to say for PMS, the management and measurement of organizational performance, rather than putting the emphasis on characteristics provided by software vendors.

Presented following the user's perspective, our results have outlined the key attributes of PMS artefacts in SMEs. They focus on the characteristics known by the user, those who play an important role in his or her use of the artefact, those relevant to his or her tasks. Moreover, this approach can reveal features that software vendors would not even imagine. Ideally, the knowledge of the designer is subordinate to that of the user for designing artefacts consistent with their function within the organization, artefacts that are also dynamic, and whose usefulness and relevance are maintained throughout the changing needs and contexts. This implies a constant exchange between the user and the designer. It is a matter of particular strategic importance for IT artefacts such as PMS and ERP whose business value depends on their alignment with the strategic objectives and requirements of the organization.

REFERENCES

Agarwal, R., & Lucas, H. C. Jr. (2005). The information systems identity crisis: Focusing on high-visibility and high-impact research. *Management Information Systems Quarterly*, *29*(3), 381–398.

Alter, S. (2003). 18 reasons why IT-reliant work systems should replace 'the IT artifact' as the core subject matter of the IS field. *Communications of the Association for Information Systems*, *12*(23), 366–395.

Alter, S. (2006). Work systems and IT artifacts - Does the definition matter? *Communications of the Association for Information Systems*, *17*(14), 299–313.

Baker, L. R. (2004). The ontology of artifacts. *Philosophical Explorations*, *7*(2), 99–112. doi:10.1080/13869790410001694462

Barley, S. R. (1998). What can we learn from the history of technology? *Journal of Engineering and Technology Management*, *15*(4), 237–255. doi:10.1016/S0923-4748(98)00016-2

Benbasat, I., & Zmud, R. W. (2003). The identity crisis within the IS discipline: Defining and communicating the discipline's core properties. *Management Information Systems Quarterly*, *27*(2), 183–194.

Bergeron, F., & Raymond, L. (1992). Evaluation of EIS from a managerial perspective. *Information Systems Journal*, *2*(1), 45–60. doi:10.1111/j.1365-2575.1992.tb00066.x

Bergeron, F., Raymond, L., Rivard, S., & Gara, M.-F. (1995). Determinant of EIS use: Testing a behavioral model. *Decision Support Systems*, *14*(2), 131–146. doi:10.1016/0167-9236(94)00007-F

Binardi, A. P., Green, J., & Kackson, G. (2013). Exploring the impact of a company's web technological development on its innovation activity: A case study of small- and medium-sized enterprises (SMEs) in North Wales. *Global Business Perspectives*, *1*(4), 488–514. doi:10.1007/s40196-013-0023-6

Bititci, U. S., Garengo, P., Dörfler, V., & Nudurupati, S. (2012). Performance measurement: Challenges for tomorrow. *International Journal of Management Reviews*, *14*(3), 305–327. doi:10.1111/j.1468-2370.2011.00318.x

Bititci, U. S., & Nudurupati, S. S. (2002). Using performance measurement to drive continuous improvement. *Manufacturing Engineering*, *81*(5), 230–235. doi:10.1049/me:20020506

Bititci, U. S., Turner, T., & Begemann, C. (2000). Dynamics of performance measurement systems. *International Journal of Operations & Production Management*, *20*(6), 692–704. doi:10.1108/01443570010321676

Boudreau, M.-C., Gefen, D., & Straub, D. W. (2001). Validation in information systems research: A state-of-the-art assessment. *Management Information Systems Quarterly*, *25*(1), 1–16. doi:10.2307/3250956

Bourne, M., Mills, J., Wilcox, M., Neely, A., & Platts, K. (2000). Designing, implementing and updating performance measurement systems. *International Journal of Operations & Production Management*, *20*(7), 754–771. doi:10.1108/01443570010330739

Brisson, L. (2001). Comment rendre compte de la participation du sensible à l'intelligible chez Platon? In J.-F. Pradeau (Ed.), *Platon: Les formes intelligibles* (pp. 55–85). Paris: Presses Universitaires de France.

Cagliano, R., & Spina, G. (2002). A comparison of practice-performance models between small manufacturers and subcontractors. *International Journal of Operations & Production Management*, *22*(12), 1367–1388. doi:10.1108/01443570210452057

Castro, H., Putnik, G., Cruz-Cunha, M. M., Ferreira, L., Shah, V., & Alves, C. (2012). Meta-organization and manufacturing web 3.0 for ubiquitous virtual enterprise of manufacturing SMEs: A framework. In *Proceedings of the 8th CIRP Conference on Intelligent Computation in Manufacturing Engineering*. Ischia, Italy: Elsevier Procedia.

Cision. (2009). *What "web 3.0" will mean to you.* Cision Executive White Paper. Chicago: Cision US. Retrieved from http://us.cision.com/assets/ whitepapers/ Cision_Whitepaper_Web3.pdf

De Toni, A., & Tonchia, S. (2001). Performance measurement systems – Models, characteristics and measures. *International Journal of Operations & Production Management*, *21*(1-2), 46–70. doi:10.1108/01443570110358459

Delen, D., & Demirkan, H. (2013). Data, information and analytics as services. *Decision Support Systems*, *55*(1), 359–363. doi:10.1016/j.dss.2012.05.044

DeLone, W. H., & McLean, E. R. (1992). Information systems success: The quest for the dependent variable. *Information Systems Research*, *3*(1), 60–95. doi:10.1287/isre.3.1.60

DeLone, W. H., & McLean, E. R. (2003). The DeLone and McLean model of information systems success: A ten-year update. *Journal of Management Information Systems, 19*(4), 9–30.

Drucker-Godard, C., Ehlinger, S., & Grenier, C. (2003). Validité et fiabilité de la recherche. In R.-A. Thiétart (Ed.), *Méthodes de recherche en management* (pp. 257–287). Paris: Dunod.

Epstein, M., & Manzoni, J. F. (1998). Implementing corporate strategy: From tableaux de bord to balanced scorecards. *European Management Journal, 16*(2), 190–203. doi:10.1016/S0263-2373(97)00087-X

European Commission. (2005). *The new SME definition – User guide and model declaration.* Brussels: Enterprise and Industry Publications.

Fernandez, A. (2005). *Les nouveaux tableaux de bord des managers: Le projet décisionnel dans sa totalité* (3rd ed.). Paris: Éditions d'Organisation.

Fine, G. (1993). *On ideas: Aristotle's criticism of Plato's theory of forms.* Oxford, UK: Clarendon Press.

Franco-Santos, M., Kennerley, M., Micheli, P., Martinez, V., Mason, S., Marr, B., & Neely, A. et al. (2007). Towards a definition of a business performance measurement system. *International Journal of Operations & Production Management, 27*(8), 784–801. doi:10.1108/01443570710763778

Gable, G. G., Sedera, D., & Chan, T. (2008). Reconceptualizing information systems success: The IS-impact measurement model. *Journal of the Association for Information Systems, 9*(7), 377–408.

Garengo, P., Biazzo, S., & Bititci, U. S. (2005). Performance measurement systems in SMEs: A review for a research agenda. *International Journal of Management Reviews, 7*(1), 25–47. doi:10.1111/j.1468-2370.2005.00105.x

Garrigos-Simon, F. J., Alcamí, R. L., & Ribera, T. B. (2012). Social networks and Web 3.0: Their impact on the management and marketing of organizations. *Management Decision, 50*(10), 1880–1890. doi:10.1108/00251741211279657

Georges, P. M. (2002). *Le management cockpit: Des tableaux de bord qui vont à l'essentiel.* Paris: Éditions d'Organisation.

Gregor, S. (2006). The nature of theory in information systems. *Management Information Systems Quarterly, 30*(3), 611–642.

Hirschheim, R., & Newman, M. (1991). Symbolism and information systems development: Myth, metaphor and magic. *Information Systems Research, 2*(1), 29–62. doi:10.1287/isre.2.1.29

Hoyle, R. H. (1999). *Statistical strategies for small sample research.* Thousand Oaks, CA: Sage Publications.

Hudson, M., Smart, A., & Bourne, M. (2001). Theory and practice in SME performance measurement systems. *International Journal of Operations & Production Management, 21*(8), 1096–1115. doi:10.1108/EUM0000000005587

Kanellis, P., Lycett, M., & Paul, R. J. (1998). An interpretive approach to the measurement of information systems success. In E. J. Garrity & G. L. Sanders (Eds.), *Information systems success measurement* (pp. 133–151). Hershey, PA: Idea Group.

Kaplan, R. S., & Norton, D. P. (1992). The balanced scorecard – Measures that drive performance. *Harvard Business Review, 70*(1), 71–79. PMID:10119714

Kaplan, R. S., & Norton, D. P. (1996). *The balanced scorecard.* Boston: Harvard Business School Press.

Kennerley, M., & Neely, A. (2003). Measuring performance in a changing business environment. *International Journal of Operations & Production Management, 23*(2), 213–229. doi:10.1108/01443570310458465

Kling, R., & Scacchi, W. (1982). The web of computing: Computer technology as social organization. *Advances in Computers, 21*, 1–90. doi:10.1016/S0065-2458(08)60567-7

Kroes, P. A., & Meijers, A. W. M. (2006). Introduction: The dual nature of technical artefacts. *Studies in History and Philosophy of Science, 37*(1), 1–4. doi:10.1016/j.shpsa.2005.12.001 PMID:16473265

Kueng, P., Meier, A., & Wettstein, T. (2001). Performance measurement systems must be engineered. *Communications of the Association for Information Systems, 7*, 1-27.

Lee, A. S., & Baskerville, R. L. (2003). Generalizing generalizability in information systems research. *Information Systems Research, 14*(3), 221–243. doi:10.1287/isre.14.3.221.16560

Leonardi, P. M., & Barley, S. R. (2008). Materiality and change: Challenges to building better theory about technology and organizing. *Information and Organization, 18*(3), 159–176. doi:10.1016/j.infoandorg.2008.03.001

Leroux, G. (2002). *Platon, la république, traduction inédite, introduction et notes*. Paris: Flammarion.

Lorino, P. (2001). *Méthodes et pratiques de la performance: Le pilotage par les processus et les compétences* (2nd ed.). Paris: Éditions d'Organisation.

Madsen, K. H. (1994). A guide to metaphorical design. *Communications of the ACM, 37*(12), 57–62. doi:10.1145/198366.198381

Malone, T. W., Lai, K. Y., & Fry, C. (1995). Experiments with oval: A radically tailorable tool for cooperative work. *ACM Transactions on Information Systems, 13*(2), 177–205. doi:10.1145/201040.201047

Marchand, M., & Raymond, L. (2008). Researching performance measurement systems: An information systems perspective. *International Journal of Operations & Production Management, 28*(7), 663–686. doi:10.1108/01443570810881802

Matook, S., & Brown, S. A. (2008). Conceptualizing the IT artifact for MIS research. In *Proceedings of ICIS 2008*. Paris: ICIS.

Merrill, G. H. (2011). Ontology, ontologies, and science. *Topoi, 30*(1), 71–83. doi:10.1007/s11245-011-9091-x

Miles, M. B., & Huberman, A. M. (1994). *Qualitative data analysis - An expanded sourcebook* (2nd ed.). Thousand Oaks, CA: Sage.

Millikan, R. G. (1999). Historical kinds and the "special sciences". *Philosophical Studies, 95*(1-2), 45–65. doi:10.1023/A:1004532016219

Neely, A. (2005). The evolution of performance measurement research. *International Journal of Operations & Production Management, 25*(12), 1264–1277. doi:10.1108/01443570510633648

Neely, A., Adams, C., & Kennerley, M. (2002). *The performance prism: The scorecard for measuring and managing business success*. London: Financial Times Prentice Hall.

Neely, A., Gregory, M., & Platts, K. (1995). Performance measurement system design: A literature review and research agenda. *International Journal of Operations & Production Management, 15*(4), 80–116. doi:10.1108/01443579510083622

Nudurupati, S. S., Bititci, U. S., Kumar, V., & Chan, F. T. S. (2011). State of the art literature review on performance measurement. *Computers & Industrial Engineering, 60*(2), 279–290. doi:10.1016/j.cie.2010.11.010

Oates, B. J., & Fitzgerald, B. (2007). Multimetaphor method: Organizational metaphors in information systems development. *Information Systems Journal, 17*(4), 421–449. doi:10.1111/j.1365-2575.2007.00266.x

Orlikowski, W. J. (2010). The sociomateriality of organisational life: Considering technology in management research. *Cambridge Journal of Economics, 34*(1), 125–141. doi:10.1093/cje/bep058

Orlikowski, W. J., & Iacono, C. S. (2001). Research commentary: Desperately seeking the "IT" in IT research - A call to theorizing the IT artefact. *Information Systems Research, 12*(2), 121–134. doi:10.1287/isre.12.2.121.9700

Orlikowski, W. J., Yates, J. A., Okamura, K., & Fujimoto, M. (1995). Shaping electronic communication: The metastructuring of technology in the context of use. *Organization Science, 6*(4), 423–444. doi:10.1287/orsc.6.4.423

Petter, S., Straub, D. W., & Rai, A. (2007). Specifying formative constructs in information systems research. *Management Information Systems Quarterly, 31*(4), 623–656.

Pinsonneault, A., & Rivard, S. (1998). Information technology and the nature of managerial work: From the productivity paradox to the Icarus paradox? *Management Information Systems Quarterly, 22*(3), 287–311. doi:10.2307/249667

Plato. (1991). The Republic (2nd ed.). (A. Bloom, Trans.). Basic Books.

Pradeau, J.-F. (2001). Les formes et les réalités intelligibles. In J.-F. Pradeau (Ed.), Platon: les formes intelligibles (pp. 17-54). Paris: Presses Universitaires de France.

Rai, A., Lang, S. S., & Welker, R. B. (2002). Assessing the validity of the IS success model: An empirical test and theoretical analysis. *Information Systems Research, 13*(1), 50–69. doi:10.1287/isre.13.1.50.96

Robson, C. (2002). *Real world research* (2nd ed.). Oxford, UK: Blackwell Publishers.

Runkel, P. J. (1990). *Casting nets and testing specimens: Two grand methods of psychology.* New York: Praeger.

Sharif, A. M. (2002). Benchmarking performance management systems. *Benchmarking: An International Journal, 9*(1), 62–85. doi:10.1108/14635770210418588

Sinclair, D., & Zairi, M. (2000). Performance measurement: A critical analysis of the literature with respect of total quality management. *International Journal of Management Reviews, 2*(2), 145–168. doi:10.1111/1468-2370.00035

Spanos, Y. E., & Lioukas, S. (2001). An examination into the causal logic of rent generation: Contrasting Porter's competitive strategy framework and the resource-based perspective. *Strategic Management Journal, 22*(10), 907–934. doi:10.1002/smj.174

St-Pierre, J., & Delisle, S. (2006). An expert diagnosis system for the benchmarking of SMEs' performance. *Benchmarking: An International Journal, 13*(1/2), 106–119. doi:10.1108/14635770610644619

Stone, E. (1978). *Research methods in organizational behavior.* Santa Monica, CA: Goodyear Publishing Company.

Strong, D. M., & Volkoff, O. (2010). Understanding organization-enterprise system fit: A path for theorizing the information technology artifact. *Management Information Systems Quarterly, 34*(4), 731–756.

Thomasson, A. L. (2009). Artifacts in metaphysics. In Handbook of philosophy of the technological sciences (pp. 191-197). Elsevier Science.

Turban, E., Aronson, J. E., Liang, T.-P., & Sharda, R. (2007). *Decision support and business intelligence systems* (8th ed.). Upper Saddle River, NJ: Pearson Prentice Hall.

Vandenbosch, B., & Huff, S. L. (1997). Searching and scanning: How executives obtain information from executive information systems. *Management Information Systems Quarterly*, *21*(1), 81–107. doi:10.2307/249743

Weber, R. (2003). Still desperately seeking the IT artefact. *Management Information Systems Quarterly*, *27*(2), iii–xi.

Weerahandi, S. (1995). *Exact statistical methods for data analysis*. New York: Springer-Verlag. doi:10.1007/978-1-4612-0825-9

Whinston, A. B., & Geng, X. (2004). Operationalizing the essential role of the information technology artifact in information systems research: Gray area, pitfalls, and the importance of strategic ambiguity. *Management Information Systems Quarterly*, *28*(2), 149–159.

Yin, R. K. (2003). *Case study research: Design and methods* (3rd ed.). Thousand Oaks, CA: Sage.

ADDITIONAL READING

Angel, R., & Rampersad, H. (2005). Do scorecards add up? *CA Magazine*, *138*(4), 30–35.

Aspelund, A., & Moen, O. (2005). Small international firms: Typology, performance and implications. *Management International Review*, *45*(3), 37–57.

Assiri, A., Zairi, M., & Eid, R. (2006). How to profit from the balanced scorecard: An implementation roadmap. *Industrial Management & Data Systems*, *106*(7), 937–952. doi:10.1108/02635570610688869

Bourne, M., Pavlov, A., Franco-Santos, M., Lucianetti, L., & Mura, M. (2013). Generating organizational performance: The contributing effects of performance measurement and human resource management practices. *International Journal of Operations & Production Management*, *33*(11/12), 1599–1622. doi:10.1108/IJOPM-07-2010-0200

Busco, C., Giovannoni, E., & Scapens, R. W. (2008). Managing the tensions in integrating global organisations: The role of performance management systems. *Management Accounting Research*, *19*(2), 103–125. doi:10.1016/j.mar.2008.02.001

Busi, M., & Bititci, U. S. (2006). Collaborative performance management: Present gaps and future research. *International Journal of Productivity and Performance Management*, *55*(1), 7–25. doi:10.1108/17410400610635471

Cagliano, R., Blackmon, K., & Voss, C. (2001). Small firms under microscope: International differences in production/operations management practices and performance. *Integrated Manufacturing Systems*, *12*(7), 469–482. doi:10.1108/EUM0000000006229

Chenhall, R. H. (2005). Integrative strategic performance measurement systems, strategic alignment of manufacturing, learning and strategic outcomes: An exploratory study. *Accounting, Organizations and Society*, *30*(5), 395–422. doi:10.1016/j.aos.2004.08.001

Evans, J. R. (2004). An exploratory study of performance measurement systems and relationships with performance results. *Journal of Operations Management, 22*(3), 219–232. doi:10.1016/j.jom.2004.01.002

Garengo, P., & Bititci, U. S. (2007). Towards a contingency approach to performance measurement: An empirical study in Scottish SMEs. *International Journal of Operations & Production Management, 27*(8), 784–801.

Georges, P. M. (2002). *Le management cockpit: Des tableaux de bord qui vont à l'essentiel.* Paris: Éditions d'Organisation.

Gomes, C. F., Yasin, M. M., & Lisboa, J. V. (2011). Performance measurement practices in manufacturing firms revisited. *International Journal of Operations & Production Management, 31*(1), 5–30. doi:10.1108/01443571111098726

Harty, C. (2010). Implementing innovation: Designers, users and actor-networks. *Technology Analysis and Strategic Management, 22*(3), 297–315. doi:10.1080/09537321003647339

Ittner, C. D., Larcker, D. F., & Randall, T. (2003). Performance implications of strategic performance measurement in financial services firms. *Accounting, Organizations and Society, 28*(7-8), 715–741. doi:10.1016/S0361-3682(03)00033-3

Kueng, P. (2000). Process performance measurement system: A tool to support process-based organizations. *Total Quality Management, 11*(1), 67–86. doi:10.1080/0954412007035

Latour, B. (1987). *Science in Action. How to follow Scientists and Engineers through Society.* Milton Keynes, England: Open University Press.

Nakayama, T., Kato, H., & Yamane, Y. (2000). Discovering the gap between Web site designers' expectations and users' behavior. *Computer Networks, 33*(1-6), 811–822. doi:10.1016/S1389-1286(00)00032-3

Pavlov, A., & Bourne, M. (2011). Explaining the effects of performance measurement on performance: An organizational routines perspective. *International Journal of Operations & Production Management, 31*(1), 101–122. doi:10.1108/01443571111098762

Purvis, R., & Sambamurthy, V. (1997). An examination of designer and user perceptions of JAD and the traditional IS design methodology. *Information & Management, 32*(3), 123–135. doi:10.1016/S0378-7206(96)01087-7

Raymond, L., Marchand, M., St-Pierre, J., Cadieux, L., & Labelle, F. (2013). Dimensions of small business performance from the owner-manager's perspective: A re-conceptualisation and empirical validation. *Entrepreneurship & Regional Development, 25*(5-6), 468–499. doi:10.1080/08985626.2013.782344

Raymond, L., St-Pierre, J., & Marchand, M. (2009). A taxonomic approach to studying the performance of manufacturing SMEs. *International Journal of Business Performance Management, 11*(4), 277–291. doi:10.1504/IJBPM.2009.030951

Rosson, M. B., Maass, S., & Kellogg, W. A. (1988). The designer as user: Building requirements for design tools from design practice. *Communications of the ACM, 31*(11), 1288–1298. doi:10.1145/50087.50090

Salleh, N. A. M., Jusoh, R., & Isa, C. R. (2010). Relationship between information systems sophistication and performance measurement. *Industrial Management & Data Systems, 110*(7), 993–1017. doi:10.1108/02635571011069077

St-Pierre, J., & Raymond, L. (2004). Short-term effects of benchmarking on the manufacturing practices and performance of SMEs. *International Journal of Productivity and Performance Management, 53*(8), 681–699. doi:10.1108/17410400410569107

Uwizeyemungu, S., & Raymond, L. (2012). Impact of an ERP system's capabilities upon the realisation of its business value: A resource-based perspective. *Information Technology Management*, *13*(2), 69–90. doi:10.1007/s10799-012-0118-9

Walsham, G. (1991). Organizational metaphors and information systems research. *European Journal of Information Systems*, *1*(2), 83–94. doi:10.1057/ejis.1991.16

Wand, Y., & Weber, R. (1990). An ontological model of an information system. *IEEE Transactions on Software Engineering*, *16*(11), 1282–1292. doi:10.1109/32.60316

Williams, M. G., & Begg, V. (1993). Translation between software designers and user. *Communications of the ACM*, *36*(4), 102–103. doi:10.1145/153571.214831

KEY TERMS AND DEFINITIONS

Designer: An individual who initially conceives and designs an IT-based information system.

IT Artefact: "The application of IT to enable or support some task(s) embedded within a structure(s) that itself is embedded within a context(s)" (Benbasat & Zmud, 2003, p. 186).

IT Artifact: The application of "IT as the integration of the processing logic found in computers with the massive stores of databases and the connectivity of communications networks. The IT artifact includes IT infrastructure, innovations with technology, and especially the Internet" (Agarwal & Lucas, 2005, p. 394).

Ontology: Specification of a conceptualization, formal framework for representing knowledge.

Performance Measurement System: An "information system based on a holistic (multidimensional / balanced / integrated) view of organisational performance, as conceptualised through a performance measurement model, in support of executive decision-making and strategic management, by producing information in a manner that reflects the performance logic (determinants/results) of the organisation" (Marchand & Raymond, 2008, p. 674).

Plato: Greek philosopher, born between 429 and 423 BCE, author of the *Republic*.

Small and Medium-Sized Enterprise: "The category of micro, small and medium-sized enterprises (SMEs) is made up of enterprises which employ fewer than 250 persons and which have an annual turnover not exceeding 50 million euro, and/or an annual balance sheet total not exceeding 43 million euro" (European Commission, 2005).

User: An individual who uses an IT-based information system in the accomplishment of an organizational task, and for whom the system is designed.

Chapter 17

IT Alignment Intelligence:
The Role of Emotional Intelligence in Business and IT Alignment

Eben van Blerk
Cape Peninsula University of Technology, South Africa

Andre de la Harpe
Cape Peninsula University of Technology, South Africa

Johannes Cronje
Cape Peninsula University of Technology, South Africa

ABSTRACT

Above average analytical and mathematical ability are highly sought-after human attributes required from IT professionals at work in the Systems Development Life Cycle (SDLC). These attributes are perceived to be ingredients for a successful career in Information Technology (IT). When companies hire IT professionals, they often focus on the "hard" skills needed to perform the work (Joseph, Ang, Chang, & Slaughter, 2010). There is a growing awareness that technical skills alone are insufficient for success in IT. Technical skills and experience are becoming an entry-level requirement. Being technically competent is no longer enough. For IT professionals, to improve business, a wider set of skills are required. This research aimed to determine what the human attributes are that contribute most to the improvement of business, namely IT alignment. It was found that Emotional Intelligence (EI) of business analysts, systems analysts, and project managers does play a role in the non-delivery of business needs by the IT department. Further, human attributes found to contribute to business-IT alignment were experience, communication skills, professionalism, and collaboration skills. A taxonomy of IT alignment intelligence for business analysts, systems analysts, and project managers is proposed.

INTRODUCTION

The well documented misalignment between business and IT strategies as well as the perceived

non-delivery of the IT department resulted in the question as to why despite all the research, there is still on-going misalignment between business and IT strategies (Belfo & Sousa, 2013; Chan &

DOI: 10.4018/978-1-4666-8147-7.ch017

Reich, 2007; Tallon & Pinsonneault, 2011). Technical skills and knowledge are essential elements but alone they are not sufficient for successful business – IT alignment. IT professionals needs IT alignment intelligence to complement their technical skills in the process of improving business – IT alignment. Despite the fact that it is the human in the IT organisation that has to ensure alignment between business and IT strategies, the non-technical skills required by IT professionals traditionally gets limited focus on the agenda of IT Managers.

Emotions influence group dynamics, occupational performance, and group effectiveness (Bar-On & Maree, 2009; Bharwaney-Orme & Bar-On, 2002; Dries & Pepermans, 2007; Goleman, 1995, 1998; Higgs, 2004; Janovics & Christiansen, 2001; Mayer & Salovey, 1997; McClelland, 1998; Sala, 2006; Salovey & Mayer, 1990; Spencer & Spencer, 1993). The world of work is emotional. Palmer, Stough, Harmer, & Gignac (2010) define EI as a "set of skills relevant to how we perceive, understand, reason with and manage our own and others' feelings". Emotions influence how we perceive and interpret information, and how we respond to others (Sala, 2006). An increasing body of research published in peer-reviewed journals suggests that developing one's emotionally intelligence can have a significant positive influence on performance in the work place. Several studies also suggest EI exhibits unique variance (incremental validity). EI was also found to be a unique forecaster of job performance independent of the effects of personality and intelligence (O'Boyle, Humphrey, Pollack, Hawver, & Story, 2010).

The purpose of this study is to establish what emotional intelligence competencies IT professionals could have to improve business – IT alignment. A taxonomy of IT alignment intelligence is proposed. Technical skills and knowledge are required of IT professionals, but on their own, they are insufficient for successful alignment of business and IT strategies (Joseph, Ang, Chang, & Slaughter, 2010; Kaluzniacky, 2004). IT align-

ment intelligence could potentially compliment the technical skills of IT professionals in improving business strategy and IT alignment. This chapter contributes towards the gap in research as far as EI and the IT profession goes. It further contributes to put forward and to highlight the need for more research on the topic and to create more debate on human factors and the alignment of business and IT strategies within organisations. In figure 1 a conceptual framework is proposed. The framework consists of 5 elements namely competencies required from industry, industry competency guidelines, approaches to EA, the Genos model and the EI profiles of IT professionals. This chapter will only address three elements of the framework namely the competency requirements from industry, the industry competency guidelines and the Genos model.

The conceptual framework seeks to assist in the exploring and understanding of the role of EI in possibly bridging the gap between business and IT in organisations. IT managers as well as human resources departments may want to use the framework and the findings of this research to be more focused on specific competencies in their efforts to improve the performance of IT professionals while delivering on the information systems requirements of business.

BACKGROUND

The growing body of literature the past two decades demonstrates the influence of emotions on occupational performance, and group effectiveness (Bar-On & Maree, 2009; Bharwaney-Orme & Bar-On, 2002; Dries & Pepermans, 2007; Goleman, 1995, 1998; Higgs, 2004; Janovics & Christiansen, 2001; Joseph, Ang, Chang, & Slaughter, 2010; Kaluzniacky, 2004; Mayer & Salovey, 1997; McClelland, 1998; Sala, 2006; Salovey & Mayer, 1990; Spencer & Spencer, 1993). Since humans are emotional, these emotions influence how humans perceive and interpret information, and

Figure 1. The conceptual framework

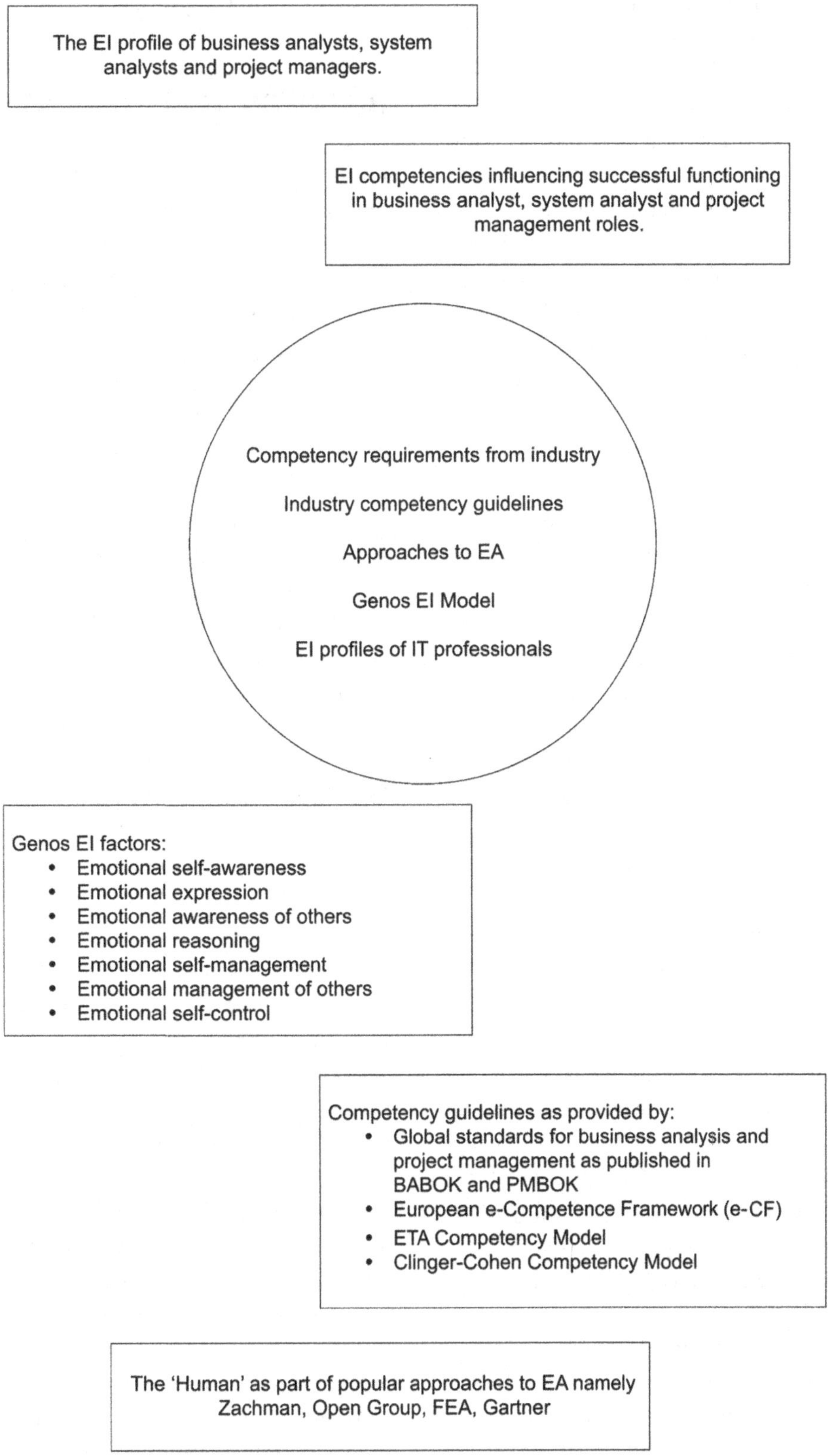

The EI profile of business analysts, system analysts and project managers.

EI competencies influencing successful functioning in business analyst, system analyst and project management roles.

Competency requirements from industry

Industry competency guidelines

Approaches to EA

Genos EI Model

EI profiles of IT professionals

Genos EI factors:
- Emotional self-awareness
- Emotional expression
- Emotional awareness of others
- Emotional reasoning
- Emotional self-management
- Emotional management of others
- Emotional self-control

Competency guidelines as provided by:
- Global standards for business analysis and project management as published in BABOK and PMBOK
- European e-Competence Framework (e-CF)
- ETA Competency Model
- Clinger-Cohen Competency Model

The 'Human' as part of popular approaches to EA namely Zachman, Open Group, FEA, Gartner respond to other humans (Sala, 2006). Developing emotional intelligence can have a significant positive influence on performance at work (Bar-On, Handley, & Fund, 2006; Gignac, 2010; Sala, 2006). Although many studies have been done on the contribution of EI in organisations, as well as on business - IT alignment (Avison, Jones, Powell, & Wilson, 2004; Belfo & Sousa, 2013; Burn, 1996; Chan, Sabherwal, & Thatcher, 2006; Henderson & Venkatramen, 1989,1990; Tallon & Pinsonneault, 2011) a gap exists in the literature on relationship between EI of IT human resources and the alignment of business and IT strategies (Joseph, Ang, Chang, & Slaughter, 2010). This research aims to contribute to research on business and IT alignment by addressing this gap.

Luftman and Brier (1999) are arguably the first to introduce the human element in business - IT alignment. They contend people management skills are critical to ensure that relationships are built and maintained. Reich and Benbasat (2000) introduced the concept of social alignment and highlight the importance of communication between business stakeholders and IT leaders. Smaczny (2001) stresses the importance of communication by suggesting a combination of business and IT functions. Silvius (2007) also supports the importance of communication and dialog, as well as a mature relationship between business and IT leaders. The concept of EI in relationship to business and IT alignment is not reported on. Enterprise architectural frameworks and models such as Zachman (1997, 1992), TOGAF and many others do not mention EI as a contributing factor for business and IT alignment. The European-eCompetence framework (e-CF) published in 2008, the ETA competency model (Employment and Training Administration, 2014), the Clinger Cohen core competencies (CIO Council, 2013) models, The PMBOK guide (Project Management Institute, 2013) and The BABOK guide (International Institute of Business Analysis, 2009) although referring to "underlying competencies"

do not refer to EI as a contributing factor towards business and IT alignment.

BUSINESS: IT ALIGNMENT

Effective and efficient IT systems to support business strategies and processes are recognised as key success factors for organisations (Silvius, 2007). Alignment between business strategies and IT strategies, defined as the degree to which the IT strategy supports or enables the achievement of business mission, objectives and plans as documented in the business strategy, has been acknowledged to have a positive impact on organisational performance (Chan, Sabherwal, & Thatcher, 2006; Hirschheim & Sabherwal, 2001; Kearns & Lederer, 2004; Kearns & Sabherwal, 2007; Reich & Benbasat, 2000).

The need for business - IT alignment has received significant attention in the literature and remains high on the agenda for business and IT leaders (Tallon & Pinsonneault, 2011). Despite substantial research over the years (Avison, Jones, Powell, & Wilson, 2004; Burn, 1996; Henderson & Venkatramen, 1989, 1990, 1993; Luftman & Brier, 1999) achieving and sustaining effective alignment between IT and business strategies remain a challenge for business and IT leaders.

Various strategic alignment models have been developed to assist business and IT executives in improving the business - IT alignment. The ground-breaking strategic alignment model (SAM) developed by Henderson and Venkatraman (1989) define business and IT alignment along the dimensions of functional integration and strategic fit between the business strategy and the IT strategy. Maes, Rijsenbrij, Truijens and Goedvolk (2000) extended the SAM model by integrating business expertise, the interpretation of information and communication, as well as technology, with strategy, structure and operations. Luftman (2000) produced a strategic alignment model based on communications, competence, governance, partnership, scope and architecture, as well as skills maturity.

There is a gap in the SAM literature with regard to the non-technical skills and competencies needed by IT professionals to align business and IT strategies. The human is neglected in the SAM literature. Scholars provide limited suggestions on which 'human' non-technical skills are needed to improve business - IT alignment. EI is not mentioned in the strategic alignment literature as a suggested element possibly contributing to business - IT alignment.

ENTERPRISE ARCHITECTURE

Enterprise architecture (EA) is usually used by IT professionals to facilitate business - IT alignment. Definitions of EA include describing an organisation in terms of its information, applications and technology systems and linking these to the organisation's business strategy (Stenzel, 2007). EA is also seen as a means of aligning business and IT strategies and used to achieve cost reduction or to facilitate change (Lucke, Krell, & Lechner, 2010). Lapalme (2012) argues that three main schools of thought on EA are present in the literature. These are Enterprise IT Architecting, Enterprise Integrating, and Enterprise Ecological Adaptation. Enterprise IT Architecting involves aligning the IT assets of an organisation through strategy, design and management activities. Enterprise Integrating as a school of thought on EA includes designing an organisation in such a way that it facilitates execution of its enterprise strategy by "maximising the overall coherency between all its facets" (Lapalme, 2012). IT is an example of one of these facets. The Enterprise Ecological Adaptation school of thought involves nurturing organisational learning by designing all the facets of an organisation to include its relationship and adaption to the environment. Enterprise strategy creation and organisation design are incorporated in this school of thought as well. The generally accepted EA methodologies include the Zachman Framework, the Open Group Architectural Framework (TOGAF), the Federal Enterprise Architecture, and the Gartner Methodology (Sessions, 2007).

The human element is absent in EA tools, EA frameworks as well as schools of thought on EA widely used by business and IT stakeholders to improve business - IT alignment. A gap in the literature exists with regard to non-technical skills and competencies. Limited suggestions are provided on which 'human' skills, characteristics or competencies business analysts, systems analysts and project managers require to build and maintain dialogue and productive relationships between business and IT stakeholders. None of the popular EA frameworks refer to EI as a suggested element potentially contributing to improved alignment between business and IT strategies.

EMOTINAL INTELLIGENCE

Palmer, Gignac, Ekermans and Stough (2008) define EI as a "set of skills relevant to how we perceive, understand, reason with and manage our own and others' feelings". The Genos EI Model resulted from a factor analytic study done of existing EI models. Gignac (2010) produced an EI model consisting of seven factors. The seven factors and their accompanying descriptions are presented in Table 1. Personality components or competencies are not included in this model.

METHODOLOGY AND RESEARCH FINDINGS

A multiple case study was done to explore the skills and competence requirements used by senior IT managers as guidelines when recruiting business analysts, systems analysts and project managers required to deliver the information systems needs of business. Semi-structured qualitative interviews

Table 1. The Genos emotional intelligence inventory (Palmer, Gignac, Ekermans, & Stough, 2008)

EI Factors	Skills
Emotional self-awareness	To perceive and understand one's own emotions
Emotional expression	To effectively express one's own emotions
Emotional awareness of others	To perceive and understand the emotions of others
Emotional reasoning	To use emotional information in decision-making
Emotional self-management	To effectively manage one's own emotions
Emotional management of others	To positively influence the emotions of others
Emotional self-control	To effectively control one's own strong emotions

were conducted with twenty IT managers from twenty organisations based in the Western Cape province of South Africa. Criterion sampling as defined by Patton (1990) was used as purposive sampling method in gathering qualitative data. The interviews were conducted over a five-month period on site at each of the twenty information systems development organisations and lasted between one and two hours each. Interviews were recorded and afterward transcribed verbatim. Coding of the qualitative data was done by segmenting the data into meaningful units (McMillan & Schumacher, 2010; Nieuwenhuis, 2010). Codes were allocated inductively.

Following the inductive coding process, related codes were combined and classified into categories. Each category was given an appropriate description. This was done in an iterative process until all coded data were combined into categories (McMillan & Schumacher, 2010). On completion of the inductive categorisation, the categories were revisited and further refined.

The IT managers interviewed in this study believed that EI influence successful functioning of business analysts, systems analysts and project managers. Experience in these roles and knowledge of the industry in which they are working was preferred over formal qualifications and certification as a project manager or business analyst. Most of the IT managers argued certification such as the Certified Business Analysis Professional

(CBAP) or Project Management Professional (PMP) was not part of their primary recruitment criteria and therefore would not influence their selection of business analysts, systems analysts or project managers. For them, behavioural competencies and EI are of greater importance than certification. Twelve categories materialized from the data, demonstrating the competency requirements for business analysts, systems analysts and project managers. These categories are presented in Figure 2.

EXPERIENCE

In terms of competency requirements for business analysts, systems analysts and project managers, experience emerged as first in priority sequence. The keyword 'experience' was mentioned 46 times by 17 of the 20 organisations (85%) as a desirable quality for business analysts, systems analysts and project managers. Experience involves a track record of functioning as a business analyst, systems analyst or project managers as well as knowing the business of their employer. Experience also includes having working knowledge of the information systems currently being utilised in their organisation. In terms of project management, it includes experience in managing specific type of projects, for example, infrastructure, insurance and retail software development projects.

Figure 2. Competency categories

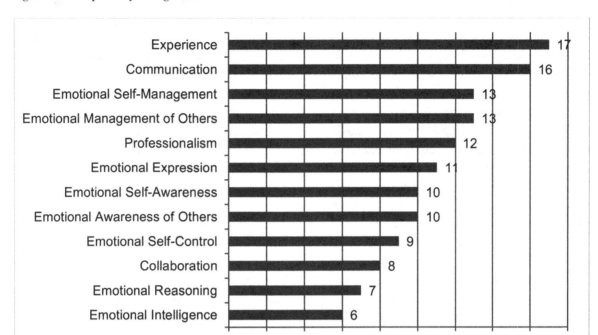

Organisation 1 requires level of knowledge, experience and technical capability that might be required for the project. In cases of a building infrastructure type project, a project manager with knowledge and experience of managing projects in the building industry is required. Generally, the participating organisations require a specific level of business knowledge and experience in project management. Certification as a project manager was considered relatively unimportant. Participant 1 stated: "I am looking for experience. I know how to do this, rather than I have the qualification. The qualification becomes secondary."

Organisation 2, a private hospital group, regarded experience in project management most important when recruiting project managers. This group recognised the value of professional certification but it did not influence their selection of project managers. When recruiting business analysts, Organisation 3 not only required business analysis experience, but also experience in working in software development surroundings. When having to pick between qualifications or certification as a business analyst, and aspects such as emotional awareness, self-awareness, empathy and communication, Organisation 3 would rather appoint the business analyst without the qualification or certification.

Experience as a systems analyst, was valued by Organisation 5 but for them understanding the business as well as its environment was of more importance. Although they value technical skills and experience when recruiting business analysts, behavioural competencies carry more weight than experience.

Organisation 6 valued organisational experience or experience. Certification was seen as important during the recruitment process, but once the business analyst or project manager was inside the organisation, certification was of lesser importance.

COMMUNICATION

Sixteen of the twenty organisations (80%) mentioned communication 48 times as a needed competency for business analysts, systems analysts and project managers. This category emerged as the second most wanted of the 12 categories. Communication comprises being approachable, having listening skills, being able to communicate effectively in written and oral form, communicating effectively at various levels in the organisation, as well as expressing oneself clearly to a technically and non-technically competent audience.

In terms of the role of the systems analyst, Organisation 5 argued: "Listening is very important and acknowledging other people's viewpoints." Participants stated: "He must have the ability to communicate a complex situation in laymen's terms. He will have to be able to present back to the business side so business can understand. It is communication."

Organisation 6 viewed communication as human skills and contended: "Ability to listen, to communicate, to interact and to steer a discussion in a logical direction. To understand what is important and what is not important. To understand who is important and who is not important [and] to extract knowledge from people. That is for me the most important, the communication skills, to understand what you are hearing, to play it back to the audience, get confirmation and to do this in a structured way and to move forward to solve a problem." The ability to listen was also stressed as pivotal in business – IT alignment. They contended that often IT professionals do not listen to what the requirement from business is. This leads to a frustrated user and wasted effort by business analysts and project managers during systems development.

Organisation 9 argued that project managers who were poor communicators, "are a deal breaker". They valued good verbal and written communication skills. Participant 10, as a business analysis competency manager, regarded the ability to communicate as an essential competency when recruiting business analysts. She stressed: "Relationship building is extremely important to us because business analysis is about relationships. It is about communication and relationships with the stakeholders and how best to get information from your stakeholders which is required for you to develop your requirements." The ability to influence and be self-confident forms part of the required communication skills for a business analyst.

EMOTIONAL SELF-MANAGEMENT

Emotional self-management was stated as desirable for business analysts, systems analysts and project managers by thirteen of the twenty organisations (65%). It is third in order of priority. This category includes how often individuals successfully manage their own emotions at work. It involves successful adjustment to negative emotional states at work (Gignac, 2010). Focus is placed on the engagement in activities to maintain a positive disposition while at work. It involves the ability to move on from an emotional setback, opposed to dwelling on the situation. Emotional self-management also includes demonstrating a passion for what one is doing, having a general optimistic outlook on life, adapting feelings and thinking to changing situations, and assertively expressing one's emotions (Gignac, 2010). The twenty senior IT managers collectively referred to emotional self-management as a key requirement 83 times.

Participant 12 felt that assertiveness was important in the media industry. They are of the opinion that optimistic IT professionals are more successful in general. Participant 13 also supported emotional self-management in the role of the project manager. Assertiveness for them was important, but they felt the project manager should express himself or herself emotionally in an appropriate way. Adaptability, flexibility, as well as a positive attitude, was highly regarded.

The necessity of emotional self-management in project management and business analysis is also clear in software development organisations. Participant 15 felt assertiveness was important and argued business analysts should have the ability to manage their emotions. Organisation 18 linked communication to emotional self-management: "Communication is managing my emotion, and therefore ensuring the way I communicate is correct both for me and the receiver as well as listening. Hearing the emotions of what they are conveying is just as important as what they are saying. That is just as important in business analysis as in project management." Organisation 20 required adaptable project managers, individuals who could change and learn new things. In software development, they argued the project manager needs to be competent at managing emotions.

The necessity of emotional self-management in business analysis was reinforced by Participant 17 (financial services) as well as by Participant 19. Participant 17 contended "Then your attitude needs to be appropriate. You cannot walk around all day complaining about the person that changed his mind again. It is that positive energy. If you are positive, it will influence all those around you. You have to be positive and have energy. By us [sic] you do not have the privilege to work on just one project at a time. You cannot really plan beforehand. With that comes flexibility and adaptability. You need structure as a business analyst but at the same time [have to] be flexible enough." Participant 19 was of the opinion a business analyst should be able to adapt to various circumstances. Emotional self-management was needed and behaviour should be adapted according to the circumstances.

EMOTIONAL MANAGEMENT OF OTHERS

Emotional management of others was mentioned as required for business analysts, systems analysts and project managers, by thirteen of the twenty organisations (65%). It is fourth in order of priority. This category involves actively and successfully managing the emotions of others. It includes deliberate actions to motivate colleagues or subordinates, as well as demonstrations of modifying the emotions of others for their own personal betterment at work. Emotional management of others also includes creating a positive working environment for others (Gignac, 2010). The thirteen senior IT managers collectively referred to emotional self-management as a key requirement 42 times.

Participant 6 required a business analyst to be able to steer a discussion in a logical direction and influence stakeholders to resolve issues triggering distress. "Then I would think the next important thing is to show the client and create a sense of confidence in that you understand the problem, you understand what the challenge is and then respond with 'there is a plan, leave it with us. We will start crafting a solution for you for this challenge'. That to me is what I expect from a business analyst in the first encounter. Much more of a listener but at the same time instilling confidence in that we can overcome this challenge and provide solutions without at that stage be all-knowing and minimising the business problem." Participant 6 firmly believed, although the project manager was more methods-based, he or she still had to be able to manage the emotions of others towards a positive project outcome.

PROFESSIONALISM

When hiring a business analyst, systems analyst or project manager, professionalism was stated as a key requirement by 60% of the participating senior IT managers. Professionalism was mentioned 33 times by twelve of the twenty organisations as a desirable quality and listed as the fifth most important competency. Among the twenty senior IT managers, three themes appeared as being essential to a true business analysis, systems analysis or project management professional. These themes are behaviour in the workplace, excellence in their craft and physical appearance in terms of dress.

Behaviour is the foremost sub-category of professionalism. IT professionals are expected to behave appropriately while at work. This involves not telling rude jokes and showing a level of respect when engaging stakeholders as well as maintaining an emotional distance. Communication is associated to professional behaviour. Participants expect project managers to speak well, concern themselves with the facts, and not become emotional in their communication with fellow colleagues and client.

In terms of excellence, IT professionals are expected to deliver high-quality output and not neglect quality standards. Being emotionally competent emerged as a prerequisite for project managers and business analysts. This involves acting appropriately in any given situation. This includes applying emotional self-management and self-control, as well as appropriate expression of emotions in daily interaction with colleagues and clients.

Appearance of business analysts, systems analysts and project managers emerged as a central component of professionalism. Participant 16, for example, argued interaction with clients becomes a problem when the project manager does not come across as presentable. How the IT professional portrayed him- or herself is critical. Participant 19 contended a business-like appearance was needed and IT professionals should always dress and operate with respect to their clients.

EMOTIONAL EXPRESSION

Emotional expression measures the relative frequency with which one expresses emotions appropriately at work. This implies in the appropriate way, at the appropriate time and to the appropriate people, in verbal and / or non-verbal form. Eleven of the twenty organisations (55%) indicated the appropriate expression of emotion as desirable for business analysts, systems analysts and project managers. In terms of competency requirements, it is sixth in order of priority and was mentioned 24 times.

The value of appropriate expression of emotion by the project manager was stressed by Participants 7, 12, 13, and 16, as well as by Participant 20. Participant 7 encouraged open communication and believed the project manager should convey the message to the client, whether it was good news or not. "To me the EI part is there to share the good news and share the bad news. Do both of them in a nice way. Do not reprimand someone, certainly not in front of his peers, ever. If you need to reprimand him, do it in a nice way." Participants 12 and 13 argued that the project manager needed to conduct him- or herself suitably. Shouting at anybody was not needed. Screaming in the workplace was not regarded as appropriate behaviour. Participant 13 contended emotions did have a role to play in the project management workplace. The project manager is responsible to respect the humanity of the team members and should ensure that the team grow from the experiences. "You need to respect their humanity and let them be better people at the end of the day. You cannot go and affect their humanity because you are angry. You do it in a way that you also develop them." Participant

16 stressed the manner in which the message is conveyed to the audience, while Participant 20 was of the opinion that inappropriate expression of emotion in the project management workplace was unprofessional.

EMOTIONAL SELF-AWARENESS

Emotional self-awareness is the ability to be aware of and understand the emotions we experience. It involves understanding what one is feeling and why, as well as how one's emotions may motivate or affect one's daily thoughts and behaviours (Gignac, 2010). Ten senior IT managers listed emotional self-awareness as a desirable competency for business analysts, systems analysts and project managers. In terms of competency requirements, it was seventh in order of priority for the twenty organisations participating in this research.

Participant 1 was of the opinion that emotions had a definite role to play in the project management environment, and as humans, we were emotional beings. It was not possible for us as humans in the SDLC to leave our emotions at the door when we walk into the workplace. It is, however, required to manage our emotions in such a way that they worked collectively to achieve our goals. "I have to manage my emotions and the emotions of those around me in such a way that they actually invite me to come back again to do the next project. That is important to me as a project manager because it means my work is sustainable. It is important to the group project office because it means we get return business. It is important to the organisation because my skills, knowledge and experience are reinvested in the organisation. So no, we can't check our emotions out." Participant 1 argued emotional outbursts and uncontrolled emotional anger does not assist the project manager. Emotions needed to be channelled and managed. In order to do that, the project manager needs to be actively aware of and understand his or her emotions.

EMOTIONAL AWARENESS OF OTHERS

Ten of the twenty participating senior IT managers (50%) reported emotional awareness of others as a desirable competency for business analysts, systems analysts and project managers. Emotional awareness of others emerged as the eighth most desirable of the twelve categories. It involves the ability of the business analyst, systems analyst and project manager to recognise emotions expressed in the workplace.

EMOTIONAL SELF-CONTROL

Emotional self-control was reported as required for business analysts, systems analysts and project managers, by nine of the twenty senior IT managers (45%). From the twelve categories, it is ninth in order of priority. Emotional self-control involves one's ability to control strong emotions reactively in the workplace (Gignac, 2010). The participating IT managers referred 16 times to emotional self-control as a key requirement for business analysts, systems analysts and project managers.

COLABORATION

Business analysts, systems analysts and project managers need collaboration skills. The project manager needs to support the client and fellow IT team members towards successful project delivery when needed. Collaboration skills were stated as required for business analysts, systems analysts and project managers by eight of the twenty participating senior IT managers (40%). From the twelve categories, collaboration was listed as tenth in order of priority.

Participant 3 contended business analysts are inherently part of the IT team and is expected to be team players. Whether working with the client or fellow IT team members, she argued one succeeds or fails as a team. Collaboration and trust were therefore key success factors for any IT team. The importance of collaboration as part of the business analysis skillset was also stressed by Participant 10.

Organisation 7 was of the opinion that collaboration skills were essential to the success of a project manager. Participant 9 had the same viewpoint and argued software development projects were highly collaborative in nature. The project manager has to understand user behaviour and needs emotional intelligence. In the absence of these competencies, participant 9 argued the project manager would fail, irrespective of applying project management processes or not. "Even if you have the process down, applying the process without understanding the emotional world, will be a problem." Organisation 14 stated the importance of the project manager's ability to collaborate in software development organisations. The respondent stated, "It is our problem and we have to try and solve it ... I want a team player that can work with people and take responsibility."

EMOTIONAL REASONING

Emotional reasoning includes the ability to consider one's own emotions and the emotions of others during decision-making (Gignac, 2010). This competency was referred to as 'emotional maturity'. Emotional reasoning was stated as required for business analysts, systems analysts and project managers by seven of the twenty senior IT managers (35%). From the twelve categories, it is eleventh in order of priority.

Participants 3, 17 and 19 confirmed the importance of emotional maturity as part of the competencies of a successful and effective business analyst. When asked what was expected from the business analyst in terms of behavioural competencies, Participant 3 reiterated "Certainly a level of emotional maturity." Participant 17 contended emotional maturity was needed to understand

reality during the business analysis process. The business analyst is pressurised from the business stakeholders as well as from IT professionals and should not take disagreements personally. "You cannot over-react if someone does not agree with you. You cannot throw your toys out of the cot if someone changes their requirement. You have to understand what the reality is and how you handle it. It is a type of maturity that comes with this." For Participant 19, maturity was a key requirement for business analysts.

SOLUTIONS AND RECOMMENDATIONS

This study highlighted that emotional competence and emotionally intelligent behaviour in the Information Systems (IS) workplace are on the agenda of senior IT managers. Analytical and mathematical ability are qualities still highly in demand in the IT workplace. They are, however, not the only ingredients senior IT managers perceive to be essential to a successful career in IT as well as successful pursuit of alignment between business and IT strategies. The EI of IT professionals does play a role in the non-delivery of business needs by the IT department, especially that of the business analyst, systems analyst and project manager. Knowledge and technical skills, however, are not enough for successful business - IT alignment. Business and systems knowledge and technical skills have become an entry-level requirement for business analysts, systems analysts and project managers in the SDLC.

We propose that technical competence and certification as IT professionals, such as Certified Business Analysis Professional (CBAP) or Project Management Professional (PMP) should not be the only requirements when recruiting business analysts, systems analysts and project managers, and allocating them to project teams. Business analysts, systems analysts and project managers should have a wider set of non-technical human emotional and alignment skills. We propose a taxonomy of IT alignment intelligence for business analysts, systems analysts and project managers comprising five dimensions, namely, experience, communication, emotional intelligence (the Genos EI model), professionalism and collaboration (Figure 3).

The taxonomy of IT alignment intelligence is unique and new to the literature on business - IT alignment. This study suggests the dimensions of IT alignment intelligence influence successful functioning in business analyst, systems analyst and project manager roles. More so, the components of the taxonomy are suggested key human attributes needed by business analysts, systems analysts and project managers to enhance business - IT alignment. EI was found to be a key requirement for business analysts, systems analysts and project managers. We recommend that IT management should incorporate Genos EI assessment as part of the recruitment and selection process of business analysts, systems analysts and project managers during project staffing. IT management should consider the impact of a lack in EI on business - IT alignment before a business analyst, systems analyst or project manager is selected as part of a project team.

We also recommend that IT organisations should assist their business analysts, systems analysts and project managers in EI development

Figure 3. Taxonomy of IT alignment intelligence

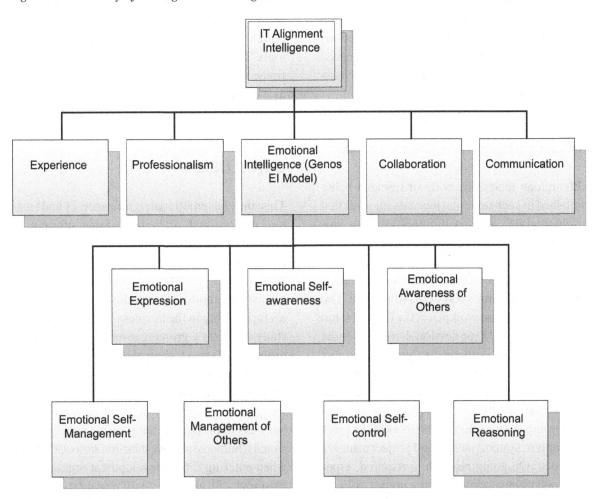

as well as the development of professionalism, communication and collaboration skills. EI should be taught along with topics such as business and process analysis, system analysis and design and project management. IT managers should identify emotionally intelligent individuals in their teams by means of formal EI assessment. These individuals as well as those competent in communication and collaboration should assist business analysts, systems analysts and project managers with developing their EI, communication and collaboration skills through formal coaching and mentoring in the workplace.

Business analysts, systems analysts and project managers should receive regular performance feedback from their managers which is based on their technical and non-technical behavioural performance. As part of performance management, specific EI, communication and collaboration related behavioural performance expectations should be incorporated into the key performance areas. The aim is to ensure that these IT professionals focus on developing these skills.

FUTURE RESEARCH DIRECTIONS

Although an increasing body of research being published in peer-reviewed journals suggests that developing one's emotionally intelligence can have a significant positive influence on performance in the work place, very little peer reviewed research is available on the impact of emotional intelligence in the information systems workplace. The information systems workplace, the IT profession and specifically IT professional roles such as business analysis, systems analysis and project management is excluded from the internationally published business cases for emotional intelligence in organisations. Further research unpacking the relationship between EI and the roles of the business analyst, systems analyst and project manager is needed. On-going research is required, especially quantitative analysis of the impact of EI on the performance of the business analyst, systems analyst and project manager. Large and diverse population samples should be part of such research, further building the business case for emotional intelligence in the IT profession.

The gap in the SAM literature with regard to the non-technical skills and competencies needed by IT professionals to align business and IT strategies need to be addressed by means of formal research. Further suggestions on which 'human' non-technical skills are needed to improve business - IT alignment are required.

Enterprise architecture frameworks are widely used by business and IT stakeholders to improve business - IT alignment. Emotional intelligence is also absent from any of the recognised enterprise architecture models. Further research needs to investigate the non-technical skills and competencies especially EI, required from business and IT professionals utilising these enterprise architecture tools. The potential inclusion of EI in popular EA frameworks needs to be investigated, unpacking EI as a contributor to improved alignment between business and IT strategies.

CONCLUSION

This study has emotional significance. IT and business professionals are reminded that information systems development is not only a technological issue but a human and social issue as well. Suggestions are provided on ways of developing competent emotionally intelligent IT professionals functioning in the business environment. This study indicates a growing awareness amongst IT professionals that technical skills alone are insufficient for improved business – IT alignment. This study highlighted that the IS industry shows some recognition of the role of EI in the delivery of business IS needs. It is not possible for IS professionals (humans) to leave their emotions at the door when entering the IS development organisation. Business – IT alignment will remain a challenge for IT professionals as long as the human in information systems development is ignored. Business analysts, systems analysts and project managers have to develop an understanding of their own emotions as well as an emotional awareness of others. As part of humanising IS work, the above IT professionals need to learn to manage their own emotions and the emotions of others. This may encourage business stakeholders to look beyond the typical stereotyping of IT professionals as "IT geeks" and prove beneficial to the collaborative delivery of business' information system needs.

REFERENCES

Avison, D., Jones, J., Powell, P., & Wilson, D. (2004). Using and validating the strategic alignment model. *The Journal of Strategic Information Systems*, *13*(3), 223–246. doi:10.1016/j.jsis.2004.08.002

Bar-On, R., Handley, R., & Fund, S. (2006). The impact of emotional intelligence on performance. In V. Druskat, F. Sala, & G. Mount (Eds.), *Linking emotional intelligence and performance at work: Current research evidence with individuals and groups* (pp. 3–19). Mahwah, NJ: Lawrence Erlbaum.

Bar-On, R., & Maree, J. G. (2009). In search of emotional-social giftedness: a potentially viable and valuable concept. In L. V. Shavinina (Ed.), *International handbook of giftedness* (pp. 559–570). New York: Springer Science. doi:10.1007/978-1-4020-6162-2_26

Belfo, F., & Sousa, R. D. (2013). Reviewing business-IT alignment instruments under SAM dimensions. *International Journal of Information Communication Technologies and Human Development*, *5*(3), 18–40. doi:10.4018/jicthd.2013070102

Bharwaney-Orme, G., & Bar-On, R. (2002). The contribution of emotional intelligence to individual and organizational effectiveness. *Competency & Emotional Intelligence*, *9*(4), 23–28.

Burn, J. M. (1996). IS innovation and organizational alignment. *Journal of Information Technology*, *11*(1), 3–12. doi:10.1080/026839696345388

Chan, Y. E., & Reich, B. H. (2007). IT alignment: What have we learned? *Journal of Information Technology*, *22*(4), 297–315. doi:10.1057/palgrave.jit.2000109

Chan, Y. E., Sabherwal, R., & Thatcher, J. B. (2006). Antecedents and outcomes of strategic IS alignment: An empirical investigation. *IEEE Transactions on Engineering Management*, *53*(1), 27–47. doi:10.1109/TEM.2005.861804

Council, C. I. O. (2013). *Clinger-Cohen core competencies*. Retrieved December 15, 2013, from https://cio.gov/wp-content/uploads/downloads/2013/02/2012-Learning-Objectives-Final.pdf

Dries, N., & Pepermans, R. (2007). Using emotional intelligence to identify high potential: A metacompetency perspective. *Leadership and Organization Development Journal*, *28*(8), 749–770. doi:10.1108/01437730710835470

Employment and Training Administration. (2014). *ETA competency model*. Retrieved December 15, 2013, from http://www.careeronestop.org/competencymodel/pyramid.aspx?IT=Y

Gignac, G. E. (2010). *Genos emotional intelligence inventory: Technical manual*. Sydney: Genos Pty Ltd.

Goleman, D. (1995). *Emotional intelligence*. New York: Bantam Books.

Goleman, D. (1998). What makes a leader?. *Harvard Business Review*, *76*(6), 93–102. PMID:10187249

Hendersen, J. C., & Venkatraman, N. (1993). Strategic alignment: Leveraging information technology for transforming organizations. *IBM Systems Journal*, *38*(2), 472–484. doi:10.1147/sj.382.0472

Henderson, J. C., & Venkatraman, N. (1990). *Strategic alignment: a model for organizational transformation via information technology*. Working Paper 3223-90. Sloan School of Management, Massachusetts Institute of Technology.

Henderson, J. C., & Venkatramen, N. (1989). Strategic alignment: A model for organizational transformation through information technology. In T. A. Kochan & M. Useem (Eds.), *Transforming organizations* (pp. 62–87). New York: Oxford University Press.

Higgs, M. (2004). A study of the relationship between emotional intelligence and performance in UK call centres. *Journal of Managerial Psychology*, *19*(4), 442–454. doi:10.1108/02683940410537972

Hirschheim, R., & Sabherwal, R. (2001). Detours in the path towards strategic information systems alignment: Paradoxical decisions, excessive transformations and uncertain turnarounds. *California Management Review*, *44*(1), 87–108. doi:10.2307/41166112

International Institute of Business Analysis. (2009). *The BABOK guide* (2nd ed.). Toronto, Canada: Author.

Janovics, J., & Christiansen, N. D. (2001). *Emotional intelligence in the workplace*. Paper presented at the 16th Annual Conference of the Society of Industrial and Organizational Psychology, San Diego, CA.

Joseph, D., Ang, S., Chang, R. H. L., & Slaughter, S. A. (2010). Practical intelligence in IT: Assessing soft skills of IT professionals. *Communications of the ACM*, *53*(2), 149–154. doi:10.1145/1646353.1646391

Kaluzniacky, E. (2004). *Managing psychological factors in information systems work: An orientation to emotional intelligence*. Hershey, PA: Information Science Publishing. doi:10.4018/978-1-59140-198-8

Kearns, G. S., & Lederer, A. L. (2004). The impact of industry contextual factors on IT focus and the use of IT for competitive advantage. *Information & Management*, *41*(7), 899–919. doi:10.1016/j.im.2003.08.018

Kearns, G. S., & Sabherwal, R. (2007). Antecedents and consequences of information systems planning integration. *IEEE Transactions on Engineering Management*, *54*(4), 628–643. doi:10.1109/TEM.2007.906848

Lapalme, J. (2012). Three schools of thought on enterprise architecture. *IT Professional*, *14*(6), 37–43. doi:10.1109/MITP.2011.109

Lucke, C., Krell, S., & Lechner, U. (2010). Critical issues in enterprise architecting – A literature review. In *Proceedings of the 16th Americas Conference on Information Systems (AMCIS 2010)*. Lima, Peru: Academic Press.

Luftman, J. (2000). Assessing business IT alignment maturity. *Communications of the Association for Information Systems*, *4*(14), 1–51.

Luftman, J., & Brier, T. (1999). Achieving and sustaining business-IT alignment. *California Management Review*, *42*(1), 109–122. doi:10.2307/41166021

Maes, R., Rijsenbrij, D., Truijens, O., & Goed-volk, H. (2000). *Redefining business-IT alignment through a unified framework*. Retrieved May 30, 2014, from http://imwww.fee.uva.nl/~maestro/pdf/2000-19.pdf

Mayer, J. D., & Salovey, P. (1997). What is emotional intelligence? In P. Salovey, M. A. Brackett, & J. D. Mayer (Eds.), *Emotional Intelligence: Key readings on the Mayer and Salovey Model* (pp. 29–60). New York: Dude Publishing.

McClelland, D. C. (1998). Identifying competencies with behavioral-event interviews. *Psychological Science*, *9*(5), 331–340. doi:10.1111/1467-9280.00065

McMillan, J. H., & Schumacher, S. (2010). *Research in education: Evidence based inquiry* (7th ed.). Upper Saddle River, NJ: Pearson.

Nieuwenhuis, J. (2010). Qualitative research designs and data gathering techniques. In K. Maree (Ed.), *First steps in research* (pp. 70–98). Pretoria, South Africa: Van Schaik.

O'Boyle, E. H. Jr, Humphrey, R. H., Pollack, J. M., Hawver, T. H., & Story, P. A. (2010). The relation between emotional intelligence and job performance: A meta-analysis. *Journal of Organizational Behavior*, *32*(5), 788–818. doi:10.1002/job.714

Palmer, B. R., Gignac, G. E., Ekermans, G., & Stough, C. (2008). A comprehensive framework for emotional intelligence. In R. Emmerling, V. K. Shanwal, & M. K. Mandal (Eds.), *Emotional intelligence: Theoretical cultural perspectives* (pp. 17–38). New York: Nova Science.

Palmer, B. R., Stough, C., Harmer, R., & Gignac, G. E. (2010). Genos emotional intelligence inventory. In C. Stough, D. Saklofske, & J. Parker (Eds.), *Advances in the measurement of emotional intelligence* (pp. 321–344). New York: Springer.

Patton, M. Q. (1990). *Qualitative evaluation and research methods*. Thousand Oaks, CA: Sage.

Project Management Institute. (2013). *The PMBOK guide* (5th ed.). Newton Square, PA: Author.

Reich, B. H., & Benbasat, I. (2000). Factors that influence the social dimension of alignment between business and information technology objectives. *Management Information Systems Quarterly*, *24*(1), 81–113. doi:10.2307/3250980

Sala, F. (2006). The international business case: emotional intelligence competencies and important business outcomes. In V. Druskat, F. Sala, & G. Mount (Eds.), *Linking emotional intelligence and performance at work: Current research evidence with individuals and groups* (pp. 125–144). Mahwah, NJ: Lawrence Erlbaum.

Salovey, P., & Mayer, J. D. (1990). Emotional intelligence. *Imagination, Cognition and Personality*, *9*(3), 185–211. doi:10.2190/DUGG-P24E-52WK-6CDG

Sessions, R. (2007). Comparison of the top four enterprise architecture methodologies. *ObjectWatch White Papers*. Retrieved July 30, 2009, from http://objectwatch.com/white-papers

Silvius, A. J. G. (2007). Exploring differences in the perception of business and IT alignment. *Communications of the IIMA*, *7*(2), 21–32.

Smaczny, T. (2001). Is an alignment between business and information technology the appropriate paradigm to manage IT in today's organisations? *Management Decision*, *39*(10), 797–802. doi:10.1108/EUM0000000006521

Spencer, L., & Spencer, S. (1993). *Competence at work: Models for superior performance*. New York: John Wiley.

Stenzel, J. (2007). *CIO best practices – Enabling strategic value with information technology*. New York: John Wiley.

Tallon, P. P., & Pinsonneault, A. (2011). Competing perspectives on the link between strategic information technology alignment and organizational agility: Insights from a mediation model. *Management Information Systems Quarterly*, *35*(2), 363–486.

Zachman, J. A. (1997). *The challenge is change: A management paper*. Retrieved January 15, 2014, from http://www.ies.aust.com/papers/zachman2.htm

Zachman, J. A. (2013). *The Zachman framework*. Paper presented at the First International Conference on Enterprise Systems ES 2013, Cape Town, South Africa.

KEY TERMS AND DEFINITIONS

Business – IT Alignment: The degree to which information systems developed by IT professionals supports the information systems needs of business.

Business Analyst: A key actors in the information systems development process involved in engaging business users, soliciting requirements and translating the requirements to functional information system requirements.

Competencies: Behavioral skills demonstrated by IT professionals during the information systems development lifecycle.

Emotional Intelligence: Abilities and traits enabling humans to recognize and understand feelings and emotions and react appropriately in the particular circumstance.

Emotions: Physical changes in the human body, including the brain, in reaction to external stimuli.

Information Systems Development: The process of planning, creating, testing and deploying manual and or computerized information system by IT professionals utilizing formal systems development methods.

Project Manager: IT professional specializing in the field of project management, including planning, orchestrating the execution and managing risk of information systems related projects.

Systems Analyst: IT professional specializing in the analysis and design of information systems.

Compilation of References

Abas, H. I., Yusof, M. M., & Noah, S. A. M. (2011). The application of ontology in a clinical decision support system for acute postoperative pain management. In *Proceedings of Semantic Technology and Information Retrieval (STAIR)* (pp. 106–112). Academic Press. doi:10.1109/STAIR.2011.5995773

Abdel-Aal, R. E. (2004). Abductive network committees for improved classification of medical data. *Methods of Information in Medicine*, *43*(2), 192–201. PMID:15136869

Abdel-Aal, R. E. (2005). Improved classification of medical data using abductive network committees trained on different feature subsets. *Computer Methods and Programs in Biomedicine*, *80*(2), 141–153. doi:10.1016/j.cmpb.2005.08.001 PMID:16169631

Abdel-Aal, R. E., Abdel-Halim, M. R. E., & Abdel-Aal, S. (2006). Improving the classification of multiple disorders with problem decomposition. *Journal of Biomedical Informatics*, *39*(6), 612–625. doi:10.1016/j.jbi.2005.12.001 PMID:16442851

Abe, H., Ashizawa, K., Li, F., Matsuyama, N., Fukushima, A., Shiraishi, J., & Doi, K. (2004). Artificial neural networks (ANNs) for differential diagnosis of interstitial lung disease: Results of a simulation test with actual clinical cases. *Academic Radiology*, *11*(1), 29–37. doi:10.1016/S1076-6332(03)00572-5 PMID:14746399

Adams, R. L. (2013). *Web 3.0 startups: Online marketing strategies for launching & promoting any business on the web*. Create Space Independent Publishing Platform.

Aditya, T., & Kraak, M.-J. (2007). Aim4GDI: Facilitating the synthesis of GDI resources through mapping and superimpositions of metadata summaries. *GeoInformatica*, *11*(4), 459–478. doi:10.1007/s10707-007-0021-4

Aditya, T., & Kraak, M.-J. (2007). A search interface for an SDI: Implementation and evaluation of metadata visualization strategies. *Transactions in GIS*, *11*(3), 413–435. doi:10.1111/j.1467-9671.2007.01053.x

Agarwal, R., & Lucas, H. C. Jr. (2005). The information systems identity crisis: Focusing on high-visibility and high-impact research. *Management Information Systems Quarterly*, *29*(3), 381–398.

Aghaei, S., Nematbakhsh, M., & Farsani, H. (2012). Evolution of the world wide web: From web 1.0 to web 4.0. *International Journal of Web & Semantic Technology*, *3*(1), 1–10. doi:10.5121/ijwest.2012.3101

Agrawal, H., DeMillo, R. A., Hathaway, B., Hsu, W., Hsu, W., Krauser, E. W. ... Spafford, E. (1984). *Design of mutant operators for the C programming language*. Technical Report SERC-TR41-P. Purdue University.

Aguilar-Luzon, M., Garcia-Martinez, J. M. A., Calvo-Salguero, A., & Salinas, J. M. (2012). Comparative study between the theory of planned behavior and the value-belief-norm model regarding the environment, on spanish housewives' recycling behavior. *Journal of Applied Social Psychology*, *42*(11), 2797–2833. doi:10.1111/j.1559-1816.2012.00962.x

Ahlberg, C., & Shneiderman, B. (1994). Visual information seeking: Tight coupling of dynamic query filters with starfield displays. In *Proceedings of the SIGCHI Conference on Human Factors in Computing Systems: Celebrating Interdependence* (pp. 313-317). Boston, MA: ACM. doi:10.1145/259963.260390

Ahmadzadeh, M., Elliman, D., & Higgins, C. (2005). An analysis of patterns of debugging among novice computer science students. In *Proceedings of the 10th Annual SIGCSE Conference on Innovation and Technology in Computer Science Education* (pp. 84-88). ACM. doi:10.1145/1067445.1067472

Ahonen-Rainio, P. (2005). *Visualization of geospatial metadata for selecting geographic datasets.* (Doctoral dissertation). Helsinki University of Technology, Espoo, Finland.

Albertoni, R., Bertone, A., & Martino, M. D. (2005). Visualization and semantic analysis of geographic metadata. In *Proceedings of Workshop on Geographic information retrieval* (pp. 9-16). Bremen, Germany: ACM. doi:10.1145/1096985.1096989

Allen, E. I., & Seaman, J. (2010). *Class differences: Online education in the United States.* Sloan Consortium. Retrieved March 19, 2014 from http://files.eric.ed.gov/fulltext/ED529952.pdf

Allen, E. I., & Seaman, J. (2011). *Going the distance: Online education in the United States, 2011.* Sloan Consortium. Retrieved March 21, 2014 from http://files.eric.ed.gov/fulltext/ED529948.pdf

Allen, E. I., & Seaman, J. (2013). *Changing course: Ten years of tracking online education in the United States.* Sloan Consortium. Retrieved September 21, 2014 from http://files.eric.ed.gov/fulltext/ED541571.pdf

Almeida, F., Santos, J. D., & Monteiro, J. A. (2013). E-commerce business models in the context of web 3.0 paradigm. *International Journal of Advanced Information Technology*, *3*(6), 1–12. doi:10.5121/ijait.2013.3601

Alpert, S. R., Karat, J., Karat, C.-M., Brodie, C., & Vergo, J. G. (2003). User attitudes regarding a user-adaptive ecommerce web Site. *User Modeling and User-Adapted Interaction*, *13*(4), 373–396. doi:10.1023/A:1026201108015

Al-Shayea, P., & Bahia, I. (2010). *Urinary system diseases diagnosis using artificial neural networks.* Academic Press.

Al–Shayea, Q., El–Refae, G., & Yaseen, S. (2013). Artificial neural networks for medical diagnosis using biomedical dataset. *International Journal of Behavioural and Healthcare Research*, *4*(1), 45–63. doi:10.1504/IJBHR.2013.054519

Alter, S. (2003). 18 reasons why IT-reliant work systems should replace 'the IT artifact' as the core subject matter of the IS field. *Communications of the Association for Information Systems*, *12*(23), 366–395.

Alter, S. (2006). Work systems and IT artifacts - Does the definition matter? *Communications of the Association for Information Systems*, *17*(14), 299–313.

Altunay, S., Telatar, Z., Erogul, O., & Aydur, E. (2009). A new approach to urinary system dynamics problems: Evaluation and classification of uroflowmeter signals using artificial neural networks. *Expert Systems with Applications*, *36*(3), 4891–4895. doi:10.1016/j.eswa.2008.05.051

Ames, M. G., Go, J., Kaye, J. J., & Spasojevic, M. (2010, February). Making love in the network closet: The benefits and work of family videochat. In *Proceedings of the 2010 ACM Conference on Computer Supported Cooperative Work* (pp. 145-154). ACM. doi:10.1145/1718918.1718946

Anderson, R. E., & Ronnkvist, A. (1999). The presence of computers in American schools: Teaching, learning and computing: 1998 national survey (Report #2). Irvine, CA: Center for Research on Information Technology and Organizations. (ERIC Document Reproduction Service No. ED 430 548).

Anderson, T., & Whitelock, D. M. (2004). The educational semantic web: Visioning and practicing the future of education. *Journal of Interactive Media in Education*, *2004*(1), 1–15. doi:10.5334/2004-1

Andersson, L., Shivarajan, S., & Blau, G. (2005). Enacting ecological sustainability in the MNC: A test of an adapted value-belief-norm framework. *Journal of Business Ethics*, *59*(3), 295–305. doi:10.1007/s10551-005-3440-x

Andreeva, T., Kianto, A., & Pavlov, Y. (2013). The impact of intellectual capital management on company competitiveness and financial performance. *Knowledge Management Research & Practice, 11*(2), 112–122. doi:10.1057/kmrp.2013.9

Andrew, C., Huy, L., & Aditya, P. (2012). Big data. *XRDS The ACM Magazine for Students, 19*(1), 7–8. doi:10.1145/2331042.2331045

Antonucci, T. (2001). Social relations: An examination of social networks, social support, and sense of control. In Handbook of psychology of aging (5th ed.; pp. 427-453). San Diego, CA: Academic Press.

Apache Axis. (2014). *Apache Axis*. Retrieved March 27, 2014, from http://ws.apache.org/axis

Apache Hadoop. (2014). Retrieved September, 2014, from http://hadoop.apache.org/

Apache Tomcat. (2014). *Apache Tomcat*. Retrieved March 27, 2014, from http://tomcat.apache.org

Armstrong, J. B., & Impara, J. C. (1991). The impact of an environmental education program on knowledge and attitude. *The Journal of Environmental Education, 22*(4), 36–40. doi:10.1080/00958964.1991.9943060

Arnould, E., Price, L., & Zinkhan, G. (2004). *Consumers* (2nd ed.). New York, NY: McGraw-Hill/Irwin.

Arora, K., & Kant, K. (2012, March). *Techniques for adaptive websites and web personalization without any user effort*. Paper presented at the Conference on Electrical, Electronics and Computer Sciences, Bophal. doi:10.1109/SCEECS.2012.6184734

Arora, N., Dreze, X., Ghose, A., Hess, J., Iyengar, R., Jing, B., & Zhang, Z. et al. (2008). Putting one-to-one marketing to work: Personalization, customization, and choice. *Marketing Letters, 19*(3-4), 305–332. doi:10.1007/s11002-008-9056-z

Asproth, V., Borglund, E., Danielsson, E., Ekker, K., Holand, I. S., Holmberg, S. C., … Öberg, L. M. (2014). *Rapport från GSS: Gränsöverskridande samarbete för säkerhet (Report from GSS. Security cooperation across the border)*. Steinkjer / Östersund: Nord-Trøndelag University College and Mid Sweden University Press.

Autorità per le garanzie nelle comunicazioni. (2013). *Relazione annuale sull'attività svolta*. Roma.

Avison, D., Jones, J., Powell, P., & Wilson, D. (2004). Using and validating the strategic alignment model. *The Journal of Strategic Information Systems, 13*(3), 223–246. doi:10.1016/j.jsis.2004.08.002

Axer, H., Jantzen, J., Berks, G., & Keyserlingk, D. G. V. (2000). *Aphasia classification using neural networks*. Academic Press.

Babitski, G., Bergweiler, S., Hoffmann, J., Schön, D., Stasch, C., & Walkowski, A. (2009). Ontology-based integration of sensor web services in disaster management. In K. Janowicz, M. Raubal, & S. Levashkin (Eds.), *Geospatial semantics* (pp. 103–121). Berlin, Germany: Springer Berlin Heidelberg. doi:10.1007/978-3-642-10436-7_7

Bailey, A., & Ngwenyama, O. (2010). Bridging the generation gap in ICT use: Interrogating identity, technology and interactions in community telecenters. *Information Technology for Development, 16*(1), 62–82. doi:10.1080/02681100903566156

Baker, L. R. (2004). The ontology of artifacts. *Philosophical Explorations, 7*(2), 99–112. doi:10.1080/13869790410001694462

Baldassar, L. (2007). Transnational families and the provision of moral and emotional support: The relationship between truth and distance. *Identities: Global Studies in Culture and Power, 14*(4), 385–409. doi:10.1080/10702890701578423

Baldassar, L. (2008). Missing kin and longing to be together: Emotions and the construction of copresence in transnational relationships. *Journal of Intercultural Studies (Melbourne, Vic.), 29*(3), 247–266. doi:10.1080/07256860802169196

Baldonado, M. Q. W., Woodruff, A., & Kuchinsky, A. (2000). Guidelines for using multiple views in information visualization. In *Proceedings of the Working Conference on Advanced Visual Interfaces* (pp. 110-119). Palermo, Italy: ACM. doi:10.1145/345513.345271

Bamberg, S., & Schmidt, P. (2003). Incentives, morality, or habit? Predicting students' car use for university routes with the models of Ajzen, Schwartz, and Triandis. *Environment and Behavior*, *35*(2), 264–285. doi:10.1177/0013916502250134

Barassi, V., & Treré, E. (2012). Does web 3.0 come after web 2.0? Deconstructing theoretical assumptions through practice. *New Media & Society*, *14*(8), 1269–1285. doi:10.1177/1461444812445878

Barley, S. R. (1998). What can we learn from the history of technology? *Journal of Engineering and Technology Management*, *15*(4), 237–255. doi:10.1016/S0923-4748(98)00016-2

Barnard, Y., Bradley, M. D., Hodgson, F., & Lloyd, A. D. (2013). Learning to use new technologies by older adults: Perceived difficulties, experimentation behaviour and usability. *Computers in Human Behavior*, *29*(4), 1715–1724. doi:10.1016/j.chb.2013.02.006

Bar-On, R., Handley, R., & Fund, S. (2006). The impact of emotional intelligence on performance. In V. Druskat, F. Sala, & G. Mount (Eds.), *Linking emotional intelligence and performance at work: Current research evidence with individuals and groups* (pp. 3–19). Mahwah, NJ: Lawrence Erlbaum.

Bar-On, R., & Maree, J. G. (2009). In search of emotional-social giftedness: a potentially viable and valuable concept. In L. V. Shavinina (Ed.), *International handbook of giftedness* (pp. 559–570). New York: Springer Science. doi:10.1007/978-1-4020-6162-2_26

Barrett, H. (2011). *Balancing the two faces of e-portfolios*. Retrieved April 15, 2014 from http://electronicportfolios.org/balance/Balancing2.htm

Barrows, H. S., & Tamblyn, R. M. (1980). *Problem-based learning: An approach to medical education*. New York: Springer Publishing Company.

Bassili, J. N., & Joordens, S. (2008). Media player tool use, satisfaction with online lectures and examination performance. *Journal of Distance Education*, *22*(2), 93–108.

Bateman, S., Gutwin, C., & Nacenta, M. (2008). Seeing things in the clouds: The effect of visual features on tag cloud selections. In *Proc. of the 19th ACM conference on Hypertext and Hypermedia* (pp. 193–202). ACM Press. doi:10.1145/1379092.1379130

Bauman, Z. (2008). *The art of life*. Cambridge, MA: Polity.

Baumeister, H., Knapp, A., Koch, N., & Zhang, G. (2005). Modelling adaptivity with aspects. In *Proceedings of International Conference on Web Engineering* (pp. 406-416). Academic Press. doi:10.1007/11531371_53

Baym, N. K., Zhang, Y. B., & Lin, M. (2004). Social interactions across media: Interpersonal communication on the internet, telephone and face-to-face. *New Media & Society*, *6*(3), 299–318. doi:10.1177/1461444804041438

Beale, R., & Creed, C. (2009). Affective interaction: How emotional agents affect users. *International Journal of Human-Computer Studies*, *67*(9), 755–776. doi:10.1016/j.ijhcs.2009.05.001

Beard, K., & Sharma, V. (1997). Multidimensional ranking for data in digital spatial libraries. *International Journal on Digital Libraries*, *1*(2), 153–160. doi:10.1007/s007990050011

Beaudoin, M. (1990). The instructor's changing role in distance education. *American Journal of Distance Education*, *4*(2), 21–29. doi:10.1080/08923649009526701

Becker, H. J. (1998). Running to catch a moving train: Schools and information technologies. *Theory into Practice*, *37*(1), 20–30. doi:10.1080/00405849809543782

Beeckman, D., Schoonhoven, L., Boucqué, H., Van Maele, G., & Defloor, T. (2008). Pressure ulcers: E-learning to improve classification by nurses and nursing students. *Journal of Clinical Nursing*, *17*(13), 1697–1707. doi:10.1111/j.1365-2702.2007.02200.x PMID:18592624

Behr, J., Eschler, P., Jung, Y., & Zöllner, M. (2009). X3DOM: A DOM-based HTML5/X3D integration model. In *Proceedings of International Conference on 3D Web Technology* (pp. 127-135). Darmstadt, Germany: ACM. doi:10.1145/1559764.1559784

Behr, J., Jung, Y., Drevensek, T., & Aderhold, A. (2011). Dynamic and interactive aspects of X3DOM. In *Proceedings ofInternational Conference on 3D Web Technology* (pp. 81-87). Paris, France: ACM.

Behr, J., Jung, Y., Keil, J., Drevensek, T., Zoellner, M., Eschler, P., & Fellner, D. (2010). A scalable architecture for the HTML5/X3D integration model X3DOM. In *Proceedings ofInternational Conference on Web 3D Technology* (pp. 185-194). Los Angeles, CA: ACM. doi:10.1145/1836049.1836077

Belfo, F., & Sousa, R. D. (2013). Reviewing business-IT alignment instruments under SAM dimensions. *International Journal of Information Communication Technologies and Human Development*, 5(3), 18–40. doi:10.4018/jicthd.2013070102

Benbasat, I., & Zmud, R. W. (2003). The identity crisis within the IS discipline: Defining and communicating the discipline's core properties. *Management Information Systems Quarterly*, 27(2), 183–194.

Bennett, S., Maton, K., & Kervin, L. (2008). The 'digital natives' debate: A critical review of the evidence. *British Journal of Educational Technology*, 39(5), 775–786. doi:10.1111/j.1467-8535.2007.00793.x

Bergeron, F., & Raymond, L. (1992). Evaluation of EIS from a managerial perspective. *Information Systems Journal*, 2(1), 45–60. doi:10.1111/j.1365-2575.1992.tb00066.x

Bergeron, F., Raymond, L., Rivard, S., & Gara, M.-F. (1995). Determinant of EIS use: Testing a behavioral model. *Decision Support Systems*, 14(2), 131–146. doi:10.1016/0167-9236(94)00007-F

Bergin, J., Eckstein, J., Manns, M., Sharp, H., & Voelter, M. (2000). *The pedagogical pattern project*. Retrieved June 12, 2014, from http://www.pedagogicalpatterns.org

Bermudez, L., Graybeal, J., & Arko, R. (2006). A marine platforms ontology: Experiences and lessons. In *Proceedings ofWorkshop on Semantic Sensor Networks (SSN 2006). Proceedings of conjunction with 5th International Semantic Web Conference (ISWC 2006)*. Athens, GA: Academic Press.

Berners-Lee, T., Hendler, J., & Lassila, O. (2001). The semantic web. *Scientific American*, 28–37. PMID:11323639

Berners-Lee, T., Hendler, J., & Lassila, O. (2001). The semantic web. *Scientific American*, 29–37. PMID:11323639

Berners-Lee, T., Hendler, J., & Lassila, O. (2001). Web semantic: A new form of web content that is meaningful to computers will unleash a revolution of new possibilities. *Scientific American*, 284(5), 34–43. doi:10.1038/scientificamerican0501-34 PMID:11396337

Berry, K., & Paulo Kushnir, L. (2013). Crossing borders: A comparison of the impact of various teaching strategies and tools in an online and face-to-face psychology course. In *Proceedings of the 25th World Conference on Educational Multimedia, Hypermedia and Telecommunications 2013* (pp. 1724-1731). Chesapeake, VA: AACE.

Berry, M. W. (2004). *Survey of text mining: Clustering, classification, and retrieval*. Berlin, Germany: Springer-Verlag.

Beyea, J. A., Wong, E., Bromwich, M., Weston, W. W., & Fung, K. (2008). Evaluation of a particle repositioning maneuver web-based teaching module. *The Laryngoscope*, 118(1), 175–180. doi:10.1097/MLG.0b013e31814b290d PMID:18251035

Bharati, P., & Chaudhury, A. (2006). Product customization on the web: An empirical study of factors impacting choiceboard user satisfaction. *Management Science and Information Systems Faculty Publication Series*, 4.

Bharwaney-Orme, G., & Bar-On, R. (2002). The contribution of emotional intelligence to individual and organizational effectiveness. *Competency & Emotional Intelligence*, 9(4), 23–28.

Bickart, B., & Schindler, R. M. (2001). Internet forums as influential sources of consumer information. *Journal of Interactive Marketing*, 15(3), 31–40. doi:10.1002/dir.1014

Binardi, A. P., Green, J., & Kackson, G. (2013). Exploring the impact of a company's web technological development on its innovation activity: A case study of small- and medium-sized enterprises (SMEs) in North Wales. *Global Business Perspectives*, 1(4), 488–514. doi:10.1007/s40196-013-0023-6

Biocca, F., Burgoon, J., Harm, C., & Stoner, M. (2001). Criteria and scope conditions for a theory and measure of social presence. East Lansing, MI: Media Interface and Network Design (M.I.N.D.) Lab.

Birkland, T. A. (2009). Disasters, lessons learned, and fantasy documents. *Journal of Contingencies and Crisis Management, 17*(3), 1–12. doi:10.1111/j.1468-5973.2009.00575.x

Bititci, U. S., Garengo, P., Dörfler, V., & Nudurupati, S. (2012). Performance measurement: Challenges for tomorrow. *International Journal of Management Reviews, 14*(3), 305–327. doi:10.1111/j.1468-2370.2011.00318.x

Bititci, U. S., & Nudurupati, S. S. (2002). Using performance measurement to drive continuous improvement. *Manufacturing Engineering, 81*(5), 230–235. doi:10.1049/me:20020506

Bititci, U. S., Turner, T., & Begemann, C. (2000). Dynamics of performance measurement systems. *International Journal of Operations & Production Management, 20*(6), 692–704. doi:10.1108/01443570010321676

Bittencourt, I., Isotani, S., Costa, E., & Mizoguchi, R. (2007). Research directions on semantic web and education. *Scientia: Interdisciplinary Studies in Computer Science, 19*(1), 59–66.

Bloehdorn, S., Cimiano, P., & Hotho, A. (2006). Learning ontologies to improve text clustering and classification. In *From data and information analysis to knowledge engineering* (pp. 334–341). Berlin: Springer Berlin Heidelberg.

Boase, J., Horrigan, J. B., Wellman, B., & Rainie, L. (2006). *Pew report: The strength of internet ties*. Washington, DC: Pew Internet and American Life Project.

Boudreau, M.-C., Gefen, D., & Straub, D. W. (2001). Validation in information systems research: A state-of-the-art assessment. *Management Information Systems Quarterly, 25*(1), 1–16. doi:10.2307/3250956

Bourne, M., Mills, J., Wilcox, M., Neely, A., & Platts, K. (2000). Designing, implementing and updating performance measurement systems. *International Journal of Operations & Production Management, 20*(7), 754–771. doi:10.1108/01443570010330739

Bourner, T. (2008). The fully functioning university. *Higher Education Review, 40*(2), 26–46.

Bourner, T., Greener, S., & Rospigliosi, A. (2011). Graduate employability and the propensity to learn in employment: A new vocationalism. *Higher Education Review, 43*(3), 5–30.

Boykov, V., Zakharov, V., Karyaeva, M., & Sokolov, V. (2013). Thesaurus poetics as a tool for information retrieval and knowledge collection. *Modeling and Analysis of Information Systems, 20*(4), 125–135.

br.ispell. (2014). *Dictionary br.ispell*. Retrieved March 27, 2014, from http://www.ime.usp.br/~ueda/br.ispell

Bra, P., Aerts, A., Berden, B., Lange, B., Rousseau, B., Santic, T., … Stash, N. (2003). AHA! The adaptive hypermedia architecture. In *Proceedings of 14th Association for Computing Machinery Conference on Hypertext and Hypermedia* (pp. 81-84). Nottingham, UK: Academic Press.

Bra, P., Brusilovsky, P., & Houben, G. (1999). Adaptive hypermedia: From systems to framework. Association for Computing Machinery Computing Surveys, 31(4).

Brekke, M. (2008). Young refugees in a network society. In *Mobility and place: Enacting Northern European peripheries* (pp. 103-114). Academic Press.

Brisson, L. (2001). Comment rendre compte de la participation du sensible à l'intelligible chez Platon? In J.-F. Pradeau (Ed.), *Platon: Les formes intelligibles* (pp. 55–85). Paris: Presses Universitaires de France.

Bristol, T. J. (2010). Twitter: Consider the possibilities for continuing nursing education. *Journal of Continuing Education in Nursing, 41*(5), 199–200. doi:10.3928/00220124-20100423-09 PMID:20481418

Bröring, A., Echterhoff, J., Jirka, S., Simonis, I., Everding, T., Stasch, C., & Lemmens, R. et al. (2011). New generation sensor web enablement. *Sensors (Basel, Switzerland), 11*(3), 2652–2699. doi:10.3390/s110302652 PMID:22163760

Brownstein, B., Brownstein, D., & Gerlowski, D. A. (2008). Web-based vs. face-to-face MBA classes: A comparative assessment study. *Journal of College Teaching and Learning, 5*(11), 41–48.

Brunsell, E., & Horejsi, M. (2013). A flipped classroom in action. *Science Teacher (Normal, Ill.)*, *80*, 8.

Brusilovsky, P. (2007). Adaptive navigation support. In P. Brusilovsky, A. Kobsa, & W. Nejdl (Eds.), *The adaptive web: Methods and strategies of web personalization* (pp. 263–290). Berlin: Springer. doi:10.1007/978-3-540-72079-9_8

Brusilovsky, P., Eklund, J., & Schwarz, E. (1998). Web-based education for all: A tool for development adaptive courseware. *Computer Networks and ISDN Systems*, *30*(1), 291–300. doi:10.1016/S0169-7552(98)00082-8

Brusilovsky, P., & Millán, E. (2007). User models for adaptive hypermedia and adaptive educational systems. In P. Brusilovsky, A. Kobsa, & W. Nejdl (Eds.), *The adaptive web: Methods and strategies of web personalization* (pp. 3–53). Berlin: Springer. doi:10.1007/978-3-540-72079-9_1

Brusilovsky, P., & Vassileva, J. (2003). Course sequencing techniques for large-scale web-based education. *International Journal of Continuing Engineering Education and Lifelong Learning*, *13*(1), 75–94. doi:10.1504/IJCEELL.2003.002154

Bucos, M., Dragulescu, B., & Veltan, M. (2010). Designing a semantic web ontology for e-learning in higher education. In *Proceedings of Electronics and Telecommunications (ISETC)* (pp. 415-418). IEEE. doi:10.1109/ISETC.2010.5679298

Bull, G., Ferster, B., & Kjellstrom, W. (2012). Inventing the flipped classroom. *Learning and Leading with Technology*, *40*(1), 10.

Bunt, A., Carenini, G., & Conati, C. (2007). Adaptive content presentation for the web. In P. Brusilovsky, A. Kobsa, & W. Nejdl (Eds.), *The adaptive web: Methods and strategies of web personalization* (pp. 409–432). Berlin: Springer. doi:10.1007/978-3-540-72079-9_13

Burke, R. (2000). Knowledge-based recommender systems. In A. Kent (Ed.), *Encyclopedia of library and information systems*. New York: Marcel Dekker.

Burke, R. (2002). Hybrid recommender systems: Survey and experiments. *User Modeling and User-Adapted Interaction*, *12*(4), 331–370. doi:10.1023/A:1021240730564

Burke, R. (2007). Hybrid web recommender systems. In P. Brusilovsky, A. Kobsa, & W. Nejdl (Eds.), *The adaptive web: Methods and strategies of web personalization* (pp. 377–408). Berlin: Springer. doi:10.1007/978-3-540-72079-9_12

Burn, J. M. (1996). IS innovation and organizational alignment. *Journal of Information Technology*, *11*(1), 3–12. doi:10.1080/026839696345388

Butts, C. T. (2008). Social network analysis with SNA. *Journal of Statistical Software*, *24*(6), 1–51. PMID:18612375

Byron, T. (2008). Safer children in a digital world: The report of the Byron Review. Department for Children, Schools and Families, and the Department for Culture, Media and Sport.

Cacioppo, J. T., Hughes, M. E., Waite, L. J., Hawkley, L. C., & Thisted, R. A. (2006). Loneliness as a specific risk factor for depressive symptoms: Cross-sectional and longitudinal analyses. *Psychology and Aging*, *21*(1), 140–151. doi:10.1037/0882-7974.21.1.140 PMID:16594799

Cagliano, R., & Spina, G. (2002). A comparison of practice-performance models between small manufacturers and subcontractors. *International Journal of Operations & Production Management*, *22*(12), 1367–1388. doi:10.1108/01443570210452057

Cai, G. (2002). GeoVIBE: A visual interface for geographic digital libraries. In K. Börner & C. Chen (Eds.), *Visual interfaces to digital libraries* (pp. 171–187). Bremen, Germany: Springer Berlin Heidelberg. doi:10.1007/3-540-36222-3_13

Cairncross, F. (1997). *The death of distance: How the communications revolution is changing our lives*. Boston: Harvard Business School Press.

Calacanis, J. (2007). *Web 3.0, the "official" definition*. Retrieved April 15, 2014 from http://calacanis.com/2007/10/03/web-3-0-the-official-definition/

Camargo, L., & Vidotti, S. (2007). Personalization: A mediating service in research environments. *TransInformação*, *19*(3), 251–264. doi:10.1590/S0103-37862007000300005

Campbell, C. (2005). The romantic ethic and the spirit of the modern consumerism. London: WritersPrintShop.

Campbell, J., Horton, D., Craig, M., & Gries, P. (2014). Evaluating an inverted CS1. In *Proceedings of the 45th ACM Technical Symposium on Computer Science Education (SIGCSE '14)*. ACM. Retrieved September 21, 2014 from http://doi.acm.org/10.1145/2538862.2538943

Campbell, J. P., Oblinger, D. G., & DeBlois, P. B. (2007). Academic analytics: A new tool for a new era. *EDUCAUSE Review*, *42*, 40–57.

Campos, S. R., Fernandes, A. A., de Sousa, R. T., Jr., de Freitas, E. P., da Costa, J. P. C. L., Serrano, A. M. R., … Rodrigues, C. T. (2012). Ontologic audit trails mapping for detection of irregularities in payrolls. In *Proceedings of the Fourth International Conference on Computational Aspects of Social Networks* (CASoN). São Carlos, Brazil: IEEE Press.

Carbone, F., Contreras, J., Hernandez, J. Z., & Gomez-Perez, J. M. (2012). Open innovation in an enterprise 3.0 framework: Three case studies. *Expert Systems with Applications*, *39*(10), 8929–8939. doi:10.1016/j.eswa.2012.02.015

Carey, T., & Trick, D. (2013). *How online learning affects productivity, cost and quality in higher education: An environmental scan and review of the literature*. Toronto, Canada: Higher Education Quality Council of Ontario. Retrieved March 5, 2014 from http://www.heqco.ca/SiteCollectionDocuments/How_Online_Learning_Affects_Productivity-ENG.pdf

Carter, L. K., & Emerson, T. L. N. (2012). In-class vs. online experiments: Is there a difference? *The Journal of Economic Education*, *43*(1), 4–18. doi:10.1080/00220485.2011.636699

Carù, A., & Cova, B. (2004). How service elements wrap the consumer's experience. The case of music consumption on the Auditorium of Milan. *Finanza Marketing e Produzione*, *2*, 5–28.

Castellanos-Nieves, D., Fernández-Breis, J. T., Valencia-García, R., Martínez-Béjar, R., & Iniesta-Moreno, M. (2011). Semantic web technologies for supporting learning assessment. *Information Sciences*, *181*(9), 1517–1537. doi:10.1016/j.ins.2011.01.010

Castro, H., Putnik, G., Cruz-Cunha, M. M., Ferreira, L., Shah, V., & Alves, C. (2012). Meta-organization and manufacturing web 3.0 for ubiquitous virtual enterprise of manufacturing SMEs: A framework. In *Proceedings of the 8th CIRP Conference on Intelligent Computation in Manufacturing Engineering*. Ischia, Italy: Elsevier Procedia.

Celentano, A., & Pittarello, F. (2004). Observing and adapting user behaviour in navigational 3D interfaces. *Advanced Visual Interfaces*, 275-282.

Center for Social Organization of Schools. (1983). *School uses of microcomputers: Reports from a national survey (Issue no. 1)*. Baltimore, MD: Johns Hopkins University, Center for Social Organization of School.

Chalmers, P. A. (2000). User interface improvements in computer-assisted instruction, the challenge. *Computers in Human Behavior*, *16*(5), 507–517. doi:10.1016/S0747-5632(00)00022-4

Chang, F., Dean, J., Ghemawat, S., Hsieh, W. C., Wallach, D. A., Burrows, M., & Gruber, R. E. (2008). Bigtable: A distributed storage system for structured data. *ACM Transactions on Computer Systems*, *26*(2), 1–26. doi:10.1145/1365815.1365816

Chan, Y. E., & Reich, B. H. (2007). IT alignment: What have we learned? *Journal of Information Technology*, *22*(4), 297–315. doi:10.1057/palgrave.jit.2000109

Chan, Y. E., Sabherwal, R., & Thatcher, J. B. (2006). Antecedents and outcomes of strategic IS alignment: An empirical investigation. *IEEE Transactions on Engineering Management*, *53*(1), 27–47. doi:10.1109/TEM.2005.861804

Charles, S., & Carstensen, L. L. (2010). Social and emotional aging. *Annual Review of Psychology*, *61*(1), 383–409. doi:10.1146/annurev.psych.093008.100448 PMID:19575618

Chau, M., Zeng, D., & Chen, H. (2001). Personalized spiders for web search and analysis. In *Proceedings of 1st ACM/IEEE-CS Joint Conference on Digital Libraries* (pp. 79-87). Roanoke, VA: ACM. doi:10.1145/379437.379454

Chen, S., Cowan, C. F. N., & Grant, P. M. (1991). Orthogonal least squares learning algorithm for radial basis function networks. *IEEE Transactions on Neural Networks*, 2(2), 302–309. doi:10.1109/72.80341

Chih-Hsiung, T. (2012). The integration of personal learning environments & open network learning environments. *TechTrends*, 56(3), 13–19. doi:10.1007/s11528-012-0571-7

Chittaro, L., & Ranon, R. (2007). Adaptive 3D web sites. In P. Brusilovsky, A. Kobsa, & W. Nejdl (Eds.), *The adaptive web: Methods and strategies of web personalization* (pp. 433–462). Berlin: Springer. doi:10.1007/978-3-540-72079-9_14

Chmiel, R., & Loui, M. C. (2004). Debugging: From novice to expert. In *Proceedings of the 35th SIGCSE Technical Symposium on Computer Science Education* (pp. 17-21). ACM. doi:10.1145/971300.971310

Cision. (2009). *What "web 3.0" will mean to you.* Cision Executive White Paper. Chicago: Cision US. Retrieved from http://us.cision.com/assets/whitepapers/ Cision_Whitepaper_Web3.pdf

Clark-Ibáñez, M., & Scott, L. (2008). Learning to teach online. *Teaching Sociology, 36*(1), 34-41.

Clawson, M. (1963). *Land and water for recreation: Opportunities, policies and problems.* New York, NY: Rand McNally.

Cleveland, M., Kalamas, M., & Laroche, M. (2005). Shades of green: Linking environmental locus of control and pro-environmental behaviors. *Journal of Consumer Marketing, 22*(4), 198–212. doi:10.1108/07363760510605317

Cloran, R. A. (2007). Trust on the semantic web. Grahamstown: Rhodes University. Retrieved from http://icsa.cs.up.ac.za/issa/2005/Proceedings/Full/025_Article.pdf

Cohen, K. R. (2005). What does the photoblog want? *Media Culture & Society, 27*(6), 883–901. doi:10.1177/0163443705057675

Collett, S. (2011). Why Big data is a big deal. *Computerworld, 45*(20), 1–6. Retrieved from http://www.computerworld.com/article/2550147/business-intelligence/why-big-data-is-a-big-deal.html

Colvin, K. F., Champaign, J., Liu, A., Zhou, Q., Fredericks, C., & Pritchard, D. E. (2014). Learning in an Introductory Physics MOOC: All cohorts learn equally, including an on-campus class. *International Review of Research in Open and Distance Learning, 15*(4). Retrieved September 21, 2014 from http://www.irrodl.org/index.php/irrodl/article/view/1902/3009

Connolly, M., Jones, C., & Jones, N. (2007). New approaches, new vision: Capturing teacher experiences in a brave new online world. *Open Learning, 22*(1), 43–56. doi:10.1080/02680510601100150

Conole, G., & Alevizou, P. (2010). *A literature review of the use of web 2.0 tools in higher education.* Milton Keynes, UK: HEA.

Cooley, R., Mobasher, B., & Srivastava, J. (1997, November). *Web mining: information and pattern discovery on the world wide web.* Paper presented at 9th IEEE International Conference on Tools with Artificial Intelligence, Newport Beach, CA. doi:10.1109/TAI.1997.632303

Cornwell, B. (2011). Independence through social networks: Bridging potential among older women and men. *The Journals of Gerontology. Series B, Psychological Sciences and Social Sciences*, gbr111. PMID:21983039

Cornwell, B., Laumann, E. O., & Schumm, L. P. (2008). The social connectedness of older adults: A national profile. *American Sociological Review, 73*(2), 185–203. doi:10.1177/000312240807300201 PMID:19018292

Cornwell, E. Y., & Waite, L. J. (2009). Social disconnectedness, perceived isolation, and health among older adults. *Journal of Health and Social Behavior, 50*(1), 31–48. doi:10.1177/002214650905000103 PMID:19413133

Cotten, S. R., Anderson, W. A., & McCullough, B. M. (2013). Impact of internet use on loneliness and contact with others among older adults: Cross-sectional analysis. *Journal of Medical Internet Research, 15*(2), e39. doi:10.2196/jmir.2306 PMID:23448864

Council, C. I. O. (2013). *Clinger-Cohen core competencies.* Retrieved December 15, 2013, from https://cio.gov/wp-content/uploads/downloads/2013/02/2012-Learning-Objectives-Final.pdf

Cova, B. (2003). *Il marketing tribale*. Milano, Italy: Il Sole 24 Ore.

Cova, B. (1995). Community and consumption: towards a definition of the "linking value" of products and services. In *Proceedings of the European Marketing Academy Conference ESSEC*. Paris: ESSEC.

Crews, N. (2008). *Comparative study of open 3D graphics standards*. Autodesk Inc.

Crook, C., Fisher, T., Graber, R., Harrison, C., Lewin, C., Logan, C., Luckin, R., Oliver, M., & Sharples, M. (2008). *Web 2.0 technologies for learning: The current landscape - Opportunities, challenges and tensions*. BECTA Research Report.

Cryptosmith.com. (2015). *Digital's RT-11 file system: Tech teaching*. Retrieved January 22, 2015 from http://cryptosmith.com/2013/10/19/digitals-rt-11-file-system/

Cummings, J. N., Butler, B., & Kraut, R. (2002). The quality of online social relationships. *Communications of the ACM*, *45*(7), 103–108. doi:10.1145/514236.514242

Czaja, S. J., Sharit, J., Lee, C. C., Nair, S. N., Hernández, M. A., Arana, N., & Fu, S. H. (2013). Factors influencing use of an e-health website in a community sample of older adults. *Journal of the American Medical Informatics Association*, *20*(2), 277–284. doi:10.1136/amiajnl-2012-000876 PMID:22802269

Dalton, R. J., Gontmacher, Y., Lovrich, N. P., & Pierce, J. C. (1999). Environmental attitudes and the new environmental paradigm. In R. J. Dalton, P. Garb, P. Lovrich, J. C. Pierce, & J. M. Whitely (Eds.), *Critical masses: Citizens, nuclear weapons production, and environmental destruction in the United States and Russia* (pp. 195–230). Cambridge, MA: MIT Press.

Das, R., Turkoglu, I., & Sengur, A. (2009). Effective diagnosis of heart disease through neural networks ensembles. *Expert Systems with Applications*, *36*(4), 7675–7680. doi:10.1016/j.eswa.2008.09.013

Daymont, T., & Blau, G. (2008). Student performance in online and traditional sections of an undergraduate management course. *Journal of Behavioral and Applied Management*, *9*(3), 275–294.

De Chenecey, S. P. (2005). Branding in an entertainment culture. *Young Consumers*, *2*(3), 20–22. doi:10.1108/17473610510701151

De Groot, J. I. M., & Steg, L. (2008). Value orientations to explain beliefs related to environmental significant behavior: How to measure egoistic, altruistic, and biospheric value orientation. *Environment and Behavior*, *40*(3), 330–354. doi:10.1177/0013916506297831

De Nicola, A., Missikoff, M., & Schiappelli, F. (2004). Towards an ontological support for eLearning courses. In *Proceedings of On the Move to Meaningful Internet Systems 2004: OTM 2004 Workshops* (pp. 773-777). Springer Berlin Heidelberg. Retrieved from http://www.starlab.vub.ac.be/events/OTM04WOSE/papers/20.pdf

De Toni, A., & Tonchia, S. (2001). Performance measurement systems – Models, characteristics and measures. *International Journal of Operations & Production Management*, *21*(1-2), 46–70. doi:10.1108/01443570110358459

Dean, J., & Ghemawat, S. (2008). MapReduce: Simplified data processing on large clusters. *Communications of the ACM*, *51*(1), 107–113. doi:10.1145/1327452.1327492

Debnath, R., & Kurita, T. (2010). An evolutionary approach for gene selection and classification of microarray data based on {SVM} error-bound theories. *Bio Systems*, *100*(1), 39–46. doi:10.1016/j.biosystems.2009.12.006 PMID:20045444

DeCandia, G., Hastorun, D., Jampani, M., Kakulapati, G., Lakshman, A., Pilchin, A., & Vogels, W. (2007). Dynamo: Amazon's highly available key-value store. *ACM SIGOPS Operating Systems Review ACM*, *41*(6), 205–220. doi:10.1145/1323293.1294281

Degenne, A., & Forsé, M. (1999). *Introducing social network*. London: Sage.

Dekker, R., & Engbersen, G. (2014). How social media transform migrant networks and facilitate migration. *Global Networks*, *14*(4), 401–418. doi:10.1111/glob.12040

Delen, D., & Demirkan, H. (2013). Data, information and analytics as services. *Decision Support Systems*, *55*(1), 359–363. doi:10.1016/j.dss.2012.05.044

DeLone, W. H., & McLean, E. R. (1992). Information systems success: The quest for the dependent variable. *Information Systems Research, 3*(1), 60–95. doi:10.1287/isre.3.1.60

DeLone, W. H., & McLean, E. R. (2003). The DeLone and McLean model of information systems success: A ten-year update. *Journal of Management Information Systems, 19*(4), 9–30.

Désilets, A., & Paquet, S. (2005). Wiki as a tool for web-based collaborative story telling in primary school: a Case Study. In KommersP.RichardsG. (Eds.), *Proceedings of World Conference on Educational Multimedia, Hypermedia and Telecommunications* (pp. 770-777). Chesapeake, VA: AACE.

Devedzic, V. (2004). Education and the semantic web. *International Journal of Artificial Intelligence in Education, 14*(2), 165–191. Retrieved from http://iospress.metapress.com/content/hr4v08qm6vy8y3t7/fulltext.pdf?page=1

Diaz, V., Garrett, P. B., Kinley, E. R., Moore, J. F., Schwartz, C. M., & Kohrman, P. (2009, May-June). Faculty development for the 21st century. *EDUCAUSE Review, 44*(3), 46–55.

Diminescu, D. (2008). The connected migrant: An epistemological manifesto. *Social Sciences Information. Information Sur les Sciences Sociales, 47*(4), 565–579. doi:10.1177/0539018408096447

Dissanayake, M. S. B., & Corne, D. W. (2010). Feature selection and classification in bioscience/medical datasets: study of parameters and multi-objective approach in two-phase EA/k-NN method. In *Proceedings of Computational Intelligence (UKCI)* (pp. 1–6). Academic Press. doi:10.1109/UKCI.2010.5625581

Dolgin, A. (2008, April). *Runet: The game in advance: What is web 3.0?* Retrieved April 15, 2014 from http://polit.ru/article/2008/04/02/web3/

Dolog, P., & Nejdl, W. (2007). Semantic web technologies for the adaptive web. In P. Brusilovsky, A. Kobsa, & W. Nejdl (Eds.), *The adaptive web: Methods and strategies of web personalization* (pp. 697–719). Berlin: Springer. doi:10.1007/978-3-540-72079-9_23

Donath, J., & Boyd, D. (2004). Public displays of connection. *BT Technology Journal, 22*(4), 71-82.

Dörk, M., Carpendale, S., Collins, C., & Williamson, C. (2008). Visgets: Coordinated visualizations for Web-based information exploration and discovery. *IEEE Transactions on Visualization and Computer Graphics, 14*(6), 1205–1212. doi:10.1109/TVCG.2008.175 PMID:18988965

Dries, N., & Pepermans, R. (2007). Using emotional intelligence to identify high potential: A metacompetency perspective. *Leadership and Organization Development Journal, 28*(8), 749–770. doi:10.1108/01437730710835470

Driscoll, A., Jicha, K., Hunt, A. N., Tichavsky, L., & Thompson, G. (2012). Can online courses deliver in-class results?: A comparison of student performance and satisfaction in an online versus a face-to-face introductory sociology course. *Teaching Sociology, 40*(4), 312–331. doi:10.1177/0092055X12446624

Drucker-Godard, C., Ehlinger, S., & Grenier, C. (2003). Validité et fiabilité de la recherche. In R.-A. Thiétart (Ed.), *Méthodes de recherche en management* (pp. 257–287). Paris: Dunod.

Drucker, P. (2011). *The age of discontinuity: Guidelines to our changing society.* Transaction Publishers.

DSpace. (2014). *Digital repository software.* Retrieved March 27, 2014, from http://www.openarchives.org

Dufresne, A., & Rouatbi, M. (2007). Ontologies, applications integration and support to users in learning objects repositories. In Proceedings of SWEL'07: Ontologies and Semantic Web Services for Intelligent Distributed Educational Systems (pp. 30-35). Academic Press.

Dumbill, E. (2012). *Planning for big data.* Sebastopol, CA: O'Reilly Media, Inc.

Dunlap, R. E., & Van Liere, K. D. (1978). The 'new environmental paradigm': A proposed measuring instrument and preliminary results. *The Journal of Environmental Education, 9*(4), 10–19. doi:10.1080/00958964.1978.10801875

Dunlap, R. E., & Van Liere, K. D. (1984). Commitment to the dominant social paradigm and concern for environmental quality. *Social Science Quarterly, 65*, 1013–1028.

Dunlap, R. E., Van Liere, K. D., Mertig, A. G., & Emmet Jones, R. (2000). Measuring endorsement of the new ecological paradigm: A revised NEP scale. *The Journal of Social Issues, 56*(3), 425–439. doi:10.1111/0022-4537.00176

Dutta, B. (2006). *Semantic web based e-learning*. Retrieved from https://drtc.isibang.ac.in/bitstream/handle/1849/223/PaperP-Biswanath.pdf?sequence=1

Dwivedi, Y., Williams, M., Mitra, A., Niranjan, S., & Weerakkody, V. (2011). Understanding advances in web technologies: Evolution from web 2.0 to web 3.0. *ECIS, 2011*, 257.

Ebner, M., Schön, S., Taraghi, B., Drachsler, H., & Tsang, P. (2011). First steps towards an integrated personal learning environment at the university level. In Enhancing learning through technology: Education unplugged: Mobile technologies and web 2.0 (pp. 22-36). Springer Berlin Heidelberg. doi:10.1007/978-3-642-22383-9_3

ECAR. (2012). *National study of undergraduate students and information technology*. Retrieved April 30th 2014, from http://www.educause.edu/ecar

ECAR. (2013). *National study of undergraduate students and information technology*. Retrieved 30th April 2014 from http://www.educause.edu/ecar

Eftekhari, M. H., & Zeynab, B. (2008). *Web 1.0 to web 3.0 evolution and its impact on tourism business development*. Working paper.

Ekker, K. (2010). Information retrieval for simulation debriefing: Statistical analysis "on the fly". In *Proceedings of World Conference on Educational Multimedia, Hypermedia and Telecommunications* (pp. 3329-3336). Academic Press.

Ekker, K., Asproth, V., & Holmberg, S. C. (2013). Debriefing with R-statistics and support for system dynamics modeling of inter regional security. In P. Kommers and P. Isaias (Eds), *Proceedings of the International Conference e-Society 2013* (pp. 3-10). Academic Press.

Ekker, K., Gifford, G., Leik, S. A., & Leik, R. K. (1988). Using microcomputer game-simulation experiments to study family response to the Mt. St. Helens eruptions. *Social Science Computer Review, 6*(1), 90–105. doi:10.1177/089443938800600109

Elias, T. (2011, January). *Learning analytics: Definitions, processes and potential*. Retrieved September 15, 2013 from http://learninganalytics.net/LearningAnalyticsDefinitionsProcessesPotential.pdf

Elliott, A., & Urry, J. (2010). *Mobile lives*. New York: Routledge.

Elmaa, Y. (2013). Horizontal training in open environments, new forms of professional development of teachers. In *Proceedings of the Information Technology for the New School Conference* (Vol. 3, pp. 15-18). St. Petersburg, Russia: Regional Centre for Education Quality Assessment and Information Technologies.

Employment and Training Administration. (2014). *ETA competency model*. Retrieved December 15, 2013, from http://www.careeronestop.org/competencymodel/pyramid.aspx?IT=Y

Epstein, M., & Manzoni, J. F. (1998). Implementing corporate strategy: From tableaux de bord to balanced scorecards. *European Management Journal, 16*(2), 190–203. doi:10.1016/S0263-2373(97)00087-X

Er, O., Yumusak, N., & Temurtas, F. (2010). Chest diseases diagnosis using artificial neural networks. *Expert Systems with Applications, 37*(12), 7648–7655. doi:10.1016/j.eswa.2010.04.078

Erragcha, N. (2014). Social networks as marketing tools. *British Journal of Marketing Studies, 2*(1), 79–88.

Escarrabill, J., Marti, T., & Torrente, E. (2011). Good morning, doctor Google. *Revista Portuguesa de Pneumologia, 17*(4), 177–181. doi:10.1016/j.rppneu.2011.03.011 PMID:21600729

European Commission. (2005). *The new SME definition – User guide and model declaration*. Brussels: Enterprise and Industry Publications.

Eurostat. (2013). *Statistics in focus*. Author.

Farquhar, M. (1995). Definitions of quality of life: A taxonomy. *Journal of Advanced Nursing*, *22*(3), 502–508. doi:10.1046/j.1365-2648.1995.22030502.x PMID:7499618

Fast, J., Gierveld, J. D. J., & Keating, N. (2008). Ageing, disability and participation. In Rural ageing: A good place to grow old? (pp. 63-73). Bristol, MA: Polocy Press.

Federal Geographic Data Committee. (1998). *Content standard for digital geospatial metadata*. Retrieved April 30, 2014, from http://www.fgdc.gov/metadata/csdgm

Feist, H. R., Parker, K., & Hugo, G. (2012). Older and online: Enhancing social connections in Australian rural places. *The Journal of Community Informatics*, *8*(1).

Feitosa, A. (2006). *Organização da informação na web: Das tags à web semântica*. Brasília, Brasil: Editora Thesaurus.

Felizardo, V., Gaspar, P. D., Garcia, N. M., & Reis, V. (2011). Acquisition of multiple physiological parameters during physical exercise. *International Journal of E-Health and Medical Communications*, *2*(4), 37–49. doi:10.4018/jehmc.2011100103

Feng, C.-C., & Yu, L. (2010). Ontology-based data exchange and integration: An experience in cyberinfrastructure of sensor network based monitoring system. In *Proceedings of International Conference on Advances in Semantic Processing* (pp. 83-90). Florence, Italy: Academic Press.

Fensel, D., van Harmelen, F., Horrocks, I., McGuinness, D. L., & Patel-Schneider, P. F. (2001). OIL: An ontology infrastructure for the semantic web. *IEEE Intelligent Systems*, *16*(2), 38–45. doi:10.1109/5254.920598

Fernandez, A. (2005). *Les nouveaux tableaux de bord des managers: Le projet décisionnel dans sa totalité* (3rd ed.). Paris: Éditions d'Organisation.

Ferrari, S. (2012). *Marketing del turismo: Consumatori, imprese e destinazioni nel nuovo millennio*. Padova, Italy: Cedam.

Fillion, G., Limayem, M., Laferriere, T., & Mantha, R. (2007). Integrating ICT into higher education: A study of onsite vs online students' perceptions. *Academy of Educational Leadership Journal*, *11*(2), 45–72.

Fine, G. (1993). *On ideas: Aristotle's criticism of Plato's theory of forms*. Oxford, UK: Clarendon Press.

Fliegenschnee, M., & Schelakovsky, M. (1998). *Umweltpsychologie und Umweltbildung: eine Ein-fuhrung aus humanokologischer Sicht*. Wien: Facultas Universitats Verlag.

Floridi, L. (2009). Web 2.0 vs. the semantic web: A philosophical assessment. *Episteme*, *6*(1), 27–37. doi:10.3366/E174236000800052X

Fogliatto, F., Silveira, G., & Borenstein, D. (2012). The mass customization decade: An updated review of the literature. *International Journal of Production Economics*, *138*(1), 14–25. doi:10.1016/j.ijpe.2012.03.002

Forghani, A., Neustaedter, C., & Schiphorst, T. (2013). Investigating the communication patterns of distance-separated grandparents and grandchildren. In Proceedings of CHI' 13 Extended Abstracts on Human Factors in Computing Systems (pp. 67-72). ACM. doi:10.1145/2468356.2468370

Forsman, A. K., Herberts, C., Nyqvist, F., Wahlbeck, K., & Schierenbeck, I. (2013). Understanding the role of social capital for mental wellbeing among older adults. *Ageing and Society*, *33*(05), 804–825. doi:10.1017/S0144686X12000256

Fox, S. (2001). *Wired seniors: A fervent few, inspired by family ties*. Pew Internet & American Life Project.

Fox, S. (2004). *Older Americans and the internet*. Washington, DC: Pew Research Center.

Franco-Santos, M., Kennerley, M., Micheli, P., Martinez, V., Mason, S., Marr, B., & Neely, A. et al. (2007). Towards a definition of a business performance measurement system. *International Journal of Operations & Production Management*, *27*(8), 784–801. doi:10.1108/01443570710763778

Franke, C., Morin, S., Chebotko, A., Abraham, J., & Brazier, P. (2013). Efficient processing of semantic web queries in HBase and mySQL cluster. *IT Professional*, *15*(3), 36–43. doi:10.1109/MITP.2012.42

Frohlich, D. (2004). *Audiophotography: Bringing photos to life with sounds*. Berlin: Springer-Verlag. doi:10.1007/978-1-4020-2210-4

Gable, G. G., Sedera, D., & Chan, T. (2008). Re-conceptualizing information systems success: The IS-impact measurement model. *Journal of the Association for Information Systems, 9*(7), 377–408.

Galkin, V., Zhuravleva, T., & Stoylik Y. (2013). Improving the quality of customer support information on technical regulations based on the technology of the Internet portal. *Transportation business in Russia, 4*, 160-161.

García-Pérez, E., Violante, A., & Cervantes-Pérez, F. (1998). Using neural networks for differential diagnosis of Alzheimer disease and vascular dementia. *Expert Systems with Applications, 14*(1-2), 219–225. doi:10.1016/S0957-4174(97)00076-6

Gardner, P. J., Kamber, T., & Netherland, J. (2012). "Getting turned on": Using ICT training to promote active ageing in New York City. *The Journal of Community Informatics, 8*(1).

Garengo, P., Biazzo, S., & Bititci, U. S. (2005). Performance measurement systems in SMEs: A review for a research agenda. *International Journal of Management Reviews, 7*(1), 25–47. doi:10.1111/j.1468-2370.2005.00105.x

Garrigos-Simon, F. J., Lapiedra Alcami, R., & Barbera Ribera, T. (2012). Social networks and Web 3.0: Their impact on the management and marketing of organizations. *Management Decision, 50*(10), 1880–1890. doi:10.1108/00251741211279657

Gatto, S. L., & Tak, S. H. (2008). Computer, internet, and e-mail use among older adults: Benefits and barriers. *Educational Gerontology, 34*(9), 800–811. doi:10.1080/03601270802243697

Georges, P. M. (2002). *Le management cockpit: Des tableaux de bord qui vont à l'essentiel*. Paris: Éditions d'Organisation.

Ghaleb, F., Daoud, S., Hasna, A., ALJa'am, J. M., El-Seoud, S. A., & El-Sofany, H. (2006). E-learning model based on semantic web technology. *International Journal of Computing & Information Sciences, 4*(2), 63-71. Retrieved from http://www.ijcis.info/Vol4N2/pp63-71.pdf

Gignac, G. E. (2010). *Genos emotional intelligence inventory: Technical manual*. Sydney: Genos Pty Ltd.

Gil, D., Johnsson, M., Chamizo, J. M. G., Paya, A. S., & Fernandez, D. R. (2009). Application of artificial neural networks in the diagnosis of urological dysfunctions. *Expert Systems with Applications, 36*(3, Part 2), 5754–5760. doi:10.1016/j.eswa.2008.06.065

Gobel, S., & Jasnoch, U. (2001). Visualization techniques in metadata information systems for geospatial data. *Advances in Environmental Research, 5*(4), 415–424. doi:10.1016/S1093-0191(01)00093-4

Godfrey, A., Conway, R., Meagher, D., & ÓLaighin, G. (2008). Direct measurement of human movement by accelerometry. *Medical Engineering & Physics, 30*(10), 1364–1386. doi:10.1016/j.medengphy.2008.09.005

Godfrey, M. (2014). Environmental infomediaries in the risk society: The behavioral impact of online environmental information communication strategies. *Stream: Culture/Politics/Technology, 5*(1), 29-36.

Golbeck, J., Parsia, B., & Hendler, J. (2003). Trust networks on the semantic web. Springer Berlin Heidelberg. Retrieved from http://pdf.aminer.org/000/674/092/trust_networks_on_the_semantic_web.pdf

Golbeck, J., & Hendler, J. (2006). Inferring binary trust relationships in web-based social networks. *ACM Transactions on Internet Technology, 6*(4), 497–529. doi:10.1145/1183463.1183470

Goleman, D. (1995). *Emotional intelligence*. New York: Bantam Books.

Goleman, D. (1998). What makes a leader?. *Harvard Business Review, 76*(6), 93–102. PMID:10187249

Goleman, D. (2009). *Ecological intelligence: How knowing the hidden impacts of what webBuy can change everything*. New York, NY: Crown Business.

Goncharov, S. A., Goncharova, O. M., & Koroleva, N. N. (2008). *Symbol, person, meaning: An interdisciplinary reflection space*. St. Petersburg, Russia: HSPU Publishing House.

González, G., Rosa, J., Montaner, M., & Delfin, S. (2007, April). *Embedding emotional context in recommender systems*. Paper presented at IEEE 23rd International Conference on Data Engineering Workshop, Istanbul, Turkey. doi:10.1109/ICDEW.2007.4401075

Gonzalez, A., Ramirez, M. P., & Viadel, V. (2012). Attitudes of the elderly toward information and communications technologies. *Educational Gerontology, 38*(9), 585–594. doi:10.1080/03601277.2011.595314

Gould, T. (2003). Hybrid classes: Maximizing institutional resources and student learning. In *Proceedings of the 2003 ASCUE Conference* (pp. 54-59). ASCUE.

Graham, C., Satchell, C., & Rouncefield, M. (2007). Sharing places: Digital content and lived life. In *Proceedings of Shared Encounters Workshop at CHI'07*. ACM.

Greener, S. L. (2009). E-modelling – Helping learners to develop sound e-learning behaviours. *Electronic Journal of e-Learning, 7*(3), 265 – 272. Retrieved 8th June 2010 from http://www.ejel.org

Gregor, S. (2006). The nature of theory in information systems. *Management Information Systems Quarterly, 30*(3), 611–642.

Grossecmk, G., & Holotescu, C. (2008). Can we use Twitter for educational activities? In *Proceedings of 4th International Scientific Conference eLSE eLearning and Software for Education*. Retrieved from http://www.cblt.soton.ac.uk/multimedia/PDFsMM09/Can we use twitter for educational activities.pdf

Grossman, R. (2009). The case for cloud computing. *IT Professional, 11*(2), 23–27. doi:10.1109/MITP.2009.40

Groves, D. L., & Slack, T. (1994). Computers and their application to senior citizen therapy within a nursing home. *Journal of Instructional Psychology*.

Gruber, T. R. (1993). *A translation approach to portable ontology specifications: Knowledge systems laboratory technical report KSL 92-71*. Computer Science Department, Stanford University.

Gupta, R. K., & Lei, S. A. (2010). College distance education courses: Evaluating benefits and costs from institutional, faculty and students' perspectives. *Education, 130*, 616.

Guzzo, R. A., Jackson, S. E., & Katzell, R. A. (1987). Meta-analysis analysis. *Research in Organizational Behavior, 9*, 407–442.

Hachisu, Y., & Yoshida, A. (2013). Generation of error correction questions for beginners of programming (in Japanese). In Proceedings of Foundation of Software Engineering XX (FOSE2013). Kaga, Japan: Academic Press.

Hachisu, Y., & Yoshida, A. (2014). A support system for error correction questions in programming education. In *Proceedings of the International Conference e-Learning 2014* (pp. 249-258). Academic Press.

Hachisu, Y., Yoshida, A., & Agusa, K. (2014). Understanding coding processes in programming exercises (in Japanese). *IEICE Technical Report 2014-CE-125(3)*. Hakodate, Japan: IEICE.

Hagel, J. III, & Armstrong, A. G. (1997). *Net Gain: Expanding markets through virtual communities*. Harvard, MA: Harvard Business School Press.

Hale, L. S., Mirakian, E. A., & Day, D. B. (2009). Online vs classroom instruction: Student satisfaction and learning outcomes in an undergraduate allied health pharmacology course. *Journal of Allied Health, 38*(2), 36–42. PMID:19753411

Halle, D. (1991). Displaying the dream: The visual presentation of family and self in the modern American household. *Journal of Comparative Family Studies*, 217–229.

Hammer, D. (1997). Discovery learning and discovery teaching. *Cognition and Instruction, 15*(4), 485–529. doi:10.1207/s1532690xci1504_2

Hansla, A., Gamble, A., Juliusson, A., & Garling, T. (2008). The relationships between awareness of consequences, environmental concern, and value orientation. *Journal of Environmental Psychology, 28*(1), 1–9. doi:10.1016/j.jenvp.2007.08.004

Harmandaoglu, E. (2012). The use of twitter in language learning and teaching. In *Proceedings of International Conference "ICT for Language Learning"*. Retrieved from http://conference.pixel-online.net/ICT4LL2012/common/download/Paper_pdf/211-IBT41-FP-Harmandaoglu-ICT2012.pdf

Haveliwala, T. (1999). *Efficient computation of PageRank*. Stanford University Technical Report.

Haveliwala, T. (2002). Topic-sensitive PageRank. In *Proceedings of 11ᵗʰ International Conference on World Wide Web (WWW'02)*, (pp. 517-526). Honolulu, HI: IEEE.

Hawkley, L. C., & Cacioppo, J. T. (2013). Loneliness and health. In *Encyclopedia of behavioral medicine* (pp. 1172–1176). New York: Springer.

Haythornthwaite, C. (2001). Exploring multiplexity: Social network structures in a computer-supported distance learning class. *The Information Society, 17*(3), 211–226. doi:10.1080/01972240152493065

Heckerling, P. S., Canaris, G. J., Flach, S. D., Tape, T. G., Wigton, R. S., & Gerber, B. S. (2007). Predictors of urinary tract infection based on artificial neural networks and genetic algorithms. *International Journal of Medical Informatics, 76*(4), 289–296. doi:10.1016/j.ijmedinf.2006.01.005 PMID:16469531

Hector. (2014). *Hector a high level java client for apache Cassandra.* Retrieved September, 2014, from http://hector-client.github.io/hector/build/html/index.html

Hendersen, J. C., & Venkatraman, N. (1993). Strategic alignment: Leveraging information technology for transforming organizations. *IBM Systems Journal, 38*(2), 472–484. doi:10.1147/sj.382.0472

Henderson, J. C., & Venkatraman, N. (1990). *Strategic alignment: a model for organizational transformation via information technology.* Working Paper 3223-90. Sloan School of Management, Massachusetts Institute of Technology.

Henderson, J. C., & Venkatramen, N. (1989). Strategic alignment: A model for organizational transformation through information technology. In T. A. Kochan & M. Useem (Eds.), *Transforming organizations* (pp. 62–87). New York: Oxford University Press.

Hendrix, C. C. (1999). Computer use among elderly people. *Computers in Nursing, 18*(2), 62–68. PMID:10740912

Hennig-Thurau, T., Gwinner, K. P., Walsh, G., & Gremler, D. D. (2004). Electronic word-of-mouth via consumer-opinion platforms: What motivates consumer to articulate themselves on the Internet. *Journal of Interactive Marketing, 18*(1), 38–52. doi:10.1002/dir.10073

Hennig-Thurau, T., Malthouse, E. C., Friege, C., Gensler, S., Lobschat, L., Rangaswamy, A., & Skiera, B. (2010). The Impact of new media on customer relationships. *Journal of Service Research, 13*(3), 311–330. doi:10.1177/1094670510375460

Henson, C. A., Pschorr, J. K., Sheth, A. P., & Thirunarayan, K. (2009). SemSOS: Semantic sensor observation service. In *Proceedings of International Symposium on Collaborative Technologies and Systems* (pp. 44-53). Baltimore, MD: Academic Press.

Herrera, V., Miguel, R., Castro-Schez, J., & Glez-Morcillo, C. (2010). *Using an emotional intelligent agent to support customers' searches interactively in e-marketplaces.* Paper presented at 22nd International Conference on Tools with Artificial Intelligence, Arrar.

Higgs, M. (2004). A study of the relationship between emotional intelligence and performance in UK call centres. *Journal of Managerial Psychology, 19*(4), 442–454. doi:10.1108/02683940410537972

Hiller, H. H., & Franz, T. M. (2004). New ties, old ties and lost ties: The use of the internet in diaspora. *New Media & Society, 6*(6), 731–752. doi:10.1177/146144804044327

Hirschheim, R., & Newman, M. (1991). Symbolism and information systems development: Myth, metaphor and magic. *Information Systems Research, 2*(1), 29–62. doi:10.1287/isre.2.1.29

Hirschheim, R., & Sabherwal, R. (2001). Detours in the path towards strategic information systems alignment: Paradoxical decisions, excessive transformations and uncertain turnarounds. *California Management Review, 44*(1), 87–108. doi:10.2307/41166112

Hirshman, E., & Holbrook, M. (1982). Hedonic consumption: Emerging concepts, methods and propositions. *Journal of Marketing, 46*(3), 92–101. doi:10.2307/1251707

Hoeber, O., Wilson, G., Harding, S., Enguehard, R., & Devillers, R. (2011). Exploring geo-temporal differences using gtdiff. In *Proceedings of Pacific Visualization Symposium (PacificVis)* (pp. 139-146). Hong Kong: IEEE.

Hogan, B. J. (2009). *Networking in everyday life.* (Ph.D. dissertation). Graduate Department of Sociology, University of Toronto, Toronto, Canada.

Homberg-Wright, K, & Wright, D. J. (2012). MBA and undergraduate business student perceptions of online courses: Experienced online students versus students who have not taken an online course. *Global Education Journal,* (1), 169-186.

Honeycutt, C., & Herring, S. C. (2009). Beyond micro-blogging: Conversation and collaboration via Twitter. In *Proceedings ofForty-Second Hawaii International Conference on System Sciences* (pp. 1-10). IEEE.

Höök, K. (2013). Affective computing. In M. Soegaard & R. Dam (Eds.), *The encyclopedia of human-computer interaction*. Aarhus: Interaction Design Foundation.

Hoorn, J., Eliens, A., Huang, Z., Vugt, H., Konijn, E., & Visser, C. (2004). *Agents with character: Evaluation of empathic agents in digital dossiers.* Paper presented at AAMAS' 04 Workshop on Empathic Agents, New York, NY.

Hopper, J. R., & Nielsen, J. M. (1991). Recycling as altruistic behavior: Normative and behavioral strategies to expand participation in a community recycling program. *Environment and Behavior, 23*(2), 195–220. doi:10.1177/0013916591232004

Hornsby, K. S., & King, K. (2008). Linking geosensor network data and ontologies to support transportation modeling. Lecture Notes in Computer Science, 4540, 191-209.

Horst, H. A. (2006). The blessings and burdens of communication: Cell phones in Jamaican transnational social fields. *Global Networks, 6*(2), 143–159. doi:10.1111/j.1471-0374.2006.00138.x

Horton, D., Craig, M., Campbell, J., Gries, P., & Zingaro, D. (2014). Comparing outcomes in Inverted and traditional CS1. In *Proceedings of the 19th ACM Technical Symposium on Innovation and Technology in Computer Science Education*. Retrieved September 21, 2014 from https://www.openconf.org/iticse2014/modules/request.php?module=oc_program&action=summary.php&id=1123

Hoyer, W., Rajesh, C., Dorotic, M., Krafft, M., & Singh, S. (2010). Customer participation in value creation. *Journal of Service Research, 13*(3), 283–296. doi:10.1177/1094670510375604

Hoyle, R. H. (1999). *Statistical strategies for small sample research*. Thousand Oaks, CA: Sage Publications.

Hristova, M., Misra, A., Rutter, M., & Mercuri, R. (2003). Identifying and correcting Java programming errors for introductory computer science students. In *Proceedings of the 34th SIGCSE Technical Symposium on Computer Science Education* (pp. 153-156). ACM. doi:10.1145/611892.611956

Huacarpuma, R. C., Rodrigues, D. D. C., Serrano, A. M. R., da Costa, J. P. C. L., de Sousa, R. T. Jr, Holanda, M. T., & Araujo, A. P. F. (2013). Big data: A case study on data from the Brazilian ministry of planning, budgeting and management. In *Proceedings of the IADIS International Conference Applied Computing 2013*. Porto, Portugal: IADIS Press.

Huang, T., Yang, Z., Liu, Q., Li, X., Wu, B., Liu, S., & Zhao, G. (2006). Semantic web-based educational knowledge service system (EKSS) for e-learning. In *Proceedings of Communications and Networking in China* (pp. 1-5). IEEE. doi:10.1109/CHINACOM.2006.344834

Huang, S., & Yeoh, B. S. (2007). Emotional labour and transnational domestic work: The moving geographies of 'maid abuse' in Singapore. *Mobilities, 2*(2), 195–217. doi:10.1080/17450100701381557

Huber, L. L., Shankar, K., Caine, K., Connelly, K., Camp, L. J., Walker, B. A., & Borrero, L. (2013). How in-home technologies mediate caregiving relationships in later life. *International Journal of Human-Computer Interaction, 29*(7), 441–455. doi:10.1080/10447318.2012.715990

Hudson, M., Smart, A., & Bourne, M. (2001). Theory and practice in SME performance measurement systems. *International Journal of Operations & Production Management, 21*(8), 1096–1115. doi:10.1108/EUM0000000005587

Hughes, S., Brusilovsky, P., & Lewis, M. (2002). Adaptive navigation support in 3D e-commerce activities. In *Proceedings ofWorkshop on Recommendation and Personalization in E-Commerce at the 2nd International Conference on Adaptive Hypermedia and Adaptive Web-Based Systems* (pp. 132-139). Malaga, Spain: Academic Press.

Hurn, J. E. (2005). Beyond point and click: Taking web based pedagogy to a new level. Paper presented at the Association of Small Computer Users in Education (ASCUE), Myrtle Beach, SC.

Hu, Y., Hu, Y., & Guo, L. (2013). Construction of C programming language based on ontology knowledge base. In *Proceedings of the Second International Conference on Innovative Computing and Cloud Computing* (pp. 23-25). Academic Press. doi:10.1145/2556871.2556877

Hwang, M. I., & Thorn, R. G. (1999). The effect of user engagement on system success: A meta-analytical integration of research findings. *Information & Management*, *35*(4), 229–236. doi:10.1016/S0378-7206(98)00092-5

Ikeda, M., Ito, S., Ishigaki, T., & Yamauchi, K. (1997). Evaluation of a neural network classifier for pancreatic masses based on {CT} findings. *Computerized Medical Imaging and Graphics*, *21*(3), 175–183. doi:10.1016/S0895-6111(97)00006-2 PMID:9258595

International Institute of Business Analysis. (2009). *The BABOK guide* (2nd ed.). Toronto, Canada: Author.

Itoh, R., Nagataki, H., Ooshita, F., Kakugawa, H., & Masuzawa, T. (2007). A fault injection method for generating error-correction exercises in algorithm learning. In *Proceedings of the 8th International Conference on Information Technology Based Higher Education and Training* (pp. 200-205). Academic Press.

Ito, M. (2005). Mobile phones, Japanese youth and the replacement of social contact. In R. Ling & P. Pedersen (Eds.), *Mobile communications: Renegotiation of the social sphere* (pp. 131–148). London: Springer. doi:10.1007/1-84628-248-9_9

Jackson, J., Cobb, M., & Carver, C. (2005). Identifying top Java errors for novice programmers. In *Proceedings Frontiers in Education 35th Annual Conference*. Academic Press. doi:10.1109/FIE.2005.1611967

Janovics, J., & Christiansen, N. D. (2001). *Emotional intelligence in the workplace*. Paper presented at the 16th Annual Conference of the Society of Industrial and Organizational Psychology, San Diego, CA.

Janowicz, K., & Compton, M. (2010). The stimulus-sensor-observation ontology design pattern and its integration into the semantic sensor network ontology. In *Proceedings of International Workshop on Semantic Sensor Networks 2010* (pp. 7–11). Shanghai, China: Academic Press.

Jansson, A. (2002). Spatial phantasmagoria. *European Journal of Communication*, *17*(4), 429–443. doi:10.1177/0267323102017004020ɪ

Jansson, J., Marell, A., & Nordlund, A. (2010). Green consumer behavior: Determinants of curtailment and eco-innovation adoption. *Journal of Consumer Marketing*, *27*(4), 358–370. doi:10.1108/07363761011052396

Jansson, J., Marell, A., & Nordlund, A. (2011). Exploring consumer adoption of a high involvement eco-innovation using value-belief-norm theory. *Journal of Consumer Behaviour*, *10*(1), 51–60. doi:10.1002/cb.346

Jazzy. (2014). *Java spell check API*. Retrieved March 27, 2014, from http://sourceforge.net/projects/jazzy

Jena. (2014). *A semantic web framework for Java*. Retrieved March 27, 2014, from http://jena.sourceforge

Jenkins, M., Browne, T., Walker, R., & Hewitt, R. (2011). The development of technology enhanced learning: Findings from a 2008 survey of UK Higher Education Institutions. *Interactive Learning Environments*, *19*(5), 447–465. doi:10.1080/10494820903484429

Jennings, G., & Nickerson, N. P. (2006). *Quality tourism experiences*. Oxford, UK: Elsevier, Butterwoth-Heinemann.

Jia, Y., & Harman, M. (2011). An analysis and survey of the development of mutation testing. *IEEE Transactions on Software Engineering*, *37*(5), 649–678. doi:10.1109/TSE.2010.62

Jinglin, Y., Li, H.-X., & Yong, H. (2011). A probabilistic SVM based decision system for pain diagnosis. *Expert Systems with Applications*, *38*(8), 9346–9351. doi:10.1016/j.eswa.2011.01.106

Jirka, S., & Nüst, D. (2010). *Sensor instance registry discussion paper*. Public Discussion Paper: Open Geospatial Consortium, Open Geospatial Consortium.

Jocker, M. L. (2009). *Executing R in PhP*. Retrieved March 7, 2014 from http://www.matthewjockers.net//?s=Executing+R+in+php&search=Go

Johansson, M., Rahm, J., & Gyllin, M. (2013). Landowners' participation in biodiversity conservation examined through the value-belief-norm theory. *Landscape Research*, *38*(3), 295–311. doi:10.1080/01426397.2012.673576

Johnson, L., Adams Becker, S., Estrada, V., & Freeman, A. (2014). *NMC horizon report: 2014 higher education edition*. Austin, TX: The New Media Consortium.

Johnson, M. W., & Sherlock, D. (2014). Beyond the personal learning environment: Attachment and control in the classroom of the future. *Interactive Learning Environments*, *22*(2), 146–164. doi:10.1080/10494820.2012.745434

Jones, S., & Fox, S. (2009). *Generations online in 2009*. Washington, DC: Pew Internet & American Life Project.

Jordan, A. (2010). *What benefit? The outcome of the "BenefIT" scheme*. Department of Communications, Energy & Natural Resources.

Joseph, D., Ang, S., Chang, R. H. L., & Slaughter, S. A. (2010). Practical intelligence in IT: Assessing soft skills of IT professionals. *Communications of the ACM*, *53*(2), 149–154. doi:10.1145/1646353.1646391

Jowett, T., Harraway, J., Lovelock, B., Skeaff, S., Slooten, L., Strack, M., & Shephard, K. (2014). Multinomial-regression modeling of the environmental attitudes of higher education students based on the revised new ecological paradigm scale. *The Journal of Environmental Education*, *45*(1), 1–15. doi:10.1080/00958964.2013.783777

Judge, T. K., & Neustaedter, C. (2010, April). Sharing conversation and sharing life: video conferencing in the home. In *Proceedings of the SIGCHI Conference on Human Factors in Computing Systems* (pp. 655-658). ACM. doi:10.1145/1753326.1753422

Juhola, M., Aalto, H., Joutsijoki, H., & Hirvonen, T. P. (2013). The classification of valid and invalid beats of three-dimensional nystagmus eye movement signals using machine learning methods. *Adv. Artif. Neu. Sys., 2013*, 16:16–16:16. doi:10.1155/2013/972412

Juhola, M., Joutsijoki, H., Aalto, H., & Hirvonen, T. P. (2014). On classification in the case of a medical data set with a complicated distribution. *Applied Computing and Informatics*. doi:10.1016/j.aci.2014.03.001

Jump, L., & Jump, R. (2006). Learning academic skills online: Student perceptions of the learning process. In *Proceedings of the First International LAMS Conference*. Retrieved from http://lamsfoundation.org/lams2006/pdfs/Jump_Jump_LAMS06.pdf

Jun, T., Kai, C., Yu, F., & Gang, T. (2009). The research & application of ETL tool in business intelligence project. In *Proceedings of theInformation Technology and Applications* (IFITA'09). Chengdu, China: IEEE Press. doi:10.1109/IFITA.2009.48

Kaluzniacky, E. (2004). *Managing psychological factors in information systems work: An orientation to emotional intelligence*. Hershey, PA: Information Science Publishing. doi:10.4018/978-1-59140-198-8

Kamahara, J., Asakawa, T., Shimojo, S., & Miyahara, H. (2005). A community-based recommendation system to reveal unexpected interests. In *Proceedings of11th International Multimedia Modelling Conference (MMM)* (pp. 433-438), Melbourne, Australia: Academic Press. doi:10.1109/MMMC.2005.5

Kanaksabee, P., Odit, M. P., & Ramdoyal, A. (2011). A standard-based model for adaptive e-Learning platform for Mauritian academic institutions. *Journal of International Education Research*, *7*(1). Retrieved from http://journals.cluteonline.com/index.php/JIER/article/view/3541/3588

Kanellis, P., Lycett, M., & Paul, R. J. (1998). An interpretive approach to the measurement of information systems success. In E. J. Garrity & G. L. Sanders (Eds.), *Information systems success measurement* (pp. 133–151). Hershey, PA: Idea Group.

Kantardzic, M. (2011). *Data mining: Concepts, models, methods, and algorithms*. Hoboken, NJ: John Wiley & Sons, Inc. doi:10.1002/9781118029145

Kapitonov, O. & Tyutyunnik, V. (2013). Logical-linguistic model of semantic markup web pages. *Fundamental Research, 1*(3), 714-717.

Kaplan, R. S., & Norton, D. P. (1992). The balanced scorecard – Measures that drive performance. *Harvard Business Review, 70*(1), 71–79. PMID:10119714

Kaplan, R. S., & Norton, D. P. (1996). *The balanced scorecard.* Boston: Harvard Business School Press.

Karger, D., Lehman, E., Leighton, T., Panigrahy, R., Levine, M., & Lewin, D. (1997). Consistent hashing and random trees: Distributed caching protocols for relieving hot spots on the world wide web. In *Proceedings of the Twenty-Ninth Annual ACM Symposium on Theory of Computing.* ACM Press. doi:10.1145/258533.258660

Karunasena, A., Deng, H., & Zhang, X. (2012). A web 2.0 based e-learning success model in higher education. In *Proceedings of 2nd International Conference on Future Computers in Education.* Retrieved from http://www.ier-institute.org/2070-1918/lnit23/v23/177.pdf

Kasimati, A., & Zamani, E. (2011). Education and learning in the semantic web. In *Proceedings of 15th Panhellenic Conference on Informatics (PCI)* (p. 338-344). Kastoria, Greece: Academic Press. doi:10.1109/PCI.2011.40

Katz, J., & Aakhus, M. (Eds.). (2002). *Perpetual contact: Mobile communication, private talk, public performance.* Cambridge, UK: Cambridge University Press. doi:10.1017/CBO9780511489471

Kearns, G. S., & Lederer, A. L. (2004). The impact of industry contextual factors on IT focus and the use of IT for competitive advantage. *Information & Management, 41*(7), 899–919. doi:10.1016/j.im.2003.08.018

Kearns, G. S., & Sabherwal, R. (2007). Antecedents and consequences of information systems planning integration. *IEEE Transactions on Engineering Management, 54*(4), 628–643. doi:10.1109/TEM.2007.906848

Kearns, L. E., Shoaf, J. R., & Summey, M. B. (2004). Performance and satisfaction of second-degree BSN students in web-based and traditional course delivery environments. *The Journal of Nursing Education, 43*(6), 280–284. PMID:15230307

Keats, D., & Schmidt, J. P. (2007). The genesis and emergence of education 3.0 in higher education and its potential for Africa. *First Monday, 12*(3). doi:10.5210/fm.v12i3.1625

Kennedy, G., Dalgarno, B., Gray, K., Judd, T., Waycott, J., Bennett, S. J., . . . Churchwood, A. (2007). *The net generation are not big users of web 2.0 technologies: Preliminary findings.* Retrieved from http://www.ascilite.org.au/conferences/singapore07/procs/kennedy.pdf

Kennedy, T. L. M., & Wellman, B. (2007). The networked household. *Information Communication and Society, 10*(5), 645–670. doi:10.1080/13691180701658012

Kennerley, M., & Neely, A. (2003). Measuring performance in a changing business environment. *International Journal of Operations & Production Management, 23*(2), 213–229. doi:10.1108/01443570310458465

Keramidas, C. G. (2012). Are undergraduate students ready for online learning? A comparison of online and face-to-face sections of a course. *Rural Special Education Quarterly, 31*(4), 25–32.

Khan, F. A., Weippl, E. R., & Tjoa, A. M. (2009). Integrated approach for the detection of learning styles and affective states. In *Proceedings of World Conference on Educational Multimedia, Hypermedia and Telecommunications* (pp. 753-761). Academic Press.

Kim, B. Y., & Park, K. S. (2000). Automatic sleep stage scoring system using genetic algorithms and neural network. In *Engineering in Medicine and Biology Society, 2000: Proceedings of the 22nd Annual International Conference of the IEEE* (Vol. 2, pp. 849–850). IEEE. doi:10.1109/IEMBS.2000.897848

Kim, W. G., Lee, C., & Hiemstra, S. J. (2004). Effects of an online virtual community on customer loyalty and travel product purchases. *Tourism Management, 25*(3), 343–355. doi:10.1016/S0261-5177(03)00142-0

Kleemann, F., Vob, G. G., & Rieder, K. (2008). Un(der) paid innovators: The commercial utilization of consumer work through crowdsourcing. *Science. Technology & Innovation Studies, 4*(1), 5–26.

Kling, R., & Scacchi, W. (1982). The web of computing: Computer technology as social organization. *Advances in Computers, 21*, 1–90. doi:10.1016/S0065-2458(08)60567-7

Kljajić, M., & Borštnar, M. K. (2011). Context-dependent modelling and anticipation the other coin in the system approach. In V. Asproth (Ed.), *Challenges for the future in an ICT context*. Mid Sweden University. Retrieved January 22, 2015 from http://miun.diva-portal.org/smash/get/diva2:478461/FULLTEXT01.pdf

Kobsa, A., Koenemann, J., & Pohl, W. (2001). Personalised hypermedia presentation techniques for improving online customer relationships. *The Knowledge Engineering Review, 16*(2), 111–155. doi:10.1017/S0269888901000108

Koch, N., & Rossi, G. (2002). Patterns for adaptive web applications. In *Proceedings of 7ᵗʰ European Conference on Pattern Languages of Programs*. Irsee, Germany: Academic Press.

Komito, L., & Bates, J. (2012). Migration, community and social media. In Transnationalism in the global city. Bilbao, Spain: University of Deusto.

Komito, L. (2011). Social media and migration: Virtual community 2.0. *Journal of the American Society for Information Science and Technology, 62*(6), 1075–1086. doi:10.1002/asi.21517

Koper, R. (2004). Use of the semantic web to solve some basic problems in education: Increase flexible, distributed lifelong learning, decrease teacher's workload. *Journal of Interactive Media in Education, 2004*(6).

Kop, R. (2011). The challenges to connectivist learning on open online networks: Learning experiences during a massive open online course. *International Review of Research in Open and Distance Learning, 12*(3).

Koskinen, I. (2004, June). Seeing with mobile images: Towards perpetual visual contact. In *Proceedings of T-Mobile Hungary 2004 Conference*. Academic Press.

Kotler, P., Kartajaya, H., & Setiawan, I. (2010). *Marketing 3.0: From products to consumers to the human spirit*. Hoboken, NJ: John Wiley & Sons, Inc. doi:10.1002/9781118257883

Kraus, L. A., Reed, W. M., & Fitzgerald, G. E. (2001). The effects of learning style and hypermedia prior experience on behavioral disorders knowledge and time on task: A case-based hypermedia environment. *Computers in Human Behavior, 17*(1), 125–140. doi:10.1016/S0747-5632(00)00030-3

Kreijns, K., Kirschner, P., Jochems, W., & van Buuren, H. (2007). Measuring perceived sociability of computer-supported collaborative environments. *Computers & Education, 49*(2), 176–192. doi:10.1016/j.compedu.2005.05.004

Krishnamurthy, S. (2009). Mozilla vs. Godzilla – The launch of the Mozilla Firefox browser. *Journal of Interactive Marketing, 23*(3), 259–271. doi:10.1016/j.intmar.2009.04.008

Krishnaswamy, S., Loke, S., & Zaslavsky, A. (2002). *Towards anytime anywhere data mining e-services*. Retrieved from http://arrow.monash.edu.au/hdl/1959.1/128540

Kroes, P. A., & Meijers, A. W. M. (2006). Introduction: The dual nature of technical artefacts. *Studies in History and Philosophy of Science, 37*(1), 1–4. doi:10.1016/j.shpsa.2005.12.001 PMID:16473265

Kück, G. (2004). Tim Berners-Lee's semantic web. *South African Journal of Information Management, 6*(1).

Kueng, P., Meier, A., & Wettstein, T. (2001). Performance measurement systems must be engineered. *Communications of the Association for Information Systems, 7*, 1-27.

Kukulska-Hulme, A., & Traxler, J. (2007). Designing for mobile and wireless learning. In H. Beetham & R. Sharpe (Eds.), *Rethinking pedagogy for a digital age: designing and delivering e-learning* (pp. 180–192). London, UK: Routledge.

Kumar, R., & Sharan, A. (2014, February). *Personalized web search using browsing history and domain knowledge*. Paper presented at Issues and Challenges in Intelligent Computing Techniques (ICICT), Ghaziabad. doi:10.1109/ICICICT.2014.6781332

Lahtinen, E., Ala-Mutka, K., & Jrvinen, H. (2005). A study of the difficulties of novice programmers. In *Proceedings of the 10th Annual SIGCSE Conference on Innovation and Technology in Computer Science Education* (pp. 14-18). ACM. doi:10.1145/1067445.1067453

Lakshman, A., & Malik, P. (2009). Cassandra: Structured storage system on a P2P network. In *Proceedings of the 28th ACM Symposium on Principles of Distributed Computing* (PODC '09). New York, NY: ACM Press.

Lancaster, F. W. (1993). *Indexação e resumos: Teoria e prática*. Brasília, Brasil: Briquet de Lemos Livros.

Lapalme, J. (2012). Three schools of thought on enterprise architecture. *IT Professional*, *14*(6), 37–43. doi:10.1109/MITP.2011.109

Lassila, O. (1998). Web metadata: A matter of semantics. *IEEE Internet Computing*, *2*(4), 30–37. doi:10.1109/4236.707688

Latha, V., Swetha, P., Bhavya, M., Geetha, G., & Suhasini, D. (2012). Combined methodology of the classification rules for medical data-sets. *International Journal of Engineering Trends and Technology*, *3*(1), 32–36.

Laurillard, D. (2012). *Teaching as a design science*. New York: Routledge.

Lavrač, N. (1999). Selected techniques for data mining in medicine. *Artificial Intelligence in Medicine*, *16*(1), 3–23. doi:10.1016/S0933-3657(98)00062-1 PMID:10225344

Lechani, L., Boughanem, M., & Daoud, M. (2009). Evaluation of contextual information retrieval effectiveness: Overview of issues and research. *Journal of Knowledge and Information Systems*, *24*(1), 1–34. doi:10.1007/s10115-009-0231-1

Lee, C. (1999). *Where have all the gophers gone? Why the web beat gopher in the battle for protocol mind share*. Retrieved from School of Information and Library Science, University of North Carolina website: http://ils.unc.edu/callee/gopherpaper.htm

Lee, M. J., & Ko, A. J. (2014). A demonstration of Gidget, a debugging game for computing education. In *Proceedings of 2014 IEEE Symposium on Visual Languages and Human-Centric Computing* (pp. 211-212). IEEE. doi:10.1109/VLHCC.2014.6883060

Lee, M. J., Bahmani, F., Kwan, I., LaFerte, J., Charters, P., Horvath, A., ... Ko, A.J. (2014). Principles of a debugging-first puzzle game for computing education. In *Proceedings of 2014 IEEE Symposium on Visual Languages and Human-Centric Computing* (pp. 57-64). IEEE. doi:10.1109/VLHCC.2014.6883023

Lee, A. S., & Baskerville, R. L. (2003). Generalizing generalizability in information systems research. *Information Systems Research*, *14*(3), 221–243. doi:10.1287/isre.14.3.221.16560

Lee, C., & Coughlin, J. F. (2014). Older adults' Adoption of technology: An integrated approach to identifying determinants and barriers. *Journal of Product Innovation Management*. doi:10.1111/jpim.12176

Leik, R. K., Carter, T. M., Clark, J. P., Kendall, S. D., Gifford, G. A., Bielefeld, W., & Ekker, K. (1981). *Community response to natural hazard warnings: Final report*. Minneapolis, MN: University of Minnesota Press.

Leonardi, P. M., & Barley, S. R. (2008). Materiality and change: Challenges to building better theory about technology and organizing. *Information and Organization*, *18*(3), 159–176. doi:10.1016/j.infoandorg.2008.03.001

Leroux, G. (2002). *Platon, la république, traduction inédite, introduction et notes*. Paris: Flammarion.

Leung, C. (2014). *Exploring the effectiveness of online role play simulations to reduce groupthink in crisis management training*. (Doctoral dissertation). University of Hong Kong. Retrieved March 18, 2014 from http://hub.hku.hk/handle/10722/196550

Ley, B., Pipek, V., Reuter, C., & Wiedenhoefer, T. (2012). Supporting improvisation work in inter-organizational crisis management. In *Proceedings of Computers and Human Interaction CHI'12*. Austin, TX: ACM. Retrieved March 15, 2014 from http://www.wiwi.uni-siegen.de/wirtschaftsinformatik/paper/2012/leypipekreuterwiedenh2012_improvisationwork_chi2012.pdf

Li, L., Cheng, L., & Qian, K. (2008, August). *An e-learning system model based on affective computing*. Paper presented at International Conference on Cyberworlds, Hangzhou, China. doi:10.1109/CW.2008.41

Liang, C. (2011, March). *User profile for personalized web search*. Paper presented at 8th International Conference on Fuzzy Systems and Knowledge Discovery (FSKD), Shangai, China.

Liang, S., Chang, D., Badger, J., Rezel, R., Chen, S., Huang, C. Y., & Li, R. Y. (2010). GeoCENS: Geospatial cyber-infrastructure for environmental sensing. In *Proceedings of International Conference on Geographic Information Science*. Zurich, Switzerland: Academic Press.

Licoppe, C. (2004). Connected presence: The emergence of a new repertoire for managing social relationships in a changing communication technoscape. *Environment and Planning. D, Society & Space, 22*(1), 135–156. doi:10.1068/d323t

Licoppe, C., & Smoreda, Z. (2005). Are social networks technologically embedded?: How networks are changing today with changes in communication technology. *Social Networks, 27*(4), 317–335. doi:10.1016/j.socnet.2004.11.001

Li, M., Tian, J., & Chen, F. (2008). Improving multiclass pattern recognition with a co-evolutionary RBFNN. *Pattern Recognition Letters, 29*(4), 392–406. doi:10.1016/j.patrec.2007.10.019

Lim, J., Kim, M., Chen, S., & Ryder, C. (2008). An empirical investigation of student achievement and satisfaction in different learning environments. *Journal of Instructional Psychology, 35*(2), 113–119.

Lin, R.-H. (2009). An intelligent model for liver disease diagnosis. *Artificial Intelligence in Medicine, 47*(1), 53–62. doi:10.1016/j.artmed.2009.05.005 PMID:19540738

Livingstone, D., Kemp, J., & Edgar, E. (2008). From multi-user virtual environment to 3D virtual learning environment. *ALT-J. Research in Learning Technology, 16*(3), 139–150.

Li, Y., & Ranieri, M. (2010). Are 'digital natives' really digitally competent? A study on Chinese teenagers. *British Journal of Educational Technology, 41*(6), 1029–1042. doi:10.1111/j.1467-8535.2009.01053.x

Lockwood, K., & Esselstein, R. (2013). The inverted classroom and the CS curriculum. In *Proceeding of the 44th ACM Technical Symposium on Computer Science Education, SIGCSE '13* (pp. 113-118). New York, NY: ACM. doi:10.1145/2445196.2445236

Logan, E., Augustyniak, R., & Rees, A. (2002). Distance education as different education: A student-centered investigation of distance learning experience. *Journal of Education for Library and Information Science, 43*(1), 32-42.

Lops, P., Gemmis, M., & Semeraro, G. (2011). Content-based recommender systems: State of the art and trends. In F. Ricci, L. Rokach, B. Shapira, & P. Kantor (Eds.), *Recommender systems handbook* (pp. 73–105). Berlin: Springer. doi:10.1007/978-0-387-85820-3_3

Lorino, P. (2001). *Méthodes et pratiques de la performance: Le pilotage par les processus et les compétences* (2nd ed.). Paris: Éditions d'Organisation.

Lucke, C., Krell, S., & Lechner, U. (2010). Critical issues in enterprise architecting – A literature review. In *Proceedings of the 16th Americas Conference on Information Systems (AMCIS 2010)*. Lima, Peru: Academic Press.

Luftman, J. (2000). Assessing business IT alignment maturity. *Communications of the Association for Information Systems, 4*(14), 1–51.

Luftman, J., & Brier, T. (1999). Achieving and sustaining business-IT alignment. *California Management Review, 42*(1), 109–122. doi:10.2307/41166021

Lui, T., Piccoli, G., & Ives, B. (2007). Marketing strategies in virtual worlds. *ACM SIGMIS Database, 38*(4), 77–80. doi:10.1145/1314234.1314248

Lund, A., & Smørdal, O. (2006). *Is there a space for the teacher in a WIKI?* Paper presented at WikiSym'06, Odense, Denmark. doi:10.1145/1149453.1149466

Lyons, A., Reysen, S., & Pierce, L. (2012). Video lecture format, student technological efficacy, and social presence in online courses. *Computers in Human Behavior, 28*(1), 181–186. doi:10.1016/j.chb.2011.08.025

Ma, X., Wang, R., & Liang, J. (2008, August). *The e-learning system model based on affective computing.* Paper presented at 7th International Conference on Web-based Learning (ICWL), Jinhua, China. doi:10.1109/ICWL.2008.27

Macon, D. K. (2011). Student satisfaction with online courses vs traditional courses: A meta-analysis. (Order No. 3447725, Northcentral University). *ProQuest Dissertations and Theses*, 88. Retrieved September 21, 2014 from http://search.proquest.com/docview/858611481?accountid=14771

Madianou, M., & Miller, D. (2011). *Migration and new media: Transnational families and polymedia*. New York: Routledge.

Madsen, K. H. (1994). A guide to metaphorical design. *Communications of the ACM, 37*(12), 57–62. doi:10.1145/198366.198381

Maes, R., Rijsenbrij, D., Truijens, O., & Goedvolk, H. (2000). *Redefining business-IT alignment through a unified framework*. Retrieved May 30, 2014, from http://imwww.fee.uva.nl/~maestro/pdf/2000-19.pdf

Maffesoli, M. (1996). *The time of the tribes*. London: Sage.

Magedanz, T., Rothermel, K., & Krause, S. (1996, March). *Intelligent agents: An emerging technology for next generation telecommunications*. Paper presented at INFOCOM'96, 15th Annual Joint Conference of the IEEE Computer Societies, Networking the Next Generation 2, San Francisco, CA. doi:10.1109/INFCOM.1996.493313

Maglaveras, N., Stamkopoulos, T., Diamantaras, K., Pappas, C., & Strintzis, M. (1998). ECG pattern recognition and classification using non-linear transformations and neural networks: A review. *International Journal of Medical Informatics, 52*(1), 191–208. doi:10.1016/S1386-5056(98)00138-5 PMID:9848416

Mahler, S. J. (2001). Transnational relationships: The struggle to communicate across borders. *Identities (Yverdon), 7*(4), 583–619. doi:10.1080/1070289X.2001.9962679

Malinowski, B. (1923). The problem of meaning in primitive languages. In C. K. Ogden & I. A. Richards (Eds.), *The meaning of meaning* (pp. 296–355). London: Routledge and Kegan Paul.

Malone, T. W., Lai, K. Y., & Fry, C. (1995). Experiments with oval: A radically tailorable tool for cooperative work. *ACM Transactions on Information Systems, 13*(2), 177–205. doi:10.1145/201040.201047

Mampadi, F., Chen, S., Ghinea, G., & Chen, M. (2011). Design of adaptive hypermedia learning systems: A cognitive style approach. *Computers & Education, 56*(4), 1003–1011. doi:10.1016/j.compedu.2010.11.018

Mandl, M., Felfernig, A., Teppan, E., & Schubert, M. (2011). Consumer decision making in knowledge-based recommendation. *Journal of Intelligent Information Systems, 37*(1), 1–22. doi:10.1007/s10844-010-0134-3

Manning, C. D. (2009). *An introduction to information retrieval*. Cambridge, England: Cambridge University Press.

Mao, B., & Ban, Y. (2011). Online visualization of 3D city model using CityGML and X3DOM. *Cartographica: The International Journal for Geographic Information and Geovisualization, 46*(2), 109–114. doi:10.3138/carto.46.2.109

Marchand, M., & Raymond, L. (2008). Researching performance measurement systems: An information systems perspective. *International Journal of Operations & Production Management, 28*(7), 663–686. doi:10.1108/01443570810881802

Markoff, J. (2006, November 12). Entrepreneurs see a web guided by common sense. *The New York Times*. Retrieved from http://dt123.com/datagrid/datagridwebsitev1a/PDFs/NYT_111306_Web30.pdf

Martinez-Garcia, A., Morris, S., Tscholl, M., Tracy, F., & Carmichael, P. (2012). Case-based learning, pedagogical innovation, and semantic web technologies. *IEEE Transactions on Learning Technologies, 5*(2), 104–116. doi:10.1109/TLT.2011.34

Martin, S., Diaz, G., Sancristobal, E., Gil, R., Castro, M., & Peire, J. (2011). New technology trends in education: Seven years of forecasts and convergence. *Computers & Education, 57*(3), 1893–1906. doi:10.1016/j.compedu.2011.04.003

Marz, N., & Warren, J. (2013). *Big data: Principles and best practices of scalable realtime data systems*. Manning Publications.

Mason, G. S., Shuman, T. R., & Cook, K. E. (2013). Comparing the effectiveness of an inverted classroom to a traditional classroom in an upper-division engineering course. *IEEE Transactions on Education, 56*(4), 430–435. doi:10.1109/TE.2013.2249066

Masoumi, D. (2006). *Critical factors for effective e-learning*. Retrieved from http://asianvu.com/digital-library/elearning/Critical_factors_for_effective_e-learning_by_DMasoumi[1].pdf

Matook, S., & Brown, S. A. (2008). Conceptualizing the IT artifact for MIS research. In Proceedings of ICIS 2008. Paris: ICIS.

Matthijs, N., & Radlinski, F. (2011). Personalizing web search using long term browsing history. In *Proceedings of 4th ACM International conference on Web Search and Data Mining* (pp. 25-34). Kowloon, Hong Kong: ACM. doi:10.1145/1935826.1935840

Mayer, J. D., & Salovey, P. (1997). What is emotional intelligence? In P. Salovey, M. A. Brackett, & J. D. Mayer (Eds.), *Emotional Intelligence: Key readings on the Mayer and Salovey Model* (pp. 29–60). New York: Dude Publishing.

Mayer, R. E. (1997). Multimedia learning: Are we asking the right questions? *Educational Psychologist, 32*(1), 1–19. doi:10.1207/s15326985ep3201_1

McClelland, D. C. (1998). Identifying competencies with behavioral-event interviews. *Psychological Science, 9*(5), 331–340. doi:10.1111/1467-9280.00065

McConatha, D. (2002). Aging online: Toward a theory of e-quality. In *Older adults, health information, and the world wide web* (pp. 21-41). Academic Press.

McCool, L.B. (2011). *The pedagogical use of Twitter in the university classroom*. Graduate Theses and Dissertations. Retrieved from Graduate College at Digital Repository (Paper 11947).

McFarland, D., & Hamilton, D. (2005). Factors affecting student performance and satisfaction: Online versus traditional course delivery. *Journal of Computer Information Systems, 46*(2), 25–32.

McKenna, K. Y., Green, A. S., & Gleason, M. E. (2002). Relationship formation on the internet: What's the big attraction? *The Journal of Social Issues, 58*(1), 9–31. doi:10.1111/1540-4560.00246

McMillan, D. W. (1996). Sense of community. *Journal of Community Psychology, 24*(4), 315–325. doi:10.1002/(SICI)1520-6629(199610)24:4<315::AID-JCOP2>3.0.CO;2-T

McMillan, J. H., & Schumacher, S. (2010). *Research in education: Evidence based inquiry* (7th ed.). Upper Saddle River, NJ: Pearson.

McMillan, S. J., & Macias, W. (2008). Strengthening the safety net for online seniors: Factors influencing differences in health information seeking among older internet users. *Journal of Health Communication, 13*(8), 778–792. doi:10.1080/10810730802487448 PMID:19051113

McPherson, M. A., & Nunes, J. M. (2008). Critical issues for e-learning delivery: What may seem obvious is not always put into practice. *Journal of Computer Assisted Learning, 24*(5), 433–445. doi:10.1111/j.1365-2729.2008.00281.x

McPherson, M., Smith-Lovin, L., & Brashears, M. E. (2006). Social isolation in America: Changes in core discussion networks over two decades. *American Sociological Review, 71*(3), 353–375. doi:10.1177/000312240607100301

Means, B., Toyama, Y., Murphy, R., Bakia, M., & Jones, K. (2009). *Evaluation of evidence-based practices in online learning: A meta-analysis and review of online learning studies*. US Department of Education. Available from https://www2.ed.gov/rschstat/eval/tech/evidence-based-practices/finalreport.pdf

Melenhorst, A. S., Rogers, W. A., & Bouwhuis, D. G. (2006). Older adults' motivated choice for technological innovation: Evidence for benefit-driven selectivity. *Psychology and Aging, 21*(1), 190–195. doi:10.1037/0882-7974.21.1.190 PMID:16594804

Melnikova, N., & Vagarina, N. (2013). The adaptation of foreign experience of semantic web technologies in education. *Engineering:Theory into Practice, 24*, 21–27.

Mering, J., & Robbie, D. (2004). Education and electronic learning-Does online learning assist learners and how can it be continuously improved. In *Proceedings of the Higher Education Research and Development Society of Australasia (HERSDA 2004) Conference.* Retrieved from http://www.google.com.au/url?sa=t&rct=j&q=how%20 did%20internet%20assist%20in%20higher%20educati on&source=web&cd=4&cad=rja&ved=0CC8QFjAD &url=http%3A%2F%2Fresearchbank.swinburne.edu. au%2Fvital%2Faccess%2Fservices%2FDownload%2F swin%3A3409%2FSOURCE1&ei=yhJxUPKHDKmh igeP_YGYAw&usg=AFQjCNHr4NurG4N_wV3eN- RG3RdiC2lerLQ

Merrill, G. H. (2011). Ontology, ontologies, and science. *Topoi, 30*(1), 71–83. doi:10.1007/s11245-011-9091-x

Merz, C. (1988). Smile, please. *New Statesman & Society, 1*(10), 42.

Mesch, G. S. (2009). Social context and communication channels choice among adolescents. *Computers in Human Behavior, 25*(1), 244–251. doi:10.1016/j.chb.2008.09.007

Micarelli, A., Gasparetti, F., Sciarrone, F., & Gauch, S. (2007). Personalized search on the World Wide Web. In P. Brusilovsky, A. Kobsa, & W. Nejdl (Eds.), *The adaptive web: Methods and strategies of web personalization* (pp. 195–230). Berlin: Springer. doi:10.1007/978-3-540-72079-9_6

Mikal, J. P., Rice, R. E., Abeyta, A., & DeVilbiss, J. (2013). Transition, stress and computer-mediated social support. *Computers in Human Behavior, 29*(5), A40–A53. doi:10.1016/j.chb.2012.12.012

Miles, M. B., & Huberman, A. M. (1994). *Qualitative data analysis - An expanded sourcebook* (2nd ed.). Thousand Oaks, CA: Sage.

Miller, A. D., & Edwards, W. K. (2007). Give and take: A study of consumer photo-sharing culture and practice. In *Proceedings of the SIGCHI Conference on Human Factors in Computing Systems* (pp. 347-356). ACM. doi:10.1145/1240624.1240682

Millikan, R. G. (1999). Historical kinds and the "special sciences". *Philosophical Studies, 95*(1-2), 45–65. doi:10.1023/A:1004532016219

Milliken, M., O'Donnell, S., Gibson, K., & Daniels, B. (2012). Older adults and video communications: A case study. *The Journal of Community Informatics, 8*(1).

Milman, N. B. (2012). The flipped classroom strategy: What is it and how can it best be used? *Distance Learning, 9*, 85.

Mine, T., Suganuma, A., & Shoudai, T. (2002). Categorizing questions according to a navigation list for a web-based self-teaching system: AEGIS. In *Proceedings of the International Conference on Computers in Education* (pp. 1245-1249). Academic Press. doi:10.1109/CIE.2002.1186203

Minocha, S., & Thomas, P. G. (2007). Collaborative learning in a wiki environment: Experiences from a software engineering course. *New Review of Hypermedia and Multimedia, 13*(2), 187–209. doi:10.1080/13614560701712667

Minton, A. P., & Rose, R. L. (1997). The effects of environmental concern on environmentally friendly consumer behavior: An exploratory study. *Journal of Business Research, 40*(1), 37–48. doi:10.1016/S0148-2963(96)00209-3

Mistilis, N. (2012). Challenges and potential of the semantic web for tourism. *E-Review of Tourism Research, 10*(2), 51-55.

Mobasher, B. (2007). Data mining for web personalization. In P. Brusilovsky, A. Kobsa, & W. Nejdl (Eds.), *The adaptive web: Methods and strategies of web personalization* (pp. 263–290). Berlin: Springer. doi:10.1007/978-3-540-72079-9_3

Monachesi, P., Simov, K., Mossel, E., Osenova, P., & Lemnitzer, L. (2008). What ontologies can do for eLearning. In *Proceedings of IMCL 2008.* Retrived from http://www.let.uu.nl/lt4el/content/files/IMCL08Final.pdf

Monahan, T., McArdle, G., & Bertolotto, M. (2008). Virtual reality for collaborative e-learning. *Computers & Education, 50*(4), 1339–1353. doi:10.1016/j.compedu.2006.12.008

Montgomery, A., & Smith, M. (2009). Prospects for personalization on the Internet. *Journal of Interactive Marketing, 23*(2), 130–137. doi:10.1016/j.intmar.2009.02.001

Moodle. (2014, March 27). *Modular object oriented distance learning*. Retrieved March 27, 2014, from http://moodle.org

Moore, J. C. (2005). *The Sloan Consortium quality framework and the five pillars*. The Sloan Consortium. Retrieved April 4, 2011 from http://sloanconsortium.org/publications/freedownloads

Moravec, J. (2009). *The role of teachers in education 3.0*. Retrieved from http://www.educationfutures.com/2009/05/10/the-role-of-teachers-in-education-30/

Moreale, E., & Vargas-Vera, M. (2004). Semantic services in e-learning: An argumentation case study. *Journal of Educational Technology & Society*, 7(4), 112–128. Retrieved from http://ifets.info/journals/7_4/ets_7_4.pdf#page=117

Morgan, M., Lugosi, P., & Ritchie, J. R. (Eds.). (2010). *The tourism and leisure experience*. Bristol, UK: Channel View Publications.

Morris, M. (2013). Collaborative search revisited. In *Proceedings of 2013 Conference on Computer Supported Cooperative Work* (pp. 1181-1192). New York, NY: Academic Press.

Mundra, P., & Rajapakse, J. (2007). SVM-RFE with relevancy and redundancy criteria for gene selection. In J. Rajapakse, B. Schmidt, & G. Volkert (Eds.), *Pattern recognition in bioinformatics* (Vol. 4774, pp. 242–252). Springer Berlin Heidelberg. doi:10.1007/978-3-540-75286-8_24

Mutton, P., & Golbeck, J. (2003). Visualization of semantic metadata and ontologies. In *Proceedings of International Conference on Information Visualization* (pp. 300-305). London, UK: Academic Press.

Nahm, E. S., & Resnick, B. (2001). Homebound older adults' experiences with the internet and e-mail. *Computers in Nursing*, 19(6), 257–263. PMID:11764717

Naik, U., & Shivalingaiah, D. (2008). Comparative study of web 1.0, web 2.0 and web 3.0. *International CALIBER*, 499-507. Retrieved from http://ir.inflibnet.ac.in/bitstream/1944/1285/1/54.pdf

Nardi, B. A. (2005). Beyond bandwidth: Dimensions of connection in interpersonal communication. *Computer Supported Cooperative Work*, 14(2), 91–130. doi:10.1007/s10606-004-8127-9

Neely, A., Adams, C., & Kennerley, M. (2002). *The performance prism: The scorecard for measuring and managing business success*. London: Financial Times Prentice Hall.

Neely, A. (2005). The evolution of performance measurement research. *International Journal of Operations & Production Management*, 25(12), 1264–1277. doi:10.1108/01443570510633648

Neely, A., Gregory, M., & Platts, K. (1995). Performance measurement system design: A literature review and research agenda. *International Journal of Operations & Production Management*, 15(4), 80–116. doi:10.1108/01443579510083622

Neri, M. A. (2005). *Ontology-based learning objects sequencing*. Dipartimento di Elettronica e Informazione, Politecnico di Milano, Italy. Retrieved from http://unikode.me/attach/Pubblicazioni/ELearn06.pdf

Neri, M. A., & Colombetti, M. (2009). Ontology-based learning objects search and courses generation. *Applied Artificial Intelligence*, 23(3), 233–260. doi:10.1080/08839510802715134

Neustaedter, C., & Greenberg, S. (2012, May). Intimacy in long-distance relationships over video chat. In *Proceedings of the SIGCHI Conference on Human Factors in Computing Systems* (pp. 753-762). ACM. doi:10.1145/2207676.2207785

Neves, B. B., & Amaro, F. (2012). Too old for technology? How the elderly of Lisbon use and perceive ICT. *The Journal of Community Informatics*, 8(1).

Nguyen, H. T., Butler, M., Roychoudhry, A., Shannon, A. G., Flack, J., & Mitchell, P. (1996). Classification of diabetic retinopathy using neural networks. In *Engineering in Medicine and Biology Society, 1996. Bridging Disciplines for Biomedicine: Proceedings of the 18th Annual International Conference of the IEEE* (Vol. 4, pp. 1548–1549). IEEE. doi:10.1109/IEMBS.1996.647546

Nicula, B., Marque, C., & Berghmans, D. (2008). Visualization of distributed solar data and metadata with the solar weather browser. *Solar Physics, 248*(2), 225–232. doi:10.1007/s11207-007-9105-4

Nieuwenhuis, J. (2010). Qualitative research designs and data gathering techniques. In K. Maree (Ed.), *First steps in research* (pp. 70–98). Pretoria, South Africa: Van Schaik.

Nimrod, G. (2012). Online communities as a resource in older adults' tourism. *The Journal of Community Informatics, 8*(1).

Nir-Gal, O. (2002). Distance learning: The role of the teacher in a virtual learning environment. *Ma'of u-Ma'aseh, 8*, 23-50.

Nordlund, A. M., & Garvill, J. (2002). Value structures behind proenvironmental behavior. *Environment and Behavior, 34*(6), 740–756. doi:10.1177/001391602237244

Normann, R. (1991). *Service management: Strategy and leadership in service business*. Chichester, UK: Wiley.

Norval, C. (2012). Understanding the incentives of older adults' participation on social networking sites. *ACM Sigaccess Accessibility and Computing*, (102), 25-29.

Noskova, T., & Pavlova, T. (2013). Electronic resources as a basis of promising professional competence. *Bulletin of the St. Petersburg University of the Russian Interior Ministry, 3*(59), 133-137.

Noskova, T. (2011). *Network educational communication.* St. Petersburg, Russia: HSPU Publishing House.

Noskova, T. (2013). *Century challenges: Pedagogy of the network environment.* St. Petersburg, Russia: HSPU Publishing House.

Noskova, T., Kulikova, S., Pavlova, T., & Yakovleva, O. (2013). *New conditions for the formation of information culture for the XXI century specialist.* St. Petersburg, Russia: HSPU Publishing House.

Noti, E. (2013, July). Web 2.0 and its influence in the tourism sector. *European Scientific Journal*, 115-123.

Nudurupati, S. S., Bititci, U. S., Kumar, V., & Chan, F. T. S. (2011). State of the art literature review on performance measurement. *Computers & Industrial Engineering, 60*(2), 279–290. doi:10.1016/j.cie.2010.11.010

Nunes, M., Bezerra, J., & Oliveira, A. (2012). PersonalitYML: A markup language to standardize the user personality in recommender systems. *GEINTEC Magazine, 2*(3), 255–273. doi:10.7198/S2237-0722201200030006

Nyqvist, F., Forsman, A. K., Giuntoli, G., & Cattan, M. (2013). Social capital as a resource for mental well-being in older people: A systematic review. *Aging & Mental Health, 17*(4), 394–410. doi:10.1080/13607863.2012.742490 PMID:23186534

O'Boyle, E. H. Jr, Humphrey, R. H., Pollack, J. M., Hawver, T. H., & Story, P. A. (2010). The relation between emotional intelligence and job performance: A meta-analysis. *Journal of Organizational Behavior, 32*(5), 788–818. doi:10.1002/job.714

OAI. (2014). *Open archives initiative*. Retrieved March 27, 2014, from http://www.openarchives.org

OAI-PMH. (2014). *Open archives initiative – Protocol for metadata harvesting*. Retrieved March 27, 2014, from http://www.openarchives.org/pmh

Oates, B. J., & Fitzgerald, B. (2007). Multi-metaphor method: Organizational metaphors in information systems development. *Information Systems Journal, 17*(4), 421–449. doi:10.1111/j.1365-2575.2007.00266.x

Office of Science and Technology Policy of the United States. (2012). *Fact sheet: Big data across the federal government*. Retrieved September, 2014, from www.WhiteHouse.gov/OSTP

Ogozalek, V. Z. (1991). The social impacts of computing: Computer technology and the graying of America. *Social Science Computer Review, 9*(4), 655–666. doi:10.1177/089443939100900409

O'Hara, K., Alani, H., Kalfoglou, Y., & Shadbolt, N. (2004). *Trust strategies for the semantic web*. Retrieved from http://eprints.soton.ac.uk/260029/1/ISWC04-OHara-final.pdf

Oliver, R. (2001). *Assuring the quality of online learning in Australian higher education*. Retrieved from http://ro.ecu.edu.au/cgi/viewcontent.cgi?article=5791&context=ecuworks

Oolun, K., Ramgolam, S., & Dorasami, I. V. (2012). The making of a digital nation: toward i-Mauritius. *The Global Information Technology Report 2012*. Retrieved from http://www3.weforum.org/docs/GITR/2012/GITR_Chapter2.2_2012.pdf

Ooms, A., Burke, L., Linsey, T., & Heaton-Shrestha, C. (2008). Introducing e-developers to support a university's blended learning developments. *Research in Learning Technology*, *16*(2), 111–122. doi:10.1080/09687760802316307

Opalinski, L. (2001). Older adults and the digital divide: Assessing results of a web-based survey. *Journal of Technology in Human Services*, *18*(3-4), 203–221. doi:10.1300/J017v18n03_13

O'Reilly, T. (2005). *What is web 2.0?* Retrieved August 29, 2013, from http://www.oreillynet.com/pub/a/oreilly/tim/news/2005/09/30/what-is-web-20.html#mememap

Orlikowski, W. J. (2010). The sociomateriality of organisational life: Considering technology in management research. *Cambridge Journal of Economics*, *34*(1), 125–141. doi:10.1093/cje/bep058

Orlikowski, W. J., & Iacono, C. S. (2001). Research commentary: Desperately seeking the "IT" in IT research - A call to theorizing the IT artefact. *Information Systems Research*, *12*(2), 121–134. doi:10.1287/isre.12.2.121.9700

Orlikowski, W. J., Yates, J. A., Okamura, K., & Fujimoto, M. (1995). Shaping electronic communication: The meta-structuring of technology in the context of use. *Organization Science*, *6*(4), 423–444. doi:10.1287/orsc.6.4.423

OWL. (2014). *OWL web ontology language*. Retrieved March 27, 2014, from http://www.w3.org/TR/owlref
PHP (2014). PHP

Padhy, R. P., Patra, M. R., & Satapathy, S. C. (2011). RDBMS to NoSQL: Reviewing some next-generation non-relational databases. *International Journal of Advanced Engineering Science and Technologies*, *11*(1), 15–30.

Pah, I., Maniu, I., Maniu, G., & Damian, S. (2007). A conceptual framework based on ontologies for knowledge management in e-learning systems. In *Proc. of the 6th WSEAS International Conference on Education and Educational Technology* (pp. 283-286). Retrieved from http://www.wseas.us/e-library/conferences/2007venice/papers/570-623.pdf

Pallof, R., & Pratt, K. (2007). *Building online learning communities: Effective strategies for the virtual classroom* (2nd ed.). San Francisco, CA: Jossey-Bass.

Palmer, B. R., Gignac, G. E., Ekermans, G., & Stough, C. (2008). A comprehensive framework for emotional intelligence. In R. Emmerling, V. K. Shanwal, & M. K. Mandal (Eds.), *Emotional intelligence: Theoretical cultural perspectives* (pp. 17–38). New York: Nova Science.

Palmer, B. R., Stough, C., Harmer, R., & Gignac, G. E. (2010). Genos emotional intelligence inventory. In C. Stough, D. Saklofske, & J. Parker (Eds.), *Advances in the measurement of emotional intelligence* (pp. 321–344). New York: Springer.

Pankratius, V., & Vossen, G. (2003). Towards e-learning grids: Using grid computing in electronic learning. In *Proceedings of IEEE Workshop on Knowledge Grid and Grid Intelligence (IEEE/WIC)* (pp. 4-15). IEEE.

Papamanthou, C., Tollis, I. G., & Doerr, M. (2004). 3D visualization of semantic metadata models and ontologies. *Lecture Notes in Computer Science, 3383*, 377-388.

Papert, S., & Harel, I. (1991). *Constructionism*. New York: Ablex Publishing Corporation.

Papp, R. (2000). Critical success factors for distance learning. In *Proceedings of AMCIS 2000*. Retrieved from http://aisel.aisnet.org/amcis2000/104/

Parkhurst, R., Moskal, B. M., Lucena, J., & Downey, G. L. (2008). Engineering cultures: Comparing student learning in online and classroom based implementations. *International Journal of Engineering Education*, *24*(5), 955–955.

Parry, M. (2010). *Colleges see 17 percent increase in online enrollment*. Retrieved April 16, 2013, from http://chronicle.com/blogs/wiredcampus/colleges-see-17-percent-increase-in-online-enrollment/20820

Patton, M. Q. (1990). *Qualitative evaluation and research methods*. Thousand Oaks, CA: Sage.

Paulo Kushnir, L., & Berry, K. C. (2014). Inside, outside, upside down: New directions in online teaching and e-learning. In *Proceedings of the 8th Annual International Conference on e-Learning (ICEL 2014)* (pp. 133-140). Academic Press.

Paxton, P. (2003). Meeting the challenges of online learning through invitational education. In *Proceedings of 2003 Educause in Australasia: Expanding the Learning Community–Meeting the Challenges*. Academic Press.

Pazzani, M., & Billsus, D. (2007). Content-based recommendation systems. In P. Brusilovsky, A. Kobsa, & W. Nejdl (Eds.), *The adaptive web: Methods and strategies of web personalization* (pp. 325–341). Berlin: Springer. doi:10.1007/978-3-540-72079-9_10

Peesapati, S. T., Schwanda, V., Schultz, J., Lepage, M., Jeong, S. Y., & Cosley, D. (2010). Pensieve: supporting everyday reminiscence. In *Proceedings of the SIGCHI Conference on Human Factors in Computing Systems* (pp. 2027-2036). ACM.

Pertierra, R. (2006). *Transforming technologies: Altered selves*. Manila: De La Salle University Press.

Peskova, O. (2011). Social media as a platform for technology PR 2.0. In *Government and business: Communication resources* (pp. 57–82). Moscow, Russia: Higher School of Economics.

Petrelli, D., & Whittaker, S. (2010). Family memories in the home: Contrasting physical and digital mementos. *Personal and Ubiquitous Computing*, *14*(2), 153–169. doi:10.1007/s00779-009-0279-7

Petter, S., & McLean, E. R. (2009). A meta-analytic assessment of the DeLone and McLean IS success model: An examination of IS success at the individual level. *Information & Management*, *46*(3), 159–166. doi:10.1016/j.im.2008.12.006

Petter, S., Straub, D. W., & Rai, A. (2007). Specifying formative constructs in information systems research. *Management Information Systems Quarterly*, *31*(4), 623–656.

phpoai2. (2014). *PHP data provider*. Retrieved March 27, 2014, from http://physnet.uni-oldenburg.de/oai

Piccoli, G., Rami, A., & Blake, I. (2001). Web-based virtual learning environments: A research framework and a preliminary assessment of effectiveness in basic IT skills training. *Management Information Systems Quarterly*, *25*(4), 401–426. doi:10.2307/3250989

Pierce, J. C., Dalton, R. J., & Zaitsev, A. (1999). Public perceptions of environmental conditions. In R. J. Dalton, P. Garb, P. Lovrich, J. C. Pierce, & J. M. Whitely (Eds.), *Critical masses: Citizens, nuclear weapons production, and environmental destruction in the United States and Russia* (pp. 97–129). Cambridge, MA: MIT Press.

Pierrakeas, C., Solomou, G., & Kameas, A. (2012). An ontology-based approach in learning programming languages. In *Proceedings of 16th Panhellenic Conference on Informatics* (pp. 393-398). Academic Press. doi:10.1109/PCi.2012.78

Pine, B., & Gilmore, J. (1999). *The experience economy: Work is theatre & every business a stage*. Harvard, MA: Harvard Business School Press.

Pinsonneault, A., & Rivard, S. (1998). Information technology and the nature of managerial work: From the productivity paradox to the Icarus paradox? *Management Information Systems Quarterly*, *22*(3), 287–311. doi:10.2307/249667

Plato. (1991). The Republic (2nd ed.). (A. Bloom, Trans.). Basic Books.

Poggio, T., & Girosi, F. (1990). Networks for approximation and learning. *Proceedings of the IEEE*, *78*(9), 1481–1497. doi:10.1109/5.58326

Poole, D. I., Goebel, R. G., & Mackworth, A. K. (1998). *Computational intelligence*. Oxford, UK: Oxford University Press.

Popescu, E., Badica, C., & Moraret, L. (2010). Accommodating learning styles in an adaptive educational system. *Informatica (Slovenia)*, *34*(4), 451–462.

Postgre, S. Q. L. (2014). *PostgreSQL: The world's most advanced open source database.* Retrieved September, 2014, from http://www.postgresql.org/

Post, T. A., & Fox, J. L. (1982). Programming experiments on a TERAK 8510/A microcomputer. *Behavior Research Methods and Instrumentation, 14*(2), 276–280. doi:10.3758/BF03202166

Pradeau, J.-F. (2001). Les formes et les réalités intelligibles. In J.-F. Pradeau (Ed.), Platon: les formes intelligibles (pp. 17-54). Paris: Presses Universitaires de France.

Prahalad, C. K., & Krishnan, M. S. (2008). *The new age of innovation: Driving co-created value through global networks.* New York, NY: Mc Graw-Hill.

Preece, J. (2000). *Online communities: Designing usability, supporting sociability.* Chichester, UK: Wiley.

Prenksy, M. (2001). Digital natives, digital immigrants. *On the Horizon, 9*(5).

Prensky, M. (2001). *Do they really think differently?* Retrieved from http://www.emeraldinsight.com/journals.htm?articleid=1532747&show=pdf

Prensky, M. (2005). Listen to the natives. *Educational Leadership, 63*(4).

Preuss, S. (1991). *Umweltkatastrophe Mensch. Ueber unsere Grenzen und Moeglichkeiten, oekologisch bewusst zu handeln.* Heidelberg, Germany: Roland Asanger Verlag.

Pritchett, D. (2008). BASE: An acid alternative. *Queue, 6*(3), 48–55. doi:10.1145/1394127.1394128

Probst, F. (2006). Ontological analysis of observations and measurements. *Lecture Notes in Computer Science - Geographic. Information Science, 4197,* 304–320.

Project Management Institute. (2013). *The PMBOK guide* (5th ed.). Newton Square, PA: Author.

Protégé. (2014). *Ontology editor and knowledge acquisition system.* Retrieved March 27, 2014, from http://protege.stanford.edu

PTStemmer. (2014). *A Java stemming toolkit for the Portuguese language.* Retrieved March 27, 2014, from http://code.google.com/p/ptstemmer

Pudaruth, S., Moloo, R. K., Mantaye, A., & Jannoo, N. B. (2010). A survey of e-learning platforms in Mauritius. In *Proceedings of the World Congress on Engineering* (Vol. 1). Retrieved from http://www.iaeng.org/publication/WCE2010/WCE2010_pp415-420.pdf

Pulvirenti, A. S., & Roldan, M. C. (2011). *Pentaho data integration 4 cookbook.* Olton Birmingham, UK: Packt Publishing Ltd.

Quan, C., He, T., & Ren, F. (2010, August). *Emotion analysis in blogs at sentence level using a Chinese emotion corpus.* Paper presented at International Conference on Natural Language Processing and Knowledge Engineering (NLP-KE), Beijing, China. doi:10.1109/NLPKE.2010.5587790

R Project. (2015). *The R project for statistical computing.* Retrieved January 22, 2015 from http://www.r-project.org/

Rai, A., Lang, S. S., & Welker, R. B. (2002). Assessing the validity of the IS success model: An empirical test and theoretical analysis. *Information Systems Research, 13*(1), 50–69. doi:10.1287/isre.13.1.50.96

Rakkolainen, I., & Vainio, T. (2001). A 3D city info for mobile users. *Computers & Graphics, 25*(4), 619–625. doi:10.1016/S0097-8493(01)00090-5

Ramadan, Z., Ropelle, K., Myklebust, J., Goldstein, M., Feng, X., & Flynn, J. (1991). A neural network to discriminate between dyslexic subtypes. In *Engineering in Medicine and Biology Society, Proceedings of the Annual International Conference of the IEEE* (pp. 1405–1406). IEEE. doi:10.1109/IEMBS.1991.684513

Ramakrishnan, R. (2012). CAP and cloud data management. *Computer, 45*(2), 43–49. doi:10.1109/MC.2011.388

Rashid, S., Khan, R., & Ahmed, F. (2013). *A proposed model of e-learning management system using semantic web technology.* Retrieved from http://www.semantic-web-journal.net/sites/default/files/swj234.pdf

Raskin, R. G., & Pan, M. J. (2005). Knowledge representation in the semantic web for earth and environmental terminology (SWEET). *Computers & Geosciences, 31*(9), 1119–1125. doi:10.1016/j.cageo.2004.12.004

Recuero, R. (2009). *Redes sociais na internet*. Porto Alegre, Brasil: Editora Sulina.

Registered Data Providers, O. A. I. (2014). *List of the registered data providers OAI*. Retrieved March 27, 2014, from http://www.openarchives.org

Reich, B. H., & Benbasat, I. (2000). Factors that influence the social dimension of alignment between business and information technology objectives. *Management Information Systems Quarterly*, *24*(1), 81–113. doi:10.2307/3250980

Reiser, R. A. (2001). A history of instructional design and technology: Part I: A history of instructional media. *Educational Technology Research and Development*, *49*(1), 53–64. doi:10.1007/BF02504506

Remy, C., & Huang, E. M. (2012). The complexity of information for sustainable choices. In *Proceedings Position Paper at Simple, Sustainable Living Workshop*. ACM.

Ren, F., & Quan, C. (2012). Linguistic-based emotion analysis and recognition for measuring consumer satisfaction: An application of affective computing. *Information Technology Management*, *13*(4), 321–332. doi:10.1007/s10799-012-0138-5

Rettie, R. (2007). *A Comparison of four new communication technologies: Research repository*. London: Kingston University.

Rettie, R. (2008). Mobile phones as network capital: Facilitating connections. *Mobilities*, *3*(2), 291–311. doi:10.1080/17450100802095346

Rheingold, H. (1993). *The virtual community: Homesteading on the electronic frontier*. Reading, MA: Addison-Wesley.

Ricci, F., Rokach, L., & Shapira, B. (2011). Introduction to recommender systems handbook. In F. Ricci, L. Rokach, B. Shapira, & P. Kantor (Eds.), *Recommender systems handbook* (pp. 1–35). Berlin: Springer. doi:10.1007/978-0-387-85820-3_1

Richardson, J. C., & Swan, K. (2003). Examining social presence in online courses in relation to students' perceived learning and satisfaction. *Journal of Asynchronous Learning Networks*, *7*(1), 68–88.

Rideout, V., & Newman, T. (2005). *E-health and the elderly: How seniors use the internet for health information: Key findings from a national survey of older Americans*. Menlo Park, CA: Kaiser Family Foundation.

Rigo, S. J., de Oliveira, J. P., & Barbieri, C. (2007). Classificação de textos baseada em ontologias de domínio. In *Proceedings of Anais do XXVII Congresso da SBC – V Workshop em Tecnologia da Informação e da Linguagem Humana*. Retrieved from http://www.nilc.icmc.usp.br/til/til2007_English/arq0169.pdf

Rincón, J. (2012). *XML y web semántica: bases de datos en el contexto de la web semántica*. Universitat Oberta de Catalunya.

Roa, D. I. J., Lapo, P. S., & Rodríguez-Artacho, M. (2010). Semantic search in institutional repositories: A case study using DSpace and Moodle. In *Proceedings of International Conference on E-Learning, E-Business, Enterprise Information Systems, & E-Government* (pp. 356-365). Academic Press.

Robson, C. (2002). *Real world research* (2nd ed.). Oxford, UK: Blackwell Publishers.

Rokou, F. P., Rokou, E., & Rokos, Y. (2004). Modeling web-based educational systems: Process design teaching model. *Journal of Educational Technology & Society*, *7*(1), 42–50. Retrieved from http://www.ifets.info/others/journals/7_1/ets_7_1.pdf#page=47

Rolfe, V. (2012). Open educational resources: Staff attitudes and awareness. *The Journal of the Association of Learning Technology*, *20*. doi:10.3402/rlt.v20i0/14395

Rovai, A. P., & Barnum, K. T. (2003). On-line course effectiveness: An analysis of student interactions and perceptions of learning. *Journal of Distance Education*, *18*(1), 57–73.

Runkel, P. J. (1990). *Casting nets and testing specimens: Two grand methods of psychology*. New York: Praeger.

Russell, C., Campbell, A., & Hughes, I. (2008). Ageing, social capital and the Internet: Findings from an exploratory study of Australian 'silver surfers'. *Australasian Journal on Ageing*, *27*(2), 78–82. doi:10.1111/j.1741-6612.2008.00284.x PMID:18713197

Russell, S., & Norvig, P. (2003). *Artificial Intelligence: A modern approach* (3rd ed.). Prentice Hall.

Russell, T. L. (1999). *The no significant difference phenomenon*. Raleigh, NC: North Carolina State University.

Russomanno, D. J., Kothari, C., & Thomas, O. (2005). Building a sensor ontology: A practical approach leveraging iso and ogc models. In *Proceedings ofInternational Conference on Artificial Intelligence* (pp. 17-18). Las Vegas, NV: Academic Press.

Russom, P. (2011). *Big data analytics: Executive summary*. Renton, WA: TDWI Research.

Sabherwal, R., Jeyaraj, A., & Chowa, C. (2006). Information system success: Individual and organizational determinants. *Management Science, 52*(12), 1849–1864. doi:10.1287/mnsc.1060.0583

Sabucedo, L., Rifón, L., Corradini, F., Polzonetti, A., & Re, B. (2010). Knowledge-based platform for e-government agents: A web-based solution using semantic technologies. *Expert Systems with Applications, 37*(5), 3647–3656. doi:10.1016/j.eswa.2009.10.026

Sadaghiani, H. R. (2012). Online prelectures: An alternative to textbook reading assignments. *The Physics Teacher, 50*(5), 301. doi:10.1119/1.3703549

Sala, F. (2006). The international business case: emotional intelligence competencies and important business outcomes. In V. Druskat, F. Sala, & G. Mount (Eds.), *Linking emotional intelligence and performance at work: Current research evidence with individuals and groups* (pp. 125–144). Mahwah, NJ: Lawrence Erlbaum.

Salcedo, C. S. (2010). Comparative analysis of learning outcomes in face-to-face foreign language classes vs. language lab and online. *Journal of College Teaching and Learning, 7*(2), 43–54.

Salovey, P., & Mayer, J. D. (1990). Emotional intelligence. *Imagination, Cognition and Personality, 9*(3), 185–211. doi:10.2190/DUGG-P24E-52WK-6CDG

Salton, G., & Buckley, C. (1998). Term-weighting approaches in automatic retrieval. *Information Processing & Management, 24*(5), 513–523. doi:10.1016/0306-4573(88)90021-0

Sandvik, B. (2008). *Using KML for thematic mapping*. Retrieved February 19, 2013, from: http://thematicmapping.org/downloads/Using_KML_for_Thematic_Mapping.pdf

Santally, M. I. (2012). *Innovative learning technologies and pedagogies*. Retrieved from http://vcilt.blogspot.com.au/2012/07/open-university-of-mauritius.html

Sappey, J., & Relf, S. (2010). Digital technology education and its impact on traditional academic roles and practice. *Journal of University Teaching and Learning Practice, 7*(1). Retrieved from http://ro.uow.edu.au/jutlp/vol7/iss1/3

Sarvas, R., & Frohlich, D. M. (2011). *From snapshots to social media: The changing picture of domestic photography*. London: Springer. doi:10.1007/978-0-85729-247-6

Sassoon, J. (2012). *Web storytelling*. Milano, Italy: Franco Angeli.

Savitzky, A., & Golay, M. J. E. (1964). Smoothing and differentiation of data by simplified least squares procedures. *Analytical Chemistry, 36*(8), 1627–1639. doi:10.1021/ac60214a047

Schafer, J., Frankowski, D., Herlocker, J., & Sen, S. (2007). Collaborative filtering recommender systems. In P. Brusilovsky, A. Kobsa, & W. Nejdl (Eds.), *The adaptive web: Methods and strategies of web personalization* (pp. 291–324). Berlin: Springer. doi:10.1007/978-3-540-72079-9_9

Schauble, L. (1990). Belief revision in children: The role of prior knowledge and strategies for generating evidence. *Journal of Experimental Child Psychology, 49*(1), 31–57. doi:10.1016/0022-0965(90)90048-D PMID:2303776

Schoenfeld-Tacher, R., McConnell, S., & Graham, M. (2001). Do no harm: A comparison of the effects of online vs. traditional delivery media on a science course. *Journal of Science Education and Technology, 10*(3), 257–265. doi:10.1023/A:1016690600795

Schwartz, S. (1999). *Normative influences on altruism*. In L. Berkowitz (Ed.), Advances in experimental social psychology (pp. 221–279). New York, NY: Academic Press.

Schwartz, S. H. (1977). Normative influences on altruism. *Advances in Experimental Social Psychology, 10*, 221–279. doi:10.1016/S0065-2601(08)60358-5

Scott, J. (2008). *jQuery edit in place (JEIP)*. Retrieved September 3, 2014 from http://josephscott.org/code/javascript/jquery-edit-in-place/

Selim, H. M. (2007). E-learning critical success factors: An exploratory investigation of student perceptions. *International Journal of Technology Marketing, 2*(2), 157–182. doi:10.1504/IJTMKT.2007.014791

Selwyn, N. (2007). The use of computer technology in university teaching and learning: A critical perspective. *Journal of Computer Assisted Learning, 23*(2), 83–94. doi:10.1111/j.1365-2729.2006.00204.x

Selwyn, N., & Facer, K. (2007). *Beyond the digital divide: Rethinking digital inclusion for the 21st century*. Bristol: FutureLab.

Serrano, A. M. R., Rodrigues, P. H. B., Huacarpuma, R. C., da Costa, J. P. C. L., de Freitas, E. P., Assis, V. L., . . . Pilon, B. H. A. (2014). Improved business intelligence solution with reimbursement tracking system for the Brazilian ministry of planning, budget and management. In *Proceedings of the 6th International Conference on Knowledge Management and Information Sharing (KMIS'14)*. Rome, Italy: SCITEPRESS. doi:10.5220/0005169104340440

Serrano, J. I., Tomečková, M., & Zvárová, J. (2006). Machine learning methods for knowledge discovery in medical data on atherosclerosis. *European Journal for Biomedical Informatics, 1*, 6–33.

Sessions, R. (2007). Comparison of the top four enterprise architecture methodologies. *ObjectWatch White Papers*. Retrieved July 30, 2009, from http://objectwatch.com/white-papers

Shaoling, D., & Fangfang, Z. (2009, August). *Intelligent agents improving the efficiency of ubiquitous e-learning*. Paper presented at International Conference on Management and Service Science (MASS), Wuhan, China.

Sharif, A. M. (2002). Benchmarking performance management systems. *Benchmarking: An International Journal, 9*(1), 62–85. doi:10.1108/14635770210418588

Shekarpour, S., Katebi, M., & Katebi, S. D. (2009). *A trust model for semantic web*. Retrieved from http://ijssst.info/Vol-10/No-2/paper2.pdf

Sheng, Z., Zhu-ying, L., & Wan-xin, D. (2010, August). *The model of e-learning based on affective computing*. Paper presented at 3rd International Conference on Advanced Computer Theory and Engineering (ICACTE), Chengdu, China.

Sheth, A., Henson, C., & Sahoo, S. S. (2008). Semantic sensor web. *IEEE Internet Computing, 12*(4), 78–83. doi:10.1109/MIC.2008.87

SIAPE. (2014). *Siape - Sistema integrado de administração de recursos humanos*. Retrieved September, 2014, in Portuguese, from https://www.serpro.gov.br/conteudo-solucoes/produtos/administracao-federal/siape-sistema-integrado-de-administracao-de-recursos-humanos

Sibbel, A. (2009). Pathways towards sustainability through higher education. *International Journal of Sustainability in Higher Education, 10*(1), 68–82. doi:10.1108/14676370910925262

Siemens, G. (2007). *Networks, ecologies, and curatorial teaching*. Retrieved 8th January 2010 from http://www.connectivism.ca/blog/2007/08/networks_ecologies_and_curator.html

Siemens, G. (2010). Teaching in social and technological networks. *Connectivism blog*. Retrieved 20th April 2014 from http://www.connectivism.ca/?p=220/

Siemens, G., Gasevic, D., Haythornthwaite, C., Dawson, S., Shum, S. B., Ferguson, R., Duval, E., Verbert, K., & Baker, R. S. (2011). *Open learning analytics: An integrated & modularized platform*. Proposal to design, implement and evaluate an open platform to integrate heterogeneous learning analytics techniques.

Siemens, G. (2013). Massive open online courses: Innovation in education? In R. McGreal, W. Kinuthia, & S. Marshall (Eds.), *Open educational resources: Innovation, research and practice* (pp. 5–15). Athabasca, Canada: Athabasca University Press.

Silvius, A. J. G. (2007). Exploring differences in the perception of business and IT alignment. *Communications of the IIMA, 7*(2), 21–32.

Šimić, G., Gašević, D., & Devedžić, V. (2004). Semantic web and intelligent learning management systems. In *Proceedings of Workshop on Applications of Semantic Web Technologies for e-Learning*. Retrieved from http://www.win.tue.nl/SW-EL/2004/ITS-SWEL-Camera-ready/SW-EL-ITS-Proceedings/SWEL04-ITS04-proceedings.pdf

Sinclair, D., & Zairi, M. (2000). Performance measurement: A critical analysis of the literature with respect of total quality management. *International Journal of Management Reviews*, 2(2), 145–168. doi:10.1111/1468-2370.00035

Singh, A., Nowak, R. D., & Zhu, X. (2008). Unlabeled data: Now it helps, now it doesn't. In D. Koller, D. Schuurmans, Y. Bengio, & L. Bottou (Eds.), NIPS (pp. 1513–1520). Curran Associates, Inc. Retrieved from http://dblp.uni-trier.de/db/conf/nips/nips2008.html#SinghNZ08

Sitnic, A., Vagarina, N., & Melnikova, N. (2011). Ontological description multimedia resources in the context of semantic web technologies. *Vestnik SGTU*, 4(60), 202–207.

Skrbiš, Z. (2008). Transnational families: Theorising migration, emotions and belonging. *Journal of Intercultural Studies (Melbourne, Vic.)*, 29(3), 231–246. doi:10.1080/07256860802169188

Smaczny, T. (2001). Is an alignment between business and information technology the appropriate paradigm to manage IT in today's organisations? *Management Decision*, 39(10), 797–802. doi:10.1108/EUM0000000006521

Smyth, B., Balfe, E., Briggs, P., Coyle, M., & Freyne, J. (2003). Collaborative web search. In *Proceedings of International Joint Conferences on Artificial Intelligence* (pp. 1417-1419). IEEE.

Smyth, B. (2007). Case-based recommendation. In P. Brusilovsky, A. Kobsa, & W. Nejdl (Eds.), *The adaptive web: Methods and strategies of web personalization* (pp. 342–376). Berlin: Springer. doi:10.1007/978-3-540-72079-9_11

Snae, C., & Brüeckner, M. (2007). Ontology-driven e-learning system based on roles and activities for Thai learning environment. *Interdisciplinary Journal of E-Learning and Learning Objects*, 3(1), 1-17. Retrieved from http://www.ijello.org/Volume3/IJKLOv3p001-017Snae.pdf

Soliman, M., & Guetl, C. (2010). Intelligent pedagogical agents in immersive virtual learning environments: A review. In *Proceedings of MIPRO, 33rd International Convention* (pp. 827-832). Opatija, Croatia: Academic Press.

Sonnenreich, W. (1997). *A history of search engines*. Retrieved from http://www.wiley.com/compbooks/sonnenreich/history.html

SourceForge.net. (2015). *ucsd-psystem-xc 0.13*. Retrieved January 22, 2015 from http://ucsd-psystem-xc.sourceforge.net/

Spanos, Y. E., & Lioukas, S. (2001). An examination into the causal logic of rent generation: Contrasting Porter's competitive strategy framework and the resource-based perspective. *Strategic Management Journal*, 22(10), 907–934. doi:10.1002/smj.174

Spence, R., & Tweedie, L. (1998). The attribute explorer: Information synthesis via exploration. *Interacting with Computers*, 11(2), 137–146. doi:10.1016/S0953-5438(98)00022-8

Spencer, L., & Spencer, S. (1993). *Competence at work: Models for superior performance*. New York: John Wiley.

Srimathi, H., & Srivatsa, S. K. (2008). *Identification of ontology based learning object using instructional design*. Retrieved from http://pdf.aminer.org/000/269/789/enhancing_learning_object_content_on_the_semantic_web.pdf

Srimathi, H. (2010). Knowledge representation of LMS using ontology. *International Journal of Computers and Applications*, 6(3). Retrieved from http://citeseerx.ist.psu.edu/viewdoc/download?doi=10.1.1.206.4163&rep=rep1&type=pdf

Stamboulis, Y., & Skayannis, P. (2003). Innovation strategies and technology for experience-based tourism. *Tourism Management*, 24(1), 35–43. doi:10.1016/S0261-5177(02)00047-X

Starostova, L. (2013). Digital technology as a factor in the transformation of aesthetic experience. In *Proceedings of the International Conference Science Culture in Perspective of "Digital Humanities"* (pp. 48-55). St. Petersburg, Russia: Asterion.

Stavrakantonakis, I., Gagiu, A., Toma, I., & Fensel, D. (2013). Towards online engagement via the social web. In *Proceedings ofWEB 2013: The First International Conference on Building and Exploring Web Based Environments* (pp.26-31). Academic Press.

Steed, A. (2012). The flipped classroom. *Teaching Business & Economics*, *16*(3), 9–11.

Stensgaard, A.-S., Saarnak, C. F. L., Utzinger, J., Vounatsou, P., Simoonga, C., Mushinge, G., & Kristensen, T. K. et al. (2009). Virtual globes and geospatial health: The potential of new tools in the management and control of vector-borne diseases. *Geospatial Health*, *3*(2), 127–141. doi:10.4081/gh.2009.216 PMID:19440958

Stenzel, J. (2007). *CIO best practices – Enabling strategic value with information technology*. New York: John Wiley.

Stern, P. C. (2000). Toward a coherent theory of environmentally significant behavior. *The Journal of Social Issues*, *56*(3), 407–424. doi:10.1111/0022-4537.00175

Stern, P. C., Dietz, T., Abel, T., Guagnano, G. A., & Kalof, L. (1999). A value-belief-norm theory of support for social movements: The case of environmentalism. *Human Ecology Review*, *6*(2), 81–97.

Stern, P. C., Dietz, T., Kalof, L., & Guagnano, G. A. (1995). Values, beliefs, and proenvironmental attitude formation toward emergent attitude objects. *Journal of Applied Social Psychology*, *25*(18), 1611–1636. doi:10.1111/j.1559-1816.1995.tb02636.x

Stojanovic, L., Staab, S., & Studer, R. (2001). eLearning based on the semantic web. In *Proceedings of WebNet2001-World Conference on the WWW and Internet* (pp. 23-27). Retrieved from http://pdf.aminer.org/000/306/170/semantic_e_learning_agents_supporting_elearning_by_semantic_web_and.pdf

Stolk, D., Alexandrian, D., Gros, B., & Paggio, R. (2001). Gaming and multimedia applications for environmental crisis management training. *Computers in Human Behavior*, *17*(5-6), 627–642. doi:10.1016/S0747-5632(01)00027-9

Stone, E. (1978). *Research methods in organizational behavior*. Santa Monica, CA: Goodyear Publishing Company.

St-Pierre, J., & Delisle, S. (2006). An expert diagnosis system for the benchmarking of SMEs' performance. *Benchmarking: An International Journal*, *13*(1/2), 106–119. doi:10.1108/14635770610644619

Strapparava, C., & Mihalcea, R. (2008). Learning to identify emotions in text. In Proceedings of SAC'08, 2008 ACM Symposium on Applied Computing (pp. 1556-1560). Ceará, Brazil: ACM.

Strong, D. M., & Volkoff, O. (2010). Understanding organization-enterprise system fit: A path for theorizing the information technology artifact. *Management Information Systems Quarterly*, *34*(4), 731–756.

Studer, R., Benjamims, V. R., & Fensel, D. (1998). Knowledge engineering: Principles and methods. *Data & Knowledge Engineering*, *25*(1-2), 161–197. doi:10.1016/S0169-023X(97)00056-6

Suganuma, A., Mine, T., & Shoudai, T. (2005). Automatic exercise generating system that dynamically evaluates both students' and questions' levels[in Japanese]. *Journal of Information Processing Society of Japan*, *46*(7), 1810–1818.

Summers, J. J., Waigandt, A., & Whittaker, T. A. (2005). A comparison of student achievement and satisfaction in an online versus a traditional face-to-face statistics class. *Innovative Higher Education*, *29*(3), 233–250. doi:10.1007/s10755-005-1938-x

Sum, S., Mathews, R. M., & Hughes, I. (2009). Participation of older adults in cyberspace: How Australian older adults use the internet. *Australasian Journal on Ageing*, *28*(4), 189–193. doi:10.1111/j.1741-6612.2009.00374.x PMID:19951340

Swartout, W., & Tate, A. (1999). Ontologies, guest editors' introduction. *IEEE Intelligent Systems*, *14*(1), 18–19. doi:10.1109/MIS.1999.747901

Swidler, A. (1986). Culture in action: Symbols and strategies. *American Sociological Review*, *51*(2), 273–286. doi:10.2307/2095521

Sycara, K., Decker, K., & Pannu, A. (1996). Distributed intelligent agents. *IEEE Expert: Intelligent Systems and their Applications*, *11*(6), 36-36.

Syiam, M. M. (1994). A neural network expert system for diagnosing eye diseases. In *Artificial Intelligence for Applications,Proceedings of the Tenth Conference on* (pp. 491–492). doi:10.1109/CAIA.1994.323624

Szpunar, K. K., Khan, N. Y., & Schacter, D. L. (2013). Interpolated memory tests reduce mind wandering and improve learning of online lectures. *Proceedings of the National Academy of Sciences of the United States of America, 110*(16), 6313–6317. doi:10.1073/pnas.1221764110 PMID:23576743

Tallon, P. P., & Pinsonneault, A. (2011). Competing perspectives on the link between strategic information technology alignment and organizational agility: Insights from a mediation model. *Management Information Systems Quarterly, 35*(2), 363–486.

Tanwani, A., Afridi, J., Shafiq, M. Z., & Farooq, M. (2009). Guidelines to select machine learning scheme for classification of biomedical datasets. In C. Pizzuti, M. Ritchie, & M. Giacobini (Eds.), *Evolutionary computation, machine learning and data mining in bioinformatics* (Vol. 5483, pp. 128–139). Springer Berlin Heidelberg. doi:10.1007/978-3-642-01184-9_12

Tao, J., & Tan, T. (2005). Affective computing: A review. In J. Tao, T. Tan, & R. Picard (Eds.), *Affective computing and intelligent interaction (ACII)* (pp. 981–995). Berlin: Springer. doi:10.1007/11573548_125

Tapscott, D. (2008). *Grown up digital: How the net generation is changing your world.* New York: McGraw-Hill.

Taskin, O. (2009). The environmental attitudes of Turkish sénior high school students in the context of postmaterialism and the new environmental paradigm. *International Journal of Science Education, 31*(4), 481–502. doi:10.1080/09500690701691689

Tasner, M. (2010). *Marketing in the moment: The practical guide to using Web 3.0 marketing to reach your customer first.* Upper Saddle River, NJ: Pearson Education.

Teahan, J. (2006). Teaching with an ever-spinning web: Instructional uses of web 2.0. *NCSSSMST Journal, 12*, 26–27.

Thiagarajan, R., Manjunath, G., & Stumptner, M. (2008). Computing semantic similarity using ontologies. In *Proceedings of International Semantic Web Conference.* Retrieved from http://www.hpl.hp.com/techreports/2008/HPL-2008-87.pdf

Thinyane, H. (2010). Are digital natives a world-wide phenomenon? An investigation into South African first year students' use and experience with technology. *Computers & Education, 55*(1), 406–414. doi:10.1016/j.compedu.2010.02.005

Thomasson, A. L. (2009). Artifacts in metaphysics. In Handbook of philosophy of the technological sciences (pp. 191-197). Elsevier Science.

Threedee.com. (2013). *The UCSD P-system museum.* Retrieved January 22, 2015 from http://www.threedee.com/jcm/psystem/

Thyagharajan, K., & Nayak, R. (2007). Adaptive content creation for personalized e-learning using web services. *Journal of Applied Sciences Research, 3*(9), 828–836.

Tkalcic, M., Kosir, A., & Tasic, J. (2011). Usage of affective computing in recommender systems. *Elektrotehniski Vestnik, 78*(1-2), 12–17.

Tomaszewski, B. (2011). Situation awareness and virtual globes: Applications for disaster management. *Computers & Geosciences, 37*(1), 86–92. doi:10.1016/j.cageo.2010.03.009

Tsandilas, T., & Schraefel, M. (2004). Usable adaptive hypermedia systems. *New Review of Hypermedia and Multimedia, 10*(1), 5–29. doi:10.1080/1361456041000 1728137

Tucker, S. (2001). Distance education: Better, worse, or as good as traditional education? *Online Journal of Distance Learning Administration, 4*(4). Retrieved from http://www.westga.edu/~distance/ojdla/winter44/tucker44.html

Turban, E., Aronson, J. E., Liang, T.-P., & Sharda, R. (2007). *Decision support and business intelligence systems* (8th ed.). Upper Saddle River, NJ: Pearson Prentice Hall.

Tussyadiah, I. P., & Fesenmaier, D. R. (2009). Mediating tourist experiences: Access to places via shared videos. *Annals of Tourism Research, 36*(1), 24–40. doi:10.1016/j.annals.2008.10.001

Tuugalei, I., & Mow, C. (2012). Analyses of student programming errors in Java programming courses. *Journal of Emerging Trends in Computing and Information Sciences, 3*(5), 739–749.

UNESCO. (2004). *UNESCO online database.* Montreal, Canada: UNESCO Institute for Statistics. Retrieved 20th April 2014 from http:// www.uis.unesco.org

United Nations Statistics Division. (2011). *Composition of macro geographical (continental) regions, geographical sub-regions, and selected economic and other groupings.* Retrieved April 30, 2014, from http://unstats.un.org/unsd/methods/m49/m49regin.htm

Urtel, M. G. (2008). Assessing academic performance between traditional and distance education course formats. *Journal of Educational Technology & Society, 11*(1), 322–330.

Vadrevu, S., Teo, C., Rajan, S., Punera, K., Dom, B., Smola, A., … Zheng, Z. (2011). WSDM'11. In *Proceedings of 4th ACM International conference on Web Search and Data Mining* (pp. 675-684). Kowloon, Hong Kong: ACM.

Vallet, D., & Castells, P. (2011). On diversifying and personalizing web search. In *Proceedings of 34th International ACM SIGIR Conference on Research and Development in Informational Retrieval.* Beijing, China: ACM.

Van Belleghem, S., Eenhuizen, M., & Veris, E. (2011). *Social media around the world 2011.* InSites Consulting. Retrieved 18-11-2011 from http://www.slideshare.net/stevenvanbelleghem/social-media-aroundthe-world-2011/download?lead=394fd930572c9 b62fb082021a-f5a6d0922046ec4

Van Dijck, J. (2008). Digital photography: Communication, identity, memory. *Visual Communication, 7*(1), 57–76. doi:10.1177/1470357207084865

Vandenbosch, B., & Huff, S. L. (1997). Searching and scanning: How executives obtain information from executive information systems. *Management Information Systems Quarterly, 21*(1), 81–107. doi:10.2307/249743

Victor, C. R., Scambler, S. J., Bowling, A. N. N., & Bond, J. (2005). The prevalence of, and risk factors for, loneliness in later life: A survey of older people in Great Britain. *Ageing and Society, 25*(06), 357–375. doi:10.1017/S0144686X04003332

Voas, J., & Zhang, J. (2009). Cloud computing: New wine or just a new bottle, "cloud computing: New wine or just a new bottle? *IT Professional, 11*(2), 15–17. doi:10.1109/MITP.2009.23

Volery, T., & Lord, D. (2000). Critical success factors in online education. *International Journal of Educational Management, 14*(5), 216–223. doi:10.1108/09513540010344731

von Kortzfleisch, H. F., & Winand, U. (2000). Trust in electronic learning and teaching relationships: The case of WINFO-Line. ECIS. Retrieved from http://csrc.lse.ac.uk/asp/aspecis/20000136.pdf

Vora, M. N. (2011). Hadoop-HBase for large-scale data. In *Proceedings of the International Conference on Computer Science and Network Technology (ICCSNT).* Harbin, China: IEEE Press.

Vygotsky, L. S. (1978). *Mind in society: The development of higher psychological processes.* Cambridge, MA: Harvard University Press.

Wagner, N., Hassanein, K., & Head, M. (2010). Computer use by older adults: A multi-disciplinary review. *Computers in Human Behavior, 26*(5), 870–882. doi:10.1016/j.chb.2010.03.029

Wahlster, W., & Dengel, A. (2006). *Web 3.0: Convergence of web 2.0 and the semantic web* (2nd ed.). Deutsche Telekom Laboratories.

Walther, J. B., & Parks, M. R. (2002). Cues filtered out, cues filtered. In Handbook of interpersonal communication (vol. 3, pp. 529-563). Academic Press.

Walther, J. B., Loh, T., & Granka, L. (2005). Let me count the ways the interchange of verbal and nonverbal cues in computer-mediated and face-to-face affinity. *Journal of Language and Social Psychology, 24*(1), 36–65. doi:10.1177/0261927X04273036

Wang, S. (2008). Ontology of learning objects repository for pedagogical knowledge sharing. *Interdisciplinary Journal of E-Learning and Learning Objects, 4*(1), 1-12. Retrieved from http://ijklo.org/Volume4/IJELLOv4p001-012Wang200.pdf

Wang, Y., & Fesenmaier, D. R. (2004). Modeling participation in an online travel community. *Journal of Travel Research, 42*(February), 261–270. doi:10.1177/0047287503258824

Wang, Y., Yu, Q., & Fesenmaier, D. R. (2002). Defining the virtual community: Implications for tourism marketing. *Tourism Management, 23*(4), 407–417. doi:10.1016/S0261-5177(01)00093-0

Warburton, J., Cowan, S., & Bathgate, T. (2013). Building social capital among rural, older Australians through information and communication technologies: A review article. *Australasian Journal on Ageing, 32*(1), 8–14. doi:10.1111/j.1741-6612.2012.00634.x PMID:23521728

Wasan, S. K., Bhatnagar, V., & Kaur, H. (2008). The impact of data mining techniques on medical diagnostics. *Data Science Journal, 5*, 119–126. doi:10.2481/dsj.5.119

We Are Social. (2014). *Global digital statistic.* Retrieved from http://wearesocial.net/blog/

Weather Underground. (2012). *The personal weather station project.* Retrieved April 30, 2014, from http://www.wunderground.com/weatherstation/index.asp

Weatherall, J. W. A. (2000). A grounded theory analysis of older adults and information technology. *Educational Gerontology, 26*(4), 371–386. doi:10.1080/036012700407857

Weber, G., & Specht, M. (1997). User modeling and adaptive navigation support in WWW-based tutoring systems. In *User Modeling: Proceedings of the 6th International Conference (UM97),* (pp. 289-300). Berlin: Springer. doi:10.1007/978-3-7091-2670-7_30

Weber, R. (2003). Still desperately seeking the IT artefact. *Management Information Systems Quarterly, 27*(2), iii–xi.

Webster, F. (2014). *Theories of the information society.* New York: Routledge.

Webster, J., & Watson, R. T. (2002). Analyzing the past to prepare for the future: Writing a literature review. *Management Information Systems Quarterly, 26*(2), 3. Retrieved from http://raptor1.bizlab.mtsu.edu/S-Drive/JCLARK/INFS6980/Articles/6980-LitReview.pdf

Weerahandi, S. (1995). *Exact statistical methods for data analysis.* New York: Springer-Verlag. doi:10.1007/978-1-4612-0825-9

Welsh, E., Wanberg, C., Brown, K., & Simmering, M. (2003). E-learning: Emerging uses, empirical results and future directions. *International Journal of Training and Development, 4*(7), 245–258. doi:10.1046/j.1360-3736.2003.00184.x

Wheeler, B., & Waggener, S. (2009). Above-campus services: Shaping the promise of cloud computing for higher education. *EDUCAUSE Review, 44*(6), 52.

Whinston, A. B., & Geng, X. (2004). Operationalizing the essential role of the information technology artifact in information systems research: Gray area, pitfalls, and the importance of strategic ambiguity. *Management Information Systems Quarterly, 28*(2), 149–159.

Wilding, R. (2006). 'Virtual' intimacies? Families communicating across transnational contexts. *Global Networks, 6*(2), 125–142. doi:10.1111/j.1471-0374.2006.00137.x

Wiley, D. A. (2003). Connecting learning objects to instructional design theory: A definition, a metaphor, and a taxonomy. Logan, UT: The Edumetrics Institute. Retrieved from http://wesrac.usc.edu/wired/bldg-7_file/wiley.pdf

Wiley, D. A. (2002). Connecting learning objects to instructional design theory: A definition, a metaphor, and a taxonomy. In D. A. Wiley (Ed.), *The instructional use of learning objects.* Bloomington, IN: Agency for Instructional Technology and Association for Educational Communications and Technology.

Wilkinson, R. G., & Marmot, M. G. (Eds.). (2003). *Social determinants of health: The solid facts.* World Health Organization.

Williamson, D. A. (2011), *Worldwide social network ad spending: a rising tide.* eMarketer.com. Retrieved 26-02-2011 from http://www. emarketer.com/Report. aspx?code=emarketer_2000692

Wood, J., Dykes, J., Slingsby, A., & Clarke, K. (2007). Interactive visual exploration of a large spatio-temporal dataset: Reflections on a geovisualization mashup. *IEEE Transactions on Visualization and Computer Graphics, 13*(6), 1176–1183.

Wright, R. K. (2010). Been there, done that: Embracing our post-trip experiential recollections through the social construction and subjective consumption of personal narratives. In M. Morgan, P. Lugosi, & J. R. Ritchie (Eds.), *The tourism and leisure experience* (pp. 117–136). Bristol, UK: Channel View Publications.

Wu, D., Im, I., Tremaine, M., Instone, K., & Turoff, M. (2002). A framework for classifying personalization scheme used on e-commerce websites. In *Proceedings of 36th Hawaii International Conference on System Sciences (HICSS)* (pp. 222-234). Waikoloa, HI: IEEE.

Wu, H., Houben, G., & Bra, P. (1998). AHAM: A reference model to support adaptive hypermedia authoring. In Van de Zesde interdisciplinaire conferentie informatiewetenschap (pp.77-88). Academic Press.

Wu, L., Liang, G., Kui, S., & Wang, Q. (2011). CEclipse: An online IDE for programming in the cloud. In *Proceedings of 2011 IEEE World Congress on Services*. IEEE. doi:10.1109/SERVICES.2011.74

Wu, S., Tsait, & Hsu, W. (2003). Text categorization using automatically acquired domain ontology. In *Proceedings of 16th International Workshop on Information Retrieval with Asian Languages* (vol. 11, pp. 138-145). Academic Press. doi:10.3115/1118935.1118953

Wuensch, K., Aziz, S., Ozan, E., Kishore, M., & Tabrizi, M. H. N. (2008). Pedagogical characteristics of online and face-to-face classes. *International Journal on E-Learning, 7*(3), 523–532.

Wu, L. (2012). Exploring the new ecological paradigm scale for gauging children's environmental attitudes in China. *The Journal of Environmental Education, 43*(2), 107–120. doi:10.1080/00958964.2011.616554

Xie, B. (2008). Multimodal computer-mediated communication and social support among older Chinese internet users. *Journal of Computer-Mediated Communication, 13*(3), 728–750. doi:10.1111/j.1083-6101.2008.00417.x

Yang, Y., Zhang, X., Liu, F., & Xie, Q. (2004). An internet-based product customization system for CIM. *Robotics and Computer-integrated Manufacturing, 21*(2), 109–118. doi:10.1016/j.rcim.2004.06.002

Yao, B., & Li, S. (2010). ANMM4CBR: A case-based reasoning method for gene expression data classification. *Algorithms for Molecular Biology; AMB, 5*(1), 14. doi:10.1186/1748-7188-5-14 PMID:20051140

Yin, R. K. (2003). *Case study research: Design and methods* (3rd ed.). Thousand Oaks, CA: Sage.

Yoo, B., & Brutzman, D. (2009). X3D earth terrain-tile production chain for georeferenced simulation. In *Proceedings of International Conference on 3D Web Technology* (pp. 159-166). Darmstadt, Germany: ACM. doi:10.1145/1559764.1559789

York, R. O. (2008). Comparing three modes of instruction in a graduate social work program. *Journal of Social Work Education, 44*(2), 157–172. doi:10.5175/JSWE.2008.200700031

Yoshida, A., Hachisu, Y., Sawada, A., Chang, H. M., & Noro, M. (2012). A source code rewriting system based on attributed token sequence[in Japanese]. *Journal of Information Processing Society of Japan, 53*(7), 1832–1849.

Zachman, J. A. (1997). *The challenge is change: A management paper.* Retrieved January 15, 2014, from http://www.ies.aust.com/papers/zachman2.htm

Zachman, J. A. (2013). *The Zachman framework.* Paper presented at the First International Conference on Enterprise Systems ES 2013, Cape Town, South Africa.

Zeithaml, V., Bitner, M. J., Gremler, D. D., & Bonetti, E. (2012). *Marketing dei servizi* (3rd ed.). Milano, Italy: Mc Graw Hill.

Zeng, H., He, Q., Chen, Z., Ma, W., & Ma, J. (2004). Learning to cluster web search results. In *Proceedings of SIGIR'04, 27th Annual International ACM SIGIR Conference on Research and Development in Information Retrieval* (pp. 210-217). New York, NY: ACM.

Zhang, G., Yan, P., Zhao, H., & Zhang, X. (2008). A computer aided diagnosis system in mammography using artificial neural networks. In *Proceedings of BioMedical Engineering and Informatics* (Vol. 2, pp. 823–826). Academic Press. doi:10.1109/BMEI.2008.93

Zhao, W., & Wakahara, T. (2011). A support system using Moodle for improving students understanding. In *Proceedings ofThird International Conference on Intelligent Networking and Collaborative Systems* (pp. 478-483). Academic Press. doi:10.1109/INCoS.2011.43

Zhu, Z., Jia, S., & Ji, Z. (2010). Towards a memetic feature selection paradigm. *Computational Intelligence Magazine, IEEE, 5*(2), 41–53. doi:10.1109/MCI.2010.936311

Zubrinic, K., & Kalpic, D. (2008). The web as personal learning environment. *International Journal of Emerging Technologies in Learning, 3*, 45–58.

About the Contributors

Tomayess Issa is a senior lecturer at the School of Information Systems at Curtin University, Australia. Tomayess completed her doctoral research in Web Development and Human Factors. As an academic, she is also interested in establishing teaching methods and styles to enhance the students' learning experiences and resolve problems that students face. Tomayess Issa Conference and Program Co-Chair of the IADIS International Conference on Internet Technologies and Society and IADIS International Conference on International Higher Education. Furthermore, she initiated the IADIS conference for Sustainability, Green IT, and Education. Currently, she conducts research locally and globally in information systems, human-computer interaction, usability, social networking, teaching and learning, sustainability, green IT, and Cloud computing. Tomayess participated in a couple of conferences and published her work in several peer-reviewed journals, books, book chapters, papers, and research reports. Tomayess Issa is a Project leader in the International research network (IRNet-EU (Jan2014 – Dec 2017)) for study and development of new tools and methods for advanced pedagogical science in the field of ICT instruments, e-learning and intercultural competences.

Pedro Isaias is an associate professor at the Universidade Aberta (Portuguese Open University) in Lisbon, Portugal, responsible for several courses and director of the master degree program in Management/MBA. Was director of master degree program in Electronic Commerce and Internet since its start in 2003 until July 2014. He holds a PhD in Information Management (in the speciality of information and decision systems) from the New University of Lisbon. Author of several books, book chapters, papers, and research reports, all in the information systems area, he has headed several conferences and workshops within the mentioned area. He has also been responsible for the scientific coordination of several EU-funded research projects. He is also member of the editorial board of several journals and program committee member of several conferences and workshops. At the moment, he conducts research activity related to information systems in general, e-learning, e-commerce and WWW-related areas. Pedro Isaias is an Adjunct Professor at School of Information Systems – Curtin University, Australia.

* * *

Raadila Bibi Mahmud Hajee Ahmud-Boodoo was born in Mauritius and in recent years moved to Sydney, Australia where she now lives with her husband and 2 children. She is currently studying for a PhD in Information Systems at Curtin University of Technology, Australia. Her current research interests are directed towards the Semantic Web, E-learning and Web 3.0 in Education. She completed a Bachelor degree in Information Systems and Technology at Curtin University of Technology and her Master's degree in Computer Science at the University of Mauritius. Raadila has several years of teaching experiences including teaching high school students in Mauritius and students from the vocational sector in Australia. Besides her research project, she also works as a Systems Officer dealing with different databases and leading a team to ensure effective database records maintenance to ensure the stakeholders' and contractual requirements are met.

Ana Paula Laboissière Ambrósio is an associate professor at Instituto de Informática of the Universidade Federalde Goiás (UFG), Brazil. She is graduated in Mathematics (UnB), with a MSc in Computer Science (UFPE) and a Ph.D. in Computer Science from the University of Paris VI/France. She is currently doing another PhD in Educational Psychology at the University of Minho/Portugal. Her current research interests are in Semantic Web, Knowledge Discovery and Computer Science Education.

Rebecca Angeles is Full Professor, Management Information Systems Area, Faculty of Business Administration, University of New Brunswick Fredericton, Canada. She has published in *Information & Management, Decision Support Systems, Supply Chain Management: An International Journal, Industrial Management & Data Systems, International Journal of Integrated Supply Management, International Journal of Management and Enterprise Development, International Journal of Value Chain Management, International Journal of Physical Distribution & Logistics Management, Logistics Information Management, Journal of Business Logistics*, among others. Her current research interests are in environmental sustainability and green supply chain management; radio frequency identification; supply chain management issues; outsourcing and its consequences on supply chains; electronic trading partnership management issues; and innovative approaches to teaching Management Information Systems.

Kenneth Berry, M.Sc., is a Research Associate working with Dr. Paulo Kushnir. His research areas include the use of educational technologies in university contexts and the design of online learning environments. He has a MSc in Information Systems, over 10 years of experience in systems administration and supporting Learning Management Systems, and is currently pursuing certification in E-Learning at the University of Toronto. He is also an Instructional and Learning Technology Specialist in the Faculty of Arts and Science, University of Toronto, providing support to faculty in using technology in teaching, focusing on both technical and pedagogical issues. He was lecturer at The University of the West Indies where he also was the IT Administrator in the Faculty of Humanities and Education.

Kouamana Bousson received a Master's degree in aeronautical engineering from the Ecole Nationale de l'Aviation Civile (ENAC) in 1988, an MSc degree in computer science (majoring in artificial intelligence) from Paul Sabatier University in 1989, and a PhD degree in control & computer engineering from the National Institute of Applied Sciences (INSA) in 1993, all in Toulouse, France. He received the Habilitation degree in aeronautical engineering in 2010 from the University of Beira Interior in Covilhã, Portugal. He was a researcher at the LAAS Laboratory of the French National Council for Scientific Research (CNRS) in Toulouse, from 1993 to 1995, and has been a professor in the Department of Aerospace Sciences at the University of Beira Interior, Covilhã, Portugal, since 1995. His current research activities include flight trajectory optimization and control, analysis and control of uncertain systems, neuro-statistical data processing, and chaotic dynamics.

Cedric Luiz de Carvalho is associate professor at the Instituto de Informática of the Universidade Federal de Goiás (UFG), Brazil. He is graduated in electrical engineering (1987), has master in electrical engineering (1990) and he obtained his Ph.D. in Computer Science at Federal University of Minas Gerais/Brasil (1999). He has been working with Applied Artificial Intelligence and is particularly interested in Intelligent Decision Support Systems, Data Mining, Virtual Communities of Practice on the Web, Semantic Web, Ontology Learning and Semantic Computing. He was director of Institute of Computer Science of Federal University of Goiás (2000 to 2004). He is currently the CIO of Federal University of Goiás.

Amit Chauhan is a PhD candidate at the Florida State University, USA. His dissertation research investigates motivation and interaction in Massive Open Online Courses (MOOCs). Amit's research interests include the design and development, use and application of instructional design and emerging technologies for learning, assessment and evaluation. These include but are not limited to the latest trends in social media, e-learning platforms, authoring tools; LMSs, LCMSs, and learning analytics. Amit is a graduate in Instructional Technology from the University of Bridgeport, USA. He has worked extensively with computer applications, tools and technology to deliver training and learning solutions to Fortune 100 companies.

Fabio M. Costa is an associate professor at the Instituto de Informática of the Universidade Federal de Goiás (UFG), Brazil. He got his PhD in computer science from Lancaster University, UK, in 2001, and his MSc and BSc, both also in computer science, from UNICAMP (1995) and UFG (1992), respectively. His current research interests are in the area of model-driven adaptive systems and middleware, based on his past contributions to adaptive and reflective middleware research. Fabio is a member of the ACM and the Brazilian Computer Society.

João Paulo Carvalho Lustosa da Costa received the Diploma degree in electronic engineering in 2003 from the Military Institute of Engineering (IME) in Brazil, his M.Sc. degree in 2006 from University of Brasília (UnB) in Brazil, and his Doktor-Ingenieur (Ph.D.) degree with Magna cum Laude in 2010 from Ilmenau University of Technology (TU Ilmenau) in Germany. Since 2010, he coordinates the Laboratory of Array Signal Processing (LASP) and since 2011, he works as a senior researcher in Business Intelligence at the Ministry of Planning. He was a visiting scholar and professor at University Erlangen-Nuremberg, at Munich Technical University, at Seville University, at Harvard University and at TU Ilmenau. Curently he coordinates a project at the National School of Public Administration (ENAP) on the development of on-line courses and also a special visiting reseacher (PVE) project on satellite communication and navigation supported by CAPES together with the German Aerospace Center (DLR).

Johannes Cronjé is the Dean of the Faculty of Informatics and Design at the Cape Peninsula University of Technology. He obtained the BA majoring in Afrikaans, English and Anthropology, the BA honours as well as a Teachers' diploma from University of Pretoria. Subsequent, he completed an MA in Afrikaans literature. He then taught English and Afrikaans at Pretoria Boys High until 1986 when he was appointed lecturer in Language Communication at Technikon Pretoria. During this time he was involved in several programmes involving intercultural communication, in both the formal educational sector and in the service industry. He obtained a Doctorate in Afrikaans Literature in 1990 and then a Masters Degree in Computer-Assisted Education from the University of Pretoria. From 1994 to 2007 he was a professor of computers in education with the University of Pretoria. He has also been visiting professor at Sudan University of Science and Technology, Addis Ababa University, Ethiopia; the University of Joensuu, Finland, and the University of Bergen, Norway. He has supervised 65 Masters and 30 Doctoral students and published more than 30 research papers.

Andre de la Harpe holds both MBA and PhD degrees. As a seasoned director of companies, IT Manager, entrepreneur and academic, Andre heads up the post-graduate Centre for CIO Research in Africa (CenCRA), backed up by 33 years leadership experience. He has substantial experience and expertise in setting strategic direction, leading, managing, coaching as well as mentoring of business professionals. Andre has been involved in academia for the past 13 years, lecturing, supervising master and doctoral students as well as facilitating skills development. He currently lectures Information Technology Management at Cape Peninsula University of Technology. He has appeared on television and radio, does frequent conferences presentations as well as leadership development programmes for clients such as Vodacom. As part of building the newly established training and development arm at CenCRA, he is responsible for the development and presentation of emotional intelligence, leadership, management and soft-skills development workshops.

Knut Ekker received the M.A. and PhD in sociology from the University of Minnesota, Minneapolis, USA. He is an associate professor at Nord-Trøndelag University College. He has worked with computerized roleplaying games for emergency response training and research since 1976. He has applied advanced research methodology and statistics in a range of projects - in particular using the open source package R statistics for the GSS project. Knut Ekker is also one of the initiators of the GSS project with Stig C. Holmberg and Viveca Asproth.

Aleteia Araujo Favacho received her B.S. in Computer Science from the Federal University of Pará (1997), and M.S. in Computer Science and Computational Mathematics from the University of São Paulo (1999) and Ph.D. in Computer Science from the Catholic University of Rio de Janeiro (2008). She is an Associate Professor II at the University of Brasilia. She has experience in the area of Computer Science, with an emphasis on Parallel Processing, Distributed Systems, Combinatorial Optimization and Metaheuristics, carrying out studies on the following topics: cloud computing, grid computing, parallel and distributed algorithms. Currently she coordinates a project at the Brazilian Ministry of Planning, Budget and Management for developing the new management system for public employees in Brazil.

Virginie dos Santos Felizardo is currently a M.Sc. Researcher in Assisted Living Computing and Telecommunications Laboratory – ALLab, a research laboratory within the Networks Group of the Instituto de Telecomunicações at the University of Beira Interior, Covilhã, Portugal. She graduated in Biomedical Sciences (University of Beira Interior, Covilhã, Portugal) and, in 2010, received M.Sc. in Electrotechnical Engineering – Bionic Systems (University of Beira Interior, Covilhã, Portugal). She is involved in researcher activities in the Department of Electromechanical Engineering at University of Beira Interior, Covilhã, Portugal. Her research interests include sensors for biomedical applications, biomedical instrumentation, Health monitoring, Medical signal acquisition, analysis, and processing.

Sonia Ferrari has been associate professor of Tourism Marketing and Place Marketing at the University of Calabria, Italy, since 2005. She has been a researcher in the same University since 1993. She has also taught Management, Service Management, Event Marketing, Marketing of Museums, and Tourism Management at the University of Calabria. At the same university she has been President of the Tourism Science Degree Course and President of Valorizzazione dei Sistemi Turistico-Culturali Degree Course since 2007. Her main fields of study and research are: service management, tourism marketing, place marketing, event marketing, wellness tourism.

Nuno M. Garcia holds a PhD in Computer Science Engineering from the University of Beira Interior (UBI, Covilhã, Portugal) (2008) and he is a 5-year BSc in Mathematics / Informatics (UBI, 1999-2004). He is Assistant Professor at UBI and Invited Associate Professor at the Universidade Lusófona de Humanidades e Tecnologias (Lisbon, Portugal). He was founder and is coordinator of the Assisted Living Computing and Telecommunications Laboratory (ALLab, Instituto de Telecomunicações, UBI). He was also co-founder and is coordinator of the BSAFE LAB – Law enforcement, Justice and Public Safety Research and Technology Transfer Laboratory (UBI). He is Head of EyeSeeLab in EyeSee Lda. (Lisbon, Portugal). He is also Chair of the COST Action IC1303 AAPELE – Architectures, Algorithms and Platforms for Enhanced Living Environments. He is the main author of several international, European and Portuguese patents. His main interests include Next-Generation Networks, algorithms for bio-signal processing, distributed and cooperative protocols.

Sehnaz Baltaci Goktalay completed her MSc on Instructional Design, Development and Evaluation at Syracuse University, NY and PhD on Instructional Technology at SUNY, Albany, NY. She has been working at Uludag University, Turkey as an assistant professor of Department of Computer Education and Instructional Technologies and the Associate Dean of the Faculty of Education. Her research interests are e-learning and integration of Web 2.0 technologies in education, social networking, clinical supervision model, and best practices in teacher education. She is involved in several national, international and European Union projects on Web 2.0 technologies and new teacher education.

Sue Greener is a Principal Lecturer at Brighton Business School, University of Brighton, UK. She conducts research in the fields of technology enhanced learning, blended learning and reflective learning and is particularly interested in developing teachers' and trainers' interest and competencies in these areas. She is editor of the journal Interactive Learning Environments. Sue leads university programmes including Foundation Degree Business, BSc Business with Enterprise, and Joint Honours Programme Business Pathway. She also teaches a fully online course in Research Methods and is Subject Examiner for a Business distance learning examination.

Yoshinari Hachisu is currently an associate professor of Department of Software Engineering, Faculty of Science and Engineering, Nanzan University, Japan. He has been working at the same university since 1999. He received the Doctor of Engineering degree from Nagoya University in 1999. His research interests include program analysis, software development environment, XML processing, and e-Learning. Especially, he has been interested in programming education recently. He is a member of the ACM, the IEEE Computer Society, the Information Processing Society of Japan, the Institute of Electronics, Information and Communication in Japan, Japan Society of Software Science and Technology, and Japan Society for Educational Technology.

Maristela Holanda received her B.S. Electronic Engineering from the Federal University of Rio Grande do Norte – UFRN, Brazil, in 1996. She completed her M.S. degree from the University of Brasilia, Brazil, in 1999. She received a PhD degree from the University of Rio Grande do Norte – UFRN, Brazil, in 2007. Since 2009 she has been working for the University of Brasilia – UnB, at the Department of Computer Science. Her current research interests include noSQL databases, transaction concurrency control systems, geographical database and biological databases. Currently, she coordinates a project at the Brazilian Ministry of Planning, Budget and Management for developing the new management system for public employees from Brazil.

Ruben Cruz Huacarpuma is a PhD student in the Department of Electrical Engineering at the University of Brasilia, Brazil. He received his M.S. in informatics (specializing in database for bioinformatics) from the University of Brasilia. His expertise is in traditional and non-traditional databases. His traditional database expertise includes Relational Database Management Systems (RDBMS), storage protocols, content management, and replication data. In addition, he has experience in new technologies such as NoSQL databases for storage and managing big data for large volumes of data. Currently he is a PhD research student at the Laboratory of Decision Making Technologies (LATITUDE) and works as a researcher in database at the Ministry of Planning. His main interests are in databases, content management, information retrieval, metadata management and the underlying technologies that support work in these areas.

Olga Iakovleva is an associate-professor at Herzen State Pedagogical University of Russia, Saint-Petersburg. Her main research interests are: network services in education, students' extracurricular activities in the field of modern virtual university, virtual communication, social media. O. Iakovleva is the author of several educational courses: Information Technology, Telecommunication educational technology, Educational activities in the modern information environment, Global information resources and the protection of intellectual property.

Lena Paulo Kushnir, Ph.D., is an Assistant Professor of Psychology at OCAD University in the Faculty of Liberal Arts & Sciences and School of Interdisciplinary Studies. Her areas of research include instructional design, online assessment, and the use of educational technologies in university contexts. More specifically, her research examines the characteristics of online learning environments, the use of educational technologies, and the effects of such environments and technologies, on perception, cognition, information processing, and learning. She also manages Teaching Technology Support, in the Faculty of Arts and Science at the University of Toronto. Previously, Dr. Kushnir taught in the Department of Psychology, University of Toronto for 16 years and has held cross-appointments at other local institutions.

Lizane Alvares Leite received her B.S. in Computer Science in 2014 from the University of Brasília (UnB) in Brazil. She was a member of the computer junior enterprise from UnB called CJR and worked on a project about sample input data at the geocronology laboratory of UnB. She is interested in studying NoSQL databases, cloud computing, and distributed system.

Marie Marchand, DBA, is a researcher at the Institut de recherche sur les PME and Assistant Professor of accounting at the Université du Québec à Trois-Rivières. Her research has been published in journal such as the *International Journal of Operations & Production Management, Entrepreneurship & Regional Development*, and the *International Journal of Business Performance Management*. Dr. Marchand's research interest center on the measurement and management of organizational performance, and on the design, use and evaluation of IT-based performance management information systems in the context of SMEs and service enterprises. She is also studying organizational performance, its ICT-based measurement and its management in the context of sustainable development and corporate social responsibility.

Tatiana Noskova is a professor at Herzen State Pedagogical University of Russia, Saint-Petersburg. She is a specialists in the field of information technology in education, carries out interdisciplinary research. She is a member of the Academy of Informatization of Education, a member of the International Academy of Higher Education. The main research interests are: virtual learning environment, information and communication technologies in education and professional pedagogical activity. T. Noskova is the author of several educational courses: High-tech educational environment design; Psycho-pedagogical bases of virtual reality; Psycho-pedagogical bases of interpersonal interaction in a virtual learning environment.

Renan Rodrigues de Oliveira is graduated in Computer Science from Universidade Católica de Goiás (2007) and Masters in Computer Science from the Universidade Federal de Goiás (2010). He is currently a professor at the Instituto Federal de Educação, Ciência e Tecnologia de Goiás and has experience in Computer Science, mainly in the following topics: Software engineering, programming languages, decision support systems, ontologies, Semantic Web, and database.

Tatiana Pavlova is an associate-professor at Herzen State Pedagogical University of Russia, Saint-Petersburg. Her main research interests are: information and communication technologies in education, formation and development of information technology competence of specialists in the field of education. T. Pavlova is the author of several educational courses: Information technology in professional activities, information technology, the resource bases of a virtual learning environment.

Nuno Pombo is CTO at Qualify Just/Innovative Prison Systems and Invited Assistant Professor at the Faculty of Engineering, Department of Informatics, University of Beira Interior. Received the Ph.D in computer science from the University of Beira Interior (UBI, Covilhã, 2014). He was also co-founder and is coordinator of the BSAFE LAB – Law enforcement, Justice and Public Safety Research and Technology Transfer Laboratory (UBI). He is member of Instituto de Telecomunicações, UBI. He is also Member of COST Actions: TD1307 "European Model Reduction Network (EU-MORNET)", TC1307 "The European Network on Integrating Vision and Language (iV&L Net): Combining Computer Vision and Language Processing For Advanced Search, Retrieval, Annotation and Description of Visual Data". His current research interests include cloud computing, big data, data fusion, machine learning, ubiquitous computing, eHealth, clinical decision support systems, and model reduction methods.

Louis Raymond, Ph.D., is a researcher at the Institut de recherche sur les PME and Emeritus Professor of information systems at the Université du Québec à Trois-Rivières. His research has been published in journals such as the *MIS Quarterly*, *Entrepreneurship Theory and Practice*, and the *Journal of Management Information Systems*. Dr. Raymond's research interest center on the measurement and management of organizational performance, and on the strategic and technological determinants of performance in the context of SMEs and service enterprises. He is also studying organizational performance and its ICT-based determinants in the context of healthcare.

Edward Ribeiro is a software engineer with more than 10 years of experience on both open source and commercial software for government institutions in Brazil. He has also contributed to open source projects (VoltDB, Cassandra, ZooKeeper, etc.) and holds an M.S. in Informatics at the University of Brasilia (Brazil). Since 2004, he has published national and international papers on distributed systems applied to bioinformatics. During the past decade, he has been a lecturer on computer science at some private colleges, and for the last five years, has been involved with the co-advising of undergraduate and graduate students, as well as lecturing on NoSQL/NewSQL at national conferences like TDC (The Developers Conference) and QCON SP, both in Brazil. He works as a Distributed Systems Engineer at DataStax.

Daniel da Cunha Rodrigues received his B.S. in Information Systems from the Euro University Center (UNIEURO). He is working on his M.S. as a graduate student in the Graduate Program for Electrical Engineering (PPGEE) at the University of Brasília (UnB), which he began in 2013, focusing on the areas of business intelligence, big data and distributed processing. Since 2011, he has been working as a research student of the Laboratory of Array Signal Processing (LASP) and the Laboratory of Decision Making Technologies (LATITUDE), participating from 2011 to 2014 as a researcher in the area of business intelligence in cooperation projects with the Brazilian Ministry of Planning. Currently he works as the senior software systems architect at the Brazilian Superior Electoral Court (TSE).

Antonio Manuel Rubio Serrano completed his M.S. degree in Telecommunications Engineering in 2012 from the Polytechnic University of Catalonia (UPC) in Spain. He completed a degree in Telecommunications Engineering and Management in 2012 also from UPC, and an M.S. in Electrical Engineering in 2014 from the University of Brasilia (UnB). Between 2008 and 2010 he worked on the development and implementation of the Shared Medical Record for Catalonia (HC3) project, the e-Health initiative for the Catalonian government in Spain. Since 2012, he has been working as a senior researcher in Business Intelligence and Predictive Analytics at the Brazilian Ministry of Planning, Budget and Management.

Rafael Timóteo de Sousa Júnior was born in Campina Grande – PB, Brazil, on June 24, 1961. He graduated in Electrical Engineering, from the Federal University of Paraíba – UFPB, Campina Grande – PB, Brazil, 1984, and got his Doctorate Degree in Telecommunications, from the University of Rennes 1, Rennes, France, 1988. He worked as a software and network engineer in the private sector from 1989 to 1996. Since 1996, He is a Network-Engineering Professor in the Electrical Engineering Department, at the University of Brasília, Brazil. From 2006 to 2007, supported by the Brazilian R&D Agency CNPq, He took a sabbatical year in the Group for the Security of Information Systems and Networks, at Ecole Superiéure d'Electricité, Rennes, France, on leave from the University of Brasília. His field of study is distributed systems and network management and security.

Declan Tuite specializes in interactive design, programming, HCI, sound design and the use of new media to maintain intimate relationships. Declan's main research is concerned with the effects of ICTs on society. Of particular interest are behaviours developed by people in maintaining and repairing personal and family relationships through ICT's particularly social media and mobile devices. He has completed a five year study on the longer term and unexpected outcomes of participation in eInclusion programmes by older adults. He has also recently taken lead on some mobile app development projects in collaboration with industry partners through the Enterprise Ireland knowledge partnership scheme. Previously, Declan has worked as a media production manager for Eircom Multimedia. In that role, he worked on web initiatives for both the general public and on the research and development of new products such as interactive telvision and news syndicaiton systems.

Eben van Blerk has 24 years corporate IT systems development experience. He started his career as a trainee programmer and has up to date, fulfilled various roles as part of the systems development life cycle. This includes system analysis, business analysis, project management and Senior IT management. He obtained a MBA from the University of Stellenbosch in 2004 as well as a Doctorate of Technology from the Cape Peninsula University of Technology in 2014. He has lectured and co-supervised in Strategic IT Management at the Cape Peninsula University of Technology. As part of his role in corporate IT, he presents emotional intelligence workshops to IT professionals. His areas of expertise include psychological factors in information systems work. His specific research focus is the role of emotional intelligence in business-IT alignment.

João Vieira is a master student in Information Systems Management at Lisbon School of Economics & Management (ISEG). He also has a degree in Geography and Regional Planning, at Faculty of Social and Human Sciences (FCSH), Nova University. His mains interests are in the areas of Information Systems Planning and Architecture, Decision Systems, Project Management, Customer Relationship Management, Information Systems Analysis and Geographic Information Systems. In special, he is interested in e-Business Models and Technologies, an area related to is thesis of empathic websites, where the main objective is to identify for a specific website type which combinations of empathic strategies are more effective.

Byounghyun Yoo is a senior research fellow of the Imaging Media Research Center (IMRC) at the Korea Institute of Science and Technology (KIST). He served the first Web3D fellow of the Web3D Consortium, the nonprofit organization that develops and maintains the international standard for 3D graphics on the Web. He has worked with the X3D Earth Working Group on scientific and engineering challenges that are particularly important for advancing the X3D standard into open geospatial computing platforms. Previously, he was a research scientist of the Center for Environmental Sensing and Modeling (CENSAM) at the Singapore-MIT Alliance for Research and Technology (SMART) Centre, the Center for Educational Computing Initiative (CECI) at Massachusetts Institute of Technology, and the Modeling, Virtual Environments, and Simulation (MOVES) Institute at the Naval Postgraduate School in Monterey California.

Atsushi Yoshida received the doctoral degree in Engineering from Nagoya University (Japan) in 1999. He worked for Toyohashi University of Technology as an assistant professor of department of Knowledge Information Engineering from 1996 to 2000 and Wakayama University as a lecturer of Center for Information Science from 2000 to 2009. He also worked for Nanzan University as an associate professor and he is now a professor of Department of Software Engineering at Faculty of Science and Engineering of Nanzan University. His research interests are primarily in the field of software maintenance. His current research includes program analysis, program pattern transformation, and aspect refactoring. He is a member of IEEE Computer Society, Information Processing Society of Japan, the Institute of Electronics, Information and Communication Engineering, and Japan Society for Software Science and Technology.

Index

Printed in the United States
By Bookmasters